Culinaria

Culinaria

European Specialties

Joachim Römer · Michael Ditter (Chief editors)

Günter Beer (Photography)

Peter Feierabend (Design)

Christine Westphal (Editor)

KÖNEMANN

Abbreviations and quantities

1 oz	1 ounce	$1/16$ pound
1 lb	1 pound	16 ounces
1 cup	1 cup	8 ounces with solids* (see below); 8 fluid ounces with liquids
1 cup	1 cup	4 ounces with flour and powdered sugar
1 cup	1 cup	6 ounces with uncooked rice
1 cup	1 cup	7 ounces with dried fruit
1 fl oz	1 fluid ounce	$1/16$ pint
1 pt	1 pint	16 fluid ounces
1 qt	1 quart	32 fluid ounces
1 gall	1 gallon	3.9 quarts
1 Tbs.	1 level table spoon	$1/2$ ounce with solids; $1/2$ fluid ounce with liquids
1 Dsp.	1 level dessert spoon	$1/3$ ounce with solids; $1/3$ fluid ounce with liquids
1 tsp.	1 level teaspoon	$1/6$ ounce with solids; $1/6$ fluid ounce with liquids
1 schnapps glass	$2/3$ fluid ounces	$1 1/2$ tablespoons
1 glass	$1/2$ cup	4 fluid ounces

Spoon measurements for solids always refer to worked ingredients e.g. 1 Tbs. chopped onions, but 1 onion, peeled and chopped.

Recipe portions
If not otherwise stated, the recipes are portioned to serve 4, with the exception of drinks (these are per person) and buffet dishes (these are for any number of people who help themselves as often as they want). To avoid any confusion, several recipes featured on a double page which are portioned for different numbers of people all state the number of servings they are calculated for, even those which serve 4.

* Where feasible, quantities in recipes have been rounded up or down for convenience. Metric conversions may therefore not correspond exactly. It is important to use either American or metric measurements within a recipe.

© 1995 Könemann Verlagsgesellschaft mbH
Bonner Strasse 126 · D-50968 Cologne

Concept and idea:	Ludwig Könemann
Studio photography:	Food Foto Cologne – Brigitte Krauth and Jürgen Holz
Food styling:	Stefan Krauth
Recipe support:	Uschi Stender-Barbieri
Picture acquisition and research:	Sally Bald, Ruth Correia, Regine Ermert
Reproductions:	Columbia Offset Group, Singapore

Original title: *Culinaria Europäische Spezialitäten*

© 2000 for this new English edition
Könemann Verlagsgesellschaft mbH
Bonner Strasse 126 · D-50968 Cologne

This present book is a new edition of the 1995
two-volume publication with the same title.

Translation from German:	Sarah Batschelet and Philip Jenkins
Editor of the English edition:	Rosalind Horton
Typesetting:	Goodfellow & Egan, Cambridge, UK
Production:	Ursula Schümer
Printing and binding:	Mateu Cromo Artes Graficas, Madrid

Printed in Spain
ISBN 3-89508-234-1

10 9 8 7 6 5 4

Contents

**Foreword
by André Dominé**

Europe is a fascinating mosaic of landscapes, climates, peoples, cultures, passions, and ways of life. But no matter where in Europe, whether in Norway, Greece, Ireland or Hungary, there is one inexhaustible aspect of everyday life that never dulls, namely the simple pleasure of eating and drinking. The characteristics of the different peoples and countries of Europe are expressed in their culinary specialties, dishes and drinks, forming an essential part of their culture. Happily, the countries of Europe have moved closer together, and once insurmountable barriers between them have been eroded away. Mutual understanding between Europeans has greatly improved, and all the regions of Europe are now accessible to visitors. This process of exchange and cooperation has never before embraced such diversity. Culinary horizons are expanding, bringing with them a wider assortment of fruits, vegetables, cheeses, meats, wines, and spirits on offer to the consumer. As we enjoy the culinary opportunities brought by this diversity, we are nevertheless in danger of succumbing to the banality of standardized foods, and the sterility of flavors developed for the international palate. This comprehensive and richly-illustrated book offsets this tendency by emphasizing the culinary characteristics of individual European countries. It presents specialties – those belonging to good, wholesome everyday dishes, as well as those reserved for festive occasions and exotic menus. Together, photographer and authors have gone in search of authentic delicacies, the products of living traditions, made with utmost regard for both ingredients and craftmanship alike. They have sought out farmers, shepherds, bakers, and pastry chefs, and the many kitchens and cellars throughout Europe to discover and record the secrets involved in each culinary masterpiece. Only those who know the details of these dishes can really appreciate them and discern the subtleties that make them so pleasurable. *Culinaria European Specialties* is a culinary encyclopaedia, to which top chefs as well as home cooks have contributed their best recipes. The wonders of the European kitchen surprise throughout. With its fascinating pictures, impressions, and detailed explanations, *Culinaria European Specialties* is intended to bridge the gap between those who delight in the intricacies of cooking and those who savor the subtleties of the finished culinary product. Only in this way can we preserve the richness and variety reflected in these pages.

Honor Moore

England

It is well known that England swims against the tide. On this island traditions have a particular standing – which not only expresses itself in the persistence with which driving continues to be on the left, but also in the dietary habits of the British, who have sealed themselves off for centuries from events upon the continent of Europe. Since 1066 England has never been subdued by arms, but with the passing of time people of differing nationalities have come again and again. The British Empire, which one hundred years ago still consisted of half the world, despite all its emphasis on tradition was willing to be influenced by foreign ideas and customs and would integrate them into daily life. When they returned home, British colonial officers would bring everyday customs and dietary habits, recipes for exotic dishes, and often enough also their Indian or Chinese cook. And when the empire turned into the Commonwealth, many Asians and Africans, Americans and Australians made their way to the country. All of them made their contribution to a varied dietary regimen.

England has, as it were, two "national dishes": roast beef with yorkshire pudding as well as fish and chips. Roast beef is regarded as a typical officers' meal, which is at home in English clubs and has even given its name to a profession, since the detachments of guards at the Tower of London, where the British Crown Jewels are kept, are called Beefeaters. Fish and chips have nourished generations of English dockers, the English equivalent of stevedores, and are generally regarded as the food of the people. The dish even became, astonishingly enough, a typical meal for yuppies, although the fish was of an exceptional quality and was served on the finest porcelain, accompanied by superior French wines.

Something that remains unchanged despite every fluctuation in culinary taste is the tradition of the English pub. The inclination to drink one's beer in the evenings in the company of others, and to drink patiently right up to the inevitable arrival of closing time, acts as a successful counterbalance to the continuous Americanization of culinary life.

Left: The team at Fortnum & Mason, one of the most distinguished London addresses for delicacies.

English Breakfast

The well-known English novelist W. Somerset Maugham once said that the best way of feeding oneself in England was to breakfast three times daily. The English Breakfast was "invented" by the architects of the British Empire – although it had already been the tradition for centuries in rural areas of England to fortify oneself thoroughly first thing in the morning before beginning the day. The English Breakfast has, without doubt, made a substantial contribution to culinary history and has become generally accepted worldwide, like the French *croissant*. There can be no discriminating hotel that manages without a breakfast buffet on the English model. However, the buffet is merely a variation – invented to save on time and staff – of the breakfast ceremony, which in its classic form is served in several courses in the same way in which a menu is presented.

First Course:
A true English Breakfast begins with a glass of orange juice or half a grapefruit, which is cut into segments, sprinkled with sugar, and then eaten with a spoon. Prunes or stewed fruit, however, are also available.

A large pot of coffee or tea, both of which are served with milk, are brought to the table.

Second Course:
Now porridge or cornflakes are on the agenda. Milk is poured onto cornflakes and they are eaten before they can become saturated. This crunchy dish is particularly popular with children. However, where the English Breakfast is concerned, for the real enthusiast nothing surpasses freshly prepared porridge, which is made by cooking oatflakes only with water and a pinch of salt, served together with a knob of butter on the plate, sprinkled with brown sugar with hot milk then being added. It is only necessary to try it once to become virtually "addicted" to this unpretentious but delicious dish.

Third Course:
There now follows the main course. This consists of eggs, preferably fried eggs, served with either lean or fatty bacon. Many people also prefer scrambled eggs. Grilled tomatoes, mushrooms, chipolatas, or sausages are popular with eggs.

If one has further culinary plans for one's breakfast it is perhaps better to eat a poached egg on toast instead of fried eggs.

Fourth Course:
Would you like a fish dish or a meat one? The favorite choice for fish devotees is the kipper, smoked herring fresh from the skillet. Also very popular are deviled kidneys ("deviled" being derived from the word "devil"), piquant lamb's kidneys, and kedgeree, which is cooked fish in curried rice.

Fifth Course:
Finally toast, marmalade, and jam are served.

How to prepare Bacon and Eggs
- Place some fat and some thinly-sliced fatty bacon in a heavy, cast iron skillet. Leave to fry gently on both sides until the bacon is crispy and brown.
- Break the eggs on the edge of the skillet and let them slide into the skillet over the bacon. Season with salt and pepper, and fry until the edges are crispy and brown. (Bacon and Eggs can also be prepared in the oven.)
- Serve with slices of white bread fried in butter.

Kedgeree
Fish in Curried Rice

8 oz (250 g) long grain rice
1 lb 2 oz (500 g) turbot, cod or salmon
Just under 1/4 cup (50 g) butter
1 Tbs curry powder, 1 pinch of cayenne pepper
4 hard-boiled eggs, sliced
2 Tbs finely chopped parsley

Cook the rice in salted water. Cover the fish with water in a saucepan, bring to the boil, remove the lid and leave to simmer for 10 minutes. Cut into large pieces and remove any bones. Put to one side.
Melt the butter, sprinkle the curry powder and cayenne pepper on to it, and brown lightly for 1 minute. Stir in the rice, add the pieces of fish and fold in. Warm everything over a low heat for 1 minute, then carefully fold in the slices of egg. Sprinkle with parsley and serve immediately with buttered toast.

Deviled Kidneys
Piquant Lamb's Kidneys

8 whole lamb's kidneys, skinned and trimmed of fat
2 tsp mango chutney
1 Tbs mustard, 1 1/2 tsp strong mustard powder
2 tsp lemon juice
1/2 tsp salt, 1 pinch of cayenne pepper

Cut the kidneys in half lengthways, without cutting through them entirely. Mix the chutney, mustard, mustard powder, lemon juice, salt, and cayenne pepper together well. Marinate the kidneys in this mixture for 60 minutes. Grease the oven's broiling pan, set the broiler's temperature on maximum. Remove the kidneys from the marinade, place in the broiling pan with the kidneys facing upwards where they have been cut, and broil for 3 minutes.
Turn and broil for a further 3 minutes. Spread the marinade on slices of toast, place the kidneys on the toast in pairs and serve immediately.

Creams
The English are well known for their cream, which is nutritious and mostly high in fat content.

Single (or light) Cream
This has a fat content of at least 18 percent and bears a certain resemblance to full fat milk. It is poured over puddings and fruit flans.

Whipping Cream
The fat content of whipping cream lies between 30 and 60 percent. Once whipped it almost has the consistency of double cream, but is considerably frothier.

Double (or heavy) Cream
This thick cream has a fat content of about 48 percent and is very well suited to whipping. It is used above all for enriching cooked food.

Clotted Cream
Cornish clotted cream is an English specialty. Originating from the county of Cornwall it is yellow and has a thick consistency that resembles butter and a fat content of over 55 percent. It is served with scones and strawberry jam or with poached fruit. Créme fraîche is used in place of this cream "on the continent" as it is only available in Great Britain.

Baked Beans from the can belong to every English Breakfast. They are eaten with toast and as a snack or at other mealtimes.

Breakfast Specialties

Baked Beans
Ten years ago the leading manufacturer of baked beans had the following advertising slogan served up on the television:
A million housewives every day
Pick up a tin of beans and say,
"Beanz Meanz Heinz."
The meaning of the rhyme is quite clear, but the skill of the advertising copywriter is to achieve an ingenious identification of product and brand through the categories' catchphrase "Beanz Meanz Heinz" which is helped by the infectiousness of the rhyme. A strong link is also created between the product and the name of this particular manufacturer, the Heinz Corporation, through misspelling the words "beans" and "means" with the closing letter "z" of the manufacturers' name.

As there are at least six other manufacturers of baked beans, we can assume that several million helpings of the pink shining beans in thick tomato sauce are heated and consumed. They are eaten for breakfast – on a slice of toast or with sausages, eggs, and bacon – as a morning snack, for lunch, for tea, or for dinner. Since it has become apparent that beans are particularly healthy, given the high portion of roughage and protein that they contain, their popularity has increased even further.

Kippers
A kipper is a herring that has been gutted and smoked over a wood fire. Kippers are popular as a breakfast dish. They are most easily prepared in the following way. A tall, narrow container is filled with hot water, the water is then poured away, the kippers placed head downwards into the container and boiling water poured over them. The carefully sealed container is subsequently left in a warm place for eight to ten minutes. Once they have been well drained the kippers are served with toast and butter.

Much More Than a Drink

Tea

The butler, the valet of an English Lord, has his first important task in the morning – he serves the early morning tea. The procedure is a ritual which unfolds as follows:

The butler knocks on the bedroom door and on a silver mahogany tray brings in the freshly brewed tea and the *Times* to the accompaniment of the prescribed formulaic greeting "Good Morning, Sir." The greeting always remains the same, whether the gentleman is lying in bed alone or with a lady. A well-trained English butler would never dare to take note of the presence of a lady in a negligee.

All English people preserve the custom of early morning tea to the present day, although with the passing of time the butler has gone. Even visitors to the island can enjoy early morning tea. All better quality hotels offer this service, even if it is by now in an automated version. A water kettle stands ready in the hotel room together with cutlery, tea-bags, milk, and sugar, so that it is only necessary to press a button in the morning to bring the water to the boil. Alternatively a "teasmade" is provided, which is activated by a timer and which, quite without the participation of the sleeping hotel guest, goes into action and rings as soon as the morning drink is ready.

Tea is certainly the most English of all drinks, and it therefore comes as a surprise that it was first fashionable in Portugal long before it came to London. Although the healing powers of this drink were extolled in the treatment of headaches, epilepsy, gallstones, lethargy, and even consumption, the first small consignment which came from Holland was received with some suspicion. It was Catherine of Braganza, the Portuguese wife of King Charles II (1660–1685) who later introduced the cult of the teapot with considerably greater success into the circles of the English Court.

Ch'a or T'e was made in those days by boiling a few tealeaves in water, sometimes for half an hour, in order to bring out the flavor. It was not long before sugar was added, so that the drink did not taste quite so bitter. Wine was often made more palatable in the same way, and a punch or fruit liqueur, which was as hot as it was sweet, was also very fashionable. However, another century was to pass before it occurred to anyone to add milk.

In the coffee houses, in which English gentlemen could refresh themselves with that newfangled drink, the company of women was unwelcome, in line with the traditions of the gentlemen's clubs of the day. It was for this reason that Thomas Twining opened the first tea house

The correct way to prepare tea: one per person, one for the pot

An essential part of the English tea ceremony is knowing the correct way to prepare the tea. There is only one proper way of doing this.

The dispute which has raged for a long time in England as to whether it is the tea or the milk which should first be placed in the cup, seems by now to have been settled. It is the milk, and it must be cold, since warm milk ruins the aroma of the tea.

- Fresh, cold water is placed in a kettle and the kettle is placed on the cooker.
- When the water boils, the pot is warmed by pouring in a small amount of the hot water, which is then poured away.

- The tea is then placed in the warmed teapot. The rule to follow is one teaspoon of tea for every cup served with an additional teaspoon for the pot.

- The pot is taken to the kettle – never the other way around, because otherwise the water might cool too much! On the other hand it should also not have boiled for very long before the tea is made.
- The tea is left to draw for five minutes, because in this time the aromatic elements best unfold without the tea becoming bitter. The tea should be stirred before being poured.

for women in the year 1717, and it immediately became a great success. The name Twining still stands today for quality of the first class in tea matters, something which is particularly true of Earl Grey, a tea which is flavored with oil of bergamot. It is this oil which gives the tea its unmistakable flavor.

In larger cities exclusive tearooms were opened, often adjoining a lending library, as well as less exclusive pleasure gardens where tea could be enjoyed and fireworks admired. Tea was an expensive luxury because it was heavily taxed. It was for this reason that tea was often smuggled in from the continent, along with brandy and wine, and unscrupulous salesmen would mix fresh or already used tealeaves with suitably colored hawthorn, ash, or blackthorn leaves. Although they can scarcely have improved the flavor of the tea, they were fortunately also not detrimental to one's health. Damage to coffee beans was a rather more serious matter, which resulted in the price of coffee remaining high. As a result of numerous crop failures beer also became more expensive, which resulted in the drinking of ever more tea. When the tax on tea was lifted shortly thereafter, the well-known English tea clippers surpassed themselves in speed every year to bring home the first products of the new tea harvest. In around 1830 the cultivation of tea spread from China as far as India, and from there to Ceylon. Kenya also made its mark as a supplier of tea.

Tea accompanies an Englishman throughout the entire day. It is not only that the day is welcomed with it at early morning tea. Amongst English working men and women it is a carefully preserved aspect of their standard of living to be allowed to have a tea break at four o'clock in the afternoon.

The custom of drinking tea has become world famous through High Tea. It is here that the English ceremony of enjoying tea reaches perfection. Heavy silver pots and containers crafted by hand, and preferably in the Victorian style, hold the tea, the milk, and the sugar whilst the characteristic, shallow teacups made of hand-finished porcelain await the guests.

High Tea is an excellent opportunity for a small snack between meals, which is the reason why cakes, cookies, and strawberry jam are served with it. On special occasions English housewives also offer sandwiches made with shrimp paste, slices of tomato, and grated cheese as well as ham rolls. There is always something baked however, such as tea scones, eccles cakes, dundee cake or shortbread, these recipes being mainly Scottish.

What You Should Know About Tea

Only black tea is real tea – herbal teas do not come into this category. This is the reason why herbal teas are sometimes called "infusions" rather than "teas" in English, as they are in French. Real tea is an infusion of dried and fermented leaves of the tea plant, whose origins go back to the Imperial Chinese Courts of 5,000 years ago. The tea plant has yellowish-white flowers and small hard-shelled, walnutlike fruits. The plant is cut back through regular pruning to create a bush about three feet (one meter) high. Its evergreen, young shoots are harvested at strictly determined intervals and according to a very specific technique. Only the tips and the first two to three leaves are cut off, they are then cut up, fermented, and dried to produce what is eventually sold as tea.

Teas often have long, strange sounding names such as Darjeeling Flowery Orange Pekoe or Ceylon Broken Orange Pekoe. These descriptions include the two important distinguishing features, firstly the country of origin and secondly the leaf size.

Countries Where Tea is Grown
A particularly aromatic tea comes from Darjeeling, the Northern Indian district on the southern slopes of the Himalayas. Darjeelings are relatively light and delicate in flavor.

In the Northern Indian province of Assam there grows a particularly heavy tea. It is strong and full-flavored, dark in color, and has a very distinct aftertaste. Assam tea is so strong that it can be brewed with any water without losing its taste. Because of this quality it is also a constituent of many blends.

Ceylon tea is aromatic and has a slightly sharp taste. From the point of view of color it lies between a Darjeeling and an Assam tea.

Teas from Africa have developed well in recent years. Kenya harvests the best quality teas during the dry season.

Green tea comes from the same plant as black tea, the only difference being that it is not fermented, or put another way it is not changed chemically. Green tea is preferred in the countries of Eastern Asia and forms, for example, the basis of the Japanese tea ceremony. Oolong tea is neither green nor black – outside it is fermented, inside, however, it is green.

A Matter of Taste: Aromatic Teas
Tea can be flavored in a number of ways. Small pieces of fruit and flowers, spices and aromatic agents assure us of variety. The most widely known aromatic tea is Earl Grey, which was already being made in the 19th century according to a recipe named after the British Foreign Minister Edward Grey. The oil of the bergamot plant is added to this tea, which gives it its characteristic flowery and slightly sharp taste. Other popular aromatic teas are flavored with vanilla, jasmine, orange, wild cherry, blackcurrant, mango, lemon, or apple.

Grades of Tea and Types of Leaf
It is not only where a tea is grown or, if applicable, which aromatic additives it comes with, which determine the taste and smell of teas, but also the grade of the tea and the type of leaf. Tea is sold as leaf tea, broken tea, fanning tea, and dust tea, although the difference between leaf tea and broken tea – tea leaves which have been cut into small pieces – scarcely plays a role any longer as most teas are imported as broken tea. So called "fannings" arise when uncut leaves are sorted and consist of very small particles, which is why fanning varieties are suitable for tea-bags. Dust, which is used for tea-bags as well, is made up of the smallest particles of all, which are left behind after sorting.

With regard to the quality of leaves there are also significant differences. The terms Pekoe Tip or Flowery Pekoe describe teas which only contain the finest leaf-buds: Orange Pekoe consists of the tender leaves directly underneath the leaf-buds; by Pekoe we understand teas which have come from the second and third leaf below the leaf-bud. Souchong First comes from the third leaf when it is coarse and long; Souchong are other large leaves. And so we see that Orange Pekoe, for example, is neither a type or grade of tea but rather a type of leaf.

Tea Scones

For about 12 scones

2¹/₂ cups (300 g) flour
2 tsp baking powder
1 pinch of salt
¹/₄ cup (50 g) sugar
¹/₃ cup (80 g) cold flakes of butter
1 egg, 1 egg yolk and 1 egg white
¹/₂ cup (125 ml) milk
Sugar crystals

Preheat the oven to 425 °F (225 °C). Grease a baking pan and put to one side. Mix together in a bowl the flour, baking powder, salt, and sugar. Add the flakes of butter, rub them into the flour mixture to obtain a crumble like consistency. Beat the egg and egg yolk until frothy, stir into the milk and pour into the bowl with the crumble. Work the dough into a firm ball and roll out on a work surface (that has been covered with flour) to a thickness of almost ³/₄ inch (2 cm). Mark out the dough in rings with a diameter of about 2 inches (5 cm) with a pastry cutter or a glass and place them on the baking tin just over one inch (2.5 cm) apart. Beat the egg white with a fork and brush the tops of the dough with it and sprinkle with sugar crystals. Bake for 15–20 minutes on the middle shelf, until the scones have browned lightly. Serve immediately. Scones are best served with butter, whipped or clotted cream and jam.

Eccles Cakes
Small Currant Cakes

For about 14 cakes

1 lb (450 g) deep-frozen puff pastry
1 cup (175 g) currants
2 Tbs (25 g) soft butter
Just under ¹/₄ cup (40 g) light brown sugar
2 Tbs (25 g) candied lemon-peel and candied orange-peel
1 pinch of nutmeg, 1 pinch of pimiento
1 egg white
Some caster sugar

Roll out the puff pastry and mark out discs of dough with a diameter of about 4 inches (10 cm).
Grease a baking tray and preheat the oven to 425 °F (220 °C).
Mix all of the other ingredients together well with the exception of the egg white and the caster sugar. Place one heaped teaspoon of each on every piece of dough. Pick up the edges of the dough and press together in the middle. Turn over and roll flat, taking great care, with a rolling-pin, until the currants can just be seen.
Make two incisions with a sharp knife in the middle and place on the baking tray. Brush the cakes with the beaten egg white and sprinkle with caster sugar. Bake for 20 minutes on the middle shelf until golden brown.

Tasting Tea According to all the Rules

Each tea plantation, as well as the large tea companies, have their own tea tasters. It is their job to assess the quality of each harvest and to produce blends in accordance with their respective house styles. Tea tasters proceed in the following way:

1. The tea sample is spread out on a sheet of white paper so that the tea can be examined with both the eye and nose.

2. The tea is brewed in a special vessel known as the tea taster's pot. The same amount of tea is made every time, exactly 5.6 grams. To measure out this amount the traditional standard weight is an old sixpenny piece.

3. After exactly five minutes the brewed tea is poured into a cup without handles, known as the tea taster's cup. The tealeaf remains on the inside of the lid which is turned upwards and laid on the pot so that the tea taster can look at and smell the leaf.

4. Then the tea is removed from the cup with a large spoon, sampled, and (as in a wine tasting) spat out.

Due to this expert tasting it is possible to create teas that are suitable for blending. This is how the large firms succeed in selling tea of a consistent quality and flavor, unaffected by fluctuations in climate and production in the countries of origin.

Professional tea tasters (see left) ensure that the quality of the tea remains at a consistently high standard.

To taste tea a very specific amount of tea (5.6 g) is always brewed with boiling water.

The tea is left to draw for 5 minutes and is then poured into the so-called tea taster's pot. The tealeaf remains under examination on the inside of the lid.

Little Scarlet
Strawberry Jam

Gooseberry Jam

Raspberry Jam

English Breakfast
Orange
Marmalade

Marmalade and Jam

Countless hedges stretch across England. They denote borders and form insurmountable barriers for cattle. Furthermore, they are supposed to hinder soil erosion by the wind and rain. However, they do have another very practical use, because a variety of berries grow in these hedges and they can be plucked on a stroll on a beautiful summer's day and enjoyed. However, they are mainly used in the making of marmalade, jam, and jelly.

The English use the word "marmalade" exclusively to describe preparations using citrus fruits. Everything else is either "jam," when the fruit pulp is used, or "jelly," if it is only the thickened juice which fills the jars. (This distinction is in accord with the appropriate EU regulation.)

Juniper and whitethorn, as well as sloes are also excellently suited to making distillates of a greater or lesser sophistication.

How Mrs Keiller Invented Orange Marmalade

Nothing is more English than a jar of orange marmalade, although in fact marmalade actually originates from Scotland. The original is called "Dundee Marmalade" and was invented in the port of Dundee on the northeast coast of Scotland, to the north of Edinburgh.

It was there that marmalade made from bitter oranges was made for the first time in the year 1770. Before then the word "marmalade" was used to describe a kind of candy which consisted of quinces, which were either indigenous or imported from Portugal (*marmelos*). When a local victualler by the name of James Keiller discovered a cargo of oranges that were being sold cheaply, he acquired all the fruit with the intention of selling it at a reasonable price in his shop. Unfortunately the oranges were bitter ones, which nobody wanted to buy. In his despair he took several of them home with him. His wife

had the idea of making them into marmalade like quinces. This was the origin of a spread which today is known worldwide.

The Keiller Company in Dundee still manufactures marmalades, which also include their famous "Black Dundee Marmalade," which is made with brown sugar and sometimes also with black molasses. There are now marmalades with thick or thin pieces of peel, flavored with whisky, Grand Marnier or ginger, only made of bitter oranges or also a mixture of citrus fruits. Marmalades of an outstanding "vintage" are left to mature for a while, in order to round off the flavor. There are now dozens of different recipes and they all have their origin in Mrs Keiller's steadfast conviction that one should waste neither oranges nor money.

Orange marmalade is a product for which the customary development towards manufacture took place the other way around. Usually products that were originally made at home are later made in factories. In the case of marmalade, however, commercial production came first. Everywhere in the British Isles today housewives make their own marmalade, either from fresh bitter oranges or from orange pulp, which is available in cans.

Lime
Marmalade

Blood Orange
Marmalade

Rose Petal
Jelly

Pink Grapefruit
Marmalade

1 Blackberry
Blackberries are made into jams and liqueur. Blackberry and apple pie numbers amongst the masterpieces of English cooking. The fruit lies heavy and sweet beneath a short pastry crust; suitable for serving with whipped cream or vanilla sauce.

2 Blackthorn (or sloe)
Ripe blackthorn berries are harvested after the first frost when they taste milder. They are used to make blackthorn wine; the berries can also be used to color and flavor gin. When preserved with sugar and vinegar, blackthorn berries make a good compote.

3 Berberis
The red, long and narrow berries of the berberis have a pleasant, slightly sour taste. Mixed with sweet fruits they are made into jams, jelly, or juice.

4 Elder
Elderberries, which are small and red-black in color, are used to make jelly, syrup, jam, and wine. A sudorific therapeutic tea is made from the flower.

5 Hawthorn and Rose-hip
Jelly, juice, vinegar, and a liqueur are made from these fruits which are rich in vitamin C.

6 Mulberry
Mulberries, which when ripe are virtually black and have a sweet and slightly sour taste, can be eaten raw or used as a cake topping.

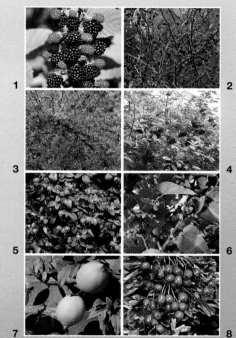

7 Quince
When picked the quince is inedible, but when made into a jelly it tastes delicious. A specialty of the West Country is quince paste, a preserve with a firm consistency, which is served as a dessert with clotted cream.

8 Whitethorn
The small red berries of the whitethorn, which have a slightly sour and sweet taste, can be made into a compote and jelly, but also into an excellent brandy.

The classic English marmalade recipe uses bitter oranges with their peel, thinly cut. Sugar is then added to the mixture.

Once a little butter has been added, the mixture is brought to the boil.

Subsequently the sugar content of the fruit mixture is measured.

Finally, the finished fruit mixture is placed in sterilized jars. These then undergo a final examination under ultraviolet light.

Roast Beef with Yorkshire Pudding

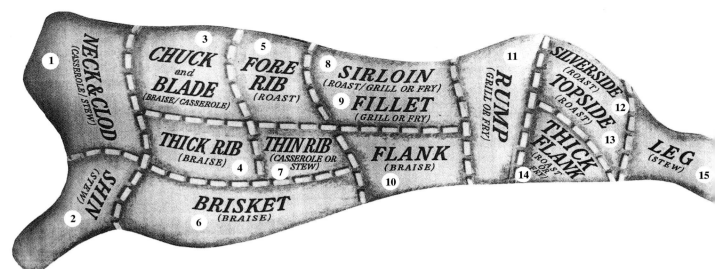

The English are passionate meat eaters. The best beef comes mainly from Scotland, with the famous Angus beef coming from Aberdeen, its meat well-known for its tenderness and characteristic flavor, which comes from the fine marbling of fat that makes cuts from it so juicy. Unfortunately, a small piece of meat off the bone is never as full-flavored as a larger one. Therefore the beef trolley in a restaurant such as Simpson's in the Strand in London, numbers amongst the special joys of good English cooking. This is a small trolley that carries enormous pieces of roast loin, from which a steak is cut before the eyes of the guest.

Since the 1980s the cattle epidemic BSE has been spreading in British herds, probably the result of using animal food inappropriate to the species. One can no longer exclude the possibility that the disease is transferable to humans. Nonetheless, *British beef*, above all, beef from the Angus breed of Scotland, remains as highly valued a delicacy as ever on the island – and at Simpson's in the Strand, which is over 150 years old and is the traditional dining place of the English upper classes, the wood panelled dining room remains occupied down to the last place at all times.

Roast beef is often the centerpiece of a Sunday meal. Normally the father of the house cuts the meat through the crisp brown crust to the middle where it is lean, pink, and juicy. It is this part which is prized above all by the connoisseur. Children rather prefer the outer, dark brown roasted slices of meat.

Roast beef is usually cooked in a hot oven, as is the yorkshire pudding that accompanies it. This is not a sweet pudding. A thick batter is made from flour, milk, and eggs and is cooked in beef suet or lard until it rises and becomes crispy and brown.

Right: The best meat for typically English roast beef comes from Scotland. That is the home of the Aberdeen-Angus, a well-known breed of cattle whose meat is of a particularly high quality.

The Most Important Cuts of Beef

1 *Neck and Clod* – Neck: for braising and stews
2 *Shin* – Shin, knuckle: for broiling and stews
3 *Chuck and Blade* – Neck and shoulder-blade: for braising
4 *Thick Rib* – Thick rib: for braising
5 *Fore Rib* – Rib: for roasting
6 *Brisket* – Breast: for braising
7 *Thin Rib* – Rib: for braising and stews
8 *Sirloin* – Steak, roast beef: for frying, or broiling
9 *Fillet* – Fillet or loin: for broiling or frying
10 *Flank* – Fleshy part of side of body between ribs and hip: for braising
11 *Rump* – Entrecote or rump steak: for broiling or frying
12 *Silverside* – Best side of round of beef: for roasting
13 *Topside* – Prime cut of beef: for roasting
14 *Thick Flank* – Fleshy cut: for roasting or stewing
15 *Leg* – Leg: for stewing

Right: The well-known London restaurant Simpson's in the Strand specializes in beef. Roast beef is served at the table there straight from the beef trolleys, which transport entire cuts of loin that are kept warm.
Roast beef is cooked in the oven. Due to the layer of fat which surrounds the meat and which is only removed on the plate, it remains tender and juicy. On the outside it is crispy brown, whilst inside it should remain pink.

Typical of a first-class Angus cut is the fine marbling effect of the fat.

The English Specialty: Variety in Preparing Meat

Beef Roll
Meatloaf English style: ground beef and ham cooked in a pudding mold and then turned out before serving.

Boiled Beef and Carrots with Dumplings
Salted and boiled breast of beef with carrots and dumplings.

Deviled Beef Bones
Ribs of beef left over from roast beef, in a spicy sauce of curry powder and cayenne pepper.

Oxtail Stew
Oxtail stew consists of braised oxtail served with the bones.

Pork and Apple Pie
Pork, onions, and apples, covered with potato purée and baked in the oven.

Potted Pork
Diced pork is slowly cooked in a covered saucepan, is then mashed and shredded and made into a spread. Eaten cold with toast.

Roast Beef with Yorkshire Pudding

Toad in the Hole
Pork sausages in a pancake mix.

Hot Pot
Lamb Stew

Serves 6

2 lb (1 kg) potatoes
6 lamb's kidneys, skinned and trimmed of fat
8 oz (250 g) mushrooms
3 onions
6 slices of shoulder of lamb about 1 inch (2 cm) thick
Salt, black pepper
6 oysters without shells
2 Tbs flakes of butter
1 Tbs chopped parsley

Peel and slice the potatoes thinly. Similarly slice the kidneys and mushrooms and cut the onions into rings. Preheat the oven to 350 °F (175 °C). Grease a deep ovenproof dish and line with a third of the potato slices. Place 3 slices of lamb on top, season with salt and pepper. Add one half of the kidneys, mushrooms, onions, and 3 oysters, then cover with a further third of the potatoes. Then add the remaining 3 slices of lamb and season too. Add a further layer consisting of the remaining kidneys, mushrooms, onions, and oysters, finishing off with a final layer of the rest of the potatoes. Add one pint (500 ml) water, cover the potatoes with flakes of butter. Cover and bake on the middle shelf of the oven for 90 minutes. Remove the lid and bake for a further 30 minutes, until the potatoes have browned lightly. Sprinkle with parsley.

Pies and Puddings

There are several differences between pies or pasties and puddings, and it is important in this respect not to confuse puddings with desserts of the same name.

1. Pies are cooked in shallow pans which are rarely taller than about 2 inches (5 cm). Puddings are cooked in deep bowls which are at least twice as tall.

2. The dough for a pie consists of plain flour, fat, salt, pepper, and cold water. For a pudding dough the fat is replaced with beef suet and self-raising flour is mainly used, because it contains a leavening agent.

3. Pies are cooked in the oven, puddings steamed.

Steak and Kidney Pudding
(See illustrations)

Dough

14 oz (400 g) self-raising flour or 14 oz (400 g) wheat flour, mixed with 1 tsp baking powder
$^1/_2$ tsp each of salt and black pepper
7 oz (200 g) beef suet, grated or chopped

Filling

2 lb (1 kg) rump steak
8 oz (250 g) veal kidneys
Salt, black pepper
2 Tbs flour
4 Tbs chopped shallots or onions
$^1/_2$ cup (125 ml) port or strong ale
$^1/_2$ cup (125 ml) beef stock
2 tsp Worcestershire Sauce

To make the dough mix the flour with the salt and pepper and knead with the beef suet and a little cold water into a smooth ball. Roll this out on a plate.
To make the filling chop the meat and kidneys into squares, season and toss in the flour.

Grease a tall pudding basin and line it with dough, keeping a little back.
Put the meat and kidneys with the shallots into the basin. Mix the port, beef stock, and Worcestershire Sauce and pour over the filling. Cover with the rest of the dough, pressing the edges together firmly so that the dough encloses the pudding completely, thus ensuring that no steam escapes during cooking.
Wrap the pudding basin in a cloth and steam for 3–4 hours in a bain-marie. The crust of dough should appear to be slightly damp at the end of cooking.
Steak and kidney pudding is best served with a strong ale.

Opposite: Hot Pot, photographed at the Riverhouse Hotel in Blackpool

An Adventure in English Taste

Sauces

"In England there are sixty different religious sects but only one sauce." This was supposedly said by Francesco Caraccioli, the very admiral who was hanged in 1799 from the mast of his frigate on Nelson's orders. He was certainly wrong, because there was and still is an abundance of sauces. The English preference for fried or boiled meat rather makes separate sauces a necessity, because both ways of preparing meat fail to provide the juices for sauces. Aside from horseradish and mustard sauces, there are a number of strong chutneys and ketchups, which were originally prepared at home in the kitchens of farmers and wealthy citizens from the surplus of either fruit or vegetables. Today they are mostly manufactured commercially.

Mustard Sauce is the British Favorite

The most widespread sauce is mustard. Since time immemorial wild mustard has grown everywhere in the British Isles, but it was the Romans who knew what use to make of it. They mixed the mustard plant with other spices, wine, and herbs and used it to season beef that had been broiled on a spit. The passion for mustard also continued following the collapse of the Roman Empire. By means of this seasoning, which is quite easy to make, salt meat and salted fish gained in flavor during the winter when other side dishes were lacking.

When the demand for mustard became ever greater people took to grinding mustard seeds (with the help of cannon balls!) into a coarse powder, and mixing it with horseradish, in order to achieve a hotter flavor. The mixture was then moistened and rolled into balls. In this way this popular item was easier to transport. It was then in kitchens that a sauce was made from these mustard balls by adding vinegar, cider or apple, and cherry juice.

To all appearances mustard powder, as we know it today, was invented by a certain Mrs Clements. She had the intelligent idea of grinding mustard seeds in a corn mill and of then carefully sifting them. The "Durham mustard" which she produced was an immediate and great commercial success.

The London firm Keens in Garlick Hill went one step further and manufactured mustard in jars for the eating houses of the city. The successor to this firm was a certain Jeremiah Colman, a miller from Norwich whose business was so successful that he dedicated himself entirely to mustard in 1814. A careful mixture of light and dark mustard seeds, to which was added turmeric, produced a mustard with a strong taste which is still available today as "English mustard."

With the passing of time a wide variety of very different mustards was developed. Today mustard comes mild, sweet, and strong, flavored with herbs, as well as packaged mustard seeds for producing one's own. Colman's in Norwich have their own mustard shop and a mustard museum, both great tourist attractions. There are also manufacturers of mustard delicacies such as the company Wiltshire Tracklements. This company began on a small scale selling their first pot of mustard in the local pub. Today four coarse grained varieties of mustard are made: strong mustard for ham, sausages, and pies; an aromatic "black" mustard; a tarragon mustard; and one which has honey added.

Worcestershire Sauce –
A Catastrophe To Begin With

One of the most famous English sauces, Worcestershire sauce, has its origins in Britain's colonial period. It is not served separately with the meal but is for seasoning during cooking. The story of how it originated is quite remarkable.

Lord Sandys, who was governor in Bengal for a while during the reign of Queen Victoria, found the local cuisine to his taste and persuaded his cook to give him the recipe for that "magic" sauce which he was constantly using. At home he entrusted two druggists with the preparation. John Lea and William Perrin from Worcester made the sauce following the recipe to the letter,

Left: Two different types of mustard seeds are ground to make mustard powder with as little heat arising during the process as possible. They are subsequently sieved to remove any remaining husks.

Left: The finished powder has a typical, luminous yellow color. This is the most widely-used form of mustard in England.

Right: Mustard powder is packed in cans. Before use, water or a little vinegar is stirred in by the cook or person eating.

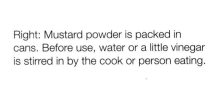

but when they sampled the result together with Lord Sandys they found that what they had prepared was undrinkable.

Lea and Perrin put the barrels containing the sauce in the furthermost corner of a stockroom where they forgot them. Several years later whilst clearing up they discovered the dusty barrels and tried the sauce anew. To their great surprise the preparation had in the meantime matured into a wonderfully spicy sauce. The two men immediately began producing the sauce on a commercial basis.

That was in the year 1837. The original Worcestershire sauce is still prepared according to the original recipe even today and is sold all over the world to lend its piquant flavor to many very varied dishes. Naturally the recipe remains a secret, but it is known that malt and spirit vinegar, sugar molasses, salt, anchovies, tamarinds, shallots, chillies, soya sauce, and garlic are all ingredients. Today Worcestershire sauce matures for three years before it is sold.

A Nation of Sauce Lovers

The classic English recipes for fish and meat, broiling and boiling, all produce no sauces. Resourceful housewives and cooks have, therefore, devised a wealth of sauces aside from mustard sauce and Worcestershire sauce.

Caper Sauce
Made from capers, butter, flour, and the juices from whatever meal is being prepared, be it lamb, beef or fish. Served with boiled meat and fish.

Cheese Sauce
A cheese specialty from Wales. Served with the Welsh national vegetable the leek, which is either boiled or au gratin.

Cream Sauce
Made from cream, flour, and butter. Shrimp in Cream Sauce, sprinkled with parmesan and baked in the oven, is a popular Welsh dish.

Cumberland Sauce
Made from orange and lemon peel and ground ginger, a reduction of red wine, port, and redcurrant jelly. Served with game, ham, and cold poultry.

Horseradish Sauce
Made from horseradish, vinegar, sugar, mustard powder, cream as well as salt and pepper. Served with roast beef and fish such as smoked trout, eel or grilled salmon.

Lemon Butter Sauce
A butter sauce which is flavored with freshly squeezed lemon juice and thickened with cornstarch. Served with boiled pike, found above all on the Devon coast.

Mint Sauce
Sugar, diluted wine or malt vinegar and finely chopped fresh mint leaves are used to make this sauce. Goes with roast lamb.

Onion Sauce
Made from onions cooked in butter and plenty of cream. Served particularly with shoulder of lamb, a London specialty.

Orange and Port Wine Sauce
A sauce made from orange juice and port, and then thickened with cornstarch. Particularly suited to fried and grilled poultry.

Raisin and Celery Sauce
This thickened sauce is made by combining chopped celery and raisins, and is flavored with dry cider. Served with freshly boiled ham.

Rhubarb Sauce
Served in Bristol with mackerel. For this reason rhubarb sauce also contains no sugar, but dry cider and lemon juice instead which gives it a slightly sharp spicy flavor.

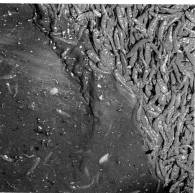

Left: An important ingredient of Worcestershire sauce are dried chillies. Other ingredients include malt and spirit vinegar, molasses, anchovies, tamarinds, shallots, soya sauce, and garlic.

Left: The chillies macerate in the stock for up to three years. The sauce is then filtered and bottled.

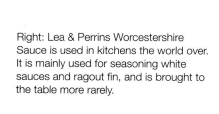

Right: Lea & Perrins Worcestershire Sauce is used in kitchens the world over. It is mainly used for seasoning white sauces and ragout fin, and is brought to the table more rarely.

Cheddar, Stilton & Co.

English monks of the Cistercian order, who moved to the valleys of Yorkshire following the Norman Conquest in 1066, are regarded as the founders of the English cheese making tradition. From these modest beginnings a highly varied culture of cheese making has developed, although the different cheeses and their variations are in the main only of local significance. English cheeses, unlike French ones, have proved unable to gain worldwide recognition – with the notable exception of Stilton.

Stilton, the only English cheese that has conquered the world, is manufactured exclusively in Leicestershire, Nottinghamshire, and Derbyshire. Blue Stilton, a blue-veined cheese made in large cylindrical shapes, is protected by trademark. It has a creamy consistency and is uniformly shot through with the blue-green veins of *penicillium roquefortii*. White Stilton is crumbly and mild, without the blue veins, but nonetheless has a quite unmistakable flavor. Seven manufacturers are members of the Stilton Cheese Makers' Association, of which one, Colston Bassett, is the producer of the only unpasteurized variety.

The most widely manufactured cheese in England is Cheddar. This hard cheese, which originates from Somerset's Cheddar Gorge, has a strong characteristic flavor and requires one to two years to mature. Mild Cheddar is sold after just three months in storage. The older the cheese is, the stronger its flavor and the deeper its color.

Cheddar is made in a way that is as unusual as the cheese's flavor. Cheddaring is an independent manufacturing process, in which cut pieces of the curd are layered in a cake-like shape, prior to the maturing process. This technique is best observed in the making of Sage Derby, where a green sage-infusion is used to create a striking marbling effect by sprinkling it upon the layers.

Although the majority of cheeses are manufactured commercially today, there are still twenty-four farms in England where Cheddar is produced in the traditional fashion, in some cases even with unpasteurized milk.

The great variety of English cheeses extends from the soft, unpressed Crowdie, which is made from sour milk or buttermilk, by way of the semi-soft varieties – to which most of the blue-veined cheeses belong – and the somewhat harder cheeses like Wensleydale or the Welsh cheese Caerphilly (which today at any rate is produced in many parts of the West of England), to the hard types, of which after Cheddar the most widely known are Cheshire, Leicester, and

Cheshire

Double Gloucester

Creamery Goat's Curd

Cheddar

Harbourne Blue

Caerphilly

Lancashire

Beenleigh Blue

Double Gloucester. Most of these cheeses are made from cow's milk, but there are by now many regional variations, which are manufactured from both goat's milk and sheep's milk.

The cheesemaking traditions of the Cistercian monks have been maintained in the countryside. Following the dissolution of the monasteries farmers continued the tradition. Hence, there are still many agricultural businesses which use the monks' methods for making cheese and this gives rise to such unusual cheeses as Swaledale or Danbydale.

However, the English cheeseboard offers yet further specialties, for example herb-flavored cheeses, smoked cheese, cheese veined with elderberry wine (Red Windsor), or that flavored with garlic, paprika, or even sweet pickles, cheese rolled in crushed oatmeal (Scottish Caboc), or rolled in ash.

A Delicacy: Stilton with Port

A small village on the route between London and York gave Stilton its name. It is regarded as the best of all blue English cheeses and can take its place self-confidently alongside the world famous Roquefort from France and Gorgonzola from Italy. Stilton is a white cheese with a light yellow hue and a strong blue-green mold culture. The rind is dark and wrinkled, the taste spicy. Connoisseurs enjoy it with a glass of fine port.

English cheesemasters are in agreement that Stilton should never be hollowed out with a spoon. Instead it is cut into wedge-shaped pieces, and in this way the consistency remains the same until the last piece. However, when hollowed out with a spoon, it dries out.

There are lovers of cheese who try to prevent this by pouring port into the hollow. This is not to be recommended – as cheesemakers like to emphasize – because it makes the cheese wet and unappetizing, as well as discoloring it. The rule of thumb is port with, but not in, the cheese.

Stilton

Pearoche

Before the finished cheeses are put into storage they are smoothed over again with a soft mass made from broken pieces, in order to obtain a uniform surface.

The whole cheeses are run through with steel needles. The resulting air holes provide the means for the mold to spread successfully inside the cheese.

Mature Stilton ready for sale in its characteristic cylindrical shape.

The Picnic

Scarcely had the English moved from the land into cities in the 19th century when they began to long for the return of country life – perhaps one of the reasons why the picnic became extraordinarily popular. There are two versions of the picnic in England. The formal, classical picnic takes place at cultural or sporting events; during the interval of an opera performance at Glyndebourne or between the acts of an open-air performance of Shakespeare in Regent's Park or Polesden Lacey; at the tennis championships at Wimbledon, horseracing at Ascot, cricket at Lords, and on Derby Day at Epsom. The informal, rather more spontaneous picnic is suited to any excursion either on water or into the country.

A formal picnic is prepared by carefully packing all of the "ingredients" in a large hamper and placing this in the trunk of the Rolls Royce. The food must be of the highest quality – for example smoked salmon, fresh strawberries, a little cold pheasant, butter, and very thinly sliced dark bread. A few bottles of champagne will ensure an atmosphere of gaiety, even when one's team is losing or the opera is proving endless.

For an informal picnic something edible is stashed in plastic bags, which are put on the back seat of a rather less noble automobile – cold chicken, sandwiches, fruit flans, cheese, and thermos flasks containing very strong tea. And don't forget the salt!

Equipment for a Classic Picnic

1 Strawberries and cream
2 Fresh fruit
3 Smoked salmon
4 Cheese
5 Fresh salad
6 Champagne
7 Sandwiches
8 A picnic hamper, equipped with plates, cutlery, glasses, cups, a can opener, salt and pepper, a thermos flask, and containers which can be kept firmly shut

Just as important is a blanket, and a croquet set is also *de rigeur*.

Fish and Chips

Fish and chips is the most popular dish amongst the English general public. It is, so to speak, the national dish of the person in the street. Fish and chips (the popular colloquial abbreviation is "fish'n'chips") is a typically English specialty, which can be bought from takeaway kiosks and can even be eaten out of newspaper according to the classic popular version.

Haddock and cod as well as sole and plaice form the basis. Typical of the meal is the thick batter which puffs up in the deep fryer and which is seasoned with salt and pepper before eating.

Fish and chip shops come from the days of the Industrial Revolution, which began at the end of the 18th century in England. They provided food that was economical, quick, and nourishing for the factory workers. Naturally, chips – actually French fries – were added as a side dish, because potatoes were cheap and available in large amounts, and the fat had already been heated up to cook the fish.

Today England is full of fish and chip shops. Newspaper has certainly had its day, but the preference is still for eating fish and chips from the paper whilst standing or sitting at bare melamine tables. As far as the refined city version goes, one can take pleasure in ordering a tasteful French dry white wine with one's meal.

In principle all potato varieties are suited to making chips but most cooks prefer varieties that are mealy and turn out firm. If the chips are soaked before frying for about half an hour, thus removing the starch, they will turn out to be especially crispy and will not stick together.

Fish and Chips

Serves 4

Batter

1½ cups (200 g) flour, 1 Tbs sugar
4 Tbs beer
¼ tsp salt, 2 egg yolks
6 Tbs milk, 6 Tbs water
2 egg whites

Sieve the flour into a bowl, add the sugar, and mix both together. Pour the beer, salt, and egg yolk into the middle. Stir everything together well. Mix the milk and water and add gradually until the batter has a thick, smooth consistency. Leave to stand for 30 minutes, then beat the egg whites until they are firm and carefully mix with the batter.

Chips

2 lb (1 kg) potatoes
Oil for deep-frying

Peel the potatoes, cut them into chips ³/₈ inch (1 cm) thick and leave them to soak. Fill the deep fryer with oil and heat to a temperature of 325 °F (160 °C). Remove the chips from the water, dry them thoroughly and place them in the deep fryer. When they are cooked remove them from the oil and leave to drain. Increase the temperature of the oil to 350 °F (180 °C) and then fry them until they are brown and crispy. Remove, leave to drain on kitchen paper and season with salt.

Fish

2 lb (1 kg) fresh white, boned fillets of sea-fish, cut into portions
Worcestershire Sauce, lemon juice, hot mustard, flour

Wash and dry the fish, sprinkle with the seasoning and dust with flour. Dip the portions in batches into the batter and place in the deep fryer after the potatoes. Fry for 4–5 minutes until they are golden brown, remove from the oil, and season with salt. Serve with malt vinegar for seasoning.

Huntin', Shootin', and Fishin'

When rich and powerful landowners appropriated enormous tracts of land in the 18th and 19th centuries, the poor people of England lost the right to either hunt (and to shoot) or to fish on land that had previously been in the public domain. Hunting, and to a certain extent also fishing, now became pastimes of the landed aristocracy. In such circles the "g" tends to be left off of the end of words ending in "ing" in everyday speech – which is the reason why "huntin', shootin', and fishin'" has generally become accepted as a *terminus technicus* for the leisure pastimes of the upper classes.

There are 825,000 hunters in Great Britain today who shoot their own Sunday lunch – mainly pheasants, partridges, rabbits, woodpigeons, and hare. Only deer hunting is reserved for marksmen. The majority of venison that is served in hotels and restaurants or sold in supermarkets actually comes from deer which has been raised on farms.

The Grouse

The most sought after game bird is the grouse, which is to be found on the Yorkshire Moors and in the marshland of north western England. The landowners there sell or rent out their hunting rights not only to shooting-parties, which pay a lot of money for a shoot that extends over several days complete with beaters and dogs, but also to locals who will perhaps pay with a bottle of whisky to go hunting for a day.

The season for hunting grouse always begins on August 12 – the so-called "Glorious Twelfth" – and lasts until December 10. It is on August 12 that a competition takes place annually to spirit the grouse as quickly as possible to the hotels and restaurants of London. Private jets as well as helicopters are used although there are competitors whose sense of tradition impels them rather to dash from Yorkshire on a horse; after a few miles a prearranged change of horses takes place.

The head chefs of the Savoy, Claridges, or the Dorchester are not exactly taken with the idea of preparing and serving a grouse that has only been shot a few hours before, since game birds should hang for two to three days, and grouse in fact for up to ten days, so that the flesh becomes tender and the flavor can fully develop. They bow to the wishes of their guests, so that on every 12th of August a grouse dish continues to be offered on the menu. Like other game birds, grouse are counted in braces, or pairs, so that the accepted way of referring to two such birds is not as "two grouse" or "a couple of grouse" but always as "a brace of grouse."

The grouse is too timid to be bred successfully. Since the main part of its diet consists of aromatic foliage, its flesh is regarded as especially tasty. Therefore the hunt for this sought-after game bird is even today quite an occasion not only for reasons of tradition.

Background: A partridge shoot in the county of Norfolk at the turn of the century.

Grouse in Red Wine Sauce

Serves 6

3 oven-ready grouse
1/2 cup (125 g) butter
2 carrots
One large onion
2 garlic cloves
1 1/4 cup (250 ml) red wine
2 cups (400 ml) bouillon
1 tsp thyme
Salt, black pepper
8 oz (250 g) small mushrooms
1 Tbs flour

Cut the grouse into portions and brown them all over in butter. Remove and put to one side.

Wash or peel the carrots, onion, and garlic, chop finely and cook in the meat juices. Add the wine as well as the meat stock, thyme, and seasoning. Place the grouse in the resulting stock, cover and cook over a low heat for about 20 minutes until done.

Meanwhile wipe the mushrooms and cook in the remaining butter.

Remove the grouse from the sauce. Reduce the sauce whilst stirring, pass through a sieve and thicken with the flour. Add the meat and the mushrooms to the sauce and leave to simmer for roughly a further 5 minutes. Served with thin slices of bread fried in butter and sprinkled with parsley.

Fishing Grounds

The best English freshwater fish are the salmon and the brown trout. The rainbow trout – which contains a lot of fat and is a product of intense breeding – rather lacks flavor and is merely regarded as a very unsatisfactory substitute. The most suitable places to fish are the Test in Hampshire (a very beautiful river rich in calcium carbonate with a rich stock of brown trout), the Lunn in Lancashire (where salmon can be caught, although this river often suffers from the attentions of poachers), and the rivers Tovey and Lyd in Devon. There are also salmon and trout in many Welsh streams. The grayling – an older and often forgotten member of the trout family – can be found in the Wharfe in Yorkshire and in the Wye in Derbyshire, where it is still much sought after, and also on the Chatsworth estate of the Dukes of Devonshire. Trout and salmon are increasingly farmed in enormous enclosures on the coast. However, these cultivated fish do not possess the unmistakable flavor of the real fish in the wild.

England's Special Beers

Ale and Stout

Burton-upon-Trent in the Midlands is regarded as the beer capital of Great Britain. It is there that the headquarters of two important breweries, Bass and Ind Coope, are located, as well as those of some smaller breweries.

It all began with ale was first brewed in Edinburgh in Scotland. Ale is milder and sweeter than beer and is often drunk directly after a whisky, to a certain extent as a chaser. Before the introduction of tea and coffee, people in rural communities drank homebrewed ale or small beer, an archaic term for weak beer, to compensate for their low daily intake of fluids, and were legitimately able to assume that there were fewer dangers concealed in such preparations than in city tapwater.

When it became possible to brew beer due to the introduction of hops and other ingredients, the initial reaction of drinkers to this bitter drink was one of scepticism. After a while, however, beer won many devotees.

There is a rich and varied selection of beers in England. One belief amongst drinkers is that the more northerly one proceeds the stronger the beer becomes. The most popular form is traditionally bitter, a strong beer with a relatively high alcohol content which is never served cold but at cellar temperature. The English swear that the flavor of bitter is shown to its best advantage when served in this way. Some English drinkers are less concerned with a full head of froth on their beer, preferring instead a full glass of frothless beer.

Text continues on p. 38

1   2   3

A Selection of English Beers

1 Thomas Hardy's Ale: Rare amongst ales, brewed in vintages
2 The Bishop's Tipple: A barley wine, a strong winter warmer
3 Bass Pale Ale: Mild in flavor, with a low alcohol content
4 Royal Oak Ale: A real full-flavored ale
5 Strong Pale Ale: Heavily hopped strong ale
6 Stonehenge Exhibition: Strong ale from the Wiltshire brewery
7 Stonehenge Ginger Beer: Beer made with ginger
8 Whitbread Best Bitter: Dark, strong bitter
9 John Smith's Bitter: Bitter with little carbonic acid and a high alcohol content

Below: Pubs or "Public Houses" are licensed premises where it is permitted to serve alcoholic drinks in public and at specific times. They have, as a result of this, turned into meeting places for people to socialize and are an integral part of English everyday life. For foreign visitors the most striking feature is the strict rule about closing time, which compels them to take their leave of the bar unusually early (11 o'clock at night), when compared with what is normal internationally.

Beer is principally drunk in the pub. The English pub is an institution, consisting as a rule of two rooms. In the Public Bar people can stand at the bar and drink their beer without paying any attention to dress codes. The second room, or Lounge Bar, will be fitted out with tables where it is possible to order something to eat.

Some old-fashioned country pubs also have a "Snug," a small cozy room where a few customers can enjoy a drink in peace and quiet.

Beer is ordered in pints or halves. The pint is the standard measure, roughly equating to a half liter, which is poured into a glass mug with a handle or a tall, straight-sided glass according to the customer's preference. It is drawn from the barrel in the cellar by pulling the traditional pumps that always adorn English bars.

Types of British Beer

Ale
Top fermented ale is one of the most well-known and oldest types of beer in England. The best ale is considered to be the so-called "Real Ale." It should still contain a little sugar after fermentation so that secondary fermentation takes place in the barrel and in this way its particular flavor can develop. The requisite type of barley only grows in the North of England. However, the term "Ale" stands more generally for an entire family of beers with various offspring.

Barley Wine
There are many versions of barley wine, a strong ale brewed for winter consumption, many of which bear the name of a bishop. These names are reminiscent of the time when many breweries still belonged to the clergy.

Bitter
This is traditionally the most popular and widely drunk beer in the whole of England. It is brewed with a high hop content. It has a strong flavor and contains much less carbonic acid when compared to German beer for example, but has a higher alcoholic content. One of the most widely known varieties of bitter is India Pale Ale. The name derives from the fact that it was originally brewed to be exported to the colonies. Having a higher specific gravity and hop content than usual, it was better able to survive traveling the long distances to faraway climes.

Bombardier Ale
A premium bitter with a distinctive rich copper color and a characteristic robust flavour.

Brown Ale
The most well-known dark ale comes from Newcastle: Newcastle Brown Ale is reddish brown and dry, and can be bought anywhere in England.

Mild
An ale that tastes like its name. It is only lightly flavored with hops and has a low alcohol content. It is particularly popular in the Midlands, with Burton-upon-Trent being regarded as the most important place for the brewing of Mild and Bitter.

Old Peculier
A strong, dark ale, sweet and heavy in taste and best when first poured.

Yorkshire Stingo
A regional specialty from Northern England: strong, particularly dry, and practically black – a dark version of barley wine.

Porter
A practically forgotten type of beer once brewed in London, which is now above all brewed in Ireland and which enjoyed a renaissance a few years ago as a lighter version of stout. Porter has a slightly sweet taste.

Stout
Stout is a malted beer – the heaviest, most full-bodied and darkest of beers, which is made from malt in the whole of the British Isles. It is amongst those beers with the highest alcoholic content. One of the most widely known varieties of stout is surely Guinness, a beer synonymous with Ireland.

Wine from Apples

Cider

In the fall, England's crop of special, bittersweet crab-apples and sour cider apples are harvested. These apples do not taste particularly pleasant but are excellent for making cider. The dry cider which they produce can contain up to eight percent alcohol.

Cider usually comes from the extensive fruit cultivating regions of south-western England. The apples are chopped into small pieces and pressed. The juice and the pulp flow into large storage tanks and enormous barrels in which the solid bodies settle at the bottom. It takes up to three weeks for cider to ferment. In the interests of maintaining quality the finished product is blended and bottled for sale. Cider bottles bear a resemblance to champagne bottles. Cider is also served directly from the barrel in English pubs.

The "history" of cider supposedly stretches back to the first century after the birth of Jesus Christ. The story is that Joseph of Aramithea came to England after the death of Christ. He founded a Christian monastery at Glastonbury in Somerset, whose ruins can still be seen today. In the Arthurian legend this place has a mysterious name – Avalon, which means nothing less than "Island of Apples." The legend has it that Joseph stood on a hill at Glastonbury and ate an apple. He spat out the pips and where they fell apple trees grew.

In fact it was the Romans who established apple cultivation in the British Isles. With them they brought the varieties from which most of today's cider apples are descended: French Long-tail, White Swan, or Slack My Girdle. The special feature of cider apples is their "internal life." Whilst they have sweet juice, their pulp is sour – which is quite important for the dry flavor and the correct acid content of the cider.

There are still farmers today who produce cider for their own consumption as used to be the case. However, the major part of production comes from the cider factories. Cider that is made in the traditional way is called "scrumpy" in the West Country – a variety particularly strong in alcohol, which many an unsuspecting drinker has underestimated in the past.

Left: Cider – fermented apple juice – is very widespread in England and available in virtually every pub fresh from the barrel. It is drunk from heavy glass mugs.

Merry Christmas

English Christmases are best enjoyed in the country. Traditional English customs are still upheld there, and the classic specialties are served for what is the most important festival of all. In past centuries the centerpiece of the banquet was the large head of a wild boar that was garlanded with laurel – reminiscent of Roman times. In the meantime it has been replaced by the turkey from the New World. This should be neither boiled nor roasted – as it says in the old English rhyme:

Turkey boiled is turkey spoiled.
And turkey roast is turkey lost.
But for turkey braised
The Lord be praised!

The highpoint of every English Christmas meal is the plum pudding – a heavy fruit cake, which is often made months before and is carried solemnly to the table for the Christmas meal covered in flaming cognac. The plum pudding is so closely bound up with the idea of Christmas in the minds of many English people that it is called "Christmas pudding."

The recipe grew out of that for plum porridge, which bore a closer resemblance to a soup. It consisted of bouillon, dried plums or raisins, seasoning, and wine and was thickened with bread crumbs. With the passing of time plum porridge had an increasingly firm consistency, and meat, of which the only remnant was beef suet, disappeared completely as an ingredient. This hardening of the texture led to the pudding mixture being wrapped in a cloth and so cooked. Once the pudding had been cooked for many hours, it was hung up somewhere in order to allow it to "mature" for several months.

On Christmas Day it was unwrapped and talismans were inserted: a silver sixpence which indicated wealth; a horseshoe for luck; a button for a bachelor or an old maid, and much more. The pudding was then cooked anew for a few hours. Today the Christmas pudding is usually steamed in a pudding bowl in a bain-marie, and the beef suet, the last remnant of the original plum porridge is usually replaced by butter or margarine.

It is generally accepted that Christmas mince pies are considerably older than Christmas pudding. They were originally rectangular in shape and consisted of dough, which enclosed a filling of chopped up meat with seasoning and dried fruit. Once the crusaders had returned from the Middle East, these pies were decorated with a small Christ figure and were served at Christmas.

Oliver Cromwell and the Puritans not only forbade all pagan festivities, such as dancing around the maypole or Halloween bonfires, but also all Christmas celebrations – including mince pies.

Following Charles II's accession to the throne in the year 1660 Christmas was restored to its rightful place, and there were mince pies again, now small, round pastry pies with a filling of dried fruit, candied lemon peel, finely chopped beef suet, seasoning, sugar, and brandy. The filling has to draw for several months before it can be used for cooking.

Christmas pudding, as well as mince pies, is served with brandy butter or hard sauce, a creamy butter sauce which is seasoned to taste with lemon juice, brandy, or whisky. Sometimes chopped almonds are also stirred into the mixture according to a tradition that dates back to the Middle Ages.

Background: A Christmas dinner in England cannot be compared with the rather more contemplative, solemn Christmas meal in continental Europe – as the paper hats and the decorations make clear.

Traditional Braised Turkey

1 oven ready turkey, weighing about 13 lb (6 kg)
1 portion of stuffing
1 cup (175 g) butter
Salt, black pepper
8 oz (250 g) sliced bacon
2 tsp cornstarch
2–3 Tbs poultry juices
Extra wide aluminum foil

Preheat the oven to 425 °F (220 °C). Stuff the turkey. Place 2 large strips of aluminum foil so that they cross each other diagonally on the baking tin and place the turkey on the foil. Rub the bird all over with butter and season with salt and pepper, place the slices of bacon upon the turkey breast.

Wrap the turkey in the foil – making sure that it is well sealed, but not too tightly. Cook for 40 minutes on the lower shelf of the oven. Reduce the temperature to 340 °F (170 °C) and cook for a further 3¼ hours. Then open the foil and remove the bacon slices, so that the skin can brown and become crisp. Increase the temperature to 400 °F (200 °C) and cook the turkey for a further 45 minutes, frequently pouring the braising juices over the bird.

Test with a skewer to see if it is cooked. Place the turkey on a preheated plate and leave in a warm place for 30–60 minutes, only after that should the meat be carved.

Pour the fat and braising juices into a skillet, skim any excess fat. Leave to simmer over a low flame, stir in the cornstarch and poultry juices, reduce the resulting sauce until it is thick.

Pork, Sage, and Onion Stuffing
Traditional Turkey Stuffing

4 heaped tsp white bread crumbs
1 heaped tsp dried sage
1 large onion, finely chopped
2 lb (1 kg) sausagemeat
salt, black pepper
2 tsp medium strong mustard

Mix the white breadcrumbs, sage, and onion in a bowl, add a dash of boiling water and stir well. Stir in the sausagemeat and season with salt, pepper, and mustard.

Chestnut and Apple Stuffing

1 can of puréed chestnuts, contents weighing 1 lb (450 g), unsweetened
1 lb 7 oz (700 g) sausagemeat
1 lb (450 g) peeled, cored and finely diced cooking apples
1 beaten egg
Salt, black pepper

Mix all of the ingredients together, then stir in the egg and season the stuffing with salt and pepper.

Christmas Pudding

Serves 8–10

½ cup (100 g) beef suet
¼ cup each of candied orange peel and lemon peel
½ cup (100 g) candied cherries
½ cup (100 g) almonds
¾ cup (150 g) each of raisins and currants
1 cup (100 g) flour
5 oz (150 g) bread crumbs
½ cup (100 g) brown sugar
Grated rind and juice of 1 lemon
2 large pinches of cinnamon, cloves and pimiento
½ tsp salt
Juice of one orange
About 1 cup of milk
3 eggs
3 Tbs Cognac

Chop the suet, candied orange and lemon peel, cherries, and almonds up into small pieces; wash the raisins and currants in hot water.

Mix the fruit and almonds together in a bowl, add the suet, flour, breadcrumbs, sugar, lemon peel, seasoning, and salt and mix everything together well. Stir in the citrus juices and milk. Mix the eggs and Cognac together with a whisk, pour into the bowl and stir in. Bring some water to the boil in a large saucepan for the bain-marie. Grease a large pudding bowl and fill the bowl with the pudding mixture to a maximum of 2 inches (5 cm) below the rim. Cover the bowl with greased baking paper and then with aluminum foil and secure both sheets all around the bowl with string. Place in the boiling water – the bowl must always be two thirds submerged in water – cover and steam the pudding on a medium heat for 4 hours. Then leave to cool and turn out of the bowl. Wrap in a cloth which has been soaked in brandy and leave in the refrigerator wrapped up in aluminum foil for at least 4 weeks. Before serving steam the pudding in boiling water in the bain-marie for a further 3 hours. Serve with brandy butter.

Honor Moore

Scotland

In Scotland they say "S mairg a ni tarcuis air biadh," which roughly translated means "He who has contempt for food is a fool." The inhabitants of the barren country in the north of Great Britain have learnt to make the best of the meagre gifts of nature. These tenacious, strong-willed mountain and farming people preserve their traditions. Here, a strong sense of loyalty exists and the clans hand their family recipes down from generation to generation. Scottish cattle-breeders have become famous for the Aberdeen Angus, a breed which in the judgment of connoisseurs worldwide provides the best meat. However, it was left to English neighbors to make from this the British national meal, roast beef. The modest and unassuming Scots, on the other hand, hold their own national dish in great esteem. This is the legendary haggis, which consists of sheep's intestines cooked in a sheep's stomach. Scottish distillers have made a great contribution through the manufacture and refinement of whisky: Scotch whisky is regarded as the quintessential whisky per se. Prized above all amongst connoisseurs is single malt whisky, which offers an unbelievable variety of aromas and flavors – to say nothing of the great number of whisky cocktails.

The small, peat-covered cottages throughout the countryside recall the art of crofting, the predominant form of cultivation over the centuries in this difficult land. The crofters, small tenant farmers, grew above all oats, barley, and root vegetables on their plots and also kept some livestock – cattle, goats, and sheep. Their diet was very simple, consisting nonetheless of tasty as well as filling dishes. Their menu offered porridge and oatcakes, salted fish and mutton, and occasionally salmon and shrimps. Many traditional Scottish dishes can be traced back to the culinary art of the farmer's wife, and some of these dishes have also found admirers outside the Scottish Highlands. The art of preparing the very tasty dish, porridge, from simple oats, owes just as much to the inventiveness of the Scots as to the country's great tradition of baking and their knowledge of making cheese.

Left: John Milroy, proprietor of a whisky business with a comprehensive selection.

Haggis

Haggis is regarded as the Scottish national dish *per se*. The Scots are fond of telling foreign guests that the haggis is a primeval, fabulous creature, which lives in the forests and is difficult to shoot because it knows how to outsmart hunters time and time again. In reality it is nothing more than a stuffed sheep's stomach – a particular kind of sausage.

Haggis is made and sold all the year round by butchers all over Scotland. However, it has two highpoints in the year, both on special days: at Hogmanay, or New Year's Eve; and on Burns' Night on January 25, when tribute is paid to Robert Burns, the greatest Scottish poet aside from Walter Scott. This day marks the anniversary of his birth. His poem addressed to a haggis (see right) is a part of a solemn ceremony. The bearer of the haggis, followed by the bearer of the whisky, accompanied by pipers, brings the dish on a silver platter into the dining room. The host makes the first incision in the haggis with a long knife, which the Scotsman traditionally carries with him in his knee-length socks, and recites the poem to it. After this ceremony the platter is carried back to the kitchen, once again to the sound of bagpipes, where the haggis is served with clapshot, which is a purée of swedes and potatoes. Whisky is drunk with the haggis out of small glasses.

Haggis

1 sheep's stomach
Sheep offal (liver, heart, lung)
8 oz (250 g) lamb suet
Salt, black pepper
3 onions
1 lb (500 g) coarse oatmeal

Wash the sheep's stomach thoroughly, turn inside out and scrape clean. Place in cold salted water and leave to soak overnight.
Wash the offal and suet, place in boiling salted water and leave to simmer for 2 hours. Remove from the water, remove the windpipe and gristle and chop everything up finely or put it through the meat grinder. Peel the onions, blanch in cooking water, and chop up finely as well. Put the water to one side.
Cook the oatmeal in a pan slowly, until it becomes crisp. Mix with the other ingredients and knead with some cooking water into a smooth mixture. Fill the sheep's stomach with it so that it is about two thirds full, expel the air, sew it up – binding it in the middle if necessary – and prick the haggis several times so that it does not burst during cooking. Cover and cook in lightly boiling water for 3–4 hours. Afterwards keep hot and remove the threads. Once it has been cut serve with a lot of butter and clapshot – a purée of swedes and potatoes.

Butchers make haggis the whole year round. However, the dish is served especially on New Year's Eve and on Burns' Night, January 25.

The main ingredients for the haggis – liver, heart, lung, and lamb suet – are finely chopped or passed through the meat grinder.

Subsequently the mixture, enriched with chopped onions and spices and bound by cooked oatmeal, is stuffed into a sheep's stomach.

The finished haggis is highly regarded as a delicacy by all Scots. It is served hot with a lot of butter and clapshot, a purée of swedes and potatoes.

To a Haggis

Fair fa' your honest, sonsie face,
Great Chieftan o' the Puddin'-race!
Aboon them a' ye tak your place,
      Painch, tripe, or thairm:
Weel are ye wordy of a *grace*
      As lang's my arm.

The groaning trencher there ye fill,
Your hurdies like a distant hill
Your *pin* wad help to mend a mill
      In time o' need,
While thro' your pores the dews distil
      Like amber bead.

His knife see Rustic-labour dight,
An' cut you up wi' ready slight,
Trenching your gushing entrails bright
      Like onie ditch;
And then, O what a glorious sight,
      Warm-reekin, rich!

Then, horn for horn they stretch an' strive
Deil tak the hindmost, on the drive,
Till a' their weel-swall'd kytes belyve
      Are bent like drums;
Then auld Guidman, maist like to rive,
      Bethankit hums.

Is there that owre his French *ragout*,
Or *olio* that wad staw a sow,
Or *fricassee* wad mak her spew
      Wi' perfect sconner,
Looks down wi' sneering, scornfu' view
      On sic a dinner?

Poor devil! see him owre his trash,
As feckless as a wither'd rash,
His spindle shank a guid whip-lash,
      His nieve a nit;
Thro' bluidy flood or field to dash,
      O how unfit!

But mark the Rustic, *haggis-fed*,
The trembling earth resounds his tread,
Clap in his walie nieve a blade,
      He'll mak it whissle;
An' legs, an' arms, an' heads will sned,
      Like taps o' thrissle.

Ye Pow'rs wha mak mankind your care,
And dish them out their bill o' fare,
Auld Scotland wants nae skinking ware
      That jaups in luggies;
But, if ye wish her greatfu' pray'r,
      Gie her a *Haggis!*

Robert Burns (1759–1796)

Opposite: Ingredients for the haggis – sheep's offal, oatmeal, and onions. In many versions of the recipe, belly of pork and a piece of rib are also used – as illustrated here.

Scottish Specialties

Hotch Potch –
Vegetable Soup with Mutton

Howtowdie –
Stuffed Braised Chicken

Lady Tillypronie's Scotch Broth
Lamb and Vegetable Soup

Serves 4

1½ lb (750 g) breast of lamb
4 onions, peeled and sliced
3 turnips, washed and sliced
2 carrots, washed and sliced
8 peppercorns
2 small leeks, washed and cut into rings
1 stick of celery, sliced
3 Tbs pearl barley

Place the breast of lamb, two thirds each of the onions, turnips, and carrots in a good 2 pints (1 l) of salted water, add the peppercorns, bring to the boil, cover, and leave to simmer for 3 hours.
Leave to cool and skim off any fat. Drain off the stock and put to one side. Bone the meat and cut into pieces, throw away the fat and vegetables.
Clean out the saucepan. Return the stock with the remaining vegetables and the pearl barley to the saucepan, cover and simmer for 45 minutes. Add the meat and warm for 5 minutes in the vegetable broth. (The recipe was taken down by Lady Clark of Tillypronie around 1880. From 1841, when her family took in refugees from the revolution in France, she collected thousands of recipes. In 1851 she married a diplomat and became acquainted with the cuisines of many European countries on her travels.)

Ham and Haddock

1 large smoked haddock
2 Tbs butter
2 large slices of smoked ham
Black pepper

Immerse the fish almost completely in water, bring to the boil and boil for 5 minutes, turning it once. Remove from the water, and remove the skin and bones.
Melt the butter in a skillet and brown the slices of ham on both sides. Then place the fish on the ham, season with pepper, cover, and leave to cook for a further 3 minutes.

Fish Tobermory
Fish Fillets on Spinach
(Illustration opposite, far right)

1 lb (500 g) blanched spinach
2 Tbs butter
Salt, black pepper
Grated nutmeg
1 lb (500 g) fish fillets
1½ cups (350 ml) milk
1½ cups (350 ml) fish stock

Sauce

3 Tbs butter
3 Tbs flour
4 oz (100 g) grated cheese
Flakes of butter

Preheat the oven to 400 °F (200 °C). Wring out the spinach in a cloth and chop. Place in a saucepan with butter, season with salt, pepper, and nutmeg, and cook over a low heat until it is dry.
Place the fish in a shallow ovenproof dish, cover with milk and fish stock and cover the dish with greased aluminum foil. Bake for about 15 minutes in the oven, then remove the fish from the dish. Strain the stock and put to one side.
Clean and grease the ovenproof dish, place the spinach in it and distribute the fish on the spinach. Cover and keep hot in the oven.
For the sauce, prepare a roux of butter and flour, add the stock and simmer for 5 minutes. Stir in half the cheese and leave to melt. Pour the sauce over the fish, sprinkle with the remaining cheese and cover with flakes of butter. Broil until the cheese has melted.

Hotch Potch
Vegetable Soup with Mutton
(Illustration top left)

2 lb (1 kg) breast of lamb with bones
10 white peppercorns
3 pimiento seeds
2 bay leaves
1 stick of celery
4 carrots
4 turnips
6 scallions
1 cauliflower
1 Tbs chopped parsley
1 Tbs chives

Put the mutton in a generous 6 pints (3 l) of cold salted water with the seasoning to boil, cover and simmer gently until soft. Then remove from the water, separate from the bones, and cut into pieces. Put to one side. Pass the stock through a sieve. Wash the vegetables, chop into pieces, and cook in the stock. Before serving, warm the meat in the soup, then sprinkle with parsley and chives.

Fish Tobermory –
Fish Fillets on Spinach

Howtowdie
Stuffed Braised Chicken
(Illustration center)

Stuffing

2 cups bread crumbs
Milk
1 onion, peeled and chopped
2 tsp chopped parsley
Salt, black pepper

1 roasting chicken, weighing 3–4¹/₂ lb (1¹/₂–2 kg)
2 Tbs butter
6 onions, peeled and sliced
1³/₄ cups (350 ml) chicken stock
2 cloves
6 black peppercorns
1 pinch of grated nutmeg
2 lb (1 kg) spinach, washed
Chicken livers from the bird
2 Tbs heavy cream
Salt, black pepper

Preheat the oven to 480 °F (250 °C).
To make the stuffing soak the bread crumbs in a little milk, then mix with the onion and parsley and season with salt and pepper to taste.
Stuff the chicken with the bread mixture. Close with a skewer or sew up with thread.
Melt 1 tablespoon of butter in a braising pan and brown the onions in it. Place the chicken in the pan, cook for 20 minutes in the oven, until it browns (turning several times). Add the stock and seasoning, cover and braise at 400 °F (200 °C) for about 40 minutes.
Cook the spinach and keep warm.
Remove the chicken from the pan and keep warm.
Pass the stock through a sieve. Chop up the chicken livers into small pieces, place in the stock and leave to simmer on the cooker for 5 minutes, then mash the livers. Add the cream and remaining butter, heat once again, but cook no further, and season to taste.
Serve the chicken on a preheated plate, making a border with the spinach and pour the sauce over the bird.

Poacher's Pot
Poacher's Stew

Serves 12

1 rabbit weighing about 2 lbs (1 kg), cut into pieces
2 pigeons, cut in half
2 pheasants, cut into pieces
¹/₂ cup (50 g) flour
2 large onions, peeled and chopped
2 turnips, washed and diced
3 large carrots, washed and sliced
2 lbs (1 kg) unsliced smoked ham
4 sprigs each of sage, thyme and parsley
1 tsp salt, 1 tsp black pepper
1 large savoy cabbage, washed and cut into quarters
1¹/₂ cups (300 ml) red wine

Dust the rabbit and game birds with flour. Place the onions, turnips, and carrots in a large saucepan, then layer the meat and then the ham. Add the herbs, salt, and pepper and cover everything with water. Bring to the boil, cover, and leave to simmer for about 2¹/₂ hours. Stir occasionally.
After 2 hours' cooking add the savoy cabbage and red wine, then season to taste.
Once everything is cooked, remove the ham, cut into thick slices, cut these slices in half and return them to the saucepan. Serve the stew with fresh, homemade bread, with which to soak up the meat juices.

Cock-a-Leekie
Leek Soup with Chicken

1 boiling fowl, weighing 3 lb (about 1¹/₂ kg)
Salt, black pepper
2 small onions, peeled and finely chopped
5 leeks, washed and sliced
1 Tbs chopped parsley

Wash the chicken, place in a generous 5 pints (2¹/₂ l) of cold water and bring to the boil. Skim any froth, season the stock with salt. Half cover and leave to simmer for 2 hours, until the chicken is practically disintegrating. Remove the chicken and leave to cool. Skim any fat from the stock and pass the stock through a sieve. Cook the onions in the fat until transparent, add the leeks and cook for a further 5 minutes or so. Skin the chicken, remove the bones and cut the meat into small pieces. Return the meat with the onion and leek mixture and the stock to the saucepan, and leave to simmer for a further few minutes. Season to taste with salt and pepper, and sprinkle with parsley to serve.

All About Oats

In the cold Scottish Highlands the most successful cereal crop is the oat because it can subsist on very little. As dishes made from oats are also very filling, the Scottish diet used to consist mainly of recipes using wholemeal oats – before the potato became indigenous – such as porridge, or oatcakes, another well-known Scottish favorite.

Porridge, which is made from coarse oatmeal, water, and salt, is eaten for breakfast. Scottish shepherds were in the habit of cooking a whole week's supply of porridge and then keeping it in a so-called porridge drawer, where it solidified. They cut it into pieces called caulders as they needed it and cooked it – this provided a quick nutritious meal when one was moving around with flocks of sheep for days.

Strict rituals were devised for preparing it. For example, porridge is always prepared stirring clockwise with the right hand. To this end a pointed stick called a spurtle is used. There is also a custom associated with porridge which dates back to the Middle Ages, namely that of eating it standing up. This derives from the fact that the Scottish Highlanders supposedly used to stab each other in the back. Porridge was traditionally eaten from a bowl made of birchwood with a deep spoon made of horn – with cold milk or cream and a little sugar, and sometimes also only with salt.

Baking Scottish Style

There is a popular saying that Scottish housewives are born with a rolling-pin under their arm since their passion for baking is boundless. Oat flour provides an excellent basis for making bread and cakes. Scottish oatcakes are typical of the baking traditions of the country, and scones must never be absent from afternoon tea. The same applies to that substantial biscuit the shortbread, which owes its pleasant aroma to a generous use of butter and sugar. And bannocks, round flat loaves made with raisins, also belong to a perfect breakfast. There is a preference today, however, for wheat flour which is finer and lighter than oatmeal.

1

2

3

4

Porridge

5 oz (125 g) medium ground oatmeal
or
7 oz (200 g) porridge oats
Salt
Butter
Brown sugar
Milk or cream

Bring just over 2¹⁄₂ pints (1¹⁄₄ l) water to the boil. Sprinkle the oatmeal or porridge oats (the amount depends on the required consistency) onto the water, stirring in constantly. Season with salt to taste. Reduce the heat and leave the mixture to simmer gently for about 30 minutes, until it has the consistency of a purée. Bring it to the boil again briefly, remove from the heat and stir vigorously. Pour into small bowls or deep plates, place a piece of butter upon each portion and sprinkle with sugar to taste. Serve milk or cream with it in a separate bowl.

Above: Shortbread is a very nutritious biscuit which is made from sugar, butter, and flour. There is a rule of thumb which states that these ingredients should have a ratio of 2:4:6 (ounces). In days gone by the word "short" was used to characterize everything that was crisp and somewhat crumbly, whilst the word "bread" in this instance meant a cake. This illogicality dates back to a linguistic usage of earlier centuries, whereby a piece of bread from a loaf would be described as a "cake of bread." The Scots have preserved this tradition and have chosen "shortbread" rather than "shortcake" to distinguish themselves from the English and the Americans.

Shortbread

**To make a shortbread with a
diameter of
7 inches (18 cm)**

2 oz (50 g) sugar
4 oz (125 g) salted butter
6 oz (175 g) flour
Caster sugar

Preheat the oven to 250 °F (120 °C). Cream the sugar and butter together, then add the flour and salt and work everything into a semifirm dough (1). Roll the dough out into a thick round circle about 1 inch (2.5 cm) thick (2) and place in a greased pie shell with removable sides and a diameter of 7 inches (18 cm) (3). Prick several times with a fork and carefully score the shortbread for individual pieces. Bake for 45 minutes in the oven, until the shortbread is golden brown (4). Once it has cooled, sprinkle with sugar.

Oatcakes

4 oz (100 g) medium fine oatmeal
1 large pinch of salt
2 tsp of melted down bacon fat
2–3 Tbs warm water

Mix the oatmeal with the salt in a bowl, make a hollow in the middle and place the fat in it. Stir the ingredients together and add as much water as is necessary to create a firm dough. Sprinkle a work surface with flour and on it knead the dough vigorously for a few minutes (1), then roll it out to the thickness of a finger. Mark out large round dough cakes (2) and cut these across into 4, 6, or 8 segments (3); sprinkle with oatmeal. Whilst baking the oatcakes should not be turned. Bake the segments on a hotplate (4) or in a heavy skillet until they bend upwards. Serve hot or cold with unsalted butter, Crowdie (Scottish cottage cheese) or another curd cheese.

1

2

Left: Porridge is traditionally eaten out of a large bowl firstly by taking a portion with a deep spoon (1) and then – with the same spoon – taking some cold milk or cream from a separate bowl (2).
Right: The classic ingredients for oatcakes are oatmeal, fat – traditionally melted bacon fat or lard, but not butter or oil (as in "modern" versions of the recipe) – and a little salt, which are made into a dough that is rolled out flat. Large round dough cakes are then marked out which are then cut into four quarters (or several segments) and baked on a hotplate. Since they are not turned over, the characteristic shape arises which makes the oatcakes somewhat difficult to package.

1

3

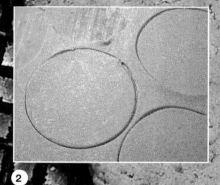

2

4

Honor Moore

Ireland

Countless peoples have left their mark on Ireland, and they have all made their own contribution to the history and culture of the country. Many aspects of Irish cooking can be traced back to them, and even the Vikings made their own, not unimportant, contribution. It is somewhat astonishing to realise that the modern method of broiling is not terribly different to the way in which the Celts used to roast an enormous Irish elk or a red deer over the open fire.

Cheese, an important part of the diet in the past, disappeared as a foodstuff at the time of Oliver Cromwell, who in the middle of the 17th century harried the original Irish inhabitants from their fertile fields in the East in the wake of the English colonialization, and drove them "to Hell or to Connaught." The Western regions of the island are, however, so barren that they could not support the Irish cattle herds, and anyway most of the animals had been slaughtered to feed Cromwell's soldiers. Moreover, the land had first to be reclaimed, mainly for the cultivation of potatoes. The countless rocks and stones that "grew" out of the ground there, were piled up to make embankments as protection against the strong winds. The resulting landscape, which makes such an impression on every visitor, has remained intact until the present day.

In those times, which were characterized by poverty and danger, a particularly penitent attitude towards food (although not towards drink) developed, the only exception being the religious feastdays at Christmas and Easter. Lent was strictly observed, although hospitality was always shown to the traveler – and due to the potato this was possible no matter how poor a household was. Home and family play an important role in the everyday lives of the Irish. Although Irish houses no longer have an open fire as a rule, the kitchen still forms the center of family life. In an Irish kitchen the activities for the day are discussed, friends entertained, music played, stories told, and harmony restored to the world through such happy company.

Left: Potato apple cakes being baked on the griddle, a flat cast iron cooking medium (recipe pp. 62–63). The photograph was taken in Omagh, the county town of County Tyrone in Northern Ireland.

An Indispensable Foodstuff

The Potato

Potatoes are a fundamental part of the diet. Their use as a foodstuff was known in Ireland considerably earlier than anywhere else in Europe. Sir Walter Raleigh, originally a pirate and later an admiral in the service of Queen Elizabeth I, is said to have brought the potato to Ireland from America in about 1585. It fundamentally transformed the eating habits of the Irish. Up until then oat-related products took pride of place upon the menu; now it was the brown potato from the New World that assumed domination.

The potato appears to have been made for Ireland for all kinds of reasons. On the one hand, the crop thrives in the damp, cool climate which protects it from viral infections, and on the other hand this simple crop will grow in virtually any soil and will also provide relatively large yields in small fields. The potato is a very healthy foodstuff. It contains many carbohydrates and minerals as well plenty of vitamin C – nutrients that are indispensable for the health of the population. It is only due to the potato that the Irish population could survive in frugal times historically.

It has been recorded what enormous amounts of potatoes were consumed in the past. Even in the last century, from a statistical standpoint, the average Irish person had a daily consumption of six and a half pounds (three kilograms) of potatoes – something which for us today appears virtually inconceivable. But when one considers that there was practically nothing else to eat, this amount just covers the normal daily energy requirement.

Since the 17th century the daily meal of an average Irish family has consisted of milk and potatoes, with the occasional addition of ham, fish, and eggs when available. Due to this clearly very healthy diet, the population doubled between 1780 and 1840 and grew to eight million. However, with the almost complete failure of the potato harvest in the year 1845 as a result of potato blight and with one very bad harvest following another in subsequent years, the population was virtually halved as a consequence of the devastation wrought by the Great Famine and an unprecedented wave of emigration.

Potatoes have remained a basic foodstuff in Ireland until today and are served at least once daily as part of a meal. They are cultivated in so-called "lazy beds," modest plots with irrigation channels. The housewife carefully selects the potatoes and is sensitive to any variations in quality. The reddish, mealy varieties are preferred and are cooked in their skins, which are only removed at the table with knife and fork – something wholly unexpected, for example, for English visitors, who have then largely to learn this way of using a knife and fork for the first time.

The cultivation of the potato is traditional in Ireland. Even in the last century the average daily per capita consumption was $6^1/_2$ pounds (3 kilograms).

Anna

Record

How Irish Housewives Cook Potatoes

New potatoes are cooked in plenty of salted water, that is already boiling when the potatoes are added to it.

Old potatoes are put on to boil in a saucepan with cold water and cooked covered.

Once the water has been poured away the potatoes must always be left to give off steam. This is best done by laying a clean cloth over the saucepan and returning the potatoes to the stove "to dry" for a few minutes.

New potatoes served with mint are a particular delicacy. The tubers are washed or brushed lightly and cooked over a low heat in a mixture of hot, generously salted water and an equal amount of milk, together with a bunch of mint. Once they have been drained a generous portion of butter is added and the potatoes are tossed in it before being sprinkled with parsley and served.

King Edward

The sequence of pictures on the right shows how Boxty Pancakes are made on a hotplate. It takes about 5 minutes for the dough, which is made from milk and raw potatoes, to turn golden brown.

Boxty – Bacstaí

Boxty, the traditional Irish potato dish, can be prepared as bread, griddle cakes, dumplings, pancakes, and puddings. Raw potatoes are used for each recipe.

It is customary to sing the "Boxty Song" to Irish children:

Boxty on the griddle,
Boxty in the pan,
if you don't eat your boxty
you'll never get a man.

Boxty, which is very similar to Swiss *rösti*, has been the subject of an unexpected revival recently. In Callaghers' Boxty House in Dublin it is possible to put together a meal for oneself consisting of sweet or savory Boxty Pancakes.

Boxty Pancakes
Potato Pancakes

1 lb (500 g) potatoes
2 Tbs flour
1 tsp baking powder
¹/₂ tsp salt
³/₄ cup (150 ml) milk

Peel, grate, and wrap the potatoes in a clean cloth, and twist the ends of the cloth tightly to squeeze out the liquid starch. Collect the liquid starch in a container. Place the potatoes in a bowl and add the flour, baking powder, and salt.
Drain the clear liquid from the liquid starch and add the remaining white starch itself to the potato mixture. Add the milk and make a light dough with a semi-liquid consistency. Spoon into a skillet containing hot fat or onto a hotplate (see left). Cook on both sides for approximately 5 minutes until the potato pancakes are golden brown. Boxty pancakes are served with butter and sugar or fruits, with fried bacon, and with meat, fish, or vegetable fillings.

Boxty Bread
Potato Bread

8 oz (250 g) peeled raw potatoes
8 oz (250 g) peeled boiled potatoes
Salt
¹/₂ cup (50 g) flour

Grate and squeeze the raw potatoes as in the recipe for Boxty Pancakes; place in a bowl.
Mash the cooked potatoes.
Cover the grated raw potatoes with the boiled and mashed ones, so that they do not discolor. Add the white starch from the grated raw potatoes, season with salt and mix well. Stir in the flour.
Make a flat round sheet of potato dough and cook in a heavy cast iron skillet until the potato bread is lightly browned on both sides (after about 30 minutes).
Cut into slices and serve.

Meat

Of Pigs and Cattle

The pig is the oldest domesticated animal in Ireland. When it was slaughtered in the Middle Ages, the prime cuts went to the local nobility and the villagers divided the rest between themselves as follows. The head, tail, and legs went to the blacksmith; the neck belonged to the butcher; two small ribs were reserved for the tailor; the liver for the joiner; and the sweetbreads for a woman with child.

Where such care was taken with the lesser parts of the animal it is not surprising to find that an extensive range of sausage specialties developed quite early on. Home-made sausages enjoy great popularity in Ireland. All year round a battle rages between the butchers over the most competitive prices for the best sausage products. Nonetheless, not many of them stock venison sausages, which have an excellent taste and contain little fat. Game as well as belly pork are the basic ingredients.

Dublin Coddle is a famous Irish dish prepared from bacon, sausages, boiled potatoes, onions, and apples, which is served to tourists as a local specialty. The meal used to be served regularly in Dublin families to the master of the house on a Saturday night.

Left: Amongst the many sausage delicacies in Ireland home-made sausages above all are especially popular. A fundamental distinction is made between uncooked sausages, sausages which are heated in boiling water, and sausages which are precooked but heated before eating, according to how they are made and what they contain. Shown here are soft smoked sausages with a beef and pork filling, sausages for frying or broiling, and sausages which are heated in boiling water – the pride of every butcher's shop.

Dublin Coddle
Irish National Dish

Serves 4

2 large onions, peeled and sliced
2 apples, peeled, cored and diced
8 oz (250 g) bacon in slices
6 large soft smoked sausages (made of ground pork and beef), cut into pieces
1 lb 10 oz (750 g) potatoes, peeled and sliced
Salt, black pepper
2 Tbs chopped parsley

Place the onions, apples, bacon, sausages, and potatoes in a saucepan and mix together. Season to taste and add 1 tablespoon of parsley.
Add about 1 1/2 cups (300 ml) of water and bring to the boil, then cover and leave to simmer for 60–90 minutes until the water has evaporated.
Sprinkle with the remaining parsley and serve.

Irish Oxtail Stew

Serves 4

1 large oxtail, cut into pieces 1 1/2 inches (4 cm) long
1/2 cup (50 g) flour
1 large onion, peeled and thinly sliced
2 large carrots, washed and sliced
2 Tbs puréed tomatoes
1 bouquet garni (thyme, parsley, bay leaf)
1 pinch each of ground mace and pimiento
3 cups (600 ml) beef stock
Salt, black pepper
2 Tbs finely chopped parsley

Dust the oxtail with flour and brown all over in hot fat. Add the onion and carrots and cook for a few more minutes. Then stir in the puréed tomatoes as well as the bouquet garni and spices.
Pour in the beef stock, bring everything to the boil, cover and cook over a low heat for 2 1/2–3 hours.
Remove the bouquet garni and any excess fat, season the stew, sprinkle with parsley, and then serve.

Irish Dishes with Pork

Black Pudding – Putóga Fola
A mixture of blood, fat, and milk, which is stuffed in sausage skins and served hot or cold.

Fried Liver and Bacon – Ae agus bagún friochta
Fried liver and bacon, also called Irish Grill.

Kidneys in their Jacket – Duáin sa tsaill
Kidneys with skin, cut into a fan shape and cooked in the oven.

Limerick Ham – Liamhás Luimneach
Ham smoked over oak shavings and juniper berries. This famous specialty from Limerick is available boiled and sliced when cold, or cooked with parsley sauce.

Pork Ciste – Ciste muiceola
Ciste means cake and refers here to the crackling of roast pork which is similar to bread, keeping it juicy and tender.

Stuffed Pork Fillets – Filleád eanna muiceola
Pork fillets stuffed with bread, onions, and spices, which are popular for Sunday lunch and on other special occasions.

Irish Dishes with Beef

Corned Beef with Dumplings and Cabbage
The favorite traditional meal of the Irish at Easter and on St Patrick's Day (March 17).

Gaelic Steaks
Juicy beefsteaks fried in a skillet, with a shot of Irish Whiskey added to the meat juices.

Spiced Beef
An old recipe with many ingredients. This dish is served especially at Christmas.

Irish Stew –
Lamb Stew with Vegetables

Irish Stew
Lamb Stew with Vegetables
(Illustration)

Serves 4–6

3 lb 4 oz (1.5 kg) neck or shoulder of lamb
1 turnip
4 onions
4 carrots
3 leeks
1 bouquet garni (thyme, parsley, bay leaf)
Salt, black pepper
6 potatoes
4 oz (100 g) white cabbage
Worcestershire Sauce
1 bunch of parsley, chopped

Trim the meat of fat and bone if necessary. Dice the meat and put the bones to one side. Cover the meat in a casserole with cold salted water and bring to the boil, then drain.

Wash the turnip, onions, carrots, and leeks and cut into bite-sized portions. Place in another casserole with the meat, bones, and bouquet garni, season with salt and pepper. Cover the ingredients with water and leave to simmer for 60 minutes, taking care to skim any scum from time to time.

Peel and cut the potatoes into pieces, add to the casserole and leave to simmer for a further 30 minutes. Wash and slice the white cabbage. Add to the casserole during the last 5 minutes of cooking. Remove the bones and bouquet garni, season the stew to taste with Worcestershire Sauce and finally stir in the chopped parsley.

How Mutton Became Lamb

Whoever travels around Ireland cannot fail to notice the many flocks of sheep. They populate the meadows just as much as the barren rocky landscape. Irish sheep are to be found almost everywhere.

Originally they were kept above all for their wool – their milk and meat were first marketed on a grand scale under English influence, because up until then these domestic animals were regarded as too precious to be slaughtered.

The fashion for eating lamb appeared a few decades ago when it was discovered how tasty the meat was from sheep that graze in salty fields near the coast, hence the classification *pré-salé*, from the French *pré* (meadow), *salé* (salt). Even just one generation ago people preferred mutton, which has somewhat fallen from favor today because of its strong, characteristic flavor. At present the demand for tender young lamb is so great that it has become rather difficult to obtain mutton.

Irish Stew – Ireland's National Dish

Ireland's national dish, Irish stew, is famous worldwide. There are countless different ways of preparing it, although the use of mutton, as stipulated in the original recipe, has become increasingly rare. The closest one gets to the original recipe is when one uses the meat of a hogget – hoggets are sheep that are one year old. Hogget meat is to be had in the early spring and in the early summer.

Opinions are also divided regarding the other ingredients. One issue, for example, is whether carrots should be used or not. The original recipe stipulates mutton, potatoes, and onions, and those who adhere to it maintain that its pure flavor is adulterated by the addition of carrots, pearl barley, or other ingredients. The modern, less heavy version of Irish stew by contrast even admits green vegetables as ingredients – an idea that for traditionalists virtually borders on the frightening. Whatever recipe is followed, a good Irish stew should always have a thick consistency rather than being runny.

Lamb's Kidneys with Mustard Sauce

Serves 4

12 lamb's kidneys
2 glasses of white wine
2 tsp chopped herbs (thyme, parsley, rosemary, chives)
2 garlic cloves, peeled and chopped
1 Tbs heavy cream
1 Tbs Dijon mustard
Salt, black pepper

Skin the kidneys, cut them longways, trim any fat, and remove any veins. Wash thoroughly and pat dry. Cook in butter in a skillet over a medium heat until they are done. Remove from the skillet and keep hot.

Add the white wine, herbs, and garlic to the skillet and leave to simmer, until the liquid has reduced by one third. Stir in the cream and at the very end of cooking stir in the mustard, season with salt and pepper.

Return the kidneys to the skillet and heat carefully in the sauce, so as not to cook them any further. Serve immediately. This dish goes well with rice and cabbage.

Cockles and Mussels

Fish and seafood play an important role in the lives of any island people, and in this respect Ireland is no exception. Since time immemorial, fish dishes have formed the basis of the diet along the country's extensive coastline. Produce from the sea, just as much as fish from the clear inland waterways, enriched the mainly sparse diet that consisted of arable crops and some meat. Before the introduction of modern refrigeration technology people made use of the methods of preserving food which were then current, such as salting, smoking, or drying.

Because they were easily accessible from land without even undergoing the perils of seafaring, it was above all cockles and mussels that enjoyed great popularity amongst the coastal inhabitants. The traditional song which follows bears testimony to this:

In Dublin's fair city,
Where the girls are so pretty,
I first set my eyes on sweet Molly Malone.

She wheeled her wheelbarrow
Through streets broad and narrow,
Crying "Cockles and mussels alive, alive, oh!"

Mussels were to be found virtually everywhere along the coast in shallow water. They were highly regarded because of their delicate flavor by folk living both by the sea and inland, where they were sold in barrels for a little money and were especially popular amongst the poor. Nowadays they are largely cultivated on mussel farms.

Cockles are also collected by hand. In their case it is not even necessary to go into the water, as one only needs to wait for the tide to turn. Then they are to be found in the wet sand, and they can be dug out with a spoon or a small spade. There is an old saying that cockles must not be collected before the third high tide in April: "They must have drunk April water three times."

In earlier times women and children with small buckets and other containers could be seen collecting cockles during the summer months all along the beaches. Cockles were very often, however, not only a source of nourishment, but were also a means of payment. They were exchanged for goods such as flour, oats, and even clothing. Even today it is most enjoyable to dig for cockles on the white sandy beaches. However, those found lying on top of the sand should be left well alone as they are already dead.

Irish oysters are popular and highly regarded, and there are several oyster farms devoted to producing them for domestic consumption as

Seaweed is very versatile, and can even be served boiled on toast.

well as export. Irish oysters are small, but particularly tasty, and a popular way of eating them is with a glass of Guinness.

A surfeit of herring and mackerel was to be found along the coast in the past. At the turn of the century mackerel were even exported to the United States of America with great success. Because of continued overfishing the stocks are largely exhausted today.

Versatile Seaweed

One unusual crop which is collected and processed is that of seaweed or sea vegetables. Several varieties are used as fertilizer, whilst others are used to manufacture medicines, and yet others such as dulse are used to make foodstuffs. Many are supposed to ensure that Guinness has its splendid head of froth once it is poured.

The most widely known sea vegetable is carrageen, which also goes by the name of "Irish Moss." In addition to its culinary use as a gelling agent in sauces and desserts, it is said to have a beneficial effect in the treatment of digestive and circulatory problems, hay fever, obesity, and – when it is mixed with garlic – coughs. It is also supposed to have its uses as an aphrodisiac.

Cod's Roe Ramekin

Serves 8

8 oz (250 g) cod's roe, cooked and skinned
$\frac{1}{2}$ cup (100 g) bread crumbs
1 pinch each of nutmeg and paprika
Salt, black pepper
2 Tbs chopped parsley
3 Tbs lemon juice
1 egg yolk, 1 egg white
$\frac{3}{4}$ cup (150 ml) heavy cream

Grease eight small soufflé dishes with butter. Chop the roe and mix with the bread crumbs, spices, parsley, and lemon juice. Beat the egg yolk with the cream and pour over the roe. Leave to stand for 10 minutes.
Preheat the oven to 400 °F (200 °C).
Beat the egg white until stiff and add to the roe mixture.
Put the resulting mix into the small soufflé dishes and bake until they have risen and turned golden brown, which should take about 15 minutes.

Cockles and Bacon Rashers

Serves 2

20 cockles
4 thick slices of bacon without the rind
Just under $\frac{1}{2}$ cup (100 g) butter
Black pepper
2 Tbs chopped parsley

Scrub the cockles under running water, taking care to throw away any open ones. Pour a little salted water into a large saucepan so that the bottom is covered and bring to the boil. Place the cockles in the saucepan and steam for about 5 minutes until they open. Then remove the shells.
Fry the slices of bacon in half the butter until crispy and brown, remove from the skillet and keep hot.
Add the cockles with the rest of the butter to the skillet and heat for a few minutes on a low flame. Sprinkle with pepper and parsley, and serve with the rashers of bacon on a preheated plate.

Mussels in Wine Sauce

Serves 4

48 mussels
³/₄ cup (150 g) butter
2 large onions, peeled and finely chopped
4 cloves of garlic, peeled and crushed
2 leeks, washed and thinly sliced
3 cups (600 ml) dry white wine
1¹/₂ cups (300 ml) water (or fish stock)
¹/₂ cup (50 g) flour
Salt, black pepper
4 Tbs chopped parsley

Scrub the mussels under running water and remove their beards, taking care to throw away any open ones. Heat two thirds of the butter in a large saucepan, and cook the onions, garlic, and leeks until they are transparent.
Add the mussels, white wine, and water (or fish stock), bring everything to the boil, cover and leave to cook for 5–8 minutes, until the mussels have opened.
Remove the mussels, divide equally between 4 soup bowls and keep warm.
Knead the remaining butter and the flour together and gradually stir into the stock. Season to taste and sprinkle with parsley. Pour the stock over the mussels and serve with bread.

Dublin Lawyer

Lobster Dublin Style

Serves 2

1 lobster weighing about 2 lb (1 kg)
¹/₄ cup (50 g) butter
4 Tbs Irish whiskey
³/₄ cup (150 ml) double cream
1 tsp lemon juice
1 tsp mustard
Salt, black pepper

Put the live lobster head first into boiling water for 2 minutes being mindful of scalding.
Remove and pour cold water over it. Detach the tail end of the lobster and slice. Cut the body in half lengthways, remove the stomach and intestines, detach the flesh and dice; put the shell to one side. Break open the claws, remove the membrane from each and dice the flesh.
Heat the butter in a large skillet and cook the pieces of lobster – they must be cooked, but must not have taken on any color. Flambé the lobster with the whiskey. Then stir in the double cream, lemon juice, and mustard, season and bring briefly to the boil.
Remove the pieces of lobster from the skillet and stuff the preheated shell. Reduce the sauce slightly and pour over the lobster. Serve immediately. (The name of this lobster dish derives from the fact that in the past only those with a higher level of income could afford this expensive delicacy.)

Oysters and Guinness

(Illustration)

For 2 people

12 fresh oysters
1 lemon, cut into quarters
Cayenne pepper
White bread, butter
Guinness

Thoroughly wash the oysters, scrub them and open. Arrange them on a plate on crushed ice, decorate with the quarters of lemon and season with a little cayenne pepper. Serve with bread, butter, and Guinness.

Oysters and Guinness

Halloween

No religious festival in Ireland is as important as the one which marks the end of the harvest, on October 31. All Hallows Eve is better known as Halloween. For many a century this festival was marked by a day of selective fasting, on which eating meat was forbidden. It is for this reason that the traditional Halloween dishes contain no meat ingredients whatsoever. Amongst them are potato apple cake, boxty pancakes and pudding or colcannon, barm brack and blackberry pies.

Whatever the choice a wedding-ring is always involved. It is carefully wrapped in grease-proof paper and hidden in whichever meal is being prepared. It was common in the past to use other small souvenirs, for example objects like a silver coin, a button, or a thimble. Whoever found such an article on their plate knew what awaited them in the coming year. The ring represented an impending marriage, the coin power and influence, the button stood for a year as a bachelor, and the thimble for a further twelve months of virginity for a woman.

Brack – A Symbolic Bread

Amongst all bakery products the brack is certainly the most Irish. The name of this fruit loaf derives from the word *breac*, which means "speckled." A distinction is made between two basic recipes: Barm Brack which is made with yeast and Tea Brack which is made with baking powder. The dried fruit used in Tea Brack is soaked in cold tea before preparing the loaf.

Barm Brack is one of the most important Halloween specialties, although this fruit loaf is also baked on countless other festive occasions. Tea Brack like other cakes is baked all year round.

Traditional Barm Brack
Fruit Loaf

1 lb (500 g) flour
1 pinch of salt
1/4 cup (50 g) butter
6 oz (175 g) raisins, soaked for 30 minutes in cold water
1/4 cup (50 g) candied orange-peel and lemon-peel
2 oz (50 g) and 2 Tbs sugar
Just over 1 Tbs (20 g) yeast
1 1/2 cups (300 ml) lukewarm water
2 beaten eggs

Knead the flour, salt, and butter into a crumble topping. Press the liquid out of the raisins, then add them and the candied peel and 1/4 cup (50 g) sugar and mix everything together well. Dissolve the yeast in lukewarm water.
Make a hollow in the flour and fruit mixture and place the eggs and the dissolved yeast in it. Work everything into a dough. Sprinkle a work surface with flour and knead the dough on it for 10 minutes and cover, then put in a warm place to rise to double its volume.
Divide the dough in two, knead each half for a few

Several ingredients for Barm Brack: flour, eggs, butter, sugar, soaked raisins, and candied lemon-peel and orange-peel.

The raisins must be soaked in cold water for 30 minutes before use.

The dough is traditionally baked in a cast-iron saucepan with hot coals placed on the lid.

Barm Brack is a nourishing, heavy fruit loaf, which is eaten at Halloween. A wedding-ring is hidden in the dough – whoever finds it, it is supposed will be married shortly.

minutes and make from both a round cake with a diameter of 7 1/2 inches (20 cm). Place on a greased baking tray. Leave to rise for a further 60 minutes in a warm place.
Preheat the oven to 400 °F (200 °C) and bake the bracks for 30 minutes.
Dissolve the remaining 2 tablespoons of sugar in 2 tablespoons of water and brush the bracks with the dissolved sugar as soon as they come out of the oven. Return to the oven to dry for a further 2–3 minutes.

Colcannon
Cabbage in Mashed Potatoes

1 lb (500 g) green or white cabbage
1 lb (500 g) potatoes
1 bunch of scallions
3/4 cup (180 ml) cream
Salt, black pepper
1 ring, wrapped in grease-proof paper
1/2 cup (100 g) melted butter

Wash the cabbage and cut into thin strips, cook in a little salted water and leave to drain well. Cook the potatoes in their skins, peel and mash.
In the meantime wash the scallions and cut them into fine rings. Leave to simmer for 5 minutes in the cream. Gradually stir the cream and scallions into the puréed potatoes. Then fold in the cabbage, season to taste with salt and pepper and place the ring in the mixture. To serve, make a hollow in the middle of the Colcannon and pour butter into it.

Potato Apple Cake
(Illustration right)

1 lb (500 g) potatoes, freshly boiled in their skins
1 good pinch of salt
2 Tbs melted butter
1 cup (about 100 g) flour
2–3 slightly sour apples
Flakes of butter
Granulated sugar

Peel and mash the potatoes, stir in the salt and butter. Knead in enough flour to make a smooth dough. Shape the potato dough into a round disc and cut into four. Peel and core the apples, then slice thinly. Cover two quarters of the potato dough with slices of apple and cover with the remaining two quarters. Press the edges down firmly.
Cook the cakes for 10 minutes each, on both sides over a low heat in a large heavy skillet. Then carefully remove the tops of the potato apple cakes. Sprinkle the apples with flakes of butter and sugar to taste. Replace the tops and return to the skillet so that the butter and sugar melt. Serve immediately.

Opposite: The Irish like to bake potato apple cakes as they have done since time immemorial, on the griddle, a heavy round, usually cast iron hotplate, which is suspended from a retractable hook over the open fire (see pp. 54–55). Due to the constant heat all kinds of bakery products cook particularly well on the griddle.

The Black Beer

Guinness

Ireland is the birthplace of one of the world's most famous drinks, a dark beer called Guinness. In the year 1759, Arthur Guinness purchased a small, disused brewery at Dublin's St. James's Gate and founded a company whose product was to become inseparable from its name. At first Guinness brewed the customary "ale," but soon a stronger beer came on the market. This was called "Porter," and was named after the men who preferred to drink it, namely the porters on the London fish and vegetable markets. Guinness introduced it to Ireland in 1799. In order to remain competitive he then brewed an even stronger beer called "Extra Stout." It was made from malted barley, hops, yeast, and purest Dublin water. Thus commenced the rise of the company and already by 1833 Guinness was the largest brewery in Ireland. From the attribute "stout" the description of a type of beer – "Stout" – has been derived. Today the company at St. James's Gate has become one of the largest breweries in the world. The visitor can trace the history of Guinness in the company's own museum and visitors' center.

Guinness is now brewed in England, Canada, Australia, Ghana, Nigeria, Sierra Leone, Malaysia, and Jamaica, but an avowed Dubliner will be sure to swear that the only true Guinness is to be found in his Dublin pub, where it is poured with due respect in such a way as to have a beautiful, creamy head of froth. (In the meantime this cask beer has also become available in cans.)

In days gone by, the brewery horses and the rafts that floated on the Liffey carrying barrels of Guinness were a familiar sight. Neither exists any longer. However, although the Irish firm has in the meantime become part of an international drinks corporation and every day ten million glasses of Guinness are drunk worldwide, there is still a member of the founder's family on the board.

At the parent company at St. James's Gate, about seventy million gallons (over 2.6 million hectoliters) of beer are presently brewed. The second largest brewery in the Guinness Group is the Harp Lager Brewery in Dundalk which has a capacity of thirty-seven million gallons (1.4 million hectoliters). Harp brews a bottom-fermented lager – a normal to high-quality light-colored beer – which has only increased in popularity in Ireland in the course of the last few years. Also located in Dundalk is the Guinness subsidiary Marcardle Moore, which brews ale. E. Smithwick & Sons Ltd in Kilkenny has a capacity of 26.4 million gallons (one million hectoliters) and is also a member of the Guinness family.

Guinness has domestic rivals in the form of Beamish & Crawford in Cork and the Murphy Brewery Ireland, also in Cork, which belongs to the Dutch corporation Heineken.

It is an Irish phenomenon that well over eighty percent of beer is consumed in pubs. The annual per capita consumption in Ireland currently stands at 260 pints (123 liters), which has been relatively constant since 1990. This places Ireland third in terms of beer consumption in the European Union (EU) behind Germany and Denmark.

When Guinness is poured it has a creamy head of froth.

The Irish are a gregarious people – 80 percent of beer is consumed in pubs.

The illustration in the background shows one of the last deliveries of Guinness from a brewers' dray to a pub in Dublin.

The essential ingredients for Guinness: hops and malt.

The wort is brewed in enormous vats from water and malt. Hops provide the flavoring.

The sugar content of the wort is measured with a pressure gauge.

After alcoholic fermentation, which takes place in tanks, the still unfiltered beer is sampled.

A Whiskey Apart

Irish whiskey is "different" to all other members of the whiskey family, something which the Irish express by spelling the word with an "e" to distinguish it from Scotch whisky. They are able to claim, with some justification in fact, that the art of distilling whiskey was invented in their own country. The skill was born in the monasteries that covered the land many centuries ago.

When Henry II – who ruled over Western France and had inherited England and Normandy from his mother (he was the king whose rash words led to the murder of Thomas à Becket in 1170) – conquered Ireland in the year 1171, his soldiers discovered the *uisge beatha*, the "water of life." What impressed the soldiers above all was the considerable increase in the fighting ability of their Irish opponents after they had consumed this drink, and since they found the word something of a tongue twister, they at first called it *uisce*, which one day evolved into the word "whiskey."

The conquest of England by Irish whiskey can, therefore, also be attributed to Henry II, as the soldiers returned home with it from Ireland. Once maritime trade between Ireland and England increased in importance, some small barrels of the water of life were always to be found on board the ships.

Irish whiskey had its heyday at the end of the 18th century. At that time the artistic and intellectual life of Dublin was thoroughly able to compete with that prevailing in either London or Paris. There were officially more than 2000 whiskey distilleries – although even then the art of illegal distillation was already widespread.

The oldest official distillery in the world is considered to be Old Bushmills in Northern Ireland, which today belongs to Great Britain. Old Bushmills received its licence for making whiskey in 1608. The John Jameson distillery was founded in the year 1780 in Dublin, and John Power arrived in 1791. Both emphasized and still emphasize quality, and their names have stood for Irish whiskey *per se* for many years.

Following the wave of emigration in the middle of the 19th century, whiskey also came to America. Murphy's Bar in New York was the meeting place for the homesick Irish, and there the whiskey flowed in abundance – something that abruptly came to an end because of Prohibition in the year 1920. This put an end to the consumption of all alcohol in the United States. The Irish, who at that time had grave problems in their mother country, were unable to create the appropriate channels for smuggling alcohol as the Scots had done, and so Irish whiskey also diminished in importance in America. When President Roosevelt abolished Prohibition in 1933, the Irish had been left behind. They did not have sufficiently mature stocks to be able to export the required amounts. In 1973 only five distilleries were still in existence, and they finally merged to form the Irish Distillers Group.

Today Irish whiskey is only produced in two locations, in Midleton and near Old Bushmills in Northern Ireland. However, the whiskey tradition is still tended to in Dublin in the Irish Whiskey Corner, a beautiful whiskey museum with a bar.

Midleton – Capital of Irish Whiskey

Midleton, County Cork is certainly the most modern distillery complex in the world. It is here that the great Irish whiskey brands are made – namely Jameson, Power's, Tullamore Dew, and Paddy, as well as the distinctive Midleton Very Rare. The history of Irish whiskey is presented in a small museum, the Jameson Whiskey Centre.

In the remote rural areas of Ireland there continues to be a tradition of "freelance" whiskey distilleries today. Home-made *poteen*, an extremely strong variation, can either be quite excellent or fatal. Should the local police, the *garda*, discover an illegal still, they will always destroy the distillate and the equipment used to make it.

Crushed malted barley is mixed in large mash tubs with hot water through constant stirring. This causes the parts of the crushed malt that contain sugar to be released. When the liquid containing sugar separates from the solid part of the malt, the result is the so-called "wort," which is placed in fermentation vats. With the help of yeast, the sugar then turns into alcohol and carbonic acid. Distillation takes place after this. Before the whiskey is bottled (see below), the alcohol content is reduced to 43% vol. to make it ready for drinking.

Irish whiskey traditionally matures for several years in oak barrels (the background picture shows Bushmills' store-room in Northern Ireland), which gives it its golden yellow color and characteristic aroma.

Whiskey Brands

Page left (from left to right): Green Spot – Tullamore Dew: a mild brand with a delicate flavor – Paddy: popular above all amongst young people – Power's: the most widely sold whiskey in Ireland – Hewitts Nut: sweet, nutty aroma – Bushmills Malt: the first Irish malt whiskey, 10 years old – Jameson 1780: an unusually mellow whiskey, 12 years old – Redbreast: produced in limited amounts, 12 years old – Midleton

Bailey's – A Liqueur of World Importance

According to an old saying, if a committee of Irishmen were asked to design a horse, the result would be a camel. Something extraordinary might have happened then when the directors of R & A Bailey and Co. got together to create a new drink. It was at that memorable meeting, however, that a man from their midst, Mr David Dand, combined whiskey, cream, and cocoa with some other ingredients to create "Bailey's Original Irish Cream Liqueur."

In the twenty years that have passed since the first sip of Bailey's, it has become one of the most widely sold liqueurs in the world – forty million people drink Bailey's. And as if enough was not enough, another liqueur was developed in Ireland in 1992 – Sheridans – which is sold in a double bottle, one side contains cream with a respectable shot of whiskey, the other a mixture of coffee and cocoa. When the drink is poured slowly into a glass it largely resembles an Irish Coffee.

Irish Fruit Delight
Red Fruit Pudding with Bailey's

Serves 4

8 oz (250 g) blackcurrants
8 oz (250 g) and 4 oz (100 g) redcurrants
8 oz (250 g) and 7 oz (200 g) raspberries
½ cup (120 g) sugar
¼ cup (60 g) cornstarch
Bailey's Irish Cream
Sponge fingers

Cook the blackcurrants and 8 oz (250 g) each of the redcurrants and raspberries with the sugar in 3¾ cups (750 ml) water until they are soft and pass through a sieve. Put to one side and leave to cool somewhat. Bind the juice with the cornstarch.
When the pudding is still lukewarm, carefully fold in the remaining uncooked redcurrants and raspberries, with the exception of a few berries which are to be put aside for decorative purposes. Place the pudding in small dessert bowls or bulbous glasses and refrigerate.
Before serving the pudding pour a layer of Bailey's Irish Cream about ³⁄₈ inch (1 cm) thick over the pudding and decorate with the sponge fingers and remaining berries.

Under high pressure such contrasting ingredients as whiskey and cream are blended with each other.

Sugar, cream, Irish whiskey, vanilla, and cocoa beans are ingredients for Bailey's Original Irish Cream Liqueur.

Bailey's is drunk on its own or on the rocks. It is said to be one of the world's most successful liqueurs.

Irish Whiskey Trifle

(Illustration below)

Serves 4–6

1 pint (500 ml) milk
1 vanilla bean, cut lengthways
3 eggs
Just under 2 Tbs sugar
1 sponge base
Raspberry jam
³/₄ cup (150 ml) Irish whiskey
1 lb (500 g) fruit (for example pears and bananas)
1¹/₂ cups (300 ml) cream

Decoration

Cocktail cherries
Blanched, sliced almonds (to taste)

To prepare the custard bring the milk and the vanilla bean to the boil, then remove from the cooker and leave to cool.

Beat the eggs and sugar. Remove the vanilla bean from the milk and gradually stir the milk into the egg mixture. Clean the milk saucepan with cold water and refill with the egg and milk mixture. Stir over a very low heat until it thickens. Put the custard to one side and stir occasionally to prevent a skin forming.

Cut the sponge base in half lengthways, spread with raspberry jam and put together again. Then cut into slices, take a large bowl made of glass if possible and cover the bottom and sides. Sprinkle on two-thirds of the whiskey in drops.

Peel and slice the fruit, sprinkle the remaining whiskey over it in drops and place on the sponge. Pour the custard on top of that.

Cover and refrigerate the bowl for several hours. Before serving top the custard with the cream, stiffly beaten. Decorate the trifle with cocktail cherries and almonds.

Irish Coffee

Per person

About 4 tsp Irish whiskey
Sugar to taste
Strong black, hot coffee
1 Tbs lightly whipped cream or double cream

Heat the whiskey and sugar in a stemmed glass over a flame. Pour the boiling hot coffee into the glass stopping about ³/₈ inch (1 cm) below the rim.
Then pour the cream onto the drink, as is being demonstrated in the illustration below. The cream should not be allowed to mix with the whiskey and coffee (therefore stirring should be avoided!). The hot drink is enjoyed through the cold cream.

Whiskey Punch

Per person

1 thick slice of lemon, cut in half
3 cloves
¹/₄ cup (50 ml) Irish whiskey
1–2 tsp brown sugar

Insert the cloves in the slice of lemon. Place together with the whiskey and the sugar in a large stemmed glass. Place a teaspoon in the glass – so that the heat does not cause the glass to crack – and pour boiling water on to the ingredients. Decorate to taste with lemon slices and cocktail cherries.
Stir well and drink hot.

Irish Whiskey Trifle
in a glass dessert bowl

The White Meat

Milk, Cheese, Butter

Written testimony and the oral tradition dating back to the early period of Irish history refer again and again to that "white meat," the *banbhianna*, which people regarded at that time as a particular pleasure. Owning cattle was synonymous with wealth and the cattle were too precious to slaughter, because the milk from the animals was necessary to make countless foodstuffs.

Sweet and sour milk and buttermilk, butter, and approximately twenty varieties of cheese are already mentioned in old manuscripts. The knowledge then prevailing concerning the manufacture of cheese has today been largely forgotten.

It belonged to the many aspects of Gaelic civilization, which were destroyed due to the reduction in economic status that befell the Irish in the wake of the English conquest in the 16th and 17th centuries.

Once again in recent times, however, a flourishing cheese industry has developed, whose products are now quite capable of competing with imported varieties of cheese. The Irish are about to rediscover their love of the "white meat," which includes butter. Businesses that manufacture cheese are distributed throughout the entire country. The majority of cheese is made from cows' milk, although some varieties of cheese made from goats' milk and sheep's milk are increasing in popularity. Most Irish restaurants are now able to create a cheeseboard consisting exclusively of cheeses from their respective parts of the country. Fresh country butter from county Kerry (hence the name "Kerrygold") is served too, as are fresh dark bread and salted crackers.

Kerry cows, grazing in the salty fields in County Kerry in south-west Ireland – in a "picture book" landscape with blue mountains, golden sandy beaches, and shimmering rivers.

Milleens, with a strong flavor and smell, is a soft cheese made from unpasteurized cows' milk. It was the first Irish country cheese in the 1980s of the "new generation" and has won many international awards. The sequence of pictures shows how milk, which has been thickened with a curdling agent, is broken down into small pieces by means of cheese wires (1). These are subsequently separated from the whey and form the basis of the cheese (2). They are then compacted in round containers (3) and placed in brine for several days, which imparts the strong flavor (4). Finally, the cheeses are stored exposed to fresh air (5) for as long as it takes for them to reach the required maturity (6).

Coolea

Cratloe Hills

Cahill's Irish Porter

Cashel Irish Blue

Gubbeen

Cooleeney

Wexford Irish Brie

Milleens

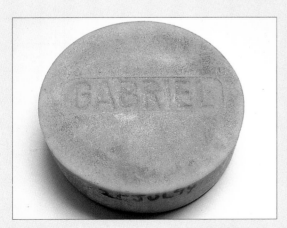

Gabriel is a hard, mild cheese that resembles Swiss cheese. It is made from the milk of sheep that graze in small herds between Mount Gabriel and the coast.

Desmond is also a sheep's cheese. Like Gabriel it is made by Bill Hogan, whose individual style of making cheese now has a virtually legendary reputation amongst connoisseurs.

Cashel Irish Blue is Ireland's only blue-veined cheese made from unpasteurized milk. Its salt content is unusually low. It tastes at its best when it is so ripe that it is extremely runny.

Bread, Cake, and Desserts

Soda Bread – Bread From The Griddle

Given the softness of Irish flour, it is difficult to bake good bread leavened with yeast. This is the reason for the development of soda bread, which is baked with baking soda. In other countries baking soda is replaced by baking powder and/or bicarbonate of soda. Until the electrification of the rural areas of Ireland, bread was baked on cast iron hotplates, so-called griddles, over the open peat fire. The quality depended upon the light touch of the baker's hand and also upon his skill in keeping the fire constant.

Gurr Cake – The Schoolchildren's Favorite Cake

Dublin bakers devised a reasonably priced cake in the last century to still the hunger of schoolchildren who were "on the gurr," or in American parlance, "playing hookey." Their Gurr Cake consisted of the leftovers of stale bread, which were mixed with sugar and dried fruit. (Cake leftovers – in this instance without dried fruit as an ingredient – were also used to good effect.) The mixture was stacked between several layers of dough. One piece of Gurr Cake cost a half-penny in those days.

Like many old recipes, Gurr Cake is also currently enjoying a renaissance. Today it is baked with a more substantial dough and a filling that is richer in fruit, and instead of leftovers from bread or cakes, highly-nutritious ingredients are used. In Dublin restaurants Gurr Cake is served together with a portion of cream as a dessert.

Puddings – Sweet Temptation

In Ireland it is inconceivable that any meal should not be rounded off with a pudding or another dessert. Wild fruits, berries, and nuts are traditionally used with honey or cream, or baked into tartlets. Milk and honey – the poets are fond of praising Ireland as the country where milk and honey flow – constantly play an important role in the preparation of puddings. However, apples also number amongst the most important ingredients, since the Normans planted the first apple trees in the 12th century.

Numerous desserts are different kinds of milk pudding, which are traditionally made with oatmeal, pearl barley, or rice. Only in the more prosperous farmhouses, the so-called "big houses," were they also served with cream, which was otherwise exclusively used to make butter. If a dessert recipe contains a large amount of cream it is, therefore, a sign that the recipe is a modern one.

Irish Soda Bread

5 cups (500 g) wholegrain wheat flour
1$^1/_2$ tsp salt
1$^1/_2$ tsp bicarbonate of soda
2$^1/_2$ cups (500 ml) buttermilk

Preheat the oven to 400 °F (200 °C). Mix the flour, salt, and bicarbonate of soda in a bowl, then stir in the buttermilk. Work everything into a crumbly dough. Sprinkle flour on a work surface and knead the dough gently and rapidly. Shape the dough into a loaf, place it on a greased baking tray and press the loaf flat so that the dough has a thickness of 2 inches (5 cm). Make the shape of a deep cross with a knife.
Bake in the oven for 30–35 minutes, until the loaf has risen well and is lightly browned. Leave to cool. Serve fresh with butter and jam.

Gurr Cake
Bread Cake

8 slices of stale bread without crusts
3 Tbs flour
$^1/_2$ tsp baking powder
2 tsp bread seasoning
$^1/_2$ cup (100 g) brown sugar
2 Tbs butter
6 oz (175 g) currants or dried mixed fruit
1 beaten egg
4 Tbs milk
8 oz (250 g) short pastry
Caster sugar

Soak the bread for 60 minutes in water, then squeeze dry. Mix with the flour, baking powder, seasoning, sugar, butter, currants, egg, and milk. Stir the ingredients thoroughly.
Line a baking pan approximately 8 inches (22 cm) square with half the pastry, place the bread mixture in the pan, distribute evenly and cover with the remaining pastry. Score through several times.
Bake for about 60 minutes at 375 °F (190 °C) in the oven. Sprinkle with sugar and leave to cool in the baking pan. Then cut the cake into 24 small square pieces (such a piece in the last century cost a halfpenny).

Blackberry Mousse

Serves 4

8 oz (250 g) blackberries
$^1/_4$ cup (50 g) sugar
Juice from $^1/_2$ lemon
Just under 2 tsp powdered gelatine
Just over $^1/_4$ cup (70 ml) heavy cream
1 egg white

Wash the blackberries. Heat them with the sugar and lemon juice over a low heat for 10 minutes. Leave to cool and pass through a fine sieve into a bowl. Mix the gelatine with 2 tablespoons of water in a cup and leave to soak for 5 minutes. Then stir in a hot bain-marie until it has dissolved. Slowly stir this into the blackberries. Beat both the cream and egg white until stiff. When the blackberry purée begins to set, first fold in the cream and then the egg white. Place in dessert bowls and refrigerate for several hours. Serve decorated with whipped cream and whole blackberries.

Jørgen Fakstorp

Denmark

Because of its geographical location, Denmark provides a bridge between Germany and Scandinavia whilst at the same time separating the North Sea and the Baltic. From the point of view of its population, history, and language, it is a very homogeneous country and for over a thousand years it has been an independent kingdom. In the 11th and 12th centuries, due to Denmark's rule over England and Norway, the country reached the greatest extent of its political influence to the west and north, whilst at the same time having sovereignty over Estonia. In 1389 Margarete, the Queen of Denmark and Norway, also became Queen of Sweden. It was only in the 19th century that Denmark's influence receded.

The Danes have the reputation for being the most generous and hospitable of the Nordic peoples. This is not surprising, as despite its northerly position Denmark is a real Cockaigne when it comes to the wealth of fish in its waters and the fertility of its land. Nowhere else in Europe is so much land under cultivation as in Denmark, relatively speaking. Raising livestock also plays a very important role in the economic life of the country, and it is rather significant that in Denmark there are twice as many pigs as people. As the Danes export the majority of their annual fish catch of approximately 1.5 million tons (1.5 million tonnes), they have mainly become meat eaters and in particular eaters of pork.

Danish cuisine developed from the Danes' need to preserve food. Fish and meat were salted and smoked, vegetables and bread were dried. Because of the relatively small size of Denmark, there are scarcely any regional variations of note. Many traditional Danish meals have existed for centuries: *Flæskesteg*, for example, the Danish version of roast pork; *rødgrød med fløde*, red fruit pudding with cream; or *æblekage*, Danish apple pie. Crabs and herring, freshly smoked eel and Baltic salmon are the produce of the sea that are loved by everyone. But above all the Danes love *smørrebrød*, an open sandwich made with sausage, cheese, or fish, imaginatively decorated and available in a hundred variations.

Left: A coffee shop in Copenhagen, where two pastrycooks proudly present their *kransekage*. The cake, which is made up of rings of pastry, is served on special occasions, above all at weddings, and is traditionally decorated with small paper flags. Sometimes the cake contains a bottle of champagne.

The salted herring are arranged in pairs, with the head of one being inserted into one of the gills of the other.

The fish are then put on to poles, with attention being paid to size and weight.

The fish are then lined up by the yard, or meter, and prepared for smoking.

The quality and quantity of the fish is important, as they number amongst the country's bestselling exports.

Bornholm's Sweet-smelling Delicacy

Smoked Herring

For many Danes a smoked herring, or bloater, is simply known as a "Bornholmer." The island of Bornholm, which lies between southern Sweden and Poland, is considered the home of the smoked herring. The chimneys of the smoke-houses are a typical feature of the island's coastal towns – even if today they are only there as a tourist attraction, as there are virtually no private businesses left.

Smoking goes on from May to October, but production is interrupted if the quantity and quality of the herring falls short of the high repu-tation that Bornholm smokehouses enjoy. Born-holmer herring are small and tender. The fish are gutted with the head left intact, and lightly salted. They are left overnight, and then made ready for smoking in pairs, the head of one fish being inserted into one of the gills of another. They are then put on to long poles and smoked over

burning, glowing alder shavings. Smoked herring, *røget sild*, can be eaten whole, but most connois-seurs prefer to fillet them and serve them with onions, chives, and radishes as well as a raw egg yolk – a dish with the poetic name *Sol over Gudhjem*, "Sun over Gudhjem."

Right: The large industrial smokehouses, which have virtually replaced the family run businesses, offer many people work. Here a herring is cleaned and then prepared for smoking.

Danish Herring Specialties

Bornholmsk Biksemad
This is a meal made from leftovers. Bloaters are mixed with fried onions, boiled potatoes, gherkins, and tomatoes and eaten hot from the skillet.

Kogt Sild
Herring that have been gutted but not filleted are cooked in a brine made with water and a little vinegar, chopped onions, and herbs, and then left to marinate in the stock overnight. The fish is eaten cold.

Ristet Saltsild
Herring broiled over an open fire, until the skin is crispy and a dark golden color.

Rullemops
Bornholmer rollmops are made from boiled, unsalted herring. The fillets are rolled up and put in a brine made with vinegar and spices.

Røget Sild
Smoked herring, or bloaters, taste best when they are warm and come straight from the smokehouse. Seasoned with salt, they are eaten with bread.

Saltsteg Sild
These are fried salted herring (really *stegt saltsild*), tossed in flour, thoroughly fried in a skillet and served with bread and dripping, red beet, and mustard.

Sildebøf
Steak of boned and puréed herring, reshaped into ground steaks with flour, salt, and pepper, and thoroughly fried. Served with a brown onion sauce.

Spegesild
On Bornholm, salt herring are called by their old name *saltsild*. The proper Danish word is *spegesild*. Herring that spawn in the fall are used.

Vindtørret Sild
Salted herring dried in the open air, fried in a skillet, and eaten with mustard.

Right: The inhabitants of Bornholm eat their bloaters warm, when they are very freshly smoked. For the fastidious islanders the fish already becomes inedible a few hours after smoking.

The coast of the island of Bornholm is dotted with smokehouse chimneys.

The herring are smoked over burning, glowing alder shavings.

During the process of smoking, heat and smoke must be kept constant.

The bloaters are ready when they have taken on a golden color.

Ål i Karrysovs – Eel in Curry Sauce

From a Popular Dish to a Delicacy

Eel

In days gone by, when fish were still plentiful and life was hard, eel was a common daily meal particularly on the coast and on the islands of Limfjord. Fishermen and daylaborers ate eel just as much as farmers and landowners. Eel was cheap, and the price for a particular night's catch was arranged in advance, rather in the manner of the commodity futures markets of today. There was a time when these heavy fish swam in their hundreds into the fishermen's nets. Even today eels are still caught in Limfjord, but no longer in the volumes seen in the past, as modern fishing equipment destroys the eels' young.

Today the eel has risen from the status of a popular dish to that of a delicacy – despite the mixed feelings that it still provokes in many people. On the one hand it has an excellent taste, whether boiled, fried, or smoked. On the other hand, it arouses a certain aversion because of its resemblance to a snake. The eel was thought to be poisonous, and it was believed that it ate drowned sailors. Eel blood does in fact contain a substance similar to snake poison, which of course is destroyed when heated. Eels play a major role in Danish myths and fairytales.

Real eel enthusiasts are prepared to pay, as the eel has become expensive. It is at its best when smoked. Another popular way of preparing smoked eel is to bake it, having skinned and filleted it first, and to serve it sliced when cold with scrambled eggs and rye bread or on a green salad dressed with oil, vinegar, and mustard, as well as a raw egg yolk.

There are many Danish recipes for eel that were much loved in years gone by, and amongst the real delicacies is *ålekage*, eel cake, or *ålebrød*, eel bread. It was only baked occasionally – in fact only when a large oven was heated to bake black bread or bread made with rye and wheatflour to be put into storage. A gutted, lightly-salted fresh eel was placed upon an expanse of dough, pressed in and then cooked in the oven. Because eel has a high fat content, the butter or cream called for in many recipes was unnecessary. Other unusual ways of preparing eel are for example *åleæggekage*, eel roe cakes – pieces of eel fried in egg and milk – and *røget ål i øl*, smoked eel in beer sauce.

Ål i Karrysovs
Eel in Curry Sauce
(Illustration left)

| 4 fresh eels |
| Salt, sugar |
| 4 large onions, peeled and sliced |
| 1 Tbs curry powder, 1 tsp paprika |
| 3 apples, peeled and sliced |
| 2 tomatoes, skinned and chopped |
| 1 bottle white wine |
| 1 Tbs chopped parsley |

Clean, skin, bone, and wash the eels. Cut them into pieces just over an inch (3 cm) long, season with salt and sugar and place in the refrigerator for 60 minutes. Melt the butter in a large skillet and fry the onions with the curry powder and paprika. Toss the pieces of eel in flour and add to the onions. Add the tomatoes and wine. Leave to simmer for 30 minutes.
Remove the pieces of eel from the skillet. Season the sauce to taste and stir in the parsley. Serve with potatoes boiled in their skins or rye bread.

Rulleål
Rolled Eel
(Illustration below)

| 1 fresh eel, approximately 2 lbs (1 kg) |
| Chopped onions, chopped parsley |
| Salt, black pepper |
| 1 bay leaf, vinegar |

Clean, skin, bone, and wash the eel, and then turn outwards. Remove the tail and chop finely. Cover the inside of the eel with the chopped tail, onions, and parsley and season with salt and pepper. Then roll the eel up from the tail end and secure it with twine, but not too tightly as the fish will expand whilst cooking.
Boil for approximately 15 minutes in plenty of water, adding a bay leaf and some vinegar.
Leave to cool in the resulting stock. Remove the twine and cut the eel into portions. Serve as an appetizer on a bed of green salad. A variation is *rulleål i gelée*, rolled eel in aspic. The recipe is identical to this one, except that a little gelatine should be added to the stock once it has cooled.

Rulleål – Rolled Eel

Pork

In Denmark farming and raising livestock are of especial importance – which is somewhat surprising as Denmark numbers amongst those countries of the European Union with the highest fish yields. The Danes are especially fond of pork, and statistics show that the annual per capita consumption of pork in Denmark is just over 150 pounds (70 kilograms). In the old days even farmers with very little land could afford to raise a pig. Today Denmark still has more pigs than people. Goose is also very popular, whilst beef and mutton have never quite found their place in the national diet.

In the past it was only the aristocracy who could afford to have fresh meat on the table outside of the time when livestock was slaughtered. The rest of the population only enjoyed fresh meat from the middle of November until Christmas – the remainder of the year saw a diet of salted and smoked meat. When the stove was introduced into Danish kitchens in approximately 1860, the possibility arose for people to cook larger cuts of meats in their own ovens. Previously meat had to be boiled or fried in small pieces in a skillet. Otherwise it was only the baker who was able to cook a large joint for a special occasion in his oven. Equipped with their own ovens, Danish housewives were henceforth better able to serve the roast pork with crispy crackling so beloved by all. This meal became the most popular choice for special occasions.

At first, roast pork was an expensive meal, which people could only afford once or twice a year. Pork has become very cheap these days, but

Sausages wrapped in bacon with ketchup

Curried sausage with mustard and ketchup

Hot dogs with mustard and ketchup

now just as much as in the past the most important thing by far is crispy crackling, hot from the oven.

Fresh meat and bacon used to be preserved in brine or by smoking. Towards spring and summer they generally tasted bitter and rancid. Meat was generally cooked in a thick pea soup. Smoked bacon and pork sausages also used to be boiled, and were served in a soup made of pearl barley and curly kale. At the coldest time of the year, the robust winter vegetable, curly kale, was the most important source of vitamin C for the people of Northern Europe. This heavy diet was offset by the introduction of mustard, vinegar, spiced wine made with honey, or pickled pitted fruit. This tradition of adding sweet and sour ingredients to salty, smoked, and fatty foods has lasted until the present day.

Peas served with bacon and sausage are still a popular winter dish. Bacon and the traditional sausage are only available nowadays in a lightly salted form, the soup is thickened with carrots, leeks, and potatoes and is heavily seasoned with thyme. The de luxe version of this vegetable soup contains salted goose or duck.

Denmark cannot compete with the selection of sausages in Central Europe. Fried sausages are eaten most widely. A Danish specialty which is a part of everyday life is the sausage stand. These small, mobile snackbars can be found on virtually every street corner and enjoy great popularity, as they not only offer a fast way of eating one's fill, but are good value too. Every conceivable hot sausage is on offer, with a variety of side dishes.

Flæskesteg med Svær
Roast Pork with Crackling
(Illustration opposite)

Half a leg of pork, approximately 6¹/₂ lbs (3 kg), boned
Coarse salt, black pepper

Preheat the oven to 300 °F (150 °C). Score the skin through diagonally at intervals of three-eighths of an inch (approximately 1 cm) to make squares and rub salt and pepper into the incisions. Place the meat on a rack in the oven with a tray below to collect the fat and cook slowly for 4 hours. Do not baste, as the skin should become crispy. Once the joint is cooked, take it out of the oven, leave it to stand briefly and then carve. Every portion should have its own piece of crackling. Serve with sweet-and-sour red cabbage and boiled potatoes. The meat juices are served as a sauce, once the fat has been skimmed off.

Left: The sausage stands, which are to be found on virtually every street corner, offer the rushed passerby hot sausages, *pølser*, in all their variations.

Opposite: *Flæskesteg med svær*, Roast Pork with Crackling, is the Danes' favorite dish. They eat more pork than any other Europeans.

Smoked Eel with Scrambled Eggs

A Way of Life

Smørrebrød

An influential New York food critic once wrote in her newspaper column that the Danes eat open sandwiches for breakfast, brunch, and lunch. She added that to make sure they do not become hungry in between meals they eat a few as snacks as well.

Of course that is an exaggeration, but it is true that the Danes eat more *smørrebrød* than any other nation. One or two slices of bread with sausage, cheese, or fish – that is the simplest and most quickly-made small meal imaginable.

The Danes have become highly accomplished at preparing this snack, both in terms of ingredients and appearance.

When people say *et stykke mad* (a bite to eat) they mean a slice of bread, mainly rye bread, spread with butter or *krydderfedt*, a Danish spiced lard, with toppings that can range from a simple slice of potato boiled in its skin with chives and sea salt, to pompous creations such as crisply roasted breast of duck, garnished with prunes, red cabbage, and small cucumbers pickled in mustard, crowned with a twist of orange peel. There are hundreds of different *smørrebrød* recipes.

Those sumptuous open sandwiches, which are piled high with various treats, even bring their own personnel with them. They are prepared by women who have their own special training in the same way that cooks, bakers, or butchers do. In delicatessens that specialize in ready to go *smørrebrød*, there is an enormous range to choose from. Such sumptuous *smørrebrød* are, in fact, a quite recent invention dating from the First World War, when it was all about dressing up the meagre selection of toppings available to give the impression of a certain level of prosperity.

A whole culture with its own terminology has grown up around the *smørrebrød* as a meal for a special occasion, with different *smørrebrød* being served in a particular order during each course. A much loved variation, which always follows the pattern of herring, salted food, meat, and cheese, is for example:

- Marinated herring
- Warm fish fillet with remoulade
- Spare ribs with savory pickled cucumbers and red cabbage
- Cheese on a slice of bread and *krydderfedt*, garnished with meat gelatine flavored with a few shots of rum
- A strong small farmer's cheese on bread and *krydderfedt*.

Beer and *sildesnaps* but not wine are drunk with *smørrebrød*. The minimum is two shots, one with the herring and one with the cheese. *Smørrebrød* with beer and schnapps chasers can be quite a debilitating experience. It is, therefore, wise to postpone the meal to a time when no great mental concentration is required.

Smoked Ham with Egg and Onion

Smoked Salmon with Asparagus

The Danish love of *smørrebrød* finds expression in the nicknames that have been given to the more popular choices:

• *Dyrlægens natmad*. "The Veterinary Surgeon's Dinner" is a slice of rye bread spread with *krydderfedt*, with toppings of liver pâté, salted meat, meat gelatine, and red or white onion rings.

• *Sol over Gudhjem*. "Sun over Gudhjem," named after a town on Bornholm, is hot smoked fillet of herring, garnished with onions, chives, radishes, and a raw egg yolk.

• *Løvemad*. "Food of Lions" is the name given by the cognoscenti to steak tartare, garnished with capers, onions, red beet, horseradish, and a raw egg yolk.

In creating *smørrebrød* the emphasis is on contrast. Garnishes of piquant, often sweet-and-sour ingredients such as pickled cucumbers, capers, onions, mustard, pickled red beet, or horseradish are popular. Herring is mainly served salted or seasoned in piquant brines or sauces.

It goes without saying that such moist toppings are not designed for either the simple or the more extravagant open sandwiches that are consumed during breaks at work and are the most widespread form of the *smørrebrød* in everyday life. For the classic Danish lunchbox, which is prepared at home and taken to work or school, a dry topping must be used.

The sense of humor of the Danes has left its mark here as well. The much loved open sandwich made with simple salami is called *Roskilde landevej*, which means "The Road to Roskilde." This type of sliced salami is said to resemble the old cobblestones of this important road that links Copenhagen with the heart of Zealand, and which have now disappeared.

Dyrlægens natmad – "The Veterinary Surgeon's Dinner"
Salted, boiled beef on liver pâté with meat gelatine, and onion rings

Fiskefilet med remoulade – Fish fillet with remoulade
Fillets of plaice deep-fried in breadcrumbs on black bread with remoulade and lemon

Rissole
Slices of rissole with a sweet-and-sour cucumber salad on black bread

Gammel ost – Mature cheese
Mature, spicy cheese on bread and *krydderfedt* with pieces of aspic; sprinkled with drops of rum

Gravlaks med rævesauce – Gravlaks (marinated salmon) with mustard sauce
Gravlaks on white bread; mustard sauce served separately

Kogt oksebryst – Boiled brisket of beef
Boiled brisket of beef with grated horseradish and vegetables in mustard pickle on black bread

Kryddersild – Pickled herring
Herring pickled in a sweet-and-sour marinade of herbs with crème fraîche, capers, chopped onions, and dill on black bread

Leverpostej – Liver pâté
Liver pâté on black bread with strips of aspic and pickled gherkin

Marineret sild på fedtebrød – Marinated herring on bread and dripping
Sweet-and-sour pickled herring with chopped red onion and dripping

Rejesalat – Shrimp salad
Cooked shrimp on a bed of mayonnaise with hard-boiled egg, dill, and lemon on white bread

Ribbensteg med rødkål – Roast pork with red cabbage
Sliced roast pork on black bread, served with boiled red cabbage, sweet-and-sour pickled gherkins, and prunes

Røget ål med røræg – Smoked eel with scrambled egg
Slices of smoked eel with scrambled egg and chives on black bread

Røget laks – Smoked salmon
Smoked salmon with slices of lemon and freshly ground black pepper on white bread

Røget sild (Sol over Gudhjem) – Smoked herring ("Sun over Gudhjem")
Fillet of smoked herring with an egg yolk in an onion ring, chopped radish and chives on black bread

Rullepølse – Sausage roulade
Sausage roulade with strips of aspic and onion rings on black bread

Russisk salat – Russian salad
Herring salad Russian style (with onions, red beet, purée of sweet-and-sour pickled herring) with a hard-boiled egg on black bread

Skinke med italiensk salat – Ham with Italian salad
Cooked ham with salad Italian style (made with peas and carrots with mayonnaise) on white bread

Tatar med garniture – Garnished steak tartare
Raw ground fillet of beef with an egg yolk, chopped onion, red beet, capers, and grated horseradish on black bread

Tradition Since the Viking Age

Beer

Beer, called *øl* in Danish, and mead have been known in Denmark since the Viking Age, which is to say from the 10th century. Barley is the basic ingredient for beer, whilst for mead it is honey. When monks brought hops to Denmark in the first half of the 13th century, beer triumphed over mead – a situation which prevails to the present day.

Annual beer consumption per capita in Denmark is approximately 275 pints (130 liters) – despite a considerable level of duty on beer, which makes it quite an expensive drink. This rate of consumption amongst European Union countries is only exceeded in Germany, where about 295 pints (more than 140 liters) per capita are drunk annually. In the Middle Ages and at the time of the Renaissance it was not unusual for a male adult in Denmark to drink between seventeen and twenty-one pints (eight to ten liters) daily. In those days, such a level of beer consumption was caused by the fact that food was heavily salted and smoked. The beer, however, unlike today, was thin and low in alcohol, top-fermented and did not keep for very long.

In 1845 the brewer J. C. Jacobsen returned to Denmark with some Bavarian beer yeast, and already by the end of 1847 was brewing the first bottom-fermented, "Bavarian" beer, which was suitable for storage. He called his new company Gamle Carlsberg after his son Carl and the location of the brewery upon a hill. Carl Jacobsen began brewing Pilsner beer in 1871 in a brewery leased by his father. When he fell out with his father, he founded the brewery Ny Carlsberg in 1880. It was the first industrial company in Denmark in which leading architects and artists became creatively involved. The plant with its monumental brewery is still well worth seeing today. The company's cultural ambitions were already clear at the beginning.

Bavarian beer declined in popularity in the course of time and had to cede victory to Pilsner. However, a bottle of beer is still called *bajer* in the vernacular.

Danish Pilsner is brewed from malted barley, starch from rice or corn, and hops. These raw ingredients produce a light, less powerful beer which is like wine in character. Some time ago an attempt was made to introduce a Pilsner beer to Denmark that had been brewed according to the strict laws operating in Germany, which allow only malt and hops to be used. Sales showed no great signs of promise.

Beer is drunk with meals, particularly with *smørrebrød* and other cold dishes. Beer is a component of the Danish lifestyle. It is drunk as an aperitif, as refreshment during the day, or on festive occasions. A soccer game, a rock concert, or

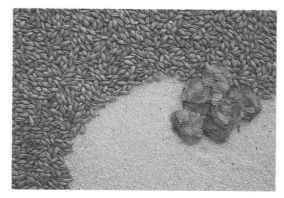

The ingredients for Danish beer are barley, hops, and corn starch.

The Carlsberg brewery in Copenhagen numbers amongst the world's largest.

Experts with a highly-developed sense of taste sample the brew and examine its quality.

an open-air political meeting, all are unimaginable without torrents of beer.

On such occasions, stronger beer is popular – Export Beer, *guldbajere*, and a stronger beer called "Elephant," which takes its name from the famous elephant gate of the Carlsberg brewery. Carlsberg also produces a porter, the equivalent of the English drink stout.

Through takeovers and mergers, for example with Tuborg, Carlsberg now controls directly or indirectly the entire Danish beer market, although there are still a few independent brewers left. Foreign brands of beer have a very small presence in Denmark. In 1887, J. C. Jacobsen left his brewery Gamle Carlsberg to a fund that he had set up in 1876. The foundation helps to support the areas of mathematics, philosophy, history, the natural sciences, and linguistics. In 1901 Carl Jacobsen also transferred his brewery Ny Carlsberg to the fund, the purpose in this case being to support the arts in Denmark.

The fund supports the Carlsberg Laboratory, an independent research institute with an international reputation, as well as the Frederiksborg Museum, a national history museum that was opened in the former royal castle at Hillerød in the north of Zealand. The fund provides, in addition, significant sums for research purposes, finances research projects, and grants scholarships. The magnificently furnished private residence of J. C. Jacobsen, with its marvelous garden, serves today as the retirement home of a Danish academic of outstanding merit.

The new Carlsberg fund, founded by Carl Jacobsen, maintains the Ny Carlsberg Museum of Sculpture in Copenhagen and awards substantial sums for art and art history, as well as for the purchase of works of art for Danish museums. The Museum of Sculpture possesses a unique collection of works of art from classical antiquity, and exhibits from the Impressionist period.

When the Danes drink their own beer they can do so with a clear conscience, as they are supporting art and culture by so doing.

Left: The most popular brands of the Carlsberg brewery (from left to right): The premium beer Elephant, the dark beer porter, Pilsner, and ordinary beer. It is noteworthy that beer bottles were already standardized at the turn of the century, which made reusing the bottles, on which a deposit is charged, easier. A Danish beer bottle makes its way from the brewery to the customer and back again about thirty times – probably a record.

Opposite: The wort is boiled along with hops in the brewing kettle during the brewing process. The photograph was taken in the Copenhagen brewery of Carlsberg.

Jørgen Fakstorp

Norway

In Northern Europe, food has kept its natural flavor. It can taste of the sea, the earth, and the mountains, and of pine and birch. The Vikings were the models for Scandinavian cooking. They knew how to practise the tradition of hospitality and served pleasing, simple dishes, namely elk in the North and lamb in the South, as well as salmon from the mountain rivers, cod, herring, and mackerel from the Atlantic and fresh mushrooms and wild berries from the forest and the fields.

It was only in 1905 that the Kingdom of Norway became an independent state. Between 1380 and 1814 it was a part of the dual kingdom of Denmark and Norway, and from 1815 onwards it formed a joint kingdom with Sweden. Despite very difficult travel conditions because of the nature of the landscape, there are no substantial regional differences in Norwegian cooking. Trading links with Europe have left their mark in the ports. Bergen is surely the only place in the whole of Scandinavia where polenta can be found. Roast pork with sauerkraut and Russian peas similarly betray a foreign influence, even if Norwegian sauerkraut is browned and seasoned with caraway seeds. The national dish, *får i kål* (mutton and cabbage stew), must be cooked in Bergen with carrots, potatoes, and kohlrabi, whilst Norwegians in the East of the country insist that only the mutton and cabbage should be cooked together and the boiled potatoes should be served separately. The tradition of preserving milk from both cows and goats by making sour milk and sour cream, rømme in Norwegian, comes from Alpine farming.

The hard life of the North has never prevented Norwegians from enjoying food and drink. Norwegians are great organizers of festive occasions. It was and is still customary to cover the table with everything that forest, sea, and field can offer. Celebrations, feasting, and eating with gusto all continue into the early morning, when oat soup, porridge with sour cream, and *dravle*, a powerful drink made of sour milk and molasses, are served. By far the most popular dish, however, is *rømmegrøt*, which is a particular kind of porridge made with sour cream and hot milk, over which melted butter is poured.

Left: On a salmon farm, where the fish are bred in enormous netted cages in the sea.

91

From a Fish of Excellence to a Mass-produced Article

Salmon

Salmon is not only found in the sea. It comes into the world in the headwaters of rivers and streams and soon makes its way to the sea, where it remains until it is time to spawn. Then it swims against the current making its way back to its birthplace once again, to lay its eggs there.

From June until August many anglers stand on the riverbanks and with the assistance of complicated baits, whose names are comprehensible only to the initiated, try to catch salmon that are making for the headwater and are ready to spawn. What they are interested in is a particular delicacy. It is precisely in this phase of its life that the salmon is endowed with strong, tasty and muscular flesh, due to its constant struggle against the river's current. But it is no easy thing to catch a river salmon, because they are wily creatures. The best way of enticing the fish is the subject of excessive discussion amongst anglers. Foreign fishermen pay a lot of money for a licence to fish in a salmon river. Strict regulations ensure that limits are set to the enthusiasm of the hunt. The angler is entitled only to the smaller fish that he catches, which he may also consume in the open, as well as one single larger salmon per day. All remaining salmon must be sold to the indigenous population.

Salmon fishermen prepare their catch in a quite simple fashion. They gut the fish, scale it from the tail towards the head, fry it in a skillet, and finally douse the cooking fat with plenty of

Gravet Laks (Gravlaks) – A Scandinavian Specialty

Most connoisseurs, and not only in Scandinavia, are convinced that the best way of preparing this excellent pink colored fish is as *gravet laks*.
The name derives from the original method of dry salt curing, in which the fish was seasoned with salt, sugar, and pepper, and was then covered with dill and buried (*gravet*) in a hole in the ground for several weeks, the pressure of the earth as it bore down upon the fish causing the spices and seasoning to flavor it.
For the modern household it is to be recommended, for example, that a plate or a thick plank of wood be used to weigh the fish down and cans of food be used as weights.

Anglers waiting for the shoals of salmon, which are swimming upstream to their spawning ground

eggs, steamed spinach, asparagus or other vegetables. In the days when there were no freezers or refrigerators salmon, as well as sea and river trout, was preserved by half-fermenting the lightly salted fish. This product, which is called *rakørret* in Norwegian, does not have that strong smell, which deters many an epicure from the Swedish *surströmming*, fermented Baltic herring. It is said that in the debate leading up to the referendum on Norway's entry to the European Union (EU), a rumor arose that if Norway became a member of the Community the production of *rakørret* would no longer be allowed, which caused lovers of *rakørret* to defect immediately to the opponents of the EU.

Most salmon available for purchase nowadays have been farmed. Salmon farms are to be found in Norwegian fjords, where salmon, salmon trout, and rainbow trout are farmed in vast netted cages in the sea and are fattened up to be sold. The fish are primarily fed on herring and capelin, an Arctic seafish which occurs in great shoals. Normally rainbow trout is a freshwater fish with very light colored flesh. By the alteration of its diet Norwegian fish farmers have succeeded in giving the rainbow trout red flesh and in fattening it to the size of salmon trout. One unfortunate consequence of salmon farming is that the wild salmon population has been badly decimated by diseases that have been spread by farmed salmon that have escaped. On the other hand, thanks to the success of such farming, salmon is available all year round and has fallen markedly in price. It is no longer the luxury item that it was even ten years ago, and is now also even cheaper than cod.

As a result of this, the salmon, which a few years ago was a sought after and expensive fish

rømme, the sour cream that the Norwegians use in virtually every dish.

After it has been gutted and cleaned a larger salmon is cooked whole and served hot with melted butter, perhaps with a little vinegar and *rømme*. Following Norwegian tradition a sweet-and-sour cucumber salad is served as a side dish,

along with the hollandaise sauce that is common to so many countries of the world. Salmon cutlets or fillets are either cooked in a skillet or in the oven and served with melted butter, lemon, and horseradish.

Particularly tasty is the justifiably famous smoked salmon, which is eaten with scrambled

that not everyone could afford, has almost returned to the status it had in earlier centuries. In days gone by it is said that there was so much salmon on the Norwegian coast, that servants and other employees would have it written into their terms of engagement that they need not eat salmon more often than twice a week.

1

1

1

2

2

2

3

3

3

Gravet Laks
Gravlaks
(Illustrations 1–3 above)

3 lb (1¹/₂ kg) fresh salmon (middle cut), scaled
2 bunches of dill, washed and coarsely chopped
2 Tbs coarse salt
1 Tbs sugar
1 Tbs white pepper

Mustard sauce
6 egg yolks, lightly beaten
1 Tbs oil
1 Tbs sugar
¹/₂ Tbs vinegar
2 tsp white pepper, 2 tsp salt
1 Tbs mustard
2 Tbs finely chopped dill

Cut the prepared salmon (1) in half lengthways and remove the central backbone. Briefly rinse the salmon halves and pat dry. Lay one fillet with the skin facing downwards in a dish and sprinkle with dill. Mix the salt, sugar, and pepper and sprinkle on the fish (2). Place the other half of the fish upon it, skin side up. Cover with

aluminum foil and weigh down with a plate upon which several cans may be placed as weights. Place in the refrigerator for 24 hours. Marinate for a further 3–4 days in the refrigerator, turning the fish several times daily, and pouring over it any liquid which collects. For the sauce mix all ingredients. Take the salmon out of the marinade, clean off the dill and spices and pat the fish dry. Cut diagonally into thin slices and serve with the sauce (3). Serve with toast and green salad.

Ristet Laks
Broiled Salmon
(Illustrations 1–3 above, center)

4 unskinned salmon fillets approximately 1¹/₂ inches (4 cm) thick
Salt
Oil and/or butter

Wash the fillets and pat dry. Cut the fillets lengthwise up to the skin, but do not separate entirely. Then fold the fillets back on themselves (2). Salt lightly, coat with oil and broil or cook in the oven. The salmon can also be fried in butter and/or oil in a skillet. Serve with broccoli and mixed vegetables (3).

Kokt Laks
Poached Salmon
(Illustrations 1–3 above)

4 salmon steaks

Stock
1 onion, peeled and cut into slices
1 carrot, washed and cut into slices
1 bunch fresh herbs (parsley, dill, thyme)
5–6 black peppercorns

For the stock place the ingredients in salted water and bring to the boil in a large saucepan, then reduce the heat and allow the stock to simmer for 10 minutes. Bring to the boil again and put the slices of salmon in the boiling water (2). Reduce the heat again immediately – the water must not boil any longer – and leave the fish to draw for 5–10 minutes in the stock, remove and serve immediately. Serve with boiled potatoes, sour cream, and cucumber salad, or alternatively with a vegetable such as cauliflower (3).

Norway's Basic Foodstuff

Cod

Several of the largest breeding grounds for cod (known as codling before it reaches maturity) and other members of the cod family are to be found off of Norway's long coast in Skagerrak, in the North Sea, in the Atlantic Ocean, and in the Barents Sea. Although ninety percent of the Norwegian fishing fleet's catch is exported, the Norwegians eat more cod than any other nation. In the coastal regions cod is so often on the

The 120 mile (190 kilometer) long group of mountainous islands called Lofoten, which is to be found off the north coast of Norway, is the center of cod fishing. It is certainly true that stocks have declined markedly in recent years, but other types of cod of similarly high quality, which had previously earned little respect, are becoming increasingly important. Amongst these above all are *sei* (coalfish), *lange* (ling), and *blølange* (blue ling).

Experienced shoppers judge cod by its color, which can range from gray, brown or green to the red of the *taretosk* variety. The color reflects the environment in which the cod has lived. The inhabitants of Western Norway prefer the dark

five to seven minutes. It can then be served simply with boiled potatoes and carrots, which are cooked together with the fish, a slice of lemon, and a small dish of *eggesaus*, Norwegian egg sauce, which is prepared with fish stock.

Stockfish and Klippfisk

Cod tastes at its best when fresh, but the Norwegians enjoy eating it dried as well. The custom of drying cod is at least one thousand years old, and the method has scarcely changed in all this time.

As soon as the trawlers drop anchor in port the fish are decapitated and gutted, although they are neither cut up nor salted. They are tied together

1

2

3

4

Norway maintains one of the largest fishing fleets in the world. Large trawlers are used to catch cod (1). As

soon as the boats drop anchor, the catch is processed into stockfish. The heads are removed from the fish (large illustration above), then the fish are tied together

at the tail and hung up to dry (illustration page right). Only the middle part of the cod is used in the recipe (2), the first stage of which is to soak the dried fish (3). The fish is then poached or fried and is served with boiled potatoes and root vegetables (4).

menu, that many people regard it as a curse rather than a blessing.

A distinction is made between cod that are seafish and offshore cod. Both belong to the genus *gadus morrhua*, but sea cod, which the Norwegians call *skrei*, is probably a separate kind of cod to be found in Norwegian Arctic areas. Strictly speaking it is only this fish which should be referred to as cod. It can be up to six feet (180 centimeters) long and weigh up to 154 pounds (70 kilograms).

The majority of North Atlantic cod are caught in the spring, when the fish is seeking out its breeding ground near the coast. It is then that the cod often follows large shoals of capelin, a small Arctic salmon, which forms the mainstay of a cod's diet.

cod that live amongst brown or green seaweed, whilst those living in Southern Norway most highly value the lighter colored fish, which has a habitat of rock or sand.

Another criterion is the method of catching the fish. According to experts the best cod is caught with rod and line. In this way it can be killed as soon as it is landed and bled white. Cod caught in trawler nets – the most widespread means of catching cod – is of the lowest quality because the fish suffocates in the process.

Preparing cod is easy. Generously salted water is brought to the boil. Once it is boiling vigorously the fish is added and left until the water comes to the boil again. Then the saucepan is removed from the heat and is left to simmer for

in pairs at the tail and hung in the open air on wooden frames. The cold Arctic wind slowly draws the moisture from them, and after six to twelve weeks they are as stiff and hard as a board. They can be piled up like pieces of firewood and stored for many years. *Tørrfisk*, dried fish, or *stokkfisk*, stockfish, as it is then called, is also a popular export item, which finds its way to the farthest countries of the world. A variation of the *stokkfisk* is the *klippfisk*. The klippfisk is split along the back, and then boned and salted. Afterwards it is hung up to dry whilst in days gone by it was left on rocks so to do.

The most popular way of preparing dried cod is the *lutefisk*. It is prepared in a lye of beech ash in which the dried fish is soaked for several days.

Strangely enough it loses its smell in the process but not its nutritional value. *Lutefisk* is not to everyone's taste. In fact, many Norwegian connoisseurs go so far as to say that this manner of treating fish is a national disgrace. The laborious and time-consuming procedure of soaking is unnecessary nowadays, since *lutefisk* that is ready for cooking is now on sale in Norway's markets and fishmongers. Deep fried *lutefisk* is regarded worldwide as a Scandinavian delicacy, and is now even available in the United States of America.

Below: Stockfish are hung up to dry in this airy construction.

Lutefisk

2 lb (1 kg) dried fish, produces 5¹/₂–6¹/₂ lbs (2¹/₂–3 kg) of fish after soaking
2¹/₂ Tbs soda (from the pharmacy)
Salt

Using a large container, soak the fish in plenty of water for one week, changing the water daily. Then dissolve the soda in a glass or earthenware container in about 2 gallons (7 l) of water, take the fish out of the water and place in the lye for another 2–3 days. Finally put the fish in fresh water for a further 2–3 days, and change the water twice daily. Season the fish with salt and bake in aluminum foil in the oven at 400 °F (200 °C) for about 20 minutes. Drain any water that has collected in the foil and serve the fish immediately.

Klippfiskegratin
Gratin of Klippfisk

1 lb (500 g) klippfisk
3 Tbs butter
3 Tbs flour
1³/₄ cups (350 ml) milk
2 eggs, slightly beaten
Pepper
1 good pinch of ground nutmeg

Soak the *klippfisk* for 1–2 days, changing the water several times. Remove the fish from the water and cut into bite-sized pieces. Preheat the oven to 350 °F (180 °C).
From the butter, flour, and milk prepare a light sauce, leave to simmer for 4 minutes and remove from the stove. Add the eggs whilst stirring constantly, season with pepper and nutmeg. Place the sauce with the pieces of fish in a greased ovenproof dish and bake in the oven for 35 minutes. Serve with melted butter.

Torsketunge
Cod Tongue

In Northern Norway, especially on the Lofoten Islands, where fishing for cod constitutes the main source of income for the inhabitants, fresh cod's tongues are regarded as a particular delicacy. They are cut out of the fishheads, from which fishmeal is made for animal feed. Cods' tongues should be absolutely fresh, because they lose their flavor very quickly.
They are prepared just as easily as fresh cod is. They are served boiled with melted butter or with a simple white sauce, flavored with curry. Cod's tongues can also be tossed in flour or breadcrumbs, seasoned with salt and pepper, thoroughly fried in butter, and sprinkled with lemon juice.

Fish, Fish, Fish

Norway numbers amongst the European countries with the largest fish catches. More than 50,000 people find employment in the Norwegian fishing industry, which has an annual turnover of more than three million tons (virtually the same in tonnes) per year. The tradition of catching fish stretches a long way back, probably to the Viking Age. Fish was always regarded as a healthy and satisfying source of protein and mineral salt.

Countless types of fish live in the fishing grounds of the Norwegian fleet, which makes for variety on the menu. It is extraordinary that coastal inhabitants have stood by the simpler methods of preparation. Boiling is the most common way to cook fish, followed by baking and broiling. This is not surprising, however, when the delicate flavor and pleasant aroma of fresh fish is taken into consideration. That infamous smell of fish which ruins the appetite of European diners all too often is only discernible when the fish is no longer fresh. This smell is very unlikely to be found in the fish markets of Norway.

The flavor of a fresh fish is best complemented by vegetables. The two side dishes that are traditionally most popular are boiled carrots and cucumber salad. However, leek, green beans, cauliflower, broccoli, and peas have become popular side dishes for fish, as stimulating to the eye as they are to the palate. Boiled kohlrabi and sweet-and-sour sauerkraut also taste excellent with herring.

For years the best accompaniment to fish was thought to be melted or browned butter. Today lower-fat sauces are preferred in the main. With boiled fish instead of butter, boiled and puréed fish livers or perhaps some fish stock with lemon juice are served.

Ål – Eel
male up to 20 inches (50 cm) – female up to 40 inches (100 cm)

Skrubbe – Flounder
up to 20 inches (50 cm)

Piggvar – Turbot
up to 40 inches (100 cm)

Rødspette – Plaice
up to 38 inches (95 cm)

Tunge – Sole
up to 24 inches (60 cm)

St. Petersfisk – John Dory
up to 24 inches (60 cm)

Knurr – Gurnard
up to 18 inches (45 cm)

Mulle – Red mullet
up to 16 inches (40 cm)

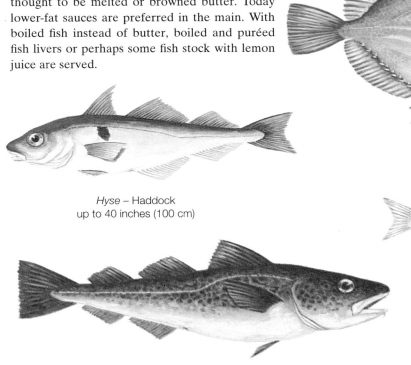

Hyse – Haddock
up to 40 inches (100 cm)

Makrell – Mackerel
up to 20 inches (50 cm)

Torsk – Cod
up to 68 inches (170 cm)

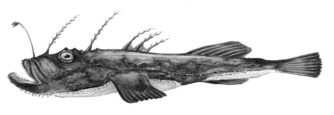

Breiflabb – Anglerfish
up to 68 inches (170 cm)

Lyr – Pollack
up to 40 inches (100 cm)

Lodde – Capelin
up to 10 inches (25 cm)

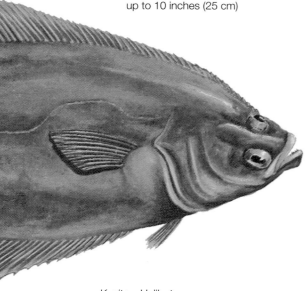

Kveite – Halibut
up to 160 inches (400 cm)

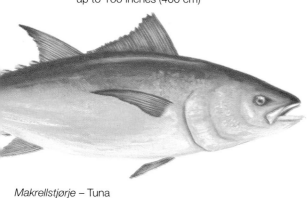

Makrellstjørje – Tuna
up to 120 inches (300 cm)

Sild – Herring
up to 16 inches (40 cm)

Fish Purée

1 fresh haddock 9 lbs (4 kg)
Salt
2 onions, peeled
Ground nutmeg
3 eggs
¼ cup (50 g) cornstarch
Just over 2 pints (1 l) milk

Prepare the fish for cooking, fillet, wash, and pat dry. Place the head, fins, tail, and backbone into salted water and boil for 30 minutes to make a stock. Put the fillets of fish and the onions through a mincer three times in succession or purée in a food-processor. Season the purée in a bowl with 1 tablespoon of salt and plenty of nutmeg. Stir the eggs in one by one (beat the purée for 5 minutes after mixing in each egg), then add the cornstarch and stir in well. Gradually add the milk and stir for a further 15 minutes.

Divide the purée into 2 portions. One portion can be used for *fiskepudding* while the other can be made into *fiskeboller*. Strain the fish stock and cover, then place in the refrigerator. Use within one week, for example for a fish soup.

Buying Fish and Preparing it for Cooking

Fresh fish is either bought whole, gutted or cut into fillets or pieces. The following criteria should be observed to ensure the best quality for all fish:

- fresh, clean aroma
- light red gills
- clear, convex pupils
- springy, firm flesh (test by touching)
- shiny, soft skin

Preparation for cooking: A whole fish is first scaled – after all the fins have been cut off with a pair of kitchen scissors – and then gutted. For scaling, a sharp knife with a suitable blade or a special fish scaler is used, whilst washing the fish frequently under running water. Scaling is best done from the tail towards the head. The belly of the fish is then cut open with due attention being paid to the innards. It is important not to damage these, but rather to detach them carefully with one's fingers and extract them from the fish. The gills are also removed. Edible organs such as roes, spleen, and liver are thoroughly washed and soaked for about an hour. The fish is washed in plenty of cold, running water, using a small brush and a small, sharp knife to remove all bloody and dark parts.

To fillet a fish take a sharp knife. Make a cut into the skin along one side of the spine from head to tail and release the flesh whilst running the knife along the central backbone. Then turn the fish over and repeat the procedure from the other side.

To remove the skin from a fillet, place it with the skin facing downwards on a work surface. With one hand hold the tail firmly and insert the knife between skin and flesh. Then move the knife, keeping it as flat as possible, in a sawing movement from tail to head, keeping the skin taut at the same time, thus gradually peeling away the skin.

Fiskeboller
Fishballs

From the purée make egg-sized balls and cook in boiling fish stock for 30 minutes. This dish is complemented by a light shrimp sauce.

Fiskepudding
Fish Pudding

Preheat the oven to 350 °F (180 °C). Spoon the purée into a well greased soufflé dish. Place the dish in a second, larger one, which has 1–1½ inches (3–4 cm) water in it, and bake the purée for 45 minutes.
A shrimp sauce or a light curry sauce will complement this well. The pudding can also be cut into finger thick slices and browned in butter.

The **cooking times** vary according to the texture and thickness of the fish:

Low-fat fish (e.g. cod)	
2 inches (5 cm) thick	13 minutes
2½ inches (7 cm) thick	25 minutes
4 inches (10 cm) thick	50 minutes
Oily fish (e.g. salmon)	
2 inches (5 cm) thick	18 minutes
2½ inches (7 cm) thick	35 minutes
4 inches (10 cm) thick	70 minutes
Flatfish (e.g. flounder)	
1 inch (3 cm) thick	13 minutes
1½ inches (4 cm) thick	23 minutes
2 inches (5 cm) thick	35 minutes

Fish Calendar
Which fish are available at which time of year?

Ål – Eel	January, April through December
Breiflabb – Monkfish	all year round
Havåbbor – Sea bass	June through September
Hvitting – Whiting	January through April, August through December
Hyse – Haddock	June through December
Knurr – Gurnard	scarce, all year round
Kveite – Halibut	all year round
Laks – Salmon	January through April, October through December
Lomre – Lemon sole	all year round
Lyr – Pollack	scarce, all year round
Lysing – Hake	June, September through December
Makrell – Mackerel	February through November
Makrellstjørje – Tuna	June through October
Mulle – Red mullet	all year round
Øyepål – Norway pout	all year round
Piggvar – Turbot	March, July through December
Rødspette – Plaice	May, November through February
Sild – Herring	January through February, July through December
Skrubbe – Flounder	all year round
Slettvar – Brill	all year round
Smørflyndre – Witch	rarely, all year round
St. Petersfisk – John Dory	all year round
Torsk – Cod	all year round
Tunge – Sole	May through December

A Liquor Travels Around The World

Aquavit

Like all Scandinavians, the Norwegians also have a relatively disturbed relationship with alcohol. The temperance movement is just as widespread as the illegal distillation of spirits. The level of taxation upon alcoholic beverages in Norway is amongst the highest in the world. This is true not only of strong liquor such as whisky, cognac, and aquavit, but also of wine and beer.

The hardy and dangerous life of Norwegian seamen and fishermen plying the Norwegian coast that created a fertile environment for revivalist movements. When the seamen spent time on land they drank away their pay, fought with each other, and caused widespread destruction. As a result the preachers emphasized the darker

over Norway is a weak form of beer which is low in alcohol.

The sale of all other alcoholic drinks is handled by the state. The state monopoly Vinmonopol imports wine and liquor and also takes on the job of selling them. Vinmonopol retails, in addition, the excellent Norwegian beer, which is made subject to the same strict brewing laws that operate in Germany. The company is also active as a producer and manufactures above all *akevitt*, literally "the water of life."

The most famous aquavit is the so-called Linie Aquavit. The word "Linie" or "Line" in English, which is used in the context of air and sea travel and which indicates a route that is traveled regularly, alerts the purchaser in this instance to the fact that this liquor is shipped once across the equator and back again, before it is bottled. Transporting it around the seas of the world and the resulting changes in temperature play a decisive role in the

had an alcoholic content of 41.5 percent. It is lightly spiced and has a subtle taste of caraway seeds and wood. Later there came the "Løiten Linje," which was more heavily spiced and sweeter. Both brands should be served at room temperature or slightly chilled, but not icy cold as is usual in the North. The label of a Linie Aquavit reveals the exact ship and exact route that saw the spirit through its expensive journey around the world.

Norwegians generally prefer to drink the simpler liquor sold by Vinmonopol. They are all to a lesser or greater extent flavored with caraway seeds. "Gilde Taffel" is the only liquor that is laid down for an indeterminate period of time, whilst most are laid down for between eight and twenty-six months. The premier product "Gilde Non Plus Ultra" is laid down in a cask for ten years and is popular as a digestif with coffee.

Distillation using a basis of grain or potatoes produces high percentage alcohol, the basic ingredient for aquavit.

Spicy ingredients give the clear alcohol its flavor: caraway seeds, coriander, aniseed, and fennel.

Old sherry casks from Jerez in Spain are prepared to store the aquavit.

The liquor, which is crystal clear at first, sets out on its journey around the world in the casks.

Having returned from its journey, it has taken on a warm amber color, which comes from the casks.

The quality and maturity are judged at a subsequent tasting.

and more punitive sides of Christianity, and stressed the notions of sin, death, the fiery sword, and damnation. The road to salvation passed only through prayer, charity, and, above all, abstinence. The only luxury consumables that did not fall prey to proscription were coffee and tobacco. In many communities, particularly on the Western coast alcohol is still prohibited and the only alcoholic drink that is available all

maturing and the mild flavoring of Linie Aquavit. After distillation, the liquor is laid down in used sherry casks made of oak and sent once around the world via Australia. Because of the constant movement of the ship the aromatic flavorings contained in the wooden casks are imparted to the spirit.

The first spirit for which this method was used was "Lysholm Linje." It was first produced in the year 1885 by Jørgen Lysholm in Trondheim and

Opposite: Linie Aquavit travels in old sherry casks once around the world by ship. As the ship pitches and tosses, the highproof drink takes on the aromatic flavorings of the cask. The map below indicates the route traveled.

When and on which ship the aquavit crossed the equator is shown on the reverse label on every bottle.

A/S Vinmonopolet | A/S Vinmonopolet
garanterer at | warrants that this
denne Aquavit | Aquavit has been
har medfulgt | carried on board
Wm. Wilhelmsen's | Wm. Wilhelmsen's

«TOURCOING»

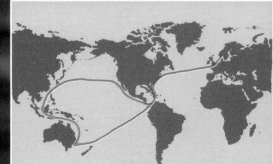

30.08.91 - 18.01.92

Raising Reindeer

In the large expanse of the tundra and the mountainous regions of Northern Norway, the Finnmark, there live about 20,000 Saami, who are descendants of an old nomadic people (the Saami were previously referred to as the "Lapps," but this word is no longer in use). The Saami language derives from FinnoUgric. Other members of this tribe live equally spread out in Sweden, Finland, and Russia, but today there are only a few left.

The life and culture of the Saami, who were originally fishermen and hunters, are closely bound up with the reindeer, which they have domesticated and which they keep in enormous herds. In days gone by, the Saami would follow the migrations of the animal as it searched for food. In winter the reindeer feeds predominantly upon lichen. With the help of its antlers, which are common to both sexes of the animal and the lowest of which has a shovel-like tip, and its powerful hooves, which are divided into two halves and have dewclaws – the name given to the two rudimentary retracted toes to the rear of the hoof – the reindeer can dig its food out from beneath the snow. The shape of its hooves enables the reindeer to roam in the snow and in boggy areas without sinking in. In past times, the Saami were entirely dependent upon the reindeer. It provided them not only with food and clothing, but they were able to make tools from its bones and antlers.

Today most Saami have settled in one place, and alongside raising reindeer they farm and keep livestock, and those at the coast fish. However, there are still a few who in the summer, just as in the old nomadic times, are forced to move with their half-wild, migrating herds and live in tents. Now as then the reindeer dictate the rhythm of the life of the Saami and their daily routine. They provide meat and milk and serve as working animals when harnessed to sleighs. The reindeer sledge races at Eastertide are a tourist attraction.

Reindeer meat was previously only known and obtainable in Northern Norway. Against the background of an improved transport network, reindeer meat is now available in the entire country. It is sold both fresh and frozen. The shoulder and leg are often dried, salted, and smoked. When fresh, the meat is prepared in a similar way to venison. For example, the saddle is a favorite dish at banquets, and is served with cranberries.

Dried or smoked reindeer meat is dark red and is considered a delicacy. It is eaten with *lefse*, potato pancakes (for recipe, see page 103), with which the Saami often eat *prim*, a whey cheese. This has the consistency of butter and is made by thickening the whey left over after making cheese from reindeer milk.

From the less tender parts of the reindeer the Saami prepare stews, which date from the time when food was prepared over the open fire. One example is *samekok*. To make this, salted or smoked reindeer meat, tongue, liver, and bone marrow are boiled in a bouillon of reindeer meat together with root vegetables, potatoes, and cabbage. Travelers in Northern Norway will come across ethnic restaurants that will prepare this regional specialty in the appropriate surroundings.

The Elk – Symbol for Europe's North

The elk, the largest member of the deer family – they can grow up to a length of ten feet (three meters) and stand six and a half feet (two meters) tall at the shoulder – live in regions with coniferous forest, and they feel particularly at home in boggy areas. They do not roam in herds, but roam around in small groups; the calves stay with their mothers until their third year. Despite their enormous, shovel-like antlers these animals can move forwards at a slow trot relatively quickly even in thick undergrowth. Because of their long forelegs and short necks they cannot reach the ground with their mouths. For this reason they only eat the upper parts of foliage and small shrubs.

In the wake of the virtual extinction of the elk's natural enemy, the wolf, the elk has increased strongly in numbers, so that every year many animals have to be shot. Whilst the hide of the elk with its fine layer of wool is very highly regarded, the meat is not of an outstanding quality because of its coarse-fibered texture and is used like ordinary beef in soups, ragouts, and forcemeat.

Bidos
Saami Reindeer Ragout

2 lb (1 kg) reindeer meat from the shin, boned
Salt, white pepper
$\frac{1}{4}$ tsp ground cloves
2 large onions, peeled and finely chopped
1 Tbs butter
3 cups (1 l) meat bouillon or meat juices
8 medium sized potatoes, peeled and chopped into cubes about $\frac{3}{4}$ inch (2 cm)
2 small bay leaves
Vinegar

Separate the meat from the skin and the principal tendons, which are white. Dice the meat into cubes of about $\frac{3}{4}$ inch (2 cm) (1) and season with salt, pepper and cloves. Cook the onions in the butter in a covered saucepan until they are transparent. Add the meat and brown on a high heat whilst stirring. Add the bouillon and cover, then leave to simmer gently for about 90 minutes. Add the potatoes and bay leaves, and add more water should it be necessary, so that everything is covered by liquid. Leave to cook gently, until the potatoes are done.
Remove the bay leaves. Flavor the ragout with a dash of vinegar and serve (2).

Røkt Reinsdyrhjerte i Fløtesaus
Smoked Reindeer Heart in Cream Sauce

1 smoked reindeer heart
1 large onion, peeled and finely chopped
Salt, white pepper
1 Tbs medium mustard
2 Tbs flour
$1\frac{1}{2}$ cups (300 ml) apple juice
$\frac{1}{4}$ cup (50 g) butter
1 pint (500 ml) heavy cream
1 good pinch of hickory smoked salt

Separate the heart from the skin, fat, and tendons with a sharp knife. Cut lengthways into thin strips and remove any visible gristle and veins. Wash the meat thoroughly, dry with kitchen paper and cut into thin slices (1). Season with salt, pepper, and finally mustard, and sprinkle lightly with one tablespoon of flour. Heat the oil in a deep skillet until it starts to smoke. Sear the meat in the oil whilst stirring constantly, remove with a strainer and keep warm. Pour half the apple juice into the skillet and reduce substantially. Add the butter, allow it to start to bubble and stir in the remaining flour. Pour in the remainder of the cold apple juice, stir together and add the cream. Allow the liquid to thicken somewhat, until the sauce has a creamy consistency. Mix in the meat of the heart and season sparingly with the hickory salt. Serve immediately (2) with accompanying rice or noodles.

1 **Jarlsberg**
A mildly spiced cheese with a slightly sweet taste of nuts
2 **Gudbrandsdalsost**
Made from heavily thickened goats' and cows' milk wheys with caramel flavor
3 **Gamalost**
A pungent hard cheese made of soured lowfat milk with a distinctive taste
4 **Snøfrisk (literally: "snow fresh")**
A curd cheese made from goats' milk
5 **Pultost – Hedemark**
A drier, crumbly variation of Pultost
6 **Pultost – Loiten**
An aromatic, almost pungent cheese made of buttermilk with caraway seeds which is easy to spread
7 **Ridder**
A very mild semisoft cheese

From Mountain Pastures to the Timberline

Cheese

The Norwegian breakfast buffet resembles a Swedish *smörgåsbord*. It offers a large and substantial selection of tasty dishes typical of the country. Herring is served in a number of different ways, as are other salted and pickled fish as well as several types of bread and crackers, hot and cold breakfast flakes, boiled and fried eggs, potatoes with bacon, fruit and fruit juices, milk, buttermilk and sour milk, coffee and tea, and much more.

Above all, it is cheese that is the most important ingredient – Alpine farming plays a large role in Norway. The mountain pastures lie mainly at the timberline or above it, a long way from the farmyards. Distances of thirty miles (fifty kilometers) between pastures are not unusual, and they can only be reached with difficulty in vehicles.

As a result of this they cannot be used for agricultural purposes and can only be used as pasture for sheep, goats, and cows. As occurs in the Alps, the livestock is driven to the pasture in the middle of June and brought down again at the beginning of September.

For the people who look after the animals and who process the milk, so-called *støl* have been built – primitive huts made of wood and boulders (*støl* means "mountain pasture," the meaning here being transferred to the hut on the area of land). Several *støl* are very often to be found close together, so that the *budeien*, the dairymaid, is able to fetch help from the neighbors in emergencies. Then there are other rooms, called the *melkebu* and the *ystarom*, where the milk is deposited for making butter (*smør*) and cheese

(*ost*). On pasture that is particularly exposed to the rigors of the weather, sheds or stalls (called *fjøs*) have been built for the animals. Alpine pastures that have several *støl* have been partly linked to the electricity supply, so that milking, churning butter, and making cheese can be done mechanically.

In order not to have to transport the intermediate products of the dairy industry unnecessarily, the Norwegians have developed ways of using all the byproducts from dairying in the manufacture

1

2

2

3

Lefse
Potato Pancakes

A Norwegian specialty, which should be tried at least once. The Norwegians eat *lefse* with butter and cream as a dessert, with butter and goats' cheese as a snack, with butter and sprinkled with sugar as a coffee cookie, as well as with dried or smoked reindeer meat.

1 lb (500 g) creamed potatoes (made from unsalted boiled potatoes)
1 cup (100 g) rye flour
1 tsp sugar
1 tsp salt

Put the creamed potatoes into a dish. Mix the flour, sugar, and salt, then add to the creamed potatoes, add some water and knead everything well to obtain a pliable dough. From the dough make little balls the size of eggs and roll these out thinly on a lightly floured work surface. Bake on a hotplate or in a skillet with a little fat, until the dough bubbles. Then turn and bake the other side. After having been baked, the pancakes should still be soft and smooth.

of butter and cheese. Soured lowfat milk, which is left over from making cream, is the basis for Gamalost. The cheese develops a specific mold on its rind that is pressed into the cheese at regular intervals and which gives the cheese its characteristic, slightly pungent taste. The easy to spread Pultost is made from buttermilk, and is a cheese flavored with caraway seeds or even aniseed.

In making Mysost (from *mys*, the Norwegian word for whey), a popular breakfast cheese, the whey becomes so thick that the lactose begins to crystallize and to caramelize in part. A brownish cheese mixture, firm in consistency and with a rather sweet flavor, is left. When the cheese is made from the whey of goats' cheese – as it was originally – it is called Gjeitost. To make Gudbrandsdalsost a mixture of wheys from both goats' and cows' cheeses is used. The slightly aromatic to pungent Jarlsberg, a cheese with a somewhat sweet nutty taste, was first developed in Oslo in 1959 and named after an old Viking settlement in Oslo Fjord.

Jørgen Fakstorp
Sweden

When the long summer evenings arrive in Sweden, before the return of winter's darkness that lasts for months and places its customary restrictions on life, the kitchens of the country houses on the lakes and at the coast are alive with baking and cooking, curing and pickling. The Swedes are particularly aware of their traditions and preserve their old customs. They celebrate with heart and soul such festivals as Midsommarafton (Midsummer Night), Luciafesten (the Festival of Lights which takes place before Christmas), and Jul, Christmas. It is particularly on occasions such as these that traditional country cooking predominates as of old. The Swedes used to be a little embarrassed by their simple fare. Today many of the gourmet restaurants in the capital offer more and more husmanskost – plain cooking – with great success, as not only the Swedes but also many foreign visitors enjoy these dishes.

Swedish cuisine has several important regional differences. In the far north they eat pitepalt, which are potato dumplings filled with pork. In the interior nyponsoppa is popular, a fruit soup made of rose-hip, which is served cold with almonds and whipped cream as a dessert. In Skåne, in the south, the "farm of Sweden," äpple-fläsk is eaten with pork, slightly sour apples, and onions, as is *pytt i panna*, a fried dish made from diced potatoes and meat or ham, served with an egg yolk or with a fried egg. As meat in general is very expensive, it is mainly ground or turned into sausages. Fish is so much the more important on the daily menu, particularly herring. Virtually nobody in the world surpasses the Swedes in their inventiveness when it comes to preparing this fish. Nonetheless, it is unusual that many Swedish herring dishes are predominantly sweet and only a few are pickled. Swedish cuisine reaches its most perfect expression in the *smörgåsbord*. It is, so to speak, the pride of the country, and its literal translation as "sandwich table" scarcely does justice to the splendor and variety of this buffet. A *smörgåsbord* offers many of the finest Swedish delicacies, which have already pleased the palate for generations.

Left: Manager Lauri Nilson and chef Karl Heinz Krücken of the Ulriksdal Wärdhus in Solna near Stockholm in front of a *smörgåsbord*.

A Swedish Institution

Smörgåsbord

Smörgåsbord: Herring

The *smörgåsbord* is a buffet offering many small dishes, from which people can serve themselves according to their appetites and personal tastes. It probably developed from the *brännvinsbord* (literally: "Spirits table"), which has been well known since the middle of the 18th century. The centerpiece was a small barrel of aquavit with small dishes of food around it, the purpose of which was to slake the appetite of a houseguest on first arriving.

The origin of the *brännvinsbord* and its evolution into the *smörgåsbord* shows parallels with the Russian *zakuski*. The richer the host and the more distinguished the guests, the greater the choice became in aquavit and tidbits. Neighbors competed with each other in demonstrating their prosperity, and in this way ever more dishes were added. In due course the choice became increasingly large and extensive, but the centerpiece of the buffet, the *brännvinskantin*, still remains a constant. In prosperous households this was a magnificent silver-plated affair with separate containers for the different kinds of spirits on a receptacle filled with ice, equipped with taps from which one could serve oneself. It was thought to be inappropriate however, to drink more than six shots of spirits with a meal. Because of the strict laws that were introduced for serving alcoholic drinks in 1917, the *smörgåsbord* diminished in significance and was only available in a smaller version – as the hors d'œuvre *smör*, *ost och sill* (butter, cheese, and herring), also known by the acronym *s.o.s.* Since the beginning of the 1960s the *smörgåsbord* has been undergoing a renaissance. However, nowadays it is practically only available in restaurants, whilst the Swedes have lost the habit of offering a *smörgåsbord* at home. In the meantime it has become a description of a meal in its own right.

A proper *smörgåsbord* consists of at least four courses:

- For the first course *sill* (herring) or *strömming* (Baltic herring) served in various ways are eaten.
- The second course consists of shrimp, salmon, egg dishes, and cold salads as well as – sometimes also as a course in itself – sliced joints of meat or ham, pâtés, and sausages. Pickled gherkins, red beets, and mixed pickles are then served as an accompaniment.
- The third course offers warm dishes, such as meatballs as well as fish and sausages browned under the broiler.
- The fourth course consists of cheese, fruit, desserts, and cakes.

To enjoy the dishes properly it is necessary to eat the *smörgåsbord* course by course, and to adhere to the proper sequence. It is customary not to fill one's plate completely, but instead to return to the buffet several times and to take a clean plate on each occasion.

Herring – Variations on a Theme

The herring is an indispensable component of the *smörgåsbord* and traditionally forms its overture. Nobody understands how to prepare herring as well as the Swedes. The fish has almost attained the rank of a refined delicacy due to the range of imaginative herring dishes that exist.

The Swedes distinguish between *sill* and *strömming*. Only those herring that are caught north of a line running from the old fortress city of Kalmar through the island of Öland to Liepaja in Estonia, are called *strömming*. As a rule this fish is smaller and not as fatty as the ordinary herring, but is nevertheless prepared in exactly the same way.

Although the Swedes do eat fresh and salted herring in hot dishes, the real culinary highpoint is formed by the cold recipes. The basis of such herring dishes are salted and seasoned herring, fresh (or green) herring pickled in sugar and salt, and dried, fried or smoked herring (a smoked *strömming* is called *böckling*, bloater).

The most popular way of preparing herring is in a marinade. Fillets of salted herring, which have been skinned, are soaked for three to eight hours and placed in a marinade of spirit vinegar, water, sugar, and onion rings as well as black pepper, pimiento, and bay leaves. When served the herring fillets are halved and garnished with red onion rings and then dressed with a little marinade.

Herring fillets that are fresh, rolled and lightly poached in a stock, can be served in a variety of ways. When prepared in a sauce made from tomato paste and onions with seasoning, they are called *tomatsill* (herring in tomato sauce), and when served in a curried mayonnaise they are called *karrysill*. Herring fillets, tossed in egg and breadcrumbs and fried, which when cool are placed in a sweetened vinegar marinade with onions, are called *ättiksill* (herring in vinegar) or *ättikströmming*.

Salted herring also form the basis for different salads. Fillets that have been soaked and cut into pieces are mixed with apples, onions, pickled red beet, sliced boiled potatoes, and sometimes even cold meat or ham and either dressed with a vinaigrette – a salad dressing made from vinegar and oil, salt, pepper, and if required Dijon mustard – or the customary sweet-and-sour marinade.

Fresh herring marinated in salt and sugar is called *gravad sill*. This has a quite different texture to salted herring which has matured in the barrel. A popular way of serving it is in a sauce of sweet mustard and dill.

Dillsill
Dill Herring
(Illustration opposite)

2 salted herring (soaked for at least 12 hours)
1 bunch of dill
1 onion
6 pimiento seeds
1¼ cups (250 ml) vinegar
5 Tbs sugar

Fillet the herring, then cut the fillets into pieces ¾ inch (2 cm) wide. Wash and chop the dill, peel the onion and cut into rings, crush the pimiento seeds. Layer the ingredients alternately in a tall jar.
Bring the vinegar and sugar briefly to the boil in 1¼ cups (¼ l) of water and stir, until the sugar has dissolved. Pour over the herring in the jar and refrigerat for 2 days.

Tomatsill
Herring in Tomato Sauce
(Illustration opposite, bottom)

2 salted herring (soaked for at least 12 hours)
4 Tbs wine vinegar
3 Tbs oil
6 Tbs tomato paste
4 tsp sugar
White pepper
4 pimiento seeds, crushed
Bunch of chives

Fillet the herring, cut the fillets into pieces and place in bowl. Stir the vinegar, oil, tomato paste, and seasoning into 4 tablespoons of water and pour over the pieces o fish. Refrigerate overnight. Before serving, sprinkle the fish with chives.

Räksallad
Shrimp Salad

4 Tbs mayonnaise
2 Tbs sour cream
Juice of 1 lemon
1 tsp sugar
1 tsp ketchup
Salt, black pepper
Cayenne pepper
1 bunch of dill, washed and chopped
1 lb (500 g) shrimp

To make the salad sauce mix the mayonnaise and sour cream together, then stir in the lemon juice. Add the sugar and ketchup, season with salt, pepper, and cayenne pepper; stir in the dill. Serve the sauce separately from the shrimp.

Räksallad – Shrimp Salad

Rödbetsallad – Red Beet Salad

Dillsill – Dill Herring

Stekt Gädda
Baked Pike
(Illustration below)

1 pike 4¼ lbs (approximately 2 kg)
1 cucumber
Salt, white pepper
2 hard-boiled eggs
About ½ cup (100 g) rice
2 Tbs chopped onions
½ cup (150 g) butter
2 Tbs finely chopped parsley
1 Tbs chives
3 Tbs cream
6 Tbs bread crumbs

Clean, gut, and scale the pike, remove the backbone and retain complete with head and tail. Peel the cucumber, remove the pith and chop into cubes. Place the pieces of cucumber in a bowl, sprinkle with salt and set aside for about 5 minutes. Drain away the water and dry the diced cucumber. Chop the eggs coarsely. Cook the rice in plenty of salted water, drain and leave on one side to cool. Braise the cucumber and onion lightly in a little butter.

Mix the cucumber, onion, eggs, rice, and herbs in a bowl, season well with salt and pepper and add the cream. Preheat the oven to 350 °F (180 °C). Wash and dry the fish and fill with the rice mixture. Close the opening well with small wooden skewers and twine. Melt the rest of the butter in a large ovenproof dish, place the pike in the dish – taking care when turning it that it remains in one piece – and then bake on both sides until golden brown. Sprinkle on both sides with bread crumbs and pour a little hot water over the pike. Bake for about 30 minutes in the oven. Serve either in the dish or carefully lift the fish on to a serving platter and decorate with hard-boiled eggs and dill.

Stekt Gädda – Baked Pike

Tomatsill – Herring in Tomato Sauce

Rödbetsallad
Red Beet Salad

1 jar of pickled red beet
1 pickled gherkin
1 apple, peeled
Grated horseradish root
7 oz (200 g) sour cream

Cut the red beet, gherkin, and apple up into small pieces. Stir the horseradish into the sour cream and stir all ingredients together well.

Smörgåsbord: Fish and Meat

The third course of the Swedish *smörgåsbord* consists of hot meat and fish dishes and the appropriate side dishes.

Köttbullar
Meatballs
(Illustration below center)

4 Tbs chopped onions
4 oz (100 g) puréed potato
3 Tbs bread crumbs
1 lb (500 g) ground beef
5 Tbs cream
1 Tbs chopped parsley
1 tsp salt
1 egg
3 Tbs butter
2 Tbs oil

Cook the onions in a little fat until they are transparent. Mix together the puréed potato, bread crumbs, ground beef, cream, parsley, salt, and egg as well as the cooked onions and stir all the ingredients thoroughly. Make meatballs from the mixture, place them next to each other on a baking tray and cover. Refrigerate for 60 minutes. Heat some butter and oil in a deep skillet and fry the meatballs in batches, stirring constantly, until they are brown. Once the meatballs are cooked, keep them warm.

Biff Lindström
Beef à la Lindström

This fine ground beef dish was allegedly named after the famous Swedish actor Carl-Gustav Lindström (1818–1893).

8 Tbs stale bread, made into bread crumbs
1¼ cups (250 ml) milk
1 peeled onion
2 slices of pickled red beet
1 pickled gherkin
1 lb (500 g) ground beef
Salt, black pepper
6 capers

Leave the bread to soak in the milk for 10 minutes. Chop the onion, red beet, and gherkin finely. Cook the onions in butter until they are transparent. Season the meat with salt and pepper, then mix with the bread and milk as well as the other ingredients. Make rissoles out of the mixture and fry them over a high heat in butter on both sides until they are brown. The rissoles can each be served with a fried egg on top if desired.

Pytt i Panna
Swedish Fry

1 lb (500 g) potatoes, peeled
1 lb (500 g) boiled or roast beef
8 oz (250 g) boiled ham
2 Tbs butter
2 Tbs oil
3 Tbs chopped onions
Salt, black pepper
1 Tbs chopped parsley
Eggs or egg yolks

Cut the potatoes, meat and ham into cubes. Heat some butter and oil in a deep skillet and cook the potatoes on a medium heat for about 15 minutes. Remove from the skillet, leave to dry on kitchen paper. Then cook the onions until they are transparent, add the cubes of meat and cook over a higher heat for about 10 minutes. Put the potatoes back in the skillet and heat. Season the dish with salt and pepper and sprinkle with parsley.
This dish should be served on plates with a fried egg or a fresh egg yolk placed in the middle of each portion.

Prinskorvar – Fried Sausages

Sweden

Sjömansbiff
Sailor's Beef

1 lb (500 g) roast beef
2 Tbs butter
2 Tbs oil
2 onions, peeled and chopped
6 medium sized potatoes, peeled and cut into thin slices
4 carrots, washed and cut into thin slices
Salt, black pepper
4 pimiento seeds, crushed
1 bay leaf
1½ pints (750 ml) dark beer

Preheat the oven to 350 °F (175 °C).
Cut the roast beef into thin slices and cook briefly in a skillet over a strong heat in fat. Remove the meat from the skillet and place in an ovenproof dish.
Reduce the heat and cook the onions until transparent. Add to the meat along with the potatoes and the carrots. Season and mix the ingredients well. Add the pimiento and bay leaf and pour the dark beer evenly over the contents of the ovenproof dish.
Cook for about 50 minutes in the oven.

Jansson's Frestelse
Jansson's Temptation
(Illustration below right)

2 lb (1 kg) medium sized potatoes, peeled
2 cans of anchovy fillets
5 onions, peeled and chopped into thin slices
White pepper
1 pint (500 ml) cream
2–3 Tbs bread crumbs
Flakes of butter

Cut the potatoes up thinly, as if for french fries. Drain the anchovies (preserving the oil) and chop them up. Preheat the oven to 400 °F (200 °C).
Layer the potatoes, onions, and anchovies alternately in a greased ovenproof dish, finishing off with a layer of potatoes and seasoning each layer with white pepper. Sprinkle with a little anchovy oil and add the cream. Top with bread crumbs and flakes of butter. Cover and bake for approximately 60 minutes in the oven, removing the cover for the last 15 minutes of cooking.

Who was Jansson?

The answer to this question is by no means straightforward. Many people believe that the Swedish bass Pelle Janzon (1844–1889) gave his name to the dish. But others maintain that the dish originates from the United States. They say that a Swedish Minister there, Eric Janson, founded a sect in Bishop Hill, Illinois and preached abstinence in all areas of life. However, one day he is said to have been discovered by a member of the sect secretly indulging in a tasty anchovy soufflé – Minister Janson had been led into temptation and succumbed. Understandably there was widespread disappointment in the community. According to the latest theory however, the dish owes its name to a Swedish film of the same title, premiered in 1929. A landlady and her cook, who are said to have considered the name "Potato Anchovy Gratin" as insufficiently attractive, are supposed to have renamed the dish, which was already known at that time after seeing the film.

Jansson's Frestelse – Jansson's Temptation

Köttbullar – Meatballs

109

Smörgåsbord: The Sweet Things

Given their marked liking for sweet things, the Swedes certainly do not forego the dessert course at the end of a meal as sumptuous as this. And who could resist when blackcurrant pudding, cakes made with different berries, baked apples, or even the famous *ostkaka* (cheesecake) await! The latter comes from the province of Småland and in fact is more like a pudding.

Today it is certainly possible to buy an *ostkaka* in most shops in Småland, but for a Swedish housewife from this province it is a matter of honor to use her own recipe, which has been handed down for generations as a well-kept secret. It is important that the *ostkaka* always looks unspoiled. Portions are taken from the center of the cake so that the resulting hole can be filled with fresh fruit the next day.

Fresh Pastries and Coffee

Braided buns and short pastry tartlets have to accompany coffee when it is served in the afternoon in Sweden. Braided buns fresh from the oven are much loved by young and old. When they rise in the oven they turn into golden yellow marvels. They can be sprinkled with sugar crystals or almond flakes, but can also be decorated with sugar icing made from confectioners' sugar and hot water.

Below left: Three variations of the Swedish *vetelängd* or braided bun – sprinkled with sugar; plain, only coated with egg before baking; with almond slices and icing

Below right: Short pastry tartlets

Ostkaka
Cheesecake

¹/₂ cup (125 g) soft butter
¹/₄ cup (70 g) sugar
1 egg
2 cups (250 g) flour,
1 tsp baking powder

Cheese mixture

¹/₄ cup (50 g) butter
3 eggs
³/₄ cup (175 g) sugar
1 lb 10 oz (750 g) low-fat farmer's cheese,
2¹/₂ cups (500 ml) sour cream
¹/₄ cup (60 g) corn starch, 1 tsp baking powder
¹/₂ cup (125 g) currants

Stir the butter, sugar, and egg well, then add to the flour once it has been mixed with the baking powder and knead quickly into short pastry. Wrap the dough up so that it stays fresh and refrigerate for 30 minutes. Preheat the oven to 375 °F (190 °C).
Fill the bottom of a spring form with half of the dough and bake for about 20 minutes in the oven. In the meantime mix together the ingredients for the cheese mixture. Make the sides of the cake from the rest of the dough and place the cheese mixture in the baking pan. Reduce the oven temperature to 350 °F (180 °C) and bake for 60 minutes. Leave to cool for 2–3 hours.

Vetelängd
Braided Bun

1 lb 2 oz (500 g) flour
2 Tbs (25 g) yeast
2¹/₂ Tbs (40 g) sugar
¹/₂ pint (250 ml) lukewarm milk
1 pinch of salt
¹/₄ cup (60 g) melted lukewarm butter
1 egg
1 egg yolk
Almond slices

Sieve the flour into a bowl and make a hollow in the middle. Stir the yeast with 1 teaspoon of sugar into 4 tablespoons of milk, place in the hollow and mix a small amount of dough. Cover the bowl with a cloth and put to one side. When the small ball of dough starts to bubble, add the rest of the sugar as well as the

Vinbärskräm med Vaniljsås
Redcurrant and Blackcurrant Jelly with Vanilla Sauce

1 lb (500 g) mixed redcurrants and blackcurrants
3–4 Tbs cornstarch
Sugar
2 cartons of whipped cream
2 packets of vanilla sugar

Wash the redcurrants and blackcurrants. Simmer in 1 cup (200 ml) water, whilst stirring, to make a liquid pulp. Strain through a sieve, remove a few tablespoons of the liquid, leave to cool and then stir in the starch. Sweeten the remainder of the liquid to taste and heat again. Stir in the dissolved starch, bring briefly to the boil and pour into dessert bowls. Refrigerate for several hours before serving. Dissolve the vanilla sugar in the cream and add to the jelly.

salt, butter, and egg and pour in about half of the remaining milk. Stir the ingredients whilst adding the rest of the milk gradually, leaving 1 tablespoon aside, to make a smooth, relatively firm dough. Cover again with a cloth and leave the dough to rise, until it has doubled in volume (after about 30 minutes). Preheat the oven to 400 °F (200 °C).
Knead the dough again briefly and divide into 3 equal portions. Make 3 strips of dough each about 20 inches (50 cm) in length. Put the strips of dough next to each other on a work surface covered with flour and starting in the middle – first in one, then in the other direction – make a braid. Press the ends flat and fold them underneath the loaf.
Put the bun on a greased baking-sheet and leave to rise for a further 10–15 minutes.
Mix the egg yolk with the remaining 1 tablespoon of milk and coat the bun. Sprinkle the bun with the almond slices and bake in the oven for 45–50 minutes.
Decorate with extra icing to taste.

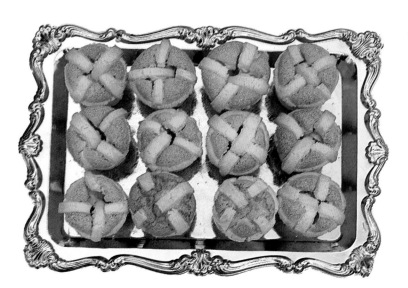

Spirits and Wine from the State

Alcoholic Drinks

The manufacture and sale of alcoholic drinks in Sweden – as with mining and forestry, sawmills and paper manufacture – are in the hands of the state. The Vin- & Spritcentraler Aktiebolag is the state owned company which produces and imports spirits and wine. This enormous concern has only one important customer, namely Nya Systemet AB (AB signifies a corporation with shares), which also belongs to the state. It runs the only legitimate sales outlets for clear spirits, wine, and beer – in grocery stores only a few brands of beer which are low in alcohol are available.

Systemet, the popular name for the sales outlets, has bureaucratic opening times that do not suit the general public. It must fulfil a peculiar double role: on the one hand it has to warn the public of the dangers of alcohol and to limit its use – above all strong spirits such as aquavit, Cognac, or whisky – whilst at the same time supposedly achieving good sales of alcoholic drinks.

Despite this restrictive attitude, which is the result of a political resolution, Vin- & Spritcentraler manufactures splendid products and imports an extensive range of good wines from many countries – even top French wines at very reasonable prices. Ordinary wine is bought in such large amounts that it is imported in tankers and bottled in Sweden.

Local production centers upon aquavit and industrially manufactured "Punsch." Aquavit is distilled from grain and potatoes and it is possible to choose between nineteen different types of flavored aquavit.

Right: Swedish Punsch numbers amongst the country's most famous specialties and is exported all over the world. This sequence of pictures shows several ingredients and stages in the manufacture of Punsch, as shown to visitors in Stockholm's Punsch Museum (from top to bottom): herbs and spices as well as exclusively natural essences and flavorings such as lemon juice number amongst the ingredients for Punsch; dry ingredients are broken down into small pieces with a mallet; alcohol is distilled from pitted fruit which has been fermented; different ingredients macerate in the alcohol, which is stored in barrels, according to the desired flavor.

Background: Greatly magnified excerpt from an old recipe for Punsch, which is preserved in the Stockholm Punsch Museum.

The Hard Bread

Crispbread

The first slices of crispbread were made around 500 years ago. Originally crispbread was made for storing. The dough was rolled out in thin, round sheets, in the middle of which a hole with a diameter of approximately two inches (which is about five centimeters) was made. Because of the relative fragility of the sheets the baking time was brief, although the temperature was very high. After baking, the individual slices were lined up on a pole and hung in the attic. During the process of drying the water content fell from an original twenty to five percent. In this way the bread could be kept virtually for ever.

Crispbread (the root of the Swedish word *knäckebröd* is the Swedish word *knäcka*, meaning "to crack") used to be baked only from rough rye flour. Today it is also manufactured from wheat flour or mixed flour. The discoveries of modern nutritional science as regards the value and function of fiber have resulted in the addition of grains and bran from different types of cereal to crispbread dough. As a result, countless variations of this tasty and healthy item are available at the retail level.

There are essentially two ways of making crispbread. Those made in thin slices have their dough cooled from room temperature to virtually 32 °F (0 °C) and are aerated with cold air. This procedure was developed by chance. In the Great Northern War (1700-1715), in which the Swedish king Carl XII had been embroiled by Augustus the Strong and Tsar Peter the Great in order to break Sweden's predominance in Northern Europe, the story goes that during a winter campaign there was no more yeast in the field kitchen. Nevertheless the bread had to be baked to feed the soldiers. The dough, according to the story, was actually ready when a violent snowstorm swept through the camp. As a result the dough was rapidly cooled. When the bad weather subsided the ice-cold dough was baked in the fire – and much to everyone's astonishment the resulting bread was light and tasty. In making other kinds of crispbread, including the dark, thicker, particularly crispy types, the yeast has to ferment to achieve a lighter dough, for which heat is necessary.

A special kind of crispbread is *skorpa* (literally "crust"). Like rusks it is baked in two stages. After a first baking, rolls are cut in half and baked again.

The Function of the Hollow

The surface of a crispbread is always covered with hollows of different shapes and sizes. They have an important function. They increase the surface of the crispbread and facilitate the greater penetration of heat during baking – a prerequisite for the extremely short baking time of only seven to eight minutes. Furthermore the air trapped in the dough can escape more quickly through these hollows. The result of this piece of cunning is that the crispbread becomes light and crispy, and the ingredients are preserved.

In days gone by special rolling pins were used to make the hollows in the sheets of dough. Today the process is fully automated.

The most widespread crispbread in Sweden today is still the one with the hole in the middle. This unusual shape in fact has a practical explanation. The individual crispbreads used to be lined up on a pole to dry after baking.

Cereals – Strength From the Whole Grain

Rye

Rye originates from the Middle East and the story of its dissemination dates back to early history. This simple plant first spread to Southern Russia and later to Central and Northern Europe. For a long time rye was regarded as the most important cereal for bread. Rye flour – also the basis for crispbread – is rich in potassium and phosphorus.

Wheat

Varieties of wheat growing wild were already being collected 8,000 years ago. This cereal was probably first cultivated in Mesopotamia. Because of its high gluten content wheat flour is regarded as the best flour for baking and cooking. Hard wheat is particularly important in making pasta. Wheat is rich in potassium, phosphorus, magnesium, and iron.

Oats

Oats are indigenous to Central Europe. In ancient Rome they were regarded as "the swill of barbarians." The Teutons, however, recognized their value and treasured them as "nourishment for strength." Oats have a high protein and fat content as well as containing essential linseed oil and are rich in B complex vitamins and in mineral salts, above all in calcium.

Barley

Barley was already being grown by the Sumerians in 5,000 BC. Barley grows all over the world as a cereal and like other cereals it is rich in vitamins and mineral salts. The most nutritious form of barley is the whole grain. Barley is an ingredient in granola and in certain types of bread as well as being important in brewing.

Roughage

Roughage – carbohydrates which cannot be broken down by the body – are not unnecessary ballast but are in fact an essential component of our diet. Above all they have an important role to play in the digestive process. They have the further advantage of exercising a positive influence upon our sugar and fat metabolism and upon the healthiness of our teeth and our body weight. Roughage from cereals is only present in the intact grain. It is therefore important to mill the whole grain and to bake it so that the essential vitamins and mineral salts remain intact. These are necessary, moreover, for the use of the carbohydrates. There is a lot of roughage in crispbread, as well as highly nutritious vegetable protein (0.8–1 g per slice) and considerable amounts of digestible and energy-giving carbohydrates.

As well as all kinds of cereal, important sources of roughage are also found in fruit, vegetables, and above all pulses.

Making Crispbread Yourself

1¼ cups (250 ml) lukewarm milk
2 Tbs (25 g) yeast
1 tsp crushed fennel seeds
1 tsp salt
8 oz (250 g) wheat flour
8 oz (250 g) coarse rye flour

Dissolve the yeast in the milk. Add the fennel, salt and flour, keeping 7 tablespoons of rye flour to one side. Knead the mixture into a dough and make 2 long narrow rolls. Divide each roll into 8 pieces, make a ball from each piece and leave to rise in a draft-free, warm place for 20 minutes.
Preheat the oven to 400 °F (200 °C). Roll the balls of dough out into circles with a diameter of 8 inches (about 20 cm) and prick several times with a fork. Bake for 10 minutes on a greased baking tray.

Rye Crispbreads
1 Rye
2 Rye Light
3 Farmhouse
4 Spicy
5 Mjölk

Wheat Crispbreads
6 Sesame
7 Soft and Crumbly

Mixed Crispbreads
8 Multigrain
9 Oat Grain
10 Granola

Swedish Toasted Rolls
11 Original Skorpa

Jørgen Fakstorp

Finland

Although they have had the terrain, climate, and history of their country against them, the Finns have succeeded in developing and preserving a society with a high standard of living. Finland was originally settled by several tribes. At a decisive moment in history the Finns migrated from the South and drove the Saami, who were settled there, to the North. Around the year 1000 the Tavastlanders migrated from the east and settled in the middle and west of Finland, as well as the Karelians who settled in south and east Finland. From the middle of the 12th century until 1809, Finland belonged to Sweden and then to Russia.

Today the country is a modern industrialized state that has joined the European Union and has oriented itself towards Central Europe. However, because of its location many characteristic features and ethnic idiosyncrasies have survived. Finnish and Swedish are official languages. Finnish and the Saami language, which is close to it, are not related to the other Nordic languages. Despite this Finland resembles other Northern European democracies from a cultural and societal point of view.

Finland's countryside is shaped by forests and lakes. Forestry plays an important part in the economy given the existence of substantial interests in manufacturing wood, cellulose, and paper. Finland lies at the northernmost level for the cultivation of cereals. Only about ten percent of the country can be used for agricultural purposes. The most important cereal crops are oats and rye; potatoes are also characteristic of genuine Finnish cooking. Farms are relatively small on the whole, the raising of livestock predominating. Mainly pork, also the smoked variety as well as sausages, form the mainstay of the meat diet which is enriched by reindeer meat, from northern Finland, and beef. Elk is relatively unimportant.

Fishing also plays an important role in the economy, although because the ports freeze over no fishing is possible for three to four months of the year. Fishing in the lakes and watercourses is not of great importance economically, but the fish caught there make their contribution to Finnish cuisine.

Left: During the last century when the Finns still traveled around with their herds of sheep they would cook lamb by burying it and kindling a fire over it. Today this method of preparation forms a tourist attraction.

115

A Finnish Way of Life

The Sauna

With a population of about five million, Finland has approximately 500,000 private saunas. The word "sauna" is the Finnish language's sole contribution to the languages of the world – except in Sweden where they insist on calling the sauna *bastu*. There are public saunas in hotels, factories, and hospitals. Even during the Second World War Finnish soldiers built their saunas on the front lines.

Since time immemorial Finnish families have taken saunas together. The sauna plays such an important part in everyday life that an invitation to visit will often include a sauna, particularly in the summer. Firstly people gather in the sauna, and then they eat and drink in a convivial circle. Sometimes the drinking spree actually starts in the sauna, though if vodka, aquavit or schnapps are poured on the hot stove then the difference between pleasure and danger narrows very quickly.

Traditionally every Finnish farm has its own sauna – often a small building in which there is a wood-fired stove that is covered with large stones. These stones give off the heat for the sauna. Every sauna has a wooden bucket containing cold water, with which the humidity can be increased, thus causing an increase in perspiration, as well as birch twigs with which people strike each other lightly. This allows the pores to open more and encourages the circulation. The ideal arrangement is for a sauna to be by a lake or by the sea so that it is possible to jump straight from the hot sauna into the water. In winter people roll in the snow to cool down.

A sauna must be well heated for a long time. Using the heat of the sauna's stove and the smoke it gives off to prepare food dates back a long way. *Savukinkku* is a type of ham smoked in a sauna (*savu* means smoke and *kinkku* ham), salted pork which is hung in the chimney of a sauna stove. When placed there it is smoked and cooked simultaneously. *Savukinkku* is a much sought after delicacy, which is enjoyed cold with a green salad or vegetables, or hot with mushrooms and scrambled eggs.

To take a sauna on a clear summer night, then to swim in the smooth sea and to eat in the open air later is such an intensive and such a Nordic experience, that Finnish *émigrés* weep with longing when they think of it.

Finnish Sauna Rituals

The first time you use a private Finnish sauna – usually a log cabin on the shore of a lake – you will notice several differences from public saunas such as are to be found in hotels. Many rules which are there for reasons of hygiene are missing in the private sauna. Preparing the sauna is usually a matter for the master of the house. Firstly he will spray the wooden walls, the floor, and the roof with a hose. Then the sauna is heated, preferably with birchwood, until a temperature of approximately 100 °C (212 °F) is reached. The stones, which are piled up on the sauna stove, store the heat.

It is customary to enter a private sauna in Finland without taking a shower, which is the rule in the public ones. Firstly you clean your body with a lot of water, which is put out in wooden buckets, or by using the hose. Then you lie down on one of the plank beds. Birch switches made from young twigs are to hand, and resemble cut flowers. They are given a good soaking in water, laid briefly on the hot stones and then used to strike the body lightly.

It is normal to remain in the hot sauna for as long as the heat is bearable. Then it is time to go outside and cool down, either by jumping into the lake or by rolling in the snow. Passionate but above all experienced sauna users also break a hole in the winter ice and jump in. The popular explanation given to baffled guests from Central Europe is that when the temperature outside is minus 20 °C (0 °F) the icy water is perfectly pleasant, being in any case 20 degrees warmer than the air.

Once the body has been abruptly cooled in this way, you rush back into the hot sauna and pour plenty of water on the hot stones on the sauna stove with a wooden spoon. The hissing *löyly*, as the steam is known, settles like millions of pins on your cold flesh and creates that special feeling for which the Finnish sauna has become famous.

It is not long before the body becomes wet – not only because of the *löyly* but also because of perspiration. It is normal to dry off from time to time and to put one's feet up in order to "roast one's toes." The next time the jump into the cold water is undertaken, it is a tremendous release.

The procedure can be repeated as many times as it remains enjoyable. At the close, however, it is important to wrap up in large towels or in a bath robe in order to avoid catching a chill.

After a sauna, the most heavily salted food is best because the body can replace the salt it has lost due to perspiration. *Lenkkimakkara*, the round sauna sausage made of pork, is either broiled on a skewer over the open fire or wrapped in aluminum foil and placed on the hot stones of the sauna stove and left to cook in its own juice.

A Highlight of Finnish Well-being

Eating Crayfish

The time for eating crayfish is in the late summer, at the end of July. This is a tradition that originates from Sweden, known there as *kräftaskiva* (literally: "a dish of crayfish"), but which has been taken over by the Finns and turned into a part of their own culture.

For hundreds of years crayfish, *rapuja* have been caught in Finland's innumerable lakes and watercourses. They were plentiful and played an important part of the daily diet as can be seen from the old records of the monasteries. Furthermore, exquisitely presented crayfish were often used as a food during Lent.

Finnish crayfish are a rarity today, and therefore eating crayfish is an expensive luxury that can only be organized with money and good connections. One alternative is to use imported boiled crayfish, something which the real gourmet would never consider. Living crayfish, flown in from Turkey, are, however, an acceptable alternative as there is scarcely any difference between them and their Finnish brethren in terms of flavor.

How to Celebrate with Crayfish

A long table is set with plates, serviettes, crayfish knives, glasses for vodka, aquavit or schnapps and beer, as well as butter and toasted bread. Garlands and posies of dill work particularly well as decorations. In the middle of the table the bowl full of crayfish is placed. Ten to twenty crayfish are allowed per person. They are boiled with a lot of dill and left to cool overnight in the stock. They are eaten cold, with the fingers, and the knife, the blade of which has a hole in the middle, is only used to break open the shell. Connoisseurs relish the tail, which is relatively easy to shell. The head and claws contain tasty small pieces of flesh, which are best extracted by sucking.

Tradition dictates that one glass of clear spirits, be it vodka, aquavit, or schnapps, is drunk after each crayfish is shelled. It need hardly be stressed that normal table manners are temporarily suspended during a crayfish feast. The sound level is high, with lots of talking, eating, and toasting.

Recently a preference has emerged amongst the Finns for drinking wine instead of clear spirits with crayfish. Wine appears to harmonize better with the delicate flavor of the shellfish – and besides, it can save the crayfish enthusiast from falling into the lake when he rises from the table.

How to Cook Crayfish

10–20 live crayfish per person
2–3 Tbs coarse salt
1–2 tsp sugar
3–4 Tbs dill seeds
5–6 dill tops
3–4 bunches of fresh dill, washed

Depending on the number of crayfish, bring 6–10¹/₂ pints (3–5 l) of water to the boil in a large saucepan with the salt, sugar, dill seeds and 2–3 dill tops.
In the meantime, wash the crayfish in running water and brush them. Put them individually – about 5 crayfish at a time – heads first into the boiling water and cover with 2 bunches of dill. When the water comes back to the boil, leave the crayfish to cook for about 10 minutes. They are cooked when the shell comes away from the tail. Arrange the rest of the dill in a large bowl. Remove the crayfish from the saucepan with a skimmer and place them on the dill. Strain the stock and pour it over the crayfish so that they are just about covered. Leave to cool, cover and refrigerate for at least 12 hours. Drain the stock before serving, arrange the crayfish on a plate and garnish with the remaining umbels of dill as well as some fresh dill. Serve with butter and freshly toasted bread, beer, clear spirits and wine.

Crayfish, dill, and clear spirits are inseparable at a crayfish feast for the connoisseur. In Finland the preferred spirit is usually an ice cold Finnish vodka and not an aquavit, in accordance with the country's Russian past.

Salmon Trout

The Finnish landscape is shaped by countless streams, rivers, and lakes. As regards the quality of their water and their ecological balance they are more intact than any other inshore waters in Europe (even if there are some dead lakes in this nature paradise because of acid rain). Angling, especially the hunt for salmon trout, is, therefore, one of the greatest passions of the Finns.

During the brief yet intensive summer it is normal to consume the freshly-caught fish immediately on the spot.

The traditional way of preparing a salmon trout in the open is by cooking on a board. A large fire is lit which simultaneously warms the air at the onset of evening. The fish is filleted and fixed to the board with wooden nails. The board is then placed vertically next to the fire, which has the great advantage that the fat can run off and so the full tenderness of the fish can be revealed. The Finns call this "nailed" fish *ristiinnaulittu lohi* (literally: "crucified salmon") or "glowing salmon," *loimulohi* (literally: "the salmon that blazes fiercely").

It goes without saying that the most appropriate drinks will be standing by. This will certainly be beer, but there will also be some *koskenkorva*, known as *koskis* for short, the Finnish vodka, which rounds off the taste of the cooked fish.

Prior to cooking the freshly caught fish are filleted.

In the crystal clear trout streams the favorite bait for the keenly sought salmon is a fly.

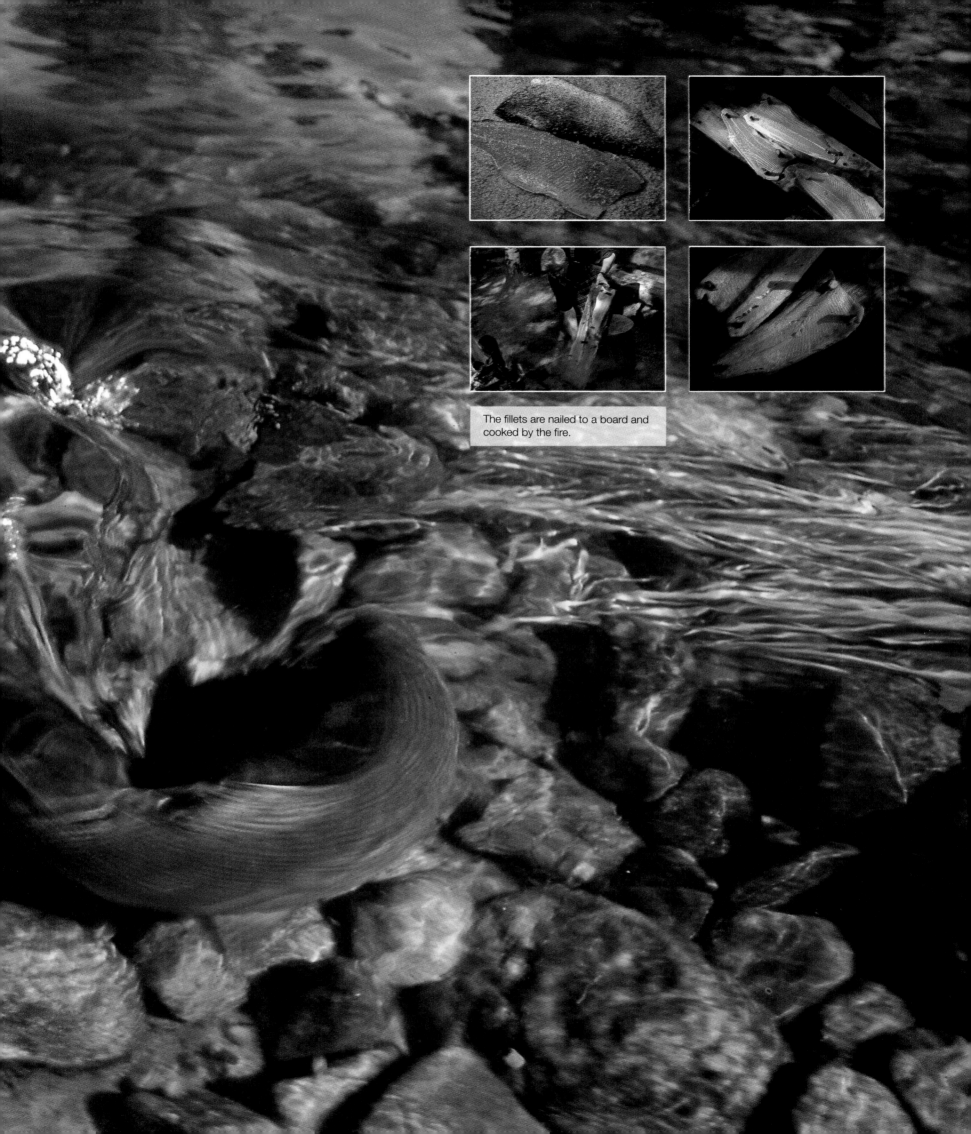

The fillets are nailed to a board and cooked by the fire.

A Special Delicacy

Roes

The meat is not the only part of the fish that is popular in Finland. The Finns also enjoy eating the roe, *mäti*, particularly that of the *muikku*, the vendace, and that of the *siika*, the lavaret. The orange colored roe, which vary in size according to the fish they come from, is salted after it has been skinned. It is eaten with onions, black pepper, and *smetana*, sour cream. At times the roe from the vendace and the lavaret are used as a substitute for real caviar, which comes from the sturgeon, unjustifiably, because the taste and texture are rather different.

Salted roe from the salmon and the salmon trout are served in the same way as the roe of the vendace and the lavaret and are used to garnish fish dishes and sauces. Particularly highly regarded is the roe of the *made*, the eel-pout, which is only to be had between November and January, like the vendace and the lavaret.

Roes as an Appetizer

Fresh roe of the vendace, lavaret or eel-pout (but also from any other suitable fish)
Salt and pepper
Thin slices of rye bread
Butter
Whipped sour cream
Chopped onions

Skin the roe. Season with salt and pepper.
First butter the slices of bread and then spread them with sour cream and round off with plenty of roe. Sprinkle with onions.

Fish Providing Roes in Finland

Ahven – Perch, up to 16 inches (40 cm)
Hauki – Pike, up to 60 inches (150 cm)
Kirjolohi – Salmon Trout, up to 55 inches (140 cm)
Kuha – Zander, up to 32 inches (80 cm)
Lahna – Bream, up to 28 inches (70 cm)
Lohi – Salmon, up to 60 inches (150 cm)
Made – Eel-Pout, up to 32 inches (80 cm)
Muikku – Vendace, up to 10 inches (25 cm)
Siika – Lavaret, up to 16 inches (40 cm)
Silakka – Baltic Herring, up to 8 inches (20 cm)
Taimen – Trout, up to 16 inches (40 cm)

Mätivoi
Roe Butter

¹/₄ cup (50 g) of freshwater fish roe
About 1 cup (250 g) of very soft butter
Black pepper

Skin the roe. Place the butter in a small bowl, add the roe and carefully fold in with a fork. Take good care that the individual eggs remain intact. Season to taste with black pepper. Serve chilled in a small glass bowl as an appetizer with white bread.

Paistettua Mätiä
Cooked Roe

About 1 cup (200 g) roe (preferably of Baltic herring)
2 Tbs chopped onions
Salt, black pepper

Skin the roe and cut into pieces. Cook the onions in a little butter until they are transparent, then add the roe and mix with the onions.
Cook for 2–3 minutes whilst stirring. Season to taste with salt and pepper.
Serve with toasted white bread.

Taimenenmätiä – Trout Roe

Lohenmätiä – Salmon Roe

Muikku – Vendace

Siika – Lavaret

Made – Eel-Pout

Siianmätiä – Lavaret Roe

Muikunmätiä – Vendace Roe

Smetana – Sour Cream

Mateenmätiä – Eel-Pout Roe

121

The Basis of the Finnish Diet

Bread

Finland is a land of bread – or to be more precise, a land of black bread. Homesick Finns who live abroad are only too happy to bring a piece of Finland into their homes in the shape of a loaf of home baked Finnish bread.

For the Finns, bread and rye are inseparable. Finnish bread is distinguished from other Scandinavian types by the use of a more coarsely ground flour and the taste of the bread, which is a little less sweet.

Bread traditionally forms the basis of the Finnish diet and must always be in the house. Should this not be the case, the old Finnish proverb is quoted: "There is nothing to eat." Another old proverb goes as follows: "Hunger which cannot be satisfied with bread must be truly great."

Finnish bread is firm and relatively hard, because the brief summer does not allow the grain to ripen fully. It must be harvested early because of this, which affects the possibilities for storage. So that it does not develop a mould, it is ground into flour straight away and then baked to make bread. Once again it then has to survive the long Finnish winter which produces so little to eat. The hole in the middle of so many unleavened Finnish loaves serves to recall the days when these loaves were hung to dry on poles in the attic.

The form, thickness, and composition of Finnish bread varies from region to region. Often a loaf will be as flat as a pizza and will be cut into pieces like a cake. Many varieties are baked without fermenting agents and a sour dough is used to make them rise. Several are baked on cast iron sheets, whilst others are actually baked in the ashes of a large oven. Loaves which have to survive the winter are baked twice, in order to dry them out.

1

2

3

Hiivaleipä
Rye Bread

2 Tbs (25 g) yeast
3 Tbs lukewarm water
2 Tbs honey
2 tsp salt
¼ cup (50 g) butter
1 cup (250 ml) hot water
2 cups (250 g) rye flour
1¼ cups (150 g) wheat flour
Melted butter

Dissolve the yeast in the lukewarm water, and dissolve the honey, salt, and butter in the hot water. Leave the honey mixture to cool, then mix the yeast and the rye flour together and work into a soft dough.
Add the wheat flour and knead the dough for about 10 minutes until it is springy. Place in a greased bowl that has been preheated and turn until the surface of the dough is covered with fat. Cover and leave in a warm, draft-free place for about 60 minutes to rise, until the dough has doubled in volume, then turn over and leave for a further 10 minutes.
Make two loaves and place them in two well-greased baking pans. Leave the dough to rise again to twice its volume (about 45 minutes) and bake in the oven for 30 minutes at 400 °F (200 °C). The way to tell if the loaves are ready is to tap the crust, and when they sound hollow, they are done. Finally brush the tops of each loaf with the melted butter.

Ruisleipä
Farmer's Rye Bread

2 Tbs (25 g) yeast
3 Tbs lukewarm water
¾ cup (150 ml) lukewarm milk
1 Tbs brown sugar
1 cup (120 g) coarse rye flour
1 Tbs melted butter
1½ tsp salt
1¼ cups (150 g) wheat flour

Dissolve the yeast in a large bowl in the water. Add the milk and sugar, then the rye flour, butter, and salt. Stir everything well. Work in enough white flour to make a firm dough. Leave the dough for 15 minutes.
Sprinkle a work surface with rye flour and on it knead the dough for 10 minutes, until it becomes soft. (Do not add too much flour, even if the dough is heavy, because otherwise the loaf will be too solid.) Place the dough in a greased bowl, turn and in this way grease it. Cover with a cloth and leave to rise in a warm, draft-free place for about 2 hours, until it has doubled in volume.
Make a round loaf and place it in a greased baking pan; leave to rise for a further 45–60 minutes, until the dough has doubled in size once again. Bake at 375 °F (190 °C) for about 50 minutes in the oven and brush with butter whilst the loaf is still hot.

Ohraleipä
Barley Bread

Just under ¼ cup (50 g) yeast
Just over 1 pint (½ l) lukewarm milk
1 tsp salt
2½ cups (300 g) barley flour
Just over 2 cups (250 g) wheat flour

Dissolve the yeast in the milk in a large bowl. Stir in the salt and barley flour, cover, and leave to rise in a warm, draft-free place for about 60 minutes.
Add the wheat flour and knead the dough until it is soft and smooth. Leave for about 10 minutes.
Make two loaves, using plenty of flour, so that the dough is relatively light.
Leave the loaves to rise, prick with a fork and bake in the oven for about 25 minutes at 475 °F (250 °C).

Näkkileipä
Flat Bread

¼ cup (50 g) yeast
1½ cups (300 ml) lukewarm water
1½ cups (300 ml) lukewarm milk
1 Tbs salt
1 egg
2 Tbs honey or brown sugar
¾ cup (100 g) wholemeal wheat flour (Graham flour)
¾ cup (100 g) wheat flour
2 cups (about 250 g) white flour
¼ cup (50 g) soft butter

Dissolve the yeast in the water in a large bowl. Add the milk, salt, egg, and honey. Gradually stir in the wholemeal wheat flour and wheat flour, and enough white flour to be able to knead the mixture. Knead into a soft dough with the butter on a work surface that has been covered with flour.
Make the dough into cakes and place these on a greased baking tray. Prick the dough cakes with a fork, leave briefly to rise and bake for about 30 minutes in the oven at 375 °F (190 °C). Brush with butter whilst the cakes are still hot.

Joululimppu
Finnish Christmas Bread

2½ cups (300 g) rye flour
4 oz (100 g) mashed potatoes
1½ cups (300 ml) water (wrung out from uncooked potatoes)
2 Tbs (25 g) yeast
¼ cup (50 g) dark molasses
3¾ cups (750 ml) lukewarm water
4 Tbs oil
5 Tbs sugar
3 Tbs salt
1 tsp anise seeds
4½ oz (125 g) currants
1 lb (500 g) white flour

Mix half the rye flour in a bowl with the mashed potatoes, the potato water, and the yeast. Stir, cover, and store at room temperature for 2 days.
Then add the molasses and water, and stir in the oil, sugar, salt, anise, currants, the remaining rye flour, and enough white flour to make a workable dough.
On a work surface that has been sprinkled with flour knead the dough until it ceases to stick. Place in a greased bowl and leave to rise in a warm, draft-free place, until it has doubled in volume.
Make the dough into a large loaf or several smaller round cakes; leave to rise further until the dough has doubled in volume again and bake in the oven for about 50 minutes at 375 °F (190 °C).

Left: For the Finns bread must not only taste good, it should also be nutritious. For this reason the general preference is for rye bread, which can be eaten at any time of day (3). Nevertheless, the variety of Finnish bread is unsurpassed: bread is made from wheat, barley or oats; then there is wheatmeal bread, black bread, crispbread, toasting bread, buttermilk bread (4), and the tasty variety which is baked a second time for several hours in the oven as it cools, bread with a crispy crust or a soft one, the flat type (1) – which is still baked according to tradition with a hole in the middle, dating back to the time when it was hung up to dry on a pole – tall loaves, sandwich tins (2), and so on ad infinitum. Finland really is a land of bread!

Joachim Römer

Russia
and Other Member States
of the Former Soviet Union

Up until recently there have been very few points of contact for Western connoisseurs with the cuisines of Russia and its neighboring states. For years the Iron Curtain and the planned economy made it difficult to take a culinary glance over the fence. The red giant has now broken into pieces, Russia is slowly turning into a democracy, and the former Soviet Republics have become independent countries once again. The halting appearance of a private economy has also created more variety as far as food is concerned, and the nationalism of the new countries is not slow to express itself by emphasizing indigenous specialties. *Zakuski*, appetizers, and *pirogi* from European Russia, *pelmeni* from Siberia and *borscht* from the Ukraine, *shashlik* from Armenia and sturgeon from the Caspian Sea are increasingly gaining the attention of the globetrotting epicure again.

Traditions are coming back to life. Under the Tsars, Russian cuisine baffled visitors with its variety and its hitherto unimagined opulence. In stark contrast to the sumptuous savoir vivre of the aristocracy the ordinary people lived modestly and often frugally. In those days they lived in poverty, as they do today, and managed with the few foodstuffs that they could cultivate and make themselves. They made the oven the center of family life, and a meal braised in the oven is probably the most important characteristic of Russian rural cooking. The highpoint of the Russian calendar is the Easter festival, which is older than Christianity and is also celebrated by nonbelievers. Together with the ceremonial masses that are said in the churches, there are also ceremonial feasts, particularly when Lent comes to an end, something which is taken very seriously in Russia. According to strict Orthodox teaching it is forbidden to eat eggs, lard, butter, and milk, as well as meat during Lent. Afterwards, however, those luxuries which have long been forgone are there to be had: beautifully painted Easter eggs, large helpings of caviar, which is called *ikra* in Russia, *kulich*, Russian Easter cake, and *pashka*, which is made with fromage blanc and eggs.

Left: A handsome feast for a special occasion in Kazakhstan.

127

A Russian Ritual

Zakuski

All civilized peoples have their ceremonies. Where the Japanese have the tea ceremony the Russians have the *zakuski* spread, a table of hors d'œuvre. *Zakuski* are the equivalent of the English appetizer, and hearty and slightly sour ingredients are used to arouse the appetite and prepare it for the dishes that follow. In terms of portions, *zakuski* are small, but the range is virtually limitless.

Russian housewives take great pains when they lay on a *zakuski* spread. The combination of colors and shapes is just as important as the range of these tasty morsels. Depending on the occasion and the financial situation of the host, the following are the constituents of a proper *zakuski* spread:

- one or several fish appetizers,
- several meat dishes,
- salads and various vegetables,
- egg dishes,
- marinated vegetables and mushrooms,
- pickled fruits,
- seasoning including mustard, horseradish, and pepper,
- fresh white and dark bread.

Figures made out of butter serve as decorations and the table is adorned with lavishly carved vegetables. Finally there is one thing which is indispensable, vodka, which comes in aromatic versions as well and is served from a rack in the middle of the table.

Selodki
Herring

2 salted herring
1 onion
1 small bunch of parsley

Leave the herring to soak at room temperature for about 8 hours, then remove from the water and skin. Fillet the herring from the top of the fish, putting the head and tail to one side. Cut the fish fillets into pieces and arrange together with the head and tail on a plate in the shape of a whole fish. Garnish with parsley and onion rings, and pieces of cucumber and tomato to taste. Dress with a marinade of vinegar, oil, salt, and pepper or a mustard sauce made from strong mustard, egg white, vinegar, oil, and a little sugar.

Salat iz Govyadiny
Beef Salad

1 lb (500 g) beef
Cloves of garlic
Salt, black pepper
1 jar of small pickled cucumbers
Grated horseradish
1 jar of pickled plums

Rub the beef with garlic, dice, but not too finely, season with salt and pepper and cook in a little fat. Leave to cool and cut into thin slices. Slice the cucumbers as well. Arrange the slices of beef on a plate with the cucumbers, garnish with horseradish and the pickled plums.

Below: The Russian *zakuski* spread consists of appetizers, not dissimilar to the lavish buffets of Scandinavian provenance. It is popular to cover a round or oval table, which can be approached from all sides. According to the social and financial status of the host a *zakuski* spread offers an abundance of delicious, small dishes and appetizers: pickled vegetables, herring, smoked salmon, stuffed mushrooms, egg dishes, chicken or beef salads, and much else besides.

Egg Zakuski

Gutap
Egg and Herb Parcels
(Illustration 1 below)

Batter
1½ cups (175 g) flour
1 pinch salt
1¼ cups (250 ml) lukewarm water
¼ cup (50 g) soft butter
Oil for deep-frying

Filling
8 eggs
Salt, black pepper
2 Tbs melted butter
1 tsp flour
5 Tbs finely chopped parsley
3 Tbs finely chopped dill
1 Tbs finely chopped coriander
3 Tbs finely chopped scallions

To make the filling whisk and season the eggs, and stir in the butter and flour as well as the herbs and scallions.
Preheat the oven to 350 °F (180 °C). Generously butter a soufflé dish and place the egg mixture in it. Bake in the oven for about 15 minutes, until the egg mixture becomes firm. Leave to cool.
To make the batter mix the ingredients and knead until a firm consistency is achieved.
Roll the batter out thinly and cut into squares about 2 inches (5 cm) across. Place 1 heaped tablespoon of the filling on each square of batter. Make batter parcels out of each square by pressing the corners together firmly. Deep-fry the batter parcels in hot oil for 3–4 minutes. Allow the oil to drain and serve immediately.

Kartofelnyi Salat po-russki
Russian Potato Salad
(Illustration 2 below)

2 lb (1 kg) potatoes
2 Tbs chopped scallions
2 Tbs finely chopped dill
5 pickled gherkins, diced
5 radishes, thinly sliced
A bunch of dill

Dressing
5 Tbs mayonnaise
2 tsp Worcestershire sauce
1 Tbs ketchup
2 Tbs white wine
A little horseradish

Boil the potatoes in their skins, peel whilst still hot, leave to cool and cut into slices. Mix carefully with the scallions, dill, gherkins, and radishes. To make the dressing mix the ingredients and add to the salad. Leave to soak for about 30 minutes and garnish with dill.

Yaitsa po-minski
Eggs Minsk
(Illustration 3 below)

10 hard-boiled eggs
⅓ cup (75 g) soft butter
1 Tbs mayonnaise
2 Tbs heavy cream
3 Tbs finely chopped dill
1 Tbs finely chopped parsley
2 tsp paprika
Salt, black pepper
4 Tbs bread crumbs
3 Tbs grated cheese
Anchovy fillets, soaked and halved

Cut the eggs in half and remove the yolks. Mix the egg yolks with the butter, mayonnaise, double cream, the herbs, and paprika, then season.
Chop 4 egg white halves finely and mix with the egg yolks as well. Fill the remaining 16 egg white halves with the egg yolk mixture.
Preheat the oven to 400 °F (200 °C). Mix the bread crumbs and cheese together. Lay the anchovy fillets diagonally across the eggs and sprinkle with the cheese and bread crumbs. Brown for about 10 minutes in the oven. Serve hot.

Yaitsa po-russki
Russian Eggs
(Illustration 4 below)

10 hard-boiled eggs
3 Tbs mayonnaise
2 Tbs Dijon mustard
5 pickled gherkins, diced
2 Tbs finely chopped scallions
Salt, black pepper
1 red pepper
Capers

Cut the eggs in half and remove the yolks. Mash the yolks and mix with the other ingredients, then return to the empty egg whites.
Decorate with star shaped slices of peppers and capers.

1

2

3

4

Zakuski with Mushrooms

Mushroom dishes not only play a large role in the *zakuski* spread, but also in Russian cooking in general. In the early fall Russia's extensive forests are rich in mushrooms. Statistically speaking, it has been calculated that approximately thirty-five pounds (fifteen kilograms) of mushrooms are consumed each year by every Russian. This gift of nature has made the Russians great admirers of the mushroom. They are to be seen in the early morning setting off into the forests on the silent hunt for mushrooms, and despite the existing damage to the environment, the yield is even today quite considerable. Mushrooms have a particular significance for the Russian diet because during Lent, which is strictly observed, even the consumption of dairy products is forbidden.

It is a natural consequence of having such a glut of mushrooms that the Russians have become adept at preserving them, even over the winter, for example by pickling. This is particularly suitable for the saffron milk cap, the chanterelle, and the honey fungus. A large barrel is thoroughly washed and treated by placing juniper bush branches in it and pouring boiling water over them. Then the barrel is sealed so that the steam cannot escape. Later a hot rock is thrown into the barrel to heat the water up again. The effect is not only one of releasing the marvellous aroma of the juniper which penetrates the barrel, but juniper also has the quality of a disinfectant, thus ensuring that the mushrooms do not go mouldy in the winter.

The mushrooms are carefully cleaned and placed in the barrel in layers. Each layer is covered with dill and the leaves of the redcurrant bush, the horseradish plant, oak and cherry, and caraway seeds and other spices are used. When the barrel is full, it is covered up with a sack of salt and a plank of wood is placed on top, which in turn is weighed down with a stone. After a while the plank sinks and mushroom juice collects upon it, which from time to time is removed. After about two months the mushrooms are thoroughly soaked and can be served. They taste quite delicious with a small glass of vodka.

Tomatoes, cucumbers, and other crops are pickled in Russia in this way. However, mushrooms are not only served pickled or dried, there are also many popular recipes for which fresh mushrooms are used, for example mushroom caviar.

Marinovannyie Griby
Marinated Mushrooms
(Illustration)

1 lb (500 g) ordinary mushrooms or oyster mushrooms
2 garlic cloves
2 cloves
1 bay leaf
3 peppercorns
1 Tbs sugar
1 tsp salt
1¼ cups (250 ml) red wine vinegar
Oil

Wash the mushrooms and remove the stalks. With the exception of the oil bring the rest of the ingredients to the boil in just over ½ cup (125 ml) of water, then add the mushrooms. Remove the saucepan lid and leave to simmer on a reduced heat, until the mushrooms sink to the bottom of the saucepan.
Remove the garlic and leave the stock to cool. Place the mushrooms in the fluid in jars and pour on the oil so that a film forms on the surface of the fluid, thus providing a seal. Cover so that the jars are airtight and refrigerate for 10 days.

Baklazhanaia Ikra
"Poor Man's Caviar"
(Illustration)

1 onion
12 oz (350 g) assorted mushrooms
½ cup (100 g) butter
1 glass of dry sherry
1 sprig each of parsley, tarragon, and marjoram
5 oz (150 g) Quark or fromage blanc

Peel the onions and chop them finely, wash the mushrooms and cook in butter with the onions in a large skillet. Add the sherry and remove the skillet from the cooker.
Wash the herbs, chop them finely and mix with the Quark. Mix the mushrooms and onions with the Quark mixture. Place in an earthenware casserole spreading them evenly, make a circle on the surface and cover. Refrigerate overnight or even better for several days. Serve with slices of rye bread.

Griby v Smetanie
Mushrooms in Sour Cream
(Illustration)

1 lb (500 g) mushrooms, washed
4 scallions, washed and chopped
½ cup (100 g) butter
1 Tbs flour
Salt, black pepper
1 carton of sour cream
1 carton of heavy cream
¼ cup (50 g) grated cheese

Cook the mushrooms with the scallions in half the butter. Stir 1 tablespoon of butter into the flour and add to the mushrooms. When the mixture has thickened, season with salt and pepper, and stir in the sour cream and heavy cream.
Preheat the oven to 350 °F (180 °C). Place the mushroom mixture in an ovenproof dish, sprinkle with cheese and the rest of the butter in flakes and brown for 20–25 minutes.

Opposite: A sumptuous *zakuski* spread in the open air at the turn of the century.

Marinovannyie Griby – Marinated Mushrooms

Baklazhanaia Ikra – "Poor Man's Caviar"

Griby v Smetanie – Mushrooms in Sour Cream

The Acid Test for the Housewife

Pirogi

The acid test for the Russian housewife is her ability to cook *pirogi*, lavish pasties which vary considerably in size. It is no accident that the *pirog* also plays an important role at weddings. Newlyweds in the country have to bake a *pirog* the day after their marriage, which they then offer to their guests with a glass of wine. Every guest is required to try the *pirog*, to sample the wine, convey their best wishes, and to place a present of money on the tray. Often a *kurnik* is served at a Russian wedding, which is a large *pirog* with several fillings, although chicken is always used.

There are countless types of *pirogi*: open and closed ones, small and large, round and square, baked and fried, sweet and sour *pirogi*. The most varied ingredients are used as fillings. A *pirog* is, therefore, always a secret – on the one hand because the pastry does not always turn out the same, and on the other because of the filling, which cannot be seen in an enclosed *pirog*. Russian housewives like to put their individual mark on *pirogi*, pricking small rows of holes in the pastry with a fork in a kind of code, so that the number of holes provides information about the filling.

The *kulibiaka* is a particularly large *pirog*. It is a huge pasty that will more than satisfy ten people at a time. The classic recipe uses a stuffing of fish and rice, but a mushroom filling is also popular.

Basic Recipe for Pirogi

1 Tbs (20 g) yeast
2 Tbs sugar
2 Tbs lukewarm water
1 lb (500 g) flour
½ cup (125 ml) milk
Salt
4 eggs
¾ cup (125 g) butter
Oil
1 beaten egg

Dissolve the yeast with the sugar in the lukewarm water and with one third of the flour make into dough. Sprinkle with flour and leave to rise in a warm place for 2–3 hours.
Add the milk, season slightly with salt and knead with the eggs, butter and the rest of the flour into a smooth, relatively firm dough. Add a little oil and knead it in, then leave for 2 hours.
Shape the dough into a tube and cut into slices of equal length. Make a ball from each slice and leave again to rise for several minutes. Roll out round pastry shapes the size of a cookie from each ball and place the desired filling in the center. Fold the dough over the filling and make a crease in it. Place on a greased baking tray and leave on one side for 20 minutes, brush with a little beaten egg and bake in the oven at a high temperature of about 480 °F (250 °C).

Pirogi iz Mjasom
Ground Meat Pirogi

1 lb (500 g) ground meat
2 onions
1 Tbs flour
Parsley, carrots, celery and leeks, washed and diced
Salt, black pepper

Brown the meat briefly in butter and then put it through the grinder. Peel and chop the onions, brown together with the flour in the meat fat and juices, add a little hot water, add the vegetables and season.
Mix with the meat and use as a filling for the *pirogi*.

Pirogi iz Tvorogom
Quark Pirogi

1 Tbs flour
1 lb (500 g) Quark
2 eggs
2 Tbs sugar
1 small packet of vanilla sugar
Salt

Lightly cook the flour with a little fat in a skillet. Mix the Quark with the eggs and sugar, add the flour and vanilla sugar, season with salt and beat until smooth. Use as a filling for the *pirogi*.

Rybnik
Large Siberian Fish Pirog

2 raw potatoes, cut into thin slices
1 lb (500 g) fish fillets, cut into pieces
Salt, black pepper
1 onion, peeled and sliced
2 Tbs of melted butter
1 beaten egg

Prepare the *pirogi* dough according to the basic recipe (left) and roll into two large sheets. Place the slices of potato on one of the sheets, then the fish, season and cover with the slices of onion. Sprinkle with butter and cover with the other sheet of pastry. Press the edges of the pastry sheets together well, leave the *pirog* to one side for about 20 minutes and brush with egg. Prick the dough case several times with a fork and bake the pasty in the oven at a temperature of 400 °F (200 °C), until the casing browns.

Siberia's Ravioli

Pelmeni

Pelmeni are small stuffed parcels of dough, which are slightly reminiscent of Italian ravioli. Although they have their origins in Mongolia, Siberia is regarded as their home, and it is there that they are mainly eaten as the main meal to the present day. The traditional filling is one of chopped horsemeat.

During Siberian winters huge amounts of *pelmeni* are prepared, an activity that involves all the women of the household. The finished parcels of dough are placed on planks and put in the open air where they freeze. They are then packed in bags and hung up in cold rooms to provide food for the entire winter.

Pelmeni were the classic provisions for Siberians on their winter journeys. When they went hunting or collecting wood they would take frozen *pelmeni* with them. When underway they would light a fire, melt snow in a cauldron and bring the resulting water to the boil. Then they would put the *pelmeni* in the water and after a short while a tasty meal would be ready for eating.

Pelmeni are today not only popular in Siberia, but also in the whole of Russia. They became famous towards the end of the last century because of the Lopachov Restaurant in Moscow, an old establishment that boasted splendid decorations of Gobelins tapestries and antique silver. It was here that the best *pelmeni* chef from Siberia worked. Rumor has it that one day the owners of the most important goldmines in Siberia alighted there and except for *zakuski* ate nothing but *pelmeni*. It is said that for twelve people around 2,500 of these small pastry parcels were served, stuffed with meat and fish. As a dessert – a premiere – *pelmeni* with a fruit filling were served in pink champagne.

The difficulty in making *pelmeni* centers upon making a dough that is as thin as possible, one that should be no thicker than a knife blade. The *pelmeni* should neither burst nor stick to each other whilst they are cooking, and they taste at their best if they were frozen before being boiled. When deep frozen they last for about three months.

Background: Pirogi and, on a plate, mushroom pelmeni

Basic Recipe for Pelmeni

¹/₂ cup (100 ml) milk
1 pinch of salt
1¹/₂ cups (200 g) flour
1 tsp oil

Mix the milk with the same amount of water and the salt. Add the flour and work into a dough. Finally, add the oil and knead it in. Roll the dough out very thinly and cut out small round shapes with pastry forms or a small glass.
Place the desired filling on each piece of dough, fold the dough into a half-moon shape and press the edges together firmly. Either cook the finished *pelmeni* in boiling water or freeze.

Pelmeni Sibirskie
Siberian Pelmeni

14 oz (400 g) beef
4 oz (100 g) calf's liver
1 onion
Salt, black pepper

Grind the beef twice through a grinder (or prepare similarly in a foodmixer), adding the liver the second time around. Peel the onion, purée it, and stir into the meat. Season, knead well, and fill the *pelmeni* with the resulting mixture.

Pelmeni iz Gribami
Mushroom Pelmeni

5 oz (150 g) mushrooms
¹/₂ onion
Salt

Wash the mushrooms, then cut the mushrooms and onion into small cubes. Cook the onion in butter until it has turned a golden yellow color, add the mushroom cubes and cook for 3 minutes whilst stirring. Then season with salt and leave to cool. Fill the *pelmeni* with the resulting mixture.

Special ships are equipped to process the sturgeon.

The catch is processed on board under clinical conditions.

The roe is removed and the grains of caviar are put through a sieve.

The caviar is salted and then packed in cans.

A Luxury Since the Time of the Tsars

The Sturgeon

The sturgeon, which has been regarded as a luxury since time immemorial, lives in the Caspian Sea and the Volga Basin. Its meat is delicate yet firm and contains virtually no bones, the fillets are rather large and the taste exquisite. In fact the sturgeon is not only highly regarded for its legendary caviar roe, but above all for its delicious meat, which can be prepared in many different ways.

The sturgeon is not only found in the Caspian Sea, but also in the rivers of Siberia and the inshore waters of Asia. It is said that this prevalence of sturgeon was one of the reasons why Russian explorers and conquerors extended the Tsar's dominion to the Pacific coast of Asia.

Even Louis XIV, who ruled France from 1643 to 1715 as the Sun King, had sturgeon delivered to his court. In the 19th century cold sturgeon with horseradish sauce was a popular dish in restaurants in Moscow, and in the banqueting rooms of the Hermitage restaurant in St Petersburg live sturgeon were presented to the guests and killed before their very eyes. It was here that grandiose banquets took place which had sturgeon dishes as the center of attention. In particular a dish by the name of *balyk* was very popular amongst the connoisseurs. It consisted of the dried back of the Sevruga sturgeon in wafer-thin slices served with a glass of vodka.

During the Soviet era the sturgeon disappeared from Russian fish markets, and it is only very recently that it has made a reappearance there – as it has also done abroad on the menus of restaurants in the West. It is regarded as the height of luxury to poach sturgeon in champagne.

Osetrina Varjonaja
Sturgeon in Champagne

| 4 sturgeon fillets |
| Salt |
| ¹/₂ bottle of champagne |
| ¹/₈ cup (30 g) of butter in flakes |
| 1 lemon, thinly sliced |

Cut the sturgeon fillets into pieces about 4 inches (10 cm) wide, season with a little salt and place in a casserole dish.
Add enough champagne to cover the pieces of fish halfway, add the flakes of butter and place the slices of lemon on top.
Put the lid on the casserole, bring the fish to the boil and cook slowly on a medium heat. Allow 30 minutes if the slices of fish are 4 inches (10 cm) thick. Remove the fish from the champagne stock, leave to drain and serve on preheated plates with a fresh green salad.
The remaining liquid makes an excellent fish stock for subsequent use.

Sevruga up to 6¹/₂ feet (200 cm)
This fish can weigh up to 175 pounds (80 kilograms). It is found in the Caspian and in the Black Sea, although it has also occasionally been sighted in the Adriatic and in the Danube as far as Bratislava. It is this fish which yields the caviar with the smallest grains.

Sevruga
Sevruga caviar: small, dark grain, diameter of ¹/₁₁ inch (2.5 mm), strong flavor.

Osetr up to 18 feet (550 cm)
This migratory fish, which spawns in the spring in rivers, can weigh up to 440 pounds (200 kilograms).

Osetr
Osetr caviar: brownish grain with a diameter of ¹/₉ inch (3 mm), nutty flavor.

Beluga
Beluga caviar: the largest grain (and most expensive), diameter ¹/₉–¹/₆ inch (3–4 mm), light gray in color.

Beluga up to 30 feet (900 cm)
This giant amongst sturgeon, also respectfully known amongst fishermen as the "elephant fish," can weigh up to 3,300 pounds (1,500 kilograms), and the roe can account for up to 15 percent of its bodyweight. Beluga caviar is the most expensive and has the largest grains.

Sterlet up to 40 inches (100 cm)
The smallest sturgeon can weigh up to 13 pounds (6 kilograms). The meat of the sterlet is excellent for making the clear fish soup *ukha* (recipe p. 141). In days gone by the sterlet could be found in the Danube even as far as Ulm, but today it is virtually extinct.

Sturgeon (*acipenser gueldenstaedti*) up to 13 feet (400 cm)
Three kinds of this migratory fish, which can weigh up to 350 pounds (160 kilograms), are well-known. They are the Pontic, the North Caspian and the South Caspian. The fish propagates in fresh water, but non-migratory varieties are found in the Volga and the Danube.

Caviar

No other Russian delicacy is so sought after in the entire world as caviar, the sturgeon's roe. As a delicacy enjoyed by the rich and powerful, it takes its place on the menu of European luxuries above champagne, truffles, oysters, and pâté de foie gras. Its price is astronomical, the pleasure it affords many incomparable. To eat caviar is to participate in luxury.

In the 18th and 19th centuries the consumption of caviar numbered amongst the passions of the *bon viveur*, and furthermore was a status symbol. It was regarded as an honor in a wealthy household to be able to keep several pounds of caviar ever ready in a *zakuski* spread, for the eventuality that unexpected guests should arrive. Today caviar – called *ikra* in Russian – is still a symbol of luxury and good living. For those lucky catches that yield a particularly beautiful and large grain, millionaires are prepared to pay top prices, and naturally at the time of the Tsars such lucky finds were first offered to the ruler.

The premium placed upon the sturgeon, the provider of caviar, has practically driven the fish to extinction. The worldwide demand for this expensive delicacy, combined with the chronic shortage of currency in the Soviet empire, coincided most unfortunately with the arrival of significant discoveries of oil in the Caspian Sea, the area with the largest stock of sturgeon in the former Soviet Union. The stocks were wiped out very quickly by overfishing, the oil took away the natural habitat of the fish. The result was ever-rising prices, which made an immensely expensive delicacy out of a fish that had once been a part of the population's everyday diet (the fishermen on the Caspian Sea ate virtually nothing else besides potatoes). It is extraordinary that ninety percent of the catch remains at home and only ten percent is exported.

There has been no shortage of attempts to find a substitute for caviar. Salmon and trout roe are regarded as an acceptable alternative, whilst the black, fine-grained roe of the lumpsucker provides an unsatisfactory substitute both from the point of view of appearance and flavor. The truth is, as admirers of caviar have always known, that nothing is better than "real" sturgeon caviar.

The Composition of Caviar

As soon as the sturgeon is caught, caviar is processed immediately on board specially equipped ships. They are distinguished by their absolute cleanliness and resemble floating operating theaters. The roe is removed from the fish, and an expert determines how the caviar will later be sold by examining the condition of the grains. The caviar is graded in the following categories.

Fresh Caviar
This is practically left untreated and must, therefore, be consumed within a few days.

Malossol
This Russian word means "lightly salted" and is therefore not an indication of a type of caviar, but rather a mark of quality. When stored correctly at 32 °F (0 °C) it keeps for a year.

Pasteurized Caviar
This is heated and placed in airtight jars like a jam and can therefore be kept virtually for ever.

Pressed Caviar
Roe which is damaged and of a lesser value is more heavily salted and made into bricks. Pressed caviar is good value, but has an intensive caviar taste.

The process of salting only lasts for ten minutes and is carried out by hand. The caviar is spread out and is rubbed with an exactly measured film of salt. In this way the grains become firm, but must not be allowed to turn hard. After this the caviar is put into large cans, which carry the number of the fish – the roe of different sturgeon are never mixed with each other. The cans are placed in the storerooms of the ship. Once on land caviar is then put into smaller cans and dispatched.

Caviar requires a constant storage temperature of 32 °F (0 °C). Frost destroys the cell structure of the roe forever and when kept at too warm a temperature the caviar spoils. For the lengthy distance from the Caspian Sea to the court of the Tsar special warming devices were required in days gone by during winter and cooling machinery was necessary in the summer. Today modern refrigeration techniques have made transportation much easier – a continuous cool chain guarantees the quality of the caviar. Buying caviar whose origin is uncertain is, therefore, not to be recommended. It may prove very attractive from the point of view of cost, but its often adventurous route around legal channels will have exposed it to considerable variations in temperature.

How to Eat Caviar

Caviar is eaten with a spoon straight from the can. A metal or silver spoon should not be used, because this can affect the taste. Spoons made of horn, mother-of-pearl or even plastic, should the need arise, are more suitable.

The Russian Tsars used a golden ball the size of a cherry to examine the quality of caviar. The caviar only passed muster if the ball remained upon the surface, which would indicate that the caviar was firm.

Caviar is served at the finest tables in crystal bowls surrounded by a silver container for ice cubes. However, it is not regarded as a breach of good manners to place a whole can of caviar whether it weighs one pound or one kilogram together with a block of ice on the table. As regards side-dishes there is much indulgence where caviar is concerned. Connoisseurs are as loath to eat chopped egg as they are chopped onion or slices of lemon. Caviar is best accompanied by *blini*, wafer-thin buckwheat pancakes, white bread and butter, or freshly-cooked potatoes, boiled in their skins. The potatoes are then peeled before they are eaten.

Caviar and potatoes cooked and eaten in this way were for centuries the principal food of the fishermen of the Caspian Sea, who distinguished themselves through their exceptional longevity – evidence that cannot entirely be dismissed out of hand that caviar must be very healthy. In fact it contains many vitamins, lecithin, and trace elements and has enormous nutritional value. It is very difficult for an unpracticed European to eat more than 100 grams of caviar in one go, even if he can afford to pay for it.

Blini with Caviar: Small Suns

The usual reaction to tasting real Russian butter *blini* is one of amazement at the pleasant aroma, which is of a quite different kind to that of a normal pancake. The main reason for this is that the dough is made with yeast. *Blini* are eaten above all in Russia during the week before Lent. This so-called "week of butter" precedes the forty days of fasting which culminate in Easter, and is the occasion of *Maslenitza*, a merry festival at which mainly *blini* are eaten.

"Blini are the symbol of the sun, beautiful days, rich harvests, happy marriages and healthy children," wrote the Russian author Alexander J. Kuprin. *Blini* represent the farewell to winter and the arrival of spring. This accounts for the round shape of *blini*, which resembles that of a small sun.

Blini
Buckwheat Pancakes

2 Tbs (25 g) yeast
Sugar
2¹/₂ cups (300 g) wheat flour
2 Tbs lukewarm water
¹/₂ cup (75 g) buckwheat flour
1 pint (500 ml) lukewarm milk
3 egg yolks, 3 egg whites
3 Tbs melted butter
3 Tbs sour cream
Salt

Dissolve the yeast with 1 teaspoon of sugar in the lukewarm water, mix with 2–3 tablespoons of wheat flour and put the dough to one side in a warm place for about 15 minutes, until it has risen. Put the rest of the wheat flour and two thirds of the buckwheat flour in a large bowl and mix. Make a hollow in the flour mix. Place half the milk and the dough that has already risen in the hollow and knead together vigorously until the dough is smooth. Cover the bowl with a cloth and leave the dough to rise for 3 hours in a warm, draft-free place.
Then mix the dough thoroughly and work in the rest of the buckwheat flour. Leave to rise for a further 2 hours, stir again and gradually mix in the rest of the milk, the egg yolks, melted butter, sour cream, as well as one pinch each of salt and sugar. Beat the egg whites until they are stiff and add carefully to the dough which has a further 30 minutes left to rise.
Cook the pancakes in a skillet on both sides until they are golden brown, brushing both sides lightly with butter. Serve hot with butter and sour cream. It is traditional to eat caviar with *blini*.

Blini, buckwheat pancakes brushed with butter, taste particularly delicious with sour cream and caviar.

Cabbage and Root Vegetables

Two types of vegetable dominate Russian cooking, namely cabbage and root vegetables. Fresh vegetables are only available for a few months in the year. White cabbage is one of the most important foodstuffs in Russia because it is possible to store cabbage heads over the winter, without necessarily having to make the renowned dish sauerkraut from them.

Farshirovannaia Kapusta
Stuffed Cabbage

1 onion
1 lb (500 g) ground beef
1 lb (500 g) ground pork
Salt, black pepper
1 cup rice
1 white cabbage, approximately 2 lb (1 kg)
5 cups (1 l) bouillon

Sauce
2 Tbs flour
2 Tbs butter
1/4 cup (50 g) sour cream
Sugar, salt to taste
1 Tbs tomato paste

Peel and finely chop the onion and cook in a little butter until transparent. Put the ground meat in a bowl, season and mix with the onion, then add the uncooked rice. Clean the cabbage and remove the stalk. Bring some salted water to the boil in a large saucepan and cook the cabbage in it for about 5 minutes. Pour ice-cold water over the cabbage, remove the leaves and place them in a circle on a clean cloth so that they overlap – firstly the outer leaves, then the next layer of leaves down to the core of the cabbage. Place some of the ground meat mixture on each layer.
Lift up the ends of the cloth and hold them together so that the cabbage reassumes its normal shape. Place in a large saucepan with boiling water, add a little bouillon to refine the taste, cover and leave the cabbage to simmer for about 15 minutes.
Preheat the oven to 400 °F (200 °C).
For the sauce, cook the flour and add the butter whilst stirring, until the mixture starts to bubble. Add a little water or bouillon, then stir in the sour cream and leave to simmer for 1 minute. Flavor the sauce with sugar and salt to taste, and bind with the tomato paste.
Remove the cabbage from the saucepan and place in an ovenproof dish. Pour the sauce over the cabbage and bake for 10–15 minutes in the oven. Pour the rest of the bouillon over the cabbage and serve with rye bread and beer.

Kapustnie Kotlety
Cabbage Cutlets

1 firm white cabbage, approximately 2 lb (1 kg)
2 beaten eggs
5 Tbs bread crumbs
1/4 cup (50 g) butter, flaked
1 carton sour cream
2 Tbs chopped parsley

Clean the cabbage, remove the stalk and cut the cabbage into six pieces. Place the pieces in boiling salted water and half cook. Leave to cool and squeeze the liquid out of the cabbage by hand so that the pieces of cabbage look like cutlets. Preheat the oven to 400 °F (200 °C).
Next dip the cabbage cutlets in egg and then toss them in the bread crumbs. Butter a braising dish and place the cutlets in it, sprinkle with flakes of butter and bake in the oven until golden brown. Pour the sour cream over them and bake for a further 10 minutes. Sprinkle with chopped parsley and serve.

Vegetables in Brine for the Winter

In Russia harvest time is short and the winter is long. In their search for suitable ways of preserving, the Russians have developed two techniques. One is that of pickling in vinegar, whilst the second involves pressing in brine. The latter is the older, albeit the more complicated method.
Kislaia kapusta, sauerkraut, is to be found in every Russian household and Russians who have cellars will be eager to make their own.

Homemade Sauerkraut

22 lb (10 kg) white cabbage
2 lb (1 kg) apples
2 lb (1 kg) carrots
Cowberries or cranberries
8 oz (250 g) salt

Clean the cabbage heads, remove the stalks and slice the cabbage. Peel and grate the apples, and repeat the same for the carrots. Add some berries and salt to taste and mix everything well.
Rinse out a large earthenware pot with hot water, place the cabbage in it and mash. Weigh down with a wooden lid, on which a stone or some other heavy object should be placed. Cover with a cloth. At the beginning of the fermentation process push a stick into the cabbage from time to time, so that the gases which build up can escape – otherwise the cabbage will have a bitter taste. Also remove any froth which collects on the surface. Leave the cabbage to ferment at a temperature of about 70 °F (20 °C) for 3 days, then place the barrel in a dry, cool cellar, where the sauerkraut must be left to mature for 2–3 weeks.

Just as old as the cabbage is the turnip, which has in the meantime been broadly replaced by the potato. Red beet has also been known since the 11th century in Russia, when it was imported from Byzantium, and from the 16th century the carrot has been established as well. Both vegetables serve as side dishes for meat and fish dishes, but can also be prepared with potatoes as a main dish in their own right.

Morkov iz Imbirem
Carrots and Ginger

1 lb (500 g) carrots
1 Tbs ground ginger
Sugar
Salt
¼ cup (50 g) butter
1 carton sour cream

Wash and slice the carrots. Place them in a bowl, sprinkle with the ground ginger, sugar, and salt, stir and leave for 30 minutes. Pour away any liquid which collects.
Preheat the oven to 400 °F (200 °C).
Heat the butter in a skillet, add the carrots and cook for about 10 minutes, stirring constantly, until they have turned a reddish golden color. Place in an ovenproof dish, pour the carton of sour cream over the carrots and then bake in the oven for about 15 minutes.

Background: A Russian family working together in a cabbage field.

Below: Sauerkraut is made by slicing white cabbage and layering it with apples, carrots, and salt in an earthenware container, mashing everything together and leaving it to ferment.

Hearty and Filling
Soups

In Russian cuisine soup is regarded as the first course and is eaten after the appetizers, because like them it stimulates the appetite. No other country in the world can offer such a wide range of soups as Russia. It was not only amongst the poor, for whom there was little choice, for even at court soups were held in high esteem. However, the Russian language had no version of our word "soup" at first, since the Russians used a range of words for soup dishes such as *shchi*, *ukha*, *borscht* or *solyanka*. It was only when Russia came under French influence through Tsar Peter the Great that the word *sup* appeared (derived from the French *souper*, meaning "evening meal"). However, it would never occur to a Russian housewife even today to refer to her *shchi* or *solyanka* as soup.

The mother of all Russian soups is *shchi*, a cabbage soup. In the summer it is made with fresh cabbage and in the winter with sauerkraut. Furthermore it contains everything which the cook finds to hand. A *shchi* is always a hearty and filling dish. The more often it is reheated, the better it becomes.

Sweshiya Shchi
Cabbage Soup
(Illustration)

1 lb (500 g) beef with bones
1 lb (500 g) white cabbage
2 potatoes
1 turnip
1 carrot
1 parsley root
1 onion
2 Tbs butter
2–3 bay leaves
Salt, black pepper
2 tomatoes
Sour cream

Put the meat in cold water and bring to the boil. Skim and leave to cook for about 2 hours.
Clean the cabbage, cut into strips and add to the meat and water. Peel the potatoes, cut into pieces and also add to the meat soup.
Wash the root vegetables and cut them up into small pieces, peel and chop the onion. Braise the vegetables and onion lightly in butter and add to the soup, leaving to cook for 20 minutes. Then add the bay leaves, as well as the salt and pepper. Skin the tomatoes, remove the pips and cut into eighths. Shortly before the end of the cooking time, add the tomatoes to the soup.
Remove the meat from the soup, dice and return to the soup. Serve sour cream with the soup separately.

Kislyie Shchi
Sauerkraut Soup

1 lb (500 g) mutton or beef
1 lb (500 g) sauerkraut
2 Tbs tomato paste
1 carrot
1 parsley root
1 onion
2 Tbs butter
1 Tbs flour
1 bay leaf
Salt, black pepper
2 garlic cloves
Sour cream

Put the meat in cold water, bring to the boil and leave to simmer for 2 hours. Press any liquid out of the sauerkraut and place in a saucepan. Add the tomato paste and some water, cover and leave the sauerkraut to cook in the saucepan for 2 hours.
Clean the root vegetables, peel the onion, chop everything up into small pieces and braise lightly in some butter. Remove the meat from the soup and dice; put to one side. Add the root vegetables and sauerkraut to the meat soup and simmer for about 30 minutes.
Mix the flour and butter to make a roux and add to the soup about 15 minutes before the end of the cooking time, and add a bay leaf, salt (use sparingly), and pepper. Press the garlic and add. Put the diced meat in the soup. Serve sour cream separately.

Borscht
Red Beet Soup
(Illustration)

1 lb (500 g) red beet
2 large carrots
1 turnip
7 oz (200 g) white cabbage
1 large onion
1 lb (500 g) beef
2 Tbs butter
7 1/2 cups (1 1/2 l) bouillon
3 Tbs red wine vinegar
2 bay leaves
1 tsp sugar
Salt, black pepper
1 bunch each of parsley and dill
Sour cream

Wash the vegetables and cut them into small pieces. Cut the beef into bite-sized portions.
Melt the butter in a large saucepan then add the meat, carrots, turnip, and onion and braise for about 10 minutes, until the meat has browned and the vegetables are done. Add the red beet, bouillon, vinegar, bay leaves, and sugar; season with salt and pepper. Stir thoroughly, cover and simmer for 45 minutes.
Wash the parsley and dill and tie in a bouquet. Place in the saucepan with the white cabbage and cook for a further 30 minutes. Remove the bouquet of herbs and the bay leaves. Stir well and serve with sour cream.

Sweshiya Shchi –
Cabbage Soup

Borscht – Red Beet Soup

"Confusion" in Russia: Solyanka

There are three variations of this soup in Russia, one being made with meat, another with fish, and a third with mushrooms. *Solyanka* means "confused," and the description dates back to the time when every participant at the large village festivals would bring something for the soup, which would be prepared in a large cauldron with all the ingredients thrown in together.

Ukha
Fish Soup

3¼ lb (1½ kg) fish leftovers
3 onions, peeled
1 bay leaf
Some peppercorns
2 sprigs of parsley
2 egg whites
Salt, black pepper
1 lb (500 g) fillets of fish
Chopped dill or chopped parsley

Place the fish leftovers in a large saucepan with some salted water, add the onions, bay leaf, peppercorns, and sprigs of parsley and cook for 30 minutes. Strain the stock through a fine sieve, taking care to squeeze any liquid out of the fish leftovers. Return the fish stock to the saucepan. Beat the egg whites until they are fluffy, add to the stock and bring to the boil whilst stirring constantly. Season and leave to cool, then strain through a cloth. Return the clear stock to the saucepan, heat, add the fish fillets and leave to simmer for 3 minutes. Serve on plates, pouring the soup over the fillets and sprinkle with dill or parsley.

Some ingredients for a Fish Solyanka: fish, pickled gherkin, green and black olives, tomato paste, and onions.

Salted water and ingredients including onions and tomatoes amongst others are brought to the boil in a large saucepan.

Then the pieces of fish are added and left to simmer in the uncovered saucepan for about 5 minutes. The flavor of the soup is rounded off with capers and black and green olives.

Rybnaya Solyanka
Fish Solyanka
(Illustrations)

1 bunch of parsley
2 large onions
2 tomatoes
1 large pickled gherkin
1 bay leaf
1 lb 12 oz (800 g) halibut, sturgeon or haddock
2 Tbs butter
Salt, white pepper
1 Tbs capers
8 black olives, stoned
4 oz (100 g) green olives, stoned
2 Tbs tomato paste

Wash the parsley, chop the leaves finely, put the stalks to one side. Peel the onions, chopping one roughly, whilst slicing the other. Skin the tomatoes, remove the pips and dice. Cut the gherkin into slices.
Place the chopped onion, bay leaf, parsley stalks, and tomatoes into some salted water in a large saucepan and bring to the boil. Cut the fish into pieces and add, reduce the temperature and leave the fish to simmer in the saucepan for about 5 minutes, having removed the lid. Remove the parsley stalks and bay leaf.
Melt the butter in a second saucepan and cook the slices of onion until they are transparent. Add the sliced gherkin and leave to braise for about 10 minutes. Add to the fish solyanka, add pepper and perhaps salt.
Remove the saucepan from the cooker, add the capers, olives, and parsley leaves to the soup, thicken slightly with the tomato paste, season to taste and serve.

Rybnaya Solyanka – Fish Solyanka

Meat Dishes

The Russians love large joints in one piece. Braising is most suited to the most important thing in the Russian household, the oven, because large pieces of meat cook better in a hot oven than smaller ones. Furthermore there are usually many people to be fed in a household, so a large joint is obligatory from the point of view of numbers as well. And so it is that we only find meat dishes that are braised amongst traditional Russian meat recipes, producing joints which are served whole with loving care and from which – according to the importance, build, and appetite of the guest – larger or smaller portions are cut.

However, when Russian meat dishes are being discussed in writing about cookery in the West outside of Russia, it is paradoxically always a dish involving meat cut into strips which is mentioned first. This is of course the famous Beef Stroganoff. It was invented in the late 19th century by a French chef for a Russian count, who has become immortal as a result. Today the dish is known and cooked worldwide – in countless variations, according to the talent and ambition of the cooks who prepare it.

Byefstroganov
Beef Stroganoff
(Illustration opposite)

1 Tbs mustard
1 tsp sugar
Salt, black pepper
1 lb (500 g) mushrooms
1 lb (500 g) onions
2 lb (1 kg) fillet of beef
2 cartons of sour cream

Mix the mustard with the sugar, one pinch of salt and one tablespoon of hot water into a thick paste and leave to simmer. Wash the mushrooms and slice. Peel and chop the onions. Brown the mushrooms and onions in oil, cover and cook gently for 20 minutes, stirring occasionally. Pour away the liquid. Cut the fillet across the grain into thin slices, dividing these into strips. In another skillet heat the oil on a high temperature and sear the strips of meat in batches. Turn and brown on all sides, using a slotted spoon to transfer the meat to the mushrooms in the other skillet. Season with salt and pepper, mix in the mustard paste and stir in the sour cream.
Cover and heat, stir and serve.

Kievskie Kotlety
Chicken Kiev

4 chicken breasts with the bones
3/4 cup (200 g) butter
Salt, black pepper
Flour
2 beaten eggs
4 oz (100 g) bread crumbs
Oil for deep-frying

Skin, bone, and cut the chicken breasts in half. Leave the short bones in the breast. Then carefully beat the meat flat.
Divide the butter into 8 portions and roll each portion out into a cylindrical shape 3 inches (8 cm) long and with a diameter of 3/8th of an inch (1 cm). Place in the refrigerator so that the butter becomes firm.
Season the meat with salt and pepper and roll a small portion of butter up in each cutlet. Toss the cutlets in flour, roll them in your hands, firstly in egg and then in bread crumbs. Refrigerate for about 2 hours, so that the butter and meat become firm. Deep-fry the cutlets for about 5 minutes so that they are golden brown.

Govyadina Tushenaia
Braised Joint of Beef

1 lb 12 oz (800 g) beef
Salt
Flour
Butter
3 onions
1 carrot
1 head of celery
4–6 raw potatoes
2 slices of dark bread
Several peppercorns
2 bay leaves
5 oz (150 g) bacon
1 cup (200 ml) bouillon
1/4 cup (50 ml) sour cream

Cut the beef into slices that are finger thick, season with salt, toss in flour and brown on both sides in a little butter. Wash the carrot and celery and chop. Peel and chop the onions. Dice the potatoes and bread. Mix everything together in a bowl, then add the peppercorns, bay leaves, and a little salt.
Preheat the oven to 400 °F (200 °C).
Cut the bacon into slices and line the bottom of a wide casserole. On top of the bacon place alternating layers of meat and vegetables. Add the bouillon and bring everything to the boil. Cover and then put the casserole in the oven and leave to cook for about 2 hours. Add the sour cream about 20 minutes before the end of the cooking time.

Bushi Hvosti iz Kashei
Spicy Oxtail with Buckwheat

4 1/4 lb (2 kg) oxtail
3 onions
4 garlic cloves
1 Tbs tomato paste
1 can of tomatoes
3 3/4 cups (750 ml) bouillon
1 bunch of parsley
1 bunch of cilantro
3 cinnamon sticks
1 tsp each of ground cumin seeds and ginger
1 tsp mustard seeds
1/2 tsp turmeric
10 oz (300 g) buckwheat groats
2 Tbs butter in flakes
3 carrots
12 oz (350 g) of turnips
1 small head of celery
2 zucchini
2 leeks
Salt, black pepper
Sprigs of parsley

Brown the oxtail in oil in a large casserole, remove and put to one side. Peel and slice the onions and brown in the oil, press the garlic and add to the onions. Add the tomato paste, the canned tomatoes with their juice, as well as the bouillon. Wash the herbs, chop finely, and stir into the onions and tomatoes along with the seasoning and bring to the boil. Add the oxtail, cover and leave to simmer for 4 hours, until the larger pieces of meat separate from the bone. Should the need arise add hot water so that the meat is constantly submerged in stock. Remove the casserole from the cooker, leave to cool and refrigerate for 12 hours or overnight. Preheat the oven to 350 °F (180 °C). Heat the buckwheat groats in a skillet whilst stirring, until the grains begin to open. Add just over 1 pint (500 ml) hot water, season with salt, add the flaked butter, cover and cook the groats for about 45 minutes until the grains are soft. Keep warm.
Remove the casserole from the refrigerator, and lift off the fat, which in the meantime will have hardened. Remove the meat, place in a large ovenproof dish and add hot water to a depth of 3/8th of an inch (1 cm). Cover with aluminum foil and heat the meat in the oven for about 30 minutes.
Pass the meat stock from the casserole through a sieve and return to the casserole. Wash the carrots, turnips, and celery, slice thinly and add to the stock. Cover and cook for about 20 minutes. Slice the zucchini, wash the leeks but do not chop. Add both vegetables to the other vegetables in the stock 5 minutes before the end of cooking.
Strain the casserole, and put the vegetables to one side. Add the liquid from the meat to the stock and bring to the boil.
Place the buckwheat groats on a serving plate, serve the vegetables upon it and arrange the meat around the vegetables. Sprinkle some of the meat juices over the vegetables, and serve the rest separately. Garnish the dish with sprigs of parsley.

Byefstroganov – Beef Stroganoff

Ingredients for kvas: rye bread, sugar, yeast, mint, and water.

The bread has to soak in hot water for 4 hours.

Then the yeast is stirred in and left to rise for about 20 minutes.

The bread mixture is then sieved and the liquid pressed out of the bread.

Bread

Bread is the most important basic foodstuff in Russia. This is not surprising, because up until the October Revolution of 1917 Russia and above all the Ukraine were the granary of Europe. The Ukraine and the southern provinces of Russia supply wheat whilst the best rye still grows in Central Russia and in the northern provinces. The consumption of bread is a part of everyday life, and a *shchi* or *solyanka* without plenty of bread represents an incomplete meal for most Russians.

Bread was already being made from sourdough in the 19th century. Today various mixed grain breads made with rye and wheat predominate. They are variously called *borodinski*, *orlovski*, and *slavianski* – according to which other ingredients they contain such as molasses, caraway seeds, or coriander.

Kasha – Symbol of Well-being

Kasha also plays an important role as a basic grain foodstuff, being groats of millet, barley or buckwheat. In the past Russians have accorded *kasha* a virtually mythical significance. *Kasha* was regarded as a houseguest who brought good fortune, and to prepare it well signified a good harvest. *Kasha* served as a meal of reconciliation between enemies, and without it no peace treaty was said to be valid. Newlyweds were given *kasha* to eat as a symbol of fertility, and on leaving the church grains were thrown over the married couple, uniting best wishes for youthfulness, beauty, and prosperity.

Today *kasha* is mainly served at breakfast or with the evening meal, but also as a side dish for various dishes.

Greshnevaia Kasha
Buckwheat Groats with Mushrooms and Onions

1/2 cup (100 g) buckwheat groats
1 egg
Salt
1/2 cup (120 g) butter
3 onions
8 oz (250 g) mushrooms

Stir the groats and egg together and dry them whilst stirring in a skillet and brown lightly. Add 1/2 tsp salt, one third of the butter and just over 1 pint (500 ml) water. Stir, cover, and leave to simmer for 20 minutes over a low heat. Remove from the cooker and keep warm.
Peel and chop the onions. Melt one third of the butter in a skillet, cook the onions in the butter until they are transparent and stir in the groat mixture.
Wash and chop the mushrooms, cook them in the remaining butter and then add to the *kasha* as well. Stir everything together well and season to taste.

A Popular Drink in Russia

Kvas

Kvas is just as popular in Russia as beer is in other countries. The name literally means "sour drink," and it is brewed from all kinds of household staples, namely dry bread, apples and pears, cowberries and cranberries, blackcurrants and redcurrants, strawberries and buckwheat. Sugar or honey are used to sweeten the brew.

In the 19th century this drink became a subject of contention between two opposing camps of opinion in Russia. One group, which was demanding greater orientation to the West, wanted beer to be imported in place of kvas. Their opponents, the Slavophiles, demanded that old Russian customs should be retained and consequently kvas as well. Today the argument has been settled and both beer and kvas are equally widespread in Russia. At any rate kvas has remained a popular drink for young and old, women and men, whilst beer is mainly drunk by men.

Homemade kvas froths up easily and contains only a little alcohol. It is still made in rural areas, where it is bottled and laid down for subsequent drinking. It plays an important role in the peasants' diet, because the yeast that it contains provides a nutritious supplement to an otherwise monotonous diet.

Kvas Domashnii
Homemade Kvas
(Illustrations below)

1 lb (500 g) rye bread
1 1/2 oz (40 g) yeast
1/2 cup (100 g) sugar
5 Tbs lukewarm water
1 bunch of peppermint
Blackcurrant leaves
1/4 cup (50 g) raisins
Rind from 1 untreated lemon

Slice the rye bread and dry in the oven, place in a saucepan and add 8 1/2 pints (4 l) of boiling water. Cover with a cloth and leave for 4 hours, then pour through a fine sieve.
Stir the yeast with a little sugar into the lukewarm water, leave to rise for about 20 minutes and add to the brew. Then carefully squeeze the moisture out of the bread mixture into the brew, add the remaining sugar, mint – putting a few mint leaves aside – and the blackcurrant leaves, and leave the brew overnight in a warm place for it to ferment.
Strain once more through a cloth and bottle. Place a few raisins, a peppermint leaf, and a piece of lemon rind in each bottle, close tightly and store in the refrigerator for 3 days.
When the raisins have risen to the surface, strain the kvas once again and rebottle. It will now be ready for drinking.

Having fermented for twelve hours the brew is strained once again.

The bottles used for the kvas have been thoroughly cleaned.

A few raisins, a peppermint leaf, and a piece of lemon rind are placed in each bottle.

The kvas is strained a third time and then rebottled.

145

Krimskoye

Sparkling wine has been made for over 200 years in the Crimea. Although as a concession to fashion a white, dry version is available, red sparkling wine from the Crimea with a smooth flavor remains the classic version. It is made from the Cabernet Sauvignon grape variety as well as from other grape varieties such as Sabernet, Saperavi, and Matrassa, which only grow near the Black Sea. A cuvée is made from the basic wines, which in the same way as champagne undergoes a secondary fermentation in the bottle thanks to the addition of yeast and continues to mature because of the yeast until delivery for at least three years. The result is a special, unmistakable flavor. Crimean sparkling wine has friends across the world and, as a result, numbers amongst the most important exports from the Ukraine.

Sweet Dishes

Whilst it is certainly true that sweet dishes and cakes play a very important role at Easter, the most important festival in the year, the Russian love of sweet things is not confined to special occasions. Everything that is regarded as pleasant is described in the Russian language with the word *sladko* (sweet). Traditional Russian sweet dishes include fruit desserts called *kissel*, Quark dishes, honey and pepper cakes, as well as sweet breads.

The *kissel*, which resembles a jelly and has a semiliqueous texture, is Russia's oldest sweet dish. Dried fruits, berries, juices, molasses, and milk are used to make it.

Kissel iz Cherniki
Blueberry Kissel

8 oz (250 g) blueberries
1/2 cup (100 g) sugar
3 Tbs cornstarch

Wash and press the juice out of the blueberries, place the juice in a bowl and refrigerate. Pour boiling water over the blueberry pulp, leave for 5 minutes and pass through a sieve.
Add the sugar to the liquid, bring briefly to the boil and skim. Stir the cornstarch in cold water, add whilst stirring constantly to the hot berry syrup, bring briefly to the boil again and add to the juice which has cooled. Serve ice cold with milk or cream.
Kissel can also be made from cranberries, cowberries, gooseberries, blackcurrants, redcurrants, cherries, rhubarb, or apricots following this recipe.

Pashka
Russian Easter Dessert

2 lb (1 kg) low-fat fromage blanc
1 cup (250 g) soft butter
1 carton of sour cream
4 eggs
3/4 cup (200 g) sugar
1/4 cup (50 g) candied orange-peel and lemon-peel
1/4 cup (50 g) chopped almonds

Place the *fromage blanc* in a conical mold with a hole in the top, hang the mold up overnight and leave so that the liquid can drain. Squeeze until it is quite dry. Pass the *fromage blanc* through a sieve and place in a bowl, then stir in the soft butter. Heat the sour cream. Beat the eggs with the sugar, slowly add them to the cream and stir over a low heat until the mixture becomes thick. Chop the candied orange-peel and lemon-peel finely and add to the egg mixture. Then add the *fromage blanc* and the almonds and heat once again, making sure the mixture does not come to the boil. Pour into a mold and refrigerate overnight until the mixture is firm.
Remove from the mold and decorate with cherries, almonds, candied orange-peel, and lemon-peel.

Charlottka
Russian Cream Cake
(Illustration)

40 sponge fingers
4 egg yolks
1/3 cup (80 g) sugar
6 gelatine leaves
1 1/4 cups (250 ml) milk
Pulp from 1 vanilla bean
8 Tbs each of heavy and sour cream
1 mandarin

Line the bottom of a spring form with sponge fingers. Cut them off at one end, so that the base of the form is completely covered. Mix the egg yolk with the sugar. Soak the gelatine in cold water.
Heat the milk in a small saucepan with the vanilla pulp. Slowly add the sugared egg to the milk whilst stirring constantly. Stir over a low heat until the mixture attains a creamy consistency. It must not be allowed to come to the boil, or the eggs will curdle.
Remove the saucepan from the heat and, having pressed the liquid out of it, stir the gelatine into the cake filling and leave to cool. Beat the heavy cream until stiff, add the sour cream and continue to beat. Carefully stir into the cake filling.
Place the cake filling in the spring form until the sponge fingers are equally covered. Put the remaining fingers in an upright position around the edge of the form and add the rest of the filling. Smooth the surface, cover with clingfilm, and refrigerate for 4 hours. Peel the mandarin and break into segments. Place the spring form on a serving plate and carefully remove the casing. Decorate the filling with the mandarin segments and several squirts of cream.

Gogol Mogol
Eggnog
(Illustration)

This egg dessert, a Russian version of *zabaglione*, was held in high esteem by the famous singer Feodor Shaliapin (1873–1938) as the best way to lubricate his vocal chords.

12 egg yolks
9 Tbs sugar
2 Tbs Cognac
1 Tbs orange liqueur
1 Tbs lemon juice

Whisk the egg yolk and sugar. Add the Cognac, liqueur, and lemon juice and beat the mixture well for as long as it takes to achieve a thick consistency. Refrigerate for at least 30 minutes and serve in dessert bowls.

Gogol Mogol

Charlottka

Hot water for tea is poured from the samovar, which is traditionally heated with charcoal.

A beautiful old Russian samovar with brass fittings, richly ornamented.

A Present from the Mongol Khan

Tea

Tea, *chai*, is certainly Russia's most popular drink, and every Russian would swear that tea is deeply Russian. In fact it first came to Russia in the 17th century. It was then that the Russian ambassador at the court of the Mongol Khan came with four pud, an old Russian measurement which equates to about 145 pounds (roughly 65 kilograms), of tea as a present from the Great Khan for Tsar Michael III (1613–45). The ambassador had originally refused to accept the present, as he feared the wrath of a Tsar who was to be offered "dried grass," but the Great Khan insisted upon his present being accepted.

As had been feared, the new drink was not at all to the Tsar's taste to begin with. However, he soon found that tea appeared to dispel sleepiness during long religious services and during the even more tedious sittings of the Duma, the assembly of the higher ranks of the nobility, which gives its name to today's Russian parliament. Once the supply was used up, tea was, however, soon forgotten.

Once again, it was envoys who brought tea to Russia a second time, and this time they came from China. Tea was now greeted as an old acquaintance. However, it remained expensive, so that only the nobility could afford it. The drink first enjoyed greater popularity in the 18th century, and it was at this time that the first samovars appeared.

Below: A modern Russian family taking afternoon tea. The samovar still takes its place upon the table, although it is electrically powered, thus showing that even the ceremony of preparing the tea has succumbed to sober pragmatism.

The Samovar – The Epitome of Russian Tea Culture

A samovar is a means of boiling water, albeit an unusual one. It comes in every possible shape: round, cylindrical, and conical, made of copper or brass. Much care is taken in engraving the individual parts, which are generously decorated with patterns and figures.

Until today there have been samovars in Russia in every size, from a mini-samovar barely larger than a single cup to the family model that can hold several pints of water. However, samovars today look rather simple when compared to their noble antecedents from better days. They are mass-produced articles made of tin, contain an electric element like an immersion heater and provide only an echo of former glories. However, they fulfill their function, and in principle that is the most important thing.

Charcoal is used to heat the classic samovar, and is placed in the heating pipe when aglow. Then an extension is added to the pipe, until the water boils. When no further smoke comes out of the flue, it is removed and the samovar is placed on the table.

The tea is brewed strongly in a small pot, which is placed on the samovar. Servings are then taken from this pot and diluted with boiling water from the samovar.

Tea is traditionally served in tall glasses with metal handles (today cups and mugs are also used) and with thin slices of lemon. In many regions of the Caucasus, in Central Asia and in Kazakhstan green tea is preferred. Russians drink tea at all times of the day. It is served with jam, cakes, sweet pirogi, croissants, and honey. In summer the fruits of the season are served with tea such as strawberries, raspberries, redcurrants, and blackcurrants.

Tea from the Forests

The original Russian tea comes from the forest. It consists of dried berries, flowers, leaves, stems, stalks, and roots of different plants. Jasmine, wild rose, and lime blossoms are popular, as are mint and cranberry leaves and cranberries, blueberries, rowan and hawthorn. The tea is made by placing one tablespoon of dried tea in about two pints (one litre) of boiling water. Forest tea has to draw considerably longer than black or green tea. It does not contain any tannin to act as a stimulant but has a pronounced flavor and an attractive aroma.

Sbitien made of Honey and Spices

In the 18th and 19th centuries *sbitien* was widespread, a hot drink made from honey and spices. It was served in market places from small wooden huts, on whose windowledges there was normally a large samovar. Nikolai W. Gogol describes such a *sbitien* kiosk in his novel *Dead Souls*: "A sbitien vendor made himself at home at the window with a samovar made of red copper. His face was just as red as the samovar. From a distance one would have thought that there were two samovars standing in the window, had one of them not had a black beard."

The name of the drink is derived from the Russian word *sbiti* (meaning "to unite" or "to mix"). Various spices such as ginger, cloves, nutmeg, cinnamon, and caraway seeds are mixed with the honey in various ratios.

The "White Magic"

Vodka

Drinking in Russia and in the neighboring countries is a serious business. Vodka is drunk neither out of necessity nor grief, a satirical writer asserted several years ago, but out of an age-old yearning for the wonderful and the extraordinary – "Vodka is a white magic." Vodka (literally "small water") was developed in the 14th century as a medicine and was originally distilled from grape must, later from rye. When the potato was introduced into Russia, it was also used to make vodka – something that came back into favor during the desperate times experienced in the Second World War, except then vodka was made from potato peelings.

Vodka is so neutral that it is not possible to taste the raw material it is made from. As a result of this it is irrelevant, as far as the law is concerned, whether it is distilled from rye, wheat, corn, or potatoes. What is important is the way it is distilled, which remains regulated by a state monopoly even after the end of the Soviet Union. Distillation is crucial to whether vodka achieves the required mellowness, clarity, and neutral flavor. It is distilled several times and eventually filtered through charcoal and asbestos, to remove the last traces of anything that would impart flavor. Storing vodka in stone or glass containers also prohibits any aroma developing, as would happen for example in wooden casks.

Vodka can be helpful in difficult situations, but can also be fatal for those with a frail constitution. As is often the case, the devil does not reside in liquor but rather in man – which does not stop the Russians from drinking rather too much on occasions. Nevertheless, at the time of the Tsars, excise duty on salt and alcohol constituted thirty percent of all tax collected.

The best vodka today is made from wheat. According to Russian tradition it is drunk ice-cold, and it is not a question of snobbery to freeze a bottle of vodka along with some glasses. It is only then that the real fire of the drink unfolds when it is drunk.

There are also aromatic vodkas, flavored for example with lemon peel, ginger, cayenne pepper, or even bison grass.

Types of Russian Vodka

There are many different types of vodka made for export from Russia, some of which are illustrated below. Where numbers appear in brackets, they refer to these illustrations.

Krepkaya (4)
This strong variety is 56 percent alcohol by volume, and only the hardened drink it pure. It is popular amongst barmen as an ingredient for cocktails.

Limonnaya
At 40 percent alcohol by volume this variety is flavored with lemon peel. It can be recognized from its bright yellow color.

Moskovskaya (7)
This is particularly mild, because soda and sodium sulphide are added to it. Its alcohol content is 40 percent by volume.

Ochotnichiya (1)
A strong vodka which is 45 percent alcohol by volume and particularly spicy, being flavored with ginger, cloves, and paprika.

Pertsovka (3)
This variety of vodka brings tears to the eyes of the unprepared, because it is not only 45 percent alcohol by volume, but is also flavored with cayenne pepper. It is highly regarded as a remedy for stomach upsets and colds.

Starka (6)
Leaves from apple and pear trees in the Crimea are added to the mash for distillation, and then wine distillate and liqueur wine are added. This vodka is 43 percent alcohol by volume.

Stolichnaya (2)
The name of this vodka, which is 40 percent alcohol by volume and contains small amounts of sugar, means "of the capital city."

Stolovaya
This is a strong vodka which is 50 percent alcohol by volume.

Ukrainskaya
This variety has a fine bouquet of lime-blossom honey and is 45 percent alcohol by volume.

Zubrovka (5)
At 40 percent alcohol by volume this vodka has a normal strength, but is flavored with bison grass. A blade of grass in the bottle acts as a reminder of this.

Vodka Liqueurs

Countless liqueurs are made at home using vodka as a basis. When herb ingredients are used the liqueurs are called *nastoika*, whereas those liqueurs flavored with berries are called *nalivka*.

It could not be easier to make them. The particular ingredients are chopped up, placed in a large bottle or a demijohn, which is then filled with vodka. The container is then put in a warm place and the infusion is left to draw for one to two weeks. It is then strained and the appropriate amount of vodka is added according to whether a milder or stronger flavor is required.

These aromatic drinks have all the more flavor the longer the ingredients are left to draw. Should a berry *nalivki* have too dry a taste, a happy redress is the addition of sugar or honey.

Background: A glass of ice-cold vodka is – and not only for Russians – a real delight.

Beata Dębowska

Poland

Poland, a country of boundless forests, expansive fields of corn, and rivers which stretch for miles, shares the same climatic conditions as European Russia, but has received more cultural influences from its Western neighbors. As a result of this, Slav and German influences have combined to create an indigenous culinary tradition – even if fifty years of socialism and the political link to the Soviet Union have allowed the Russian element to predominate. Hospitality and an attachment to tradition have great significance in Poland. Certainly, over the centuries several of the old customs have been forgotten, but the virtue of hospitality has survived. However, anyone who does not have a healthy appetite and cannot tolerate alcohol, should be warned. That goes above all for baptisms, weddings, and name days. There is no need for any reason or pretext whatsoever to meet for coffee, tea, or a glass of vodka. Vodka is considered to be "a liquid form of nourishment" and belongs to the small number of Polish specialties that are known beyond the country's confines. It is a general misapprehension concerning Poland that the goose falls into the same category. In fact Poland exports a considerable number of geese but the bird is no longer as popular at home as it is, for example, in neighbouring Germany. The Poles much prefer the pig as a provider of meat and everything that can be prepared from it – from ham to pig's snout, from cutlets to sausages.

Cabbage, root vegetables, mushrooms, and cucumbers, which are plentiful in the summer, are pickled in salt or vinegar for the winter, even salted berries are served with meat dishes at that time of year – a quite piquant flavor which is peculiar because it is unusual.

Because in the past Poland was often subject to occupation, annexation, and division, the vicissitudes of history have inevitably left behind various traces, including culinary ones, and so it is possible to tell from the dishes that people prepare from which area of Poland they come. These differences become particularly clear at Christmas – a religious festival celebrated very formally in Poland, which is a Roman Catholic country and deeply religious.

Left: Some of the famous Cracow sausages are hung up for smoking.

Boczniak ostrygowaty – Oyster Mushroom

Borowik szlachetny – Penny Bun Boletus

Czubajka kania – Parasol Mushroom

Gąsówka naga – Wood Blewit

Delicacies from Poland's Forests

Mushrooms

Mushrooms traditionally provide the basis for many Polish dishes as they have been collected in Poland since time immemorial. A wide range of mushroom species is to be found in Poland's extensive forests. Ceps and morels, milk caps and agarics are particularly sought after. Mushrooms were regarded by the wealthy as delicacies and were served as side dishes to meat, whereas poor people struggled to earn a little extra money by collecting them.

Today Polish forests are equally still a gold mine for mushroom gatherers. Moreover, for several years mushroom collecting in Poland fulfilled a remarkable role in society, particularly in the years after the war. Nothing could bring people more alive than to spend their leisure time together at the weekends going mushrooming. Such an excursion often culminated in a picnic, accompanied by plenty of alcohol, and it was in this way that many a problem could be settled informally.

In Poland thirty-one species of mushroom are authorized to be sold and used when fresh. Unofficially there are far more – including those which can only be found in particular areas and which are, therefore, merely of local importance. There is a particularly abundant occurence of mushrooms in the administrative districts of Zielona Góra, Piła, and in the Masurian Lakeland.

Fifteen species have been approved for sale in dried form. Only caps with stems are allowed for use in this way. Such highly aromatic dried mushrooms are used for sauces, soups, and stuffing and as side dishes for such classic Polish dishes as *zrazy*, a meat olive stuffed with mushrooms, *bigos*, steamed sauerkraut with many different types of meat, *barszcz*, a soup made from red beet, roast duck, and roast beef, which is enriched with sour cream.

Tips on Using Mushrooms

Mushrooms are rich in protein, mineral salts, and trace elements. The protein contained in a mushroom is particularly important, because it has a higher value than normal plant protein and can virtually replace animal protein. Ceps in particular contain protein of a high quality.

At the same time forest mushrooms should not be eaten all that often. A weekly maximum of just under eight ounces (200 grams) is advisable, because forest mushrooms store poisonous heavy metals and other harmful chemicals from the air. They are only to be recommended for eating if they come from areas that have escaped intense damage to the environment. To be absolutely sure, it is best to cook mushrooms as soon as possible after they have been picked. They can then be either consumed or dried and kept for up to one year.

Raw mushrooms should not be washed as far as is possible, because they tend to absorb too much water. On the whole, it is sufficient to wipe them with a damp cloth. If they are very dirty, they can be rinsed briefly in cold water.

Mushrooms should only be peeled if their skin is tough or discolored. In such cases the skin should be removed with a small sharp knife. Fresh mushrooms are best kept in an open plastic container in the refrigerator where they keep for a few days.

As a rule, mushrooms are steamed or fried. When frying mushrooms, it is best to remove them from the skillet when any liquid that has escaped – after all, 90 percent of mushrooms is water – has evaporated. Mushrooms should not be eaten when raw, as they contain poisonous substances, which are destroyed when the mushroom is heated up. (Even cultivated mushrooms have now fallen under suspicion for being carcinogenic when eaten raw, for example in salads.)

One should also exercise caution when making use of leftovers from mushroom dishes. If they show the slightest change compared to how they were when first served after cooking, the mushrooms are no longer edible. Mushroom dishes with eggs or mayonnaise, or mushroom dishes made from deep frozen mushrooms should on no account be kept. In order to avoid all of these problems the best course of action is to cook only as many mushrooms as one can consume.

The classic way of preparing fresh mushrooms is to braise them in cream. Milk caps, which are regarded as a particular delicacy, are cooked in butter or in a firmly closed clay utensil. Pickling is also customary. To pickle, pour salted water over the mushrooms and season with pepper, pimiento, and bay leaves. It first became fashionable to marinate things at the beginning of this century. A marinade can be made from vinegar and water as well as onions, a bay leaf, and pimiento, in which mushrooms can be left to soak for a while. Marinated mushrooms are popularly served with vodka.

Zrazy duszone z grzybami
Beef Rolls with Mushroom Stuffing

1 onion
4 oz (125 g) mushrooms
1 Tbs breadcrumbs
1 egg yolk
Salt, black pepper
4 thin slices of beef
Mustard
2 oz (50 g) fatty smoked bacon
1 Tbs flour
1 glass of red wine
1/2 cup (125 ml) sour cream
Bay leaf

Peel and chop the onion. Clean, wash, and chop the mushrooms into small pieces. Brown the onion lightly in hot oil, add the breadcrumbs and fry them as well. Add the mushrooms, cook briefly and leave the mixture to cool. Stir in the egg yolk and season to taste with salt and pepper.

Season the beef slices with salt and pepper and brush with mustard. Spread the mixture of mushrooms and onion between them, roll up the slices of meat and close with a toothpick and twine.

Dice the bacon and cook until transparent in a braising saucepan, then add the beef rolls. Brown them all over and dust lightly with flour. Add the red wine and some water. Add the bay leaf and leave the meat to braise for about 60 minutes.

Remove the bay leaf, mix the sauce with sour cream, and pour over the beef.

Koźlarz babka – Brown Birch Boletus

Koźlarz czerwony – Poplar Boletus

Lejkowiec dęty – Horn Of Plenty

Maślak żolty – Larch Boletus

Maślak sitarz – Shallow-pored Boletus

Maślak pstry – Sand Boletus

Mleczaj rydz – Saffron Milk Cap

Muchomór czerwonawy – The Blusher

Opieńka miodowa – Honey Fungus

Pieczarka polna – Field Mushroom

Pieprznik jadalny – Chanterelle

Piestrzenica kasztanowata – Turban Fungus (Warning! This mushroom can only be used for eating in certain circumstances. See p.123)

Podgrzybek brunatny – Cep

Podgrzybek złotawy – Yellow-cracked Boletus

Smardz stożkowaty – Large Morel

Smardz jadalny – Common Morel

155

A Traditional Polish Dish

Kasha

Poland's specialty is *kasza*, groats. They are made from several different types of grain, above all from wheat, oats, barley, maize, millet, and buckwheat. Strictly speaking, buckwheat is not a grain but rather a plant whose seed is processed like corn, above all in its ground form. Buckwheat is particularly important in preparing kasha, because it provides the groats with their typical flavor.

Kasha's quality does not only depend upon the types of grain used, but also on how they are processed. It is particularly important how the grain is ground. The result should be not too coarse and not too fine, and the correct consistency is only to be had by persistent experimentation.

Kasha is eaten at all levels of society, it can be found upon the tables of the wealthy as it can be upon the tables of the poor. For a while it diminished in popularity because potatoes were being eaten more. In the wake of a return to traditional dishes, kasha once again became socially acceptable. Even renowned restaurants serving Polish

In Poland landscapes of corn hold the attention – here we see the waving corn of a field of barley. It therefore comes as no surprise that grain products play an important role in Polish cooking and that kasha is widespread in many different forms.

specialties consistently offer kasha on their menus – above all kasha made from buckwheat.

The blossom of the buckwheat smells of honey and is, therefore, much sought after by bees. This gives rise to the dark buckwheat honey, which is regarded, and sought out, as a delicacy. Buckwheat grains cook quickly, and in order to protect the grain, it is roasted before shelling. As a result, a brownish protective layer forms, which prevents the grain from bursting when it is cooked. This "burnt" buckwheat kasha is very highly regarded for its characteristic flavor. It is an irreplaceable addition to many meat dishes with sauce. It also tastes wonderful with hot bacon crackling that has been melted down and with buttermilk.

Buckwheat kasha from Cracow is regarded as the finest and most delicious. It is prepared with an admixture of salt, but sometimes it is also sweetened. Pearl kasha is made by polishing grains of barley to produce a smooth surface. It is from this type of kasha that another typically Polish dish is made, namely pearl barley soup. It has a pleasant taste and is extremely nutritious. In several regions of Poland kasha is used as a filling for pirogi.

1 Jęczmien – Barley
2 Pęczak – Pearl barley
3 Plathi jęczmienne – Barley flakes
4 Kasza perłowa gruba – Coarse pearl kasha
5 Kasza perłowa drobna – Fine pearl kasha

1   2   3   4   5

1

2

3

4

5

6

Kasza krakowska
Cracow Kasha
(Illustrations 1–6)

1 cup buckwheat groats
Salt
$^1/_2$ cup (100 g) butter
1 cup pearl barley
10 oz (300 g) onions, peeled and chopped
5 cups (1 l) bouillon

Wash the groats (1), dry them in a skillet whilst stirring and brown slightly (2). Add $^1/_2$ tsp salt, half the butter and most of the bouillon (3). Stir, cover, and leave to simmer for 20 minutes on a low heat. Remove from the cooker and leave to stand.

In the meantime cook the pearl barley in a small saucepan in the remaining bouillon (4), drain and mix with the groats. Melt the remaining butter in a skillet, cook the onions until they are transparent and stir into the kasha (5). Mix everything together well and season to taste.

Budyń gryczany
Buckwheat Pudding

Just over 1 pint (500 ml) milk
Pulp of 1 vanilla bean
$^1/_2$ cup (100 g) butter
1 cup buckwheat
4 egg yolks, 4 egg whites
$^1/_3$ cup (80 g) sugar
Grated peel from 1 untreated lemon
$^1/_2$ cup (100 g) raisins
Flaked butter
Cherry jam

Bring the milk to the boil with the vanilla pulp in a medium sized saucepan. Remove the milk from the cooker, add two thirds of the butter and melt. Preheat the oven to 375 °F (190 °C).

Add the buckwheat to the milk, return the saucepan to the cooker and cook the buckwheat mixture whilst stirring constantly until it thickens. Place in an ovenproof dish with a tight lid and bake in the oven for about 45 minutes. Leave to cool.

Beat the egg yolks with the sugar until they are fluffy, add the lemon peel and raisins, and mix with the buckwheat. Beat the egg whites until they are stiff and fold in.

Smooth the surface and edge with flakes of butter. Bake for a further 30 minutes in the oven and serve together with the cherry jam.

Krupnik
Pearl Barley Soup

10 oz (300 g) beef for making soup
4 oz (100 g) mushrooms
1 bunch of vegetables for making soup
(e.g. carrot, leek, turnip)
3 medium-sized potatoes
1 cup pearl barley
Salt, black pepper

Place the beef in a large saucepan with salted boiling water and simmer on a low heat for about 30 minutes until the meat is cooked.

Remove, leave to cool and cut into bite-sized portions. Wash the mushrooms and cut them into quarters, peel and dice the potatoes. Wash the rest of the vegetables and chop them up.

Put some of the bouillon in a small saucepan and cook the pearl barley in it. Drain the pearl barley and place in the remaining bouillon. Add the potatoes and cook them until done, then add the beef, mushrooms, and remaining vegetables.

Bring to the boil once again and season to taste with salt and pepper.

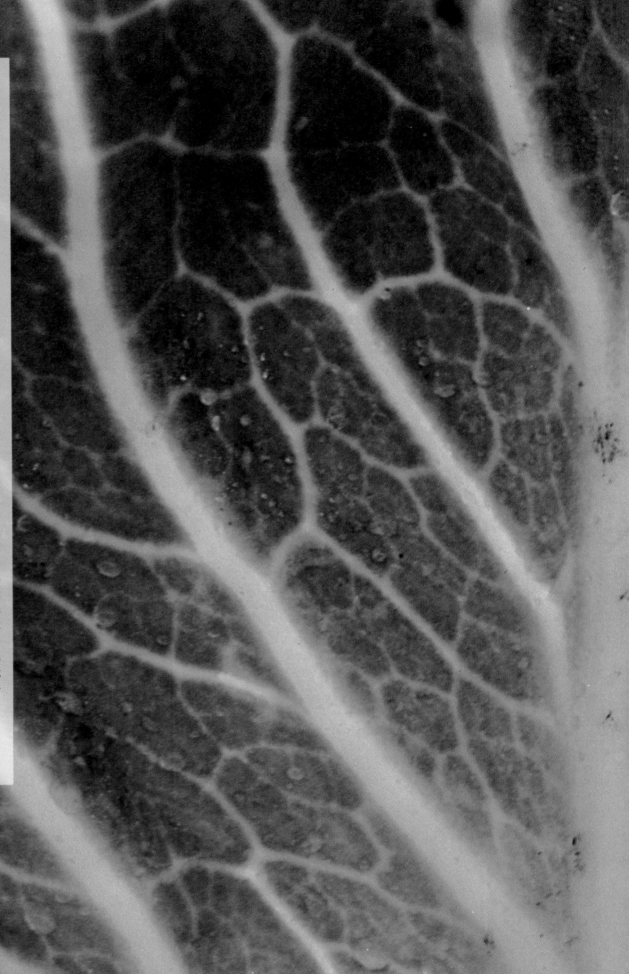

King of Vegetables

Cabbage

In Poland the climate for the "king of the vegetables" – as the Poles like to describe cabbage – is particularly favorable, and as a result it can be cultivated in large numbers and is available all year round. Cabbages are stored until the end of winter, then people get by until the next harvest with cabbage pickled in vinegar.

The heavy and fatty cabbage dishes of old Polish cooking, such as cabbage with peas, cabbage with potatoes, or cabbage with mushrooms, are no longer prepared today – they were also somewhat difficult to digest. For this reason another cabbage dish has become all the more popular, namely *bigos*. The tradition of making bigos stretches far back into the Polish past. It was prepared as an accompaniment for traveling, to be eaten on hunts, as an everyday meal and for banquets. It used to be kept in wooden barrels or large clay jugs. Bigos belonged to every well-stocked larder. It was eaten at Lent, at Christmas, but also at every other opportunity.

The dish is a composition with many variations and every housewife will have her own recipe. The greater the number of different types of meat, sausage, and bacon that it contains, the better it is. It is also popular to make bigos with dried mushrooms and prunes, and it is common to round off a bigos served on a feast day with either dry red wine or madeira.

Bigos tastes at its best after it has been reheated a third time. It is best served piping hot, with rye bread and a small glass of ice-cold vodka.

1　2　3　4

5　6　7　8

Bigos
(Illustrations 1–8)

1 Tbs dried mushrooms, to produce 5 oz (150 g)
1 lb (500 g) meat (of different kinds)
6 oz (200 g) fatty bacon
2 Cracow or other kinds of sausage
1 lb (500 g) sauerkraut
1 Tbs lard
1 onion
1 pint (500 ml) bouillon
Caraway seeds
Sugar
Red wine
Salt, black pepper

Soak the mushrooms for 30–60 minutes in lukewarm water according to their size.
Cut the meat into bite-sized portions (2), dice the bacon into small pieces. Chop the sausages up coarsely. Loosen the sauerkraut, cutting it up into small pieces if necessary (3). Squeeze the moisture out of the mushrooms (4).
Heat the lard in a saucepan, brown the meat, bacon, and sausages in it on all sides (5). Peel and chop the onion, add to the meat in the saucepan and cook until transparent.
Then add the sauerkraut and mushrooms (6) and fill up with bouillon. Add the caraway seeds and a little sugar, as well as a dash of red wine (7). Leave the ingredients to simmer for about 30 minutes, season (be sparing with the salt, as the sauerkraut already contains salt) and serve the dish (8).

Gołąbki
Stuffed Cabbage
(Illustration right)

1 white cabbage
1 cup rice
1 large onion
1/3 cup (80 g) butter
10 oz (300 g) ground meat (half beef, half pork)
1 egg
Salt, black pepper

Sauce

2 tsp butter
2 tsp flour
1 can tomatoes
1 garlic clove
1/2 cup (125 ml) chicken stock
Dried thyme
1 pinch of sugar
Salt, black pepper

Wash the cabbage. Cook it whole in boiling salted water for about 30 minutes. Remove from the water, drain and leave to cool. Cook the rice so that it is still grainy. Peel and chop the onions and cook lightly in the butter. Add the ground meat and brown. Add the rice and egg and season. Leave to cool.
Preheat the oven to 375 °F (190 °C).
Lay the cabbage leaves out, divide the ground meat between the leaves, roll them up and place in an ovenproof dish. Add a little hot water, cover and cook for about 30 minutes in the oven.
For the sauce make a roux of butter and flour and simmer with the sauce ingredients for 20 minutes. Arrange the stuffed cabbage leaves on the sauce.

Meat Dishes

Nóżki wieprzowe w galarecie
Pig's Shanks in Aspic
(Illustration)

1 lb 10 oz (750 g) pig's trotters (feet)
10 oz (300 g) pork
Salt, black pepper
Wine vinegar
2 carrots
1 stick of celery
2 egg whites

Place the pig's trotters, the meat, and vegetables in a large saucepan in cold water, bring to the boil and leave to simmer for 2 hours. Skim, add salt, pepper, and a dash of vinegar and leave to cook for a further 2 hours. Pass through a sieve, retaining a part of the stock. Separate the meat on the pig's trotters from the bone, and dice the pig's trotters and pork. Wash the carrots and celery and slice. Bring the meat stock to the boil and add the egg whites, stirring vigorously, until a thick froth is formed. Bring to the boil several times and strain into a bowl, which has been lined with a clean cloth. Leave to cool, place a part of the mix in a round baking pan and refrigerate until it sets. Decorate with the slices of carrot and celery, once again add some of the liquid to the pan and refrigerate again. Mix the diced meat with the remaining liquid and fill the pan with it. Refrigerate for at least 4 hours, until it sets, and turn out.

Wolowina z grzybami
Fillet of Beef with Mushrooms

Just over 1 Tbs dried ceps, to produce about 1 cup (about 250 g)
1 lb 12 oz (800 g) potatoes
1 lb (500 g) fillet of beef
1/4 cup (50 g) butter
Salt, black pepper
1 tsp flour
1 carton crème fraîche
1 carton light cream
2 Tbs chopped parsley

Soak the mushrooms for about 30 minutes in lukewarm water. Peel and slice the potatoes. Cut the fillet along the grain in the middle and brown on all sides in a cast-iron saucepan in butter, season with salt and pepper. Squeeze the liquid out of the mushrooms and put the liquid to one side. Cover one half of the fillet with mushrooms, and lay the other half on top. Pour on the liquid from the mushrooms and bring to the boil. Season the slices of potato and arrange them around the fillet. Cover and leave to braise for about 20 minutes. Shake the saucepan gently from time to time so that the potatoes do not stick to the bottom. Mix the flour with the crème fraîche and cream and carefully place beneath the potatoes. Leave to simmer for a further 10 minutes. Before serving sprinkle the fillet and potatoes with parsley.

Nadziewany rostbef
Stuffed Roast Beef

1/4 cup (50 g) butter
2 lb (1 kg) loin of beef
Flour
Approximately 1 cup (150–200 ml) bouillon
Thyme
Black pepper

Stuffing
3 onions
1/4 cup (50 g) butter
3–4 slices of bread
1 Tbs chopped parsley
1 tsp chopped thyme
1 egg
Paprika
Salt, black pepper

Heat the butter in a heavy saucepan. Dust the meat lightly with flour and brown on all sides in the butter. Add the bouillon and the thyme and season with pepper. Cover and cook the meat on a moderate heat for about 45 minutes, turning from time to time. If necessary add more bouillon or hot water. Remove the meat from the saucepan and keep hot.
For the stuffing, peel the onions and chop them finely and cook in butter until transparent, break the bread into bread crumbs and add to the onions together with the other ingredients; stir well.
Cut the meat in several places, put some stuffing in each incision and close again. Cook the meat for a further 40 minutes. When it is tender, remove from the saucepan and serve. Reduce the meat juices to a syrup-like consistency and pour over the meat.

Nóźki wieprzowe w galarecie –
Pig's Shanks in Aspic

Kaczka pieczona
Duck in Caper Sauce
(Illustration)

1 duck
1 garlic clove
Salt, black pepper
¼ cup (50 g) butter
Just over ½ cup (125 ml) chicken stock
1 tsp sugar
Vinegar
1–2 tsp cornstarch
6 Tbs capers

Gut, wash, and dry the duck. Press the garlic and rub the duck with it and season with salt and pepper. Put to one side. Heat some oil in a heavy oval pan suitable for braising, add the butter and brown the duck in fat all over. Add the chicken stock, cover and cook the duck for about 90 minutes.
Dissolve the sugar in a little water in a small saucepan and thicken until it caramelizes. Remove from the cooker, add some of the meat juices and a splash of vinegar and bring to the boil over a medium heat whilst stirring. When the duck is cooked, remove from the saucepan and keep warm. Skim the surplus fat from the meat juices. Dissolve the cornstarch in a little cold water and bind the meat juices with it. Add the capers and stir over a strong heat until the sauce thickens. Stir in the dissolved sugar. Serve the duck with the meat juices poured over it.

Rossolnik
Duck Stew

1 duck
Salt, black pepper
10 cups (2 l) veal stock
1 cucumber
2 egg yolks
1 carton of heavy cream

Gut and wash the duck, rub the skin with salt and pepper and cook until golden brown on all sides in an oval dish suitable for braising. Heat the veal stock and add to the duck, cover and cook for about 60 minutes. Carve the duck and dice the meat; put to one side. Peel the cucumber, remove the pith and dice. Blanch in boiling water and pour cold water over it. Mix the egg yolks with the cream in a bowl, add a little of the meat juices and pour everything into the hot juices from the duck. Season with salt and pepper. Before serving add the duck meat and the pieces of cucumber.

Kaczka pieczona – Duck in Caper Sauce

Drink from the Middle Ages

Mead

This drink, which resembles wine and is made from fermented honey, was already known in large parts of Europe in prehistoric times. Mead has been made in Poland since the Middle Ages and is, therefore, the oldest popular drink in the country, beer and vodka being of a much later date. Over the centuries there was scarcely a Polish kitchen where mead was not distilled – in the houses of the nobility just as much as on farmyards.

Mead used to be produced in large amounts. In those days its most important constituent, honey, was available in abundance. Large swarms of wild bees lived in the country, which had extensive forests, and the arrival of domestic beekeeping made its own contribution. Following the clearance of the forests and the transformation of many fallow fields into farmland, the natural conditions for bees worsened and as a result of this the production of mead declined.

Mead resembles wine. It is made by fermenting alcohol, specifically by diluting honey with water and adding hop extract. Spices or fruit juices are used for flavoring.

A distinction is made between unsaturated and saturated mead. Unsaturated mead is made from a cold mixture of honey and water, whilst the saturated variety is made by boiling the mixture. Boiling sterilises the drink and facilitates quicker fermentation. Whilst this results in an improved and healthier quality the accompanying disadvantage is that saturated mead is not as aromatic as the unsaturated variety. In the case of saturated mead the quality of the honey is of secondary importance, whilst for the unsaturated variety only the best honey with excellent flavoring, such as limetree or clover, is used. The most popular and widely produced variety is made with one part honey to two parts water, and attains an excellent quality after being laid down for between one to two years.

Mead is served at room temperature, and in winter is served hot with the addition of spices. Mead is kept in the same way as wine – in a dark and cool place, at a temperature of 41 °F to 50 °F (5–10 °C).

Types of Mead

The crucial factor in determining the quality of mead is the extent to which it is diluted with water. A distinction is made between the following types:

Sweet Mead
2 pints (1 liter) honey and 1 pint ($^1/_2$ liter) water
Semi-sweet Mead
2 pints (1 liter) honey and 2 pints (1 liter) water
Threefold Mead
2 pints (1 liter) honey and 4 pints (2 liters) water

Background: This photographic enlargement shows a fascinating view of a honey bee and the chamberlike honeycombs of its hive.

A beekeeper with a hive. Domestic beekeeping is traditional in Poland.

Mead is made from fermented honey to which hop extract is added.

Mead is laid down like wine: in barrels and at a temperature of between 41 °F and 50 °F (5–10 °C).

Mead is served at room temperature. In winter it is served hot and seasoned with spices.

Thomas Veszelits

Czech Republic · Slovakia

Formerly united in the Federation of Czechoslovakia and subject to Communist rule from 1948-198 for over 70 years, The Czech Republic (Bohemia) and Slovakia (Moravia) founded two independent countries on January 1, 1993. Logically, their foods are similar. Both are robust, partial to pork and sweet desserts. The Bohemian Czechs prefer beer, however the Moravians and Slovaks, wine. Another difference is that Moravia produces a more varied assortment of cheese because of its bounty in sheep. To digest their heavy and fatty meals, the Czechs enjoy herb schnapps, becherovka. The Slovakian preference is for slivovica, plum schnapps. While more than forty years of Socialism threatened to make a culinary desert of both countries' flourishing kitchens, the end of Communist rule in 1989 and the subsequent privatization of grocers and restaurants, spurred a reappearance of the traditional delicacies: the *knedlík* (dumpling), the *povidla* (plum purée), carp from Třeboň, sheep's milk cheese from Slovakia, and Pilsner beer. Then there is the singularly renowned Prague Ham, *Praœská πunka*, which reassumes its place among great hams like Parma and Bayonne. Sweets like kipferl and buchteln take up their place of honor also, having had to defer to those in neighboring Austria for decades. Likewise, *povidla*, or plum purée, took lengthy exile in Austria, although it is quintessential Bohemian. Plum purée is prepared at the end of the harvest beginning September 28, or Wenceslas Day, the day Bohemia celebrates its patron saint. While the Czech Republic and Slovakia cultivate their own national identities today, they maintain good neighborly relations, not uncommonly over the same pot.

Left: On a small farm in Slovakia, sheep's milk cheese is squeezed and pressed into molds.

Prague Ham

Fate is sometimes unfair. From the meat of pigs that thrive in Bohemia and Moravia, the clever butchers around Prague know how to produce excellent *Pražská šunka*, the world renowned Prague Ham. Socialism meant passing its first-rate reputation on to similar specialties in the years after the Second World War: to Italian Parma, French Bayonne, and Spanish Serrano.

One might deduce that Prague Ham was simply cooked ham; it survived in the consciousness of the western European gourmet in a popular form: "Prague Ham in Bread Dough." On the contrary, the ham at its best is pickled with skin and bones in a brine spiced with pepper, coriander, and bay leaves, then smoked over a beech wood fire. It takes on a mildly salty taste and smoky aroma. Thinly sliced and served with creamy horseradish, it is a delectable appetizer.

Every Prague Ham recipe is guarded by its butcher like a state secret. The Italians modeled its history in the same way that Prague's architecture was influenced by Southern prototypes. By comparison, however, butchers in Prague refined the technique of air-drying more than the Italians. And it goes without saying that a primary ingredient as fine as this opens doors to a whole array of dishes.

Prague Ham in Burgundy Wine

1 Prague ham about 5½ lbs (2½ kg)
7 oz (200 g) root vegetables (carrots, celeriac, leek)
1 bottle of white Burgundy
Powdered sugar

Let the ham cook about 50 minutes in water, cool, and remove the rind and excess fat.
Preheat the oven to 400 °F (200 °C).
Clean and finely chop the vegetables; sauté them in a little butter in a large ovenproof casserole. Add the ham, pour in the wine, cover the pot and continue to stew in the oven for 45 minutes. Shortly before the end of the cooking time, remove the cover and sprinkle the ham with powdered sugar. Then quickly glaze the meat at high temperature. Reduce the juices for gravy and embellish with Madeira or finely chopped mushrooms.

Šunka lesnická
Forester's Ham

7 oz (200 g) Prague ham in thick slices
¼ cup (50 g) butter
4 oz (100 g) mushrooms
2 oz (50 g) bacon
2 Tbs red wine
1 Tbs tomato paste
Herb butter

Braise the ham slices briefly in the butter. Cut, clean, and quarter the mushrooms. Chop the bacon, and cook in a pan. Add and sauté the mushrooms, red wine, and tomato paste. Arrange the ham slices on plates, cover with the mushrooms and garnish with herb butter.

Zapečená šunka plněná chřestem
Baked Ham with Asparagus

7 oz (200 g) Prague ham in thick slices
⅓ cup (80 g) butter
7 oz (200 g) asparagus
2 Tbs bread crumbs
⅓ cup (80 g) grated cheese

Braise the ham slices in a third of the butter, lay in a deep, ovenproof casserole and garnish with the asparagus. Sprinkle with bread crumbs and cheese, and dab the ham with the rest of the softened butter. Bake at 400 °F (200 °C).

Opposite: Prague Ham in Bread Dough
A Prague Ham, *Pražska šunka*, at the center of a festive buffet, is particularly appealing when baked in bread dough. Crucial to success are a high performance oven or a baker who makes the dough.
A Prague Ham of 5½ pounds (2½ kg) will bake through in about 50 minutes. Then the cook lets it cool, removes the rind and superfluous fat, and wraps it in a rye flour bread dough. Baked as if it were a loaf of bread, and sliced at the table, the ham produces an inimitable aroma.

King of the Bohemian Kitchen

Carp

As long as recorded time, carp has been a traditional Czech Christmas dish. Even when the sea was still considered ominous and full of mysterious creatures, or explorers Columbus and Marco Polo had still to tell of the harmless delights of eating salt-water fish, carp was a popular food. At that time, it was caught in the fisherman's bare hands or knocked out with a heavy stone.

"Duckling, pork, and hare are pleasant tastes, but the king of the kitchen, the carp, reigns with grace" goes the proverb (loosely translated). The natural habitat of the *Třeboňský kapr*, the Bohemian Carp, is Třeboň in Southern Bohemia, a landscape of lakes, ponds, pools, and swamps. The bottom soil determines the fish's distinctive taste. If the brackish water the carp inhabits is boggy, then its flavor will be slightly unpleasant, whereas in waters above a sandy bottom, the fish finds clean food easily and will taste far better.

While the carp is fondly called "pig of the water," it hardly takes to mud. Nor does it hang about lazily in the water like the perch, who lies in wait for its prey and then suddenly attacks. No, the carp is industrious and swims tirelessly behind its catch, and it covers vast distances. The Svět, a Southern Bohemian lake with a surface area of about 200 hectares, for example, is three miles (five kilometers) long, but a full-grown carp easily covers its length twice a day. It is in the Svět that the oldest (thirty-three years) and largest (sixty-six lbs or thirty kilograms) carp have been caught.

At best, carp is either roasted or boiled. Comparable to the lobster, whose shell will turn bright red, the golden scales of the carp change color in boiling water. The Viennese confectioner, Sacher, owner of the hotel and inventor of the famous Sachertorte, devised a special dressing technique in 1832 for Count Metternich; carp, too, was coated in egg, flour, and fine bread crumbs. In Prague, understandably, baked carp was far preferred to Wiener Schnitzel. The Třeboň fishermen have their own special method of preparation: turned in mud and packed in green leaves, the fish is baked beneath hot embers and ashes. Then the crust is opened and the white tender meat is eaten with the fingers.

Třeboň in South Bohemia is the home of the Czech carp. The sandy bed, in which the fish live, provides the inimitable taste.

Carp are an easy catch. In the brackish waters near the banks, they can be netted effortlessly. This fish is one of Central Europe's oldest "pets."

The Scaly Carp (bottom of page) is the wild version. Mirror carp (below), which have just a few scales along the fins, are bred.

Kapr marinovaný
Marinated Carp

1 carrot
¹/₂ celeriac (root celery)
1 onion
¹/₄ cup (50 g) green peas
1 sour pickle
1 lb (500 g) mayonnaise
1 glass of white wine
Juice of one lemon
Salt, black pepper
Sugar
1 carp, gutted and cleaned about 2 lbs (1 kg)

Clean or peel the carrot, celery root, and onion and slice them all into thin strips. Blanch in boiling water, drain and cool. Simmer the peas in salted water and cut the pickle into narrow strips before adding both to the vegetables. Toss in mayonnaise, white wine, lemon juice, and season with the salt, pepper, and sugar to taste.
Simmer the carp in salted water. Remove the skin and bones, cut the fish into small portions and marinate for several hours.

Kapr v aspiku
Carp in Aspic

12 gelatine leaves
2 Tbs vinegar
1 tsp salt
1 bouquet garni
1 bay leaf
A few peppercorns
2 lemons
1 carp, gutted and cleaned about 2 lbs (1 kg)
1 egg white
An assortment of fresh vegetables

Soften the gelatine in a little water. Brew 5 cups (2 l) of water with the vinegar, salt, bouquet garni, bay leaf, peppercorns, and the lemon juice. Slice the second lemon.
Divide the fish into portions and poach them before removing to a casserole.
Sieve the liquid, press out the gelatine and add it to the pot. Add the slightly beaten egg white, sieve again, and let cool.
Garnish the pieces of fish with slices of lemon and decorative vegetable cut-outs. Pour the gelatine mixture over the carp before refrigerating.

Kapr smažený
Carp in Fine Bread Crumbs

1 lb (500 g) carp fillets
Salt
Flour
1 egg, beaten
Fine bread crumbs
1 lemon
Grated horseradish

Salt the carp portions lightly. Turn them in flour, then egg, finally bread crumbs. Boil or fry the fish pieces in a generous amount of oil. Allow to dry on paper towels. Slice the lemon, top each slice with a tablespoon of horseradish, and serve as a garnish to the fish.

Slovakian Dishes

Sheep's Milk Cheese

Agriculture and animal husbandry are highly important in Slovakia. As in Greece, there are still many shepherds. Contrary to the Greeks, however, the Slovakians do not produce olive oil; at the outer reaches of the Carpathian range, in the High Tatra, olive trees cannot thrive. There is an abundance of sheep's milk cheese in Slovakia, however. Because in many places there is no way to pasteurize the milk, Slovakian *bryndza* (soft cheese) is not exported to the European Community countries.

The sheep are the livelihood of the *bačas*, the Slovakian shepherd: a herd counts about 400 sheep, and the ewes are milked three times a day. Sheep's milk is higher than cow milk in fat and protein content. A sheep produces about one cup (200 ml) of milk, which is poured into a cotton sack to make cheese. The soft, moist mass dries in about a week, and a cheese manufacturer processes it into *bryndza*, refining it and adding salt. After a short fermentation period, the cheese acquires its characteristically sour taste. It can be eaten alone or spread on bread in combination with red pepper, butter, or onions. *Bryndza* is also the primary ingredient for *strapačky* and *halušky*, two traditional Slovakian dishes.

Sheep's milk is often smoked so it will keep longer. The pressed cheeses look lovely when removed from their molds and hung decoratively around the smoking chamber.

The ewes in the herd are milked three times a day.

The milk is collected in large wooden vats and rennin is added.

The milk is stirred to prevent any settling of contents.

Then it goes into cotton sacks.

The sheep's milk cheese is smoked in a smoking hut.

Cheeses removed from molds hang in the smoking hut.

Halušky

1 lb (500 g) potatoes, raw and grated
½ cup (100 ml) milk
Salt, flour
1 lb (500 g) sheep's milk cheese
Dripping

Knead the grated potato, milk, salt, and flour into a loose dough and drop in small amounts in boiling water. Simmer a minute, then remove the dumplings from the water and turn them in the cheese. Melt the dripping and pour over the potato-cheese mixture.

Strapačky

1 white cabbage
2 onions
Ingredients for halušky

Clean and shred the cabbage, and simmer in salted water. Peel and finely chop the onions. Sweat the onions in the dripping until transparent, stir into the cabbage and serve with the *Halušky*.

Liptovský syr
Liptauer Cheese

¼ cup (50 g) softened butter
1 cup (200 g) sheep's milk cheese
1 onion, peeled and finely chopped
Paprika, capers, caraway seeds, anchovy paste, mustard, chives

Whip the butter until creamy, press the cheese through a sieve and add to the butter. Add the remaining ingredients to taste before refrigerating. Garnish with chives before serving.

The sacks are hung so that the milk can trickle out slowly.

What remains is a soft, moist mass that must dry.

Bryndza is derived from ground and salted soft cheese.

After a period of fermentation, the cheese acquires its sour taste.

PLZEŇ 12°
Malé pivo 24,-
Kořalka 40,-
Víno 40,-
Whisky 100,-
Košher slív 60,-
Minerálka 25,-
Becherovka 40,-
ČESKÝ TALÍŘ 300q

Mandle 42,-

Background: An original tavern in Prague where various beers can be enjoyed.

Pilsner Beer

Czech beers, particularly Pilsner Urquell, command great respect among beer connoisseurs. Beer for the Czechs is at once politics, religion, and cult, but above all, it means controversy: "Urquell or Budweiser, that is the question." In fact, while these are the two most popular national beers, most Czechs would swear on their more local varieties. Experts from the Czech Beer Academy and a lay jury inspect them and confer awards on the occasion of the Annual Beer Fair "Pivex" in Brno. Beer has been brewed in Prague since 1082. In the 13th century, new cities were founded in Bohemia, which, as royal settlements, enjoyed certain privileges, among them the right to brew beer. Every citizen had the right to produce beer and sell it. Pilsen, Budweis, and Saaz, the city of hops, counted among the most privileged areas.

Breweries in other areas were not as fortunate: some were razed to their foundations so fortifications could be built with the stone.

Until 1842, beer was always dark or opaque. Every year, though, Pilsner produced a light and clear variety. Its unusual

A good heady Pilsner is some time in the making. Only then will it have the right amount of carbon dioxide and the typical frothy crown.

taste made it popular overnight. It is not quite certain how it was invented. Perhaps master brewer Josef Groll, who came from the neighboring Bavarian city of Vilshofen, discovered the beer purely by accident – or so goes the story on a plaque in Pilsen. His beer became more and more popular, in no small part because it was drunk from clear glasses instead of wooden and ceramic tankards. In glass, the golden-colored liquid looked far more attractive, and more importantly, it tasted better. To this day, breweries all over the world strive to imitate the original Pilsner, but in producing that unique spicy flavor, they come up short every time. The original Pilsner beer, *Plzeňský Prazdroj* has a bit more aroma, more the taste of malt, more hops, and is a little drier.

Prazdroj, the original, is brewed from Bohemian and Moravian oats. Connoisseurs argue that a true Pilsner must always be produced with hops from Saaz, and breweries all over Europe import it for that reason.

It was here, in the "Bourgeois Brewery" – today restored to the ownership of descendants of the original brewer – that in 1842, the original Pilsner beer was produced quite by accident by the Bavarian master brewer, Josef Groll.
Due to its incomparable dry full-bodied taste it has become known worldwide, and many other breweries even import the hops used here in an attempt to imitate the taste.

How Pilsner Beer is Brewed

The oats are soaked to soften for thirty-six hours and sprout six days in the malthouse; before malt is produced, the process of drying and germination takes twenty-four hours. The malt is cooked for twelve hours, and is fermented for twelve days with hops and original wort in huge vats, where it ferments another twelve weeks before it is bottled.

The original Pilsner always had twelve hops, just like Budvar, the Budweiser. Both are among the lager beers in the Czech Republic, and differ from barreled beers (that can also be of milder strength). While barreled beers are made with only six or seven degrees wort, they have a fresh, clear taste and are only mildly alcoholic. For that reason, steel workers and mountain folk are permitted to drink them while on the job. The ten-degree-beers, also called "black beers" offer better quality, produced as they are in the Bavarian tradition with aromatic, dark malt.

Pilsner beer was first awarded a prize at the International Exhibition in Hamburg in 1863.

In spite of the accolades about Pilsner beer, there are many Czechs who would go to great lengths to defend Budvar, the beer from Budweis. King Ferdinand had it delivered to his court as early as 1531, and ever since then, the beer has been advertized as "The Beer of Kings." Budvar is lighter than Pilsner and has a slightly sweet flavor.

Sprouting oats are dried.

The oat malt produced makes the base for beer production.

The malt is boiled in huge tubs to produce the wort.

Yeast is added to the mixture.

The amount of yeast determines the characteristic Pilsner flavor.

The alcoholic fermentation occurs in open vats in special cellars.

The degree of maturity of the still unfiltered beer is checked.

Ultimately, the beer is stored in wooden barrels.

Specialty Beers

A country with as highly developed a beer culture as the Czech Republic would hardly be happy with "common" beer. Many breweries produce special beers that markedly differ from the classic Pilsners in hop content and taste.

The most renowned of these is the darkbeer from the U Fleků, a popular restaurant with a huge beer garden. The beer has a light caramel taste and thirteen degree original wort. Similar specialty beers are produced in Western Bohemia under the name *Chodovar* and in Slovakia as *Čierny Bažant* (Black Pheasant).

Even stronger beers are the bock beer *Velkopopovický Kozel* from Central Bohemia and *Konžel* (Bureaucrat) from Litomerice. In addition, there are about a dozen light beers with fourteen degree wort. *Diplomat* from the Gambrinus Brewery in Pilsen, has eighteen degree wort, but is made for export or found only in exclusive restaurants. *Martinský Porter*, the strongest beer with twenty degree wort, comes from the city of Martin in central Slovakia.

Dishes to Have With Beer

Topinky
Fried Garlic Bread

4 slices of wholewheat bread
8 garlic cloves
Salt

Rub the garlic over both sides of the bread and fry in a pan. Salt and serve warm.

Pivní guláš
Meat in Bohemian Beer

1 lb (500 g) pork shoulder
1 Tbs rose paprika
2 large onions
½ cup (50 g) pork fat
1 tsp caraway seeds
1 bottle Pilsner Urquell
1 slice of black bread
Salt, black pepper

Cube the pork and mix with the paprika. Peel the onions, chop them coarsely and fry in the fat. Add and brown the meat, stirring for about 10 minutes.
Add the caraway seeds and half the beer, cover and simmer for about 45 minutes.
Crumble the bread and add it to the meat with the rest of the beer, simmer for a further 15 minutes, and season with salt and pepper before serving.

Bramborová polévka
Potato Soup

2 Tbs (20 g) dried mushrooms (expands to about 1 cup)
1 lb (500 g) potatoes (floury variety)
1 bunch bouquet garni
6 strips (150 g) smoked bacon
5 cups (1½ l) bouillon
Caraway seeds
Marjoram
1 large onion
1 garlic clove
¼ cup (50 g) butter
¼ cup (50 g) flour
Salt, black pepper
6 oz (container) sour cream
1 egg yolk
Chopped parsley

Soften the mushrooms in water overnight. Peel and cube the potatoes, clean and finely chop the bouquet garni and cube the bacon.
Bring the mushrooms, potatoes, bouquet garni, bacon, caraway seeds, and marjoram to a boil and simmer for 20 minutes.
Peel the onion and garlic clove, and fry them to a golden brown in the butter. Sprinkle in the flour and stir to a roux. Add the roux to the soup, stirring constantly, and pass the soup through a sieve. Season with generous amounts of salt and pepper.
Combine the egg yolk and the sour cream, remove the soup from the heat, and stir in the egg-cream mixture.
Garnish with parsley and serve.

Specialty and lager beers:
1 Velkopopovický Kozel
2 Radegast
3 Budvar (Budweiser)
4 Gambrinus
5 Topvař
6 Zlaty Bažant

1   2   3   4   5   6

Zoltán Halász

Hungary

Hungary's oldest cooking utensil, the *bogrács*, or cast iron pot, was the vessel brought by migrant people into the Carpathian lowlands. It serves as a reminder today that Hungary was once made up entirely of nomadic folk. To a native, a goulash is authentic only if cooked over an open fire as was the custom of the ancient Magyars. During Turkish occupation in the 17th century, Hungarian cuisine adopted many Turkish recipes. Later, when the counts in Siebenbürgen employed French cooks, a French flair became evident, decidedly so when Emperor Napoleon III's premier chef became the director of the Casino Pester. In the 19th century, there were reciprocal culinary currents between Hungary and the Austro-Hungarian Empire.

In addition to paprika, a certain mild onion is an integral part of Hungarian cuisine. So too is sour cream, an essential ingredient in countless dishes. In numerous variations, smoked bacon – from the fine pigs Hungary has bred for centuries – is also a hallmark of national cuisine. As a rule, Hungarians like their meats fatty and fried. Making pork sausages around slaughter time has a long tradition among farmers, and Hungarian salami counts among the finest anywhere: both are coveted export articles and generate a significant income. The same can be said of goose liver, which satisfies a demand of the French that exceeds that country's own production. *Fogas*, or pike-perch, from Lake Balaton, counts among the other renowned Hungarian specialties, as does Tokajer wine from the northern part of the country, and *barack pálinka*, the apricot schnapps produced from fruit harvested in the great Hungarian plains. The Hungarians, a life- and pleasure-loving people, produce superior quality products from the gifts Nature has given them. While its dimensions within Europe and its population are small, Hungary is indeed a culinary giant.

Left: Two workers in a Kalocsa paprika mill.

179

Ruler of the Balaton

The Pike-Perch

It is with a touch of irony that the Hungarians call the Balaton the "Hungarian ocean." But people are serious when they talk about the fish which inhabit it, in particular when the issue is *fogas*, or pike-perch.

As a fish of prey, the pike-perch is the king of the lake. Only king, though, when weighing more than three pounds (1.5 kilograms), for smaller perch are called *süllő*. A full-grown Balaton pike-perch reaches a weight of between thirteen and eighteen pounds (6–8 kilograms).

The fish's habit of moving quickly and steadily lends a slightly nutty taste to its delicate meat. The pike-perch keeps to deep water as a rule and comes to the surface only in pursuit of smaller prey, those *Alsen* or the whitefish that make up most of its diet. Owing to the filter of fine grains of sand, sunlight cannot penetrate to the depth of three to four meters (about the same in yards) where the fish lives. Because of this, its meat is almost white.

The female pike-perch lays her eggs between April and May. She can lay as many as 40,000, but as she and her partner consume a great number of the eggs during gestation, hardly a third actually hatches into young fish. At a year, the young *süllő* weigh about two pounds (approximately a kilo); the name *fogas* is given from about two years old.

Scientists have argued for centuries about the relationship of the Balaton pike-perch to the salmon. Naturalist Otto Herman settled the dispute by proving that the *fogas* belongs to the salmon family, but is of a kind unique to the Balaton, and is not to be found anywhere else.

Hungarian master chefs have experimented with countless and unusual perch recipes. Among connoisseurs, however, there is a preference for the whole fish pan-broiled, head and tail curling up from the platter when the fish is served. Broiling the perch on a open grill or spiking it on a cooking stake are two earthier ways of preparation.

A fisherman proudly shows his fine catch: a mature pike-perch at several pounds.

The pike-perch has white meat and counts among the tastiest of fish.

Background: A fishing boat on Lake Balaton, plentiful in fish and home to the pike-perch.

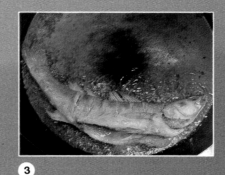

1

2

3

4

Fogas, egészben sütve
Whole, Broiled Pike-perch
(Illustrations 1–4)

1 pike-perch (about 4½ lbs (2 kg))
5 oz (150 g) smoked bacon, sliced in strips
Salt
Flour
½ cup (100 g) butter
1 small onion
1 cup (200 ml) sour cream
½ cup (100 ml) heavy cream
1 tsp sweet paprika
1 slice of lemon

Scale, gut, and wash the pike-perch (1). Cut back the gills, oil and score the fish on both sides to prevent contraction while broiling (2). Salt the fish, turn it in flour and baste in a large part of the butter in a cast iron pan (3). Broil at the highest possible temperature for about 15 minutes, then remove the fish from the heat and keep it warm (4).
Peel and finely chop the onions, turn them in butter until transparent. Add the sour and sweet cream, cook a short time, and sprinkle with the paprika. Combine the flour and remaining butter and add them, stirring constantly, to the onion cream. Once the sauce has thickened, pass it through a sieve. Arrange the fish like a crescent on the platter and garnish with the lemon slice in its mouth.

Fogas Gundel módra
Pike-perch Gundel

Devised by the illustrious Hungarian master chef, Károly Gundel.

1 small pike-perch
4 eggs
4 oz (120 g) flour
8 oz (250 g) fine bread crumbs
1 cup (200 g) butter
1 lb (500 g) spinach
10 oz (300 g) potatoes
4 oz (100 g) grated cheese
6 oz (container) cream
Salt, black pepper

Scale and gut the pike-perch and cut into portions. Beat 2 eggs. Turn the fish in flour, egg, and bread crumbs alternately. Heat 6 oz of the butter and fry the fish. Wash, blanch, and purée the spinach. Add 2 tablespoons of cooking butter. Boil and peel the potatoes, grate them while they are still warm, and add the remaining eggs and a little butter to them. Butter an ovenproof casserole. Using a decorator's bag, garnish its edge with the potato and spoon the spinach into its middle. Lay the fish on the spinach, stir the cheese into the cream and pour all over the fish. Either bake in the oven or broil.

Hungary's Bouillabaisse: Halászlé

It is fishermen who take the credit for a fish soup that rivals the best French bouillabaisse: the *halászlé* fish chowder. Paprika lends great appeal to the tasty and satisfying dish, which can readily be eaten as a main course, given the heartiness of its ingredients.

To make the true *halászlé*, the original recipe asks for the widest possible variety of fish, cooked in a large cooking pot that hangs over a fire. The fate of those of us who are city-folk or non-Hungarians is to settle for a smaller variety of fish and a stove.

Halászlé
Fish Soup

About 1 lb (500 g) each of carp, pike and pike-perch
5 onions, peeled and sliced
Salt
2 Tbs sweet paprika powder
1 Tbs rose paprika

Gut and clean the fish, and cut into inch (3 cm) cubes. Layer the various kinds of fish in a large casserole, separating each layer of fish with one of onions, ending with fish on top. Cover all with water, add salt, and bring to the boil. Then sprinkle on the two types of paprika and simmer for about an hour. Shake occasionally (but do not stir, or the fish will fall apart).
Serve the *halászlé* with fresh white bread.

Goose Liver

Whoever buys goose liver terrine in Strasbourg will probably purchase the liver of a Hungarian goose. Hungarian goose liver, in fact, was already a profitable article for export to the West during the Socialist Regime, primarily because the demand for the delicacy far exceeded the amount the French could produce.

While geese are raised practically all over Hungary, the real roots of goose liver production are the Southern Hungarian plains. The soil in the region between Kiskunhalas to Orosháza is optimally suited to geesé-farming as the birds prefer sandy to muddy ground, and a temperate, sunny climate.

Equally important is that over many generations expertise in breeding and fattening the birds has been accumulated on small private farms, where success depends entirely on the knowledge and the care taken by the breeder. The type of corn used as feed and the soil in which it grows, for example, are crucial to fattening the birds optimally. Drinking water also has an influence, so every farmer has a method of improving its quality with white clay and other elements.

In addition to the *hungaviscomb* and the *babut*, two kinds of white-feathered geese raised in Hungary, the gray-feathered bird of French origin is also popular. As it grows to be a heavier bird, its liver is correspondingly larger. At nine or ten weeks on the average, and in the care of specially trained geese-farmers, the geese are fed generously four or five times a day with corn. Over two or three weeks, this method gives their livers a golden color.

Every goose keeper has a secret formula for the feed he uses. The corn is either cooked or softened with vegetable oil and Vitamin C. It is vital that feedings be given gently, so that the birds do not incur undue stress. Artificial additives and antibiotics are forbidden, as are any elements the birds cannot break down naturally.

The feedings raise the cholesterol level in the goose, and blood is transported to the liver and absorbed in great quantity there, such that the liver swells to about three pounds. A quality goose liver is golden yellow and is soft and silky to the touch. According to the experts, Hungarian goose liver tastes its very best when submerged in garlic milk and stored in the refrigerator overnight, then rinsed and braised in goose fat at high heat. In Orosháza the liver is softened in milk, turned in flour, and cooked without fat in an open skillet.

Opposite: The gray-feathered geese of French origin are particularly popular for fattening. It is a heavier bird and therefore has a larger liver.

The formula for the feed is crucial in fattening geese – this formula being a closely-guarded secret of the goose keeper. Artificial additives and antibiotics are forbidden, as are any elements the birds cannot break down naturally. During the two-week fattening period, the geese are fed four or five times a day, but gently and incurring no undue stress.

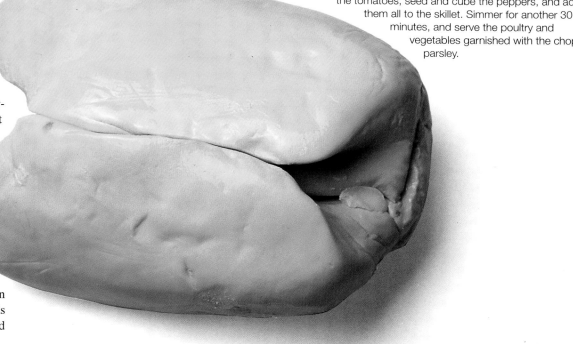

Hungarian goose livers are well known for their high quality. They weigh around three pounds and get their golden color from the corn with which the geese are fed.

Libamáj
Braised Goose Liver

1 goose liver
1/2 cup (100 g) goose fat
Salt
2 onions
1 tsp sweet paprika powder

Slice the goose liver into 1/2 inch (1.5 cm) thick medallions. Salt, remove them from the pan and keep warm. Peel the onions, slice one into rings, and set aside. Finely chop and brown the other onion in the fat. Remove from the heat, sprinkle with paprika and slowly heat a second time. Arrange the liver on a platter, pour over the sauce and garnish with the onion rings.

Libacomb
Goose Thighs

4 goose thighs
Salt
3 oz (80 g) goose fat
1 onion
1 Tbs sweet paprika powder
1 garlic clove
Caraway seeds
2 lbs (1 kg) potatoes
2 tomatoes
2 green peppers
Chopped parsley

Rinse, dry, and salt the goose thighs. Heat the goose fat in a large skillet and braise the thighs quickly on both sides. Remove them from the pan and keep warm. Peel and finely chop the onion; brown in the fat. Remove from the heat, sprinkle with paprika and add a little water. Return the goose thighs to the skillet, add the crushed garlic clove and some caraway seeds, cover and simmer over medium heat for about half an hour. Peel and make sticks of the potatoes, wash and chop the tomatoes, seed and cube the peppers, and add them all to the skillet. Simmer for another 30 minutes, and serve the poultry and vegetables garnished with the chopped parsley.

Not Just Any Old Goulash

Pörkölt

While "goulash" is a catch-all word outside Hungary, native Hungarians make a careful distinction between *gulyás*, *pörkölt*, *tokány*, and *paprikás*. *Gulyas* once stood for sheep herders, and *gulyashus* was the name for the meat dish they carried on their long journeys. They cut beef, mutton, or pork in large cubes and cooked the meat in an iron kettle, a *bogrács*, until all the liquid had evaporated. They dried meat in the sun and preserved it in sacks made out of sheep's stomach. If they were hungry, they extracted a piece, added some water and heated it up. A larger amount of water produced *gulyás leves* or goulash soup.

Pörkölt translates literally as "roasted," and differs in consistency from *gulyás*. With its dark red, thick sauce, the dish corresponds to the Western notion of "goulash."

Tokány is related to *pörkölt*, but rather than paprika, the spices used are marjoram and black pepper. It is a dish of many meats, sometimes in combination with vegetables or mushrooms.

Paprikás are dishes whose small pieces of meat – traditionally, fish, chicken, veal, or lamb – are refined with sweet or sour cream.

Bográcsgulyás
Kettle Goulash

Serves 8

2 onions
2 Tbs fat
2 lbs (1 kg) beef (shoulder or shank)
7 oz (200 g) heart (beef)
1 garlic clove
1 tsp caraway seeds
Salt
1 tomato
2 peppers
1 lb (500 g) potatoes
Rose paprika

Peel and chop the onions into large pieces. In a large stewing pot, melt the fat and fry the onions until they are transparent. Cube the meat and heart, add to the onions and brown.
Add the garlic, caraway, and some salt. Remove the pot from the heat and distribute the spices evenly. Add 2 quarts (about 2 l) of warm water, cover and simmer for about an hour over low heat.
Skin, seed, and cube the tomatoes, wash the peppers and slice them into rings. Peel and cube the potatoes. Add the tomato and the peppers to the meat, as well as a little more water and salt. Simmer for another 30 minutes, then add the potatoes and heat through. Season to taste with the pungent rose paprika and serve in deep soup bowls.

Borjúpörkölt
Veal Goulash

Serves 4–6

2 lbs (1 kg) veal
1 large onion
1 Tbs sweet paprika powder
1 garlic clove, crushed
Salt
1 tomato
1 pepper
2 Tbs fat

Cube the meat, peel and chop the onion.
Melt the fat in a stewing pot and lightly brown the onions in it.
Remove the pot from the heat and add the paprika powder, garlic, a pinch of salt, and finally the meat. Stew over low heat, adding water as the liquid evaporates.
Skin, seed, and cube the tomatoes, wash, seed, and cut the pepper into small pieces. After about 15 minutes' cooking time, add them to the uncovered pot, and allow most of the liquid to evaporate before serving.

Csirskepörkölt
Chicken Goulash
(Illustration)

Serves 4–6

1 stewing chicken
3 onions
1 Tbs fat
1 Tbs sweet paprika powder
1 Tbs tomato paste
1 garlic clove, crushed
Salt
2 tomatoes
2 peppers

Cut the chicken into pieces. Peel and chop the onions and fry them in the fat until transparent.

Turn the meat in the paprika, tomato paste, crushed garlic, and salt, and add it to the onions. Let it stew, covered, for about 15 minutes.

Skin, seed, and cube the tomatoes. Wash, seed, and cut the peppers into small pieces. Let everything simmer until the meat is tender, and add as little liquid as possible for the chicken to stew in its own extremely tasty juices.

Unquestionably *the* Hungarian specialty: paprika, here packed in burlap

Csirskepörkölt – Chicken Goulash

Nothing is More Typical

Paprika

Fiery, spicy, and temperamental – attributes associated as much with paprika as with the Hungarian national character. Not only is paprika the Hungarian kitchen's most important spice, but it is also the main ingredient of countless dishes – indeed, without paprika, Hungarian cuisine would be unthinkable.

The origins of paprika are unclear. Possibly Columbus brought it from America, as the vegetable shows up first in Spain in the Middle Ages. Some contend Hungarian paprika came through Persia from India, and was brought into Hungary by the Turks at the beginning of the 16th century. That paprika was called "Indian pepper" for centuries supports this thesis – one made tenuous again when we recall that "Indian" also meant "American Indian" to early botanists.

To follow the course of paprika's expansion after Spain is to find it in Italy, where the Turks acquired it and brought it to the Balkans. In the 16th century, Bulgarian gardeners came to Hungary in great number, and it is likely that they planted paprika there.

Over the centuries Hungarian planters cultivated the plant such that, in time, its desirable characteristics were able to develop fully. Its pungent taste, which is derived from the alkaloid capsaicin contained in the cavity of the fruit, was moderated.

A century earlier, the Pálffy brothers, paprika farmers from Szeged, thought to extract the ribs from the paprika fruit, thereby considerably reducing the pungency of the spice. It was in this way *édesnemes paprika*, or sweet paprika evolved. It eventually came to enjoy renown all over the world. Another paprika farmer cultivated the plant so long that the fruits were devoid of pungency – as such, the highly-colored, yet completely mild *csemege paprika* evolved.

Manufacture of Paprika Spice

For the manufacture of paprika spice, the dried, red fruits are washed and dried in modern industrial plants. In the Szeged and Kalocsa regions, the paprika is ground and processed with stone and steel rollers. Paprika millers expertly determine how many of the separately selected seed kernels should be ground with the fruits. The high temperatures reached in the milling process releases the fruits' color and cause seed oil to exude from the kernels, which determines the degree of pungency. The milling temperature must also be set exactly; the slight caramelization of the paprika's natural sugars rounds out the aroma of the spice.

After the spice is ground, the mixture undergoes a careful quality control and classification. So much for laboratory testing. In the final analysis, the taste buds of the paprika gourmet determine whether the spice mixture meets all requirements successfully and the packaging should carry the coveted name. Today, paprika is used all over the world. Even hobby cooks who are browning onions in oil, know that a sprinkling of sweet paprika stirred carefully into the mixture calls up an entirely new palette of aroma and taste. In Hungary, the preparation of many delicacies begins right there.

In Hungary, the word paprika is used only to denote the actual spice, and is distinguished from

It is likely that the plant came from America, as it shows up first in Spain after the journeys of Columbus.

After the harvest, the fruits are washed and dried.

The paprika is ground and processed with stone and steel rollers.

A number of seed kernels are added when milling. These determine color and pungency.

vegetable peppers, or "tomato peppers," whose greenish-yellow fruits characteristically turn red in the process of ripening.

Paprikás csirke
Chicken Paprika

1 kitchen-ready chicken (about 2 lbs, 1 kg) with innards
Salt
5 oz (150 g) smoked bacon
1 onion
1 tsp sweet paprika powder
Chicken broth
Chicken liver
6 oz (container) sour cream

Wash the chicken and pat it dry. Salt and separate into large pieces.
Chop and cook the bacon, then peel and finely chop the onions and add them to it. Remove the pan from the heat and sprinkle the onions with the paprika.
Put the chicken pieces in the pan, brown and add a little stock. Cover and simmer for about 60 minutes over low heat, turning the pieces occasionally.
Chop the liver into small pieces and add for the last few minutes, then spoon in the sour cream, cover briefly to heat through, and serve.

Lescó
Tomatoes and Peppers Paprika

1 onion
2 Tbs fat
5 small peppers
3 tomatoes
1 Tbs sweet paprika
Sugar
Salt

Peel and slice the onions. Heat the fat in a casserole and fry the onions until they are transparent.
Wash, seed, and slice the peppers into rings, add to the onions and fry another 15 minutes. Skin, seed, and chop the tomatoes, and add them to the onion–pepper mixture with a little sugar and salt. Simmer for another 20 minutes before serving.

Peppers are processed in many ways: crushed to a powder for spice, packed in aluminum cans (above), or conserved in glass (below).

Below: The mild, finely-crushed Hungarian delicacy paprika is exported all over the world. While it undergoes strict quality control, it is ultimately the palette of the gourmet that determines its success.

Hungarian paprika spice

There are five grades of pungency, but the rule of thumb is this, that the redder the color, the milder the spice.

Delicacy paprika
Dark red, medium-fine texture, very mild

Sweet paprika
Dark red, medium-fine texture, mildly pungent

Semi-sweet paprika
Red, matte color, strong spice aroma and medium-fine texture, should never be fat-fried

Rose paprika
Piquant and very pungent, medium-fine texture
Mild: shiny light red, medium-fine texture, less pungent but spicy to the taste
Pungent: yellowish to light red, medium-fine texture and as hot as they come

Töltött papriká
Stuffed Peppers

8 medium-sized green peppers
1/2 cup (100 g) fat
1 onion
1 lb (500 g) chopped pork
Juice of one garlic clove
Salt, black pepper
1/2 cup (100 g) cooked rice
1 egg
4–5 tomatoes
Flour

Remove the stems, cut off the tops, and seed the peppers. Wash and allow to dry.
Heat half the fat. Peel and finely chop the onion and fry to golden in the fat. Add the pork and brown slightly, stirring all the while. Spice with garlic, salt, and pepper. Add the rice to the meat, drop in the egg and work into a shiny filling for the peppers.
Cook and sieve the tomatoes before seasoning with salt and pepper. Make a roux of the remaining fat and the flour and add it to the sieved tomatoes.
Put the peppers in a buttered, ovenproof casserole, and pour the tomato sauce over them. Cap each stuffed pepper with its top, and bake for 20 minutes at 400 °F (200 °C).

The Finest Pancakes

Palacsinta

Ask four cooks, French, Austrian, Bohemian, and Hungarian, to speculate on the origin of the pancake, and each one will lay claim to the paper-thin delicacy. While the French cook will defend the *crêpes*, the Austrian the *Palatschinken*, the Bohemian the *palatcinky*, and the Hungarian the *palacsinta*, each of them will be discredited in the end, as the origins of the dish are actually Roman. In Roman times, so-called *placenta* were the round cakes eaten in lieu of bread, a custom that Roman Legionnaires spread as far as their Empire.

The Hungarian *palacsinta* can be traced back to its inventor, Károly Gundel. It was he invented – albeit under French influence – the "Pancake Gundel" with its delicate walnut filling.

Palacsinta Gundel módra
Pancake Gundel
(Illustration opposite, top)

Batter
3 eggs
1 cup (250 g) flour
1 cup (200 ml) milk
1 tsp sugar
Pinch of salt
Butter
1 cup (250 ml) soda water

Combine the eggs, flour, milk, sugar, and salt to a shiny, well-blended batter, and let it stand for 2 hours. Warm a large pan and add some butter, and while the butter is melting, stir the soda water into the dough.
Pour a little batter into the pan and distribute evenly. Flip the pancake when bubbles appear.

Walnut filling
6 oz (container) cream
1 cup (200 g) ground walnuts
¼ cup (50 g) chopped raisins
½ cup (120 g) sugar
2 Tbs rum
Peel of 1 untreated orange

Warm the cream and add the other ingredients. Let it simmer for about a minute. Spread one tablespoon of filling on each pancake before rolling up.

Chocolate Rum Sauce
1 large bar of semi-sweet chocolate
1 cup (200 ml) milk
3 egg yolks
2 Tbs cocoa powder
1 Tbs melted butter
2 Tbs sugar
2 Tbs light rum

Melt the chocolate in the warmed milk. Remove the pan from the heat and stir in the egg yolks, cocoa, butter, sugar, and rum, in that order. Stir until uniform and thin with a little milk if necessary. Pour the sauce over the filled pancakes.

Töltött körte
Stuffed Pears
(Illustration below)

2 Tbs lemon juice
½ cup (120 g) sugar
4 firm pears
½ cup (50 g) ground walnuts
1 Tbs sour cream
1 packet of vanilla sugar

Combine one tablespoon of lemon juice with 2¼ cups (500 ml) water and bring to a boil. Peel and halve the pears, remove the cores and cook them almost through in the syrup. They should stay slightly firm.

Combine the remaining lemon juice with the nuts, sour cream, and vanilla sugar, and form little balls with the mixture. Remove the pear halves from the syrup and garnish each with one ball.

As in the illustration, the filled pears can also be served on a bed of whipped cream and decorated with chocolate sauce.

Background: A café in Budapest at the turn of the century.

The picturesque town of Tokay, in the heart of vineyards of the same name, produces wines of international renown.

The Secret of "Ausbruch" Wine

Tokaji Aszú

Wine is produced all over Hungary, but only one, Tokay, has achieved a reputation worldwide. The picturesque village which lends the wine its name lies at the foot of the Tokajer Mountains. Over and beyond their slopes, however, the grape grows in and around twenty-eight villages in the surrounding Tokaj-Hegyalja area, Hungary's most north-eastern region.

The renowned *tokaji aszú*, "Ausbruch" wine, is a Hungarian specialty that dates back to the 17th century. A landowner postponed his harvest, and his grapes began their fermentation on the vine: they began to dry and to shrivel, their sugar content increased, and their acidity was reduced.

The wine pressed from these grapes eventually found its way to the court of Louis XIV in France, and there competed so successfully with French wines that the sun-king granted Tokay the honorable title "King of Wines – Wine of Kings." That noble recommendation made the wine popular at other European courts. Catherine the Great of Russia, for example, employed a buyer in the Tokajer vineyards who exchanged Siberian fur pelts for the wine she needed at court. Archduchess Maria Theresa of Austria, too, thought so highly of the wine that she once had it sent to Pope Benedict XIV (1740–58). The Pope thanked the Archduchess, who was also the Hungarian queen, with the following: "Blessed be the earth that makes you, blessed be the woman that sends you, and blessed be I, Benedict, who drinks you." Three kinds of grape are cultivated in the Tokaj-Hegyalja region: the *furmint* foremost, second, the *hárslevelü* ("the linden leaf"), and to a lesser extent, the yellow muskatelle.

The wine harvest begins traditionally on Simon Judas' Day, or October 28. It extends all the way through November, and sometimes even into December. The burst grapes are collected in small buckets whose bases are eventually coated by a small amount of juice. Pressed by the sheer weight of the grapes themselves, it is this essence that becomes the rare and costly specialty. Tokay is produced only in very small quantities, is high in sugar content, flowery, and highly aromatic.

The burst grapes are pressed into a paste, the so-called "burst mush," and the remaining juice is bottled.

To make Aszú, "burst mush" is added in quantities to normal wine. The eight-gallon (thirty liter) collection buckets, which are known as *puttonyos*, are used as measures. One refers to a Tokay with three, four or five *puttonyos* depend-

Opposite: An assortment of the renowned Hungarian burst wines, *Tokaji Aszú*, purportedly of "biblical" age. The noble rot of the grapes on the vine is the secret of the wine's special flavor.

An old barrel in which Tokay is stored: and a *puttony*, the 8 gallon (approximately 30 liter) bucket in which the grapes are collected.

The cellar walls are covered with a black fungus whose aroma affects the wine.

Owing to the controlled micro-climate in the cellars, the Tokay burst wine keeps its characteristic taste, which has the hint of fresh bread.

Tokaji Aszú is produced from yellow muskateller, furmint, and the hárslevelü grapes.

ing on how many buckets are added to a thirty-six gallon (about 136 liter) barrel of juice, and this notation usually appears as the number of stars on the label.

One is apt to find wine cellars that have been dug out of the vineyard hillside in Tokaj-Hegyalja. A coal-black covering of fungus, which collects on the walls, helps maintain a micro-climate highly favorable to the Tokay's development. The air, reeking of fungus, absorbs the acidity of the wine, and makes development of its full aroma possible.

As the high sugar content delays fermentation, the ripening process is particularly slow. To reach full maturation, the Tokay requires from six to eight years.

Barack pálinka

The most popular Hungarian schnapps is undoubtedly the apricot *Barack pálinka*. Two kinds of apricot are used to make it, the *kajszi* or common apricot, and the *rakovszky*, a juicy fruit of particularly full taste. During distillation, the crushed apricot pits are added to intensify the flavor. Later, *barack pálinka* matures in oak barrels for at least a year.

Joachim Römer

Austria

Whoever thinks German is the language spoken in Austria must be prepared to hear otherwise, at least when it comes to culinary matters: the tomato, cauliflower, horseradish, and plum purée all have entirely and uniquely Austrian names. And whoever orders a "coffee" in a Viennese coffeehouse, points unmistakably to himself as an outsider, as every coffee specialty has its own Austrian name.

Linguistic peculiarities such as these are rooted in the long culinary tradition of the alpine country that was once a world power. All of Hungary, Bohemia (the Czech Republic today), parts of Northern Italy (Southern Tyrol and Trieste), and Istria, some of today's Croatia, once belonged to the Austrian Empire. Wars against the Turks were hard and long, but the Turks never succeeded in taking Vienna thanks to "the noble knight," Prince Eugene. Instead, they left an indelible mark on the Austrian taste for coffee.

The whole world was entertained at Austrian court. Swedish and Prussian, English and Russian, French and Greek guests all feasted there. For centuries, the Austrian Emperor was also King of Spain, and a strong Iberian influence on Austrian cuisine is still evident to this day.

After the last victory over the Turks in 1697, the spirit of the baroque spread out over Austria in all its glory. While the former imperial capitol reflected the glory of the past, Vienna today, as capitol of a small alpine republic, is almost ostentatious. Its palaces and imposing ring architecture, however, do make an impressive, cosmopolitan backdrop for cuisine whose "royal" dimensions have survived to this day, and Austrian taste passes readily over national borders. The Austrian kitchen avails itself freely of the ethnic foods of the former Danube monarchy, the strong presence of the rural provinces. Not only are cooking, dining, and the appreciation of food long-standing Austrian traditions, they are graces which, to the Austrian, markedly increase the quality of life.

Left: Herr Hawelka, owner of the Viennese coffee house of the same name, behind the counter. The Hawelka is one of the illustrious literary coffee houses where the intelligentsia met.

Myth and Legend

The Viennese Coffeehouse

A host of legends and stories revolve around the Viennese coffeehouse. In Emperor Franz Joseph's era and in the 1920s, during the early years of the Austrian Republic, it was the meeting point of intellectuals, artists, and the literati. Perhaps this was less for the pleasure of drinking coffee and round marble tables, than for the lack of a roof over their heads: not uncommonly, a Viennese artist or man of letters lived in appalling conditions or had at best, just a little bedroom. The coffeehouse was inviting – on one hand, one could sit there, warm and dry, on the other hand, because of the "people," the company of kindred spirits. Mail could be delivered there, writing craft could be exercised, the latest gossip exchanged, or one could simply immerse oneself in thought. Purportedly, there were even professors who called doctoral candidates into the coffeehouse to take examinations.

The Viennese coffeehouse is more myth than reality today. While more than 500 coffeehouses still open their doors to the public, they mostly do so to tourists. And there are so few literati anyway, the Jews among them having been persecuted and killed under Hitler. Between the two wars, 200,000 Jews made Vienna their home. Of the 174 editorial posts at daily newspapers, Jews held no fewer than 123. Yet after the war, the Jewish community had been reduced to a mere 5,000 people.

Some Jews returned after the war, but the coffeehouse as an institution began to decline. The valuable property of the downtown café gave way to dress shops and fast-food restaurants. What is more, Italian Espresso, the powerful "enemy" of Austrian coffee, came into its own.

In the interest of tourism, Vienna renovated the traditional Landtmann, Sperl, and Schwarzenburg coffeehouses in the 1980s. While they feature the typical coffeehouse trademarks: the newspaper table, the window seats, mirror, and billiards table, and serve coffee, they have become commercial enterprises and are now professionally managed. Every table is expected to generate a certain turnover, so whoever bides their time nursing a glass of water is likely to get the evil eye. In addition to these showy establishments, there are also a few of the old-world kind that have survived and are less well-known to tourists. Classics of literature are no longer written in them, but the young Viennese have discovered them as meeting points. In their somewhat dusty, less than elegant interiors, the visitor who accidentally enters is able to sense what a Viennese coffeehouse of yesteryear was like.

All of Vienna's coffeehouses, whether of the revitalized or nostalgic kind, are fully-fledged restaurants. A broad assortment of coffees is offered with cake, yes, but one can also order warm meals – anything from veal dishes to a *Fiaker* goulash. The latter is made with a small sausage, fried egg, and a pickle cut and spread out like a fan, and was the traditional "hold-me-over" meal of the cabby or coachman.

Coffee Specialties
(Illustration left)

1 **Einspänner ("Hitch")**
Sweet black (demi-tasse) in a glass with whipped cream and sprinkled with chocolate powder
2 **Fiaker ("Coachman")**
Sweetened demi-tasse served in a glass
3 **Kapuziner ("Monk")**
Coffee with lots of milk
4 **Grosser Brauner ("Big Brown")**
Large cup with a dash of milk
5 **Kleiner Schwarzer ("Small Black")**
Demi-tasse without milk
6 **Kleiner Goldener ("Small Gold")**
Demi-tasse with milk
7 **Kleiner Brauner ("Small Brown")**
Small cup of coffee with a dash of milk
8 **Melange ("Mélange")**
Coffee and fresh milk in equal parts with a crown of froth

The Cutting Edge

Beef

In Austria, the preferred meat is beef, contrary to Germany, where pork is so popular. Cooked beef is found everywhere in the world, true, but only in Austria has its preparation into dishes like *Tafelspitz*, *Beiried*, or other specialties been developed to such a fine art. Indeed, there are no fewer than twenty-six specialized beef cuts. Emperor Franz Joseph relished beef greatly and his subjects happily shared his culinary weakness. Before the war, Vienna's Meissl & Schaden Restaurant offered twenty-four kinds of beef on its menu. Afterwards, the renowned Hietzinger Brewery picked up on the same predilection. Today, the Viennese frequent Restaurant Plachutta in the city's first district, where almost all the dishes on the menu are beef. Despite its massive size, you can simply forget about getting in unless you have a reservation. If you do, you will enjoy the *Zwiebelrostbraten* or *Beuschel* with dumplings, *Fiaker* goulash and shoulder, and the famous *Tafelspitz* cooked to absolute perfection.

It is fair to say that *Tafelspitz* has achieved world renown. Preparation includes cutting a particular part of beef in a way done nowhere else outside Austria. Only this allows for the tender end of the rump (at the outermost end of the tail) from which, according to regulation, the *Tafelspitz* can be prepared. It is incomparably tender – everything else is meat for making soup. Served in finger-thick slices, cut across the grain, *Tafelspitz* is served with a little hot beef broth ladled over it and decorated with chives. While even in the finest Austrian restaurants, no side dishes are served with it, one can always depend on *Apfelkren* (apple horseradish) and chive sauce.

Schulterscherzel mit Wurzelgemüse
Shoulder with Root Vegetables

1 lb (500 g) marrow
2 lbs (1 kg) shoulder
Root vegetables, cleaned (carrot, celery, leek, parsley root)
Salt
Chopped chives

Wash the marrow, put in a pot with 7 cups (1 1/2 l) water and bring to a boil. Rinse the meat and add it with the (whole) root vegetables to the boiling broth. Simmer 30–40 minutes.
Remove the meat and the vegetables. Slice the meat and chop the vegetables into bite-sized pieces. Garnish with the chopped chives and serve with the broth.

Wiener Tafelspitz
Viennese Sour Boiled Rump

1 lb (500 g) marrow
3 lbs (1 1/2 kg) Tafelspitz (rump)
1 onion, peeled and sliced in rings
Root vegetables, cleaned (carrot, celery, leek, parsley root)
Black peppercorns
Salt
Chopped chives

Wash the marrow, put in a pot with a generous amount of cold water and bring to the boil. Rinse the meat and add to the boiling broth. After about 30 minutes, fry the onion and add it to the meat with the (whole) root vegetables, the peppercorns, and a little salt. Let the dish simmer for about 2 hours.
Remove the meat, cut into thick slices across the grain and add a little liquid. Garnish with the chopped chives. Serve with crunchy potatoes and *Apfelkren*, a mixture of grated horseradish, grated apples, and cream.

Austrian Beef Cuts
(given in the closest name used abroad to the specialized cuts)

1	Loin roast	14	Porterhouse
2	Roast beef	15 and 16 Short	
3	Roast	Ribs	
4	Rump (used for Tafelspitz)	17, 18, and 19 Chuck	
5	Round	20	Ground
6, 7 and 8	Wedge, Flat and Pin Bone	21	Foreshank
		22	Skirt
9	Shank	23	Short Plate
10 and 11 Tip		24	Brisket
12	Shoulder	25	Porterhouse
13	T-Bone	26	Flank

Wiener Schnitzel

Nobody really knows how long a history the *Wiener Schnitzel* has. It is traditionally a veal dish, but there are serious connoisseurs who contend that if pork is used instead, it is less dry and more flavorful. Pork, however, cannot be sold as *Wiener Schnitzel*, and is advertised as "Schnitzel in the Wiener (Viennese) fashion" instead.

Let us stay for a moment with the original. The renowned Field Marshall Count Joseph Radetzky, one of the most personable of Austrian military men, was at war in Italy in the middle of the last century. He reported back to Vienna that the Milanese turned their Schnitzel in bread crumbs before baking. The Viennese were quick to try the new recipe, unaware that the Italians had adapted the recipe from the Spaniards, who in turn had seen the Moors prepare it during Moorish occupation. The Moors had brought the technique from Byzantine. In effect, then, the *Wiener Schnitzel* is a Byzantine Schnitzel and an offshoot of the North Italian *costoletta milanese*, which the tourist simply calls *piccata*.

Whether to either the Italian mother or the Austrian daughter, both Schnitzels suffer enormous injustices at the hands of cooks all over the world. *Piccata* is sometimes served with egg noodles, drowning in tomato sauce or worse.

An authentic *Wiener Schnitzel* is made of the finest veal, sliced thinly and baked dry. Made to perfection, it has a loosely attached bread crumb crust and is made of extraordinarily tender meat.

Wiener Schnitzel

(Illustrations 1–9, left)

7 oz (200 g) flour
2 beaten eggs
7 oz (200 g) fine bread crumbs
4 veal Schnitzels
Salt
1¼ cups (250 g) pork fat or oil
1 untreated lemon
1 bunch of parsley

Get ready the flour, eggs, and bread crumbs in three separate bowls. Illustrations 1 and 2 show the special cut of the Schnitzel across the grain. Lightly pound them, prick them all over with a knife point (3), lightly salt, then turn alternately in flour (4), eggs (5, 6), and fine bread crumbs (7).

Heat the fat in a large skillet and brown the Schnitzels for 3–4 minutes on both sides (8). Take care that the Schnitzels neither touch each other nor the edge of the skillet – if necessary, brown each singly – and keep the pan moving during the browning. In addition, be sure not to puncture the meat when turning.

When the Schnitzels are golden brown, drain them on paper towels and serve with lemon wedges and parsley on a pre-heated plate. Potato salad goes well with Schnitzel. In Vienna, the classic accompaniments are new potatoes, an orange wedge with a cranberry sauce garnish, and green salad.

1

2

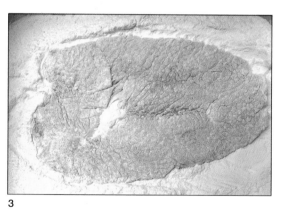

3

4

5

6

Game

The dense Austrian forests make the country an Eldorado for hunters. The landscape varies from meadows and valleys, to hilly and the high alpine regions. Two-thirds of the land mass is covered by mountains, and the *Grossglockner* at 3,979 meters is its highest peak. In the lime soil of the mountains there are primarily beech and spruce forests, while in the Central Alps, pine predominates.

In hunting, one distinguishes big and small game. To the first belong red-deer, fallow deer and wild boar, mountain goat, moufflon, chamois, bear, lynx, wolves, and wood grouse. All the other sorts of game, among them the roedeer, belong to the designation small game.

Big game are taken with bullets as a rule. However, wood grouse, lynx, and wolf may be taken with buck shot, as small game is usually taken. The roedeer, however, must be shot.

In Austria, hunting rights fall under property rights. The property owner may hunt as long as his property is larger than 116 hectares and he is in possession of a paid license, which proves he has passed a state-approved examination.

Every hunt is an effort to protect the animals. Measures taken for caring for the game include feeding them in emergencies, as well as discouraging poachers, marauders, and disease.

Austria is a favorite hunting ground for chamois, stag, wood grouse, and small game. There are private and public areas, and native, professional hunters conduct hunting trips for guests.

Background: A European red deer "family." The antlers of the stag are a coveted trophy.

Below:

1. **Field hare:** now rare in Europe. Dark reddish meat with typical game flavour
2. **Moufflon:** the meat from the young moufflon is a delicacy
3. **Deer:** smallest variety of stag. For culinary purposes, the most popular game
4. **Wild boar:** tender, lean meat beneath a thick bacon rind
5. **Pheasant:** originally from Asia. Firm, light-colored meat; preferred when prepared whole
6. **Graylag goose:** predecessor of the domestic goose
7. **Partridge:** rare. Moderate hunting permitted only where stocks are stable
8. **Wood pigeon:** large pigeon easily identifiable by the ring markings around its neck
9. **Snipe:** rare delicacy – only really available directly from the hunter
10. **Mallard:** considerably leaner than its domestic relatives

2 3 4

Hunting Seasons for the most Important Game

Fallow deer	September 1 through January 15	**Wood pigeon**	July 16 through April 15
Pheasant	October 1 through December 31	**Red deer**	June 1 through December 31 (Stag: August 1 through December 31)
Field Hare	October 1 through December 31		
Chamois	July 1 through December 31	**Snipe**	September 1 through April 15
Greylag Goose	August 1 through January 31	**Wild boar**	Year round (apart from leading sow)
Grouse	June 1 through January 15	**East Asian stag**	August 1 through January 15
Partridge	Widely protected in Austria, staggered hunting season	**Mallard**	September 1 through December 31
Roe deer	August 16 through October 15 (Buck: May 16 through October 15)		

5

6

7   8   9   10

Game Dishes

From the Forest to the Table – Handling Game

Stag and deer must be gutted as soon as they are taken. And they must cool down before the meat travels any distance. The carcass is hung up for a time to be sure that the flavor is sweet and develops the right way. The best parts for cooking are the saddle (*Ziemer*) and the haunches. The venison of younger game should never be marinated, as the delicate taste would be affected. The meat of more mature game, on the other hand, becomes more tender when marinated.

Venison contains little fat and water but a lot of protein. Before preparation, fat should be applied in the form of a hearty, fatty bacon that one can draw through the meat with a bowed game prong. Hares and wild rabbits are often sold with their pelts intact. The cook can hang a rabbit a few days in a refrigerated room before skinning and disembowelling it. The blood can be collected and stirred with a few drops of vinegar for use in rabbit stew. Hare meat is usually dark, whereas that from wild rabbits is white. Ribs and haunches are the best meat, head and neck, forelegs and heart make a good ragout.

Game birds must be plucked as soon as possible after the hunt. Game birds must be hung in a refrigerated room for 8 to 10 days. The once-popular practice of hanging the birds outdoors for longer periods has been abandoned for reasons of hygiene. Piercing the bird's breast with fat is no longer common with the larger birds such as the pheasant. Instead, a thin layer of bacon is wrapped around the bird.

Fasan im Speckhemd
(Illustration)
Pheasant in Bacon

Even in Antiquity, pheasant was considered a great delicacy. In Austria, the bird is hunted primarily in the marsh meadows near the Hungarian border.

2 kitchen-ready young pheasants
Salt, black pepper
10 oz (300 g) fatty bacon
2 oz (50 g) butter
4 oz (100 g) black grapes

Rinse the pheasants inside and out and then salt and pepper them generously. Cut the bacon into thin strips and lay it around the bird. Secure with kitchen twine, also binding the haunches. Preheat the oven to 450 °F (250 °C).
Sear the pheasant in the butter and cook in the oven for 60 minutes, occasionally turning and basting.
Reduce the fat and add the grapes to the sauce.
Serve the pheasant with red cabbage and potato croquettes.

Pheasant in Bacon

Wildschwein nach Lainzer Art
Lainz Wild Boar
Lainz is a district of Vienna.

3 lbs (1¹/₂ kg) young wild boar
8 oz (150 g) fatty bacon strips
Salt
Flour
1 lb (500 g) venison
2 cups (500 ml) game broth
Root vegetables (carrot, celery, leek, parsley root), cleaned
Peppercorns
Bay leaf
2 sprigs of thyme
¹/₄ cup (50 g) cranberries
¹/₂ cup (125 ml) red wine
¹/₂ cup (125 ml) sour cream
Lemon juice
5 oz (150 g) sweetbreads
5 oz (150 g) goose liver
5 oz (150 g) mushrooms

Slice about six steaks from the meat. Lightly pound with a mallet, brush with lard, salt, sprinkle one side with flour and sear in a little hot oil. Prepare the venison in the same way. Hack the bones of the boar into small pieces. Skim off the fat and dilute the drippings with a little broth. Fry, sprinkle with flour and the diluted gravy. Roast the bones, meat, and bacon with the vegetables in the fat. Lightly flour and cook with the rest of the broth, the rest of the stock, the spices, thyme, cranberries, and red wine. Add a little sour cream and some lemon juice and pass the mixture through a sieve. Simmer the Schnitzel until cooked through.
Quickly sear the sweetbreads and cube them, spice the liver and then sear and cube it, too. Slice the mushrooms and fry in a little butter. Thicken all with a little sauce. Arrange the boar Schnitzel on a plate, cover them with the ragout and lay the stag schnitzel on top. Pour a little sauce over them both.

Montafoner Hirschrücken
Montafon Rack of Venison

Derived from *mont*, "mountain" and *davo*, "behind," Montafon is the name of the Ill Valley in the Vorarlberg mountains.

1 rack of venison
Salt, black pepper
4 oz (100 g) fatty bacon, in strips
Juniper berries
¹/₂ cup (100 g) butter
8 oz (200 g) chanterelles
1 bunch of parsley

Rub salt and pepper into the game and lard evenly. Put it in a suitable baking dish with a handful of juniper berries. Melt the butter and pour half of it over the meat. Cook over medium heat, and occasionally baste with the butter. As soon as the underside of the meat is browned, turn it over and simmer until the whole piece is tender.
Clean the chanterelles, wash and finely chop the parsley. Turn them in a little butter until soft, and season to taste.
Carve the venison and serve with the chanterelles. Spätzle and cranberries are nice accompaniments.

Hirschkoteletts mit Steinpilzen
Venison with Mushrooms

4 venison cutlets
Oil
Salt, black pepper
¹/₂ cup (100 g) butter
Juniper berries
¹/₂ cup (100 ml) Madeira
¹/₂ cup (100 ml) game broth
4 oz (100 g) Steinpilze mushrooms
Lemon juice

Marinate the cutlets in oil, salt, and pepper for a couple of hours. Heat about a third of the butter and brown both sides of the cutlets. Crush a couple of juniper berries, add them to the juices and dilute with Madeira. Add the game broth and let the liquid simmer until it is somewhat reduced, pass it through a sieve and smooth by adding a pat of butter.
Clean, salt and pepper the mushrooms, douse them in lemon juice, and cook in the remaining butter.
Serve the cutlets covered with the mushrooms.
Sweet chestnuts, red cabbage, and poached pears are delightful accompaniments.

Gamsschlegel in Weinsauce
Chamois in Wine Sauce

1 leg of chamois
8 oz (200 g) fatty bacon in strips
¹/₄ cup (50 g) butter
2 Tbs (30 g) flour

Marinade
2¹/₂ cups (500 ml) red wine
10 oz (300 g) root vegetables (carrot, celery, parsley root)
1 onion, peeled and sliced
1 bay leaf
A few peppercorns
1 twig of sage

To make the marinade, add the ingredients with 2¹/₂ cups (500 ml) water to a cooking pot, heat and cool. Coarsely chop the root vegetables, and arrange half in a ceramic casserole.
Wash the game meat, pat it dry, put it in the casserole and cover with the remaining half of the root vegetables. Pour enough marinade over the game to cover, then put the covered casserole in a cool place for 3 days.
Remove the meat, garnish with the bacon and sear it all over in butter. Add more marinade and root vegetables and simmer until tender. Sieve the drippings and thicken to a gravy by adding flour. Serve with caraway dumplings, chanterelles, and cranberries.

Gefüllte Hasenfilets in Madeira-Sauce
Stuffed Fillet of Hare in Madeira Sauce

4 hare fillets
Salt, black pepper
4 oz (100 g) mushrooms
2 oz (50 g) shallots
1 garlic clove
Chopped parsley
Chopped peel of one lemon
1¹/₂ cups (300 ml) "demi-glace," reduced gravy with veal broth
3 oz (80 g) fatty bacon, in strips
¹/₂ cup (100 g) butter
Flour
¹/₂ cup (100 ml) Madeira
1 Tbs tomato paste

Rinse and dry the fillets. Cut them lengthways into *Schnitzel*, and pound each with a meat mallet, then salt. Clean and slice the mushrooms, peel and chop the shallots and chop the garlic. Combine all three with the parsley and lemon peel and fry in a little oil. Salt, pepper, and add 1 tablespoon of *demi-glace* to thicken. Spread the mixture on each fillet, then roll up and garnish each with bacon. Turn the rolled fillet in flour, quickly sear in oil, then pan fry in butter. Remove the fillet from the heat and keep warm.
Add Madeira, and then the remaining *demi-glace*, to the pan drippings. Season to taste with a little tomato paste and the remaining butter. Serve the fillets with the sauce and rice or dumplings.

Towards Universal Acclaim

Wine

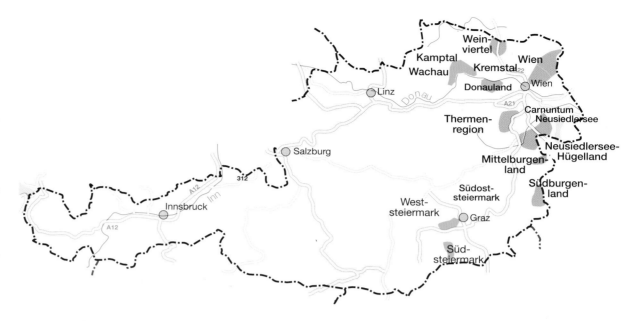

The glucose scandal which broke in 1985 was devastating: unscrupulous businessmen used antifreeze on grapes, and the reputation of Austrian wine was severely threatened.

The shock hit hard. Then in that same year, a new law was passed, and the vine-growers resumed work according to the principles of organic grape cultivation. Since then, an impressive culture of premier wines has been produced in Austria, and they also enjoy acclaim abroad. Indeed, the best *Veltliner, Riesling,* and *Zweigelt* can compete with the finest wines from Germany and Italy.

In total, thirty-three kinds of grapes are used to manufacture quality and special quality wines. Green *Veltliner* accounts for 36.7% of the vineyards in Austria, and as such dominates the white wines. It is fruity white wine with a piquant tartness. Its hallmark is what is called *Pfefferl,* a tart aroma that some connoisseurs contend is not unlike the aroma of roast beef. The elegant, mildly acidic *Riesling* (2.6% of the vineyards) is unquestionably the finest of the Austrian whites. Its subtle rose, peach, and apricot taste overtones have earned it acclaim.

Müller-Thurgau, Welschriesling, Weissburgunder, Chardonnay, the *Neuburger, Muscat-Ottonel,* and other white grape varieties, each account for less than one percent of cultivated production. Among the red wines, fruity-austere *Zweigelt*; *Blaufränkisch,* which holds its own in international competition; and the *Blauer Portugieser,* a light, mild red wine that is enjoyed chilled, are the most popular.

While Austria's white wines count among the best in the world, its reds have recently had international acclaim as well. This owes much to new regulations which mean more and more stringent quality control and better consumer protection.

A differentiation is made among *Tafelwein* (table wine), *Landwein* (country wine), *Qualitätswein* (wine of certified origin and quality), and *Kabinettswein* (high quality whites) as well as among the *Prädikatsweine* (special quality wines). These include *Spätlese* (late vintage), *Auslese* (from selected grapes), *Beerenauslese* (another from selected grapes), *Ausbruch* (burst wine), *Trockenbeerenauslese* (made from choice grapes that are left on the vine at the end of the season), and *Eiswein* (sweet wine made from grapes that have been exposed to frost). Vine-growers in the Wachau Valley have designated categories that reflect typical conditions of their indigenous grapes.

Austrian Wine-Growing Regions

Burgenland – Neusiedlersee-Hügelland, Mittelburgenland, Südburgenland

While *Müller-Thurgau* once dominated production here, red grapes do so today. *Zweigelt, Saint-Laurent, Spätburgunder,* and *Blaufränkisch,* among them, the last being Austria's second most popular wine overall. The climate along the west shore of the *Neusiedlersee* is humid and warm, and a sweet or so-called *Ausbruchwein* (burst wine) is produced there from naturally dried grapes.

Niederösterreich – Donauland-Carnuntum, Kamptal-Donauland, Thermenregion, Wachau, Weinviertel

Collectively, these regions make up half the vineyards in Austria. *Grüne Veltliner* is grown here primarily, a grape unique to this area. The grape is somewhat similar to the German *Silvaner,* particularly in that it, too, takes on the aroma of the soil. This is also the region of robust reds and light, mild wines from the blue Portuguese grape. In the Wachau Valley, *Riesling* is of a special quality. It is argued that the grape originated here, not in the Rhine Valley. Distinctions among the special quality wines include *Steinfeder* (an un-enriched quality wine), *Federspiel,* and *Smaragd* ("Emerald," a superb late vintage).

Steiermark – Südost-Steiermark, Südsteiermark, Weststeiermark

The sweet wines produced here were once consumed in rural areas. Meanwhile, the fine, dry whites have received wider acclaim, among them: *Chardonnay, Weissburgunder,* and *Sauvignon blanc. Schilcher-Rosé* is pressed from *Blauer Wildbach* grapes in West Steiermark.

Vienna

The more than 700 hectares of vineyards around Vienna exceed those in the Middle Rhine area in number. The different grapes of the *Heuriger* thrive here, but there are also respectable *Grüne Veltliner, Weissburgunder,* and *Rheinriesling* (the designation for a true Riesling in Austria and other countries). They are fruitier and more spirited than those of the Burgenland, but fall short in comparison with wines from the Wachau Valley.

In a wine cellar in the Wachau region.

The new vintage is sampled.

Austria's white wines are world renowned.

Opposite: The sunny climate of the Wachau Valley, along the Danube, makes for first-class wine.

Eaten with *Heuriger*, a proper snack, like the "board snack" illustrated here, includes home-made sausages, smoked meats, warm, pickled meat, sliced cold pork, cheese, sour pickles, and a *Laberl* or bread roll.

Young Wine and Age-Old Hospitality

Heuriger

Whoever visits Vienna is sure to pass through the towns Grinzing and Heiligenstadt, two little vineyard villages on the edges of the city. In high season, the merrymaking there begins as early as in the afternoon. In a cozy setting, people sit at big tables and drink new *Heuriger* wine from glasses no less large. Because of its effect on the digestive system, *Heuriger* is commonly known as *Sauser*, "buzzer," loosely translated. The pleasant ambience with tavern band and song, an occasional *Jause* or snack from the bar: these are the hallmarks of the Austrian way of life the tourist enjoys. The wine grower may share his wine without being charged a concession, a privilege that goes back to Emperor Franz Joseph ll (1765–1790), who first granted it in 1784. When the vine-growers offer their own wines and simple meals, a pine branch is hung like a tavern sign to signal that the young wine is ready. As such, the four month moonlighting *Heuriger* businesses are alluded to as "twig operations" or "pine closets." In Vienna, the word *Heuriger* connotes both the new harvest wine and the locale which serves the wine along with homemade cold dishes. The name originated in an era when vine-growers were less keen on storing their wine and more interested in selling at market as soon as they could.

Opposite: An old *Heuriger*-locale where new wine and snacks can be enjoyed in good company.

Today, the *Heuriger* Edens around Vienna have little to do with that tradition. There are wine bars open all year that even buy wine from the trade. Friends of the true *Heuriger* have their reservations about these operations, which cater largely to tourists. The songs which belong to the true *Heuriger* tradition have become world famous, but the devotee today knows that the wine is usually better in a place where no music is played and will go to a favorite *Heuriger* locale on a side street in Nussdorf or Sievering where no tourist bus stops, where *Schmalzbrot* with onion rings, Liptauer cheese, and *Brezn* (large pretzels) are tasty accompaniments to the wine. And whoever comes with his own snack gets a plate and silverware without problem.

Vienna – City of Wine

The Roman Emperor Marcus Aurelius Probus laid out the first Viennese vineyards, and the city street Probusgasse reminds us of that still today. In Gaul, as well as in Vienna, Probus kept his soldiers from the temptations of idleness by keeping them busy planting grapes. Due to the foresight of the Roman Emperor and the generous spirit adapted by Habsburgs who succeeded him on the throne, the outskirts of Vienna bustle with sociability, such that there is hardly any night life left in the center of town. And when the *Heuriger* locales close at midnight or one in the morning, the Viennese are tired and tumble off to bed.

At a traditional Viennese sausage stand, there is much more than "Frankfurters," as the Viennese sausages are called. In addition to a snack, one may engage in a bit of conversation.

Delicious, aromatic *Buren* sausages, so-called "*Häuterl*," tempt a hungry passer-by.

Snacks with Heuriger

Geselchtes
Smoked bacon and other pork parts cut not too thinly, with crusty bread
Heurigenplatte ("board snack")
Sausage, cold, sliced pickled meat, cheese, chopped onions, sour pickles and bread
Liptauer
Soft cheese generously spiced with paprika
Quargel
Little cheese with chopped onions
Saumeise
Ground meat in pig's net, smoked and boiled
Saure Blunzen
Slice of blood sausage marinated in vinegar
Schmalzbrot
Crusty bread spread with dripping
Schweinebraten
Sliced cold pork, with bread
Surbraten
Meat that has been pickled three weeks and is then cooked, eaten warm
Verhackerts
A spread made of minced sausage and meat

The Sausage Stand

Viennese sausages, made of beef and pork, a little bacon, and a variety of spices, are famous worldwide. Oddly enough, in Vienna, the city that gave them their name, they fly under a foreign flag and are called "Frankfurters."

The sausage stand is a Viennese institution. They are there to appease the stomach, certainly, but also for talking with every Tom, Dick, and Harry about God and the world if the mood strikes. In the colloquial, the sausage stand is known as "little trifle" for the uncomplicated contact with people and the tendency to philosophize it promotes.

A Viennese sausage stand offers a wide variety: *Liverwurst*, the fatty, piquant *Burenwurst*, the Hungarian *Debrecziner* (a raw sausage with middle-sized pieces of meat), *Bratwurst*, and *Käsekrainer*, which actually contains a large piece of cheese.

Other than that, one can get pickled herring spiced with enough sharp paprika that it is called "devil's roll." There are also bread, pickles, pearl onions, and an assortment of drinks, as well as desserts, including the *Mannerschnitten* or "man's cut": hazelnut-chocolate waffles.

Whatever Tastes Good Puts on Pounds

Desserts

While they are indeed flour-based, flour takes a back seat to the other ingredients in Austrian desserts. Apple strudel is the classic example. Many Austrians contend that only the experienced housewife knows how to roll the strudel dough out thinly, draw it carefully out from its middle and up over the fruit. The dough should be transparent enough to read a newspaper through it. The quality of apples used, too, together with rum, raisins, and bread crumbs, is crucial. Very tart apples, Russett or Gravenstein, for example, make the true strudel. The apples must be fresh, of course.

Like many dishes in the Austrian cuisine, the apple strudel claims many fathers. The paper-thin dough is of Turkish origin and the apples themselves can be traced to Hungary. But it was in Vienna that apple strudel became a masterpiece of culinary art.

Below: Apple Strudel – masterpiece of Viennese culinary art. The paper-thin dough is filled with the apple-raisin filling (recipe right, whose numbers refer to the illustrations here).

1

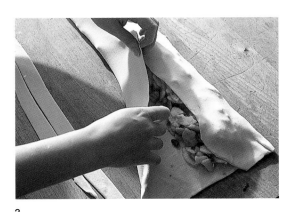

2

3

4

5

6

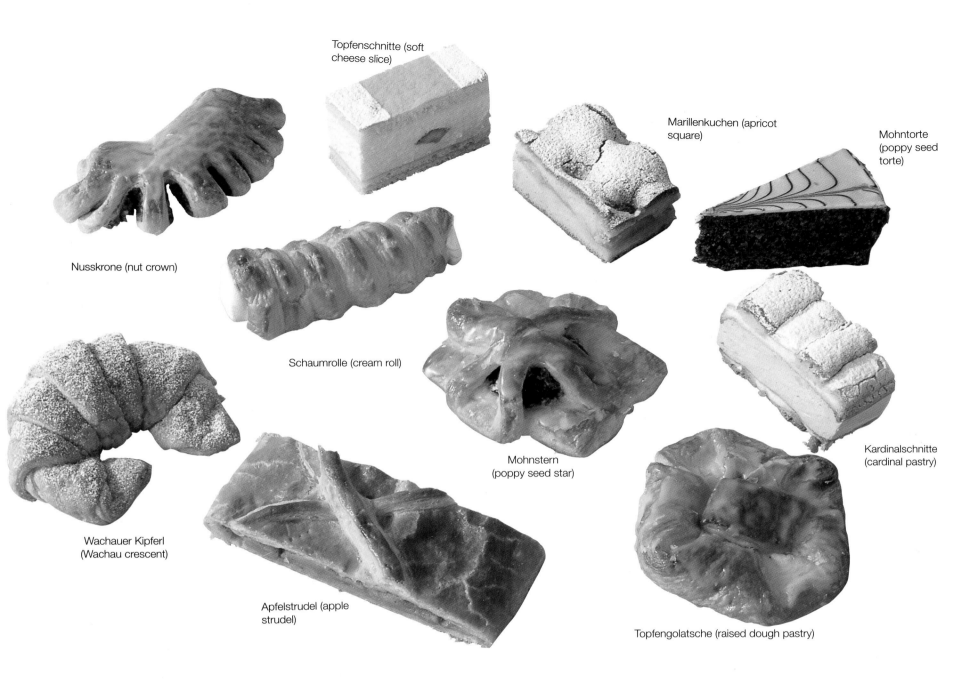

Topfenschnitte (soft cheese slice)

Marillenkuchen (apricot square)

Mohntorte (poppy seed torte)

Nusskrone (nut crown)

Schaumrolle (cream roll)

Wachauer Kipferl (Wachau crescent)

Mohnstern (poppy seed star)

Kardinalschnitte (cardinal pastry)

Apfelstrudel (apple strudel)

Topfengolatsche (raised dough pastry)

Apfelstrudel
Apple Strudel
(Illustrations 1–6 opposite)

Dough
2¹/₂ cups (300 g) flour
1 pinch of salt
1 egg
Oil
Powdered sugar

Filling
¹/₃ cup (80 g) raisins
2 Tbs rum
¹/₃ cup (80 g) bread crumbs
¹/₂ cup (100 g) butter
3 lbs (1¹/₂ kg) sour apples
¹/₃ cup (80 g) chopped nuts
¹/₂ cup (100 g) sugar
Cinnamon
Lemon juice

Combine the flour, salt, egg, and one tablespoon of oil with ¹/₂ cup (125 ml) lukewarm water to make a soft dough and leave alone for 30 minutes. Then roll out in a floured kitchen towel and brush with oil. With flour-covered hands, reach under the dough and draw it out from the center until it becomes very thin. Remove the thicker edges and save. For the filling, douse the raisins in rum, roast the bread crumbs in butter, and strew over the dough. Peel the apples (1) and remove their seeds, slice them thinly and combine with the raisins, nuts, cinnamon, and lemon juice before spreading the mixture out over the dough (2). Roll up the strudel (3) and fasten the ends by pressing them firmly. Decorate the top with the remaining dough and pierce several times with the tines of a fork (4).

Preheat the oven to 350 °F (180 °C). Melt the remaining butter. Put the strudel on an oiled cookie sheet (5), baste with the melted butter, and bake for 30–45 minutes. Baste with the butter a few times while the strudel is baking.

To serve, slice the strudel (6), decorate with powdered sugar, and bring it warm to the table.

Kaiserschmarrn
Deep-fried Raisin Pancake

1 cup (200 g) flour
1 pinch of salt
4 egg yolks, 4 egg whites
¹/₄ cup (40 g) sugar
1 cup (250 ml) milk
¹/₄ cup (40 g) raisins
Powdered sugar

Make a smooth batter by combining the flour, salt, egg yolks, sugar, and milk. Beat the egg whites until stiff and fold into the mixture.

Heat a little butter in a pan, pour in about half an inch of the batter and let it bake just a little before strewing the raisins over it. When the batter is golden brown, turn it and bake it on the other side.

Finally tear it into bite-sized pieces with two forks, sprinkle with powdered sugar and serve. Cranberry compote is a nice accompaniment.

A Sensory Pleasure

Dumplings

Austrian dumplings actually have Bohemian origins. It was both there and in Moravia that there were large grain fields and the cooks took to making those wonderful, soft, fluffy round dumplings from flour and other ingredients. It is just that lightness that distinguishes them from their northern European cousins, *Klössen*. It has been documented that in the Battle of Norhastedt in 1404, women's regiments used *Klössen* as ammunition against the enemy. Such an incident would have been unthinkable in Austria: its native tender dumpling would fall apart as soon as it were shot.

There are seven basic ingredients for Austrian dumplings: flour, potatoes, semolina, bread rolls, ricotta, cheese, and yeast, which allow for a great variety. Dumplings come to the table either as side-dishes, simple main dishes, or desserts.

The method of preparation is always the same: generously salted water is brought to a boil in a large pot, a dough of precisely the right consistency is separated into pieces and formed, with wet hands, into balls. The balls go into the boiling water and rise to the surface when they are cooked through.

The great appeal of the Austrian dumpling is the many-faceted ways it can be filled: with croutons, bacon or pieces of meat in the hearty variation; plums or pitted cherries or with *Powidl* – plum purée; or with the famous *Marillen*, the apricots that grow in the Wachau Valley region.

The crowning glory of the dumpling art is the *Serviettenknödel*, "napkin dumpling" that is actually cooked in a linen napkin. Formerly, it came to the table in its entirety and one cut a single portion from the larger piece.

Naturally, the delicious results of this Bohemian wizardry are hardly figure-friendly; the beauties who once promenaded along the avenues of Vienna were indeed quite portly. Nowadays, for the dieting rage, dumplings are less appreciated as throw-backs to opulent times than they are considered to be a symbol of solid native cuisine. The dumpling has regained its place of honor.

Serviettenknödel
Napkin Dumpling
(Illustration below)

6 bread rolls
1/2 cup (125 ml) milk
3 eggs
1 onion
1 1/2 oz (40 g) bacon
3/4 cup (150 g) butter
1 bunch of parsley
Salt
Flour

Cube the bread rolls, combine the milk and eggs briskly and pour the mixture over the bread cubes. Peel and chop the onion, chop the bacon and fry both in a skillet. Beat the butter until creamy, finely chop the parsley. Add the bread-egg mixture, onion, bacon, parsley, a little salt, and a tablespoon of flour to the butter. Put the mass on a moist, buttered, and lightly floured linen napkin, roll this into a sausage shape and bind the ends firmly.
Attach the roll to a cooking spoon and hang it in generously salted water, allow to cook for 30–45 minutes. Run under cold water quickly, remove the dumpling from the napkin and serve in half-inch thick slices.

Several bread rolls must be cubed to make the Napkin Dumpling specialty.

Then the eggs and milk are whisked together.

The egg-milk mixture is poured over the bread cubes.

Then butter, onion, bacon, flour, and parsley are added.

The mixture is formed into a sausage and put in a moist, buttered, and floured linen napkin.

The napkin roll and its contents are hung in boiling water to cook.

A Slice of Dumpling Life

1 Strawberries as filling for strawberry dumplings
2 Raised Dumplings
3 Napkin Dumplings sliced
4 Flat parsley, a must for raised and napkin dumplings
5 Wheat meal
6 White bread cubes for bread and pan dumplings
7 Butter for dumpling batter
8 Lemon for the pan dumpling batter
9 Milk for napkin and bread dumplings
10 Onions for napkin and bread dumplings
11 Eggs for the basic dumpling batter
12 Filling for meat dumplings
13 Raised dumpling dough

Strawberry dumplings are prepared in the same way as apricot dumplings (*Marillenknödel*). The smooth dough is cut into portions.

Then the dough pieces are flattened, a strawberry is laid on top, and the dumplings are formed around the fruit.

The dumplings are cooked in boiling water. They are done when they rise to the surface.

The finished dumplings are turned in browned bread crumbs and sprinkled with powdered sugar.

Marillenknödel
Apricot Dumplings

The dough is made of jacket potatoes and flour. In the Wachau Valley region where apricots are so prolific, some recipes call for a yeast dough, others for a cooled sweet dough.

2 lb (1 kg) potatoes	
2¼ cups (300 g) flour	
1 pinch of salt	
1 egg	
½ cup (120 g) butter	
1 lb (500 g) apricots	
Cube sugar	
4 tsp of apricot brandy	
½ cup (100 g) bread crumbs	

Boil the potatoes in their skins until they are soft. Make a dough of the potato, flour, salt, egg, and half the butter. Cut the dough into portions and form each piece to a sausage, press flat, and top with an apricot. Dip a sugar cube in apricot schnapps and put it in the center of the fruit, then form the dough into dumplings. Place the filled dumplings in boiling water and cook until they rise to the surface.
Heat the remaining butter and lightly brown the bread crumbs. Turn the drained apricot dumplings in them, sprinkle with powdered sugar and serve. While one variation is strawberry dumplings as shown here in the illustrations, any fruit can be used at the center, plums, for example.

Topfenknödel
Sweet Pan Dumplings

½ cup (100 g) butter
½ cup (100 g) sugar
Vanilla sugar
3 eggs
Lemon juice
Salt
3–4 slices (120 g) white bread
2 cups (500 g) soft white cheese (Quark)
2 Tbs sour cream
½ cup (100 g) bread crumbs
Powdered sugar

Cream half the butter with the sugar, vanilla sugar, eggs, a splash of lemon juice, and a little salt. Cube the bread and add the *Quark* combined with the cream. Stir well, and then let the dough cool for about 60 minutes.
Make small dumplings from the dough, and put them in boiling, salted water to simmer for about 10 minutes. Remove and let them dry on a paper towel. Fry the bread crumbs in the remaining butter and turn the dumplings in them before sprinkling them with powdered sugar.
Serve with a compote of fresh plums that have been laced with sugar and cinnamon.

Germknödel
Raised Dumplings

2 cups (250 g) flour
1 Tbs (10 g) yeast
1 Tbs sugar
2–3 Tbs lukewarm milk
½ cup (100 g) butter
1 pinch of salt
1 egg yolk
½ cup (100 g) plum purée
1 tsp rum
Generous pinch of cinnamon
¼ cup (50 g) ground poppy seeds
Powdered sugar

Put the flour in a large bowl. Dissolve the yeast and the sugar in the milk and add it to the flour. Melt 2–3 tablespoons of butter and add to the flour with the salt and egg yolk, then knead vigorously to a smooth dough. Let it rise for 60 minutes.
Add the rum and the cinnamon to the plum purée. From the risen dough, cut 12 equal-sized pieces, put 1 tablespoon of the plum mixture in the middle of each and then form into dumplings. Let the dumplings rise another 30 minutes and then in salted water over low heat, cook for 6 minutes, turn and cook another 6 minutes. Brown the rest of the butter. Sprinkle the dumplings generously with poppy seed and powdered sugar, pour the butter over them, and serve.

Peaks of Cream

Salzburger Nockerln

Salzburg, the elegant festival town on the Bavarian border, differs from the other Austrian regions in a number of ways. The state of Salzburg, which has belonged to Austria only since 1805, prides itself on its worldly image even outside the festival season. Rather than wine, beer is preferred by the people of Salzburg, and their cuisine is largely cosmopolitan. As a result of this, there are only a handful of typically Salzburgian recipes – with one grand exception: Salzburger Nockerln.

Nockerln are little more than hills, and the dish itself consists of heaped peaks of foam, a type of soufflé, in fact. The dessert should be "as sweet as cream and tender as a kiss," or at least so is sung in an operetta. Tourists, particularly, marvel at and relish gigantic portions of the sweet dish. And whoever does not like it will never be an Austrian, or so the story goes.

Salzburger Nockerln
Salzburg Meringue
(Illustration)

4 egg yolks, 4 egg whites
1 pinch of salt
1 oz (30 g) sugar
1 packet of vanilla sugar
Peel of one untreated lemon
4 tsp (20 g) flour
Powdered sugar

Beat the egg whites and the pinch of salt in a bowl until they are stiff. Gradually add the sugar and vanilla sugar. In a second bowl combine about a third of the beaten egg whites with the egg yolks and the lemon peel. Fold it into the larger portion of egg whites slowly, and carefully add the flour.
Preheat the oven to 425 °F (220 °C).
Generously butter an oven-proof, oval casserole and spoon in the meringue, forming little hills (Nockerln) before the dessert goes into the oven. Bake for about 10 minutes until the peaks are golden brown.
Sprinkle with powdered sugar and serve immediately. The meringue should be crisp outside and creamy inside (so be sure not to open the oven door while it is baking).

Linzer Torte
Linzertorte

Like the meringue, Linzertorte is known well beyond the Austrian border.

1¼ cups (150 g) flour
¾ cup (150 g) chilled butter
¾ cup (150 g) ground almonds
¾ cup (150 g) sugar
Cinnamon
Ground cloves
2 eggs
Juice of ½ a lemon
1 jar of red currant jam
4 oz (125 g) sliced almonds
Vanilla sugar
Powdered sugar

Sift the flour on a flat surface and make a dent in the centre. Flake the butter and add it into the flour indentation with the ground almonds, sugar, cinnamon, cloves, one egg, and the lemon juice. Knead the ingredients to a smooth dough.
Halve the dough and cool it in the refrigerator for 30 minutes.
Preheat the oven to 350 °F (180 °C).
Butter a springform pan with a 10 in (24 cm) diameter and lay in half the dough, pressing it flat with the fingers until the bottom of the form is completely covered. Spread the redcurrant jam on top. Cut the remaining dough into strips and lay a basket-weave over the jam layer. Beat the second egg, paint the weave crust and sprinkle the top with almond slices.
Bake the torte for about 60 minutes until it is golden brown. Combine the vanilla and powdered sugars and sprinkle on top before serving.

Salzburger Nockerln – Salzburg Meringue

Still a Cult Pastry

Krapfen

There are two schools of *Krapfen* in Austria. The one prefers *Tiroler Krapfen*, made in the farm kitchens of the mountain regions, the other, the Viennese Winter Carnival *Krapfen*, baked only around that season.

The word "Krapfen" is used in Austrian dialect for all the kinds of deep-fried pastries. Old cookbooks include dozens of these doughnut recipes. In Baroque times, the habit of filling the doughnut with jam became popular – and this led to a rage in Vienna in the 18th and 19th centuries. *Krapfen* were even noble enough for court: they were served at the Court Ball, the grandest social event of the Habsburg Monarchy. In one part of Salzburg, the doughnuts are traditionally served on New Year's Day; in Salzkammergut they appear on January 5 before Twelfth Night as "bell-ringer doughnuts." During Lent, one eats "confessor's doughnuts" and on Midsummer's Day, June 22, farmers should bake nine different kinds: with juniper berries, clover, stinging nettle, herbs, and butter and those with odd names like "cord," "snowball," "lead," and "punishment." At harvest time, field workers had "mowing doughnuts," and at church consecration and at farmers' weddings, *Krapfen* were always served – never, however, at a funerary meal.

Whatever kind they are, all have this in common: they are baked in hot fat, usually in melted butter. The jam-filled Carnival Krapfen has a light ring around its middle. The *Tiroler Krapfen*, on the other hand, is a triangular piece of dough filled, originally, with fat, milk, flour, sugar, butter, and honey. While there was indeed a Viennese cook named Cäcilie Krapf, her invention of the Krapfen is most likely legend.

Tiroler Krapfen
Tyrolean Doughnuts

¹/₂ cup (125 ml) milk
¹/₂ cup (150 g) butter
1 lb (500 g) flour
1 pinch of salt
7 oz (200 g) jam, to taste
¹/₄ cup (50 g) bread crumbs
Frying oil

Warm the milk and let the butter melt in it. Make an indentation in the flour, add the salt, the lukewarm milk-butter mixture, and knead to a dough.
Let the dough stand 30 minutes, then roll it out thinly and cut out about ten 4-inch (10 cm) squares. Combine the jam and bread crumbs. On each square, spoon out one teaspoon of the mixture and fold the dough into a triangle. Press the edges well. Fry in hot oil, drain on paper towels and serve warm.

Faschingskrapfen
Winter Carnival Doughnuts
(Illustration)

¹/₂ cup (125 ml) milk
1 heaped Tbs (20 g) yeast
¹/₄ cup (50 g) sugar
2¹/₂ cups (300 g) flour
¹/₄ cup (50 g) butter
1 pinch of salt
3 egg yolks
1 Tbs rum
Peel of ¹/₂ an untreated lemon
5 oz (150 g) apricot jam
Frying oil
Powdered sugar

Warm the milk. Knead half the milk, the yeast, one tsp of sugar and a little flour to a dough, and let it rise until it has doubled in size.
Melt the butter and remaining sugar in the rest of the warm milk. Combine the salt, egg yolk, rum, lemon peel, and the remaining flour with the butter-sugar-milk mixture and knead into a smooth dough until it makes bubbles, then let it stand for 20 minutes. Roll the dough out to a thickness of ³/₈ inch (1 cm) and use the diameter of a large 4¹/₄ inch (6 cm) glass to cut out circles. Spoon one teaspoon of apricot jam onto one half of the circle, cover with another circle and lightly press around the circumference. Cut out the finished *Krapfen* by using a glass with a smaller, 2 inch (5 cm) diameter. Lay the *Krapfen* on a floured kitchen towel, cover, and let them rise another 20 minutes.
Fry 3 minutes each side in hot oil, drain, cool, and serve sprinkled with powdered sugar.

Faschingskrapfen – Winter Carnival Doughnuts

Austrian Schnapps

Schnapps has been distilled in Austria for centuries. Almost every farmer has a still in which to distil fallen fruit and other windfall farm products, and almost every schnapps drinker has an insider's source, which he will swear is better than any other.

Close to a dozen Austrian distillers have begun to produce first-rate schnapps in the past few years. Every year, others with wares of equally high quality join the ranks. One of them is the Tyrolean Günther Rochelt. He produces schnapps with an alcoholic content of fifty percent, which is unusually high. His products –

Gravenstein Apple, Elderberry, Apricot, Quince, Morello, and Pear Williams – are put in special bottles that look like perfume bottles, a form that is adapted from the Tyrolean *Zangenflasche*. Connoisseurs swear by the products of the Freihof Distillery in the Voralberg, a family operation with over one hundred years' tradition in distilling. The kind called "Vom ganz Guten" (from the very best) and "Gebhard Hämmerle – Herzstück" (from the heart) both enjoy coveted reputations in the finest restaurants. "Herzstück" is the middle process of distillation in which the aromatic composition of the fruit comes into its own most distinctly.

Wachauer Apricot Brandy has a superior reputation. The fruit pulp mash combined with a selected amount of fruit pits make an aromatic drink that is clear and colorless, and viable competition for the Hungarian apricot schnapps *Barack Pálinka*.

Liquor has been distilled from the root of the gentian flower in all the alpine nations for over a hundred years. The gentian is known to moun-

tain people as a plant with healing properties. It is among the oldest of such plants and is not bitter in any way, rather, has a unique earthy tone and a suggestion of sweetness. The blue alpine blossoms pictured on the label have little to do with the schnapps. It is distilled exclusively from the root, which can grow to fourteen pounds (six kg) weight and reach a yard's length. Gentian only grows in the wild, and all attempts to cultivate it have proven unsuccessful to date.

Other specialties are the Austrian liqueurs, which have a uniquely rural nature. Among them the "Wachauer Gold Apricot Liqueur" and a liqueur made from green walnuts, "Nujuki," are the finest. "Mozart Liqueur" has a taste which recalls the world-famous chocolate truffles, *Mozartkugel*, which are also made from nougat, chocolate, and cherry brandy.

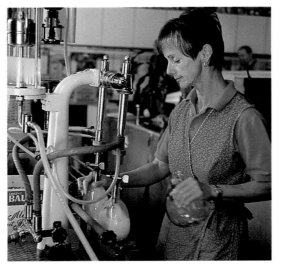

Wachauer Apricot liqueur of the famous brand Bailoni is filled in bottles.

Clear apricot brandy enjoys no less of a grand reputation.

Apricot liqueur in the "Bugelflasche," with its distinctive wire clip fastening, and in the typical round bottles.

The Apricots of Wachau Valley

The Wachau Valley – Austria's "bread basket" – picturesquely located along the Danube between Melk and Krems – has achieved fame not only for the beauty of its landscape and excellent wines, but for its apricots, or *Marillen*.

The warm-climate loving fruit came originally from China. It was cultivated there for profit as long as 4,000 years ago. Its early blossom (the name is derived from the Latin *praecox*, meaning premature) is whitish-pink, the orange-yellow fruit sweet-sour and aromatic. Apricots only thrive in sunny climates, such as those of California, Spain, France, Hungary, and Israel – and indeed the sun-soaked region described here. A broad assortment of delicacies are made from the fruit, including the renowned apricot liqueur and apricot schnapps amongst others.

Schnapps is produced from apricot pulp that contains a certain amount of ground pits.

The Torte Royal

Sachertorte

In front of the long-established Hotel Sacher in Vienna, tourists stand in long lines in the summer season. They wait in hopes of sitting at one of the tiny tables where the same treat is always ordered: a piece of Sachertorte accompanied by a Viennese coffee.

Butter, egg yolk, chocolate coating, egg white, sugar, flour, and apricot jam are the ingredients of the noble Sachertorte. Originally created for Count Metternich, the press called attention to it after the Second World War when the hotel, suffering financial difficulties, sold the recipe to a pastry chef Demel, who subsequently advertized "original Sachertorte."

Later, when Sacher became solvent once more, he brought the case to court. For decades, the struggle persisted and even to this day, the famous Viennese Torte War has not been settled.

Sachertorte
(Illustration)

5 oz (150 g) chocolate
³/₄ cup (150 g) soft butter
¹/₂ cup (100 g) powdered sugar
6 egg yolks, 6 egg whites
¹/₄ cup (50 g) sugar
1¹/₄ cups (150 g) flour
1 pinch of salt
Apricot jam

Icing

7 oz (200 g) chocolate
³/₄ cup (200 g) sugar

Melt the chocolate over a double boiler and mix with the butter until creamy. Gradually add the powdered sugar and, one by one, the egg yolks. Beat the egg whites with the sugar to form semi-stiff peaks, fold in the flour (to which the salt has been added), and turn into the chocolate-butter mixture.
Preheat the oven to 350 °F (180 °C). Butter and flour a springform pan with a 10 inch (24 cm) diameter, slide in the mixture and bake for 45–60 minutes. Let the torte cool completely in the pan before attempting to remove it.
Warm the apricot jam and brush it over the torte with a pastry brush. Let it cool for a few hours.
To make the icing, bring the chocolate, sugar, and half a cup of water to the boil, stirring constantly. Then reduce the heat and continue cooking for another 5 minutes, until the icing begins to thicken. Spread the icing quickly and evenly over the whole torte, and serve, once it has cooled, with unsweetened whipped cream.

Joachim Römer

Switzerland

In her 700-year history, Switzerland has earned a reputation as a peace-loving and solidly neutral insular nation situated in the middle of the European continent. With a decidedly nationalistic consciousness – complemented by savvy in worldwide trade – the Swiss have kept themselves at bay from political unrest, intrigues, and alliances.

The country is divided into four linguistic and cultural areas. While the French-speaking part of the country leans towards the habits and customs of France, the culinary arts established around the French court were never to have much effect on Switzerland. The German-speaking Swiss look across the Rhine to their northern neighbors, but enjoy a tradition based on the potato rather than on German Spätzle and dumplings. The Italian-speaking Swiss in southernmost Ticino, on the other hand, openly acknowledge the Mediterranean delights of their Italian neighbors and have readily adopted its abundant pasta. In the southeast, the solid people of the Graubünden stand strictly on their own. Some 40,000 Rhaeto-Romanish Swiss speak no other language than their own and keep their traditional alpine farming culture intact – both in their language and at church.

Whoever tries to expound on "typical" Swiss cuisine is quick to run aground. Had Swiss cheese and Swiss chocolate failed to achieve worldwide renown, one would down-scale and talk about cantonal cuisine. An understanding of what one can call Swiss, however, is gleaned readily if one steps into a small alpine restaurant. Whatever is served at that table has a century-old tradition and usually bespeaks the poverty of what was the annual production on the farm. These are simple preparations from a few products: milk, meat, and fruit, and in some areas, wine.

Left: Preparing a cheese fondue in Zurich's "Raclette Stube."

After the *Bündner Fleisch* is pickled, it is air-dried for several months. As a snack, it goes extremely well with wine.

Bündner Fleisch

What better snack with wine than the famous *Bündner Fleisch* that the old farmers of Graubünden used to take as food on their mountain wanderings? Made of the tender and rich muscle of beef shank, it is rubbed with a herbed brine and then dried over several months in the fragrant mountain air. In time, it loses more than half its water weight. Called *bresaola* in Italian, the air-dried beef is sliced paper-thin, rolled, and served on a wooden board with hearty brown bread and butter, and lots of pepper.

Bündner Fleisch is pressed at the beginning of the drying process, which gives it its typical corners.

Cut paper-thin, *Bündner Fleisch* is served with lots of freshly ground pepper.

Sweets Precisely to the Millimeter

Basle Leckerli

The Swiss love confections and cakes of all kinds. The German-speaking Swiss, particularly the people of Basle, have the biggest "sweet tooth."

The honey-rich Leckerli of Basle have a 600 year-old tradition that has made them world-renowned.

Basle Leckerli

2 cups (400 g) honey
1 cup (250 g) sugar
2 tsp (10 g) potash
1 glass Kirsch
$^{1}/_{4}$ cup (50 g) candied orange and lemon peel
$^{1}/_{2}$ cup (100 g) almonds
1$^{1}/_{2}$ lb (700 g) flour
Cinnamon, ground cloves, nutmeg

Bring the honey to the boil, add the sugar and cook again before removing to cool. Dissolve the potash in the Kirsch and add to the honey-sugar mixture. Chop the almonds and the candied orange and lemon peel and add them and the spices to the flour. Gradually add the flour to the honey mixture and knead the dough. Let the dough rest overnight. Preheat the oven to 400 °F (200 °C). Roll out the dough and place it on a buttered baking sheet. Bake for about 20 minutes, allow to cool, and then cut into small squares.

Below: The Swiss are considered conscientious and precise – during production, they adhere to the dimensions of the Leckerli exactly.

Above: Ingredients for Leckerli – honey, chopped almonds, flour, candied orange and lemon peel, spices, potash, a leavening agent, and sugar.

1

2

3

4

5

6

7

8

Sweet Specialties

Aargauer Rüeblitorte
Aargau Carrot Cake
(Illustration below)

The canton of Aargau is famous for a torte that never fails to get accolades. It is made of raw, grated carrots that lend the torte a piquant-sweet taste.

6 egg yolks, 6 egg whites
1¼ cups (300 g) sugar
Peel of one untreated lemon
2 Tbs Kirsch
10 oz (300 g) carrots
1 cup (300 g) ground almonds
½ cup (50 g) flour
Powdered sugar
Marzipan

Beat the egg yolks and sugar until creamy. Add the lemon peel and the Kirsch. Clean and grate the carrots, then add them, along with the flour and almonds, to the egg-sugar mixture. Beat the egg whites until stiff, and fold them into the mixture.
Preheat the oven to 350 °F (180 °C). Pour the mixture into a spring form and bake for about 60 minutes. Sprinkle the cooled cake with powdered sugar and garnish with marzipan carrots.

Aargauer Rüeblitorte –
Argau Carrot Cake

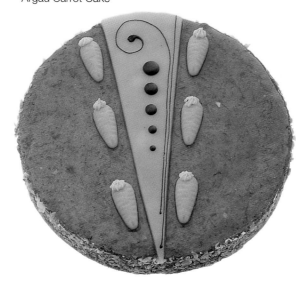

Zuger Kirschtorte
Zug Cherry Torte
(Illustrations 1–8 above)

A cherry torte without cherries? Yes, but between the pastry layers of this nut and biscuit torte, the butter cream is generously flavored with Kirsch.

Nut layer
4 egg whites
½ cup (125 g) or a little more powdered sugar
½ cup (100 g) ground hazelnuts
2 Tbs cornstarch

Biscuit layer
3 egg yolks, 3 egg whites
⅓ cup (75 g) powdered sugar
½ cup (50 g) flour
½ cup (50 g) cornstarch
½ tsp baking powder
Peel of ½ an untreated lemon

Butter cream
⅔ cup (150 g) butter
1½ cups (150 g) powdered sugar
1 egg yolk
4 Tbs Kirsch

Finishing
4 Tbs Kirsch
½ cup (125 g) chopped hazelnuts
1 cup (100 g) powdered sugar

To make the nut layer, beat the egg whites until stiff and fold in half the powdered sugar. Combine the remaining sugar, nuts, and cornstarch and fold this into the stiff egg whites. Bake two layers from the mixture, using a spring form.
To make the biscuit layers, beat the egg yolks with 3 tablespoons of warm water until creamy, and add half the powdered sugar. Beat the egg whites with the remaining sugar until stiff, fold into the yolks and add the flour, cornstarch, baking powder, and lemon peel to make a batter. Using the same sized spring form, bake for 20 minutes in a moderate oven.
For the butter cream, beat the butter until creamy, add the sugar and egg yolk, and the Kirsch last. Divide into three portions. To finish, spread one third of the butter cream on a nut layer (1), stack a biscuit layer on top (2), and sprinkle with Kirsch (3). Spread on the next portion of butter cream, and lay the second nut layer on top (4). Spread the remaining butter cream (5), sprinkle the edge and the top with nuts (6) and dust with powdered sugar (7). Mark the torte into diamond shapes (8).

Made with Swiss Alpine Milk
Chocolate

As a result of the explorations of Christopher Columbus and Hernán Cortés, the cocoa bean came from America to Europe in the 16th century. As a drink, chocolate enjoyed great popularity among the bourgeois and at court. In 1828, the Dutchman C. J. Houten made a breakthrough: he devised a way to extract the oil from the cocoa bean and produce cocoa powder. Two decades later, the Englishman Joseph Fry manufactured the first edible chocolate, and in 1825, a Swiss named Daniel Peter added condensed milk to produce the first milk chocolate bar. A few years later, his countryman Rudolph Lindt invented a refinement known as "conching" (from the Spanish *concha* or shell): heated and constantly moving shell-shaped drums crushed the chocolate between two rollers and removed the lumpiness and grittiness that had characterized the product up to that time. This led the way to the manufacture of chocolate figures in which a smooth liquid mass was poured into a form. Not only did Lindt's invention give chocolate the mellowness that makes it so delicious, it promoted its use in further processing.

In manufacturing chocolate, the Swiss were always the strongest presence in development at all stages. Names like Kohler and Cailler, Sprüngli and Lindt, Suchard and Tobler mark Swiss chocolate's road to glory. Today, Swiss chocolate is a world-renowned delicacy. The names are of the competent industrialists who, at the end of the 19th and beginning of the 20th centuries, shared the common goal of marrying the cocoa bean with fine Swiss alpine milk.

Opposite: Double layered sweet-dough cookie with a strawberry jelly filling. On the lid, a geometric cross is punched out so that the filling is visible, making a play on the Swiss national flag, a white cross on red ground.

From Bean to Cocoa

The cocoa bean grows primarily in Africa, South America and Asia. The ripe, seven to nine inch (fifteen to twenty-five centimeter) long beans are cut down and split open. The white seed kernel, the cocoa beans and the fruit pulp are retained, piled on top of one another, covered and cooked. The beans turn "chocolate brown" in the process and develop that unmistakably enticing aroma. Then the beans are dried, and sacked for export to

Europe, where they are cleaned, roasted, and ground into cocoa powder. Grinding and pressing force the extraction of cocoa butter, which is particularly valuable. Cocoa butter's low melting temperature is comparable to the temperature of the human body, which makes it profitable in a range of cosmetics and pharmaceutical products. When the remaining chocolate mass is ground again, cocoa powder for use in syrup, beverages, icings, and puddings is produced.

In a complicated manufacturing process, cocoa powder and cocoa butter are combined with milk powder to make chocolate. Just the right combination of these three ingredients is the secret of every chocolate manufacturer. Nuts, almonds, and grapes can be added to increase appeal. Strict regulations control the purity and contents of the various brands. We differentiate between melting and cream chocolate, full-milk and skim-milk chocolate, glaze and white chocolate, made of cocoa butter alone.

The Praliné – Queen of Chocolates

Pralinés, or assorted chocolates, are known in three versions depending on method of production: glazed chocolates with a hard or semi-hard filling, hollow chocolates with soft or liquid fillings, and solid chocolates. The first category makes up the widest variety, as the center may be marzipan, nougat, truffle, or crisp. Almonds or other nuts may top the praliné, and the applied decorations in bitter chocolate and other garnishes demand a high degree of dexterity and skill.

Swiss Confectionery

1. Orange slice (candied orange slice with sugar and chocolate icing)
2. Princesses (orange truffle with powdered sugar)
3. Pineapple triangle (candied pineapple pieces)
4. Little Kirsch drops (cherries in schnapps)
5. Whisky – Truffles (with whisky filling, turned in cocoa)
6. Little crowns (a marzipan confection modeled on Danish crown cake)
7. Florentines (in miniature)
8. Calissons (little boats with sugar icing)
9. Schiesser Rum (invented by Café Schiesser in Basle)
10. Baisers du jour ("daytime kisses")

Nougat is at the top of the popularity charts. It is produced like chocolate, except that ground hazelnuts or almonds are used instead of cocoa beans. The most costly fillings are truffles in their multiple variations. They are made of chocolate whipped with cream and select ingredients, like butter, liquor, nut, and almond pastes, as well as fruit products. *Krokant* is the crispy delicacy made of candied sugar and chopped nuts. Rose water has been added to the mixture of chopped almonds and powdered sugar we call marzipan. Other delectable treats are the fruits in alcohol and liquid fillings based on schnapps or liqueurs that are indispensable to any grand chocolate assortment.

Cigars

Geneva, the respected seat of international organizations on the lake of the same name, is also the hub of cigar culture. Closely connected to it is a name almost synonymous with cigars, Zino Davidoff. Born in Kiev, the Russian Davidoff was able to emigrate with the rest of his family to the safety of Geneva before the October Revolution. He died in 1994 at the age of eighty-eight, but his life's work continues. During the Second World War, Davidoff skilfully managed to trade from Cuba to France and Germany through Geneva, and his business became a familiar meeting point of passage for friends of the cigar worldwide. He introduced a climate-controlled cellar for the cigar as early as 1929,

and after 1945, he brought the famous Château Cigar onto the market, imported from Cuba and named after the great Bordeaux wines. He broke off with Cuba in 1990, and since then, Davidoff Cigars have been manufactured in the Dominican Republic. Davidoff cigars are lighter than Havanas: the Davidoff Grand-Cru series includes five sizes between four and six inches (10.2 and 15.5 centimeters) long.

The Cohiba – Cuba's Answer to Davidoff

The long-lasting quarrel between Cuba and Davidoff, which finally led to the break-up, was in no small part due to the priority treatment the Cubans gave their own Cohiba cigar, by reserving the best tobacco leaves for its production.

The Cohiba, which means "cigar" in the language of the native Taino Indians, is known today, hands down, as the finest of Havana cigars.

The revolutionary Che Guevara, who was responsible for the cigar industry, called on the expertise of his countryman and tobacco expert Avelino Lara to encourage production. The excellent quality of the Cohiba can be attributed to its inclusion of only the finest tobacco leaves – the best selected from ten different cultivated plantations – as well as the fact that the leaves are fermented three times. The cigars also have to pass stringent quality control. Around twenty percent of the daily production are tested according to various criteria: length, weight, degree of firmness, wrapper and the cut at the end. Expert smokers, or *catadores,* have the last word.

Cohibas are the most expensive of all Havanas. Annual production, at about 3.5 million cigars, amounts to about one percent of Cuba's total output. The noble Cohiba has also been exported since 1982.

10 9 8 7 6 5 4 3 2 1

Above: Standard formats for Havana cigars – the numbers relate to the descriptions in the yellow box at the right. The ruler illustrated measures about 8 inches (20 cm).

Left: Cohiba formats – see the yellow box right. The cigar inaugurated by the revolutionary Che Guevara is considered *the* Havana. Favorite cigar of Fidel Castro, it was once reserved for foreign dignitaries, royalty, and dictators. Since 1982, however, it is also exported to "lay" smokers. It was designed by Avelino Lara, the top-notch expert who began his career as a cigar maker in the 1920s. Nobody questions the leading position of the Cohiba in terms of quality and price.

11   10   9   8   7   6   5   4   3   2   1

Cigar Formats

There are about sixty different cigar formats, however many brands use their name for their own standard formats. The length and thickness of a cigar is given in inch units (1 inch = about 25.5 mm) In addition, the valid measurement is 1/64 inch. A cigar with a ring measurement of fifty, for example, has a diameter of 50/64 inches. The following chart shows the measurements in inches/mm for length and ring measures.

Standard Formats for Havana Cigars
(small illustration left)

1	Double-Corona	7⁷/₈"/200 mm	49
2	Especial	7¹/₂"/191 mm	38
3	Churchill	7"/178 mm	47
4	Corona Grande	6"/152 mm	42
5	Corona	5¹/₂"/140 mm	42
6	Small Corona	5"/127 mm	42
7	Pyramide/Torpedo	6¹/₈"/156 mm	52
8	Robusto	5"/127 mm	50
9	Panetela	4¹/₂"/114 mm	26
10	Demi-Tasse	4"/102 mm	30

Cohiba Formats
(large illustration left)

1	Siglo I	4"/102 mm	40
2	Siglo II	5"/127 mm	42
3	Siglo III	6"/152 mm	42
4	Siglo IV	5⁵/₈"/142 mm	46
5	Siglo V	6³/₄"/171 mm	43
6	Robusto	5"/127 mm	50
7	Panetela	4¹/₂"/114 mm	26
8	Exquisito	5"/127 mm	36
9	Coronas Especial	6"/152 mm	38
10	Lancero	7¹/₂"/191 mm	38
11	Esplendido	7"/178 mm	47

The formats of the siglo series were named *siglos* for the centuries after 1492, the year in which Columbus discovered America and the habit of smoking came back to Europe.

Right: a stack of renowned Havana cigars. Handmade cigars are packed and stored in cedar wood boxes, as cedar promotes ripening and prevents drying out. With the beginning of growth at the middle of the last century and the increasing number of manufacturers, a system of definitive markings became advisable. Henceforth, every cigar box was sealed with the emblem of its maker. A guarantee also appears (in Spanish) on the boxes: "Guarantee of the Cuban Government for cigars exported from Havana." (The lowermost box in the stack carries the official seal of the Republic.) Among the best known and most popular brands in the middle to high cost range are the *Bolivar*, one of the strongest and heaviest Havanas, and the *Montecristo*, which remains one of the best, despite over-production. Its name, incidentally goes back to the time when reading aloud to cigar makers was customary, and one of the favorite novels was Alexander Dumas' "The Count of Monte Cristo." Other highly popular brands are the *Romeo y Julieta* with its assortment of over forty formats; and the *Partagas*, which is produced in large quantities and counts among the oldest of all Havanas.

One of the exclusive air-conditioned cigar shops which stocks the complete range of Havana cigars. The temperature at which cigars are stored is kept constant (at 60 °F/16 °C), as is humidity (80%).

The Cigar Maker – Most Important Fellow

Cigars are hardly rolled on the thighs of Cuban beauties – and the legend is refuted if one watches a cigar maker at work. His work comes at the end of a long process that begins with tobacco planting in August, continues through the harvest in January, and even with fermentation and the three- to four-year storage of tobacco balls is not completed.

Cigar makers, *torcedores*, work primarily with their hands; their only tools are a sharp knife and a wooden template. Their cigars are made up of three parts: the wrapper (*capo*), the binder (*capote*), and the filler, rolled of single leaves lengthways to form a kind of canal for the flow of smoke, which can only be done by hand.

The cigar maker's art depends on the choice of three kinds of leaves for the filler: *seco* (from the center of the plant) for aroma, *volado* (from the foot) to insulate properly, and *ligero* (from the tip) for the perfect combination of spiciness and robustness.

The fresh cigars undertake their trans-Atlantic crossing, and are stored again in Geneva for over a year. They undergo another quality check before they land in the climate-controlled cellars of specialty shops.

How to Smoke a Cigar

A so-called "humidor," a temperature- and moisture-controlled box or cupboard made of fine wood, is basic equipment for every friend of cigars. Optimum humidor conditions are not unlike those of wine cellars, which is why cigars can also be stored successfully there: about 60 °F (16 °C) and moisture of about eighty percent. As cigars are made up of living material, they are green while being made, and only lose their color a few weeks later.

A properly stored cigar should not rustle when one holds it up and turns it at the ear. The cigar is stored moist, and its outer leaf should be smooth and elastic. With a sharp knife, or better yet, special cigar scissors, one snips off the round end of the cigar and lights the cigar slowly and carefully with a long match or a sandalwood "fidibus" chip.

A cigar is smoked with care. The wrapper must never get hot and the cigar should never go out. Smoking a cigar lasts about ninety minutes, which merited this from the French film director François Truffaud: "Just as long as a good film – and that is life."

Joachim Römer

Germany

The range of culinary specialties in Germany extends from the famous Printen gingerbread in Aix-la-Chapelle (Aachen) to the meat balls known as Buletten in Berlin, from sprats in Kiel to white sausage in Munich. The cuisine of the sixteen German states is as varied as the different regions – there is no "typically German" or "national" dish. The mess kitchen of Prussian soldiers at the end of the 19th century may have roughly defined what German meals had to be: bread and potatoes, pork and sauerkraut, pea soup and meat balls. These were meagre meals for hardened men to whom victory in battle meant much more than culinary pleasure.

For centuries, German cuisine was considered spartan. Those with savoir vivre always knew better than that, and whoever could afford it could always eat well. The less fortunate concocted surprising achievements with the most humble of ingredients: delicious cabbage in the North, imaginative preparation of innards in the Baden area, the soul-warming delights of a Bavarian roast pork with dumplings, or Allerlei (the "hodge-podge" whose true form includes crabmeat, a delicacy often forgotten today), Swabian pasta squares, Sauerbraten from the Rhineland, Thüringer Bratwurst, or – from day one of creation – the ever-delectable fried potatoes some gourmets would climb over the finest Lobster Bisque to get.

Today's German wants foods of quality and natural products. Bio-gardening and humane animal husbandry make for better results in the pan and skillet than the commonplace product. German wine, too, has made a name for itself: competent wine-growers offer vintages that are fine and light, dry and fermented. German beer, the national drink, is also superb. Nobler brands, the so-called "premiums" have conquered the market and competed with the simple "lights." Such that German cuisine, once rather wanting for imagination, has come into new culinary diversity.

Left: Grape harvest in the vineyards of the "Bürgerspital" near Würzburg.

233

Above: Fresh *Bauernbrot* with its uneven, rustic crust is among the most delectable bakery products. Hearty "farmer's" breads, for the most part, ryes, are among the breads formed in single loaves and then baked in the oven close enough to one another to form their characteristic crust.

Bread Dishes

Cooking with Bread

Because the Germans so love their bread, they use it as a basis for a variety of other dishes. Many regional recipes embellish "yesterday's" bread rather than simply reduce it to breadcrumbs. In the olden days, when the "bread basket" was harder to obtain, cooks were particularly imaginative with their remainders.

Stale Bread Is Not Old Bread

Stale bread is not necessarily old. Independent of the way it is stored, bread is subject to a continuous process of the dehydration of its starches. As it "ages" it smells and tastes a little stale. White bread is high in starch, and as such, this process affects it readily. On the other hand, in breads that contain sourdough as the leavening agent, this chemical reaction is delayed. Rye bread, for example, rarely tastes stale.

Brotsuppe
Bread Soup

4 slices of stale bread
2 1/2 cups (500 ml) bouillon
1 cup (200 g) fresh vegetables of the season
1 potato, peeled and cubed
1 egg yolk

Fry the bread in the butter and pour in the broth. Add the vegetables and potato and simmer before passing through a sieve and thickening with the egg yolk.

Frikadellen
Fried Patties

Stale breadrolls are an essential ingredient in the preparation of an economical meat dish called *Frikadelle*, or *Hacksteak* in Northern Germany, *Bulette* (in Berlin) or *Fleischpflanzerl* in Munich.

2 stale rolls
1 lb (500 g) ground meat (half beef, half pork)
1 egg
1 onion, peeled and chopped
1 bunch of parsley, washed and finely chopped
Salt, black pepper

Soften the rolls in water. Press out and combine with the ground meat. Add the egg, onion, and parsley, spice with salt and pepper and stir thoroughly. Form the meat dough into balls, flatten them and fry in a skillet.

Strammer Max (Egg and Ham)

Winzer-Vesper ("Wine-grower's Evening")

Armer Ritter ("Poor Knight")

Armer Ritter auf Weinschaumsauce
"Poor Knight" in Wine Cream Sauce
(Illustration)

8 slices of stale white bread
1½ cups (300 ml) milk
2 eggs
1 pinch of salt
1 Tbs sugar
Fine bread crumbs
Cinnamon and sugar

Wine Cream Sauce

2 egg yolks
¼ cup (50 g) sugar
½ cup (125 ml) white wine

Lay the white bread slices over one another on a large plate. Whisk the milk, eggs, salt, and sugar, pour over the bread and leave to soak. Turn the milky bread slices in bread crumbs and fry in butter, then sprinkle with cinnamon and sugar.
For the sauce, stir the egg yolks with the sugar until smooth. Add the wine and beat with a whisk to a thick and creamy sauce over a double boiler. Spoon the sauce out onto a plate, arrange the bread slices on top and serve.

Strammer Max
Egg and Ham
(Illustration)

Especially in countries once under Prussian rule, this dish has always been a simple and tasty pick-me-up.

1 slice of wheat or rye mixed bread
Butter
2 slices cooked ham
1 egg
Salt, black pepper

Butter the bread and top it with the ham. Fry the egg, salt and pepper it and serve it on top of the ham.

Hamburger Kraftbrot
Hamburg High-energy Bread

For years, this Northern German specialty was a standard meal in the railway's restaurant cars.

1 slice of whole-wheat or rye bread
Butter
1 thick slice of raw or smoked ham
1 egg, beaten
Salt, black pepper
Chopped parsley

Butter the bread, cube the ham into small pieces and arrange on the bread. Season the egg with salt and pepper and scramble. Put it over the ham, garnish with parsley and serve.

Winzer-Vesper
"Wine-grower's Evening"
(Illustration above)

Mixed wheat or rye bread slices
Butter
Sliced blood- and liverwurst sausage and raw or cooked ham, in slices
Soft farmer's cheese (Quark) seasoned with chives
Mustard
Baby onions
Pickles

Every guest at the table selects what he or she likes. Served at best with a glass of German country wine.

237

Important Pork Cuts

1	Head	8 Shank
2	Shoulder butt	9 Foot
3	Loin	10 Bacon belly
4	Fat back	11 Hock
5	Loin	12 Picnic
6	Fillet	shoulder
7	Ham	13 Cheek

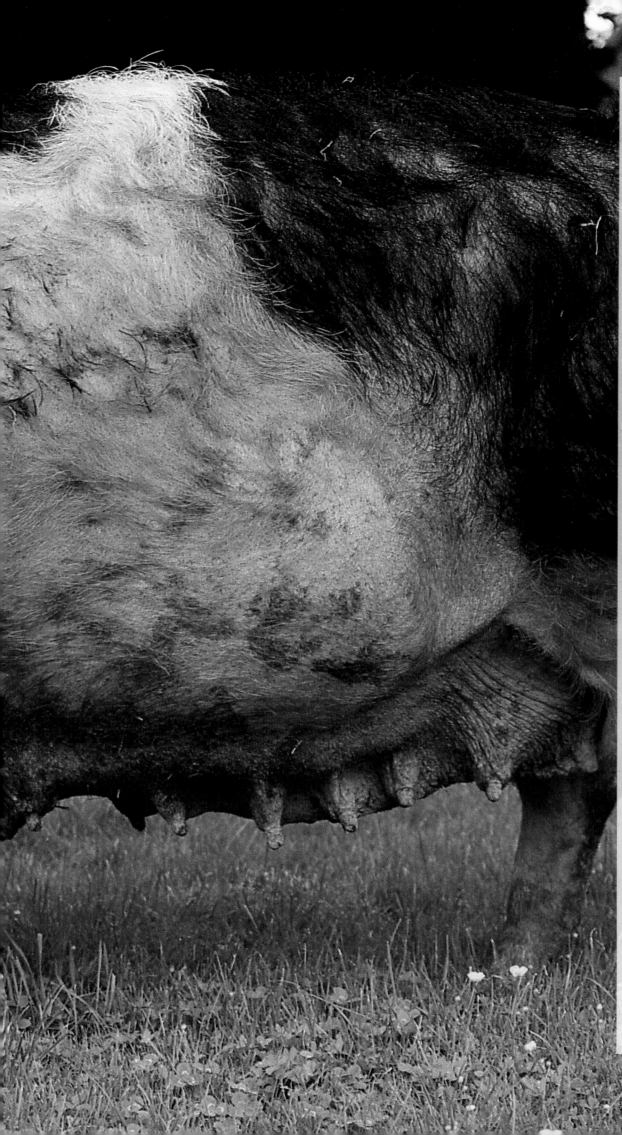

The Pig

No other domestic animal – barring the dog, perhaps – has been as assured of German loyalties through its history as the pig. Through the centuries, it has been a living meat reserve and also an appreciative disposal system. In the Middle Ages, pigs were left to roam freely in the meadow and around the farmyard, but they have been penned since the 19th century. They were to be fattened up for desirable pig fat. Only after the Second World War did leaner pigs begin to be bred in accordance with changing market demands. They had only half the fat bacon as their predecessors, but more meat and sixteen instead of twelve ribs. Today we know that lean pigs cannot satisfy the demands of taste, so once again, pigs with fattier muscle and marbled meat are preferred. The fat ensures a juicy roast.

Deutscher Schweinebraten
German Roast Pork

2 lbs (1 kg) leg of pork with rind
Salt, black pepper
Spices to taste
Pork fat
1 bouquet garni
1 tsp dried marjoram
Cornstarch

Preheat the oven to 325 °F (160 °C). Rinse and dry the meat, criss-cross the skin with a knife. Season the roast on all sides with salt, pepper, and any other spices desired. In a large roasting pan, heat the fat and brown the meat in it until crisp.
Add a cup of water, the bouquet garni and stir in the marjoram. Cover the pan and put it in the oven, bake for 90 minutes to 2 hours, after one hour baste the roast with the pan juices, and add more water if needed. Sieve the pan juices, add boiling water to increase the amount, and thicken with cornstarch. Slice the roast and pour juice or sauce over it, and serve with potatoes or dumplings.

Above: Butchers making bratwurst.
Large photograph: The tied, small and thick sausages called *Knacker* or *Regensburger*.

In many parts of Germany, roast pork is the Sunday or special meal. Every region has its own special method of preparation, which differs primarily around the treatment of the skin to make it crunchy. The Bavarians, for example, rub it in beer, the people of Rhineland with garlic, and in still other recipes, horseradish, juniper berry, or nutmeg are used.

Pork available in markets comes from young mast pigs, slaughtered at 7–8 months. The pink to light-red meat is fine and tender. Pork meat only requires a short "ripening period" and needs no hanging. It contains thiamine, a B-group vitamin, that affects metabolism as well as the nervous and muscular systems.

Almost Everything can be Eaten

- Its most delectable parts are the cutlet, fillet, and ham.
- Fatty bacon is taken from the back.
- The neck yields juicy cutlets.
- The belly is valued for its economical stew and broiling meat.
- Pork knuckles and shoulder are taken from the legs.
- The head meat is used in jellies, stews and hearty pea soups.
- Pork cheek, *Schweinebacke* – a favorite in Northern Germany – is also used in stews and hearty broiled snacks.
- The hooves, fresh or pickled, are delicious when dredged in bread crumbs and then broiled or baked. As hoof has a high gelatine content, it is used in jellies as well.

Sausage – Quality and Variety

Wurst is a staple in the German household. Sliced on bread, sausage is most popular, and butchers never tire of finding new ways of preparation, including the thin slices in animal shapes created for children. Among snacks, *Bratwurst* is a classic. There are hundreds of kinds throughout Germany – too many to know all of them. It is helpful to know that there are three different classifications of sausage, depending on ingredients and production: raw, steamed and cooked. Hams constitute a fourth group.

Wurst is made of muscle, bacon, innards, salt, and spices as a rule. The ingredients are refined, combined and stuffed into sausage skins according to strict regulations. The minimum amount of lean meat each must contain is pre-determined.

Nuremberg broiling sausages count among Wurst delicacies. They go nicely with sauerkraut.

Munich white sausages are known far and wide. The Wurst is sucked ("zuzzelt") out of the skin.

Currywurst in spicy sauce is a Berlin invention, and is eaten with wooden forks from a cardboard plate.

Regional Wurst Specialties

The spirit of invention in the various regions has made for the variety of *Wurst* preparation. Among the *Bratwurst* – almost a popular culture item at markets and shooting competitions, but which holds its own at every snack stand – those from Thüringen and Nuremberg are especially tasty. The finger-length Nuremberg broiling sausages are cooked over beechwood. The custom is to eat six or a dozen from a tin plate with horseradish rather than the usual mustard. Potato salad or sauerkraut are accompaniments.

Another "cult dish" of the working class is *Currywurst* that a still-unidentified butcher in Berlin invented in the 1930s. The sausage is sliced (by a machine made for that purpose), generously sprinkled with curry powder and covered in a spicy sauce. The sausage is eaten from a cardboard plate with a little two-pronged fork or a toothpick.

Among the regional sausages known far beyond their regions, is the Munich white sausage (*Weisswurst*), steamed and made from veal, beef, and pork, that is served hot and sucked from its skin.

Differences among Wurst

Raw sausages (about 550 kinds)
They are made of raw meat, bacon, and spices. The ingredients are chopped, salted, spiced, and filled into the skin. Pickling and slow drying or smoking ripens them and gives them their typical taste. This group includes all long-lasting and hard sausages.

Stewing sausage (about 750 kinds)
Most *Wurst* belong to this group. Stewing sausages are made of raw pork or beef and bacon, with the addition of egg, pickling salt, and spices. Once stuffed in their skins, they are stewed in water at 200 °F (75 °C) and some are briefly smoked. They must be eaten right away.

Cooking sausage (about 350 kinds)
Of cooked meat, intestines, and spices, which is cooked a second time once they have been stuffed. Most are fresh sausage that must be eaten quickly. Their shelf-life can be extended by a short period of smoking.

Ham
Mostly from the highly valued ham leg. Its firmness and good taste come from pickling, smoking or cooking. Special attention given to the Holstein, Schwarzwald, and Westphalian hams make them particularly good.

Regional Meat Specialties

Rheinischer Sauerbraten
Rhineland Sauerbraten
(Illustration)

One of the favorite dishes of Rhineland cuisine uses a combination of sweet and sour for special appeal. The Rhineland Sauerbraten, which was horsemeat in the original, tastes best with potato dumplings.

3 lbs (1½ kg) beef brisket
Fat and butter
2 onions, peeled and finely chopped
2 oz (50 g) raisins, softened in water
4 pieces of gingerbread, crumbled
1 cup (250 ml) heavy cream
1 Tbs red currant jelly
½ cup (125 ml) red wine

Marinade

2½ cups (500 ml) water
1¼ cups (250 ml) vinegar
1 tsp salt
10 crushed peppercorns
10 crushed juniper berries
5 cloves
½ tsp mustard seeds
3 onions, peeled and sliced
1 carrot, cleaned and sliced
2 bay leaves
1 cup (250 ml) red wine
Coriander, marjoram and rosemary

Rinse the meat in cold water and pat dry. Put in a bowl. For the marinade, combine the ingredients and heat quickly. Cover the meat with the marinade, and put in a cool place, covered, for 3–4 days. Turn it several times daily.

Heat the fat in a heavy skillet and braise the beef on all sides for about 5 minutes. Add the onions and cook for another 5 minutes, stirring constantly, then pour in the marinade. Cover and allow to simmer for about 2 hours over low heat. Occasionally turn, and add more water or marinade to keep the amount of liquid constant. At the end of the cooking time, take out the meat and keep warm. Pass the pan juices through a sieve. Squash the raisins and add them with the gingerbread and cream to the pan juices. Stir and simmer for 10 minutes and season with salt and pepper. Finally, add the red currant jelly and red wine.

Accompany the sauerbraten with dumplings, cooked fruit, and applesauce.

Mecklenburger Lammkeule
Mecklenburg Leg of Lamb

1 leg of lamb (about 3 lbs or 1½ kg)
1 lb (500 g) scallions
1 lb (500 g) green peppers
1½ oz (40 g) butter
1 Tbs sugar
Flour
3½ cups (750 ml) lamb broth
Salt, black pepper

Rinse the lamb and pat dry. Peel the onions and clean the peppers. Chop the vegetables into small pieces. Fry the onions in the butter until transparent, add the sugar and sprinkle on a little flour. Dilute with the broth. Add the peppers and simmer for 10 minutes. Season the lamb and fry it in hot oil. Add the vegetables, cover, and simmer over medium heat for about 90 minutes.

Cut the meat in slices and serve with the vegetables and a cabbage salad.

Abgebräunte Kalbshaxe
Browned Leg of Veal
(Illustration)

This dish is a southern German specialty. In some recipes, the meat is turned in bread crumbs before it is fried.

I leg of veal
1 bouquet garni
1 onion
1 carrot
Salt, black pepper
Butterfat

Rinse the meat in cold water and then put in boiling salted water on the stove. Cut the carrot in half and add these and the onion to the pot together with the bouquet garni. Let the meat cook over medium heat for about 60 minutes, then remove it from the cooking pot, drain and season with salt and pepper.

In hot butterfat, cook the veal for about 60 minutes until it is crispy brown all over. Add more water periodically. At the end of the cooking time, arrange the meat on a platter and cover with the pan juices. Potato salad is a good accompaniment.

Rhineland Sauerbraten

Browned Leg of Veal

Pfälzer Saumagen
Pfalz Pig's Stomach
(Illustration below)

In the Pfalz it was the custom at the slaughter to gather the remains together with potatoes in a pig's stomach and cook it. Once a meal for poor people, it has found its way upstairs through a number of refinements, none the least of which is that German Chancellor Helmut Kohl, a native of Pfalz, calls it his favorite meal.

1 pig's stomach
1 stale bread roll
Milk
8 oz (250 g) spare rib
8 oz (250 g) belly of pork
2 onions
1 lb (500 g) cooked potatoes
Pork fat
10 oz (300 g) sausage filling
2 eggs
Salt, black peper
Marjoram, thyme, caraway seeds, nutmeg
carrot, leek, parsnip, parsley

Put the pig's stomach in salted water overnight, then rinse it thoroughly. Soften the bread roll in the milk. Slice the spare rib and belly meat in ³/₄ inch cubes. Peel and coarsely chop the onions, cube the potatoes, fry the meat and onions in the fat followed by the potatoes. Let the meat mixture cool. Press out the bread roll and combine it with the Wurst filling, eggs, and seasoning, knead the mass and fill the stomach with it. Stitch closed and lay it in a linen napkin. Wash and chop the remaining vegetables and parsley. Add them and the filled pig's stomach to a pot of salted water and let them simmer for 3–4 hours.

Then remove and fry in pork fat until it is crispy brown all over.
Dilute the pan fat with a little boiling water and season to taste. Slice the pig's stomach and pour over the sauce. Sauerkraut and crusty brown bread are nice accompaniments.

Kaninchenbraten
Rabbit Roast

In Southern Europe, rabbit is a popular meat. In Germany, and particularly in the Ruhr Valley, rabbits were raised in harder times and kept in sheds behind the house.

2 lbs (1 kg) rabbit meat
1 cup (250 ml) game broth
1 glass of white wine
1 glass of red wine
Salt, black pepper
6 oz (container) sour cream

Cut the rabbit meat into portions, rinse and pat dry. Fry the meat in hot fat and season with salt and pepper, then pour in the game broth and the white wine. Simmer for about 40 minutes. Remove the meat, dilute the juices with the red wine and spoon in the sour cream. Bring up to heat and serve with the meat, along with potatoes, *Spätzle*, or dumplings.

Martinsgans
St. Martin's Goose

This dish is traditionally served in many areas on St. Martin's Day, November 11, which coincides with the beginning of Carnival in Rhineland.

1 ready-to-eat goose (about 9 lbs or 4 kg)
1 lb (500 g) potatoes
2 onions
2 apples
1 bunch of parsley
Marjoram
Salt, black pepper
I bay leaf
Mugwort
Sage
1 tsp cornstarch

Clean the goose thoroughly, in and out. Peel, cube, and blanch the potatoes in boiling, salted water. Peel and cube the onions and apples, having removed the seeds. Wash and chop the parsley. Turn the onions and apples in butter until soft, combine with the potatoes, parsley and marjoram and fill the goose. Stitch the bird closed with kitchen thread and rub with salt and pepper. Preheat the oven to 425 °F (220 °C).
In a large roasting pan, boil a little water and lay the goose, breast down, into it. Add the bay leaf, mugwort, and sage, push the pan in the oven and roast the goose for about 2¹/₂ hours. Turn the goose 30 minutes before the end of the cooking time.
Remove the bird from the pan and keep warm. Sieve the broth and skim off the fat. Add a little cold water to the cornstarch and use it to thicken the gravy. Serve the sauce separately. Potato dumplings and apple red kraut or Brussels sprouts with chestnuts are tasty accompaniments.

Pfalz Pig's Stomach

Lined up on rods at the head, the sprats go into the smoking chamber.

Before being packed, the sprats get a generous pinch of salt.

Kiel sprats are exported to all parts of the world in small wooden crates.

The photograph shows the relative sizes: above, a large smoked mackerel, a smoked herring, about a foot (30 cm) long in the center, and below, two small Kiel sprats.

Below: After the catch, the fish are staked through the gills for smoking.

Northern Germany's Specialty of Worldwide Renown

Kiel Sprats

Schleswig-Holstein, Germany's northernmost state, abuts the North Sea and the Baltic Sea, and its count of fish is bountiful.

A special smoked delicacy are *Kieler Sprotten* (Kiel Sprats). Related to the herring, the sprat grows to only about six inches (fifteen cm). Unlike the herring, it lives in waters near the coast and in river mouths. It has tender meat with a high fat content, which makes it particularly well suited to smoking.

The only true Kiel sprats are those caught in the Bay of Kiel. There are no restrictions, however, on where they are smoked. So most sprats come from waters north of Schleswig-Holstein rather than from Kiel itself.

Centuries ago, fishermen along the coast smoked their fish to preserve it. Their recipes were kept secret and were passed from generation to generation. Only with the building of the railroads at the beginning of this century did chances for the easily-spoiled fish open up in the interior. As such, a smoking industry that steadily improved its technology was built up along the coast and today employs great numbers of people.

Left: In the north-German smoking plants, fish is processed in a variety of ways. This photograph shows rolled fish fillets being smoked. Every smoked fish specialty has an appetizing golden brown color.

Rührei mit Kieler Sprotten
Scrambled Eggs with Kiel Sprats

About 8 oz (250 g) Kiel Sprats
2 oz (40 g) butter
Black pepper
6 eggs
4 Tbs light cream
Salt
Chopped chives

Gut the sprats, fillet them and remove the head and tail of each. Heat the butter in a pan, braise the fish in it and season with freshly-ground pepper.
Mix the cream with the eggs, pour over the fish and stir until thickened. Garnish with the chives and serve with roast potatoes and green salad.

Fish from the North and Baltic Seas for Trade

1 Eel: smoked (80% of the catch), fresh, in aspic or marinade
2 Mackerel: fresh, smoked and canned
3 Sprats: fresh, smoked (Kiel Sprats) and canned
4 Herring: fresh (green herring), smoked *(Bückling)*, pickled in vinegar as Bismarck Herring, among others
5 Plaice: fresh and whole, or as fillet, frozen

The trout, a favorite eating fish, is bred primarily on trout farms today. The farm shown here is one in the Eifel region.

For trade, the trout farm's fish are caught and sold alive as fresh fish, smoked, or frozen.

Many fish farms, in addition to rainbow and brook trout, stock other sweet water fish like eel (above) and carp (below).

Trout smoked over a juniper berry fire, are a special delicacy.

Forelle blau
Blue Trout

4 fresh trout
1 cup (250 ml) vinegar
Juice of ½ a lemon
Parsley
Lemon slices

Rinse the trout quickly under cold running water, taking care not to damage the viscous layer of skin which ensures the "blue" hue.
Together with the vinegar and lemon juice, bring 5 cups (1 liter) of lightly salted water to a boil.
Steam the fish in the broth for about 8 minutes (do not boil!). Serve with the parsley and lemon slice garnish, melted butter, and green salad.

From the Interior and the Coast

Fish Specialties

The Rhine, as Germany's largest river, has been an important source of fish over the centuries. Whitefish, mostly in the month of May ("May-fish") counted among the most popular of common foods up until the 1950s. The King of Rhine fish, however, was salmon, which was always listed as "Rhine salmon" on menus in Cologne. In light of the increased pollution in the 1950s, it became harder to find, and a little later, the fish disappeared altogether.

Those who live on the shores of lakes and rivers in Southern Germany, on the other hand, are in an enviable position; the waters in the interior continue, even today, to host an endless supply of delicious fish. Fine trout swim in the cold waters of rivers and streams whose sources are in the mountains: whoever has once had the chance to enjoy the taste of a freshly caught brook trout will find eating those bred on trout farms much less appealing. Southern Germany offers a wide variety of fish taken from the still waters of its many lakes. Undoubtedly, the most popular fish is carp, common in the winter months at Christmas or New Year, which first lands in the family bathtub and then – providing the children do not protest – on the festive holiday table.

Plaice – Germany's Flat Fish

The year's first plaice come from the sea in May, and while they are still small, they are especially tender and tasty. The best recipe for them is named after the small fishing village of Hansestadt, west of Hamburg. Like the *Steinbutt* and the flounder, plaice belongs to the flatfish family. It is called *Goldbutt* if taken from the Baltic Sea.

Flatfish are remarkable inhabitants of the sea. As larvae, they have a normal fish form, while, when they develop, one eye moves to the edge of the body, later the upper side of the fish. As camouflage, the upperside is dark and the underside

light. The fish often buries itself in the sand to the point where only the eye is visible. It is difficult for any predator to attack at eye level, more so because of the confusion of eye-like red dots the fish has on its upper side.

Finkenwerder Maischollen
Finkenwerd May Plaice
(Illustrations 1–4 below)

4 plaice
Lemon juice
Salt, black pepper
1 Tbs flour
5 oz (150 g) fatty bacon
1 Tbs butterfat

Fillet the fish (1), rinse and season with lemon juice (2), season with salt and pepper and turn in the flour (3). Cut the bacon into small cubes and put them in a pan with the butterfat. Remove the bacon bits and drippings and set aside.
Fry the fish in hot fat on both sides (4) and arrange on a platter. Reheat the bacon bits and spoon them over the fish. Parsley potatoes and green salad are nice accompaniments.

Herring – a Story of its Own

Prince Otto von Bismarck, founder of the German Reich in 1871, gave us this: "If only herring were as costly as caviar and oysters, it would be considered a rare delicacy."

Since then, it has been proven true: in the 1960s, German fishermen caught 100,000 tons of the popular food annually. Then the oceans were practically exhausted of their stock and a six-year moratorium on herring fishing went into effect. Now permitted again in the Baltic, it is only done so according to the strict regulations of the European Union catch quotas. In the beginning of the 1980s only about 18,000 tons of herring were taken. What Bismarck purportedly said seems to be becoming true.

Bismarck also gave a name to a herring specialty which was particularly popular. His doctor had advised the Chancellor to eat herring as often as possible for reasons of health. For the politician to also be able to enjoy his "prescribed" fish on his retreat in East Elba, his cook devised this kind of "conserve" recipe: the head

Rollmops

and bones are removed and the fish is marinated with onion rings and spices in vinegar for two to three days.

Rollmops
(Illustration above)

This variation on Bismarck Herring was created inland. Especially in Berlin, but elsewhere, too, rollmops are eaten at the bar or for brunch.

6 fresh herring
1 cup (250 ml) white wine
1/2 cup (125 ml) vinegar
1 onion
1 carrot
1 leek
Peppercorns
Bay leaf
Juniper berries
Dill
Thyme
1 jar of salted or spiced pickles

Fillet the fish. Clean and finely chop the vegetables. Put the white wine and vinegar in a pot, add the vegetables and spices, bring to a boil and simmer for 5 minutes. Lay the herring fillets in an ovenproof dish, cover with the liquid and allow to cool. Cut the pickles lengthways and wrap each fillet around a pickle slice. Secure with a toothpick. Return the rollmops to the marinade and leave for 4–6 days before serving.

1

2

3

4

The "Krauts"

Perhaps the favorite vegetable in Germany is the cabbage, and as such, it is the derogatory name given to Germans abroad. All kinds of cabbage are rich in vitamin C, mineral and ballast stuffs, and low in calories. Tasty and economical, cabbage has long been considered a classic among army folk. The white cabbage in particular plays a leading role as it is the primary ingredient in sauerkraut.

In Northern Germany, the wrinkly-leafed green cabbage is almost like a cult-dish. A few evenings of light frost will bring it into its full flavor. The frost converts its starch into sugar and makes it more tender.

Sauerkraut

Sauerkraut is made from strips of salted white cabbage. In the fermentation process, lactic acids develop and give the dish full flavor. It is best bought ready-made, but the Offenburg refinement is well worth trying.

2 onions
2 sour apples
2 Tbs (30 g) goose fat
1 lb (500 g) fresh sauerkraut
6 juniper berries
10 peppercorns
$^1/_2$ tsp caraway seeds
1 garlic clove
1 cup (250 ml) dry Riesling
1 carrot
A pinch of sugar
Salt
1 potato, peeled and grated

Peel the onions and apples. Chop the onions, core the apple, and cube it finely. Fry them both in the fat until golden brown. Add the sauerkraut and stir over heat for about 5 minutes. Crush the juniper berries, peppercorns, caraway seeds, and garlic in a mortar and add them to the skillet. Pour in the Riesling, lay the carrot on top, cover the skillet and simmer for about 90 minutes. Remove the carrot, sprinkle in the sugar and salt to taste. Thicken a little with the potato.
Sauerkraut is popular with *Eisbein* and *Schweinshaxe* but also with sausages or the famous Pfalz Pig's Stomach.

Background: A prime white cabbage, one of the adaptable German cabbages, and basis for *Sauerkraut*.

1

2

3

4

German Cabbages

Cauliflower (illustration 1)
Stalk and leaves are removed. It is cooked either whole or as florets.

Broccoli (illustration 2)
Green or (less often) purple sort of cauliflower relative, also called "asparagus cabbage". The tender buds of the stalk taste best when steamed.

Green Cabbage
Also known as "wrinkled" or "winter cabbage," it is especially tasty after the season's first frost. Popular with sausage and game.

Kohlrabi
There are white and blue kohlrabi, both with delicate tasting tubers. The vitamin-rich leaves are also often chopped finely for use.

Brussels Sprouts
Small cabbages so-called because they are cultivated in Belgium. The little rosettes grow like grapes in the axis of the stem's stalk-like leaves.

Red Cabbage (illustration 3)
Similar to white cabbage, it has a dense round or oval head, but as it tastes sweeter, is often prepared with sour apples.

Pointed Cabbage
This nutritious cabbage has a pointed head and smells of cabbage only mildly. It is only available in spring and summer.

Savoy Cabbage (illustration 4)
A delicious winter vegetable with wrinkled leaves which are green outside and yellow inside. The leaves are well-suited as a vehicle for stuffing.

Stewards' Meal of Fellowship

Green cabbage with *Pinkel*, a fatty sausage, is an important part of the traditional Stewards' Meal of Fellowship in Bremen. *Schaffer*, the name for the steward of provisions aboard ship, is also the name of the meal of fellowship which has been shared annually on the second Friday in February since 1545 at Bremen's City Hall. It commemorates the festive last meal of ship-owners and sailors who set off on new sea journeys after the winter break. Outsiders, who according to regulation may only be invited once, come in formal dress tails.

The meal recalls the traditional sailors' fare. It begins with chicken soup, includes stockfish, and is washed down with beer brewed for the occasion.

The main course, *Grünkohl mit Pinkel* (recipe p. 256), is accompanied by smoked meat with chestnuts and baked potatoes. Whoever dislikes either of those can have veal and baked plums instead. Cheese and smoked flounder follow, and in addition to the sailors' beer, guests enjoy Rhine and Bordeaux wines. Every guest has a silver sack at his place for salt, a gold one for pepper – to recall the time when both spices were so costly that guests were asked to bring their own.

At the end of the meal, which lasts from 3 through 8 p.m., collection boxes for the *Haus Seefahrt* circulate. Guests' generous contributions are used to support former sea captains and their widows.

Variety of Greens

Vegetables

German cuisine has a countless variety of vegetable dishes. From the time it was proven that vegetables had to be carefully cooked to retain their vitamin and mineral content, the vegetable plate has advanced markedly to the status of delicacy.

Vegetables are usually served in Germany as accompaniments to meat or fish, but in many regions, vegetable dishes which serve as main courses in their own right have been devised. *Lübecker National* is one such dish, a carrot casserole with pig's belly, the mixed vegetables with bacon dish called *Holsteiner Dickmusik* is another. *Westfälische Blindhuhn* is made of beans, carrots, potatoes, and apples, and the other all-in-ones include *Pichelsteiner Topf*, Berlin's *Teltower Rübchen*, Brandenburg pea soup, and famous "Thick Beans with Bacon" dish from the Rhineland. The so-called "Leipzig Hodgepodge" from Sachsen has achieved world renown.

Grünkohl mit Pinkel
Green Cabbage with Pinkel Sausage
(Illustration)

The people of Bremen are the biggest fans of this dish (which they call "brown cabbage") and it is associated there with a dubious honor: whoever is the last to stop eating at a Green Cabbage with Pinkel Sausage "orgy" gets the *Fressorden*, the Order of the Feast. Such contests are held in the rural surroundings of the city: country inns advertise for them in winter with their offerings, and whole parties seat themselves around the rustic tables. To aid digestion, Schnapps or other liquor is consumed.
A sociable meeting of an entirely different kind is the Stewards' Meal of Fellowship (see preceding page).

3 lbs (1½ kg) green cabbage
5 oz (150 g) smoked bacon
1 Tbs fat
5 oz (150 g) pig's stomach
1½ cups (350 ml) bouillon
2 Pinkel sausages
Salt, black pepper, nutmeg

Clean the cabbage by removing the limp and spotted leaves as well as ribs. Wash thoroughly and boil in salted water for 1–2 minutes, allow to dry and chop coarsely.
Cube the bacon, fry in a large pot and add the fat. Add the cabbage and the pig's stomach, pour in the broth and simmer in the pot for about 45 minutes.
Slide in the sausages, add a little water if the vegetables are still too hard, and cook for an additional 15 minutes, stirring occasionally so that the cabbage does not stick to the bottom. At the end of the cooking time, remove the sausages and keep them warm. Season the cabbage with salt, pepper, and nutmeg and serve with the warm sausages.

Pichelsteiner Topf
Pichelstein Stew

8 oz (250 g) mutton
8 oz (250 g) veal
8 oz (250 g) pork
8 oz (250 g) beef
Just under 8 oz (200 g) beef marrow
8 oz (250 g) carrots
8 oz (250 g) celery
8 oz (250 g) onions
8 oz (250 g) potatoes
1 small Savoy cabbage
3¼ cups (750 ml) bouillon
Salt, black pepper, nutmeg
1 bunch of flat parsley, washed and chopped

Cube the washed and dried meat. Rinse the marrow, pat it dry and slice it. Peel or clean and chop the vegetables. Wash and chop the parsley.
Melt the marrow in a large cooking pot, and heat the stock in another.
When the marrow has melted, layer the vegetables and meat over it. Pour in the stock, cover and simmer for about 60 minutes. Stir, season with salt, pepper, and nutmeg and garnish with parsley.

Leipziger Allerlei
Leipzig Hodgepodge
(Illustration below)

1 Tbs dried morels
Lukewarm milk
Bouillon
Butter
8 oz (250 g) carrots
8 oz (250 g) green beans
1 cauliflower
8 oz (250 g) asparagus
8 oz (250 g) peas
Salt, black pepper
Finely chopped parsley

White sauce

1/4 cup (50 g) butter
1 Tbs flour
1 cup (250 ml) bouillon
1 cup (250 ml) light cream

Soften the morels in the lukewarm milk and water for 30 minutes, rinse thoroughly and drain. Simmer them for 10 minutes in the meat stock, to which a pat of butter has been added.
Wash and chop the vegetables. Put them in a large pot of water with 1 teaspoon of sugar and bring to a boil. Gradually add the vegetables: first the carrots, then the beans, followed by the cauliflower florets, the asparagus, and the peas. When the vegetables are cooked through, drain them, then butter and season to taste. Slice the morels and combine with the vegetables.
To make the sauce, heat the butter in a saucepan, stir in the flour and add the stock, stirring constantly. Add the cream and season with salt and pepper.
Serve the vegetables in a bowl and garnish with parsley, and offer the sauce separately.

Erbsensuppe
Pea Soup

For centuries, Prussian soldiers enjoyed pea soup as a main meal.

1 lb (500 g) dried peas
10 oz (300 g) ham hock
10 oz (300 g) pickled pork
1 1/2 lbs (750 g) potatoes
Celery, leek, carrot, parsley
Salt
Marjoram

Soften the peas overnight in a generous amount of water. The next day, bring the water to a boil and drop in the meat. Skim off the husks and fat.
Peel and cube the potatoes, clean, wash, and chop the celery, leek, carrot, and potato. After 60 minutes' cooking time, remove the meat and cut it into bite-sized pieces.
Add the potatoes to the peas. Let the soup simmer for about 2 hours until the peas are beginning to soften. Then add the vegetables and continue cooking for 30 minutes. Season with salt and marjoram and return the meat to the soup before serving.

Linseneintopf
Lentil Stew
(Illustration bottom)

1 lb (500 g) lentils
10 oz (300 g) smoked bacon
Tomato paste
2 1/2 cups (500 ml) bouillon
2 carrots
2 onions
2 leeks
1/4 of a celery stick
10 oz (300 g) potatoes
1 bunch of parsley
1 branch of lovage
4 smoked sausages
Vinegar
Salt, black pepper

Wash the lentils. Add them to the stock with the tomato paste and bacon and a generous amount of water. Cook for about 60 minutes.
Peel, clean, and chop the vegetables, and add them to the lentils to cook for about 20 minutes. Wash and chop the herbs, slice the sausages, remove the bacon and cut it into bite-sized pieces. Add everything to the lentils and slowly bring up to heat. Season with vinegar, salt, and pepper to taste.

Seasonal Vegetable

Asparagus

Asparagus is eaten with great gusto in Germany between April and June. The white variety is preferred to the green asparagus eaten in Italy and France. Its heads, for lack of light, have not turned blue, and it is harvested before sunrise for that reason, then transported along the shortest possible route to market and traded immediately. Asparagus has an ancient culture: it was known as early as 200 BC as a costly vegetable. The Roman Emperor Diocletian (284–305 AD) issued an imperial decree relating to its price.

The plant was first cultivated in Germany near Stuttgart in 1568. Still a culinary luxury, asparagus is more or less subject to a "rule of thumb": the whiter and thicker the stalk, the more costly it will be. Scratch it with the thumbnail, and fresh asparagus will exude a little liquid.

It is prepared in the simplest way: calculate a pound per person, cook and serve with melted butter, new potatoes, and ham. An assortment of sauces and of fresh-baked egg cakes also go well with asparagus. In the areas where asparagus is grown in quantity, hosts of restaurant specialize in simple methods of preparation to attract an annual influx of tourists. It is also served in season as an accompaniment to roast beef, smoked salmon, or poached fish.

Below: German – as a rule, white – asparagus is primarily grown in the country's southwest region and is one of the most noble of vegetables. It is planted in raised beds and harvested when its head has just come up through the soil. Asparagus is rich in Vitamins A and C and many minerals. As it is made up of 90 percent water and low in calories, it is the perfect vegetable for someone slimming.

Stangenspargel
Asparagus

4 lbs (2 kg) white asparagus
1 small glass dry white wine
¹/₂ tsp salt
¹/₂ tsp sugar
1 Tbs (20 g) butter

Peel the stalks lengthways with a small, sharp paring knife or asparagus peeler. Lop off the bottoms so that all the stalks are the same length. In a large cooking pot – or a special asparagus pot – bring the water to a boil with the wine, salt, sugar, and butter. Bind the asparagus and drop it carefully in the pot, and cook for 20 minutes, covered, in the boiling water. Drain, and then serve with melted butter or hollandaise sauce from a folded fabric napkin.

Cream of asparagus soup can be made from the broth by adding hot milk and thickening with egg yolk and cream.

Sauce Hollandaise
Hollandaise Sauce

1 cup (250 g) butter
2 egg yolks
3 Tbs white wine
Salt, white pepper
Lemon juice

Melt the butter, skim the fat and allow to cool.
In a small and heavy saucepan, and over low heat for 2–3 minutes, beat the egg yolks with the wine until creamy. Take care that the bottom of the pan does not get so hot that the eggs congeal. Remove the pan from the heat and gradually, drop by drop, whisk the melted butter into the egg mixture. Season with salt, pepper, and lemon juice.
The basic hollandaise sauce recipe allows many variations: adding fresh whipped cream results in a *sauce mousseline*, for example. Adding shallots, white wine, and chopped tarragon make a *sauce béarnaise*, while tomato paste makes a *sauce Choron*.

The German Noodle
Spätzle

German children love "Pagetti," or the wheat noodles of Italian origin. One easily forgets that there was always a highly-developed noodle culture in Germany, particularly in *Swabenland*, the area of the Swabian Jura where *Spätzle* was invented. Those familiar with Italian noodles will have trouble understanding this variety. Producing them depends on a handiness developed around them which is unique to this part of the world. Their high egg content means that *Spätzle* are softer and juicier than other noodles. While they are available ready-made, there is no reason for cooks not to make their own.

Traditionally, the southern Germans have been, and are the great noodle consumers. Almost one half of the noodles produced in Germany are consumed in Bavaria and the region of Baden-Württemberg. While half the population lives in the North, it enjoys only twenty-eight percent of the country's noodles.

Noodles count among the oldest of man's basic foods. Even prehistoric peoples ground their grain, kneaded dough from it in combination with liquid, and left the flatcake to dry in the open air before cutting it into thin slices and serving the noodles in a warm broth. The most ancient recipe for noodles, in combination with chicken, appears in a culinary guide from China which is 4,000 years old. At that time, noodles were made from eggs, wheatmeal, and water – a combination somewhat like German egg noodles today.

In Europe, pasta recipes are found as early as the first century AD in the cookbook of the Roman Apicius. The Germans may not be far wrong when they contend their noodles are throwbacks to the time of Roman occupation.

1

2

3

4

5

6

Spätzle
(Illustrations 1–6)

3 ½ cups (400 g) flour
4 beaten eggs
1 tsp salt
¼ cup (50 g) butter

Sift the flour into a bowl. Add the eggs with the salt and 2–3 tablespoons of water. Combine the ingredients thoroughly, gradually adding an additional ³/₄ cup (150 ml) water and kneading the dough until it forms bubbles (1). Bring the salted water to a boil in a large cooking pot. Dip a wooden board with a handle, better yet, a *Spätzle* board, into the water briefly, smooth the dough over the board (2) and with a large, flat knife or *Spätzle* scraper, scrape the dough in thin strips into the water (3). Repeat the procedure as long as it takes to use up the dough. The *Spätzle* are done when they rise to the surface (4). Skim with a large skimming spoon (5) rinse with cold water and drain.
Heat the butter and turn the noodles in it until they are hot and puffy. Serve immediately with a roast or chopped meat.
Spätzle can also be "melted" by covering them with buttered bread crumbs just before serving.

Käse-Spätzle
Cheese-*Spätzle*

A delectable variation on the *Spätzle* prepared on the left are Cheese-*Spätzle*. Grate 2 cups (400 g) Gruyère cheese and layer it with *Spätzle* in a pre-warmed large bowl. Pour a mixture of melted butter and roasted onions over the dish.
In some parts of Germany, *Spätzle* are made round in the so-called *Knöpli* ("little heads"). Emmental, Romadur, and Limburger are the cheeses popularly used, as all three have a relatively short time of ripening and lend a piquant, salt-spicy taste to the dish.

Vitamins from the Garden

Fruit

Almost every German landowner, and no fewer city dwellers, have a little kitchen garden in which to grow fruit and vegetables for their own use. In season, there is a zealous exchange of products among gardeners and non-gardeners, and in order to make it through the winter comfortably, the excess fruit and vegetables are preserved and conserved. The country woman's greatest pride is a cellar stocked with glass jars and filled with fruit and vegetables, jams and juices. While the vitamin content of these conserved goods can be argued, they do serve the guest as a pleasant reminder of the summer past and spark his enthusiasm for the season to come.

German Country – Apple Country

Talk about fruit in Germany, and the apple will come up. The ancient fruit, so closely tied to many myths and legends, is the favorite of the German people. Adam and Eve had to leave Paradise because of it; and Hercules stole three golden apples. When Paris chose Helen as the most beautiful of all Greek women, an apple was at issue. In Norse mythology, the apple was symbol of love, fertility and eternal youth. And it even had a role to play in politics: as the imperial orb with the cross, it was a symbol of Christian dominion and has been among the German national insignia since the 12th century.

Apples are in season in Germany all year round. Some sixteen million apple trees in 24,000 orchards ensure a profitable harvest. Of the 1,000 different kinds – one hundred traded regionally and fifteen to twenty traded farther afield – there is something for every taste: apples with fresh-sour, tart, mild, or aromatic taste and fruit flesh which is either sweet, crunchy, juicy, delicate, or hard.

The apple can be used in many ways in cooking, especially in combination with other foods. Apples go with liver as well as herring, with pork as well as lamb. Duck and goose are stuffed with apple, and sauerkraut and red cabbage come into their own flavors with its addition. In the Rhineland, apples are combined with potatoes in a dish called "Heaven and Earth." Among baked goods, apple cake is a leader – whether baked in sweet dough or fried in an apple pancake.

Alkmene
Sweet-fruity, slightly sour, aromatic
Picked: beginning through mid-September
Best eaten: September through end of November

Berlepsch
Slightly sour, very aromatic
Picked: end of September through beginning of October
Best eaten: November through March

Glockenapfel
Tart, refreshing
Picked: mid-October
Best eaten: February through June

Gloster
Delicate fruity, sour
Picked: mid-October
Best eaten: November through May

Holstein Cox
Slightly sour, spicy
Picked: mid-September through mid-October
Best eaten: October through March

Ida Red
Mildly sour
Picked: mid-October through end of October
Best eaten: January through July

Jonagold
Sweet to slightly sour
Picked: end of September through mid-October
Best eaten: October through May

Jonathan
Sweet, mildly sour
Picked: end of September through mid-October
Best eaten: December through July

Russet
Fruity, sour
Picked: end of September through mid-October
Best eaten: December through April

Cox's Pippin
Sweet-sour, typically sharp and highly aromatic
Picked: mid- through end of September
Best eaten: October through March

Elstar
Delicately sour, sharp, refreshing
Picked: end of September through beginning of October
Best eaten: end of September through March

Golden Delicious
Sweet-sour, refreshing
Picked: beginning through end of October
Best eaten: November through July

Goldparmäne
Sweet-fruity, nut-like aroma
Picked: mid- through end of September
Best eaten: October through December

Gravenstein
Refreshingly tart, particularly aromatic
Picked: end of August through beginning of September
Best eaten: September through November

Ingrid Marie
Delicately sour, mild
Picked: mid- through end of September
Best eaten: October through March

Jamba
Mildly sour, aromatic
Picked: mid-August through the beginning of September
Best eaten: mid-August through end of October

James Grieve
Sour-sweet, sharp
Picked: end of August through beginning of September
Best eaten: end of August through end of October

Klarapfel
Mildly sour to sour
Picked: beginning of July to beginning of August
Best eaten: mid-July through mid-August

McIntosh
Sweet-aromatic, mild
Picked: mid- through the end of September
Best eaten: September through April

Apples are the most popular fruit in Germany, and are prepared and presented in a variety of ways: as in a jelly, sauce, or compote, or as an accompaniment to cabbage dishes, as filling, juice, preserved in rum, or fermented to make apple wine. The palette of apples here shows those known far and beyond their own orchards and gives a brief description of their characteristics.

261

Apfelgelee mit Mandeln
Apple Jelly with Almonds

Juicy, tart apples, or crabapples have a high pectin content that makes them well suited to use in jellies or compotes. Crabapples, most probably the ancestor of eating apples, are so sour that they cannot be eaten raw. The little red fruits are only available for a short time in the fall.

4 lbs (2 kg) untreated apples
Preserving sugar with pectin in an amount relative to liquid
Grated zest of 1 untreated lemon
3 oz (100 g) sliced almonds

Wash and quarter the apples, leaving the core and peel. Put the fruit into a large cooking pot, cover with water and bring to a boil. Simmer until the fruit is soft – the time will be variable depending on the density of the fruit. Put the fruit mash in a linen towel or special juice towel and let the juice drip into a bowl overnight. Avoid wringing or squeezing, as this will discolor the jelly. Measure or weigh the juice and use exactly the same amount (1:1) of sugar. Add them both to a large saucepan with the lemon juice. Bring to a boil and cook for 5 minutes, stirring constantly.
Remove from the heat, leave to cool slightly and stir in the almonds. Spoon the jelly into prepared jars and seal immediately.

Bratäpfel mit Aprikosensauce
Baked Apples with Apricot Sauce
(Illustration bottom)

4 large, untreated apples
1 can of apricots
2 Tbs raisins
5 oz (150 g) raw marzipan
Just under 1/2 cup (80 ml) apricot liqueur
6 oz (200 g) heavy cream
1 packet of vanilla sugar
2 Tbs sugar

Wash the apples and remove the cores.
Drain the apricots, cube three of them and purée the rest. Combine the apricot cubes with the raisins, marzipan and half the apricot liqueur, and press the mixture down into the apples with a spoon.
Place the apples on a tin baking sheet and bake in a hot oven at 425 °F (220 °C) for about 20 minutes.
In the meantime, beat the cream until stiff. Combine the beaten cream with the apricot purée, the sugar, vanilla sugar, and the rest of the liqueur.
Divide the dish into portions, pour the sauce over the fruit and serve.

Strawberries and Plums

After the apple, the second most-loved fruits are the strawberries of spring and early summer and the late summer harvest of plums and damsons. Strawberries are cultivated under glass starting in March and April. However, when the season begins – end of May through the beginning of July – strawberries are to be found growing in fields all over Germany. Signs by the side of the road invite you to "pick your own." Everybody gets a basket, strolls into the field, and has a good time of the usually tiresome bending and picking. Eating as you go is part of the fun, as you only weigh and pay for the berries that you collect in the basket.

Most plums are available from mid-July through September, some varieties into October. Plum cake (recipe opposite) is a treat that is anticipated for months.

Erdbeerquark
Strawberry Soft Cheese

2 lbs (1 kg) fresh strawberries
2 containers cream Quark (farmer's cheese)
1 packet of vanilla sugar
2 egg yolks
Juice of 1 lemon

Wash and quarter the strawberries and put a few whole berries aside. Combine the Quark, vanilla sugar, and egg yolks thoroughly in a bowl. Purée the berries and fold into the cheese mixture. Serve in small bowls with the whole berries as garnish.

Sommerlicher Obstsalat
Summer Fruit Salad
(Illustration far left)

1 untreated apple
1 untreated pear
Lemon juice
8 oz (250 g) purple grapes
4 oz (125 g) blueberries
4 oz (125 g) strawberries
4 Tbs sugar
1/2 cup (100 ml) Port

Rinse and dry the fruit. Quarter the apple and pear and remove their cores. Slice the quarters and sprinkle immediately with lemon juice to avoid discoloring. Halve the grapes and strawberries.
Put all the fruit in a bowl. Mix the port and sugar and pour over the fruit, and let it chill in the refrigerator for about an hour before serving in a decorative glass bowl.

Summer Fruit Salad

Baked Apple with Apricot Sauce

Cake

Because sugar had to be imported and was beyond most people's means, cake in the Middle Ages was reserved for the rich, not only in Germany. It was traded at prices similar to those of exotic spices needed for cake-baking. While commoners used honey as a sweetener and had to do without sugar for the most part, a lively culture of confections developed in the royal courts. The pleasure of sweets at court was so taken for granted that the French Queen Marie Antoinette, confronted with starving demonstrators in front of the royal palace in Paris declared: "They have no bread? Then let them eat cake."

The unstoppable ascent of the confectioner's art began with the chemist Andreas Sigismund Marggraf, Director of the Chemical Laboratory of the Academy of Scientists in Berlin. It was he who discovered beet root as a sugar source and thereby established the basis for a German sugar industry. The resulting lower prices meant sugar became a favorite culinary treat, and the establishment of coffeehouses at the beginning of the 19th century helped its reputation along even more. The coffeehouses were the meeting places of the rising bourgeoisie – and before long, a first step towards the emancipation of women who got out and about to enjoy their coffee and cake. This is not to suggest that home-baking lost any of its attraction. In fact, many of today's cake recipes have their origins in that era.

Quark-Streuselkuchen
Moist Streusel Cake

Streusel cake is *the* cake eaten with coffee in Germany. Its simplicity is what makes it so good.

Dough

3 1/4 cups (400 g) flour	
2 Tbs (25 g) yeast	
1 cup (250 ml) lukewarm milk	
1/3 cup (80 g) sugar	
1/3 cup (80 g) butter	
2 eggs	
Peel of 1 untreated lemon	
Pinch of salt	
Pinch of allspice	

Filling

1 cup (250 ml) milk	
1/3 cup (90 g) sugar	
1 oz (30 g) cornstarch	
1 cup (250 g) Quark soft cheese	
Juice and grated peel of 1 untreated lemon	
1 Tbs rum	

Streusel

3 cups (350 g) flour	
1 cup (200 g) butter	
1 cup (200 g) sugar	
Drop of vanilla essence	

To make the dough, sift the flour into a large bowl, make an indentation in the middle and crumble the yeast into it. Add half the milk and a little sugar and stir down some of the flour from the sides before putting it aside, covered, for 15 minutes in a warm place. Dilute the butter in the remaining milk, and stir in the rest of the sugar, the eggs, lemon peel, salt and allspice. Add the milk mixture to the flour dough and beat the dough to a loose, smooth consistency. Let it rise again for 20 minutes.
Preheat the oven to 400 °F (200 °C). Roll out the dough, lay it on a baking sheet, and prick it several times with the tines of a fork.
For the filling, bring the milk and sugar to a boil. Add the cornstarch to a little milk and thicken, then set aside to cool. Stir in the *Quark*, lemon juice, lemon peel, and rum, and spread the mixture in a layer over the dough.
To make the streusel, work the flour, the butter, sugar, and the vanilla between the fingers and distribute evenly on top of the *Quark* layer.
Bake for about 25 minutes, and allow to cool before cutting to serve.

Pflaumenkuchen
Plum Cake
(Illustration above)

Early fall in Germany heeds the call of plum cake, whose Bavarian origins are in Augsburg. Heavily sprinkled with sugar and eaten warm, plum cake counts among the most special of the pastry chef's seasonal delicacies. Some prefer a yeast dough for the bottom layer, others a baking powder cookie dough, as is given in the recipe here.

Dough

3 1/4 cups (400 g) flour	
2 tsp baking powder	
Pinch of salt	
3/4 cup (150 g) sugar	
3/4 cup (150 g) butter, at room temperature	
2 eggs	
4–5 Tbs chilled milk	

Fruit Layer

3 lbs (1 1/2 kg) plums or damsons	
5 Tbs sugar	
Cinnamon (optional)	

Combine the baking powder and salt with the flour. Cream the sugar, butter and eggs and add them to the flour mixture. Pour in the milk and work to a smooth and fairly thick dough. Spread the dough onto a large, buttered baking sheet.
Preheat the oven to 400 °F (200 °C). Rinse, core, and halve the fruit. "Tile" the surface of the dough with the upright fruit, and bake for about 30 minutes. Remove the sheet from the oven and cool for a few minutes. Before cutting, decorate with sugar, and cinnamon if desired.
Variation (as in the illustration): make a streusel dough from 1 1/4 cups (150 g) flour, 1/2 cup (125 g) sugar, 1/2 cup (125 g) butter, and a pinch of cinnamon worked through the fingers. Before baking, decorate the fruit layer. Once it is done, serve quickly and warm from the pan to avoid the streusel absorbing all the fruit juice.

But with Cream, If You Please

Tortes

A German torte may well look too pretty to eat. The pastry chef imagines all sorts of refined combinations and ornamental finishes which might easily be called works of art. Children have eyes like saucers when a torte comes to their festive table, decorated with candles for a birthday or a bride and groom for a wedding.

While the most popular torte is undoubtedly the Schwarzwalder Kirschtorte, the other tortes are equally beautiful. All are substantial, too, as cream and buttercream are their basic ingredients. Their far healthier relatives, the fruit tortes, can be considered more humble, yet even they come "with cream" for maximum satisfaction.

Schwarzwälder Kirschtorte
Black Forest Cherry Torte
(Illustration below)

1½ lbs (700 g) sour cherries (2 jars)
1 Tbs cornstarch
½ cup (100 g) sugar
1 cinnamon stick
1 chocolate cookie cake layer, diameter 10 in (26 cm)
3¼ cups (750 ml) cream
2–3 Tbs Kirsch
Chocolate shavings

Drain the sour cherries. Add a little juice to the cornstarch and boil about a cup (250 ml) of juice with ¼ cup (40 g) sugar and the cinnamon stick. Remove the cinnamon stick and thicken the liquid with the cornstarch. Boil again, add the cherries, reserving a few for the decoration, stir carefully with a wire whisk, then remove from the heat and allow to cool.
Slice the cookie layer twice through, combine the remaining sugar with the cream and beat until it forms stiff peaks. Spread a thin layer of cream over the first chocolate cookie layer, use a pastry bag to make 4 concentrated cream stacks on the layer, and fill the remaining surface with half the sour cherries. Add the second cookie layer, press lightly and sprinkle with Kirsch (diluted with sugar water if desired). Cover with the remaining cherries and a thick layer of cream. Add the third layer and again, sprinkle with Kirsch. Cover the top and sides with cream, make cream rosettes using the pastry bag, and garnish them with the whole cherries. Garnish the center and sides with the chocolate shavings.

Frankfurter Kranz
Frankfurt Crown

A crown baking form is needed to make this popular specialty. A cookie dough is baked, left alone to cool over 24 hours, and sliced three times horizontally. Each of the layers is dunked in liqueur or Kirsch and spread with buttercream before the torte is reassembled. The outer layer is evenly spread with cream and sprinkled with burnt sugar, then garnished with buttercream rosettes and candied cherries.
Making the cake is demanding and time-consuming, so most buy their *Frankfurter Kranz* at a good pastry shop.

Schwarzwälder Kirschtorte

Buttercreme
Buttercream

The tortes with the highest calorie counts are the buttercream varieties. They were especially appreciated after the Second World War as symbols of economic recovery and well-being.
There are many ways to make buttercream. This German vanilla version contains relatively little sugar.

½ cup (150 g) sugar
2 heaped Tbs (40 g) cornstarch
3 egg yolks
2 cups (500 ml) milk
2 cups (350 g) butter
Pulp from a vanilla bean

Put half the sugar and the cornstarch in a small bowl, add the egg yolks and pour in half the milk. Using a wire whisk, combine the ingredients thoroughly. Bring the remaining milk, sugar, and vanilla bean pulp to a boil. Add the cornstarch mixture gradually and stir constantly over a high heat.
Cream the butter and add the vanilla cream, making sure they are both at the same temperature, otherwise the cream will curdle.

Käsekuchen
Cheesecake

Cheesecake is one of the most popular German tortes, although every cook knows its pitfalls: baked at too high a temperature, it will crack and fall apart. The art of the cheesecake is in choosing both the right ingredients and baking temperature.

Crust
1 cup (200 g) flour
½ cup (50 g) confectioner's sugar
1 egg yolk
Pinch of salt

Filling
3 oz (80 g) raisins
2 Tbs Kirsch
1 lb (500 g) Quark
4 egg yolks, 4 egg whites
¾ cup (160 g) sugar
Zest of 1 untreated lemon
½ cup (100 g) soft butter
½ cup (50 g) flour
Confectioner's sugar

To make the crust, sift the flour onto the work surface, and make an indentation for the butter, confectioner's sugar, egg yolk, and salt. Add more and more flour to make a crumbly dough. Cut the mixture through with a large knife and knead to a smooth consistency. Wrap the dough in aluminum foil and put in the refrigerator to cool for 1–2 hours.
Roll out the dough into a large circle, lay it in a spring-form, and prick it several times with the tines of a fork. Pre-bake at 375 °F (190 °C) for 10 minutes.
For the filling, soften the raisins in Kirsch, sieve the Quark and add the egg yolks and half the sugar to it. Stir the mixture well, and then add the lemon peel, butter, flour, and raisins.
Beat the egg whites until they form stiff peaks and sweeten with the remaining sugar. Fold carefully into the Quark mixture and spoon onto the top of the pre-baked bottom layer. Smooth the surface, reduce the oven heat to 325 °F (160 °C) and bake for about 45 minutes. Sieve powdered sugar through a stencil over the hot surface so that the caramelized sugar forms a decorative pattern.

Obsttorten
Fruit Tortes

Fruit tortes are amongst the classic baked goods. They were made economically at harvest-time, when fruits were abundant. Every region has its own specialty.

Apple torte is probably the most popular – not the least because it is available all year long. There are other fruits equally well suited to use, however. It is most convenient to buy a ready-made sweet dough or pastry dough crust and top it with blanched, fresh fruit. A simple glaze serves as icing. To protect the delicate fruits in baking, a crust is sometimes baked separately and decorated with either whipped cream or buttercream.

Apfeltorte mit Rum
Apple Torte with Rum

Crust
1 package of frozen puff pastry dough
4 lbs (2 kg) apples
2 oz (60 g) currants
2 Tbs rum (or Calvados)
¼ cup (50 g) sugar

Cream Filling
4 gelatine leaves
3 egg yolks
⅓ cup (70 g) sugar
1 cup (250 ml) milk
Pulp from 1 vanilla bean
3 Tbs rum (or Calvados)
1 cup (250 ml) cream

Icing
1 cup (250 ml) dry white wine
¼ cup (50 g) sugar
1 Tbs cornstarch
2 oz (50 g) sliced, roasted almonds

Thaw the frozen dough and roll out two circles of 11 in (28 cm) diameter. Using a template (dinner plate or pot lid) cut the two to exactly the same size. Rinse a baking sheet with cold water, dry and lay on the two crust circles. Prick each several times with fork tines and bake at 425 °F (220 °C) for 15 minutes.
Peel, core, and wedge the apples. Sprinkle the currants with rum and sugar and leave to stand for 1 hour.
To make the cream filling, soften the gelatine in cold water. Stir the sugar into the egg yolks. Bring the milk and the vanilla to a boil and stir into the egg-sugar combination while the milk is still hot. Press out the gelatine and add to the filling and set aside to cool. Then stir in the rum, beat and fold in the cream.
Spread three quarters of the cream filling between the first and second crust layers. Cover the top and sides with the remaining cream. Drain the apple wedges and generously cover the top of the torte with them. Sprinkle the currants evenly over the apples.
For the icing, boil the wine with the sugar. Add a little water to the cornstarch, spoon it into the wine and heat again. When the liquid is clear, spread it with a pastry brush over the fruit and decorate the edge with the sliced almonds.

Lebkuchen and Printen

There were gingerbread and *Lebkuchen* as early as the Middle Ages. In 1296, "Lebzelter" was recorded as a patrician name, and the invigorating and health-promoting properties of *Lebenskuchen* ("Cake of Life") have been known just as long.

Probably the best of these varieties are the *Oblaten-Lebkuchen* from Nuremberg. The wafers, originally one of the blessed sacraments of the mass, were spread out on hot iron plates and served the monastic bakers of the Middle Ages as a practical baking aid when handling the sticky and sweet gingerbread dough. Thanks to the wafers, the dough did not stick to the baking tin and the finished little cakes remained fresh much longer.

Even today, there is something mysterious about *Lebkuchen*. No wonder, as in addition to flour and honey, they are made with spices from every corner of the world: anise and ginger, cardamom and coriander, nutmeg and cloves, allspice and cinnamon, all of which were rare in medieval times. The ancient imperial and commercial city of Nuremberg took advantage of being at the crossing of trade routes that handled exotic spices. It inaugurated a tradition of gingerbread that has survived without interruption up to this day.

Background: Nuremberg *Lebkuchen* and *Printen* from Aix-la-Chapelle (Aachen) have a long tradition and are world renowned. While there are many variations on both themes today, they still stand for choice taste.

Elisen-Lebkuchen
Gingerbread Elise

Elisen-Lebkuchen, commonly baked at Christmastime, are the highest quality among the so-called Oblaten cakes. The dough must be made of at least 25 percent almonds and/or hazelnuts.

Just under 1 cup (200 g) sugar
1 cup (200 g) ground almonds
1 heaped Tbs candied orange
1 heaped Tbs candied lemon
½ cup (50 g) flour
Pinch of baking powder
Grated peel of 1 untreated lemon
Pinch of salt
1 packet of vanilla sugar
1 tsp cinnamon
3 eggs
1 Tbs rum

Combine all the ingredients, and spoon the dough by teaspoon onto small Oblaten molds which measure 1½ in (4 cm). Bake for about 20 minutes at 350 °F (180 °C), then cover with chocolate or sugar glaze.

Aachener Printen
Printen from Aix-la-Chapelle (Aachen)

Printen are one gingerbread variation. The "original" is not unlike Spekulatius, as its dough is pressed into a wooden mold, while *Printen* takes its name from the pressing process.

At the time when, in 1806, Napolean levelled a sanction against England that permitted no imports, German bakers were left without raw sugar or American wildflower honey. They made do with beet sugar and syrup. The dense, coarser dough could not be made in the usual way, and thus the flat, rectangular cut sweet cake evolved – an emergency solution with whose discovery the baker Henry Lambertz of Aix-la-Chapelle (Aachen) is credited. Their characteristic flavor comes from the crumbs of the candied sugar.

1 cup (250 g) brown candied sugar
1 cup (250 g) candied syrup
1 cup (200 g) candied orange
1 cup (200 g) candied lemon
½ tsp anise
1 tsp Lebkuchen spice (gourmet shop)
4 cups (500 g) flour
1 tsp baking powder
Chocolate glaze

Crush the candied sugar. Warm the syrup with 3 tablespoons of water, and add the sugar, candied orange, candied lemon and spices. Allow to cool. Mix the flour with the baking powder, add the syrup and work into a dough. Let the dough stand 24 hours. Roll out the dough until it is quite thin and cut out strips measuring 1½ by 4 in (3 x 10 cm). Bake at 400 °F (200 °C) for about 15 minutes.
Paint the baked strips with a chocolate glaze.

Marzipan from Lübeck

Whoever strolls through Lübeck will see the sign that has become synonymous with marzipan all over the world: two crossed rings and the stylized doorway with the superimposed monogram JGN. Johann Georg Niederegger was a pastry baker from Ulm who opened his business in Lübeck in 1806.

Niederegger was so successful that, in 1922, he was able to build an establishment across from the City Hall steps in one of Lübeck's most prestigious locations. The Café Niederegger still stands there today, and is an El Dorado for marzipan lovers who select from over 300 kinds of wares – breads and tortes, pralines and filled pastries, fruits and figures, as well as seasonal confections for Christmas and Easter. Marzipan is made of almonds, sugar, and rosewater, and the photographs on the right document production at the historic firm.

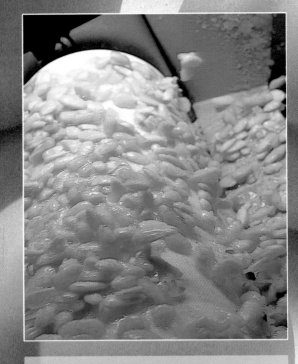

To manufacture marzipan, almonds are covered with fluid sugar before both are ground.

The ground almonds are turned with sugar and rosewater in large copper kettles.

Marzipan

8 oz (250 g) peeled, sweet almonds	
2 cups (250 g) confectioner's sugar	
2 Tbs rose water	

Finely crush the almonds and make a dough by adding them to the sugar and rosewater. Cover and leave in a cool place for 12 hours to blend the flavors.
Form the mass into little figures and dry out in a 250 °F (120 °C) oven for about 30 minutes. Marzipan has a limited shelf-life.
To make it last longer, heat the mass, and stir it constantly in a copper bowl until the candy no longer sticks to the bottom.

How Much Sugar Can Marzipan Contain?

The marzipan purchased in shops contains mostly sugar. According to German food consumer regulations, 1 pound (500 grams) of raw marzipan – which already contain 35 percent sugar – may be combined with an additional 1 pound (500 grams) of sugar. Although the heavy sugar content qualifies it as a candy, the mixture may still be called marzipan. The so-called "Noble Marzipan from Lübeck," on the other hand, contains 1 lb 12 oz (900 g) raw mass and only 4 oz (100 g) added sugar. Niederegger uses strictly raw marzipan in production without additional sugar.

Figures or small blocks are formed from the marzipan mass, and some are covered with chocolate.

Then the articles are dried.

Sweet-smelling marzipan from Lübeck – beautifully packaged – is famous for quality and shipped all over the world.

Marzipan apples – greatly enlarged in the background photograph – are much-loved treats.

Germany – Source of Riesling

Wine

In many parts of Germany, wine has determined the rhythm of life among the simple farming folk for centuries. It gives them work and bread – as well as worldly pleasure after the harvest. Its credit goes back to the Romans, who used the waterways to reach Germania and showed the barbarian people along the route how to plant grapes.

So evolved a wine culture that enjoys world renown today. German wine is delicate and light, has plenty of acidity and little alcohol. Above all, it has made a name for itself through the Riesling, which is derived from the Meriten grape.

The thirteen wine-growing regions count among the most northerly in the world. Germany lies east of the humid and warm Gulf Stream and west of the dry continental climate of the east. It is seldom too hot in the summer, seldom too cold in the winter. While farther south, there are countries which get little or no rainfall, the German vineyards have regular downpours between May and September. So the grapes thrive even in high summer, and the warm fall climate allows a much longer period of ripening, which sometimes stretches as far as into November.

The long ripening period makes a fresh and fruity acidity, a reduced alcohol content and a delicate bouquet. Germany's premier grape, the Riesling, embodies the best of these qualities. No other country has such vast Riesling vineyards nor offers the connoisseur superior white wines quite as elegant.

The Sylvaner is also widespread in Germany. Its wines are more neutral in taste, and it is sometimes called heavy and common, but its grape can thrive in stony or gravel soil. The Müller-Thurgau combines the mildness of the Sylvaner with the flower of the Riesling, a combination devised more than one hundred years ago. Wines of this kind should be consumed when immature, as with age, they lose their typical nutmeg-overtone.

The *Ruländer* (Pinot Gris), which is another important grape in German vineyards, is used to produce heavy wines with a full-bodied bouquet.

If the Riesling takes first place among the whites, then it is the *Blaue Spätburgunder* among the reds. Other favorites among German wines are *Kerner* (a cross between Trollinger and Riesling), *Scheurebe* (of Sylvaner and Riesling), *Blauer Portugieser*, *Trollinger*, and *Gewürztraminer*.

How It Presents Itself

Being cultivated so far north, it can be difficult for German grapes to reach the specific gravity of the must that makes for a harmonious, high-profiled wine. In the final analysis, it is the sugar content in the grape juice that determines the alcohol content of the wine. Sugar may be added to the juice during the process of fermentation, which makes for a higher alcohol content rather than a "sweetening" of the product. During fermentation, the natural and added sugars are converted into alcohol and carbohydrates. The latter disappears, but the alcohol remains and lends substance and aroma to the wine.

Sugar converted into alcohol during fermentation is the measure of ripeness. It determined the specific gravity of the must, or Öchsle-degree, whose name commemorates the apothecary, goldsmith and mechanic Ferdinand Öchsle (1774–1852) in Pforzheim. He invented the *Mostgewicht*, the measuring instrument whose principles are still in use today.

The Öchsle-degree, now measured with a refractory device, show how much heavier a liter of juice is at 69 °F (20 °C) than a liter of water. The sugar content in grams pro liter is extrapolated from the difference, and the potential alcohol content of the wine after fermentation can be estimated.

Background:
Wine harvest in Rhenish Hesse

Apple Wine in Sachsenhausen

Ebbelwoi

Applewine, or *Ebbelwoi* as it is called in Hessan dialect, hails from the picturesque quarter of Frankfurt known as Sachsenhausen. In Munich, the custom is beer and good company in the shade of the summer trees; the custom in Sachsenhausen is for *Ebbelwoi*. It is served from large stoneware pitchers called *Bembel* into ribbed glasses that hold no less than nine fl oz (a third of a liter). The glasses are covered by a wooden lid decorated with carvings, mounted coins or coats of arms, even photographs of relatives. Nobody, even the people of Frankfurt, really understands why this is done. To prevent an insect or a leaf falling in the glass? Perhaps, but then again, the lids are used indoors as well.

Whoever tastes applewine for the first time will find it acerbic and dry, and will most likely decide to dislike it. But the second or third glass will dispel this prejudice. All to the good, as the refreshing thirst-quencher, made of specially selected apples, contains 5.5 percent alcohol and as a natural combination of organic acids and mineral stuffs, is a valuable food product.

Production of applewine begins at the harvest in the beginning of September. Most often, pressing-apples are shaken from the tree and bagged by hand to this day. The hard, juicy fruit must contain the right combination of fruit sugar and fruit acid. During the first process, the apples are reduced to a mash and pressed of their fresh – non-alcoholic – juice, the so-called "sweet juice." Before fermentation, the liquid is measured on the Öchsle-scale to determine fruit sugar and acid content. In the subsequent fermentation, lasting four to six weeks, the fruit sugar is converted into alcohol and carbohydrates.

Then the applewine is removed to large vats or tanks and undergoes fermentation that is completed only in December. A harmonious flavor is conferred to the liquid, but it retains its fizziness thanks to its natural carbohydrates. When drunk at about 50 °F (12 °C), or lightly cooled, apple wine's natural freshness can be best appreciated.

Several culinary specialties are traditionally accompanied by applewine: *Handkäs mit Musik* is a small hand-sized cheese embellished with the "musical" marinade of chopped onions, vinegar, oil, and spices. In Sachsenhausen, *Handkäs* is served only with a knife – no fork, no napkin. Simple: butter your bread, cut off a piece of cheese, and top it with the onions.

Frankfodder Gebabbel
Frankfurt Babble

Ribs with sauerkraut is the other favorite meal served with applewine. In Frankfurt, the ribs are pickled rather than smoked. As it is generally assumed that applewine promotes babble, the drink is also called "babble water" there.

1¹/₂ lb (750 g) pickled ribs
2 onions
2 cloves
5 peppercorns
2 apples
Fat
1¹/₂ lb (750 g) sauerkraut
1 bay leaf
4 juniper berries
1 glass of apple wine

Together with the peeled, coarsely chopped onion, peppercorns, and cloves, cook the ribs in a little water for about 30 minutes. Remove and slice. Peel and chop the second onion; peel, core and slice the apple. Sweat the apple and onion in the fat in a large pot, add the sauerkraut and cook with the bay leaf and juniper berries. Pour in the apple wine and lay in the ribs. Cover and cook through over low heat.

Frankfurter grüne Sauce
Frankfurt Green Sauce

To be served with cooked beef.

4 hard-boiled eggs
Salt
1 bunch of chives
1 bunch of parsley
2 sprigs of dill
1 bunch of mixed herbs
¹/₂ cup (125 ml) oil
Lemon juice
Black pepper
Sugar
Mustard

Peel and halve the eggs, remove the yolks, and press and salt them. Wash, pat dry, and finely chop the herbs, combine with the egg yolks and add in the oil. Chop the egg whites and add them to the mixture. Season with lemon juice, pepper, salt, sugar, and mustard.

Background: In Frankfurt's Sachsenhausen quarter, people crowd around to enjoy *Ebbelwoi* in a relaxed atmosphere.

In Frankfurt, *Ebbelwoi* is served from a *Bembel* or stoneware pitcher.

Pure Quality

German Beer

The World's Biggest Beer Festival

There is a gigantic folk festival in Munich every September: the *Oktoberfest*. Many of the millions of visitors go for one reason alone – to indulge in some hearty drinking.

For its jolly effects to kick in as soon as possible, the beer is drunk from glasses that actually hold a full – or what should be a full – liter of the brew. Tackling the enormous handle of the *Masskrüg* is a skill that must be acquired, as is the drinking rhythm: "A toast, a toast to Gemütlichkeit (good cheer)" that the band leads in the enormous tents to promote sales. Then the solidly-built, spirited service personnel – cross them, and they will give you a piece of their minds – jump to bring re-orders, and carry their loads of up to twelve glasses with aplomb. These might be women you would not want to cross.

Beer is a cult drink not only in Bavaria, but all over Germany. The per-capita consumption is more than 290 pints (140 liters) per year, children and the elderly included. Wine (5½ gallons; 20 liters) figures in second place, and it is only coffee (55 gallons; 200 liters) that the Germans drink more.

Beer in Germany is not just any beer. Whichever kind one prefers can be likened to a philosophy of life, and will spur lengthy discussions and justification. Because it is not only at the *Oktoberfest* that beer is in the limelight. There are plenty of other occasions to pander to the weakness – whether by day in any of the hundred thousand restaurants across the country, or at one of the whole host of festivals that are scheduled in places all over Germany throughout the year.

An Oath to Purity for 500 Years

German brewmasters have been committed for centuries to making beer according to the purity regulations the Bavarian Duke William IV established on April 23, 1516. (A similar regulation had been in effect in Cologne since 1412.) Despite its reversal by the European Court in 1987, which defined limitation to hops and malt, yeast and water in beer as an impediment to European trade, German brew masters do not use any other than these four ingredients. Nevertheless, there are about 5,000 different kinds of

Opposite: In Cologne "top fermented" Kölsch is drunk from "rods" which hold only a half pint (0.2 l). It tastes best on tap as shown here in Brauhaus Päffgen.

beer produced in the country, from the simple beer to the *Maibock*. The important determinants are kind of hops, the yeast cultures used, and the taste of the water in the brewing locale. German beer drinkers honor the brewer's commitment: in 1992, ninety-two percent of 3,000 people surveyed said that they felt the purity regulations ensured quality and wholesomeness of the drink.

In Bavaria, beer is drunk from liter glasses – a challenge not only for the waitresses.

At the *Oktoberfest* in Munich, the band adds more good mood to the beer tent.

Top Fermented and Bottom Fermented

Strictly speaking, there are only two kinds of beer. These are differentiated according to brewing practices and depend on the yeast used in fermentation. Even in 1516, when the Bavarian Purity Regulation was admitted, brewer's yeast was still unknown, so success or failure more or less fell to chance. Only in the 17th century was the effect of yeast documented, and in the 19th century, the Dane Emil Christian Hansen discovered several different sorts of yeast, many of them effective on beer. Having successfully cultivated special yeast, brewers consciously top- or bottom fermented. Most brewers cultivate their own yeast from a single controlled yeast cell, so that all the cells share the same characteristics, and a certain standard of taste is ensured.

Top fermented beer is brewed at a temperature of 60–79 °F (15–20 °C). The added yeast builds additional colonies that rise to the top of the brew at the end of the fermentation process – hence the name – and can be skimmed off. This is the older of the two brewing procedures. And it is hardly by chance that it was in the regions with mild climate and temperatures, such as the Lower Rhine – where a long hard winter is the exception – that a sophisticated top fermented brewing process developed, that used for *Altbier*. Among other top fermented beers, also of limited shelf-life, are *Kölsch*, *Berliner Weisse*, wheat, and malt beers.

Bottom fermented beer presupposes temperatures lower than 50 °F (10 °C). Before the invention of refrigeration in 1876 by Bavarian engineer Carl Linde, bottom fermented beer could only be made in the winter months. Regions with cold, long winters, Bavaria among them, were well-suited for its production. Bottom fermented yeast ferments the malt sugar slowly in about a week, and then attaches to the bottom of the vat. Beer brewed in this way can be stored longer (all lager beers are bottom fermented). Pils, Export, Stout, and bock beer of this type account for eighty-five percent of beer sales and, as such, dominate the market.

Variety from North to South

It is safe to say that beer has been brewed all over Germany since the Middle Ages. Once the task of the housewife, brewing beer became its own business in the last century, primarily as family-owned operations. Most have disappeared in the meantime: first bought up by larger, more worldly competition and eventually closed down. In the big breweries, little of the brewing process is still visible. Impressively large, polished vats, switchboards with electronic lamps and massive stainless steel storage tanks, hundreds of cylinder-formed aluminum vessels in the dispatching department and highly complicated bottling areas the size of football fields that seem to operate magically, have dispelled the old brewery nostalgia.

It is another story in the small and smallest of the private breweries, still extant in Bavaria. They have refused modern technology in the name of tradition – technically less perfect, but still using the old manual means. The native beer drinker will swear by his "own" and have nothing to do with the "premiums." And the smaller brew masters move readily into the niches left empty by the larger breweries – bringing back clamp closures, wooden cases, and even the old wooden vats to the market. Some of them have even become famous beyond their areas and send

Hops, barley malt, yeast, and water are the ingredients for German beer.

their beer to nostalgia-loving customers at great distance. They preserve a tradition that would otherwise disappear.

Beer brewing is a tradition that stems from the numerous medieval monasteries in Germany. It was a privilege reserved for monks who zealously undertook the task and raised the skill of brewing to an art. The most renowned of the monasteries is Weihenstephan, where even today, the aspiring brew masters acquire their credentials in brewing at the University of Munich.

The hub of German beer production lies where most people live: in the Ruhr Valley, Dortmund, and its surrounding areas where the quality of water is good. Among these are the primarily "premium" Pilsner beers; fine brand beers, which are exported – other than to Bavaria – which clings with conviction to its light beers. They include a variety from the top fermented *Weissbier* to bock, to May bock, and to the dark bock beers to the strong *Märzen* specially brewed for the *Oktoberfest*.

Islands of Beer Consumption

When beer plays such a dominant role as a beverage, regional specialties inevitably crop up. It is no wonder that the German beer map looks like a patchwork quilt.

In Berlin, there is *Berliner Weisse*: low in alcohol, a top fermented draft beer based on lactic acid and a third wheat malt, embellished with a "shot" of green juniper or red raspberry syrup and served with a straw.

In Hanover, it is the *Lüttje Lage*. Just as the miner in the Ruhr Valley likes a glass of

The malt and water are cooked in brewing vats. The so-called wort – basis for the subsequent fermentation – develops.

Schnapps with his beer, the citizen of Hanover brings the beer glass and Schnapps glass carefully to his lips so that he can enjoy the flow of the two together.

Alt is a spicy, dark, and top fermented bitter popularly drunk from simple cylindrical glasses in Düsseldorf and the Lower Rhine Valley. Owing to a special roasting process of the grains,

Alt tastes a little like malt. In Düsseldorf's old town, fondly known as "the longest bar in the world," everybody has to drink *Alt*.

Cologne is the city with the most breweries (twelve within city limits, another twelve in the surrounding areas), and it is *Kölsch* which is the favorite there. A "light top fermented full beer with a flavor of hops" consumed from the slim, cylindrical glasses called "rods" (*Stangen*) is also a unique document in the history of German beer. The Kölsch Convention in 1986, specifically regulated origin and markets: *Kölsch* must come

To give a dry flavor, hops are added to the cooking brew.

from Cologne as readily as *Lebkuchen* comes from Nuremberg.

Bamberg's *Rauchbier* ("smoke") has a story in its own right. Its smoky flavor comes from the beech wood fire used to dry its malt.

German Beers

1 Flensburger Pilsner
2 Altenmünster Premium Bier
3 Dom Kölsch
4 Diebels Alt
5 Aecht Schlenkerla Rauchbier
6 Augustiner Bräu München
7 Warsteiner Pilsner
8 Weltenburger Kloster Asam-Bock
9 Ayinger Maibock
10 Königliches Festtagsbier
11 Erdinger Dunkler Weizenbock
12 Münchner Kindl Weissbier
13 Weihenstephan Hefeweissbier
14 Lauterbacher Brotzeitbier
15 Kloster Andechs Doppelbock

1   2   3   4   5

Ingredients and Brewing of German Beer

There are about 5,000 different beers in Germany, all brewed from four ingredients. The basis is barley malt, occasionally also wheat malt. The starch is the springboard for alcohol and carbohydrates, and as such, basis of the beer. The hops are added to give a delicate bitter taste and to increase the drink's shelf-life. Foremost, however, it is the hops that determine the type of beer: depending on which one and what amount is used, a milder or drier beer is produced.

The third ingredient is yeast. Top fermented is the older method with fermentation temperatures between 60 and 70 °F (15–20 °C). Bottom fermented, done at lower temperatures, was brewed during the winter until the advent of refrigeration.

As for water, that with a high calcium content is best suited to dark beers, spring water for light beers. Today, water may be softened industrially before use.

The most important processes in brewing are mashing, cooking the wort, fermentation, and maturing in storage cellars.

"Mashing" denotes the heating and cooking of the shredded malt with water. The "wort" develops and is cooked subsequently with hops.

Yeast is added and the fermentation process, which lasts four to ten days, can begin. Then the immature beer goes into storage tanks where it matures for a few weeks before being transferred to barrels or bottles. At every phase of production, the brew master is able to intervene in order to personalize his beer. Not only the choice of ingredients, but also the length of each process and the final filtering determine a given beer's distinguished taste.

Regional Snacks with Beer

Not only the beers, but also the snacks enjoyed with them, differ according to region.

Berlin

- *Aal jrün mit Jurkensalat*
  Eel steamed in vinegar with cucumber salad
- *Berliner Bierkarpfen*
  Carp in an aromatic gingerbread crumb coating
- *Bollenfleisch*
  Mutton with onions and caraway
- *Bulette*
  Fried beef and porkmeat patty
- *Gänseweisssauer*
  Goose in vinegar gelée
- *Hackepeter*
  Spiced pork patty eaten raw with bread
- *Hoppel-Poppel*
  Leftover meat, potatoes, eggs, and onions
- *Rollmops*
  Roulade of sour herring with cucumber and onions
- *Soleier*
  Pickled hard-boiled eggs
- *Stolzer Heinrich*
  Bratwurst with onions and gravy, served with mashed potato

Bavaria

- *Beuscherl*
  Cooked lung, heart, and spleen
- *Fleischpflanzl*
  Finely ground beef and porkmeat patty
- *Knöcherlsulz*
  Pickled pork knuckles
- *Leberkäs'*
  Baked puréed beef
- *Milzwurst*
  Sausage with tidbits of spleen
- *Obatzter*
  Dressed Camembert
- *Presssack*
  Sausage and collared pork head
- *Radi*
  White radish, decoratively cut in spirals and salted

- *Tellerfleisch*
  Cooked beef with horseradish
- *Wammerl*
  Pig's stomach
- *Weisswurst*
  Mild sausage of veal purée

Rhineland

- *Hämmche*
  Pickled and cooked upper pork shank
- *Halve Hahn*
  Half a rye roll with a slice of Dutch cheese
- *Himmel un Äd*
  Potato and apple sauce with roasted blood sausage
- *Hirringschlot*
  Herring salad
- *Klatschkies met Musik*
  Farmer's cheese with onions
- *Knabbeldanz*
  Meat turned in buckwheat flour and fried
- *Kölsch Kaviar*
  Sliced and fried blood sausage with onions
- *Rievkooche*
  Grated Potato Pancake (recipe p. 252)
- *Suurbrode*
  Beef sauerbraten, originally horsemeat
- *Zizies*
  Fresh sausage

The Ruhr Valley

- *Blindhuhn*
  Potato, bean, bacon, carrot, apple and pear stew
- *Pfefferpotthast*
  Goulash from Westphalia: braised beef cubes in sauce thickened with bread crumbs
- *Pillekuchen*
  Egg pancake with potatoes
- *Potthucke*
  Potato bread with sausage baked inside
- *Töttchen*
  Cubed veal in a light white sauce

6   7   8   9   10   11   12   13   14   15

Elke Meiborg

Netherlands

Were it not for the dunes and dikes, half of Holland would be submerged in water. Large parts of the small and predominantly flat country in the northwestern part of the European continent lie either at or, in fact, under sea level. Confrontation with the waters has determined the Dutch rhythm of life for centuries. Even today, the country is predominantly influenced by agrarian structures – barring the industrial development in the large city agglomerations in its north and west.

Colloquially, the country is divided into areas "above" and "below" the river. The Waal and Lek, the Maas and the Rhine separate it into two parts, and the residents on one side are quick to mock those of the other. Sober, reserved, and parsimonious Calvinists live in the north; "Burgundian" Catholics and lively bon viveur inhabit the south. While such characteristics are exaggerated for the most part, they do contain a kernel of truth. Moreover, they show how, in each of the twelve provinces of a small country, there is a definite regional consciousness. It is reflected in the culinary offerings of each, and almost every nook and cranny prides itself on its traditional specialties.

As in most European nations, the standard of living rose in this century in the Netherlands. But there are dishes that prevail date from "poorer" times – simple and wholesome stews of legumes, potatoes, vegetables, and meat, as well as hearty pancakes so big that they extend over the edge of the plate. Along the coast, the favorites are herring and Maatjes, as well as mussels, which are cultivated in large underwater beds.

Kaas, or cheese, is one of the most important foods. Dutch cheese is world-renowned. The "Holland" seal always stands for The Netherlands, and butter, milk, and milk products are the most important agricultural products for export that carry it. Flowers, fruit, and vegetable cultivation are also crucial to the economy.

Left: The team at the van de Lei cheese shop, Groningen, in front of their extensive assortment of cheeses.

Dutch Cheese

Stone containers for cheese found in archeological excavations testify to milk production in Holland more than 2,000 years ago. Edam cheese was one of the country's leading export articles in the Middle Ages. Edam was a port city at the time, and its cheeses traveled as far as Germany, France, and over the Alps into Italy. The waterway passage to Zuider Zee, Ijsselmeer today, dried up when land was reclaimed in the 1920s

cheese production: in sour milk cheese, lactic acid bacteria thickens the milk; and sweet milk cheese – most cheeses are this kind, the famous Dutch cheeses among them – and so called rennin cheeses. For the latter, the cheese maker adds rennin – an enzyme taken from the stomach of suckling calves – to separate the solids in the milk from the fluid. The rennin causes the milk's proteins to build up and the milk to curdle without turning sour. In this method, other solid parts, like fat, mineral stuffs, and vitamins, are encapsulated.

When the process is completed, the whey is poured off. The so-called *Bruch*, a soft curd cheese, remains. It is cut through and through with a fine-wired and rake-like stirring utensil called a "cheese harp." More whey drains off and the mass becomes harder. The dripping wet

at least four months, and a mature Gouda, ten months or longer. The older the cheese, the more intensive and sharp its taste. During the ripening process, the cheese is turned and brushed many times, usually with a porous plastic that protects the rind from mold.

Contrary to industrial production, cheese is produced from raw milk on Dutch farms and smaller agricultural operations. The raw milk contains some bacteria that is destroyed during pasteurization. Raw milk cheese, which is ready to eat after a three-month ripening period, is markedly different from its industrially-produced relatives.

In order to identify their own cheese products, farmers apply an oval *Boerenkaas* sticker to each; by contrast, the stickers on industrially-produced cheeses are round.

1

2

3

4

5

6

7

8

and 1930s, and the traditional cheese market had to be stopped. Only the historic cheese scale reminds us that this was once a city steeped in that trade.

Today, Gouda counts as the most important cheese. The enormous rounds can weigh as much as sixty-six pound (thirty kg), and the varieties of flavor offer a culinary delight for any occasion.

Steps in Cheese Production

Cow milk is eighty-seven percent water and thirteen percent dry mass. Around ten quarts (about ten liters) of milk are needed in order to make a kilogram of cheese. There are two methods of

Bruch is kneaded in wooden cheese forms (today primarily plastic is used). The cheese is stamped with the *Rijkskaasmerk* (cheese seal) which is the "passport" of every Dutch cheese, the form closed with a lid, and put under the cheese press. After some four to six hours, the cheese goes from there into brine, where it develops a specific aroma and the rind hardens. After a few days, the cheese round is removed from the brine and goes into a temperature and humidity-controlled storage area to ripen. The ripening process can last a few weeks to as much as over a year. An immature Gouda, for example, is stored between four and eight weeks, a somewhat mature Gouda

Above: The production of Gouda is illustrated in this series of photos. After the addition of rennin, the hard and liquid parts of the milk are separated, and a soft curd mass or *Kaasbruch* results (1). It is cut through and through with a "cheese harp," in order to drain more whey (2). Then the *Käsebruch* is kneaded and laid into forms (3) before being pressed for several hours (4). The cheese is removed from the form (5) and put in a salt brine (6), where the aroma develops and the rind hardens (7). Finally, the cheeses are stored in a cool cellar (8) until the desired degree of ripeness has been reached.

Dry Mass and Fat Content

The fat and protein contents of cheese are about equal. Milk protein is particularly nutritious and easily digestible, as it has a biological constitution comparable to that of the human being. Cheese also contains lactose, plentiful vitamins, and mineral stuffs. The latter become more concentrated in the process of cheese production. Indeed, two thick slices of cheese cover the daily requirements for calcium and phosphorus.

The fat content in cheese is given in percent "% fat in the dry mass" on packaging. The dry mass consists of all the parts of the cheese except the water content. During the ripening process, some of the water evaporates. An immature Gouda, for example, contains forty-two percent water, which is reduced to thirty-four percent at the end of the process. The higher the (relative) part of the dry mass, the harder the cheese will be. A so-called "hard cheese" contains more than sixty percent dry mass, a soft cheese between thirty-four and fifty-two percent, or a low-fat farmer's cheese about twenty percent.

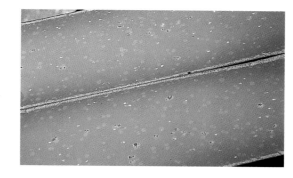

Kaasaardappelen
Cheese Potatoes

8 large potatoes, cooked in their skins
¹/₄ cup (50 g) butter
³/₄ cup (150 g) mature Gouda
Pepper, caraway seeds, paprika, basil

Cut the potatoes in half lengthways and put them face up on a buttered baking sheet. Grate the cheese and strew it over the potatoes. Bake in the oven for about 10 minutes at 450 °F (250 °C). Season with herbs and spices, if desired.

1 Commisie Kaas – Wholesale Cheese
The large round cheese is similar in taste and aroma to Edam. In earlier days, it was ordered and delivered to France "wholesale," and from that was given its name.

2 Maasdammer (Leerdammer) Kaas – Leerdammer Cheese
Belongs to a new group of so-called "Goutaler" cheeses, which combine the firm cut and smoothness of Gouda with the aroma of Emmentaler. It is sold after a ripening period of five weeks, has cherry-sized holes and a mild, nut-like taste.

3 Friese Nagelkaas – Fresian Clove Cheese
Spiced with caraway seeds and cloves, this cheese was once produced on farms in the area of Leyden. It ripens for three months.

4 Kernhemmer Kaas – Kernheimer
This semi-hard cutting cheese, has an especially high fat content (more than sixty percent), an orange-colored rind, and a creamy taste.

5 Goudse Boerenkaas (oud) – Farmers' Gouda (mature)
Produced from raw milk, sometimes with the addition of spices, this cheese is stored at least ten months. As with industrially-produced Gouda, it is available both in an immature and a more mature form.

6 Drentse Kruidenkaas – Drent Herb Cheese
This is a hard, not a cream cheese. It has a relatively high fat content of fifty percent.

7 Geitekaas – Goat's Milk Cheese
Goat's milk cheese is still widely produced by hand on small farms, primarily as a soft cheese. In Holland, it is best known as Limburger when it is spiced with herbs.

8 Edammer Kaas (belegen) – Edam (semi-mature)
The cheese with the typical round form and red or yellow paraffin rind ripens in two to four months. It can be cut, but is softer than Gouda.

9 Leidse Kaas – Leyden Cheese
The mild hard cheese contains twenty or forty percent fat. Like all the Leyden cheeses, it is spiced with caraway seeds.

10 Mon Chou – Dutch White Mold Cheese
This soft cheese, covered with a thin layer of mold, is the Dutch variation on French Neuchâtel. It has a hard, but smooth consistency and a mildly sour taste.

Solid and Long-Established

Stews

The Dutch themselves are often characterized as solid and long-established, and many of their dishes reflect this – the *stamppot*, or stew, foremost among them. This pungent and filling family meal has it origins in the rural countryside, where hard work was always done on the farm, and rarely was there enough food to satisfy. Not surprisingly, the potato is the main ingredient.

The oldest and most popular Dutch stew is the substantial *hutspot*. Made of beef, onions, carrots, and potatoes, the cooked combination takes on a unique taste. The dish is thought to have come from Spain. Evidently the story that the people of Leyden like to tell visitors to their city is authentic: in the 16th century, Leyden was occupied by the Spanish. The half-starved and morally defeated people of Leyden were all but ready to surrender when, on October 3, 1574, the *Geusen* – Dutch freedom fighters – who had joined forces against Spanish rule, chased them away. In their rush to retreat, the defeated Spanish left a earthenware pot that contained a thick bubbling soup made with different meats, root vegetables, and chick peas. The Dutch adapted the dish, calling their vegetable stew with beef and potatoes a *hutspot*, shed pot. Even today, when on the third of October, the day of liberation from the Spanish is celebrated in Leyden, the *hutspot* is the meal, whose story is even marked with a commemorative stone.

Many other stews, too, are prepared from potatoes, butter, and a kind of vegetable one works into a coarse and thick purée. Green cabbage, endive, or sauerkraut can be used for this with *rookworst*, a smoked sausage, or bacon – the possibilities for variation are endless.

Dutch cuisine without its traditional legume dishes would be unthinkable. Most popular among these is *snert*, a pungent soup of green peas and pork, a whole and tasty meal which can be easily prepared.

Ingredients for the *hutspot*: potatoes, carrots, onions, and beef, and in some variations also bacon and *rookworst*, a smoked sausage.

The vegetables are cut into cubes. When cooked they are puréed or mashed.

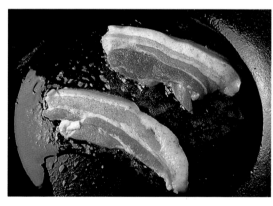

To serve, the meat – either in thick slices or bite-sized pieces – is arranged on a bed of vegetables.

Hutspot met klapstuk
Leyden Vegetable Stew
(Illustrations left)

1 lb (500 g) beef (brisket)
4 onions
1 lb (500 g) carrots
1 lb (500 g) potatoes
Salt, black pepper
Butter
Chopped parsley

Rinse the meat and bring it to a boil in salted water. Let it simmer for 90 minutes.
Peel and slice the onions, clean and cube the carrots, and peel and cube the potatoes. Add the vegetables to the beef brisket in the cooking pot and simmer for another 45 minutes.
Remove the brisket and cut it into cubes. Purée the vegetables and season them with salt and pepper. Arrange the meat on a vegetable bed, spoon brown butter over them and strew generously with parsley before serving.

Snert
Pea Soup

1 lb (500 g) dried green peas
1 lb (500 g) smoked pork/beef sausages, bacon, pickled pork shank or cured pork chop
1 lb (500 g) leeks
2 celery sticks
1 small piece of celeriac (root celery)
Salt, black pepper
2 Tbs chopped parsley

Wash the peas and soak them overnight in cold water, then cook in that liquid for 60 minutes. Clean and finely chop the leeks and celeriac. Add the meat, the celery stalks and the leeks to the peas and simmer for another 30 minutes until the peas are a thick mush. Season heartily, and right before serving, add the celeriac to the soup and garnish with parsley.

Stamppot
Cabbage Stew

Butterfat
1¼ lb (600 g) pork shoulder
5 cups (1l) meat stock
1 lb (500 g) each of white and red cabbage
1¾ lbs (800 g) potatoes
Salt, black pepper
¼ cup (50 g) butter

Heat the fat in a large cooking pot and brown the meat in it on all sides. Pour in the stock and simmer, covered, for 15 minutes.
Clean and quarter the white and red cabbage, remove the stalks, and slice lengthways. Add to the pot and cook for another 20 minutes. Peel, wash, and quarter the potatoes, add to the meat, salt and cook another half hour.
Remove the meat and cut into cubes. Stir the vegetables vigorously to break up the potatoes. Add the butter, and season with salt and pepper. Serve the meat on top of the vegetables.

Holland's Gugelhopf

Poffert

The Dutch bake a delicious small raisin cake that serves four with coffee, as a dessert, or simply as a treat in its own right. While the *poffert* looks like, and has the consistency of the Gugelhopf, it is made without yeast or butter. It requires only a few – readily available – ingredients and is easy to make. The Dutch cut the little cake into slices and spread it with butter, candied sugar, and syrup – indeed a calorie-rich affair. A variation on the cake are the *poffertjes* one finds offered everywhere as a snack. Often, the little portions are made of simple pancake batter.

Poffert
Raisin Cake

1 lb (500 g) flour
1 tsp baking powder
2 cups (400 ml) milk
2 eggs
¾ cup (150 g) raisins and currants
1 packet of vanilla sugar
A pinch of salt

Combine all the ingredients to make a semi-solid batter. Butter two small tins (7 in or 18 cm in diameter) and fill them with the batter. Bake in the oven at about 250 °F (120 °C) for about 60 minutes. Allow to cool before slicing and arranging on a plate.
  In small bowls, serve butter balls, crushed candied sugar and syrup with the cake.

Depends on the Size

Pancakes

Pancakes in the Netherlands, or *pannekoeken*, are legendary because of their size and golden crispiness. Loved by children and adults alike, pancakes are served almost all over Holland in what is called the *pannekoekenhuis*, a restaurant which makes nothing else. They are usually so large that they hang over the plate's edge.

Pannekoeken
Basic Pancake Batter

1 cup (200 g) flour
1/2 tsp baking powder
A pinch of salt
2 eggs

Combine the flour with the baking powder and salt, and add enough cold water to make a thick batter. Stir in the eggs. Heat a little butter in a skillet and spoon in the batter, cooking it both sides to a golden brown. Continue until all the batter has been used.

Spekpannekoek
Bacon Pancakes

Basic recipe for pancake batter (left)
7 oz (200 g) fatty bacon, thinly sliced

Of all the pancakes in Holland, whether sweet or piquant, this is by far the most popular one – a crispy, aromatic delicacy.
Brown the bacon lightly and add only enough batter to cover both it and the bottom of the skillet. Cook the pancake on both sides to a golden brown and enjoy immediately.

Strooppannekoek
Pancakes with Syrup

Basic recipe for pancake batter (left)
Syrup

This is the uncomplicated pancake recipe that children seem to like the best.
The pancake is cooked in the usual way, and the light-brown syrup, which is derived from the sugar beet, is spooned over it. It tastes especially good when the syrup is added to the pan itself and allowed to caramelize a little.

Appelpannekoek
Apple Pancakes

Basic recipe for pancake batter (left)
2 apples
Lemon juice
Granulated sugar

Peel and core the apples and slice them thinly. Turn them in lemon juice so they retain their color, and arrange them like tiles on top of the pancakes. Sprinkle with sugar and cook until the pancake is brown. Using a dinner plate or pot lid, carefully turn the pancake over so that the apples cook and the sugar caramelizes.
Turn once again and serve hot.

Gemberpannekoek
Ginger Pancakes

Basic recipe for pancake batter (left)
1 little pot of preserved ginger

Preserved ginger is sold in the Netherlands in small, oriental blue jars.
Every pancake is strewn with small chunks of ginger and a little of the ginger syrup – which caramelizes – while still in the pan.

A stack of golden brown, crispy Dutch pancakes. They are often eaten with *stroop*, a light brown syrup. Made with bacon (as here), ginger, apples, or other ingredients, pancakes are served all over Holland.

Things Worth Knowing about the Herring

Herring is easily digestible and is an important dietary food. Like the salmon and carp, it belongs to the group of fish that has a twenty-five percent fat content, and is particularly valuable for its essential vitamins and unsaturated fatty acids. The herring, whose existence has long been threatened by over-fishing, has valuable proteins and mineral stuffs like iodine and the B group vitamins vital to metabolism.

Herring live in large schools in open waters, from the Bay of Biscay to the polar cap, primarily in the North and Baltic Seas. They are fished in three stages of development: *Maatjes* are young fish before they spawn, caught primarily in May and June. *Volle haring* are caught in July and August, and from December to April. They have not spawned and are fairly fatty. *Ijle haring* (fish that have spawned and contain much less fat than the other two) are caught in September and October.

Most herring on the market come ready to eat and preserved.
- Green herring are fresh fish well suited to baking and broiling.
- Fried herring are whole fish that have been fried with their bones and are preserved in a vinegar marinade.
- Smoked herring are salted, hot-smoked fish.
- Kippers are cold-smoked herring that must be fried or heated in another way before consumption.

Head First into the Mouth

Maatjes

Herring thrive in the waters along the coast of Holland – particularly in early summer when the young fish have their season. Many Dutch people are absolutely convinced that the only correct way to eat the *maatjesharing* is practiced here: the fish is held at its tail and lowered into the mouth. *Maatjes* are the young fish that have not yet spawned, and their name is derived from the Dutch *maagdekensharing*, virgin herring.

The most important harbor for the Dutch herring fleet is the old holiday and fishing town of Scheveningen. At the end of May – the season begins officially on the 31st with numerous herring festivals – the herring boats head out for the first time, and every year begins with a competition to see who can bring in the first catch of *Hollandse Nieuwe*. The first ton of that catch traditionally belongs to the Queen. The young fish are gutted right after the catch. As such, a part of the pancreas stays intact, and it contains the enzyme which gives the *Maatjes* their incomparable taste. So, too, does the special method with which they are preserved: frozen in salt brine (of a concentration between six and twenty-one percent) in oak barrels. As a result, the fish are mildly spicy. They can be caught, incidentally, until the end of June, at which time they can spawn.

Naturally, fishing in Holland is enormously important. It has an age-old tradition. Until the 12th century, Holland was the leading fishing nation, and there are reports in the 16th century of bitter disputes over fishing grounds and markets with the Norwegians. At that time, as many as 20,000 fishermen were busy in the North Sea. Today, herring is fished primarily by the Danes, because the fish numbers are greatest in the part of the North Sea where Denmark has fishing rights. But the trade of the fish continues to be done by the Dutch to this day.

The name "herring" is said to be of Dutch origin. During the golden age of the herring trade, the Dutch introduced quality control, sealing each wooden crate of saleable fish with a wood-burned ring. The ring is supposed to have inspired the term *haring* itself.

Salting as a preservation technique has been known since early history. Only by using this method was it possible to transport the fish inland or load them as provisions into ships sailing to foreign ports. The Dutchman, Willem Beukelsz, is credited with the invention of pickling, and it is from his name that the term *pekelen*, or to pickle, is derived. We cannot be completely sure of his dates, but he probably worked at the end of the 14th century, at which time the Dutch made enormous strides in herring preservation methods.

The Dutch maintain a large herring fleet whose most important harbor is the old holiday and fishing town of Scheveningen.

The herrings are gutted right after the catch. The first ton of herring *Hollandse Nieuwe*, are traditionally offered to the Queen.

The lightly-salted herring matured in oak barrels are a greatly valued delicacy amongst connoisseurs.

The fish market is the most important trading place for both buyers and sellers.

Maatjes met groene Bonen
Maatjes with Green Beans

8 maatjes fillets
1 lb (500 g) potatoes
½ tsp caraway seeds
Chopped parsley
1 lb (500 g) green beans
1 Tbs (about 20 g) butter
1 cup of stock
Salt, black pepper
Dried savory
6 oz (150 g) fatty bacon
2 onions

Rinse and dry the fish.
Put the potatoes – in their skins – in salted water with the caraway seeds, and cook them through. Peel them while they are still hot, put them in a bowl and garnish with parsley.
Rinse the beans, heat the butter in a pan, and add the stock. Season the stock with salt, pepper and savory, and then cook the beans in it for about 15 minutes. Cube and fry the bacon, and then drain the beans and serve them with the bacon bits on top.
Peel and ring the onion, and use it as a garnish for the *maatjes*.

Maatjessla
Maatjes Salad

8 maatjes fillets
1 small cucumber
2 apples
Lemon juice
2 carrots
1 bunch each of scallions, chives and dill
6 oz (container) of sour cream
6 oz (container) crème fraîche
Salt, black pepper
Sugar

Rinse and drain the fish fillets, and cut them into bite-sized pieces. Peel and halve the cucumber lengthways. Remove the seeds and slice thinly. Peel and core the apples, and sprinkle them with lemon juice so they do not lose their color. Peel and grate the carrots. Slice the onion finely.
Wash and finely chop the chives and dill.
Combine the sour cream and crème fraîche, season with salt, pepper, sugar, and lemon juice and the herbs. Put the fish fillets in a bowl, add the vegetables and the herbed-cream sauce and stir. Serve the *maatjes* salad chilled and with bread, if desired.

Mussels

The Dutch speak of the culture of mussels they farm on the sea floor as their single "natural resource." The annual harvest amounts to about 100,000 tons and is almost all exported to France, Belgium, and Germany. The center of the mussel farms is Yerseke at the mouth of the River Schelde, and those who tend them are called "mussel farmers." In fact, mussel farming has little to do with fishing – only the sowing of the mussel seed and the harvesting of the mature shells is done by boat.

The Dutch method of cultivating mussels is considered one of the most progressive in the world. The small immature shells are sowed in shallow water in parcels that every licensed fisherman leases from the government. When the mussels are about one to one and a half inches (some three to four centimeters long), they are transferred into deeper water and dropped onto nutrition-rich subterranean banks. (In earlier times, the mussels attached themselves to piers, which is why they are also called "pier mussels.") They are harvested twice a year, in May and September. If they have reached their market-ready size – two to four inches (about five to ten centimeters) – they are raised from the sea floor with drag nets and brought to shore in special sea water-storage containers. The containers keep out sand and other impurities until the mussels can be packed and shipped. Thanks to these storage containers and modern refrigeration, it is possible to deliver to both wholesale and smaller markets.

These sophisticated and strictly controlled farming and marketing techniques make it possible to still eat mussels in the months whose names contain an "r" – according to an old rule, while between June and August mussels should not be eaten because of a possible poisoning. In the summer months the animals, filtering the sea water currents, may release the so-called "water blossom," a poison which develops because of a concentration of certain red algae. Today, as almost without exception, only cultivated mussels are available on the market, so the danger of encountering it is small.

The mussels are harvested from the sea banks with large nets.

Later the mussels are transported and flushed with water in special sea water storage containers.

Mosselen in witte Wijn
Mussels in White Wine

4 lbs (2 kg) mussels
2 onions
2 carrots
$\frac{1}{4}$ celeriac (root celery)
1 bunch of parsley
$\frac{3}{4}$ cup (150 g) butter
1 garlic clove
1 bay leaf
Black peppercorns
1 cup (250 ml) dry white wine

Rinse the mussels under running water and remove the "beards" (1). Toss out any open mussels (they have died). Peel the onion, clean the carrots and celery, and chop all the vegetables into small pieces; wash and chop the parsley. Melt the butter in a large pot and lightly braise the vegetables with the parsley, garlic, bay leaf, and peppercorns (2,3). Dilute with the white wine and add the mussels to the stock. Cover and cook over high heat until the mussels open (4). Remove the pot from the stove and serve them from it.
An empty mussel shell can be used to pry out the meat.

Background: Cooked, open mussels greatly enlarged

1

2

3

4

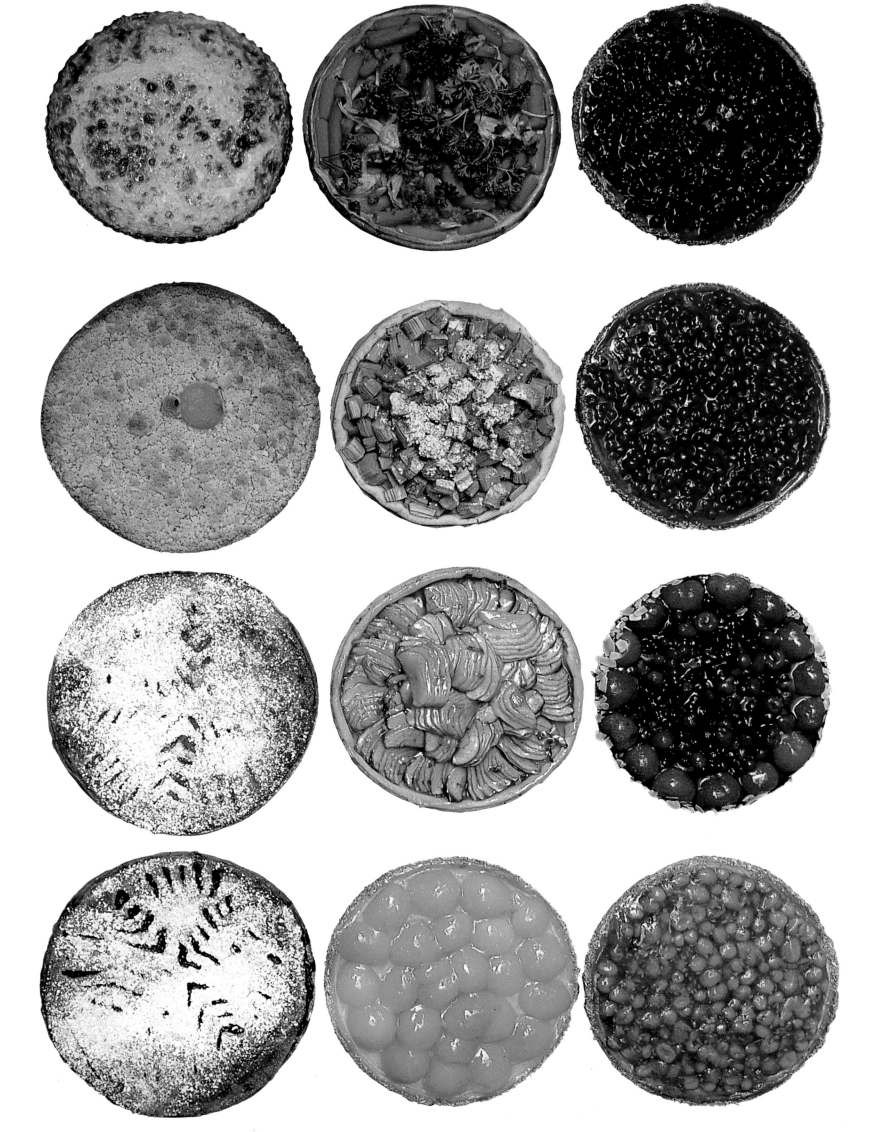

The Delicate Little Torte

Limburger Vlaai

Limburg is not especially typical of The Netherlands. The southernmost province is marked by hills and woods, old monasteries, and cross-timbered houses – one might think to be more in Belgium than in Holland. The Limburger mentality is also different than in the northern parts of the country, where one often confronts puritanism. The specialty of the region is its much-appreciated *Limburgse vlaai.*

According to an old dictionary, a *vlaai* is a "flat, round bread cake topped with fruits or creamed rice." In the Middle Ages, it was baked as an offering to give thanks for the harvest. The *vlaai* of today is more of a cookie. No longer baked from bread dough, it is made, instead, from dough with more butter. The filling or topping can be of native strawberries, cherries, gooseberries, or plums, and even exotic fruits. Occasionally the little torte is topped with a dough lattice or streusel.

A popular variation is the *rijst-vlaai* with sweet, creamy rice pudding as a filling. The native enjoys the *vlaai* simply from the hand, not without a *kopje koffie*, or little cup of coffee.

Krentewegge for New Mothers

Some baked goods are closely tied to old Dutch traditions. The rural, wooded area of Twente, close to the German border, is abundant with these. From time immemorial, relatives and friends have brought gifts to new mothers and their babies, among them the *krentewegge*, a flat, long raisin roll. Visitors who are well-to-do show off their means by presenting an especially long roll. Even today, there are competitions among bakers to see who can bake the very longest *krenteweggen*, and some measure up to two meters long.

Vlaai with streusel

Limburgse Vlaai
Small Limburg Tortes

1 cup (250 g) flour
Generous pinch of salt
¹/₂ cup (100 g) sugar
1 egg
2 Tbs (25 g) yeast
1 cup (250 ml) lukewarm milk
¹/₃ cup (80 g) butter, melted

Sieve the flour into a large bowl, and add the salt and sugar. Make an indentation in the flour and drop the egg into it. Stir the yeast with a little warm milk and add it, too, to the flour. Combine the remaining milk with the melted butter and knead it into the dough to make a soft mass. Cover, put in a warm place, and let it rise for about 60 minutes.
Pre-heat the oven to about 400 °F (200 °C). Butter little torte forms and roll out the dough. Dress the forms with the dough and prick through with the tines of a fork, then bake for about 15 minutes. Allow to cool and decorate with the desired topping.

Krenteweggen
Raisin Rolls

Yeast dough
¹/₂ cup (100 g) raisins

Prepare the yeast dough (left). Knead in the raisins and form the dough into long thin loaves. Set them on a buttered baking sheet and allow to rise for 30 minutes. Brush with egg yolk and bake at high heat for about 20 minutes until they are golden brown.
Krenteweggen are eaten spread with butter for the traditional *koffietafel* (coffee hour), but they also taste good with a slice of Gouda cheese.

Opposite: *Limburgse vlaai*, little tortes originally made of bread dough, come in many variations – filled with fruit, with sweet or piquant fillings, as a rice or farmer's cheese torte, or baked as a quiche.

Licorice and Ginger

The Greatest Licorice Consumers

Nowhere else on earth is as much licorice or *drop* consumed as in The Netherlands, and nowhere else is licorice available in so many variations. Over 30,000 tons of it are enjoyed by the Dutch annually, and their partiality to the jet-black, glutinous, saltier than sweet "stuff" sometimes perplexes foreigners. Licorice, which is made from the thickened extract of the licorice root, was cultivated as a medicinal plant and grows in southern Europe and Asia Minor. The base product for licorice is imported in large blocks from the Mediterranean. With the addition of water, sugar, cornstarch, flour, glucose syrup, and flavorings like sal ammoniac, bay leaf, menthol, anise, eucalyptus, and honey, the sweet is processed further in Holland. Sometimes a gelling agent is used to lend further elasticity. The bonbons, or *drops*, are shown in large vitrines behind the counter at the confectioner's shop. A scale on the counter weighs the wares. It is not uncommon to see a customer leaving the shop, one of the triangular, often transparent, candy bags in hand, with an expression full of pleasurable anticipation on his face.

Ginger: Something Sweet from the Far East

As early as 2,000 years ago, the young, tender and juicy roots of Chinese ginger were candied – a delicacy that even Marco Polo lauded. Ginger was a popular spice in the Middle Ages, but was lost to subsequent history until sailors brought it back from their expeditions to Asia in the 18th century. Since then, ginger has been used in Holland, not only as a refinement to many exotic dishes, but also in ginger snap cookies, candied ginger (made by cooking ginger pieces in a concentrated sugar formula until it turns glassy) and ginger bonbons.

Drops, licorice bonbons in the form of hats...

as *toverballen* or "magic balls"...

as *brikett* pieces...

as little discs with imprints, etc.

In a confectioner's shop in Groningen, the licorice bonbons are kept behind the counter in glass jars.

The Pastry from Nicholas

Speculaas

Every December 6, Saint Nicholas Day, brings *speculaas* to Holland. Nicholas offers the cookies to children who have behaved well throughout the year.

In Dutch families, it is a tradition to spend the evening before the 6th at the home of grandparents, where little gifts are exchanged and *speculaas* cookies and hot chocolate are enjoyed in cozy company.

The basic *speculaas* dough – which is also a popular Christmas cookie in Germany and Belgium – is a relatively hard, sweet dough, spiced with cinnamon, nutmeg, cardamon, cloves, and ginger. The dough is pressed into figured, carved wooden molds and baked in the oven. It is always astounding to see how artistic and imaginative the molds can be, and the affection for the cookie stems not only from its spicy taste, but from the delightful forms it takes.

Ontbijtkoek, honey cake and *janhagel*, spiced almond cookies, are also associated with Christmas.

Speculaas

The cook will need special wooden *speculaas* molds. Today, they are also found in ceramic.

1 cup (250 g) flour
1 tsp baking powder
1/2 tsp each of cinnamon, nutmeg, cardamon, cloves and ginger
1/2 cup (100 g) softened butter
1/2 cup (125 g) sugar
1 egg
Grated peel of 1/2 an untreated lemon
1/2 cup (50 g) ground almonds

In a large bowl, combine the flour with the baking powder and spices. In another bowl, cream the butter and sugar, then add the egg and the lemon peel. Stir half the flour mixture and the ground almonds into the butter-sugar mixture. Gradually add the remaining flour and knead the mass to a hard dough.
Wrap the dough in transparent paper and cool for 3–4 hours in the refrigerator.
Pre-heat the oven to 400 °F (200 °C). Grease the molds liberally and lightly flour them. Press the dough into the forms and remove the excess at the edges. Then carefully remove the imprinted dough from the molds and bake them for 10–15 minutes. Let them cool on the baking sheet before transferring them with a knife to a cooling rack.

Ontbijtkoek
Honey Cake

2½ cups (350 g) flour
1 packet of baking powder
Pinch of salt
3 tsp honey-cake spice (specialty shop)
¼ cup (50 g) each candied orange and lemon
½ cup (125 g) brown sugar
¾ cup (150 ml) milk
¾ cup (175 g) honey
2 Tbs (25 g) candied sugar

Grease the cake form and lay waxed paper over the bottom. Combine the flour, baking powder, salt, spice, candied orange and lemon, and the sugar. Add the milk and honey and knead to a smooth dough. Preheat the oven to 325 °F (175 °C). Put the dough into the molds, crush the candied sugar and strew it on top of the dough. Bake for 60–70 minutes in the oven. Remove from the form and cool on a rack.
The honey cake is cut like a loaf of bread, the slices spread with butter.

Janhagel
Spiced Almond Cookies

1 cup (200 g) flour
Just under ½ cup (100 g) sugar
1 tsp cinnamon
Generous pinch of allspice
Pinch of salt
⅓ cup (80 g) cold butter
1 egg white
¾ cup (150 g) almond slices or halves

Combine the flour, sugar, spices, and salt. Cut the butter into small pieces and work into the flour mixture. If the dough crumbles, gradually add a few teaspoons of cold water until it sticks together.
Form the dough into a ball and roll out to a rectangle of even thickness on a greased baking sheet.
Pre-heat the oven to 325 °F (160 °C). Beat the egg white with a little water and brush it on the upper surface of the dough. Strew with almonds and press them in lightly. Then cut the dough into 2 × 3 in (5 × 6 cm) rectangles and bake for 20 minutes until the almonds are brown. Allow to cool, separate the rectangles, and let them cool further on a cooling rack.

Left: *Speculaas* is a favorite St. Nicholas and Christmas cookie. The dough is pressed into decorative wooden molds and then baked on a baking sheet. The imaginative designs appeal to children of all ages, and the aromatic spice cookies are also part of the Advent tradition in Belgium and Germany.

Distilled in the Interior

Genever and Liqueurs

A *Borrel* of Genever

Genever is indisputably Holland's national drink. It was developed around 1600 by a Leyden professor, Franzikus de Bove, at the dawning of the Golden Age. After a long period of Spanish occupation, the Dutch had liberated themselves and begun, with their illustrious fleet, an ascendancy to a world trade power. Their wealth grew exponentially as sailors were able to sell the rare items they brought from abroad at a high profit.

The professor from Leyden was looking for a medicine to counter the unhealthy symptoms of a high standard of living – medical concerns originally prompted almost all distilled products – and he concocted a digestive schnapps from barley, rye, corn, and juniper berries that he called *genièvre*, French for "juniper." The drink met with an enthusiastic reception and its name in the colloquial was changed to "Jenever."

The juniper taste is negligible today, the corn, much more obvious. The Dutch distinguish between mature and immature Genever – which leads to confusion as the difference has nothing to do with age. The immature, *jonge* Genever is simply a distillation with or without juniper aroma, while the mature *oude* Genever is manufactured according to an old process and based on *moutwijn*, malt wine, distilled three times out of corn, rye, and shredded barley malt. During the third distillation, the aroma is added, be it juniper berries, or spices like caraway and anise. Even fruit, apples or cherries, for example, can lend a special taste to the Genever. For the Dutchman, five in the afternoon is the fond hour of bitters. He enjoys his glass of schnapps, *borrel*, and adds a couple of drops of bitters to it. He snacks on a little piece of Gouda or some salted peanuts. If there is convivial conversation and the *borrel* drinking is extended, one talks about the *borreluur* in the same way Americans do about the cocktail hour. According to the latest statistics, the Dutch drink about 150,000 gallons (about 50 million liters) of *borrel* a year.

For Genever production, malt wine, *moutwijn*, is distilled from corn, rye, and barley malt.

Once distilled, the malt wine is given aroma by the addition of juniper berries or spices.

Before proceeding with another distillation, one checks to see whether the aroma has blossomed adequately.

During the *borreluur*, the *borrel* hour, a glass of Genever can be enjoyed at a favorite haunt.

Famous Liqueurs

In earlier times, it was primarily monks who, from liquor, spices, herbs, fruits, and certain "secret" ingredients, concocted liqueurs in countless new variations. In a wooden shed near Amsterdam, Dutch liqueur was born in 1575. It was then that a certain Lucas Bols distilled – outside the city walls because of the danger of fire – liqueurs that the people of Amsterdam walked out to try. With an array of original inventions, he was always able to attract his fellow citizens, and gave them liquor with lacing of caraway, anise, orange, or bitter orange that came from Curaçao, one of the islands among the Dutch Antilles in the Caribbean. Sometimes Bols' patrons would bring home his liqueur in an earthenware jug. His son, Jen Jacob Bols, enjoyed enough prosperity to build a grand house and his descendants were among the patrician families of the city of Amsterdam.

Then, as now, the Bols liqueurs are distilled in 200-year-old copper kettles. The most famous is the apricot. At thirty-one percent proof, it has a relatively high alcohol content and mixed with gin and orange juice (equal thirds), makes a delicious cocktail known as "Paradise." Other Bols specialties are the dry Curaçao Triple-Sec with its hallmark bitter orange, and the sugar, egg, spice, and Genever egg cognac known as "Advocat."

Liqueurs are well-suited for use in cocktails, both to sweeten them and add aroma. There are some mixed drinks made by real experts in the field, and the possibilities for creativity are limitless. Even the small house bar should have a standard assortment of liqueurs. As each of them has a high sugar content, they can be stored a long time. Fruit juice liqueurs, however, will – once opened – lose their fresh aroma after a time.

To whet the appetite, here is a drink made with the popular apricot brandy.

1 tsp (5 ml) Grenadine
2 Tbs (30 ml) apricot brandy
1 Tbs (15 ml) lemon juice
1 Tbs (15 ml) dry gin
2–3 ice cubes
Stemmed cherries to garnish

Shake all the ingredients on ice in a shaker and strain into a chilled cocktail glass. Garnish each cocktail with the cherry.

From left to right: *Jonge Genever*, *Genever met Appel* (apple), *Kersen* (cherries), *Frambozen* (raspberries), and *Bessen* (currants).

André Dominé

Belgium

The Belgians look with enthusiasm to their French neighbors and their wine-cellars. Almost all French wines are appreciated in Belgium, particularly Bordeaux and Burgundy. Indeed, French influence on Belgian restaurants is so strong that some gourmets refer to the Belgian and the French cuisine in one and the same breath. This is, of course, not to say that the Belgians do not hold their own specialties in high esteem. A good example is beer, of which Belgium boasts more than a hundred different types, including some that are rated amongst the best in the world. It is always a good time to drink beer, and each sort has its own particular moment: the pale, lighter ones make ideal lunch time drinks or thirst-quenchers, whilst the darker, full-bodied, stronger beers are usually enjoyed in the evening. As regards the enjoyment of their food, the Belgians are flexible. They treat themselves to only one long meal a day, which may last a good two hours. Moreover, an evening dinner with friends may extend over five hours. For lunch, on the other hand, Belgians are often quite content with a simple one-course meal, or with one of the well-filled baguettes that are available everywhere. Belgium is regarded as the land of the very best French fries; but equally famous, and justifiably so, are Belgian mussels. The Flemish people in particular are blessed by the close proximity of the sea. The Walloons, on the other hand, benefit from the forests of the Ardennes with their abundance of game, and from the numerous specialties of Liège. More restraint is displayed when it comes to sausages and cold meats, although there is a fine range of pâtés and boiled ham. Vegetables are enjoying an increase in popularity.

Belgium is home to some excellent cookies and an enormous variety of chocolates. Nevertheless, the Belgians are not such great consumers of sweets as it might seem. They do not often indulge themselves, preferring to leave that to others: chocolates are the most popular small present to take along to a dinner party. Occasionally however, Belgians do give in to temptation when faced with freshly baked waffles. The more solid Liège version can provide a complete family supper, whereas the light Brussels waffles are served only as a dessert.

Left: One of the monks who brews the beer in the famous Trappist monastery of Chimay.

Waterzooi

If Flemish fishermen were unable to sell all their day's catch they used to share out the unsold fish amongst the crew. Then all the men would carry home this so-called *Waterzooi* – which can be translated freely as "hodgepodge" – for their wives to cook the sole, turbot, cod, whiting, crab, or whatever there happened to be. She would use the seasonal vegetables she had at hand, braising them lightly and adding water and perhaps some white wine. Then she would add the fish, gutted and boned and cut into large chunks, and simmer it slowly. The meal was served by simply putting the pot on the table, and letting everybody help themselves to what they wanted. This simple kind of fish stew exists in innumerable variations in fishing communities throughout the world.

It is the fresh North Sea fish that gives *Waterzooi* its regional character. Over the centuries the Flemish people, with their instinct for refined cuisine, have created a number of variations, including one exquisite recipe using only turbot and lobster. The vegetables used nowadays tend to be leeks, potatoes, and celery and chopped much more finely than they used to be. The fairly thin sauce is enriched with cream and butter.

Waterzooi
North Sea Fish Stew
(Illustrations 1–4 and main photograph)

Serves 8

4 lbs (2 kg) various North Sea fish, mussels, and other shellfish
4 oz (125 g) shallots
2¹/₂ cups (500 ml) fish stock
2¹/₂ cups (500 ml) dry white wine
14 oz (400 g) leeks
¹/₂ stick celery
14 oz (400 g) carrots
¹/₂ cup (150 g) butter
2¹/₂ cups (500 ml) cream
2 Tbs finely chopped parsley
Salt, black pepper

Gut and fillet the fish, thoroughly wash and scrape the mussels and other shellfish. Peel and finely chop the shallots and poach together with the fish, mussels and other shellfish in the fish stock and white wine (1). Wash or scrape the remaining vegetables, cut into fine strips and braise lightly in 3 tablespoons of butter. Strain through a sieve and retain the liquid (2). Remove the fish and shellfish from the stock, add the vegetable stock and reduce the liquid (3). Pour in the cream and bring to the boil, then add the remaining butter.
Remove the shellfish from their shells and put them in an oven proof tureen together with the vegetables; pour the sauce over the ingredients. Bring briefly to the boil once more and serve sprinkled with parsley (4).
Chardonnay is a good accompaniment to this dish.

The main ingredient of *anguilles au vert* is of course eel, but important also are spinach and a lot of green herbs to make a green sauce.

First braise the eel chunks in butter, together with the finely chopped shallots, until the flesh turns white.

Then add the fish stock and white wine and simmer the eel until done.

The herbs add a fresh aroma to this dish, which can be eaten hot or cold.

Eel in Green Sauce

It was not necessary to be a fisherman to catch the eels for *anguilles au vert*, another Belgian specialty. When eels left their rivers or lakes for their spawning grounds in the far-off Sargasso Sea, they would occasionally take a shortcut and slither across the meadows. This is indeed how the dish acquired its name. To ensure that the eel appears green when cooked, plenty of spinach and herbs such as sorrel, parsley, tarragon, and sage are added. In Belgian cooking, fish stock and white wine are generally added to the lightly braised eel and onion; alternatively, the Flemish often use beer instead.

Anguilles au Vert
Eel in Green Sauce

Serves 4

2 lbs (1 kg) eel
3 oz (100 g) shallots
3 Tbs (50 g) butter
1¹/₂ cups (400 ml) dry white wine
2 cups (400 ml) fish stock
7 oz (200 g) spinach
1 Tbs chervil
1 Tbs finely chopped parsley
1 tsp finely chopped pimpernel
1 tsp finely chopped savory
1 tsp finely chopped tarragon
1 tsp finely chopped thyme
2 leaves of finely chopped mint
1 egg yolk
¹/₂ lemon
Salt, black pepper

Skin, gut, and wash the eels and cut into pieces about 3–4 inches (6–8 cm) long. Peel and finely chop the shallots and lightly braise them in the butter. Add the eel chunks and cook until the flesh turns white. Add white wine and fish stock and simmer until done.
Remove the eel and put aside. Reduce fish stock to one quarter. Thoroughly wash, prepare and finely chop the spinach. Add the spinach and herbs to the fish stock. Bring to the boil, season to taste and thicken with egg yolk.
Serve the eel pieces in the green sauce either hot or cold, and garnished with lemon wedges.
The Belgians like to accompany this dish with a bone-dry Riesling from Luxembourg or a Pilsner beer.

Opposite: North Sea fish, shellfish and shrimps are the main ingredients of Belgium's famous fish stew *Waterzooi*. The combination can vary – it is important for the fish to be fresh.

French Fries

The French like to challenge the notion that it was the Belgians who first invented *french fries*. It is, however, a fact that a large part of the Belgian population nourished itself on the potato which had originated on the American continent, but which at that time was completely unknown to most of the French. North European countries were generally slower in developing a taste for potatoes. The nutritious tubers, first noticed by a comrade-in-arms of Pizarro's, were introduced to Spain in the first half of the 16th century. They reached Italy in 1565 when the Spanish King Philip II sent some as a gift to Pope Pius IV, allegedly as an effective remedy for rheumatism. Whatever the true story, the *tartufolo*, or little truffle, was received very well by the Italians.

In 1601 the Flemish botanist Charles de Lescluse, active in Vienna, Frankfurt, and Leyden, published his history of plants, "Plantara Historia." It was in large measure due to his book and his studies that the potato spread in the countries north of the Alps. In Belgium, potato cultivation increased quickly thanks to good soil and favorable climatic conditions. By about half a century later, farmers in what is today known as Belgium had converted so many cereal fields over to growing potatoes that the monasteries' income from the "cereal tax" had decreased. Monasteries, therefore, began to impose a tithe on potatoes as well. And it was probably towards the end of the 17th century that the first french fries sizzled in a Belgian frying pan. The historian Jo Gérard found a manuscript in his family archives that dated back to 1781 and from which

his colleague Léo Moulin quotes as follows: "The inhabitants of Namur, Andenne, and Dinant especially the poor, are in the habit of fishing for all sorts of small creatures in the River Meuse and frying them in fat in order to enrich their everyday diet. But when the streams and rivers are in the grip of the frost and fishing becomes too risky, the inhabitants cut potatoes in the shape of small fish and fry them in fat in the same manner as the fish. I am told that this custom goes back over one hundred years."

At almost every street corner you can find *fritures*, chip stalls, where you can buy french fries; with a variety of dressings, for instance:
• Mayonnaise – presumably it was the Belgians who discovered what a felicitous taste is achieved by a combination of mayonnaise and french fries
• Sauce andalouse – mayonnaise with pepper purée
• Sauce tartare – a sauce of egg and herbs with chopped gherkins
• Mixed pickles – vegetables such as cocktail onions, cauliflower florets, gherkins pickled in vinegar.

Stoemp

Another Belgian national dish that is made from potatoes is *Stoemp*, mashed potatoes with vegetables. Peeled potatoes are boiled in salted water with one or two kinds of vegetable at a time, for instance with carrots, leeks, spinach, chicory, or endives. Both are then mashed with a fork, seasoned with pepper, salt, and nutmeg, and some butter added to the purée. *Stoemp* is usually eaten with a tasty sausage or slices of smoked bacon.

Mussels

Along the Belgian coast and in Brussels, mussels are served in pots in which they have been steamed in their own juices or with various other ingredients. Served with the mussels is a large plate of chunky french fries. Both mussels and french fries are eaten with an empty mussel shell that is used like a pair of pincers. Ever since mussels have been produced in the extensive mussel beds of the Dutch coast land the season has started as early as mid-July and ended at the beginning of April.

Methods of Preparing Common Mussels

Moules natures – steamed in their own juice
Moules à l'ail – with garlic butter, similar to snails
Moules à la crème – steamed in white wine and prepared with cream
Moules à la poulette – with mushrooms, white wine and crème fraîche (recipe opposite)
Moules à la provençale – with tomatoes, tomato paste, garlic, thyme, and bay-leaf
Moules au beurre – mussels removed from their shells and served in a sauce of butter, egg yolk, and herbs
Moules au champagne – cooked in champagne, served in only one half of the shell and with a champagne-cream sauce poured over it
Moules au curry – mussels removed from their shells, served in a curry sauce
Moules au vin blanc – steamed with white wine (recipe opposite)
Moules parquées – raw mussels, opened, with lemon and pepper or a mustard vinaigrette
Moules sauce tartare – cooked mussels served cold with *sauce tartare*

French fries with ketchup seasoned with curry powder

French fries with *sauce tartare*, a sauce made from egg, herbs, and chopped gherkins

French fries with mayonnaise

French fries with *sauce andalouse* – mayonnaise mixed with pepper purée

Moules au Vin Blanc
Mussels in White Wine
(Illustrations 1–4)

Serves 2

4 lbs (2 kg) mussels
2 onions
1 stick celery
³/₄ cup (150 ml) dry white wine
Black pepper
2 Tbs (30 g) butter

Scrub the mussels under cold running water and wash thoroughly; discard open and damaged ones (1). Peel and chop the onions, wash and prepare the celery and cut into pieces. Put onions, celery, and mussels into a large saucepan and add the white wine and plenty of pepper (2).
Cover and bring the mussels to the boil. They are ready when the shells open.
Add the butter and shake the saucepan several times to ensure the butter is well distributed (3). Serve the mussels in the saucepan immediately (4).
Serve with a Luxembourg Rivaner.

Moules à la Poulette
Mussels Chicken-style

Serves 2

4 lbs (2 kg) mussels
1 shallot
Juice of 1 lemon
1¼ cups (250 ml) dry white wine
Salt and black pepper
1 lb (500 g) mushrooms
1½ cups (300 ml) crème fraîche

Scrub the mussels under cold running water and wash thoroughly; discard any open and damaged ones.
Peel and finely chop the shallot and put in a large saucepan together with the white wine and lemon juice; season well with pepper. Add the mussels and bring to the boil.
Wash, prepare and finely slice the mushrooms. Add mushrooms and crème fraîche to the mussels; simmer for 10 minutes. Add salt to taste and serve.
A Muscadet is a fine accompaniment to this dish.

Huîtres au Champagne
Oysters in Champagne

Serves 2

12 flat oysters
1 shallot
1 cup (200 ml) champagne
1 cup (200 ml) crème fraîche
3 Tbs (50 g) butter
Salt and black pepper

Open the oysters with a special knife (see p. 59), taking care to catch any liquids in the oyster and not to damage the deeper half of the oyster shell which is needed for serving.
Peel and finely chop the shallot and put into a saucepan together with the champagne, oysters and liquid; poach the oysters over a low heat.
Remove the oysters from the saucepan, put them back into their shells and keep warm in a preheated oven.
Reduce the stock to a quarter, add the crème fraîche and bring to the boil again. Remove from the heat, stir in the butter and season the sauce.
Pour the sauce over the oysters and serve immediately with a glass of champagne.

1

2

3

4

Above and left: Mussels are eaten by using the two, still connected, shells as pincers. Freshly made french fries are an ideal accompaniment.

Chicory

Chicory, as we know and value it today, was discovered in around 1830 in the Botanical Gardens in Brussels. It was by no means the result of an experiment. Rather, the head gardener had set aside a corner of the extensive cellars in order to grow vegetables and lettuce in the winter. There he discovered that chicory formed lovely, firm spindles if covered by a thick layer of loose soil. It took another two decades or so before this method was perfected and word had spread around. Once introduced, however, chicory quickly established itself in the Belgian cuisine as a winter vegetable or salad ingredient.

The stronghold of chicory cultivation used to be the area between Brussels, Leuven, and Mechelen; but now most of the soil there has been exhausted. Chicory is sown in the open field in May and June. The plant develops long, floppy leaves and big roots and in September and October the farmers pull up the roots and cut off the leaves. Nowadays, these roots are kept in cold storage at a temperature of just below 32 °F (0 °C), before they are induced to grow under hydroponic conditions at a constant temperature.

The traditional way of growing chicory, in which the fields are fertilized with manure and the second stage of vegetation is allowed to take place outdoors, has almost died out. It requires the farmer to prepare beds heated by warm-water pipes. The roots are arranged in rows and driven into the soil very closely together at an angle, before being covered by more loose soil containing clay. Insulated with straw, and usually also protected against rain by a sheet of corrugated metal, it takes about a month for the shoots to appear: they form the *chicon*. The roots, dug out by the farmers on their hands and knees, are broken off and later used as animal feed. Next the outer leaves are removed until the white *chicons* appear. When grown in soil, they are particularly firm, regular in shape, and sweet-tasting. If kept at 43 °F (6 °C) in dark and dry conditions they keep for up to three months. Exposure to light causes the formation of chlorophyll which turns the leaves green and makes them taste bitter.

If chicory is washed it should not be left in water for too long since this will impair both aroma and consistency. An iron saucepan should not be used to steam chicory. The leaves should be sprinkled immediately with lemon juice; otherwise they will lose their immaculate paleness.

Les Chicons au Gratin
Chicory au Gratin

Serves 2

1/2 cup (120 g) butter
4 heads chicory
Salt, black pepper
1 Tbs chopped parsley
1/3 cup (40 g) flour
Pinch of nutmeg
3 oz (100 g) Greyerzer (Gruyère)
4 slices cooked ham

Melt 3 tablespoons (50 g) of butter in a saucepan. Cut out in a wedge-shape the bitter core at the root end of the chicory head, add the chicory to the butter, season with salt and pepper and sprinkle with parsley.
Cover and simmer for 20 minutes.
For the sauce, prepare a roux from the flour and 3 tablespoons (50 g) of butter and add the milk, stirring constantly; simmer for 5 minutes. Season sparingly with salt, pepper and nutmeg, and stir in one third of the grated cheese.
Preheat the oven to 400 °F (200 °C).
Grease an ovenproof dish with the remaining butter. Remove the chicory from the saucepan and drain well. Wrap up each piece of chicory in a slice of ham and put them in an ovenproof dish. Pour over the sauce and sprinkle with parsley. Bake in the oven until brown and serve immediately.
The Belgians serve this dish with creamed potatoes and either Pilsner beer or a Sauvignon from the Touraine or Sancerre.

Stoemp aux Choux de Bruxelles et Carottes
Mashed Potatoes with Brussels Sprouts and Carrots

Serves 2

1 lb (500 g) Brussels sprouts
7 oz (200 g) carrots
4 Tbs (60 g) butter
Salt, black pepper
1 bouquet garni
10 oz (300 g) potatoes
Pinch of nutmeg

Wash and prepare the Brussels sprouts and cut into halves; peel the carrots and cut into thirds. Cook the vegetables in 2 tablespoons (30 g) of butter for 10 minutes. Cover with cold water, add salt and pepper and the bouquet garni. Bring to the boil and cook for 5 minutes.
In the meantime, peel the potatoes and cut them into large cubes. Add them to the vegetables and boil for another 15 minutes. Pour off any remaining water that has not evaporated.
Mash everything roughly with a fork. Season to taste and add nutmeg and the remaining butter. Mix well and serve.
This dish may be accompanied by Pilsner beer or a Coteaux de Tricastin.

Background: Chicory – elegant paleness and bright yellow tips. Top quality varieties taste sweet.

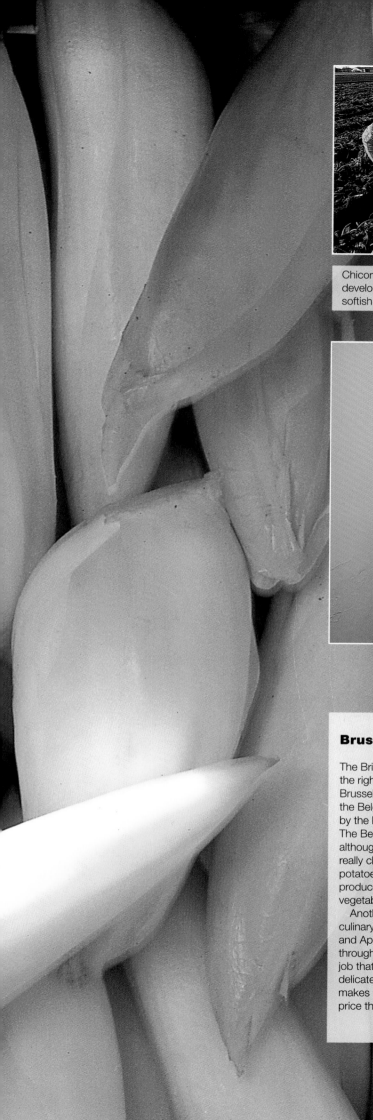

Chicory is sown in the open field where the plants develop long, floppy leaves and put down large, softish roots.

The edible spadix sprouts from the freshly-dug roots. The outer leaves are removed by hand (see below).

Brussels Sprouts and Hop Shoots

The British name for this vegetable (illustrated on the right) originates from their conviction that Brussels sprouts were first grown in the vicinity of the Belgian capital. This idea is also lent credence by the French who call them *choux de Bruxelles*. The Belgians themselves also use that name, although not altogether sure whether they can really claim to be the originators. Brussels sprouts, potatoes, and carrots can be combined to produce a version of the extremely popular vegetable purée called *Stoemp*, a real specialty.

Another kind of shoot, hop shoots, are a rare culinary peculiarity. Their proper season is in March and April. As soon as the young shoots break through the soil they are pulled out – a laborious job that has to be performed kneeling down. The delicate taste of the shoots, however, more than makes up for the effort and, indeed, for the high price that hop shoots command.

Poultry

The Belgians love poultry. The classic Sunday menu consists of chicken and french fries or chicken and stewed apple. Chicken is also important as the main ingredient of the meat version of *Waterzooi*. Poultry is frequently used in vol-au-vent fillings and in croquettes, or cold with mayonnaise and salad. So popular has poultry been in the Belgian capital over the centuries that the Flemish would call the inhabitants of Brussels *Kiekefretters*, chicken eaters.

Flanders is home to most of the traditional poultry breeders. They are, however, declining in numbers since the profession demands a great deal of manual work and time, mainly because of all the plucking involved.

The quality of the poultry depends, of course, on the proper husbandry of the birds, since the conditions in which they are kept will influence the structure and taste of the meat. But another, crucial factor with regard to the quality of the poultry is whether it has been plucked by hand, *plumé à sec*, plucked dry. The usual mechanical method involves the chicken being immersed in hot water in order to widen the pores before plucking. Only then can a chicken be plucked successfully by machine. This method has the disadvantage that water penetrating under the chicken's skin impairs the roasting process and the juices. In contrast, a chicken which has been plucked in the traditional manual way can roast normally in its own fat and the meat does not lose any of its succulence or intensity of taste.

Types of Poultry

The figures refer to the illustrations on the right-hand page.

1 **Coucou de Malines** – Belgium's national poultry comes from the district of Malines, a town in the Brabant near Antwerp. What the Bresse fowl is to the French, the "Cuckoo" is to the Belgians. It is descended from the Dutch Blaue race and has gray plumage and black and white claws. This very demanding fowl does not tolerate intensive fattening methods. It has to be reared with a lot of loving care and given time to put on fat. The best specimens come from small breeding farms where the fowl are fed on grain. After ten to twelve weeks they reach their optimum slaughter weight of $2^1/_2$ to 3 pounds (1.3 to 1.4 kg). The meat is succulent with a delicate flavor and tastes best when simply roasted.

2 **Poularde de Bruxelles** – This imposing fowl is a larger and older bird of the Coucou de Malines family.

3 **Poussin** – A rare specialty, chickens which are plucked when they weigh about a pound (450 grams).

4 **Pintadeau** and **Pintade** – Guinea-fowl used to come onto the market according to seasonal availability. Male specimens appeared at the age of eleven weeks in the poultry shops, around Whitsuntide, when they had reached the size of a young partridge. Young guinea-hens, however, had to weigh in at a minimum of just over two pounds (1 kg) and were, therefore, spared until the fall. But today guinea-fowl weighing between $1^1/_2$ and 2 pounds (800 to 1000 g) are available throughout the year.

5 **Pigeon belgique** – In contrast to the reddish meat of the French pigeon, the Belgian pigeon has pale meat. It breeds only once a year. If there are too many young pigeons, the pigeon lovers dispose of the surplus. The pigeons are not bred for consumption and the earliest they can be obtained is around Easter when they weigh between 10 oz and a pound (300 to 350 g); but they are very rare.

6 **Oie** – In Belgium, the demand for geese is increasingly concentrated around the festive days at the end of the year.

7 **Caille** – Both the French and the Belgians share a love of quails. These partridges are actually migratory birds and are barely the size of a hand. Nowadays they are bred for consumption.

1

5

2

6

3

7

4

Background: The Maison Matthys & Gaever in Brussels is a paradise for poultry lovers, as the shop gets its supplies from the best breeders.

Ardennes Ham

The Ardennes region has, since time immemorial, been famous for two things: the game from its forests, and its ham. Originally the reputation of the ham rested on a regional breed of pig. These animals were adapted to their wild surroundings, with long legs and robust, undemanding natures. The ham produced from them has probably got little in common with today's ham, for their meat must have been very lean and of extremely distinctive flavor. These were, however, not qualities that the farmers wanted: they crossbred their Celts with more domesticated breeds that produced a greater amount of meat and fat.

It is always astonishing to realize just how much patience past generations invested in the production of their ham. The meat would often be left to marinate for days on end in herbs, vinegar, and salt before it was put in the brine – the Ardennes people use a wet curing method. After that the ham would be hung in the chimney for several months, as high up as possible so that the smoke would already be cold by the time it passed the ham. Then they were left to mature in a drafty attic, a process that would take about eighteen months to be completed. This lengthy preparation inevitably brings to mind the top quality hams of southern countries.

The hams which have the best aroma have been smoked over juniper and thyme twigs as well as beech and oak chips.

Jambon d'Ardennes is the only product of the Belgian meat and sausage industry to carry an official quality mark. It always refers to a ham on the bone, in contrast to ham off the bone which is known as *Cobourg*. The production process has long been adapted to modern requirements. Today the ham is cured in brine for twelve to twenty-one days, after which it is stored in a cold store or air-conditioned room. Depending on the kind of smoke chamber and the flavor desired, it takes between twelve hours and one week for the ham to absorb enough flavor in the cold smoke. Beech or oak chips are used for the smoking process, sometimes combined with some twigs of juniper and thyme which impart additional aromatic qualities to the ham.

The most important requirement for a top quality ham is that the pig was raised in a natural way and was fed well, so that it was able to put on fat. If a ham is too lean it becomes dry and loses some of its taste.

Of course ham can be consumed after about a month, but its flavor and quality improve considerably if left to mature for three or four months. Once started, a ham should be consumed within two weeks.

Below: A correct, well-balanced proportion of fat and lean meat is the key – when this balance is right, ham from the Ardennes is a succulent delicacy.

Opposite: The hams hang in the smoking chamber for up to one week in order to absorb the delicate flavors.

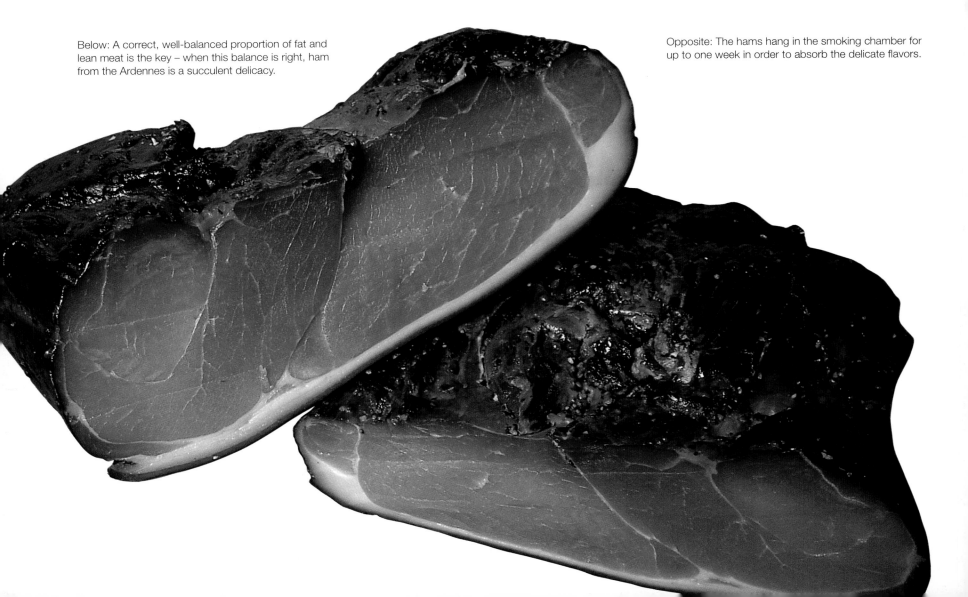

Cooking with Beer

Belgium's beer brewing tradition goes back about a thousand years. It is, therefore, not surprising that beer is an ingredient in many Belgian recipes. Astonishingly, however, only very few of this store of traditional dishes were cooked after the Second World War. The revival of the beer cuisine was led by the chef Raoul Morleghem in the 1950s with the publication of a substantial cookery book which attracted great popular acclaim. Since then, *ballekes à la bière*, rissoles in a beer sauce, has not been the only Brussels specialty. One often finds that *à la Bruxelloise* stands for a sauce prepared with beer.

Occasionally *à la flamande* also implies that beer is an ingredient. This label is used, for instance, in most menus to refer to the famous *carbonnades*. In the meantime, every region has developed its own variation. The only thing on which the cooks agree is that the cubes of beef shoulder have to be cooked in beer with plenty of onions. But opinions differ as to which kind of beer should be used. Some people keep to Braunes, whereas of course in Brussels, Lambic or Gueuze are used. The subtle sweet-and-sour flavor of this dish, which is left to stew for two and a half hours, is achieved by the addition of mustard, a dash of vinegar and some brown cane-sugar.

There are hardly any restaurants specializing exclusively in cooking with beer, although the best-known dishes have found a firm place in the Belgian cuisine. It is indeed still mainly in private households and through books that the extensive variety of cooking with beer, from soups to desserts, is disseminated.

Côtes de Porc à la Leffe
Pork Chops with Leffe Beer

Serves 2

2 pork chops
Salt, black pepper
2 Tbs (40 g) bacon fat (or butter)
1 onion
1 apple (Reinette)
1/2 bottle Leffe beer (see pp. 29–30)
1 cup (200 ml) crème fraîche

Sprinkle the chops with salt and pepper. Finely cube and melt down the bacon fat (or butter). Quickly brown the chops on both sides, then cover and cook until tender; remove from the pan and keep warm.
Peel and finely chop the onion and apple and braise lightly in the bacon fat. Skim off the fat. Loosen the meat residue from the bottom of the pan, add the beer and then simmer to reduce the liquid. Add the crème fraîche and cook for about 5 minutes. Season the sauce with salt and pepper to taste and pour it hot over the pork chops.

Carbonnades Flamandes
Flemish Beef Casserole
(Illustration opposite)

Serves 4

2 lbs (1 kg) beef shoulder
1/4 cup (60 g) butter
Salt, black pepper
3 large onions
1 Tbs brown cane sugar
2 1/2 cups (500 ml) Gueuze, Lambic or brown beer (p. 29)
1 slice of bread
1 bouquet garni
1 Tbs white wine vinegar
1 Tbs mustard

Cut the meat into large cubes, about 2 oz (50 g) and fry in the butter until brown on all sides. Add salt and pepper and remove.
Peel the onions and cut them into rings and braise them lightly in the meat juices. Add the cane sugar and the beer and bring to the boil.
Crumble the bread and add to the gravy together with the bouquet garni, the vinegar, and the chunks of meat. Cover and cook at a low temperature for 2 1/2 hours, stirring occasionally. The best accompaniment is *stoemp aux carottes*, mashed potato and carrot.

Ballekes à la Bière
Rissoles in Beer Sauce

Serves 6

2 slices white bread
2 onions
1 lb (500 g) ground pork
1 lb (500 g) ground veal
1 Tbs finely chopped thyme
1 Tbs finely chopped parsley
2 eggs
Pinch of nutmeg
Salt, black pepper
1/3 cup (70 g) butter
2 shallots
2 garlic cloves
1 Tbs flour
2 pints (1 l) beer

Soak the bread in water and then squeeze well. Peel and finely chop the onions and mix with the ground meat, bread, thyme, parsley, eggs, nutmeg, salt and pepper. Shape the meat mixture into large round rissoles.
Heat 3 tablespoons (50 g) of the butter in the pan and fry the rissoles until brown all over. Peel and finely chop the shallots and the garlic and fry lightly in the remaining butter. Sprinkle with the flour and season with salt, and pepper, then add the beer and bring to the boil.
As soon as the rissoles are browned, add the beer sauce and cook everything on a low heat for 30 minutes, turning the rissoles several times. Serve them in the sauce with french fries.

L'étuvée de Westmalle
Westmalle Stew

Serves 6–8

2 lbs (1 kg) leg of lamb
2 lbs (1 kg) lean pork
1/4 cup (50 g) butter
1 lb (500 g) onions
Salt, black pepper
Pinch of nutmeg
1 Tbs flour
2 bottles Westmalle or brown beer (see pp. 30–31)
1 tsp finely chopped thyme
1 bay leaf
2 lbs (1 kg) mealy potatoes

Cut the meat into one inch (3 cm) cubes. Heat the butter in a large stewing pan.
Peel and quarter the onions and brown in the butter together with the meat. Season with salt, pepper, and nutmeg, sprinkle with flour and add the beer. Add the thyme and bay-leaf, and stew for 60 minutes.
Peel the potatoes, cut them into large cubes, and add to the meat. Stew for another 20–30 minutes.

Lapin du Brasseur
Beer-brewer's Rabbit

Serves 3

1 cup (200 g) currants
1/4 cup (50 ml) Genever (juniper schnapps)
1 1/4 cups (250 ml) Lambic beer (p. 29)
1 ready-to-cook rabbit, about 4 lbs (2 kg)
8 oz (250 g) smoked bacon
1/4 cup (50 g) lard
20 pearl onions
Salt, black pepper
1 garlic clove
1 bouquet garni
1 Tbs flour
1 Tbs cane sugar

Soak the currants in the Genever and a dash of Lambic. Cut the rabbit into pieces that are roughly the same size.
Cut the smoked bacon into cubes and, using a cast iron pot, brown them in the lard. Remove and put aside. Remove the skin from the pearl onions, braise them lightly in the fat, remove them and put them aside. Brown the rabbit portions on all sides; then drain off the fat. Season the meat with salt and pepper. Add the remaining beer and add just enough water to make sure the meat is covered. Stir gently, making sure to loosen the meat gravy from the bottom of the pot. Bring to the boil.
Add the onions and smoked bacon and simmer for 30 minutes. Should the gravy still be too liquid, remove the meat, onion, and bacon, boil the sauce until reduced. Arrange the rabbit portions on a pre-heated serving dish and pour the hot gravy over them. Serve with boiled potatoes or creamy mashed potatoes.

Carbonnades flamandes –
Flemish beef casserole

317

Belgian Beers

The Belgians are proud of their beers, of which there are basically three types:

• Bottom-fermented beers, which are brewed at a low temperature (below 50 °F, 10 °C). They are pale and yellowish in color and, because of the hops, slightly bitter and dry in taste. The best-known brands in Belgium are Jupiler, La Stella, and La Maes.

• Spontaneously fermented beers, a process which is triggered by bacteria and yeasts which naturally occur in the Senne valley.

• Top-fermented beers, which can be brewed at higher temperatures (59–68 °F, 15–20 °C). Their color is usually copper to dark brown and their taste sweet and fruity (see "Trappist beer," pp. 320–321).

Furthermore, Belgium is famous for its specialist beers. As well as the Trappist beer, there are another five categories:

• Strong beers, such as the Duvel (meaning "devil"), a beer of golden color with a very distinctive aftertaste, which is served in iced glasses.

Other strong beers of similar character are Gouden Carolus, Gauloise, Lucifer, Verboden Vrucht, and the very strong Bush Beer. Kwak, a strong beer of a most distinctive taste, is served in a special glass with a wooden stem and base.

• Brown beers, the most renowned and most widespread of which is Roodenbach, available in three versions: the plain, rather bitter one which goes well with crab and is often drunk with a dash of Grenadine; the very fruity and refined Cuvée Alexandre; and the excellent Grand Cru.

• Beers of the Ale, Scotch, Christmas, or Stout type. These beers are dense, dark and often very strong, and are imported from England.

• Seasonal beers; these top-fermented beers are brewed at certain times of the year in Wallonia and are often very refreshing with a slightly sour taste.

• Weiss beer; at one time the best-known brand was Blanche de Louvain, which was served in earthenware or porcelain jugs. Today Hoegaarden in Flanders is the capital city of Weiss beers, which are brewed from wheat, and are light, cloudy and very refreshing. Two very good brews are Brugs Tarwerbier from the Bruges brewery, De Gouden Boom, and the Weiss beer from Namur. Weiss beers usually come in two varieties: Standard and Grand Cru, the latter having a higher alcohol content and subtler flavors.

Lambic and Gueuze

The inhabitants of Brussels have every reason to believe that their air is special, for it is thanks to this air that they are able to brew the only beer in the world produced by spontaneous fermentation. Lambic, as it is known, is brewed in Brussels itself and the immediate area, above all in the Senne valley.

Nowadays, Lambic is mainly used as the raw material for Gueuze, Kriek, and Faro. The slightly sour, non-effervescent Lambic is served only in bars in the Pajotten country, the favorite haunt of the painter Breugel the Elder; it was here that he painted the "Peasants' Dance," for example. It may also be found in cafés in the capital. From the original fifty breweries only the Brasserie Cantillon has survived, a true living museum. In the city's environs about a dozen are still in production. The law demands a minimum of thirty percent whole wheat. This is ground together with malted barley and poured into the mash tub. While mechanical arms mix the cereals for two and a half hours, hot water is added (122–167 °F, 50–75 °C). Then the mixture is left to settle and the wort drawn off and pumped into a boiler where it is mixed with hops. The hops used by Lambic brewers are two years old, and impart their subtle bitter taste to the beer. At the same time the hops

Hoegaarden – From the village of the same name in Flanders, the center of the refreshing Weiss beers brewed from wheat

Jupiler – One of the best-known bottom-fermented blonde beers with a slightly bitter and dry taste

Bellevue – Producer of spontaneously fermented beers, such as this Kriek which is flavored with cherry juice

Duvel – The "devil" amongst beers, a stro beer of golden color a lingering after-taste

protect against harmful bacteria. During the three to four hours that the boiler is bubbling away, some of the water evaporates, making the wort more concentrated.

It is then that the future Lambic proceeds towards its unique development. It flows into a low open cooling basin made from copper or stainless steel where it is exposed to fresh air and allowed to react with the microorganisms of the *Pajottes* country.

Overnight, the liquid's temperature gradually falls to about 70 °F or 21 °C. The wort is now filled into barrels, usually so-called *pipes* which have a volume of about 175 gallons (650 liters). Before each new filling they are scrupulously cleaned using only mechanical means and pure water. Otherwise the precious bacteria and yeasts might be destroyed. Layers of dust and cobwebs found in the cellars are further proof that only natural means are employed. Fermentation sets in after only a couple of days and lasts for two to three months. Subsequently, Lambic is generally left to mature for at least a year, sometimes even two or three, according to its destination.

The brewing of Lambic is seasonal, for in the summer there are too many bacteria and not enough yeast cells. Brewed in such conditions, the beer would taste awful. The most successful

The secret of Gueze lies in the spontaneous fermentation triggered by naturally occuring bactera in the Senne vally near Brussels.

results are achieved in the coldest conditions. This is why brewing is restricted to the period from mid-October to mid-May. Lambic provides the basic ingredient for a variety of specialty beers. Candied sugar is added to produce Faro, a beer which had its heyday around the turn of the century. For Kriek, the farmers originally had to wait for the harvest of the local sour cherries. These were then left to macerate in the Lambic for up to six months, by which time they had more or less dissolved. Nowadays cherry juice is usually added.

The crowning glory of spontaneously-fermented beers is Gueze. To produce the "Champagne of Brussels," the brewer uses a concoction of Lambic of different ages, using beers that have already matured in the barrel for two or three years, and mixing them with twice the amount of fresh, as yet immature Lambic. This results in further fermentation inside the bottles that are stored at the brewer's for a whole year before they go on sale. After buying Gueze it is advisable to store the bottles on their side for at least a fortnight to allow the yeast residue to resettle. The beer is drunk at cellar temperature, around 53 °F (12 °C). Its taste is best developed after maturing for two years, although Gueze can be stored for another three years without a noticeable deterioration.

A dark, slightly top-fermented tery beer brewed by pendent brewery

Ciney – Another *bière d'abbaye* or monastery beer is this dark, slightly sweet, and top-fermented variety

Rochefort – A fruity, top-fermented Trappist beer from the Abbey of Saint-Rémy, about a mile from Rochefort

Trappist Beer

Of the more than one hundred varieties of beer in Belgium, the most famous ones are brewed by monks. The brewing of beer in monasteries dates back to the 9th century. Its nutritional value aside, the beverage was more reliable than water: in the 11th century Saint Arnold was declared patron saint of the brewers' guild after ordering his flock in Oudenburg to drink consecrated beer instead of the contaminated water from the river. Because the wort was left to boil for several hours, the beer was free of any germs. At first, monks produced only enough beer to quench their own thirst, but soon they started selling it to their neighbors. The business flourished, and continued its expansion, filling the coffers of the Benedictine monasteries. In the 17th century, most of them joined the movement that had been initiated by the abbot Bouthillier de Rancé who had stepped up the discipline of the order in the French monastery of La Trappe. Of the six Trappist monasteries in Belgium, five brew beer: Westvleteren, Westmalle, Rochefort, Orval, and Chimay.

Despite their long tradition, the monks have managed to reconcile respect for nature with the latest in modern know-how and the most progressive technical developments. Founded in 1850, the Abbey de Scourmont near Chimay in the south of Belgium is regarded as the pioneer in this development. When they had to overhaul their brewery after the war they did so on the basis of state of the art know-how provided by the renowned school of brewery of the Catholic University of Leuven, and sought the advice of the school's director Jean de Clerck.

Of course, the Trappists have not abandoned their top-fermented beer. They use malted barley and mash it with pure groundwater. When the boiling process is finished they add selected hops. The wort is cooled down to no lower than 68 °F (20 °C). Fermentation is then left to the yeast, which the monks themselves isolate, and which has a decisive influence on the character of the beer. Inside the new stainless steel tubs with a capacity of 1,300 gallons (500 hectoliters), the fermentation process takes one week. After purification in the centrifuge the beer is left to mature in storage tanks.

The Trappists do not share the custom of other breweries of simply adding carbon dioxide to the beer when it is bottled. Instead, they have returned to the traditional method of providing each bottle with an exact dose of yeast which causes re-fermentation after bottling. It is to this fermentation within the bottle that Trappist beers owe their head and their fine, full-bodied, rich flavor. The beers are not offered for sale until bottle-fermentation is completed and the yeast residue has settled on the bottom. Their rich brown color, reminiscent of copper, is a result of the high temperature of the malt. When the temperature is lower amber-colored beers are produced in which the character of the hops is more evident. The strongest beers, such as the blue cap from Chimay which bears its vintage year, improve with age. They should always be stored in an upright position and at cellar temperature.

A number of Belgian abbeys belonging to different orders granted the right to breweries to use their names. The majority of beers brewed under this system are also top-fermented, for example the *spéciales* or *brunes* from small breweries, which are generally of excellent quality. However, anyone who insists that their beer must be brewed by a monk has to stick to the five *trappistes* mentioned above.

Brewing beer is an ancient tradition and an art that is cultivated in Trappist monasteries. Here, a monk checks whether the barley has germinated properly.

Beer has been brewed since 1862 in the abbey of Notre-Dame-de-Scourmont near Chimay in the south of Belgium.

The stainless steel vats are fitted with a porthole to allow for the optical supervision of the fermentation process.

Trappist beers, like champagne, undergo a second process of fermentation inside the bottle and therefore have to be secured with adequately wired corks.

With justifiable pride the master brewer presents his product: the fine head and the natural carbon dioxide of the beer are the result of bottle fermentation.

Trappist Breweries

Chimay – In the abbey of Notre-Dame-de-Scourmont south of Chimay, the following beers have been brewed since 1862: 1. Red Cap, the monks' premier beer, copper colored and very smooth; 2. White Cap, distinguished by its amber color, delicate bitterness and refreshing quality; 3. Blue Cap, a dark, fruity, strong, full-bodied beer with a thick creamy head. They also have the special brews: Première, Cinq Cent, and Grande Réserve.

Orval – Founded in 1070 and rebuilt in 1948, this is the most visited abbey and it produces only one type of beer. The Orval in the skittle-shaped bottle has an orange color, plenty of flavor and a slightly bitter aftertaste, and is made from three varieties of malt. It keeps for up to five years but is best enjoyed aged four months to one year.

Rochefort – Rochefort beer comes from the abbey of Saint-Rémy founded in the 13th century and situated about a mile from Rochefort. There are three different types of beer: 1. The red with its mild and fruity taste; 2. The green with its distinctive aftertaste; 3. The blue which is dry and bitter.

Sint Sixtus de Westvleteren – This is the least known of the monasteries, which brews four interesting varieties of dark beer which are rarely found on beer menus: 1. The popular Double; 2. The stronger and more full-flavored Spécial; 3. Extra which has a fruitier, livelier quality but also a higher alcohol content; 4. The velvety and full-bodied Abbot, one of the strongest beers brewed in Belgium.

Westmalle – This monastery near Antwerp produces three types of beer: 1. Simple beer which is reserved for the monks themselves; 2. Westmalle Double which is brown in color and distinctly malty in taste; 3. Westmalle Triple which is golden in color, fruity and full-bodied in taste, and for which demand is greatest.

Bières d'abbayes – monastery beers – Amongst the monastery beers that are now produced by independent breweries, the following are the most famous varieties: the very well-known Leffe; the Cuvée de l'Hermitage which comes from the Charleroi area; Grimbergen; Maredsous; Floreffe.

Herve

You cannot hide a Herve. Its intense aroma permeates everything. Its soft, brownish-pink, shimmering rind alone seems to promise spicy and delicious enjoyment. The first cut will reveal to the connoisseur what he can expect: the creamier it is and the further this creaminess extends into the center of the cheese, the stronger will be its taste. The best are allowed to use the label *traditionnel mûri à coeur*, "ripened unto the heart."

This celebrity amongst cheeses comes from the eastern Belgian region near Aix-la-Chapelle (Aachen). Its characteristic but decidedly mild flavor is very striking. Nowadays, Herve is usually sold when it is about four weeks old and still mild in taste. At two-months old its flavor is much stronger. The hardest cheeses which are only turned when dry, the Remoudous, demand extra patience. Several factors contribute to the unique character of Herve. The Pays de Herve is an elevated plain with a clay and chalk soil at an altitude of around 650 feet (200 m) where even the grasses that grow here have a character of their own and influence the taste of the milk. The climate ensures that the conditions in the cellars are of an even humidity and constant temperature. These factors provide ideal conditions for the bacteria and yeast fungi which have conquered the whole plateau. Indeed, they are everywhere: in the air, the water, the dairies as well as in the maturation cellars.

Milk fresh from the cow is heated in the usual way and mixed with rennet. Once the whey is drained off, the dairy farmer places the curd between wooden planks on a steel table. The curd is left for two days to allow any remaining moisture to drip off, during which time it is turned over several times and begins to set and harden. The cheese is then cut into cubes weighing seven or fourteen ounces (200 or 400 g). There follows a soaking of between three and five hours' duration in salt brine, after which the *fermier* has fulfilled his duty. Unless, that is, he also wants to be responsible for the maturing of the cheese, a job normally done by the *affineur*. At this stage the cheese is already infected with the special enzyme. The cellars are the source of these enzymes which are to be found even in the water with which the cheeses are wiped three times a week. They spread on the cheeses' surface and are responsible for its maturation, gradually penetrating deeper and deeper into its core. During this process they break up the acidity of the fresh cheese and develop their flavor components.

The curdled milk is broken up so that the whey can drain off.

The dairy farmer cuts the cheese mass into cubes and puts it into the salty brine.

Firms or cooperatives take charge of the remainder of the maturation process which involves the regular washing of the cheese.

Herve always has a "scent" – and the taste of the cheeses varies from mild to strong, depending on the extent of its maturation.

Background: On the plateau of Herve near Liège the cows graze in particularly rich meadows.

Cheese

With over 300 varieties available, the Belgians might well be proud of their cheeses. Nevertheless, they have only just started to appreciate all that abundance. It is thanks to a handful of *affineurs* (who are in charge of the final stages of cheese maturing) that the best restaurants at last serve fine cheeses. Even so, it is still an exception for Belgians to eat cheese after the main course of a meal. They prefer to eat their cheese at home, cut into slices and wedged between two slices of bread, in a baguette, or in pistolets (the small round bread-rolls that are often eaten for the weekend breakfast). Cheese is popular cut into small cubes to accompany a special beer or an aperitif. Cheese is also eaten at breakfast time, on bread as an afternoon snack, or in the evening. A light dinner may consist simply of soup, bread with cheese spread, stewed fruit, and some hard cheese.

It goes without saying that cheese is also used in numerous recipes, and in particular in sweet or savory cheesecakes such as *tarte au blanc stofé* and *tarte au maton*, which is made of soft gel, the curdled milk. Their tradition goes back a long way: the famous *tarte al Djote*, a chard cheesecake with full-fat cheese, was offered to the Emperor Henry III on May 4, 1046 on the occasion of the consecration of the new abbey of Saint Gertrude.

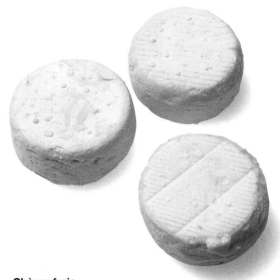

Chèvre frais
The Fromagerie d'Ozo in the Ardennes region produces particularly good curd cheeses from goats' milk.

Petit Lathuy
An excellent, creamy cheese from Jodoigne; somewhat reminiscent of Reblochon.

Clairieux
A hard cheese from the Mont de l'Enclus in the Tournai district.

Chimay
Five types of cheese are produced by the Trappist monastery, including one made from unpasteurized milk and a beer cheese with a very delicate flavor.

Herve
A cube with a reddish rind, intense aroma, and a mild to spicy flavor, which depends on its age.

Boû d'fagne
Made from unpasteurized milk like the Trou, this square, tasty soft cheese is matured by the Fromagerie Vanderheyden and has a washed rind.

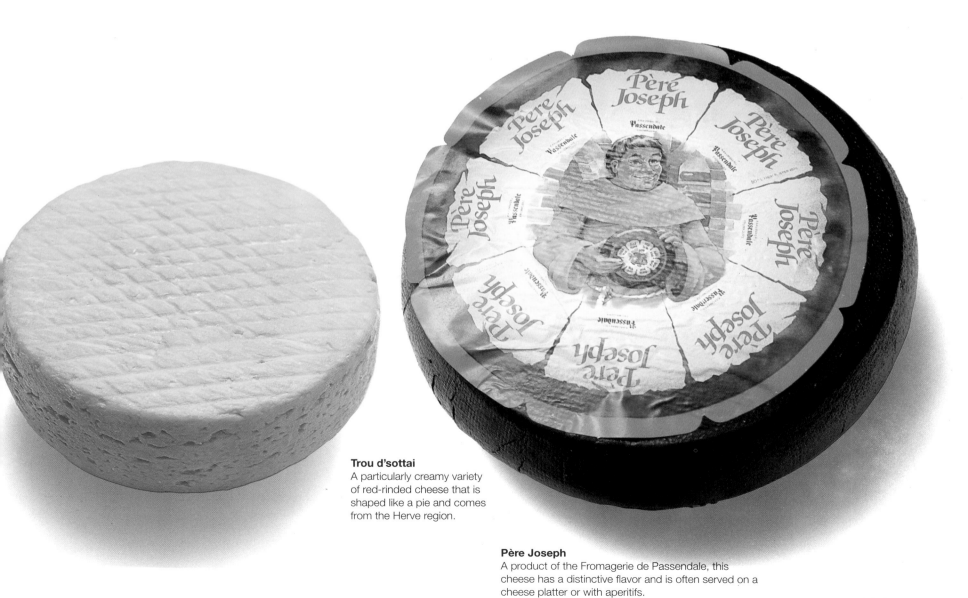

Trou d'sottai
A particularly creamy variety of red-rinded cheese that is shaped like a pie and comes from the Herve region.

Père Joseph
A product of the Fromagerie de Passendale, this cheese has a distinctive flavor and is often served on a cheese platter or with aperitifs.

Liège Waffles

The New Year in Liège has always begun with waffles, although both families and bakers are now equipped with modern electrical waffle-makers. In the past, long-handled cast iron molds were kept in nearly every house to be used for those special occasions when waffles were called for. The molds were suspended above the red-hot coal in the fireplace or oven, and great care had to be taken that they did not become too hot. When one side was cooked, the mold was turned to cook the other side. It could take several hours before the cravings of both young and old for this spongy delicacy were satisfied.

These delicious cakes were simply too tasty for their consumption to be confined to one single day. Since everybody could not or would not go to the trouble of making the waffles, women took basketfuls of homemade waffles to the markets on festive days, or waffle bakers prepared their delicious wares on the spot. Poets would go into raptures about these culinary delights, even in the Middle Ages.

The first principle is that of freshness. Therefore, even large waffle bakers produce their goods only to order and do not keep stocks, although waffles can be kept for at least two weeks and even up to three months. The best flavor is achieved if the flour, sugar, and egg-yolk are kneaded into a dough with only butter or cream. In Brussels, where waffles can be up to two inches (5 cm) thick, fluffiness is most important, this depending on the amount of stiffly beaten egg-white added. In Liège people are more restrained in this matter: although fluffiness is appreciated, the people of Liège generally prefer the easily manageable compactness of the traditional small square. The waffles are ready to eat when, on opening the iron, they are golden brown and smell of vanilla or cinnamon.

Specialties from Belgian Bakery and Pastry Shops

Couque de Dinant
A dry, hard cookie from the small town of Dinant in the province of Namur.

Cramique
A rich currant bread with eggs and butter.

Craquelin
A Liège specialty, this round bread is made from the same dough as Cramique but uses sugar instead of raisins.

Faluche
A small, round bread that looks like a mini pizza. You cut it open, spread it with butter, sprinkle with cane sugar and heat through in the oven for five minutes.

Gaufre de Bruxelles
A very fluffy waffle that contains plenty of beaten egg-whites. It is eaten with sugar, whipped cream, or chocolate.

Gaufre de Liège
A sweet waffle in the traditional square shape, flavored with vanilla, cinnamon, and small pieces of sugar.

Pain à la grecque
Made from bread dough rolled in coarse sugar (but has nothing to do with Greek bread). The heart-shaped version is called *coeur de Bruxelles*.

Pistolet
These rolls are available freshly baked from bakers' shops on Sundays, and are consumed with sausage, cheese, eggs, or, if you live near the coast, with fresh gray crabs.

Speculaus
The Belgian national cookie, containing rock candy and numerous spices. It is available in various shapes and sizes and is particularly popular in the shape of St. Nicholas.

A portion of dough is placed on each waffle-iron before being transported through the oven on a conveyor belt.

The small lumps of sugar in the dough are a characteristic of Liège waffles.

With waffles, freshness is the first priority. Fresh waffles give off a delicious scent of vanilla and cinnamon.

Above: pear and apple syrup is a delicious specialty of eastern Belgium – wonderfully dark, thick in consistency, and yet easy to spread.

Right: The press, which is filled with crushed fruit, squeezes out the fermented fruit juice which is later boiled down to a concentrate.

Syrup

Sugar remained a luxury good well into the 19th century. In the late Middle Ages it was sold only in apothecaries. Although sales in Europe increased with the beginning of large-scale sugar cane cultivation in the West Indies in the 17th century, most people were only rarely able to afford sweets. Those with a sweet tooth decided to remedy this situation.

From time immemorial there have been apple and pear trees in the eastern part of Belgium on the edge of the Hautes Fagnes. For about 400 years the local people have boiled down each season's fruit to a glutinous, almost black, and wonderfully sweet syrup. It became a favorite of children and grown-ups alike, but was always associated with people who lived in humble circumstances, until, that is, cooks started using it in sauces for game and meat. Since then, its gastronomic name has been established. There are, however, only a few enterprises left where syrups are produced by hand; one example is the Siroperie Nyssen in Aubel.

As soon as the fruit harvest begins in the middle of September, local farmers bring mountains of pears and apples to the Siroperie Nyssen. Every day at about two in the afternoon, both father and son are busy with their shovels filling their three large copper kettles to the brim. They hold a combined volume of six thousand pounds of fruit (2,800 kg). Then the gas burners are lit, and the fruit is left to boil for ten to twelve hours.

For the Nyssens, the day begins much earlier, at four o'clock in the morning. This is when father and son carry the fruit pulp to the press in barrows. Each layer of fruit is covered with a layer of sacks: the jute retains the pips and the fruit pulp. Thus the fruit-juice is already filtered when it flows into the tank, while the press applies gradual hydraulic pressure of up to 3,800 pounds per square inch (250 kg per sq. cm). The residue is fed to the cows and helps them to produce milk of a particularly high fat content.

From eight o'clock onwards, the Nyssens run between 350 and 500 pints (200–300 liters) of fruit-juice into each of the freshly cleaned vats. Now the refining process begins. The juice is concentrated by boiling it until the water it contains is evaporated. Once it has reached the required consistency it is put into the mixing tank for homogenization, and the vats are filled with the next load. At two in the afternoon, the whole process starts again from the beginning. The wide surface of the filling funnels allows the syrup to cool to 104 °F (40 °C) before it flows into the jars.

The traditional production of syrup uses exclusively pears and apples. Eight pounds of fruit yield one pound of syrup. The most delicious combination contains four parts of pears to one part of apples, although nature does not always allow for this proportion. Nature is rather fickle in any case, sometimes providing an abundance of produce in one year, and a very meager harvest the next. Each syrup vintage therefore varies, just as wine does. Likewise, pear and apple syrup improves if left to mature in a cool cellar.

Chocolates

Belgian chocolates are a world apart from the simple sugared almonds that in his time the Count Graf von Plessis-Praslin used to seduce the ladies. Chocolates comprise a whole range of sweet temptations. Belgian *chocolatiers* are proud of the huge variety of chocolates they have on offer and are constantly occupied developing new recipes. Even chocolate factories produce more than sixty different types of chocolates, while independent master *chocolatiers* effortlessly notch up a hundred or so varieties in dark, milk, or white chocolate. The latter is not chocolate at all, strictly speaking, but simply a mixture of cocoa butter, sugar, and powdered milk, and contains no cocoa. To make filled chocolates, the dark variety is best since it blends in harmoniously with almost any other ingredients and flavorings. Belgium's total production of chocolate per annum amounts to 250,000 US tons (220,000 tonnes), with more than sixty percent being exported. 200,000 US tons (180,000 tonnes) of the total are however used for the coating of filled chocolates.

There are two main categories of filled chocolates: glazed and molded. In order to produce the former, the *chocolatier* creates a chocolate paste with a distinctive flavor, such as that well-known classic, Praliné. This consists of ground roasted almonds or hazelnuts and sugar. The paste is put into a frame and pressed into a layer from which various shapes are cut such as thalers (coins), lozenges, and squares. They are then coated with liquid chocolate.

The second category benefits from a wide variety of shapes. These are produced by pouring melted chocolate coating into large sheets with the corresponding molds. They are then shaken to remove any air bubbles, and cooled down. The confectioner makes the filling by mixing creams with a sugar and butter base. Guided by their imagination or sense of taste, they add other ingredients such as chocolate, cream, fruit, caramel, liqueurs, or liquor, to name but a few. Nuts, chestnuts or marzipan may also be included. Once the filling is in the mold, the base is covered with chocolate. Marzipan allows the confectioners to display their humorous and artistic sensibilities, enabling them to form, by hand, whole basketfuls of bananas, plums, kiwis, apples, lemons, tomatoes, and carrots, for instance, or cute little piglets performing amazing contortions. Anyone purchasing a pound box of chocolates from a Belgian chocolatier can expect about forty little surprises inside – and all of them fresh and delicious.

Chocolate figures are formed by means of molds, a process that is also used for many filled chocolates.

The chocolate has to cool down before the figure can be removed from the mold.

Background: Belgian chocolatiers are constantly devising new shapes and fillings for their delicious products.

For glazed chocolates, the melted chocolate is poured over a delicious paste.

Not only is dark chocolate used for casting chocolates, but also milk and white varieties.

The filling for many chocolates consists of creams, the basic ingredients of which are butter and sugar.

André Dominé

France

Surely there is no other country in the world where eating and drinking represent such a strong expression of culture. In France the instinct for good food is so widespread that even the most unsophisticated person will talk about it with passion and knowledge. By according it such a high value, the French have developed highly discriminating tastes which form the foundations for their cuisine and its numerous specialties. Every traveler to France will know that the shops and places of work close for two hours at midday: time is vital, mealtimes are not just about eating. They allow relaxation and communication, and even the simplest meal consists of at least three, mostly four courses: hors d'œuvre, main course, cheese, and dessert. This variety at the same time allows a diverse and balanced diet. Every country is endowed with mouthwatering specialties, but France is well known for having more than its fair share of such delights. Some are of course an acquired taste, such as andouilles and andouillettes, sausages made of bladder and stomach. The French appreciate a variety meats (offal), just as they prefer mature and correspondingly strong-tasting cheeses. Wine with food is a matter of course. It used to be regarded simply as a food and those who did physical work had the right to consume several liters a day. In France the art of combining aromas and textures has achieved an unprecedented level of refinement and no vintner or wine dealer will recommend a bottle of wine without also recommending the type of food it should complement. There has been an ever greater appreciation of the importance of the taste of the ingredients. High quality suppliers are vital if the chefs are still to produce those masterpieces of haute cuisine. In an age when ever more banal products are influencing eating habits, the hope must be that specialties will escape this sterile standardization and maintain their high quality and character.

Left: Poultry breeder with a Bresse chicken.

The Baguette

If the French had to choose from amongst all their food specialties the one that was most typical of their home country, the largest vote would go to the most modest of them: the baguette. The French are very particular about their bread; it accompanies everything they eat. Nevertheless it is only exceptionally used as a sandwich. The delicate *canapés* are just small snacks and the overflowing half baguettes are simply inventions for emergencies and tourists.

Whether at home or in the restaurant, it is always the bread that comes first onto the table, helping perhaps to relieve the most desperate hunger. Its true purpose, however,

The dough, made of wheat flour, yeast, and sour-dough, is divided into 7 oz (200 g) portions.

The dough is shaped into lengths of just over two feet (70 cm) and laid on the baking tray.

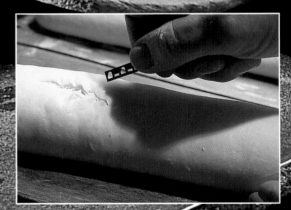

Before the baguettes are baked, the surface is slit so the crust produces the well-known surface pattern.

is to complement the meal, from the initial hors d'œuvre right through to the final cheese platter.

Its origins do not go that far back in time. After the ancient Egyptians had perfected sourdough, the Greeks had developed the use of wine yeast, and the Romans had refined the grinding of grain, little happened in the world of baking for the next one and a half thousand years. The bakers' problem was how to obtain flour rather than worry about technical refinements. The unpredictable supply was their main concern, not only in terms of quantity but also quality.

The bakers would roll their dough into balls, *boules*, hence their name *boulanger*, to produce the main source of food for the people. In order to both regulate supply and prevent abuse, a whole range of rules was introduced very early on in order to regulate the weight, composition and price of bread. Bakers were only allowed to purchase flour

when the people had satisfied their needs. The bread was baked from wholemeal flour and without salt. The latter was in too short supply and too expensive. White bread only became possible when, in the reign of the Sun King, it was discovered how to separate off the bran. Louis XIV indeed preferred white bread. In addition to sourdough, beer yeast also came to be used. A slit was made along the top of the loaf to obtain a more attractive crust.

The popularity of the crispy crust eventually stimulated the appearance of the baguette. Even today the crust is the criterion of quality. It must be golden or at least light brown. The consistency must be even in structure. Today's best quality baguettes often come from bakeries where progress has not yet made significant inroads. The best bread is produced where a minimum of yeast is used, where plenty of time is allowed for rising, and where the machine kneads slowly.

Butter from Unpasteurized Milk

Although butter has been known for thousands of years, it is really only in the last hundred years or so that it has been available in any significant quantity. Until then it was an expensive and very rare product. Butter remained everywhere the preserve of the landed gentry and served as a means of paying taxes, or generally as a method of payment. It was only with developments in agriculture, which relieved the ox from its responsibilities of pulling the plough, that changes occurred. There was a greater emphasis on breeding cows for milk production and the resulting increase in milk herds made the raw material for butter production widely available.

Really good butter is only obtained from the milk of cows kept in a mild climate and grazed on succulent, herb-rich meadows. To date, the butter from only four regions has been awarded the prestigious Appellation D'Origine Contrôlée (AOC):
- Beurre d'Isigny,
- Beurre des Charentes,
- Beurre Charentes-Poitou,
- Beurre des Deux-Sèvres.

Nevertheless its fine, nutty and scented taste only comes to the fore with butter from unpasteurized milk. It requires particularly careful and rapid processing and is a rare specialty. Isigny-sur-Mer in the Département of Calvados is particularly famous for its butter from unpasteurized milk and the only cream with the Appellation D'Origine Contrôlée. Most other sorts of butter, in contrast, are pasteurized.

Background: Fresh baguettes with the crisp golden-brown crust and delicious moist center

Ficelle – string
3–4 oz (100–125 g) in weight, almost as long as a baguette, but thinner

Flûte – flute
5–6 oz (150–175 g) in weight, somewhere between baguette and ficelle

Baguette – drum stick
7–8 oz (200–250 g) in weight, just over two feet (70 cm) in length

Couronne – crown or wreath
Loaf in the shape of a wreath

Pain – loaf
Elder brother of the baguette, just under one pound (400 g) in weight

The wreath is a popular shape for country bread and hearty rustic loaves

Pain au fromage blanc – loaf with farmer's cheese
Bread specialty made out of dough enriched with curd cheese

Bâtard – bastard
Oval, uneven shape, approximately one foot (30 cm) in length, 10 oz (300 g) or more often one pound (500 g) in weight

Pain au son – bran loaf
Wheat bread containing 20 percent bran

Pain au noix – nut loaf
The proportion of nuts is 15 percent

Pain anglais – English loaf
Bread for toasting made of wheat or whole meal

Pain Graham – Graham loaf
Whole meal bread made of coarsely ground wheat

Pain de seigle – rye loaf
Rye bread with dough containing wheat

Pain rond – round loaf
Flat, round loaf; spherical shape in northern France, *pain boulot*, weighing up to four pounds (2 kg)

Small loaves of 3–4 oz (100 g)

Pain à la bière – beer loaf
Robust bread made with beer

Fougasse – antipersonnel mine
Pretzel made of bread dough; sometimes with bacon or sweetened

Croissant

The croissant is the favorite breakfast food of the French and is well known and loved throughout the world. Yet, although it appears archetypically French, it actually originates from Hungary. *croissant* literally means *waxing moon*. At the end of the 17th century the Turks were besieging Budapest. They hoped to bring down the city by digging a tunnel under the defensive walls. The bakers, who pursued their profession in the early hours of the morning, noticed something suspicious and raised the alarm in time. The Turks, thus thwarted, had to withdraw. As a symbol of their triumph, the bakers recreated the emblem of the Ottoman Empire, the waxing moon, out of puff pastry.

The croissant caught on in Vienna too, and it was Marie-Antoinette, Austrian by birth, who introduced it to France on her ascension to the French throne in the 18th century.

In order to avoid disappointment, always order *croissants au beurre*, butter croissants, at the baker's. And do not dunk them in your coffee. That will spoil the pleasure of the nice crispy crust!

Making croissants requires a puff pastry with a lot of butter.

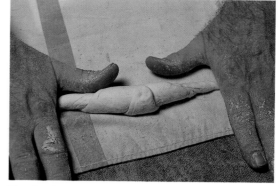

The dough is rolled out thinly and triangles are cut. Each triangle is then rolled up towards its apex.

The dough is folded several times and spread with butter between each folding.

The cloth is lightly sprinkled with flour, allowing the croissants to be lifted easily onto the baking tray.

Bretzel au flan – pretzel with filling. Puff pastry pretzel with vanilla custard

Brioche – bun made of a rich yeast dough containing eggs and butter

Chausson aux pommes – apple turnover made with puff pastry

Pain aux noix – yeast dough "snail" with nuts

Croissant au beurre, the "de luxe model" made with butter

Gugelhupf – made with yeast dough

Crémontaise – breakfast cake

Pain au raisin – raisin "snail"

Pain au chocolat – pastry containing pieces of chocolate

Pastis

It is for two reasons that the most popular French aperitif evokes Provence, its balmy air and the sun beating down on a blue sea. The first is historic, the second economic. Pastis is an aperitif with an aniseed base, and it is above all around the Mediterranean that aniseed is to be found. The Egyptians, Greeks, and Romans held it in great value, particularly for its many medicinal properties. Nowadays it is used to season fish, baked foods, and desserts. Most popular of all is its liquid form, whether as Arrak, Raki, Ouzo, Sambucca, Aniseta or, of course, as Pastis. The farms in the wine villages of Provence used to produce it with various herbs for consumption at home.

It was from an old native of Provence that Paul Ricard, the *promoter* of Pastis, obtained the basic recipe. In 1932, when aperitifs with an aniseed base were legalized, he began production in Marseilles.

It was not only Ricard who enjoyed success, for aniseed-based drinks became generally popular. With its typically spicy, licorice taste, it is reminiscent of the notorious absinthe. The latter, an extract of vermouth and generally administered as a cure-all, had begun to develop into a liquor in Switzerland around the end of the 18th century. The first distillery in France was opened by a certain Henri-Louis Pernod. During the empire of Napoleon III (1852–70) it was regarded as chic to meet in the late afternoon in the cafés for the *green hour*. It owed its name to the color of the absinthe, diluted with sugar water. However, its reputation was soon destroyed for it was ruining the health of thousands and it was finally banned in 1915. From 1951 many of the old absinthe manufacturers began to market Pastis, their labels often evoking its forbidden forerunner.

The essence of aniseed, which is much kinder to the stomach and whose basic ingredient is oil of aniseed, is usually distilled from star anise, the fruit of the Badian tree, a type of Chinese magnolia. Anethol can also be obtained from the

The storeroom holds Pastis ingredients from Provence and far-off countries. Star anise, the main ingredient, is the fruit of the Badian tree, a type of Chinese magnolia.

Herbs and spices are distilled in alcohol and water.
Below: The five best-known brands of Pastis in France.

Below: You never drink Pastis neat. It is diluted with ice-cold water, but never ice. The mint oils crystallize when water is added, giving the Pastis its typical cloudy appearance.

seed of the anise plant, fennel or tarragon. Other legally stipulated ingredients of Pastis are sweet root and Provençal herbs, which are prepared in water and alcohol. These ingredients give the alcohol (forty-five percent by volume) its characteristic aroma. Finally, in order to improve taste and color, a finely judged amount of sugar and caramel is added. Pastis is drunk diluted with water. The connoisseur only adds ice-cold water, but never ice, since this would cause the anethol to separate out. Bottles should also not be allowed to stand in the cold, as this will cause the Pastis to become cloudy.

Traditional Aperitifs

Amer Picon
A bitter flavored with the bark of the cinchona tree, gentian roots, and distillate of orange. Today it is usually drunk added to beer, Picon Bière.

Byrrh
Ingredients are very strong red wine must, extracts of the bark of the cinchona tree, herbs, and fruits.

Dubonnet
An aperitif *à base de vin*, with a wine base, made of red or white wine must. The original recipe specifies flavoring with the bark of the cinchona tree.

Noilly Prat
Dry Vermouth made of a white wine which is oxidized and reminiscent in taste of a Madeira wine. It is the base for the famous cocktail, Martini Dry, and is excellent in fish sauces.

Rivesaltes
Vin doux naturel, a wine with Appellation d'Origine Contrôlée (AOC), whose fermentation is completed by the addition of wine spirit, so that the natural grape sugar is preserved.

Saint-Raphaël
Aperitif made of a mixture of must and wine, also flavored with the appetizing bark of the cinchona tree.

Suze
Its taste is largely determined by the gentian. It is served with ice and soda.

Ingredients for noble Pastis
1 mint – 2 birch leaves – 3 vervain –
4 sapwood – 5 licorice – 6 maize –
7 currant leaves (cassis leaves) –
8 poppy seeds – 9 thyme –
10 chamomile – 11 cinnamon –
12 star anise – 13 caraway –
14 aniseed – 15 savory – 16 parsley –
17 fennel – 18 coriander

Crème de Cassis

Crème de Cassis, a blackcurrant liqueur (*cassis* is the botanical name for blackcurrant), would not have been so familiar to us if it had not been for the Chanoine (canon) Félix Kir. The priest (born in 1878) was well known as a fervent opponent of the Nazis, helping thousands of resistance fighters to escape. At the age of over sixty, he was elected Mayor of Dijon. Since the Dijon liqueur factories were fighting for survival after the war, he would always give every guest a glass of white wine and Cassis, in line with the old tradition. Even the Blanc-Cassis, an aperitif that was made of dry white wine with plenty of fresh acidity and a shot of Crème de Cassis, had become a victim of the war.

In prewar France the café had always been the second living room, at least for the men. This custom had died out during the Occupation, not because alcohol was rationed, but because careless talk in the café could lead to trouble with the authorities. Thus, many a famous aperitif became forgotten, including Blanc-Cassis. Revived by

The blackcurrants are packed in foil and kept in refrigerated storage. They are then processed as and when needed throughout the year.

Fully ripe blackcurrants keep their taste qualities, fresh color, and high vitamin C content when frozen rapidly.

Left: To make Kir, the Crème de Cassis is poured first into the glass, followed by an acidic white wine.

Good blackcurrant liqueurs contain more than a pound (500 g) of berries.

Father Kir, the drink took on his name, a rare honor indeed in France.

Originally Blanc-Cassis had been more of a Parisian affair. Nevertheless it was two Dijon businessmen who first came upon the drink in Neuilly. Enthused by the experience, they started its production in their native town in 1841. There was only one problem: almost nobody grew blackcurrants. That was to change quickly however. The fruit liqueur became very popular, so much so that in 1914 around eighty liqueur factories were founded. Demand for it encouraged wine-growers to plant blackcurrant bushes around the edges of their vineyards and thereby boost their income.

It is still Burgundy, as well as parts of the Loire and Rhone Valleys, that supply the blackcurrants. The farmers in these areas have specialized in the growing techniques required. The blackcurrants need ten weeks of temperatures below freezing, for only then do the plants develop plentiful buds. Once the berries achieve their optimal taste, they only retain this for a day, and so they are processed rapidly by machine. The value of the blackcurrant lies in its rich store of vitamin C, but this can also pose a problem, as the berries oxidize quickly. The most modern method of retaining the taste and fresh violet black color, consists in shock freezing them to –22 °F (–30 °C). In this way the fruit can be processed as and when required. When this is done, the fruit is brought up to a temperature of 23 °F (–5 °C) and sprayed with alcohol. This acts as a solvent for color and taste, and at the same time prevents fermentation. For five weeks the fruit macerates (softens) in an alcohol–water mixture in rotation vats. The first juice, which will be reserved for the top quality Cassis, is then drawn off. Fruit liqueurs with the label *Crème* are exclusively produced by maceration.

Blackcurrants naturally have a high acid content. In order to obtain a liqueur with harmony and strength of taste, the three main components, acid, sugar, and alcohol, must be perfectly balanced. At a percentage by volume of twenty, it has taken up the maximum amount of fruit, and the sugar has reached saturation at a weight of one pound (520 g). The alcohol measure is an indicator of quality, for at a percentage by volume of sixteen the Crème de Cassis has absorbed only half as much fruit, but contains only 2 oz (60 g) less sugar. Crème de Cassis used to stand on café tables and be used like mustard as seasoning. In France it is not drunk neat, but is used to flavor wine, champagne, vermouth or mineral water. It is also delicious with cake or ice cream as well as duck or pork. Once opened, it should be kept in a refrigerator and consumed within three months.

Opposite: The Crème de Cassis, a specialty of Burgundy and almost syrupy in consistency, flows into the bottles.

Félix Kir, Mayor of Dijon, became so popular that a drink was named after him.

Edible Snails

Antoine Carême (1784–1833), effectively the founder of fine French cuisine, was responsible for the elevation of the edible snail to gourmet status at the beginning of the 19th century, *à la bourguignonne* – Burgundy style, with butter, garlic, and parsley. So popular did these bite-sized animals become that little plates with special compartments were developed together with pincers that could grip their hot shells and a two-pronged fork to extract the flesh. The gourmet, however, little realizes how meticulous the preparation of this gristly little animal is. Before consumption snails must undergo a starvation diet for at least ten days. This is strictly adhered to everywhere except in the South of France where the snails are allowed a diet of thyme. This is essential to rid the snail of any poisonous leaves it may have consumed. For reasons of cleanliness the snail is subjected to three washes with water. The first cleans the outside, whilst the second, with salt and vinegar added, concentrates on the insides. Finally the snail is bathed in clear water. The snails are then generally blanched, cooled, removed from their shells, and usually cooked in a well-seasoned bouillon. Once cold, they are replaced in the shells which have in the mean-time been sterilized. They are sealed with snail or herb butter and are then ready for consumption.

Our distant human ancestors did not take long to discover the delights of these gastropods, as prehistoric waste tips will testify. The Greeks devoted careful attention to them whilst the Romans pioneered snail breeding. They grilled them much as the natives of Catalonia and Provence do today, without cooking them beforehand. In the rest of France, however, the upper class considered snails as food for the poor, and at most would perhaps pick at them during Lent, until, that is, the Cook of the Kings and the King of Cooks adopted them. Since then, the French have positively exaggerated their passion for snails. The large Burgundy snail, whose shell is up to two inches (5 cm) in diameter, fell victim to the gourmets (and modern agriculture) and has now become very rare. Chefs often substitute them on the menus with *petits gris*, the smaller variety of the edible snail with a gray body in a white or speckled yellow shell. They are a native of Gascony, Provence, Languedoc, and Roussillon and are more suitable for domestic breeding, *héliciculture*, than their larger cousins.

Canned snails are often Eastern European imports, or Turkish snails, which are recognized by their dark flesh and black edge to the shell, or imported deep-frozen Chinese snails which are half-pound giants from the family of Achat snails. Although snails contain a large amount of mineral salts, they are in fact quite indigestible and should, therefore, only be consumed in extreme moderation.

Beurre d'escargot
Snail Butter

1 shallot
2 garlic cloves
2 tsp finely chopped flat-leaved parsley
$1/2$ cup (125 g) butter
Salt, black pepper

Peel the shallot and garlic and chop finely.
Mix with parsley and butter and season with salt and pepper to taste.
The butter is spread in the opening of the snail shells. The snails are then heated in the oven until the butter has melted. The snails are immediately removed from the oven – the butter should not become brown – and served with a baguette or simple bread.

Snails as a Commercial Product

Escargot achatine – the Achat snail
The Achat snail originates from East Africa and is widespread in Asia, where it is also commercially bred. These giant snails, weighing up to a pound (500 g), are mainly imported from China. They are increasingly being used as a substitute for the Burgundy or edible snail. Shells of the latter species are filled with pieces of the flesh of the Achat snail and then marketed under the simple label *escargot*.

Escargot de Bourgogne – edible snail
This central European snail has a shell of over an inch (3–4 cm) in diameter. Generally it is precooked and deep-frozen or canned.

Petit gris – small edible snail
The southern European edible snail, with a shell of just under an inch (2–3 cm) in diameter, occurs in various varieties as far away as Asia Minor. It is also bred in captivity. It is sold live in markets in the South of France and elsewhere in cans.

Snail farm in the South of France, where these tasty mollusks are bred in wooden boxes under the open sky

The snails, which feed on lettuce and greens, take a year to reach a marketable size

Special cutlery for the classical preparation: Snails in herb butter

Background: *Petit gris*, the *small gray* southern European edible snail, is largely replacing the now rare Burgundy snail.

Lobsters

If you want to enjoy completely fresh seafood in general, or *homard*, lobster, in particular, then a journey to Brittany is a must. Saint-Brieuc is the French capital for lobsters, langoustes (spiny lobsters), crabs, scallops, and other shellfish. Even oysters, indispensable on any seafood platter, are available in Brittany. When lobster catching was still a profitable business for the fishermen of ports such as Erquy or Saint-Quaynoch, Breton chefs would proudly serve *homard à l'armoricaine*, "Armorica" being the old name for Britanny. The lobster was split up, flambéed, and served with a red sauce which included tomatoes to add extra taste and color. However, the stocks on the Breton coast are now practically exhausted, and today fresh lobsters are landed from Ireland or the west coast of England.

The catching of lobsters is an arduous job. Lobster pots are laid in the sea at depths of up to 220 feet (70 m). These contain bait – salted fish for lobsters, fresh fish for crabs. Every day the fishermen put out to sea to haul up the pots and check the catch – lobsters, crabs, langoustes or spider crabs – it is a question of potluck. Being caught is a shock for the lobsters, and they require several days in the aquarium to recover. If they are bought alive, they may be kept for at least two days in the lowest compartment of the refrigerator, covered with a damp cloth. Dark blue is the color of live lobsters and it is only when cooked that they assume their characteristic red pigment. Cooking will also bring out the true taste, but care must be taken not to simmer the lobster for more than a quarter of an hour as it will otherwise lose its flavor and the flesh will become tough. The summer, the main catching season, is of course the time when lobsters are at their freshest and best value for money.

Background: A fine specimen of a lobster, the ten-footed crab of the European seas.

Famous Lobster Recipes

Homard à l`armoricaine
Flambéed lobster pieces in fine tomato sauce

Homard à la crème
Pieces of lobsters fried quickly and then cooked in cream

Homard à la nage
Whole small lobster cooked in white wine stock

Homard au court bouillon
Cooked and served whole in a seasoned clear bouillon

Homard cardinal
Cooked with truffles and mushrooms in a *sauce béchamel* flavored with the shell of the lobster

Homard grillé
Halved, brushed with olive oil, and broiled

Homard Thermidor
Lobster ragout in piquant mustard sauce gratinéed with cheese. (Thermidor corresponds to the month of August and is the eleventh month in the calendar of the French Revolution, which applied from 1792 to 1806)

Oysters

Oyster fishermen consider themselves as the farmers of the sea, for their work has a distinctly agricultural character, even if they are dependent on the tides and can only tend their land when the tide is out. In France, the oyster beds are to be found on the Brittany coast, at Marennes and Arcachon, and on the Mediterranean at Bouzigues in the lagoon of Thau. The beds at Marennes cover fourteen square miles (3,500 hectares). They are located on the sand banks between the estuaries of the Rivers Seudre and Charente and on the east side of the offshore island of Oléron. There the oysters are able to live on the right mixture of sea and fresh water and can flourish in summer water temperatures of more than 70 °F (22 °C). The native flat European oyster species was completely decimated by disease in 1922. Fortunately there was a substitute, for in 1868 a ship in distress was forced to ditch its load of Portuguese oysters overboard, which then flourished on the Marennes coast until they too succumbed to the epidemic. Help was on hand however in the form of the Pacific rock oyster, *crassostrea gigas*, which has dominated the French coastal area and its restaurants ever since.

In July the oysters breed on strictly protected, natural banks. These invertebrate mollusks reproduce by producing millions of larvae that swim freely for a time before finding a firm place on which to anchor themselves and develop. The *ostréiculteur* (oyster breeder) is able to take advantage of this process by putting down wooden pots, slates or, more commonly nowadays, ribbed plastic pipes at strategically favorable points. The larvae attach themselves and immediately begin to develop their shells. After about two months they are roughly the size of a pea, although only around a dozen offspring per oyster ever survive the perils of this first stage of their life.

In the spring the fishermen relocate the young oyster colonies, since, if they are to grow quickly, they need more nourishing food than the sea is able to provide. The fishermen of La Tremblade, for example, place them on wooden frames in the Bay of Ronce-les-Bains. Even in their second year of life, the oysters are threatened by fish, snails, starfish, other shellfish, and by the storms. If they survive these dangers, they are stripped from their pipes, sorted by size and their future decided by the fishermen. Some continue their growth in *poches*, black plastic nets, on iron frames in the sea, whilst others are selected for further breeding. Those which are too small are spared for another year.

Each fisherman rents parcels of land from the state. Some parcels offer good nourishment and the oysters grow correspondingly quickly. Others are poor and the oysters stagnate. These natural

Conditions for oyster cultivation are ideal between Marennes and the island of Oléron, on the Atlantic coast to the north of Bordeaux and the Gironde estuary.

The oysters are harvested after temporary storage in the old salt basins, where they gain in weight and taste by consuming the algae on the gravel.

Whether a lean-to shed or a decorated house, all the oysters have a home of their own, the *bourriche,* the original packaging, which keeps them fresh.

How to open an oyster (see illustrations on right-hand page)
1. Oysters are not washed, since they are supplied already cleaned.
2. Lay out the oyster on a cloth which has been folded several times, so that the flat side is uppermost.
3. Grip firmly with the left hand and hold straight. Work over a flat bowl to catch any water spilling from the oyster.
4. With the short, strong oyster knife cut into the so-called hinge and separate the closing muscle.
5. Now draw the knife horizontally between the shells, and then use it as a lever to open up the two halves. Remove the upper shell.

Varieties of Oyster

Belons
Flat oysters from Brittany with a very delicate, nutty taste

Bouzigues
From the large inland lake of Thau on the Mediterranean between Sète and Agde

Gravettes d'Arcachon
Mostly known as *Arcachons*; flat oysters from the southwestern Atlantic coast of France at Bordeaux

Marennes
Rock oysters from the area between the Charente coast and the island of Oléron; they are fattened and refined in natural basins, the *claires.*
• *claires* have been refined in the basins for a short time
• *fines de claires* are those which have spent four weeks in the breeding basin at 20 to the square yard (square meter) and contain at least six percent flesh.
• *spéciales de claires* are entitled to their name when they have spent at least two months at 10 to the square yard (square meter). Then they should contain at least nine percent flesh

conditions have to be exploited to manage the development of the oysters. After three years the oysters can be harvested and consumed, but in Marennes-Oléron there is still one more stage. In the marshes on the coast and twelve miles (20 km) up the Seudre valley there are basins in which salt used to be produced. The Romans, great oyster gourmets themselves, discovered the unique advantage of these basins. Each high tide the *claires* (breeding basins) are supplied with fresh water by means of a system of channels, and are eminently suitable for temporary storage of the oysters. They do not grow any more, but their shells harden, making them more resistant and stronger. They feed on the algae, the blue Navicula, causing them to gain weight, fineness, and acquire an astonishingly green color. Furthermore they develop glycogen, a carbohydrate, and a rich stock of mineral salts and vitamins. If kept in their original packaging, the *bourriche*, at a temperature of between 40 and 60 °F (5–15 °C), the *fines de claires* and the *spéciales de claires* (see explanation above) remain fresh for eight to ten days, even in summer. At this time the smaller and more solid oysters taste best. Otherwise the gourmet should choose according to the size of his mouth. Be careful not to fill your mouth too full, especially when sipping the oyster!

Oyster Sizes

Ostrea edulis, huître plate
European Oyster

Nr. 4	=	1.3 oz (40 g)
Nr. 3	=	1.7 oz (50 g)
Nr. 2	=	2.0 oz (60 g)
Nr. 1	=	2.5 oz (75 g)
Nr. 0	=	3.0 oz (90 g)
Nr. 00	=	3.3 oz (100 g)
Nr. 000	=	3.7 oz (110 g)
Nr. 0000	=	4.0 oz (120 g)
Nr. 00000	=	5.0 oz (150 g)

Crassostrea gigas and *crassostrea angulata, huître creuse*
Pacific and Portuguese Oyster

Très grand (TG) – very large	= 3.3 oz (100 g)
Grand (G) – large	= 2.5 to 3.2 oz (75 to 99 g)
Moyen (M) – medium-sized	= 1.7 to 2.4 oz (50 to 74 g)
Petit (P) – small	= 1.7 oz (50 g)

Below: Before being sent all over the world, the oysters are sorted and packed strictly according to size. To enable them to survive for about ten days out of water they are subjected to a process called *expédition*.

Races of oyster common in Europe

Ostrea edulis, huître plate, European Oyster
Named after their areas of cultivation: Belons, Marennes or Gravettes d'Arcachon; delicate mineral taste, not widespread

Crassostrea angulata, huître creuse, Portuguese Oyster or Rock Oyster
Dome-shaped oyster, cultivated particularly in Marennes-Oléron, where their taste is refined in *claires*, development basins; less important than previously

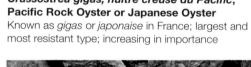

Crassostrea gigas, huître creuse du Pacific, Pacific Rock Oyster or Japanese Oyster
Known as *gigas* or *japonaise* in France; largest and most resistant type; increasing in importance

How to open an oyster

The knife is inserted into the closure muscle, the so-called hinge.

The closure muscle is separated by horizontal movements with the knife, which is then used as a lever.

By turning the knife, the shells are separated.

After removing the upper shell, the oyster is sipped or served on ice.

347

Seafood

Oyster
(See pp. 346–347)

**Grande cigale de mer –
Flat Lobster**
Has delicious tail meat,
just like langoustes and
lobster.

Clam
Originates in America; eaten
raw in France.

Bigorneau – Winkle
About one inch (3 cm)
long; generally cooked
quickly and served with
other seafood.

Langouste – Langouste or spiny lobster
With long feelers, but no pincers; has
become rare in the Mediterranean. The
best are red and come from the Brittany
coast or the British Isles. If bought alive,
they should still be agile. When lifted, they
will move their tail.

Moule – Mussel
Known as *bouchot* on the Atlantic coast;
best in fall and winter.

Amande de Mer – Dog Cockle
Generally from the Atlantic coast;
throughout the year in the
Mediterranean. It is not particularly tasty.

Praire – Warty Venus
With ridged shell; occurs almost
everywhere in European seas. They
are eaten raw, steamed or broiled.

**Coque, bucarde –
Cockle**
Has little flesh and must
be thoroughly cleaned.

**Clovisse, palourde – Venus
shell**
Has tender flesh; throughout
the year.

Bulot, buccin – Whelk
About two inches (10 cm)
in size; should be cooked
in *court bouillon* and
served with mayonnaise,
vinaigrette dressing or
other seafood.

Varech, algues marines – Seaweeds
Popular for presenting shellfish dishes.

Crabe tourteau – Edible crab
Has very fine-flavored meat; highly prized in France, essential to every good seafood platter.

Homard – Lobster
Most well known are the deep blue Breton lobsters. They can weigh up to 20 pounds (10 kg) and reach 10 inches (50 cm) in length. They should be bought live, preferably from a tank in which they have been able to recover from the stress of being caught.

Crevette rose – Shrimp
Somewhat larger shrimp species which is popular as an hors d'œuvre.

Ecrevisse – Crayfish
Popular as the base for a sauce; mostly imported nowadays.

Coquille Saint-Jacques (p. 352)
The firm muscle (*noix*) is delicious, but the softer reddish roe sack (*corail*) also tastes good when fresh. Season: October through April, best at the beginning of the year.

Fish

Anchois – Anchovies
This small herring from the Mediterranean is particularly tasty; in the summer it is best eaten quite fresh, quickly marinated, and raw.

Anguille – Eel
The best time for fresh eel is from April through October. In Bordeaux and the Charente it is very popular as *matelote*, stew, braised in red wine.

Brochet – Pike
In France pike is used for the popular *quenelles de brochet*, pike dumplings. Otherwise it is usually cooked in fish stock.

Cabillaud, morue – Cod
The popularity of stock fish has also promoted a renaissance of fresh cod. It can be prepared in numerous different ways and is best from October through March.

Congre – Conger Eel
The almost black conger eel, which occurs in coastal waters throughout the year, can reach a length of ten feet (3 m). Because of its many bones, it is mainly used for soups and sauces.

Dorade – Sea Bream (4)
The many species of bream are not exclusive to the Mediterranean, although bream is particularly popular in Provence, whether eaten whole or as fillets, baked in the oven or grilled. Available throughout the year.

Eglefin – Haddock
The haddock, a member of the cod family, is also known in France as the *morue noire*. It is caught in the Atlantic and is prepared in the same way as cod.

Grondin – Gurnard (5)
The firm flesh of the gurnard is very tasty. However, the very prickly scales and large head produce a lot of waste, for this reason it is best suited to making soups.

Lieu jaune – Pollack
Only recently has this close relative of the cod been found on French fish stalls. Its white flesh is somewhat more succulent than the *lieu noir*, the coley or coalfish.

Lotte, Baudroie – Angler or Devil Fish (8)
Because of its heavy, ugly head, the fish is always marketed skinned and with the head removed. It lives in the deep waters of the Mediterranean and the Atlantic. Its firm flesh is often rolled up and roasted, *rôti*, in the oven.

Loup de mer – Sea Perch (1)
It is known under this name in the Mediterranean, where it has become rare, whereas on the Atlantic it is called the *bar*. A very fine, delicate, but overpriced fish, which is often eaten whole, either broiled, roasted or baked in a crust of salt. Good in the spring and summer.

Maquereau – Mackerel
The mackerel has plenty of taste, but is fatty. Therefore it is usually broiled, cooked in lemon juice or vinegar, or marinated. The best come from cold waters. In spring it is known as the *lisette*.

Merlan – Whiting
This delicate fish has very tender flesh. It is mainly caught in the Atlantic, having become rare in the Mediterranean.

Plie, Carrelet – Plaice (6)
The plaice, easily recognized by its orange spots, also occurs in the Mediterranean. It has tender flesh and is fried or baked.

Raie – Ray
Ray is popular in France. Only its *ailes*, wings, are eaten. The common ray comes mainly from the Atlantic whilst the spotted ray also often occurs in the Mediterranean.

Rascasse – Scorpion Fish
Neither its shell nor its prickles protect the fish from its role as a valued ingredient in Bouillabaisse, its white flesh having a very pleasant taste.

Rouget-barbet – Red Mullet (2)
Although red mullet is caught on the French Atlantic coast, it belongs predominantly to Mediterranean cuisine and marries well with the herbs and olive oil of the area. It should never be poached.

Saint-Pierre – St. Peter's Fish
Because of its tasty fine flesh, the St. Peter's Fish is in great demand and correspondingly expensive. It is found in most seas, but is nevertheless uncommon.

Sandre – Zander
This predatory freshwater fish, popular in Burgundy, is reminiscent of the fine taste of young pike.

Sardine (3)
The very fatty relative of the herring has a powerful taste, popular above all in the South of France. Here they are broiled in large quantities, fanned out on a grid made of vine sticks.

Saumon – Salmon
The French are very partial to salmon. Often it is cooked, fried or broiled as *darne de saumon*, slice of salmon, marinated, or served as salmon tartar.

Sole
One of the finest fish of all, it has many enthusiasts worldwide. The best sole come from Normandy. Available throughout the year.

Thon – Tuna Fish
The tuna is caught in the Mediterranean. It is sold in slices, broiled or fried and served with Mediterranean herbs and vegetables. Best season: early summer.

Truite – Trout
Numerous fish farms supply trout. One of the favorite dishes is *truite aux amandes*, trout with almonds (recipe p. 352).

Turbot (7)
Because of its firm, delicious flesh, the turbot is a much sought after and expensive flat fish. It can be prepared in a variety of ways.

Vive – Weever
Because it is so delicious, it is highly valued in the South of France, where it flavors the Bouillabaisse. Nevertheless it is only rarely caught in the Mediterranean nowadays.

Dishes for Gourmets

Fish, Shellfish, and Crustaceans

Truites aux Amandes
Trout with Almonds

Serves 2

2 trout
Salt, black pepper
2 Tbs flour
3 Tbs (40 g) butter
1 oz (30 g) sliced almonds
2 Tbs crème fraîche
Slices of lemon

Clean the trout, rinse and pat dry. Add salt and pepper and dip in flour. Heat the butter gently and fry the fish in it for 7 minutes on each side. Turn the fish very carefully. Remove the fish and keep warm.
Briefly roast the almonds and stir in the crème fraîche. Pour the almond sauce over the trout and decorate with the slices of lemon.

Coquilles Saint-Jacques sautées –
Sautéed pilgrim cockles

Coquilles Saint-Jacques sautées
Sautéed Pilgrim Cockles
(Illustration)

16 Coquilles Saint-Jacques
1 Tbs lemon juice
A pinch of cayenne pepper
Salt, black pepper
1 Tbs flour
1 Tbs olive oil
3 Tbs (40 g) butter
2 garlic cloves, finely chopped
2 Tbs finely chopped parsley

Open the Coquilles Saint-Jacques with a knife, remove the white flesh and orange roe, wash thoroughly, and pat them dry.
Cut the white flesh in half horizontally.
Stir the cayenne pepper in with the lemon juice, season the *coquilles* with salt and pepper, and sprinkle some lemon juice and flour on them.
Heat the oil and butter. Fry the white flesh for about a minute on each side and then add the roe. Spread with garlic and parsley. Cover and allow to cook on a gentle heat for four minutes. Serve immediately.

Dorade Rose à la Provençale
Red Sea Bream à la provençale
(Illustration)

1 pink sea bream about 2 lbs (1 kg)
3 Tbs olive oil
1 sprig fennel
2 sprigs parsley
2 tomatoes
1 onion
1 green pepper
2 garlic cloves
1/2 tsp finely chopped thyme
Salt, black pepper

Rôti de Lotte
Roast Angler Fish

2 garlic cloves
1 angler fish about 2 lb (1 kg) ready for cooking
5 Tbs olive oil
Salt, black pepper

Preheat the oven to 470 °F (240 °C)
Chop the garlic and insert it into the fish. Brush with oil and season.
Grease a roasting dish with the remaining olive oil, and lay the fish in it.
Bake in the oven for about 25 minutes. Pour the juices over the fish several times during cooking.
Cut in slices and serve with *ratatouille* (recipe p. 103) or white wine sauce.

Mouclade Charentaise
Charentais Mussels

4 lbs (2 kg) mussels
3 shallots
2 oz (50 g) butter
1 cup (200 ml) white wine
3 garlic cloves
1 Tbs flour
1 egg yolk
4 oz (125 g) crème fraîche
1 tsp curry powder
2 Tbs finely chopped parsley
Salt, black pepper

Thoroughly wash and scrub the mussels, removing any strands attached. Peel the shallots, chop them finely and fry in a tablespoon of butter. Pour in the wine and bring to the boil. Add the mussels, cover the pan and stir occasionally.

As soon as the mussels open (after about 7 minutes), pour off the stock through a cloth into a container. Remove the mussels from their shells and keep warm. Fry the garlic in the remaining butter, sprinkling on the flour (do not allow it to get brown) and gradually pour in the mussel stock. Remove the saucepan from the heat. Mix the egg yolk, crème fraîche, and curry powder together and stir into the sauce, at the same time adding the parsley. Season with salt and pepper to taste and carefully heat the mixture up again, stirring it continuously.
Arrange the mussels on the plate, pour sauce over them and serve with a well-chilled vin de pays Charentais or Muscadet.

Dorade rose à la provençale -
Red sea bream à la provençale

Sardines grillées – Broiled sardines

Sardines Grillées
Broiled Sardines
(Illustration)

12–16 sardines
1¹⁄₂ cups (250 ml) olive oil
1 tsp finely chopped thyme
1 tsp finely chopped rosemary
1 Tbs finely chopped fennel
3 Tbs lemon juice
3 garlic cloves, finely chopped
Salt, pepper

Prepare the bream for cooking, rinse in cold water and pat dry. Add a few drops of olive oil, and the fennel and parsley to the fish.
Preheat the oven to 40 °F (200 °C).
Remove the skin from the tomatoes, remove center and cube. Peel and chop the onions finely. Clean the green pepper and cut in rings. Put the vegetables in an oven proof dish with the remaining olive oil and season with salt and pepper. Slit the fish on both sides, season, and lay it on the bed of vegetables.
Cook for about 20 minutes and serve in the dish.

Prepare the fish and marinade for at least 30 minutes with the other ingredients.
Remove the sardines, season and grill for 3–5 minutes according to size.

Bouillabaisse

Fantastical stories seek to explain the origin of this Mediterranean specialty. One tale says that Venus used it to make her husband Vulcano sleepy, another that it was an abbess who devised the recipe as a Friday meal, and yet another that a Bordeaux man, by the name of Baysse, was its originator. The latter theory, related by Robert J. Courtine, is particularly misleading – why should someone from the Atlantic coast have thought up the most famous dish in the Mediterranean?

The truth is simple: *Bouillabaisse* is formed from the words for boil *bouillir* and waste *baisse*. It became the name for the soup that the fishermen prepared from the remains of their catch. Above all, they used the rock fish of the Mediterranean coast, which had gone into their nets, such as the scorpion fish, conger eel, gurnard, St. Peter's fish, angler fish, sea bream, and whiting. These used to be the cheapest fish, although one or two other fish or crustaceans might also be added if no buyer could be found. Once the stew was ready, the fish and shellfish were piled up on a platter and the soup stock poured into a bowl on the table. Proof of its humble origins is also the slice of bread which is put into each plate and then covered with the soup. In Marseilles, which lays claim to the classical version of Bouillabaisse, a peasant bread, *Marette*, is used, which is neither toasted nor rubbed with garlic, as is the present custom elsewhere. In Marseilles neither mussels nor butter are put in the Bouillabaisse. Instead, lobsters or langoustes are often used to transform it into a gourmet meal. On the coast between Menton and Cerbère yet other variations are to be found. By tacit agreement, only those recipes which contain Mediterranean fish, and at least half a dozen species, are entitled to the name of *Bouillabaisse*.

Opposite: Ingredients for a Bouillabaisse – various sorts of Mediterranean fish, crabs if desired, as well as various vegetables, herbs, and spices.

For a Bouillabaisse, the vegetables are first fried in olive oil with the herbs. Then the fish with the firmer flesh is added.

Since the original dish used leftovers, the basic recipe allowed for many variations, and potatoes were a common ingredient.

When the ingredients have cooked for about 10 minutes, the softer fish is added to the stock and allowed to cook for a further 10 minutes.

The crabs and fish are arranged on a platter and the soup is served up in separate dishes.

Bouillabaisse
Provençal Fish Stew

Serves 10

6 lbs (3 kg) fresh fish from the Mediterranean scorpion fish, conger eel, gurnard, St. Peter's fish, angler fish, sea bream, whiting and squid)
2 large crawfish
2 leeks
2 large onions
1/2 cup (100 ml) olive oil
5 tomatoes
4 garlic cloves
1 bay leaf
3 sprigs fennel
1 sprig savory or thyme
1 Tbs chopped parsley
1 strip of untreated orange peel
A pinch (1 g) of saffron strands
Salt, black pepper
Slices of southern French peasant bread

Prepare and rinse the fish and crawfish for cooking, cut the larger fish into portions. Clean or peel the leeks and onions, cut into small pieces and fry with the garlic and half the olive oil in a large saucepan, but do not allow to brown. Remove the skins from the tomatoes and dice them. Wash the herbs. Add the tomatoes, herbs and seasoning to the leek/onion mixture. Allow to cook for 10 minutes. First put the crawfish and then the fish with the firmer flesh on to the vegetables. Season and pour over the remaining olive oil. Add boiling water to the mixture until the fish is just covered. Allow it to bubble for 10 minutes. Add the softer fish and boil vigorously for no more than 10 minutes. Arrange the fish and crawfish on a warmed platter. Place a slice of the peasant bread in each plate and pour the soup over it. Serve with *rouille* or *aïoli*.

Rouille
Spicy Sauce for Fish Soups

2 ripe red paprikas
5 garlic cloves
1 small fresh red pepper
A pinch (1 g) saffron strands
1 tsp sea salt
1 large mealy potato, peeled and cooked
1 cup (200 ml) olive oil

Cook the paprika in the oven and remove the seeds and skin. Pound it with a pestle and mortar with the garlic, red pepper, saffron, and salt. Stir in with the potato to produce a thick paste. Whilst continuously beating the mixture, add olive oil drop by drop, until the sauce has the consistency of a stiff purée.

Aïoli
Garlic Paste

10 garlic cloves
2 egg yolks
1/2 tsp salt
2 1/2 cups (500 ml) fine provençal olive oil
1 tsp lemon juice

Crush the garlic. Add egg yolks and salt and stir vigorously. Whilst continuously beating, add the olive oil drop by drop, until a firm paste is obtained. Finally stir in the lemon juice according to taste.

Anchovies

Collioure is the most famous fishing and bathing resort of the Côte Vermeille, and a mere stone's throw from the Spanish border. In the summer its quay is lined with the easels of artists and hobby painters. Over and over again the sheltered bay with its fortified church, and the one time summer residence of the kings of Majorca is captured in oil or water color. Collioure appears to have lost none of the drawing power it must have exerted on the Phoenicians, Greeks, and Romans in times gone by. Indeed, today it lives primarily from tourism. Only its distinctive red wine, the naturally sweet Banyuls, and its anchovies – the famous *anchois de Collioure* – still bear witness to the once flourishing economy.

For centuries Collioure was an important trading port. Already by the Middle Ages the salted fish produced here, the anchovies, sardines, cod or tuna fish, had a good reputation. When Collioure fell to France in the Treaty of the Pyrenees in 1659, the king freed it from the salt tax, the *gabelle*. Whilst Collioure may have lost its importance as a trade center, its fishing began a golden age.

The fishermen of Collioure would put out to sea in their *catalanes*, the thirty feet (ten meters) long sailing boats with their six-man crews. They would cast out their *sardinal*, the 400 yard (400 m) long net. Even then the anchovy was the principal catch. These slim, longish herring fish occur in all warm seas, but those in the Mediterranean are a particular delicacy, above all those from Collioure. Their preservation by salting was a traditional trade in the small harbor at the foot of the Pyrenees, and many of the fishermen's wives were amongst its workforce. At its

peak there were around thirty businesses, of which only four have survived. It is about thirty years since the fishermen of Collioure last put out to sea in their *catalanes*. Only the neighboring Port-Vendres has retained a small fleet of these old fishing boats.

The freshly caught fish are immediately mixed with salt. The insides and heads are removed and the fish put in layers in barrels, with a generous dose of salt between each layer. Weighed down with large stones, they must then mature for three months in order to acquire their distinctive taste. The fish are then washed to remove the salt, sorted according to size, and placed in jars which are filled with brine. Preserved in this way, they keep for more than a year. When taking out the fish to eat, care must be taken that the remaining fish stay covered with brine.

Collioure, the picturesque fishing port at the foot of the Pyrenees, is famous for its anchovies.

The anchovies are caught in 400 yard (400 m) long nets and processed immediately.

Today there are only four firms left which prepare the fish for commercial sale.

Anchovies as a Commercial Product

Anchois – Anchovies

Whole fish mostly preserved and sold in glass jars. To remove the salt they must be soaked for an hour in water which is changed frequently. They are then cut in half along their length and the bones removed. Wipe dry. Sprinkle them with olive oil and garnish with *persillade* (finely chopped parsley and garlic). Serve with hard-boiled eggs.

Filets d'anchois – Anchovy fillets

Mostly preserved in oil in small glass jars, they are popular for salads and pizza.

Crème d'anchois – Anchovy paste

Made of pieces of fillet and oil stirred together, this paste is used as a seasoning for grilling or as a spread for toast or bread. *Anchois de Collioure* will give any meal a distinctively Mediterranean feel.

The freshly caught fish are immediately mixed with salt.

After salting, the insides and heads are removed and the anchovies put in layers in barrels.

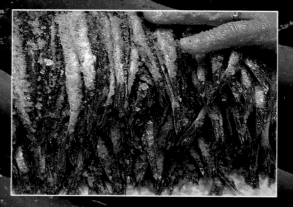

Salt is scattered between the layers. The anchovies then mature for three months.

Terrine de foie de volaille – Poultry liver
terrine

Pâté de campagne – Country paté

Pâté en croûte – in a pastry case

Pâtés and Terrines

The French love of pâtés goes back to the Middle Ages. At that time it was the *pâtissiers*, the pastry cooks and confectioners, who made them. Their delicious pâtés were always cased in *pâte*, pastry, and were thus served *en croûte*, in a crust. In the 14th century, in the lifetime of the gourmet Taillevent (1326–1395), who wrote the first French cookery book *Le viandier* (the butcher), the crusted pâtés were filled with all kinds of ingredients, for example, eel or mackerel, pigeon or goose, sucking pig or venison. The attractive exterior of the pâtés was important and was often made in the shape of poultry, the animal on the family coat of arms or some other spectacular shape. Even in the 20th century no feast is complete without pâtés.

Today the labels *pâté* and *terrine* are largely interchangeable. There are pâtés without *pâte* and terrines with the pastry casing. However, when prepared with good, fresh ingredients, they are always a delightful hors d'œuvre. Their advantage is of course that they may be prepared in advance.

Pâté en Croûte
Paté in a Pastry Case
(Illustration opposite)

Serves 10–12

2 lbs (1 kg) pie pastry
1 heaped Tbs (20 g) butter
14 oz (400 g) fresh belly of pork
1 lb (500 g) spare rib of pork
1½ oz (30 g) shelled pistachios
2 garlic cloves, finely chopped
½ tsp marjoram, finely chopped
Salt, white pepper
14 oz (400 g) knuckle of pork
6 sheets gelatin
2½ cups (500 ml) veal stock
1 large pinch nutmeg
1 large pinch ground cloves
¼ cup (50 ml) Madeira

The firm pastry is made from flour, butter, lard, oil, egg, a little salt, and cold water. Roll out the dough; grease a rectangular tin with the butter and line it completely with the pastry.
To make the stuffing, grind half of the belly of pork and half of the pork, and mix it thoroughly with the garlic, pistachios, marjoram, a little pepper, and 2 tsp salt.
Cut the knuckle of pork into largish cubes and the remaining belly of pork and spare rib into smaller cubes; season well with salt. Starting with the stuffing, put alternating layers of stuffing and meat cubes evenly into the lined tin. Fold the pastry slightly inwards at the top, but without covering the filling.
Bake in the oven at a temperature of 400 °F (200 °C) for about 90 minutes.
Soak the gelatin in cold water. Heat up the veal stock, season to taste with Madeira, nutmeg, and cloves and then thicken with the gelatin. Pour over the pâté and leave to cool.

Pâté de Campagne
Country Paté
(Illustration opposite)

Serves 10–12

8 oz (250 g) pig's liver
14 oz (400 g) pork (shoulder or spare rib)
10 oz (300 g) fat bacon
1 tsp parsley, finely chopped
1 tsp each of finely chopped thyme and marjoram
1 bay leaf, crushed
1 Tbs shallots, finely chopped
1 tsp garlic, finely chopped
1 Tbs salt
½ tsp black pepper
2 Tbs Armagnac
2 eggs
Stomach membrane of pork

Process the liver, meat, and bacon to a coarse purée and put it into a large bowl. Add the herbs, shallots, garlic, salt, pepper, and Armagnac. Mix everything together well and leave overnight in the refrigerator. Now mix in the eggs and put the mixture into an oven proof dish, taking care to distribute it evenly. Smooth out the top and cover with the pork membrane.
Cover and bake in the oven at a temperature of 350 °F (180 °C) for about 90 minutes. Allow to cool and keep in the refrigerator for 24 hours before cutting.

Terrine de Foie de Volaille
Poultry Liver Terrine
(Illustration opposite)

Serves 6–8

8 oz (250 g) turkey liver
7 oz (200 g) chicken liver
1 tsp Banyuls vinegar
1 Tbs shallots, finely chopped
4 bay leaves
½ tsp thyme, finely chopped
½ tsp white peppercorns, crushed
5 Tbs (80 ml) Banyuls or port
5 oz (150 g) chicken breast
5 oz (150 g) veal
2 tsp salt
3 oz (100 g) fat bacon, thinly sliced

Sprinkle the livers with the vinegar and marinate them overnight in Banyuls together with the shallot, one bay leaf, the thyme and the pepper.
Now purée the turkey liver, chicken breast, and veal, season with salt and mix with the marinade. Line an oven proof tureen with the slices of bacon and fill it with one third of the stuffing. Cut the chicken livers into cubes, mix them with another third of the stuffing and put it into the tureen over the first layer. Put the remaining stuffing on top and garnish with the remaining bay-leaves.
Cook the terrine in a bain marie in the oven for 60 to 90 minutes at a temperature of 350 °F (175 °C). Allow it to cool and leave it in the refrigerator for at least 24 hours so that the flavors can develop.

Terrine de Lapin
Rabbit Terrine

Serves 10–12

10 oz (300 g) rabbit meat
3 oz (100 g) chicken liver
7 oz (200 g) veal
7 oz (200 g) spare rib of pork
10 oz (300 g) fat bacon
1 tsp each finely chopped marjoram and thyme
2 Tbs Cognac
Salt, black pepper
1 egg
4 oz (125 g) fat bacon, cut into strips

Cut the rabbit meat into narrow strips. To make the stuffing, purée the liver, the remaining meat and the fat bacon. Mix the purée with the herbs, Cognac, pepper, salt, and egg.
Line an ovenproof tureen with the bacon strips. Fill the tureen with alternate layers of the stuffing mixture and the rabbit meat, finishing with a layer of rabbit and the bacon strips.
Cover and cook in a bain marie in the oven for about 90 minutes at a temperature of 350 °F (175 °C). Place a heavy weight on top of the tureen and keep in a cool place for 6 hours.

Foie Gras

As Christmas approaches the shelves of the *épiceries fines*, the delicatessens, fill up with cans of *foie gras*, pâtés made from the fattened livers of goose or duck. Even in supermarkets and hypermarkets mountains of the expensive cans tower over the customer. What would the greatest feasts of the year be without this delicacy, a byword for luxurious living. Although *foie gras* is also produced in Poland, the Czech Republic, Luxembourg, and Belgium, as well as many French provinces, the capital of these "waddling" birds is Gascony, west of Toulouse. It is there that we find acres of undulating corn fields across hill and valley. Whilst in the Département of Gers, ducks hold the ascendency, in the Landes it is the geese that rule. The reverence in which these fattened livers are held is very evident between November and April at the

marchés au gras, the markets for the stuffed geese and ducks at Samatan, Gimont or Aire sur l'Adour.

During the first three to four months the birds enjoy a carefree life. Then the fattening begins. Corn mash is literally funneled into the birds. Today it is mostly done by machine with electronically weighed amounts. The good quality of the liver depends on the carefully staggered increase in the daily dose. Ducks can swallow up to thirty-six pounds (eighteen kg) of corn in three weeks whilst geese can cope with around fifty pounds (thirty-six kg) in four weeks. The forced overfeeding induces an over-dimensional growth of the liver. Finally they become so big (up to almost two pounds or 900 grams in the case of geese) that the birds can hardly move. Whilst most of these birds are now close to breathing their last, the finest breeders now prescribe a diet for a few days in order to purify the gall bladder.

It has been proven that the ancient Egyptians practiced this activity 4,500 years ago. The Romans, especially the despotic Nero, were obsessed with foie gras. Nobody knows how this technique spread to France, but it was widespread in 16th century Gascony, and further stimulated by the expansion in corn growing. The culinary breakthrough however took place in Strasbourg. It was there that a chef by the name of Clause created the pâté de foie gras in order to delight his employer, the Maréchal de Contades. It was he who gave the king some to taste, and thereafter this delicacy became a favorite in the royal household.

In the meantime the production of duck liver has far exceeded that of goose liver. In 1993 the annual total for the latter stood at a modest 600 tons (607 tonnes) compared with around 7,500 tons (7,629 tonnes) for duck. Goose liver is nevertheless of higher quality and keeps its finer taste for a longer period when canned. Duck livers have a stronger taste and are therefore more suitable when freshly prepared. Preparation involves the removal of all the veins and nerves and the green parts colored by the gall bladder.

Since foie gras is so valuable, chefs used to go to great lengths to combine it with other culinary delights and integrate it into complex recipes. These efforts were of dubious value, for the joy of foie gras is its texture – it almost literally melts on the tongue. It is best eaten in its pure state, accompanied only by a slice of good lightly toasted bread. Its qualities are at their finest when freshly made in a terrine. Canning makes the foie gras slightly dry, and chefs today often serve fresh duck's livers. They are at their most authentic when simply grilled on vine twigs.

Left and opposite: Pierrette Sarran is a culinary institution in France. Her foie gras broiled on vines is considered a delicacy which has inspired many chefs.

Goose and duck foie gras are amongst the most sought-after delicacies in France. Nowadays ducks dominate a market that once belonged to the geese.

The fattening process speeds up and intensifies the growth of the liver which finally becomes so large that the animals can hardly move.

The foie gras of a goose can reach a weight of nearly two pounds (900 g).

Each Bresse fowl can enjoy nearly ten square yards (ten square meters) of land to itself.

The fowl are fed on a healthy diet of milk and corn.

Volaille de Bresse

Nature has granted France's most noble poultry, *volaille*, the honor of sporting the national colors. The hens of the Bresse, therefore, walk around on blue feet, boasting shiny white plumage and wearing a fire-red comb. Moreover, they lead a charmed life, strutting around on their succulent green meadows and pecking away to their heart's content.

The day-old chicks are kept in one of the approximately 600 farms which are licensed to breed this species. After at most thirty-five days the doors are opened and they are allowed out onto the green grass. The law prescribes ten square yards (10 m²) for each hen, and each enclosure must be at least an acre (half a hectare) in area. No more than 500 of its fellows are allowed in any one enclosure. All this surely represents a true paradise for hens! The Bresse

old half-timbered houses. Without this tradition the Bresse hens would not be so unique.

In 1957 the French parliament decided to ennoble the hens of the Bresse with the Appellation d'Origine Contrôlée, the first feathered animal to be given the award which is normally reserved for wines and a few other delicacies. The intention was to protect the species, for the regulation ensures their well-being from their first day to their last, and follows age-old traditions.

The Bresse hen is a race on its own, and strenuous efforts are made to maintain its purity. The breeding is often in the hands of women, as the farms are often primarily dairy concerns. This benefits the hens since their food consists mainly of corn soaked in milk. There are indeed many pigeons, ducks, and turkeys in the Bresse, but it is only the hens which receive the "VIP" treatment. The *poulet* enjoys its freedom for nine weeks, the *poularde* eleven, whilst the castrated *chapon* is granted twenty-three.

This noble bird is not however allowed to grace the exquisite tables of the world without first undergoing further preparation. It undergoes its *finition*, the final preparation, in small

and sewn in a linen cloth. What was once a method of preserving is now done for the sake of presentation. When the cloth is removed two days later, the now evenly formed body is ready for its great stage appearance.

Shortly before Christmas the Bresse summons the best of them. In Bourg-en-Bresse, Montrevel, and Veaux-le-Pont hundreds of the fine birds line the exhibition tables. Above all it is a matter of honor. Every year since 1862 judges have solemnly inspected the waxen bodies and granted this eagerly sought-after award to the best. Then it is the turn of the chefs and dealers. For the breeders this is the financial reward for all their efforts. Up to 400 US dollars are offered for the top birds.

Anyone taking a Bresse bird home should pay it the proper care and respect. Its renown rests on the tasty meat which melts on the tongue. Its special taste comes from the fat which permeates the meat. The simplest method of cooking is to roast it in the oven, frequently pouring its own juice over it to prevent drying out. The chicken is then cut in pieces, browned in butter, and cooked in cream – pure poetry.

Opposite: An exemplary bird. Since the French Revolution (1789) the French cockerel has been the heraldic animal and symbol of France.

The seal vouches for quality: only after a strict inspection is it awarded to France's most famous poultry.

Bresse fowl sport the national colors of red, white, and blue, starting from their heads via their plumage down to their feet.

The fowl is treated with utmost care before it reaches the consumer: the precious birds are displayed and presented like chocolates.

extends from the first slopes of the Jura in the east to the Saône in the west. Anyone traveling through this region at the warmest time of year with its cheerful, healthy and rich farming landscape can truly believe himself in paradise. There are still the old trees standing in the meadows, the rambling hedges and bushes, the flowering shrubs and the climbing plants blooming on the wells, and the picturesque and somewhat fragile

cages. There it partakes of the best food, without of course having to walk around and scrape the ground for it. As a result it puts on a highly desirable extra layer of fat. The *chapon* and the *poularde*, which crown the feasts at the end of the year, must have put on sufficient fat. The *chapon*, capon, receives royal treatment and requires the sensitive hands of a woman: after careful plucking and a bath of milk, it is enclosed

The Traiteur

The French expect their traiteur to pamper them and pander to their tastes. When they enter his delicatessen then they have, firstly, no time to cook, secondly, no desire to cook, and, thirdly, the desire for foods whose preparation requires too much time. In addition they would like to eat at home, either alone or with friends. They may even want to put on a reception or function. For all these needs, the traiteurs are willing to oblige. Even if nowadays there are delicatessens which serve up unusual and exotic dishes, the traiteur on the corner is valued above all for the familiar cuisine and the well-known classics. For over 500 years there have been specialists in the cooking and roasting of meats: *chair-cuitiers* and *rôtisseurs*. The *pâtissiers*, who cased many different sorts of food in pastry, may also be included in this tradition. Thus it was that consumers early on developed the custom of buying ready-prepared meals. Today it is primarily the *charcuterie* (fine butcher's) which provides a wide selection of dishes. The label *traiteur*, which has no legal definition, can also be applied to quite large enterprises which cater for sizable companies.

Delicacies from the Traiteur

Tomates Farcies
Stuffed Tomatoes

Serves 4

8 medium-sized, firm tomatoes
Salt, black pepper
1 piece of dry baguette
½ cup (100 ml) milk
1 onion
2 garlic cloves
1¼ oz (40 g) butter
14 oz (400 g) ground pork
1 egg
2 Tbs parsley, finely chopped
1 tsp thyme, finely chopped

Wash and pat the tomatoes dry. Cut a lid off each one and carefully remove the seeds with a spoon. Season the inside with a little salt.
Crumble up the dry baguette and soak it in the milk. Peel and chop the onion and fry it lightly in a little butter with the garlic. Add the onion and garlic to the soaked baguette.
Preheat the oven to 350 °F (180 °C).
Add the ground meat, egg, parsley and thyme and knead everything together well. Stuff the tomatoes with the meat mixture. Grease an oven proof dish with butter. Put a flake of butter on each tomato and replace the cut-off lids on top. Bake the stuffed tomatoes in the oven for about 45 minutes and serve them hot.

Champignons à la Grecque
Mushrooms Greek Style
(Illustration on p. 374)

Serves 4

1 lb (500 g) fresh mushrooms
2 Tbs olive oil
1 Tbs tomato paste
2 garlic cloves
1 Tbs parsley, chopped finely
1 tsp coriander and fennel seeds
1 Tbs lemon juice
2 Tbs Cognac
Salt, black pepper

Clean and prepare the mushrooms and cut bigger ones in half. Heat up the oil in a saucepan, add the mushrooms, cover and stew for 8 to 10 minutes. Now add the remaining ingredients, season well with salt and pepper and leave to simmer briefly over a low heat. Take out the mushrooms and allow them to cool. Champignons à la grecque are served cold.

Bouchées à la Reine
The Queen's Vol-au-vents

Serves 6

1¼ lbs (600 g) calf sweetbreads
1 onion
2 baby carrots
1 bay leaf
7 oz (200 g) mushrooms
Lemon juice
1½ oz (50 g) butter
Salt, black pepper
2 shallots
2 Tbs flour
2 Tbs port
3 Tbs crème fraîche
6 ready-made puff pastry vol-au-vent cases
2 Tbs chopped parsley

Soak the sweetbreads in water for 60 minutes, changing the water several times. Then carefully remove any bits of skin, blood-vessels and meat. Peel or clean the onion and carrots and chop into small pieces. Add the bay leaf and bring to the boil in 2 pints (1 l) of salted water. Then add the sweetbreads and simmer for 8 minutes. Remove the sweetbreads, allow to cool and cut into slices. Pass the stock through a sieve.
Clean and prepare and slice up the mushrooms and sprinkle them with a little lemon juice to avoid discoloration. Fry them lightly in a little butter, season, add a little water, and cook over a low heat for 5 minutes.
Peel and finely chop the shallots. Fry them lightly in the remaining butter, and add the flour. Gradually add enough stock to form a thick sauce. Stirring constantly, add first the port and then the crème fraîche. Season to taste with salt and pepper.
Now add the mushrooms and sweetbreads to the sauce and heat everything through. Crisp up the vol-au-vents in the oven, fill them with the sweetbreads mixture and sprinkle them with parsley.

Salade Niçoise
Niçoise Salade
(Illustration opposite)

Serves 4

8 smallish, firm tomatoes
Salt, black pepper
1 green pepper
2 onions
1 cucumber
2 boiled potatoes
4 oz (100 g) cooked runner beans
24 black olives
1 can tuna in olive oil
6 Tbs olive oil from Provence
2 Tbs red wine vinegar
1 Tbs chopped basil
2 hard-boiled eggs
12 anchovy fillets

Wash, quarter, and lightly salt the tomatoes. Wash and clean the pepper and cut it into strips; peel and slice the onion and the cucumber. Peel the potatoes and cut them into cubes, and cut the beans in half. Put the vegetables and the olives in a large salad bowl. Break up the tuna and add it to the other ingredients. Mix everything together well. Prepare a vinaigrette from the oil, vinegar, pepper, salt, and basil, and pour it over the salad. Allow to cool. Before serving, mix the salad up once more, and garnish it with egg quarters and anchovy fillets.

Langue de Boeuf Madère
Ox Tongue in Madeira

Serves 10

1 ox tongue about 4 lbs (2 kg)
1 onion
2 cloves
3 baby carrots
2 leeks
1 stick celery
1 bouquet garni (p. 107)
2 garlic cloves
Salt, black pepper
2 shallots
1½ oz (50 g) butter
1½ oz (50 g) flour
¾ cup (150 ml) Madeira

Leave the tongue overnight in salted water; rinse and cook for 10 minutes in boiling water. Let it drain and put into a clean saucepan.
Stick the cloves in the onion; prepare and chop up the carrots and leeks. Add the vegetables and the herbs to the tongue and season with salt and pepper. Cover everything well in water and let it simmer for about 3 hours.
To prepare a sauce, remove 2½ cups (500 ml) of the stock about 40 minutes before the end of the cooking time. Strain and allow it to cool. Peel and finely chop the shallots and fry them lightly in the butter. Sprinkle in the flour and, stirring all the time, gradually pour on the stock and the Madeira. Season to taste and simmer over a low temperature for about 20 minutes.
Remove the skin from the tongue. Cut the meat into thin slices, arrange it on a pre-warmed plate and pour the Madeira sauce over it.

Salade niçoise – Niçoise salad

Blanquette de veau – Veal fricassee

Lapin à la moutarde – Rabbit in a mustard sauce

Blanquette de Veau
Fricassee of Veal
(Illustration top right)

Serves 4

1 lb (500 g) veal shoulder
Salt, white pepper
1 onion
2 cloves
2 carrots
1 leek
1 stick of celery
1 bouquet garni (p. 107)
1¹/₂ oz (50 g) butter
2 Tbs flour
1 egg yolk
¹/₂ cup (100 ml) heavy cream
Juice of ¹/₂ lemon
1 Tbs parsley, finely chopped

Cut the meat into large cubes, put in cold water and bring to the boil. Skim off and season with salt. Bring to the boil again.

Stick the cloves in the onion. Wash and prepare the carrots, leeks and celery and chop into pieces. Add the vegetables and the herbs to the meat and cook over a low heat for about 20 minutes.

Now remove the meat and leave it to drain thoroughly. Season it with pepper and keep it warm in a shallow dish. Pass the stock through a sieve.

Melt the butter, sprinkle in the flour and, whilst stirring continuously, pour in the stock and let it boil briefly. Then leave it to simmer for 10 minutes.

Mix together the egg yolk and the cream. Add the sauce whilst stirring briskly, then stir in the lemon juice. Season to taste and then pour over the meat. Sprinkle with parsley and serve at once.

Lapin à la Moutarde
Rabbit in a Mustard Sauce
(Illustration above)

Serves 4

1 ready-to-cook rabbit (minimum weight 2³/₄ lbs/1.3 kg)
Salt, black pepper
2 Tbs Dijon mustard
3 oz (100 g) streaky bacon
1 oz (30 g) butter
2 Tbs peanut oil
1 Tbs flour
2 onions
1 cup (250 ml) dry white wine
1 tsp thyme, finely chopped
3 Tbs crème fraîche

Cut the rabbit into pieces, season with salt and pepper and brush with 2 tablespoons of the mustard. Cut the bacon into cubes.

Heat up the butter and oil in a cast-iron pot. Brown the bacon cubes in it, then remove and set them aside.

Add the meat to the fat, dust it with flour and brown lightly from all sides.

Peel and finely chop the onions, add them to the meat and fry them until transparent.

Now pour on the wine, cover the pot and let the meat stew for about 35 minutes, then add the bacon and the thyme. After another 10 minutes' cooking, remove the rabbit meat, arrange it on a serving plate and keep it warm.

Fold the crème fraîche into the sauce and remove the pot from the fire. Now stir in the remaining mustard. Pour the sauce over the meat and serve immediately.

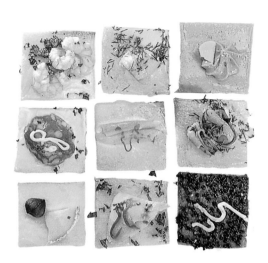

Canapés
Little open sandwiches, appetizers

Champignons à la grecque
Mushrooms cooked with garlic, olive oil and tomatoes
and served cold (for recipe see p. 372)

Confit de canard
Pieces of duck preserved in their own fat (for recipe see
p. 371)

Couscous
An Oriental dish made with merguez, spicy sausages

Fromage de tête de porc
Pork brawn

Gallantine de volaille
Pie filled with poultry cooked in bouillon

Gâteau de poisson
Fish terrine

Lapin à la moutarde
Rabbit in a mustard sauce (for recipe see p. 373)

Mousse de foie de volaille
Fine jellied chicken liver purée

Quenelles de brochet
Pike dumplings

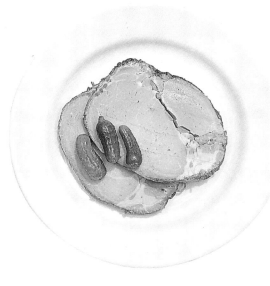

Rôti de porc
Rolled roast pork

Rôti de veau
Thinly sliced roast veal

Salade de lentilles
Lentil salad with fried bacon cubes

Salade niçoise
Salad with tuna fish, hard-boiled eggs, potatoes,
tomatoes and anchovy fillets (for recipe see p. 372)

Saucisson en brioche
Pork sausage baked in a brioche pastry case

Taboulé
A salad seasoned with mint; prepared from cold
couscous and raw vegetables; of Lebanese origin

Tomate grillée avec boudin
Broiled tomato with blutwurst

Tourte à porc
Pork pie

375

The andouillette – a sausage made of veal tripe, pork belly, and stomach – is a specialty of the French who are very partial to variety meats.

Background: A *charcuterie*, butcher, presents its choice selection of sausages, hams, terrines, and ready-to-eat dishes.

Ham and Sausage

As is amply demonstrated by the sheer variety of sausages and hams, the pig is sacred to the butcher. The old adage is proved over and over again: *Dans le cochon, tout est bon*, everything to do with the pig is good. Even in the time of the Gauls, it was held in high esteem. They dried hams which made many a Roman mouth water. Above all the *Celtic hams* of the mountain regions of the Pyrenees, the Massif Central or the Jura as well as the wooded hills of the Ardennes were highly prized. Even today the best air-dried raw hams and sausages come from these regions and from Corsica. But as far as cooked and smoked sausages, cooked hams and brawns, liver pâtés and terrines are concerned, there is not a single area in France which does not boast its own specialties. Particularly renowned are Alsace, Brittany, Lyon and the south-west of the country.

Ham

Jambon cru
The delicate flavor of air-dried, raw ham develops slowly over a maturing period of more than seven months. The ham should be neither too dry nor too moist. The most well-known is the Jambon de Bayonne. The following can be particularly recommended: Ibaïona from the Basque country, and hams from the Auvergne, Lacaune, Morvan, and Corsica.

Jambon cru fumé
This type of raw smoked ham comes mostly from the Alsace, the French Ardennes, the Jura, the Haut-Savoie, or from Sancerre where it is smoked over vine sticks.

Jambon cuit or Jambon choix
Cooked ham of the lowest grade.

Jambon cuit supérieur
Good quality cooked ham which must not have been frozen prior to selling.

Jambon cuit à l'os
A whole ham cooked and then cut from the bone.

Jambon d'York
A ham slowly matured in brine, then steamed in a smoky atmosphere, and finally cooked, with bones, fat and rind, in a finely seasoned broth. This ham is sold only freshly cut. No label of origin.

Jambon supérieur maison
Cooked ham produced by the butcher himself; has to be cut by him on the day it is sold.

Saucisson de porc
An air-dried salami-type sausage that comes in various shapes; it consists exclusively of lean and fat pork more or less finely chopped. The flour coating prevents the melting of the fat in high temperatures.

Saucisson de Lyon nature
A stout, raw sausage made from lean and fat pork; boiled it is eaten with potatoes and sauerkraut and is also used in stews.

Saucisson à la cendre
A sausage that contains 100 percent pork and is rolled in ash; during drying it acquires its subtle smoky flavor.

Montbéliard
A smoked sausage containing three parts of lean and one part of fat pork; used in stews, especially with lentils.

Grelot aux noix
A small, hard salami sausage with nuts; a specialty of Savoy.

Boudin noir
A black pudding made of cubes of white bacon fat, onions, pig's blood, and crème fraîche.

Baguette
An air-dried, salami-type pork sausage in the shape of a baguette.

Saucisson de Lyon aux pistaches
The Lyon sausage is also prepa[r]ed using pistachios.

Mourteau
A slightly smoked pork sausage that can be eaten hot or cold, often with pulses, cabbage or sauerkraut.

Saucisse de foie
An air-dried sausage specialty containing chopped liver and bacon.

Fouet
A completely or semi-dry sausage as thin as a finger; made from 100 percent lean and fat pork, and usually seasoned only with salt and pepper; mini version of the *saucisse sèche*.

...cisse sèche
...ard, medium-coarse sausage made ...n raw, salted pork which is filled in ... natural skins and air-dried in long ...ing loops; a specialty from the ...h of France.

Saucisson de sanglier
An air-dried salami containing either 100 percent wild boar meat, or with some fat and lean pork added.

Andouillette
A sausage made of fat-free chitterlings of pork or veal, or both, stuffed, marinated and boiled in broth. It is usually broiled or baked in the oven.

379

Beef

Two excellent breeds of cattle dominate the French steak scene: Charolais and Limousin. The ancestors of the Charolais, which originate in the Jura, used to graze on the Saône and the Loire. They thrived on the lush meadows and were known for being heavy fast-growing plow oxen. The Charolais is a completely white beast, although it now occurs in a cream color. It has a broad forehead, round white horns, protruding cheeks, a wide mouth, and a short neck. It is characterized by a completely straight muscular back, powerful hips and loins, and strong limbs.

The Limousin, on the other hand, used to graze on the slopes and high meadows of the western Massif Central. It had to contend with a rougher climate and sparse meadows. Because it was so robust and undemanding, the farmers would harness it to their plows. Its hair color is always a light or dark shade of red. On its short compact head it has slightly tinted horns which twist upwards at their ends. It is endowed with a very long neck and an almost straight back. It has very muscular hindquarters with round fleshy haunches and relatively short legs.

The Charolais and Limousin developed into pure meat-producing breeds as soon as technology made them superfluous as plow animals. Both are very suitable for calving. In Burgundy, west of Mâcon, the classical Charolais area, the cows and their calves live out in the meadows from the beginning of April. Right into the summer the lush grass promotes an astonishing increase in weight. In the fall at the Thursday market in Saint-Christophe-en-Brionnais, the traditional center of the trade, there is always a lively turnover in sales. Young bulls are fattened up to the age of fifteen to seventeen months, compared to twenty-four to thirty-six months for oxen. Charolais meat is very tasty and low in fat. With around 1.4 million breeding cows, the Charolais is the most important meat producer in France.

With just under half this number, the Limousin is in second place, although its share is increasing. It has proved itself, not only as a breeding cow, but also as a producer of meat whose quality and taste has consistently proved superior to all other breeds in national and international competitions. Initially it became famous through the milk veal and the *veau de Lyon*, Lyon veal, which is produced by smaller farms. If slaughtered young, the pink meat is extraordinarily tender and fine-tasting. It is the young fattened cattle between fifteen and twenty months old which are currently the most popular. Even the cows, however, yield tender and excellent-tasting meat. Although the customer must dig deeper in his pocket to purchase Charolais or Limousin, once he has tasted the difference, the choice is clearcut.

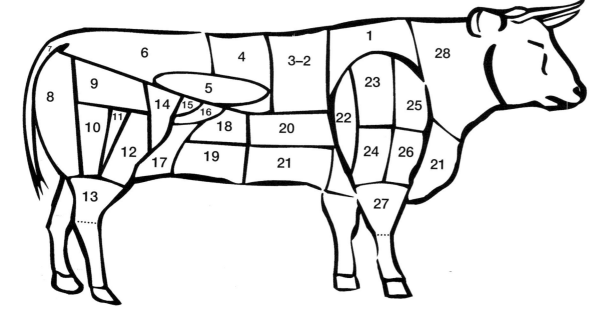

French cuts of beef
1. Basses côte – lower rib
2. Côtes – rib
3. Entrecôte – entrecôte steak, rib steak
4. Faux-filet – sirloin
5. Filet – fillet, loin steak
6. Rumsteck – rumpsteak
7. Queue – tail
8. Rond de gîte – round steak, standing rump
9. Tranche grasse – silver side
10. Gîte à la noix – topside, bottom round
11. Araignée – middle part of round steak
12. Tranche – lower part of round steak
13. Gîte et jarret arrière – shank, shin
14. Aiguillette baronne – aiguillette (top part of the eye)
15. Onglet – prime cut of beef
16. Hampe – flank
17. Bavette d'aloyau – undercut of sirloin (colloquial)
18. Bavette de flanchet – undercut of flank
19. Flanchet – flank
20. Plat de côtes – middle rib, best rib
21. Poitrine – plate
22. Macreuse à bifteck – lean shoulder
23. Pabron – upper shoulder
24. Macreuse – shoulder of beef
25. Jumeau à bifteck – front upper part of shoulder, false loin
26. Jumeau à pot-au-feu – front lower part of shoulder
27. Gîte et jarret avant – knuckle and front shank
28. Collier – chuck shoulder

Aubrac
Southern Massif Central. A very hardy breed that can subsist on very little and spends all the year out in the open. It is often crossed with Charolais bulls and produces good quality meat.

Bazadaise
Northern Landes and hills of the Bazadais. A robust breed that adapts well to its surroundings; has a beautiful gray coat and produces very tasty veal.

How to Store and Prepare High-quality Beef

- Do not store the meat in cling film or aluminum foil.
- The beef has to be taken out of the refrigerator one hour before it is prepared, or it will become tough.
- Do not buy a rolled meat joint tied in a net: it usually consists of several pieces of meat – often of rather low-grade quality – with bacon wrapped around it.
- Always ask for a *rôti nature,* a joint in one piece.
- To make sure the meat retains its juiciness, always brown and seal it on all sides in hot fat.
- Never salt the meat until immediately before, or during, cooking.
- Do not prick meat with a fork during the cooking process.
- Allow the meat to rest for a moment before serving.
- Do not serve up slices of a meat roast in gravy as the meat becomes discolored; serve the gravy separately.
- Brown the steaks only in very hot oil.
- Steaks must be turned over only once.
- If blood appears on the surface, the steak is cooked *à point* (medium); if a *saignant* (rare) steak is required, fry the meat for a maximum of two minutes on each side.
- Be careful never to overcook high-grade beef.
- Put a lump of butter on the cooked steaks when they are ready to eat.

Cattle breeds

Maine-Anjou
Maine-Anjou. At the turn of the century, the indigenous Mancelle breed was crossed with the Shorthorn cattle renowned for their meat to produce these red-and-white animals. Their meat is dark and finely marbled.

Normande
Normandy. A black-and-white spotted mixed breed well suited for extensive farming. Produces creamy milk and remarkable quantities of meat.

Blonde d'aquitaine
Hilly southwestern regions. This muscular breed is the result of crossbreeding Garonnais, Quercy, and Blond des Pyrénées cattle in 1962. It is bred particularly for its veal.

Gasconne
Central Pyrenees. These extremely hardy animals are well adapted to rough and difficult terrain at high altitudes, making them the obvious choice for keeping on mountain pastures. Distinctively flavored meat.

Parthenaise
Brittany to Charente. Most animals of this breed are a medium brown color; these prolific cows are the original suppliers of the milk used to make the famous butter. High-quality meat.

Charolais
Saône-et-Loire. A very hardy and adaptable breed with lean, tasty meat.

Limousin
Western Massif Central. Large animals that can subsist on very little and produce very tender, delicate, and tasty meat.

Salers
Auvergne. Tall, reddish-brown, very robust animals that supply quality milk and dark, very tasty meat.

Beef Dishes

Pot-au-Feu
Beef Stew
(Illustration opposite top right)

Serves 6

1 small knuckle of veal
1½ lbs (750 g) beef (neck)
1½ lbs (750 g) shank of beef
3 marrowbones
1 onion
3 cloves
2 large and 6 baby carrots
1 stick celery
6 white turnips
6 small leeks
2 garlic cloves
1 bouquet garni (p. 107)
Salt

Rinse the meat and bones. Put all the meat in 6 pints (3 l) of cold water and bring to the boil. Cook for 30 minutes and skim off the fat several times.
Stick the cloves in the onion. Clean and prepare the vegetables. Cut the two large carrots into pieces. Add the onion, carrot pieces, and the stick of celery to the meat, together with the garlic and the bouquet garni. Cover and leave to simmer for 2½ hours. Then remove the bouquet garni, the celery, and the onion from the saucepan and season the stock.
Now put the baby carrots, the turnips, the leeks and the marrowbones in with the meat and the stock. Cover and cook for a further 20 minutes. Then remove the meat, let it drain well and cut it into slices. Pass the stock through a sieve and drain the vegetables. Arrange the meat and vegetables on a pre-warmed serving plate. Serve the gravy separately in a tureen.

Entrecôte Bordelaise
Entrecôte Bordeaux Style
(Illustration below)

Serves 2

4 Tbs olive oil
1 entrecôte about 1 lb (500 g)
Salt, black pepper
4 shallots
1 garlic clove
1 oz (25 g) butter
1 cup (200 ml) red Bordeaux

Heat up the oil. Brown the entrecôte until droplets of blood form on the surface (entrecôte is a slice of roast beef cut thicker than rump steak). Sprinkle with salt and pepper, turn the meat over and also season the browned side with salt and pepper. Brown the second side for the same amount of time as the first, then remove the meat and keep it warm.
Peel and finely chop the shallots and the garlic and fry them lightly in the butter. Pour on the wine and reduce the liquid.
Cut the meat across the grain into thick slices and arrange them on a plate; serve the gravy separately. This dish goes well with a mature Saint-Emilion, a wine from the little medieval town east of Bordeaux.

Entrecôte bordelaise –
Entrecôte Bordeaux style

Boeuf à la ficelle –
"Beef on a thread"

Pot-au-feu – Beef stew
This dish has derived its name from the fact that in the past the stewing pot used to be hung over an open fire. Everything inside the pot stewed slowly for hours so that all the flavors of the different ingredients blended together perfectly.

Boeuf à la Ficelle
"Beef on a Thread"
(Illustration left)

Serves 4

1 onion
2 cloves
1 carrot, 1 leek and 1 stick celery
1 sprig each of thyme and savory
½ tsp black peppercorns
1 bay leaf
1³/₄ lbs (800 g) fillet of beef
Sea salt, black pepper, mustard, gherkins

Stick the cloves in the onion. Clean and prepare the vegetables and cut them into large chunks. Put them in a high-sided saucepan together with the onion, herbs, and spices. Pour on about 4 pints (2 l) of water and bring everything to the boil. Cook for about 30 minutes. Tie some fine string around the fillet of beef so that it resembles a rolled roast, leaving enough string at the ends to allow the meat to be tied onto a wooden stick or spoon. Now suspend the beef over the saucepan so it is completely immersed in the boiling liquid.
Boil the meat at not too high a temperature for 16 minutes if you want it *saignant* (rare), or for 24 minutes if you prefer it *à point* (medium).
Remove the fillet from the saucepan and let it rest for a moment before cutting into slices. Make sure that sea salt, pepper, mustard, and gherkins are at hand for seasoning at the table.

Pork and Lamb

In France pork is essentially a family affair. It is eaten at home or in simple restaurants. *Choucroute* (sauerkraut with assorted cooked meats and sausages), whole braised ham, milk sucking pig or those solid hearty meals which have once again become popular, such as ragout of pig's ear and shanks, are all exceptions which prove the rule. The huge range of excellent sausages which enrich the menus of many restaurants also fall into this category. On the other hand, simple *côtes de porc*, chops, *saucisses*, the often truly excellent sausages, or *rôti de porc*, rolled roast pork, are generally prepared at home. Chops and sausages are broiled whilst the roast is simply put in the oven. In this way a simple and reasonably-priced meal can be conjured up quickly after a busy day at work.

With a pig population of around 11.5 million, France is the third biggest pig producer after Holland and Spain. Almost two-thirds of these are bred in Brittany and the Pays-de-la-Loire, whilst in the whole of eastern France, from Alsace to Provence, pig breeding is relatively unimportant. The time has gone when families in the country would fatten, slaughter, and process their own pig, although this change has perhaps only happened in the last ten or twenty years.

Whilst only four breeds of pig dominate pig farming, there are over thirty breeds of sheep in France. The sheep population is around 12.5 million. Amongst these are the Merinos, famous for their wool, Lacaunes, which provide the milk for Roquefort, and Bleu de Maine, whose fine meat is a delight to the gourmet. Lamb is extremely popular in France and there is scarcely a restaurant that does not offer several lamb dishes. Although lamb is nowadays available throughout the year, January through May is the main season for *agneaux de lait*, milk lambs, which are slaughtered when three to four months old.

A distinction is made in breeding between *agneaux de bergerie*, which are kept indoors, and *agneaux de l'herbe*, which are kept outside and feed on fresh grass. The living conditions of the latter are more natural and the meat is leaner, firmer, and tastier.

Rôti de Porc
Rolled Roast Pork

Serves 4

2 lbs (1 kg) rolled roasting pork
Salt, white pepper
1 tsp Dijon mustard
1 tsp lard

Pre-heat the oven to 470 °F (250 °C).
Rub the salt and mustard into the pork and season with pepper.
Grease a casserole with the lard, put in the pork and cook in the oven for 25 minutes. Turn the meat over once or twice and baste it with the meat juices.
Now reduce the heat to 400 °F (200 °C) and cook the meat for another 25 minutes, turning and basting it as before. Switch off the oven, open the door and let the pork joint rest for 5 minutes.

Grillades de Porc
Broiled Pork

Serves 4

4 pork chops
1 Tbs olive oil
Salt, black pepper
1 tsp Provençal herbs
1¼ lbs (600 g) fresh broiling sausage

Heat up the broiler. Rinse and dry the pork chops and brush them with olive oil. Season them with salt and pepper on both sides, broil for 7 minutes. Sprinkle the broiled side with herbs and then turn them over. Cook this side for another 7 minutes.
At the same time, or immediately afterwards, place the sausage under the broiler, prick it several times with a fork, and grill it on each side until the whole sausage is done (about 7 minutes). Serve on pre-warmed plates with broiled tomatoes or a salad.
Tip: Fresh sausage for broiling is a specialty of the Midi where a lot of lean meat is used in its preparation. It is also a custom there to broil over the embers of vine twigs. This gives the meat a particularly distinctive flavor.

Breeds of Pig

Landrace français
An early cross between the Large White and northern European Celtic breeds, this breed was imported from Denmark around 1930. Prolific animals and good mothers. These long-bodied pigs are close relatives of the Landrace belge breed.

Large White
Imported from Yorkshire around the turn of the century, this breed adapts well to its environment and provides 55 percent of breeding sows. The animals grow fast and are not prone to stress; they are muscular, with little fat and good quality meat.

Pietrain
This breed originated in Belgium in 1920 but did not spread until 1950; it is important in the north, but is also farmed in the Alsace, Burgundy and Picardie. These muscular and lean animals supply good quality meat but are prone to stress.

Breeds of Sheep

Berrichonne du cher

A popular breed found in central and southwestern France, kept mainly indoors. Provides good legs for roasting. The lambs gain weight quickly and weigh between 40 and 55 lbs (21 and 27 kg) when they are 70 days old.

Bleu de Maine

Large animals from the western regions with characteristic blue heads; good breeding ewes. Kept mainly out on open pastures; provide delicate, lean meat. 70-day old lambs weigh between 45 and 55 lbs (22 and 27 kg).

Charmoise

A very hardy and undemanding breed that accounts for the majority of all the flocks in western central France. Kept out of doors. After 70 days, the lambs weigh between 30 and 37 lbs (15 and 18.5 kg).

Ile de France

Sturdy, broad-headed animals that gain weight quickly and supply good quality wool, although they are relatively demanding with regard to their environment and husbandry. Kept outdoors or in pens. At 70 days old, the lambs weigh between 45 and 55 lbs (22 and 27 kg).

Lacaune

The most popular breed for sheep's milk, used for making Roquefort. Robust animals, used to being outdoors; also provide good meat. At the age of 70 days, the lambs weigh between 50 and 60 lbs (25 and 30 kg).

Mouton charolais

A traditional breed from Burgundy and Morwan which is, as it were, the equivalent of the Charolais cattle. The robust animals are kept largely out of doors and provide good meat. The 70-day-old lambs weigh between 45 and 55 lbs (22 and 27 kg).

Mouton vendéen

A robust and adaptable breed which will even tolerate damp winters and is usually kept out of doors. Good dairy sheep. At 70 days old, the lambs weigh between 40 and 48 lbs (20 and 24 kg).

Rouge de l'est

Large, adaptable animals that are becoming increasingly popular and are kept either out in the pastures or in pens. They put on weight quickly, with 70-day-old lambs weighing between 45 and 56 lbs (22.5 and 28 kg); they are sold when they are 100 days old.

Côtes de porc en papillote –
Pork chops in aluminum foil

Côtes de Porc en Papillote
Pork Chops in Aluminum Foil

Serves 2

2 pork chops
4 oz (100 g) cooked ham
1 heaped Tbs (20 g) butter
1 small onion
1 shallot
1 garlic clove
5 oz (150 g) mushrooms
1 tomato
1 tsp thyme, finely chopped
Salt, white pepper
Aluminum foil

Preheat the oven to 450 °F (220 °C).
Trim the fat off the cutlets and chop it up finely together with the ham; fry both lightly in the butter. Peel and finely chop the onion, shallot and garlic. Clean, prepare and slice the mushrooms. Skin and remove the seeds from the tomato. Add the vegetables and the thyme to the ham mixture, fry everything lightly and season. Remove the vegetables from the frying pan and keep warm. Brown the pork chops only briefly in the hot frying pan on both sides to seal in the juices.
For each pork chop, spread out a sheet of aluminum foil, arrange a quarter of the vegetable-ham mixture on it, place a pork chop on top, and wrap everything up in the aluminum foil (*papillote* means "hair curler"). Place the aluminum parcel on the grill in the oven and cook for 18 minutes. Serve in the aluminum foil.
Tip: The same method can be used to prepare lamb or veal cutlets or sweetbreads. In the past, flavorless grease-proof paper was used instead of aluminum foil.

Choucroute

Even if other Frenchmen mock Alsace for its love of *choucroute*, pickled cabbage or sauerkraut, it is widely available in the rest of France together with the hearty dishes in which it features so prominently. It is by no means only on the Rhine that the annual production of 28,000 tons (25,000 metric tons) is consumed. The huge white cabbages, the best specimens of which may weigh up to fourteen pounds (7 kg), are grated or cut into strips and salted in large containers or, if done at home, in earthenware pots. After crushing, the cabbage is weighted down, covered, and allowed time to ferment and become sour. The lactic acid fermentation needs three to seven weeks, by which time the cabbage has been transformed. It now not only keeps well, but is also easily digestible and healthy to eat, thanks to the various trace elements and vitamins. This ability to keep for long periods together with its vitamin C content made it an ideal food for sailors on their long voyages of discovery. It helped to prevent scurvy and protected their teeth.

Little is known of its origin. In Asia it has been known for thousands of years, whilst in the Balkans fermented vegetables are an ancient tradition. Sauerkraut is best when eaten fresh and not pre-cooked. It must be crunchy, as light as possible in color, and have a pleasant acidic aroma. Alsace has known and loved sauerkraut since the Middle Ages, but one cannot help but suspect that it is appreciated because it provides an ideal platform for pork products of all kinds. *Choucroute*, namely, goes well with smoked or unsmoked bacon, smoked loin of pork, known as *schiffala*, liver dumplings

Choucroute à l'Ancienne
Sauerkraut in the Traditional Style

Serves 8

4 lbs (2 kg) fresh raw Sauerkraut
2 whole bacon rinds
2 carrots
2 onions
$^1/_2$ tsp peppercorns
$^1/_2$ tsp caraway seeds
2 garlic cloves
4 cloves
12 juniper berries
2 bay leaves
1 sprig thyme
1 knuckle of pork
2 finger-thick slices of smoked streaky bacon
$^1/_2$ bottle dry Riesling
4 smoked sausages from Montbéliard
About $1^1/_4$ lbs (600 g) smoked loin of pork
4 pairs of Strasbourg knackwurst
1 boiling sausage from Mourteau

Wash the sauerkraut in a colander under running water, separate the strands and squeeze it out. Line the bottom of a large cast-iron pot with the bacon rinds.
Arrange half the sauerkraut on top of the bacon rinds. Wash, prepare and peel the carrots and onions, cut them into chunks and distribute them over the sauerkraut. Sprinkle evenly with the peppercorns. Tie the remaining spices and the thyme into a little muslin bag and add the bag to the vegetables. Put the knuckle of pork and the bacon slices on top and cover with the remaining sauerkraut. Pour in the wine and $1^1/_4$ cups (250 ml) of water.
Cover the pot tightly, put it in the oven and stew the meat at a temperature of 350 °F (180 °C) for about $2^1/_2$ hours.
Now put the smoked sausages and the smoked loin of pork in with the sauerkraut and cook everything for a further 30 minutes. Place the Strasbourg sausages and the Mourteau sausage on top of the sauerkraut and cook for another 20 minutes.
Remove the bag with the spices. Arrange the sauerkraut with the meat and sausages.
A well chilled Sylvaner or Riesling goes well with this dish.

(essential!), boiled belly pork, or knuckle of pork. Sausages are of course an indispensable ingredient. Strasbourg sausage is compulsory, but smoked, grilled, blood or liver sausages are all a welcome addition. As the white cabbage is harvested from mid-August through November, the sauerkraut is nicely fermented just at the time when the traditional celebrations and feasts that accompany the slaughtering of the animals take place.

A dish with assorted cooked meats, sausages, and Choucroute (sauerkraut) should include the following:

1 Sausage for frying or grilling
2 Strasbourg knackwurst
3 Smoked piece of shoulder
4 Knuckle of pork
5 Fatty bacon
6 *Schiffala*, smoked loin of pork
7 Meat ball made from liver, onions, eggs and flour
8 Smoked sausage
9 Pork sausage
10 Potatoes

Vegetables and Potatoes

The French have a peculiar relationship with vegetables. On the menus of many restaurants a vegetable of the day is recommended to accompany the meat course. The French will not be surprised if this vegetable turns out to be potato, rice or pasta. In many a French cookery book, rice and pasta recipes are to be found in the chapter on vegetables. It is not uncommon for men to turn up their noses when served with freshly prepared vegetables. If at all, some may accept them in the form of *crudités*, raw with a vinaigrette dressing as a simple hors d'œuvres or side salad.

In regional cuisines the vegetables do come into their own as traditional ingredients in hearty stews. Cabbage and haricot beans would be the main ingredients, but onions, carrots, and leeks would also be included. Particularly popular on the Mediterranean coast are tomatoes and peppers.

Potatoes were introduced comparatively late to France, in the reign of Louis XVI (1774–92). Nevertheless, French cuisine is well endowed with a plethora of potato recipes. Mealy and firm sorts predominate, which are used depending on the consistency required: whether for purées, soups and stews or salads, or for boiled potatoes, with or without their skins.

Céleri – celery
A popular vegetable particularly to add flavor to broths, soups, and sauces.

Epinards – spinach
Normally prepared as leaf spinach.

Aubergine – eggplant
Hardly any taste of its own, but delicious when cooked with tomatoes and other vegetables or when prepared with a tasty stuffing.

Poireau – leek
Used in sauces or soups or gratinéed; also as a starter, cold or warm with vinaigrette.

Petits pois – garden peas
Prepared mostly by simply boiling them in water, *à l'anglaise*, and serving them with a little butter. Available fresh from quite early in the spring.

Artichauts – artichokes
From Brittany, Provence, Roussillon. Only the tender tips of the leaves are eaten. Served with vinaigrette or *sauce béchamel*, but also *à la barigoule*, "mushroom style," fried with bacon.

Carottes – carrots
Raw as *crudité*; otherwise a basic or flavoring ingredient for sauces, soups, and stocks.

Haricots blancs – white beans
Highly valued in many parts for hearty casseroles or as a side-dish.

Haricots verts – runner beans or French beans
Available fresh from May through October. Blanched in salads, or with garlic and parsley tossed in butter.

Poivron – pepper, capsicum
A typical ingredient in the cuisine of the Midi. In salads, steamed or grilled.

Tomates – tomatoes
Used in many dishes when ripe; but for salads they have to be firm and pale-red; also stuffed and broiled.

Chou-fleur – cauliflower
Famous export article of Brittany. Can be used in a variety of ways for salads, crème, purée, soufflé, or gratin.

Oignons – onions
The most widely used vegetable. For salads, however, the French prefer to use scallions or *oignons rouges* (red onions).

Navet – white turnip
Used as a traditional ingredient in many regional recipes; a specialty of Nantes.

Ail – garlic
One of the most widely used flavoring agents of the French cuisine; used for meat and vegetable dishes as well as in salads.

Fenouil – fennel
A tasty tuber vegetable with an aniseed flavor; a Midi specialty.

Courgette – zucchini
Used for gratin or steamed with tomatoes.

Asperges blanches et vertes – white and green asparagus
The green variety is preferred in France; used mainly in salads.

Crudités
Raw Vegetables

Combine the quantities of the vegetables and seasonings according to requirements and taste, for example:
cucumber – celery or celeriac – carrots – cooked red beet – firm tomatoes – onions – radishes
salt, black pepper – finely chopped tarragon – finely chopped parsley – basil leaves – olive oil – vinegar – mayonnaise – Dijon mustard – hard-boiled eggs

Wash and prepare or peel the vegetables and cut them into bite-sized pieces. Add a dressing of vinaigrette or a mayonnaise-mustard sauce. Arrange on a serving plate.

Ratatouille
Vegetable Stew

2 eggplants
Salt, black pepper
4 small zucchini
1 red and 1 green pepper
1 lb (500 g) tomatoes
2 large onions
4 Tbs olive oil
1 tsp thyme, finely chopped
1 tsp rosemary, finely chopped
1 tsp savory, finely chopped
1 Tbs parsley, finely chopped
1 tsp garlic, finely chopped

Cut the eggplants into chunks, sprinkle them with salt and leave on one side for 20 minutes; then rinse and pat them dry. Wash and prepare the zucchini and the peppers and cut the zucchini into pieces and the peppers into strips. Skin and remove seeds from the tomatoes and cube; peel and cube the onions. Lightly fry the vegetables in the oil, and season with salt and pepper. Then add the herbs and the garlic to the vegetables. Cover and cook over a low heat for about 20 minutes.
Served hot, Ratatouille makes a tasty accompaniment to meat or rice; but it may also be served cold as a starter or a side-dish.

The versatile potato
The French cuisine abounds in different ways of preparing potatoes. These are the most important ones:

Croquettes Duchesse
Croquettes made from mashed potato, coated with flour and fried
Pommes à la vapeur
Steamed potatoes
Pommes de terre à l'anglaise
Boiled potatoes
Pommes de terre au gratin
Potatoes au gratin (baked with cheese)
Pommes de terre en papillote
Potatoes baked in aluminum foil
Pommes de terre en purée
Mashed potatoes
Pommes de terre sautées
Fried potatoes
Pommes en robe des champs
Potatoes boiled in their skins
Pommes frites
French fries, chips
Pommes soufflées
Souffléd potato chips baked two or three times.

389

Salads and Oils

Varieties of oil

Huile d'arachide – peanut oil
Imported from the principal peanut-growing countries Senegal, Brazil, and India. For deep-frying and frying, has a pleasant flavor; also used for salad dressings.

Huile d'olive – olive oil
From Provence, a region whose oils are refined and fruit flavored. The quality of the cold-pressed oil is determined by its acid content which is determined by the pressing – first pressing: *vierge extra*, second pressing: *vierge fine*, third pressing: *vierge* (*semifine* or *courante*, medium fine). Olive oil marked as *huile d'olive* is a (less high-grade) blend of native and refined olive oil. For practical reasons, independent oil producers, or *oléiculteurs*, usually label only *huile d'olive vierge*.

Huile de colza – rapeseed-oil
Over the last few decades, rapeseed-oil has been widely available in France and has gained popularity as a flavor-neutral all-purpose oil.

Huile de mais – corn oil
Used mainly for frying; not so popular in France for salad dressings.

Huile de noisette – hazelnut oil
Its flavor is reminiscent of roasted nuts; its use is reserved for seasoning crudités and fine salads.

Huile de noix – walnut oil
In France, over 123,000 acres (almost 50,000 hectares) is planted with walnut trees. A popular salad oil.

Huile de pépins de raisin – grape-seed oil
With the aid of solvents, this oil is extracted from the little seeds that are left behind in the grape marc, and then refined. It has a high content of polyunsaturated fatty acids; it is neutral in taste and well suited for flavoring with herbs. Suitable for deep-frying.

Huile de tournesol – sunflower oil
In its neutrally flavored form, by far the most widely used edible oil; has a high vitamin E content.

Scarole – smooth endive
Endive variety with a pale heart, broad leaves and a milder taste compared to that of other endive varieties. Popular as a salad, or steamed as a vegetable.

Romaine – Cos lettuce
A variant of the small lettuce, with elongated, broad, dark leaves. Best season is early spring to early summer.

Sucrine – small lettuce
A specialty from southern France; grown outdoors in nurseries, it is sold by weight; nice firm heads with a slightly sweetish taste.

Endive belge – chicory
Very popular in France both as a starter salad and as a steamed vegetable. Prior to its preparation the very bitter center has to be cut out. Its main season is during the winter, that is from October through March.

Huile à l'aneth – oil with sprig of dill

Huile d'olive vierge extra – extra virgin olive oil

Huile de noisette – hazelnut oil

Huile de noix – walnut oil

Huile d'olives – olive oil

Huile de pépins de raisins – grape-seed oil

Huile de tournesol arôme truffé – truffle-flavored sunflower oil

Huile d'arachide – peanut oil

Feuille de chêne – oak-leaf lettuce
Oak-leaf lettuce belongs to the cut-leaved lettuces; it is grown in the greenhouse and picked from November through April; outdoors it is grown from April through October; not often available.

Laitue – lettuce
The most widely available and cheapest green lettuce; in France it is also steamed or used in soups. If grown outdoors, its main season is summer and early fall, if grown in greenhouses from October through May.

Iceberg – iceberg lettuce
Firm heads with very crisp leaves. Originally bred and cultivated in California, it has become very popular in Europe, too. Grown mainly outdoors; its season is from mid-May through the end of November in the north, and does not include the hottest months in the south.

Chicorée frisée – curly endive
A variety of endive lettuce with narrow, serrated leaves, a yellow heart and a slightly bitter flavor. Available in the winter from outdoor cultivation in the Midi; in the north only in October and November if grown outdoors, or in February and March if grown in the greenhouse.

Vinegar

Varieties of Vinegar

Vinaigre à la framboise – raspberry vinegar
The most popular fruit vinegar made from raspberry juice and vinegar; variations are available made with other berries and cherries. Suitable for both sauces and salads.

Vinaigre à l'estragon – tarragon vinegar
Flavored with sprigs of tarragon; other varieties include vinegars flavored with thyme, rosemary, savory, fennel, or other herbs. Used for the preparation of *sauce béarnaise* as well as fish and salad dressings.

Vinaigre de vin blanc – white wine vinegar
Used for cooking purposes and for preparing *sauce béarnaise*, mayonnaise, and for potato or seafood salads; a good basis for herb vinegars.

Vinaigre de vin rouge – red wine vinegar
An indispensable ingredient of the most widely used salad dressing, the vinaigrette. The best qualities, which improve in flavor and refinement the longer they mature, are supplied only by the winegrowers. They are based on good red wines or sometimes a liqueur wine such as the Banyuls from the south of France.

Vinaigrette

1 Tbs red wine vinegar
3 Tbs oil
Salt, pepper
According to taste:
1 tsp Dijon mustard and/or 1 Tbs finely chopped herbs

Mix all ingredients together thoroughly.
Tip: The classic quantities for a vinaigrette are 3 parts of oil to one part of vinegar. Apart from the addition of optional ingredients such as mustard or herbs, the taste may also vary according to the type of oil and vinegar used.

Vinaigre à l'estragon – tarragon vinegar

Vinaigre aux herbes de Provence – vinegar with herbs from Provence

Vinaigre de Banyuls – vinegar made from the sweet Banyuls liqueur

Vinaigre à la framboise – raspberry vinegar

Vinaigre de vin blanc – white wine vinegar

Herbs of Provence

The herbs of Provence owe their power, fame, and influence to the agricultural no man's land on which they grow. Two thousand years ago there were lush green woodlands here. Then the Romans came and felled, cleared and cultivated, and built on the land, finally leaving behind an impoverished soil. Herbs and heathers invaded and colonized these bare, stony areas. There the sun and the searing heat concentrate the aromatic essences and herbal powers. *Farigoule* is the name that the inhabitants of Provence have given to the *thymus vulgaris*, which is considered and valued as the king of all the kitchen herbs. There is no other aromatic herb that combines so readily with such a large variety of foods. On the one hand, thyme can lend a very piquant flavor to sausages and ham, and on the other, endow figs or plums with an exotic, refined taste. Medically it has a beneficial effect on the stomach, bladder, and lungs. Its most charming effect, however, must be that on the girls of Provence, who used to know themselves loved by a young man when they found a bouquet of thyme on their doorsteps.

Thyme is very much at home in the whole of the Mediterranean area, although it flourishes nearly everywhere. Its mild, almost sweet flavor, was already appreciated by the ancient Greeks. By the Middle Ages, at the latest, it was lending a delicious flavor to Anglo-Saxon stews and German roasts, and pervading their meat stuffing and thin soups. It is cultivated in rows and grows in low globular bushes. Its pale red flowers are open from the end of April through June. In spring the soil between the rows is turned over and the weeds removed by hand. Once the harvesting is taking place, it is too late to separate the "chaff from the wheat," the weeds from the *herbes de provence*.

It is only since the beginning of the eighties that the cultivation of thyme has acquired significance, when two farmers in Drôme invented a harvesting machine. The harvest is brought into the drying chambers in the form of a ten cubic yard, five foot thick mattress of herbs weighing about two tons. Warm air is blown through the herbs from below and, once dried, the leaves are removed, sorted, packed, and dispatched.

Background: A lavender field in Provence – a sea of fragrant blue flowers that evoke the taste of sun, light, and air

1 Basilic – basil
The fresh leaves have a mild taste while the dried ones have a peppery piquancy. A very versatile herb.

2 Estragon – tarragon
A very popular herb in France which is used in *sauce béarnaise*; also often used in fish dishes and salads and put in mustard and vinegar.

3 Laurier – bay leaf
Distinctive, slightly sharp tasting leaf which goes well with all meat roasts, stews, and sauces; also used in stocks and marinades.

4 Lavande – lavender
Haute-Provence in midsummer is a particular feast for the eye, for at that time the lavender fields are in full bloom. For this extremely barren and harsh landscape, its perfume has become its elixir of life. Lavender is the only cultivated plant that enables the farmers to earn a sufficient income.

5 Marjolaine – marjoram
Its intense aroma makes this herb particularly suitable for ground meat, poultry, and meat and tomato sauces.

6 Marjolaine sauvage – oregano
Wild marjoram has a stronger flavor than its cultivated variety; bushes of oregano grow wild throughout the Mediterranean region.

7 Romarin – rosemary
The intense and resinous flavor of this herb makes it an excellent accompaniment for lamb and Mediterranean meat dishes.

8 Sauge – sage
Has a strong and individual flavor and so should be used with caution and in small doses with white meat and in stuffings.

9 Thym – thyme
The king amongst the herbs of Provence, thyme is the herb with the greatest variety of culinary uses, be it with vegetables, sauces, soups, fish, or meat.

10 Bouquet garni – bouquet garni
A small bunch of herbs in a muslin bag which usually includes thyme and bay-leaf and often parsley; rosemary or marjoram are also present, depending on the region or on the dish.

Herbes de Provence – herbs of Provence
A mixture of usually three or four herbs which always includes thyme and rosemary and often marjoram and lavender; may also include sage and bay leaf. Commercially available.

Moutarde de Dijon

It is almost as if Rabelais, that restless satirist of the 16th century, had suspected it – what does he have administered to the giant Gargantua? Shovelfuls of mustard, one after the other, between the dozens of hams, ox tongues, blood, and liver sausages, which the glutton swallows as an hors d'œuvre. Mustard, as has now been proven scientifically, strongly stimulates the stomach and digestive juices. Already in ancient Alexandria the spicy hotness of the mustard seeds were valued highly and they were crushed like cloves or coriander seeds. Columella, a Roman farmer and author on agriculture, whose twelve volume work "Dere rustica" around 60 AD described the agriculture and cattle breeding of his time, noted down in 42 AD the first traditional recipe for mustard. It was named *mustum ardens*, burning juice. The French word *moutarde*, the English *mustard*, and the German *Mostrich* were of course all derived from it. Over the last 2,000 years mustard has indeed brought many tears to European eyes, particularly the best quality mustards. After Charles the Great suggested the growing of mustard to the farmers in "Capitulare de villis," it flourished everywhere in the France of that time. In around 1300 ten *moutardiers* were at work in Paris and by 1650 this figure had risen to 600. Elsewhere the Dukes of Burgundy residing in Dijon saw fit to ensure the quality of their mustard by means of a decree. They prescribed that the seed should be dipped in quality vinegar. Despite a solid reputation, Dijon mustard only really acquired its premier status when in 1752 Jean Naigeon replaced the vinegar with the must of unripe grapes, the *verjus*. This lent it additional acidity. Thereafter the *moutarde de Dijon* became a byword for the best mustard quality. Since 1937 this label has guaranteed the type of production, in which the mustard must contain at least twenty-eight percent of dry extract and not more than two percent husk. It is not, however, an indication of the place of production, although ninety percent of French mustard production is in or near Dijon.

Biologically mustard is part of the crucifer family, which also includes radish and cress. Two species are used in the production of mustard and these are mixed according to the desired strength. The milder, yellowish *sinapis alba* gives the fine aroma whilst the reddish brown *brassica nigra* supplies the sharpness which is contained in the seeds. It is Canada, the largest mustard producer in the world, that supplies France with nearly all its requirements. The seeds, often slightly crushed to crack the outer husk, are soaked in brandy vinegar, water, and salt for several hours, before being weighed, mixed with spices, and ground. It is the protein-type enzyme myrosin and water that bring out the ethereal allyl mustard oil and causes the biting sharpness. This, however, disappears if it is carried out in industrial mills, which generate heat with their 3,000 revolutions a minute. Mustard cannot tolerate heat, for its taste is highly volatile. Horseradish then has to be used to replace the sharpness. France's most renowned mustard miller operates in Beaune, only 200 yards from the famous hospices. The firm Edmond Fallot supplies most French three-star chefs with both powder and their own ready-prepared mustards. The young mustard maker, Marc Desarmeniens, whose grandfather took over the mill around the turn of the century and gave his name to it, shows his secret with pride. "We cherish and maintain the old stone mills because they do not heat up the paste and so preserve the essential essence of the mustard," he says. The separation of the paste from the husks is carried out in a centrifuge. Only in the *moutarde à l'ancienne* do the husks remain. Finally citric acid, anti-oxidizing agents and turmeric are added, the latter to provide the strong yellow color. Irrespective of which spice or herb Fallot uses, the mustard is always the same: strong in taste and with a powerful bite. Although mustard is served with warm or cold meats, its true purpose is in the kitchen where it is used to provide subtle background flavors. Mustard is the universal seasoning par excellence. It intensifies taste generally, but is particularly effective in salad, meat, and fish sauces. A good chef will always use it with subtlety and sensitivity.

Background: The mustard seeds must not be overheated during grinding, or the mustard oil which provides the hotness of the mustard will evaporate.

Types of Mustard

Moutarde de Champagne – champagne mustard
This coarse-grained mustard derives its especially mild flavor from the wine of the Champagne. It goes well with roast or broiled meat and is good in salad dressings.

Moutarde à l'ancienne – traditional style mustard
A coarse-grained mustard in which the seed-skins have not been removed. It is used for marinades or for vinaigrette and is served with cold or hot meat.

Moutarde à l'estragon – tarragon mustard
Popular for fish sauces and vinaigrette.

Moutarde au poivre vert – mustard with green pepper
The green pepper goes well with broiled dishes.

Moutarde de Dijon – Dijon mustard
A classic, refined mustard particularly suitable for cooking purposes, it can be used in sauces of all kinds and for rubbing into meat roasts and meat fried quickly and on a high flame.

Tip: Always seal mustard well and keep it in the refrigerator. Mustard should always be added to cooked dishes when the cooking is completed, otherwise it will lose its character.

After grinding, mustard must be allowed to mature for several hours in wooden vats. During this process the mustard loses its initial bitter flavor.

Yellow seeds produce delicate flavours, while reddish-brown seeds provide the hotness. The seeds are slightly crushed and soaked before grinding.

Quiche Lorraine

Lorraine's contribution to the culinary delights of France lies above all in the realm of cakes, flans, biscuits, macaroons, jams, and confectionery, all of which can tap a rich supply of butter, cream, eggs, and fruit from this western side of the Vosges. Nevertheless it is Quiche Lorraine, a savory delicacy, which has become its best-known specialty. This recipe is very old and finds mention in 400-year-old cookery books. Smoked bacon, another specialty of this province, is the most important ingredient, as this is vital to the characteristic taste of Quiche Lorraine. Salt, also an important ingredient, is a valuable commercial product which has been obtained from Lorraine's salt works since the Middle Ages, and was also put to good use in the conserving of Lorraine's excellent sausage and other meat products. When the popularity of Quiche Lorraine spread to the other regions of France, grated cheese found its way into the recipe. Originally this was not an ingredient, for the first Quiche Lorraine built its reputation on the quality of the butter, eggs, and bacon. A dry Riesling or a fruity Beaujolais is the best accompaniment.

Quiche lorraine
Quiche Lorraine
(Illustrations 1–4)

Serves 2–4

1¼ cups (150 g) flour
Salt, black pepper
3 eggs
¼ cup (75 g) butter
5 oz (150 g) fine, lean, smoked bacon
4 oz (125 g) crème fraîche
1 pinch nutmeg

Sieve the flour into a bowl and make a hollow in the center (1). Add a pinch of salt, one egg, and the butter cut in small pieces. Knead together the ingredients and the flour and form the dough into the shape of a ball. Squash the pastry flat again and knead it once more into the shape of a ball. Wrap the dough in airtight cling film and put it in the refrigerator for 2 hours.
Preheat the oven to 425 °F (220 °C).
Roll out the dough very thin. Grease a flan or quiche tin with butter (the classic size is 7 ins/18 cm diameter). Line the tin with the pastry (2) and trim off any surplus. Prick the dough several times with a fork. Bake for 10 minutes and then remove from the oven.
Cut the rind off the bacon and remove any gristle. Cut the bacon into small cubes and brown them slightly in a frying pan. Beat the two remaining eggs, stir in the crème fraîche and season the mixture with nutmeg, pepper and a very little salt.
Distribute the bacon cubes evenly over the flan case (grated cheese may also be sprinkled in if required [3]). Pour the egg-cream mixture over the bacon (4). Bake in the oven for about 25 minutes. Serve hot.

1

2

3

4

Cheese

"Comment est-il possible de gouverner un pays qui produit plus de trois cent soixante-dix fromages différents?" – "How is it possible to govern a country which produces more than three hundred and seventy different cheeses?" With this heartfelt groan General de Gaulle's intention was to point to the numerous regional differences in France. The variety of landscapes, climates, vegetation, animal breeds, traditions, and character of the people are all reflected in the cheeses – from Coulommiers to Munster, from Roquefort to Saint-Maure, from Saint Nectaire to Comté, to mention but a few of the terrific range of high and top quality cheeses available. Thirty-two types of cheese have to this date received the seal of quality – *Appellation d'Origine Contrôlée.* Cheese may be soft, partially hard or hard in consistency; it may have rind or no rind; it may have blue mold inside or a reddish mold outside; it may be young or matured; it may be seasoned, washed or steeped. The variety is infinite. Cheese in France is classified according to the following methods of production: curd cheese, industrially-processed curd cheese, soft cheese with white or red mold rind, blue-veined cheese, goats' cheese, and hard cheese pressed either from cooked or un-cooked curds. It almost goes without saying that any good French meal must have a cheese course.

Background: Roland Barthélemy, chairman of the Paris cheese guild, in his delightful shop *"Specialitées Fromagières."*

Fromage Frais – Soft White Cheese

There is a huge number of products that are associated with the production of farmer's cheese, or *fromage blanc* as it is called in French. Such specialties are to be found wherever cheese is produced by hand. It is a cheese that has had no time to form rind or develop in color. Depending on the fat content its consistency varies from light to creamy.

Also included in this category are young goats' cheese and special preparations of soft cheeses, which have spices, herbs, chopped onions or other ingredients added. Often they are left in their natural state as an alternative to the cheese platter, or offered as a dessert. In the latter case sugar, honey or jam may be added.

Camembert

Whilst many cheeses were already being produced in the Middle Ages, often in abbeys, Camembert's history only dates back 200 years. Moreover, it is the only cheese type whose "inventor" is known: Marie Harel from the village of Camembert in Normandy. During the Revolution she was lodging a priest from the Brie area who would lend her a hand with the cheese making. This cooperation benefited from the knowledge of the guest and, so to speak, the help of the flourishing bacteria of the Pays d'Auge, also the home of the finest Calvados. The result was a particularly delicate cheese which Marie formed into hand-sized rounds of about half a pound in weight. From 1880 they were packed in thin wooden packets which helped spread the fame of Camembert, especially as the cheese fitted so neatly into them.

Background: To make Camembert, the broken cheese curds are poured into the little cheese molds with a ladle, *à la louche*.

The Normandy pastures provide lush grass for the cows, and ensure the richness of their milk.

The raw milk is put into metal churns, where it curdles after rennin is added.

The final weight of the cheese is determined by the ladle. A Camembert usually weighs around half a pound (250 g).

Camembert is a sweet milk cheese, which is curdled by means of rennet, an enzyme from the stomach of a cow. The cheese mixture is then scooped into molds. The cheese matures with the help of salt. To produce the typical downy outer coating, the cheese maker promotes the process by adding a fine dose of the mold. Before the Camembert can be enjoyed, it must have matured for three weeks. The downy, pleasantly reddish exterior will conceal a soft yellow cheese which is almost, but only just, beginning to flow, and which radiates a pleasant aroma. The best seasons are summer and fall.

Fromages à Croûte Fleurie – White Mold Cheese

This type of cheese enjoys great popularity and is available in many varieties. Every supermarket sells a variety of popular, Camembert imitations with white downy mold rinds as well as neutral-tasting, often plaster-like Bries made of pasteurized milk. If it is a high-quality cheese that you are looking for, make sure to ask for *fermiers*.

Vacherin Mont d'Or

When the French prepare a cheese platter for the Christmas or New Year menu, the Mont d'Or takes the place of honor. Although this cheese specialty from the French Jura is produced between August 31 and March 31, its actual season does not really begin until December. Because of the huge demand for it, it often happens that the Vacherin de Haut-Doubs is not sufficiently mature. It is a joy to eat when the ivory-colored cheese flows out from under its yellowish or gray, wrinkled and folded rind. Indeed a spoon may be needed to serve it out. In this state it has a creamy, fruity, fragrant, and seductive taste.

The cows, which are of the Montbéliarde or Pie rouge de l'Est breeds, graze on the meadows of the Doubs at an altitude of over 2,100 feet (700 meters), and supply all their milk for the Vacherin cheese. The cheese is exclusively produced from non-pasteurized milk, which is curdled by means of rennet and then lightly pressed. The flat round cheeses, which weigh either one or two pounds (a half or one kilogram), or four or six pounds (1.8 kg or 3 kg), initially mature on spruce wood boards. They are turned regularly and rubbed with salt water. The *affinage*, the final refinement when they acquire their mature taste, occurs in the spruce or fir match wood boxes in which they are sold.

Fromages à Croûte Lavée – Soft Cheese with Red Mold

These soft cheeses from the northern half of France are frequently rubbed with a damp cloth during the maturation process. As a result a smooth, initially slippery rind develops, and it is on this that the red mold grows. In the course of the maturation process the cheese takes on a stronger and stronger reddish-orange coloration. At the same time it becomes stronger in taste. The last phase of the *affinage* may be carried out with beer, wine or brandies. Although their smell is often very intensive and marked, many are surprisingly mild, creamy or elastic cheeses. They should never be biting or bitter in taste. Most *washed* cheeses are nowadays supplied by the large dairies.

Once the whey has drained off, the cheeses are removed from the molds, salted, and stored in maturation cellars.

The Camembert cheeses are administered a dose of mold. Within three weeks the cheeses develop their characteristic pale downy skin.

Camembert has reached its optimum maturity when reddish blotches appear on the white down. The inside of the cheese is now yellow and soft.

Roquefort

It looks like marble, for its noble paleness is patterned with blue veins and patches. Its taste is legendary. Roquefort is a sheep's cheese made of pure full cream unpasteurized milk. It originates in Roquefort-sur-Soulzon, a village of 900 inhabitants in the south of France, a classic sheep area. It lies on the edge of the bare Causse de Larsac, a windswept limestone high plateau, on which only gnarled bushes and wild herbs can eke out an existence. Herds of the thin-coated Lacaune sheep struggle to find the meager nourishment, which gives their milk its fine taste. Shepherds from the whole of Aveyron as well as other regions in the south and even the Pyrenees, nowadays work for the large cooperative and ten other cheese firms in the area between Millau and Saint-Affrique. That the most famous blue-veined cheese in France can mature only there is due to a primeval catastrophe: the north eastern edge of the limestone massif of the Combalou collapsed and formed a gigantic heap of rubble. In its interior, however, natural caves remained, in some cases of considerable size. The porous limestone guarantees ninety-five percent humidity in the caves, and the cool air penetrating through the cracks in the rock maintains a constant low temperature. All this means ideal conditions for the *penicillium roqueforti*, which spreads across the walls of the caves. Nowadays minute quantities of this mold are introduced into the thousands of gallons of milk in the dairies themselves, before the cheese production even begins. The cheeses are therefore infected before they reach the maturation cellars. Before the unwrapped cheeses are loaded onto solid oak frames for their first phase of maturation, they are perforated by means of nail boards. In this way a system of air passages is created within each cheese, allowing space for the mold to develop unhindered for a month. Before it can gain too much of an upper hand, however, the cheeses are covered with their familiar coats of tin foil. They are then transferred to the cooler climes of the Combalou. The mold has at least another three months to spin its web of veins, although higher quality cheeses may be allowed up to a year or more. The younger Roquefort cheese is paler, whereas its mold is darker in color and less in quantity. As the maturity increases the cheese takes on an ivory tone. The mold gains more and more ground and assumes that highly desirable bluish-green hue. The cheese has now acquired its full taste. It is delicious when eaten with a naturally sweet muscatel wine from the South, especially the Muscat de Rivesaltes.

It is from raw sheep's milk that the cheese acquires its distinctive flavor.

The *penicillium roqueforti* mold thrives in the caves of the limestone mountains of Combalou.

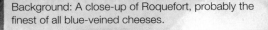

Background: A close-up of Roquefort, probably the finest of all blue-veined cheeses.

Nails are used to drill evenly distributed air channels in the cheeses to ensure development of the mold.

During the first stage of maturation, the uncovered cheeses are left on wooden tables.

Each individual cheese is checked as to its stage in the ripening process by the *maître de chai*.

Now the cheeses are wrapped in tin foil ready for their second phase of maturation.

Chèvre – Goats' Cheese

Goats are modest animals. They do not need lush grass and are equally satisfied with herbs, stalks, and the leaves of bushes and trees. For this reason goats are kept nearly everywhere in France. They mostly belong to the small agricultural concerns, which have little or only barren land at their disposal. Over the centuries various regions, such as Poitou, Berry, Quercy, Provence, and Corsica, have acquired a reputation for their goats' cheese. After the Second World War when agriculture was mechanized, many farmers turned away from goat breeding, which had been an important part of a traditional and varied, but uneconomic way of farming.

It received a boost however after the students' revolt of May 1968. Many young people moved to the country to try out a more natural way of life. Their emblem became the goat. Even if most of the '68 generation eventually returned to the towns, those alternative people who stayed, gradually gained a deeper appreciation of their new métier. *Fromage de chèvre*, or Chèvre for short, became their staple product and no weekend market was complete without at least one stall selling goats' cheese.

On average a goat can supply a gallon (four liters) of milk a day, or 200 gallons (800 liters) a year. Goat's milk is richer in fat than either cow's or sheep's milk. The milk is heated up in a vat to about 90 °F (33 °C). Rennet is then added at a rate of about one fluid ounce to twenty-five gallons (thirty milliliters to one hundred liters). After a good half hour the milk curdles and the casein is transformed into a pudding-like mass. This is divided carefully into pieces with a so-called cheese harp, so that the whey can drain away. The cheese mass is now poured into containers with holes in the base. In the case of hand-made cheeses, the small format, made from about two pints (one liter) of milk, is the most popular. Tradition may on the other hand demand pyramid, rod or cylinder molds. When the goats' cheese comes out of the mold it is soft, white, very creamy, and has little taste.

After a week, during which it loses considerable volume through drying, it begins to develop its typical aroma. By the end of the second week it has become considerably firmer and a soft yellowish, or light bluish crust has begun to form. A clear but mild aroma has started to develop. After twenty to thirty days it has completed the drying process. The crust now shows cracks and often has patches of mold. The longer it remains exposed to the air, the harder, drier, and stronger-tasting the cheese will become.

Goats have established themselves in areas too barren for other livestock. The goat provides the French with some of their best cheeses.

Fromages à Pâte Pressée non Cuite – Firm and Semi-firm Uncooked Cheeses

In France a distinction is made between hard and firm cheeses which are pressed, but not cooked, and those in which the broken curd is additionally warmed up (see below). When the *fromages à pâte pressée non cuite* are produced by hand, the milk obtained in the morning and the evening is immediately warmed up to 90 °F (32 °C) and rennet added. After thirty to sixty minutes of thickening, caused by curdling and the formation of a jelly-like consistency, the cheese is broken up with a cheese harp. The broken curd is then pressed for the first time and left to settle. It is then broken up again, this time into smaller pieces. It is salted and filled in a mold wrapped in a cloth, and pressed for a second time for forty-eight hours. The resulting large cylindrical cheeses are then taken out of the mold and brought into cool damp maturation cellars. Depending on the type of cheese, they then undergo a process of *affinage,* refinement.

The most well-known types of cheese in this family, the Cantal and its cousins Salers and Laguiole, originate from the volcanic landscape of the Auvergne. The cows, which are of the rustic breeds Aubrac and Salers, graze on the fresh aromatic herb-rich meadows in the mountains at altitudes of between two and three thousand feet (700 to 1000 meters). These herbs, which include clover and gentian, give a distinctive taste to the milk, and hence the cheese.

Fromages à Pâte Pressée Cuite – Cooked Hard Cheeses

The method of preparing cheese with a press and cooked curds was above all developed in the Alpine regions. It is particularly typical of large hard cheeses such as Emmental, also produced in France, Beaufort, and Comté (also called Gruyère de Comté). These two latter are protected by law and only cheese produced in these respective areas may bear these names. The semi-cooked Abondance, which has been produced since the Middle Ages, also belongs to this family. After the milk has been thickened by the addition of rennet and curdled to a jelly-like consistency, it is broken into small grain-sized pieces with the cheese harp. Under constant stirring, the broken curd is heated, first slowly and then more strongly until the curd grains become harder. After it has been stirred for a further thirty minutes the broken curd is poured into perforated containers covered in cloths, and the whey allowed to drain off. It is then put in molds and pressed. In the case of Beaufort these molds contain beech hoops. Once the cheese has become firm it is salted, rubbed down, and allowed to mature for three to six months.

Rennet is added to the goats' cheese to make it curdle; the broken curds are then poured into molds.

The bottoms of the molds are perforated, allowing the whey to drain away and the cheeses to take shape.

After only one hour the cheeses have become so firm that they can be removed from the molds and start their maturation process.

Well-ripened goats' cheeses with a firm rind and a creamy-white center.

French Cheeses at a Glance
(Illustrated on pages 406–409)

The types that are marked with * have been awarded the seal of quality Appellation d'Origine Contrôlée and are produced exclusively from raw unpasteurized milk.

Fromages à croûte fleurie – white mold cheese
Brie de Meaux*
Brie de Melun *
Brillat-Savarin
Camembert*
Chaource*
Coulommiers
Neufchâtel*
Saint-Marcellin

Fromages à croûte lavée – soft cheese with red mold
Epoisses*
Langres*
Livarot*
Maroilles*
Mont d'Or, Vacherin de Haut-Doubs*
Munster, Munster-Géromé*
Pont l'Evêque*

Chèvre – goats' cheese
Cabécou
Chabichou du Poitou*
Charolais, Charolles
Crottin de Chavignol*
Montrachet
Pélardon
Picodon de l'Ardèche, Picodon de la Drôme*
Poivre d'âne
Pouligny-Saint-Pierre*
Saint-Maure*
Selles-sur-Cher*

Fromages à pâte persillée – blue-veined cheese
Bleu d'Auvergne*
Bleu des Causses*
Bleu du Haut-Jura, Bleu de Gex, Bleu de Septmoncel*
Fourme d'Ambert, Fourme de Montbrison*
Roquefort*

Fromages à pâte pressée non cuite – firm and semi-firm cheeses
Ardi-gasna
Bethmale
Cantal*
Laguiole*
Mimolette
Morbier
Ossau-Iraty*
Reblochon*
Saint-Nectaire*
Salers*
Tomme de Savoie

Fromages à pâte pressée cuite – hard cheeses
Abondance*
Beaufort*
Comté, Gruyère de Comté*

Wine

In France wine is closely linked with a very particular concept, which is impossible to translate – *terroir*. Although the idea of soil and ground is inherent, *terroir* means much more. It encapsulates all the conditions which cause a wine to flourish in a particular place: structure and stoniness of the ground, slope and orientation, sunshine and rain, frost, heat, and wind, in short, all the natural elements. Everywhere where wine has acquired a high prestige, it is due to a terroir combining all the favorable factors.

The cleverly devised system of French labels of origin is based above all on these conditions. In all, around 320 different growing areas have been elevated to the level of Appellation d'Origine Contrôlée, the highest category. These range from a couple of acres to areas of a thousand or more. It guarantees the authenticity of the wine, whether it be Sauternes or Chablis, Margaux or Pommard, Châteauneuf-du-Pape or Saint-Emilion, Beaujolais or Hermitage. It also includes other factors that the producers are obliged to respect, such as, for example, the types of grape, whose choice and methods of growing are dependent on old traditions.

Apart from the work in the vineyard, all the processes in the wine cellar influence the wine, from the wine-making to the filling. Nevertheless, the most decisive factor is still the human one. The vintner impresses his character on the wine, as he also does his cultural and historical background, his philosophy and ethics, his insights and intentions. So it is that within one appellation, even in an excellent year, there can be both disappointing wines and wines that give unique expression to their terroir.

In the last two decades French wines have made much progress. Their incredible variety has become even greater as more and more wine growers successfully produce more and more great wines within their appellations – living proof of a cultural development that began with the Phoenicians and the Romans.

Categories of Wine

Vin de table, VdT
Table wine, lowest category, mostly mass-produced wines without character.

Vin de pays, VdP
Ordinary local wine but subject to regulations; this category may include pleasant, tasty wines and occasionally wines of a single grape variety.

Vin délimité de qualité supérieure, VDQS
Limited wines of superior quality; this regulated category applies to wines between vins de pays and AOC wines and has become rather rare; may include good quality wines.

Vin d'appellation d'origine contrôlée, AC or AOC
Wines with controlled labels of origin; these are the highest quality wines and subject to strict regulations with regard to grape types and yield; all top-range wines belong to this category and should always guarantee superior quality.

Bottle Shapes

Some wine-growing regions have developed their own characteristic bottle shapes. The best-known amongst them are the following:

1 Burgundy
2 Bordeaux
3 Alsace
4 Provence
5 Châteauneuf-du-Pape

Below: France is a veritable treasure-house for gourmets and wine lovers alike. Sealed away under foil caps and corks, an incredible abundance of the most varied French wines are waiting to be discovered.

Wine Language – a Basic Vocabulary

Acidité	acidity
Barrique	oak cask holding 70 gallons (225 liters)
Bouche, goût	palate, taste
Bouchon	cork
Bouquet, nez	bouquet, aroma, scent, nose
Cave	cellar
Caveau	tasting cellar
Caviste	cellar man, Master cellarer
Cep, souche	vine stock
Cépage	type of vine
Chai	premises where wine is stored
Chaptalisation	adding sugar to the must before fermentation;
Charpente	structure
Couleur, robe	color
Cru	vineyard; growth
Cuvaison	period for crushing grapes
Cuve	(fermentation) vat
Cuvée	special vintage or blend
Degré	percentage of alcohol
Dégustation	wine-tasting
Elévage	development, maturation
Equilibre	balance, harmony
Fermentation	fermentation
Fermentation maloctique (malo)	biological breakdown of acids
Fût	barrel, cask
Garde	maximum length of storing or maturation
Grape	bunch of grapes
Lie, lies	yeast sediments, lees
Macération	maceration
Millésimé	vintage date
Mise (en bouteille)	bottled
Nez, bouquet	nose, aroma, scent, bouquet
Persistance	lingering on the palate,
Pièce	cask, barrel (Burgundy)
Pigeage	immersing of the marc, remains of grapes after pressing
Pressurage	pressing
Puissance	intensity, strength
Raisin	grape
Rendement	yield
Robe, couleur	color
Souche, cep	vine stock
Taille	pruning of the vine stocks
Tastevin	wine-tasting cup
Tri	selection, sorting out of the grapes
Vendange	grape harvest
Vigne	vineyard
Vigneron	wine grower
Vignoble	all the vineyards of an area or country
Vinification	wine-making process
Viticulteur	wine grower, viticulturist

4 5

411

Bordeaux

Gironde
Médoc
Saint-Estèphe
Pauillac
Côtes de Blaye
Haut-Médoc
Saint-Julien
Listrac
Côtes de Bourg
Moulis Margaux
Bordeaux
Côtes de Francs
Libournais
Graves de Vayres
Côtes de Castillon
Sainte-Foy-Bordeaux
Pessac-Léognan
Premières Côtes de Bordeaux
Entre-Deux-Mers
Graves
Cérons
Barsac
Loupiac
Sainte-Croix-du-Mont
Sauternes
Saint-Macaire
Bordeaux
Montlieu
Montpon-Ménestrol
Marmande
Bordeaux

Lalande-de-Pomerol
Lussac Saint-Émilion
Fronsac et Canon-Fronsac
Pomerol
Montagne-Saint-Émilion
Puisseguin-Saint-Émilion
Libourne
Saint-Émilion

Bordeaux

Around the southern French port city of Bordeaux lies the largest continuous area of vineyards in the world with an area of almost 400 square miles (100,000 hectares). Bordeaux offers a whole range of wines apart from the reds: dry, semisweet and very sweet white wines, rosés and even sparkling wines. The range varies from the simplest tipple to the world-famous *Châteaux* wines. The label Château rarely implies some castle-like building, for in the Bordeaux area this term is synonymous with a vineyard.

This area, which borders on the Atlantic, has a mild climate and the forests protect it from the storms blowing in from the sea. The fall often brings sunny days, during which the grapes achieve their optimal ripeness – a prerequisite for any good vintage. The area is divided by the rivers Dordogne and Garonne, which join together just north of the town in the Gironde. This creates three zones which provide highly distinctive and diverse wines.

• To the west of the Garonne, a strip of wine growing land, twelve miles at its widest, runs around Bordeaux and along the left bank of the Gironde to its mouth. This is the famous Graves, which adjoins the Haut-Médoc and Médoc to the north of the town. Gravel with good drainage properties and, in some areas, deep layers of limestone determine the character of the soil in this area. Sweet, golden-colored wines acquire extremely complex bouquets, particularly Sauternes. Graves supplies the best dry white Bordeaux wines. The red wines, dominated by Cabernet Sauvignon, whether Graves, Margaux, Saint-Julien or Paulliac are the stuff of legend, with their often youthful bashfulness that later develops into a distinguished and complex character.

• Between Garonne and Dordogne lies the beautiful hilly area of Entre-Deux-Mers, with its Premières Côtes de Bordeaux and its powerful red wines on the right bank of the Garonne. Here it is predominantly clay on limestone-rich deposits. Entre-Deux-Mers is a white wine appellation, in which the Sauvignon grape provides a fruity taste.

• On the right bank of the Dordogne, in the Libournais, excellent deposits of gravel on limestone are again to be found. This is also the case in some areas of Saint-Emilion and Pomerol. In this area the Merlot grape is dominant in a mixture of grape varieties and produces particularly velvety, harmonious red wines. In the surrounding appellations heavier soils predominate, suitable for good, robust red wines. Bourg and Blaye, to the north west of Libourne, produce both fruity red wines and dry, often perfumed, white wines on mixed soils.

Opposite: The Cabernets are the dominant varieties of the Médoc, whilst the Merlot grape is the one most widely cultivated on the right bank of the Dordogne, in Saint-Emilion and in the Libournais region.

Grape Varieties of Bordeaux

Cabernet Sauvignon
Dominant amongst the great wines of the Médoc. The wine is dark and strong, with an aroma of black currants. It requires maturation due to its distinctive tannins.

Cabernet Franc
Closely related to Cabernet Sauvignon; a familiar feature of the traditionally mixed vine cultivation of Bordeaux. The wine is complex and less full-bodied, tangy and with more subtle tannins.

Merlot
A variety that ripens early in the season and often produces enormous yields; it is an important part of the Bordeaux wine industry, particularly in Pomerol and Saint-Emilion, but is also popular in the Midi. The sensual, velvety wine is distinguished by a lot of body and mild tannins and needs less time to mature.

Petit Verdot
Excellent but awkward Médoc grape. The wine is dark and spicy, with a lot of volume and very distinctive tannins. Excellent for blending.

Malbec, Auxerrois, Cot, Pessac
The main varieties of Cahors but rarely grown in the Bordeaux region. The wine is dark, dense, with very strong tannins.

Sémillon
A variety that is prone to attack by noble rot and can then be used as the basis for Sauternes and other sweet and medium sweet white wines; it is added to Sauvignon grapes to produce dry Bordeaux wines; grown in the southwest. It takes over-ripeness or long maturation times for the wine to develop its fascinatingly complex aromas.

Sauvignon
A vine with a very good yield that forms the basis of the dry white Bordeaux wines; it is cultivated all over the world but has its stronghold in the Loire region. The highly aromatic wine is very fruity and somewhat acid, with a bouquet of blackcurrants.

Southwest France

The strong climatic influences of the Atlantic are the only common denominator in the otherwise very varied wines of the rest of south western France. The wine enthusiast will discover a wealth of pleasures at very reasonable prices. To the east of Bordeaux, the Bergerac region, with its almost fifty square miles (12,000 hectares) of vineyards, offers the same variety of wines as its famous neighbor. Its sweetest star is called Monbazillac, whereas in Cahors it is the Malbec which determines the character of the red wines, which in good years possess considerable character and age well.

Wine appellations such as Côtes de Duras or Buzet are founded above all on red Bordeaux grapes, even if there are some white and rosé wines. On the other hand, Côtes du Frontonnais exploits a richer variety of grapes to obtain its often very aromatic, lighter style red wines. The rare Negrette imbues a wine with the greatest strength and character. Gaillac is a melting pot of Mediterranean and Atlantic influences with numerous grape varieties – whether sparkling or still, dry or sweet, white, rosé or red, everything is available in abundant diversity.

Madiran has attracted a lot of attention because of the young generation of wine-growers led by Alain Brumont. They demonstrate that the traditional Tannat as an almost pure-raced wine shows considerably more depth and greatness than Cabernet. Even Jurançon, to the south west of Pau, enjoys a strong demand for its excellent semisweet or dry white wines, which are pressed from Manseng. Finally, Irouléguy is well worth sampling, the Basque wine which is harvested from sometimes quite spectacular vineyards.

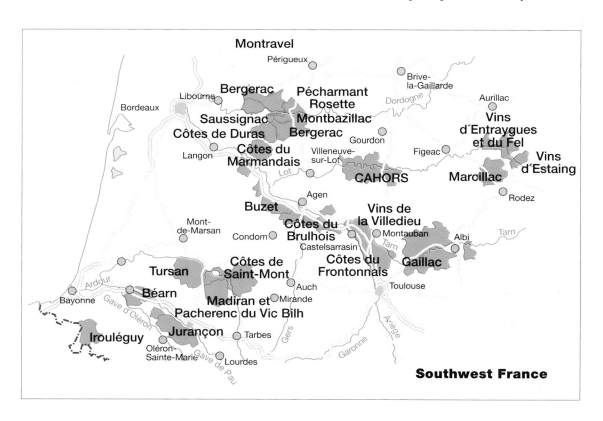

Southwest France

Burgundy

No other wine region has such a cleverly thought-out method of dividing the individual parcels of vineyard one from another, and assigning quality categories to them. The heart of the area, the Côte d'Or, the Golden Slope, which extends over thirty square miles (8,500 hectares) from Dijon southwards via Beaune out to Chagny, can boast almost seventy different appellations alone. Even this is a simplification when one takes into consideration the further categorization of Premiers Crus. The division of the land by ownership is equally complicated and results in very small parcels of land. In all, Burgundy comprises over ninety square miles (24,000 hectares) of vineyards, which like the Crus de Bourgogne, have the claim to the status of AOC Bourgogne.

Whilst the geology surprises by its sheer variety, there are many factors in common in Burgundy, which combine to create its distinctive character. One example of this is the continental climate, whose considerable variability from year to year is reflected in the nature of the vintages. Another is the types of grape. Burgundy is home to two excellent sorts: the white Chardonnay and the blue Pinot noir. It is in the Grands Crus of Burgundy that they find their deepest and most noble expression. However, the numerous and differing vineyards play many fascinating variations on these two basic themes.

Burgundy can be divided into four growing areas:
• Chablis lies in the north west, in the Yonne. It is exclusively white wines that come from this soil – limestone formed from seashells and it is this which gives the Chardonnay its very fresh mineral taste. There are 6,000 acres (2,400 hectares) of Chablis, and a further 4,600 acres (1,900 hectares) of regional wine appellations such as Irancy.
• Côtes d'Or:
1. Côtes de Nuits, beginning south of Dijon, it accounts for twenty-three (nearly all red) of the thirty Grands Crus, which flourish on slopes whose foundations are mixtures of gravel earth, clay and limestone. Generally their wines are full-bodied, have striking tannins and age well.
2. Côtes de Beaune – home of the famous full-bodied white wines Meursault and Montrachet. Here the ground marl plays its part in the wine, producing mainly more supple, young and very fruity red wines, with the exception of Pommard.
3. At a higher altitude are to be found the Hautes-Côtes de Nuits and de Beaune with fresh Chardonnays and lighter Pinot noirs;

• Côte Chalonnaise where the high limestone and marl concentrations in some parts produce often very tangy and elegant wines. The best-known appellations are Bouzeron, Rully, Mercurey, Givry, and Montagny.
• The Mâconnais in southern Burgundy begins to the north of Tournus and reaches as far as the cliffs of Solutré and Vergisson, where Pouilly Fuissé and Saint-Véran, its best whites, are grown. Otherwise very varying soils, pleasant, fresh, young white and red wines. Total area: 22,000 acres (8,800 hectares).

Beaujolais

Beaujolais is one of the most charming of all red wines. Its 56,000 acres (22,500 hectares) directly adjoin the Mâconnais and Burgundy and stretch almost down to Lyon. The ten top areas in the north of Beaujolais have the right to sell their wines under the "Appellation Bourgogne." Historically, however, Beaujolais was never part of Burgundy, and its red wine based on Gamay stands in its own right.

Grape Varieties of Burgundy

Chardonnay
The outstanding white grape variety in France, used in Burgundy to produce one of the most famous white wines in the whole world. Depending on the soil and the wine making process, the wine may be fresh, steely, fruity or smooth, full-bodied, and strong.

Pinot noir
An excellent red variety which is the basis for great, very fine red wines, and is also used for rosé or champagne in the Alsace. When young, the wine has the delicate aroma of berries.

Gamay
A robust variety which can produce interesting wines if grown on granite and if yield is restricted; otherwise the wines tend to be ordinary. The wines are fresh on the palate, fruity, and very drinkable, with a pleasant fruity or flowery aroma.

Aligoté
This white Burgundy variety is little cultivated today and, because of its earthy acidity, is mixed with blackcurrant liqueur to make Kir. Handled with care, as in Bouzeron or Saint-Bris, it can produce fine, interesting white wines.

Recommended wines
• Chablis will reward the wine connoisseur with regional appellations such as Saint-Bris, Irancy or Tonnerre.
• Good quality Pinot noirs can be obtained at less expense from all less well-known appellations along the Côte d'Or, such as Marsannay, Chorey-lès-Beaune, Monthélie.
• The red Premiers Crus from the AOC Beaune are often of great quality and are comparatively cheap.
• Good Chardonnays are grown in Clessé and Viré in the Mâconnais region; the rare late vintages are excellent.
• Chénas and Cru des Beaujolais offer the same character as Moulin-à-Vent, but at lower prices.

One of the most famous vineyards of Burgundy is the Clos de Vougeaut with its Château and wine cellars dating back to the 12th century.

Burgundy

Dijon

Côtes
de Nuits

Arnay-le-Duc

Hautes Côtes
de Nuits

Nuits-Saint-Georges

Beaune

Côtes
de Beaune

Hautes Côtes
de Beaune

Rully

Mercurey

Chalon-sur-Saône

Côte
Chalonnaise

Givry

Montagny-
Buxy

Tournus

Mâconnais

Cluny

Pouilly-
Fuissé

Mâcon

Pouilly-Loché

Saint-Véran

Pouilly-Vinzelles

Jovinois

Armaçon

Tonnerois

Chablis

Saint-Bris-
le-Vineux

Auxerrois

Irancy

Yonne

Clamecy

Vézelois

Beaujolais

Mâcon

Beaujolais-
Villages

Saint-Amour

Juliénas

Chénas

Moulin-à-Vent

Chiroubles

Fleurie

Beaujolais-
Villages

Morgon

Beaujolais-
Villages

Régnié

Côtes de
Brouilly

Brouilly

Beaujolais-
Villages

Azergues

Villefranche-
sur-Saône

Saône

Beaujolais

Beaujolais

Azergues

Beaujolais

L'Arbresle

Coteaux
du Lyonnais

Rhône

Lyon

Rhône

Côtes du Rhône

The Rhône valley boasts a whole range of wines along the 120 miles (200 km) from Vienne to Avignon. They can be divided into two families, those of the northern and those of the southern Rhône. In the north the vines often grow on steep terraces. The vineyards are very small and range from the eight acres (3.4 hectares) of Château-Grillet to the Crozes-Hermitage, which extends over 2,500 acres (1,000 hectares). Red wines owe their great character exclusively to the Syrah grape. White wines are pressed from the original Viognier or Marsanne and Roussanne grapes. The yields are low, and the wines very concentrated in good years. The very deep reds age well.

In the south with Châteauneuf-du-Pape and its thirteen authorized grapes the range is more extensive. The generous sun makes for good powerful wines, although many wine-growers or cooperatives prefer to produce lighter and simpler reds and rosés. White wines are relatively rare, the exception being the naturally sweet Muscat de Beaumes-de-Vénise and the sparkling Clairette de Die.

Provence

Even if it is the rosé of Provence that enjoys great popularity as a summer wine, the best of the six appellations in the 57,000 acres (23,000 hectares) of its vineyards are its reds and rare whites. In the Coteaux d'Aix-en-Provence or the Côtes de Provence, Cabernet Sauvignon, and Syrah often combine to produce powerful, full-flavored red wines. The Mourvèdre, which is grown in Bandol, develops great refinement after several years' maturing in the bottle. Cassis, on the other hand, is well-known for its white wines.

Corsica

6,000 acres (2,400 hectares) of Corsica's 30,000 acres (12,000 hectares) of vineyards have been granted appellation status. The indigenous vines, Nielluccio and Sciacarello, are cultivated here together with a mixture of other Mediterranean types. Alongside the rosé and other traditional simple wines, there are now some very intense, full-blooded, and complex red wines that are being produced.

Languedoc-Roussillon

The vineyards of this stretch of land, which extends from the Spanish border to the Rhône, are blessed with a Mediterranean climate. A whole variety of grapes are grown here, but the southern varieties predominate amongst the quality wines. Although the whole area, including the parts which produce table and country wines, is still the biggest wine producer, the proportion accounted for by vin de table is decreasing strongly. On the other hand, its thirty or so quality wines account for only about fifty-three million gallons (two million hectoliters), a third of the production of Bordeaux. Their quality has, however, significantly increased. Nowadays the new generation is exploiting the climatic advantages, the poor soils and southern grape varieties to develop Mediterranean wines full of strength and refinement.

One of the specialties is the Vins Doux Naturels, naturally sweet wines, such as Banyuls, Maury or Muscats, in which the natural grape sugar is retained. They are extremely distinctive and, when aged for several years, they possess highly subtle flavors.

Inside the fermentation tubs, the men use their feet to break open the grape skins so that fermentation can begin.

The quality of the wine's aroma is determined when it is bottled.

Special wines are still often labeled by hand.

Once the wine has completed its fermentation process, it is left to mature in oak barrels.

A good wine deserves a first-class cork.

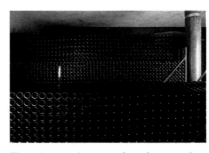

The wine needs to rest for a few months before it can be enjoyed at its best.

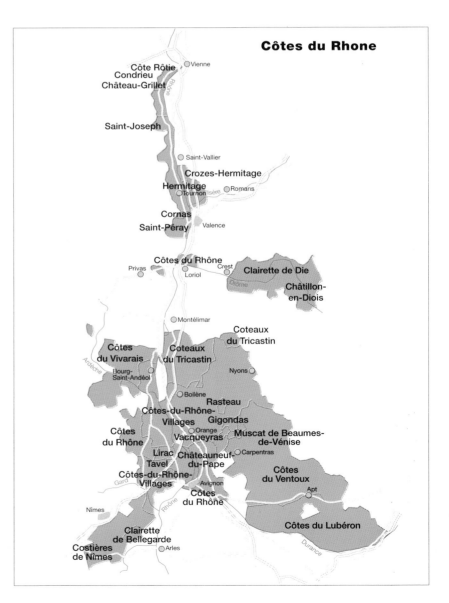

Côtes du Rhone

Grape Varieties of Southern France

Syrah

A superb red grape variety from the Rhône region widely grown all over the Midi and also popular in Australia, California etc. The dark wines are marked by a spicy and exciting bouquet with hints of cherry and other berries, and with excellent tannins.

Grenache

Originally from Spain, this grape variety is resistant to drought. It forms the basis of voluminous red wines, good rosés and numerous Vins Doux Naturels. The wine is strong, very fruity, and well-rounded.

Mourvèdre

This very demanding grape has its origins in Catalonia and ripens very late in the season; it is magnificent in the Bandol. The wines are dark and spicy with superbly strong and yet subtle tannins.

Carignan

Also originating from Spain, this grape variety has been misused as a basis for mass-produced wines. It is now on the decline, although still widely grown. It provides plenty of character at low yields.

Cinsault

A traditional variety that needs heat and develops few tannins or acidity; used for rosé and blends. The wines are pale, flowery and elegant.

Viognier

A variety of the famous white Condrieu which is gaining popularity in the Midi; produces very low yields. Makes fine, fragrant wine.

Macabeo

This white grape variety is used for Cava and Rioja and is widely cultivated in Spain; elsewhere it is above all grown in the Roussillon region. The potential of this grape has been underestimated, as its qualities only come to the fore when it is picked ripe and the wines are well matured.

Roussanne and Marsanne

Two varieties from the north of the Rhône region where they complement each other in blends. Marsanne brings structure to the wine, while Roussanne gives it refinement.

Muscat

A white grape variety with small fruits which is excellent for naturally sweet wines (or dry Vins de Pays). The wine is of pale golden color and great intensity, sweet, with hints of nutmeg, candied citrus fruit or fennel.

Recommended wines

• The most famous red wines of the northern Rhône, such as Côte Rôtie or Hermitage, are rare and expensive and should undergo a long period of maturation. Bargains can be found in Saint-Joseph and Crozes-Hermitage.
• Cairanne in the Côtes-du-Rhône-Villages is distinguished by some first-class wine growers.
• Highly interesting prestige wines at reasonable prices can be obtained from Coteaux d'Aix-en-Provence.
• The Languedoc is home to many first-class wine estates such as Château des Estanilles, Mas Jullien, Domainen l'Hortus, Peyre Rose, d'Aupilhac, and Coopérative Embres-Castelmaure.
• The top estates in the Roussillon region are Domaine Gauby, Château Casenove, Mas Crémat, Banyuls L'Etoile, and Vial Magnères, Collioure La Rectorie, Muscat from Cazes Frères.

Illustrated below: The Muscat de Rivesaltes is a naturally sweet specialty from the Roussillon region. Drinking this wine is somewhat reminiscent of eating fresh grapes.

Provence

Corsica

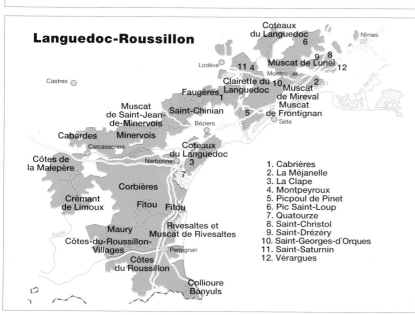

Languedoc-Roussillon

1. Cabrières
2. La Méjanelle
3. La Clape
4. Montpeyroux
5. Picpoul de Pinet
6. Pic Saint-Loup
7. Quatourze
8. Saint-Christol
9. Saint-Drézéry
10. Saint-Georges-d'Orques
11. Saint-Saturnin
12. Vérargues

Loire

The vineyards extend for over 600 miles (1,000 km) along the Loire and its tributaries. In Anjou and Touraine there are grand cellars in former quarries in the cliffs, where the wines can age for an eternity. The area along the river can be divided into four large regions:

• Muscadet, whose capital is the port city of Nantes, is grown on 27,000 acres (11,000 hectares) of the lower part of the Loire; a light crisp white wine, whose best qualities mature on the yeast, the lees – *sur lie*.

• Anjou extends over 39,000 acres (14,500 hectares) of vineyards, well-known for its simple medium-dry rosés. Red Anjou-Villages and Saumur-Champigny can be very good, delicately aromatic wines. Excellent also are the white wines such as the dry racy Savennières or semi-sweet Coteaux du Layon or Bonnezeaux.

• Touraine is the home of the Cabernet Franc variety, which finds subtle expression in Chinon, Bourgueil, and Saint-Nicolas-de-Bourgueil. Also notable is the white Chinon grape which achieves perfection in Vouvray and Montlouis, whether as a dry, sweet or sparkling wine. Amongst the AOC wines in Touraine are aromatic Sauvignons, fruity Gamays, and powerful red wines, especially in Mesland and Amboise.

• Sancerre and Pouilly, the strongholds of the Sauvignon; nowhere else does it attain such finesse and complexity as here, and in nearby Ménétou-Salon, Quincy, and Reuilly.

Alsace

The slopes of Alsace on the left bank of the Rhine are protected against bad weather by the Vosges mountains. With 33,000 acres (13,500 hectares) of vineyards, they stretch over 60 miles (100 km) between Mulhouse and Strasbourg. Their heart lies within a twelve mile radius to the north and south of Colmar. Fifty classified slopes are listed on the labels as Grands Crus and are subject to much more stringent regulations. This applies also to *Vendange tardive* (Auslese) and *Sélection des Grains Nobles* (Beerenauslese).

Otherwise, and in contrast to other appellations, there are seven grape varieties which determine the nature of the wines. Four of these are also authorized as Grands Crus:

• Riesling, the finest with a delicate bouquet, racy, elegant and exquisitely acidic

• Gewürztraminer, highly aromatic, spicy white wine with pink-colored grapes

• Pinot gris (Tokay), Gray Burgundy, known in Germany as Ruländer, very powerful

• Muscat, dry, very intense, aromatic, light white wine with hints of muscatel.

Other sorts include:

• Pinot noir, Spätburgunder in Germany, either a pleasant rosé wine or a bright, finely aromatic red wine

• Sylvaner, very dry, high-yielding grape, weakly aromatic dry wine

• Pinot blanc, also known as Klevner, high yields, wine with little character.

Jura and Savoy

Both of these small mountainous wine areas lie near the Swiss border. The Jura vineyards with their 3,500 acres (1,400 hectares) form a single area, whilst the 3,700 acres (1,500 hectares) of Savoy consist of fragmented vineyards strewn about the sunny slopes. Savoy produces crisp white wines such as Roussette, Crépy or Seyssel or fruity and lighter red wines. In contrast the Jura offers wines of great character. As well as full bodied red wines and rosés, produced with Trousseau and Poulsard, there are excellent white Savagnin wines. These find their greatest expression in the sweet vin de paille (straw wine), whose grapes dry on mats, as well as in the vin jaune. It ages for at least six years in the barrel, during which a protective yeast flora forms, and develops sherry-like aromas. It is a wine of unsurpassed refinement.

Grape Varieties of the Loire Region

Melon
A variety that originated in Burgundy and is now often named after the Muscadet wine which it produces. The very dry wines are distinguished by light aromas and their subtle fruitiness.

Gros Plant
Strictly speaking Folle Blanche; only the lower-growing varieties present no problems with rot; famous as base wine for liquor. The wines are extremely dry, have little body, and not very strongly developed aromas.

Grolleau
A very high-yielding variety, also known as Groslot, especially used for rosé wines. The pale wines are light and slightly fruity.

Cabernets, Gamay, Malbec
See Bordeaux, p. 413

Chenin Blanc
The great white grape from the Loire is now cultivated all over the world and can be put to a variety of uses, but is prone to frost; it has a high acidity content and the wines produced from Chenin Blanc vary according to the degree of ripeness of the grapes. The late vintage wines are complex but beautifully balanced, very fruity, with a hint of honey and a delicate sweetness, and age very well.

Recommended wines
• The Muscadet des Côtes de Grand Lieu is a new appellation; strong but flighty.
• In a good year, Coteaux du Layon produces excellent late vintage wines which age well.
• Savennières is rare and expensive, but it has no peer amongst dry white wines.
• A red wine with a delicate character of spicy fruitiness is the Chinon.

Recommended wines from Alsace
• Some of the old established wine-producing families are Léon Beyer, Trimbach, Hugel, Josmeyer, Dopff, Wolfberger, Zind-Humbrecht etc.
• Bargains can often be picked up from wine producers' cooperatives.
• Highly interesting wines can be obtained from "newcomers," such as Kreydenweiss or Ostertag.

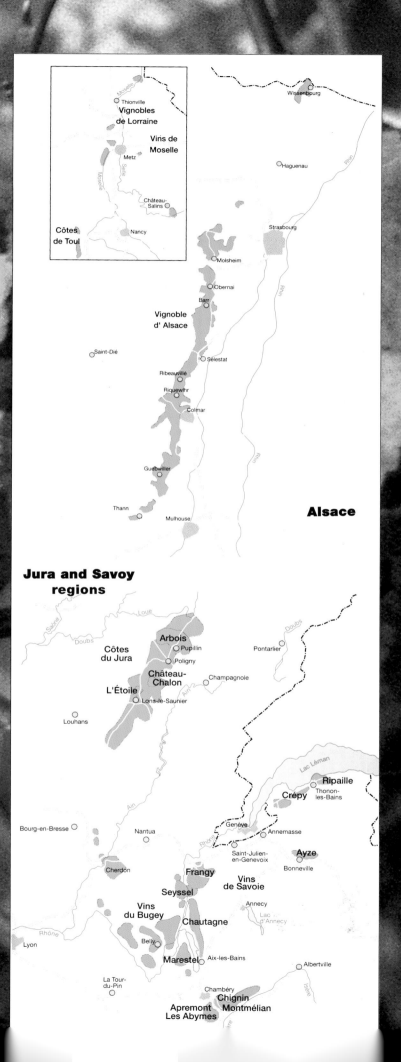

Every wine grower in the Alsace produces a large range of wines based on a variety of different grapes, degrees of ripeness, and processes.

Vignobles de Lorraine

Thionville

Vins de Moselle

Metz

Wissenbourg

Haguenau

Côtes de Toul

Château-Salins

Nancy

Strasbourg

Molsheim

Obernai

Barr

Vignoble d'Alsace

Saint-Dié

Sélestat

Ribeauvillé

Riquewihr

Colmar

Guebwiller

Thann

Mulhouse

Alsace

Jura and Savoy regions

Arbois

Pupillin

Pontarlier

Côtes du Jura

Poligny

Champagnole

Château-Chalon

L'Étoile

Lons-le-Saunier

Louhans

Lac Léman

Ripaille

Crépy

Thonon-les-Bains

Bourg-en-Bresse

Nantua

Genève

Annemasse

Ayze

Saint-Julien-en-Genevoix

Bonneville

Cherdon

Frangy

Vins de Savoie

Seyssel

Annecy

Lac d'Annecy

Vins du Bugey

Chautagne

Lyon

Belly

Aix-les-Bains

Marestel

La Tour-du-Pin

Albertville

Chambéry

Chignin

Apremont Les Abymes

Montmélian

Loire

Le Mans

Orléans

Coteaux du Vendômois

Vins de l'Orléannais

Châteaubriant

La Flèche Jasnières

Blois

Coteaux du Loir

Muscadet des Coteaux de la Loire

Ancenis

Angers

Cheverny

Saint-Nazaire

Nantes

Coteaux du Layon

Anjou

Tours

Touraine

Gros plant du Pays Nantais

Muscadet de Sèvre et Maine

Bourgueil

Vierzon

Cholet

Anjou-Villages

Saumur

Chinon

Loches

Valençay

Muscadet

Touraine

Indre

Châteauroux

La Roche-sur-Yon

Parthenay

Haut-Poitou

Creuse

Fiefs Vendées

Poitiers

Coteaux du Giennois

Les Sables-d'Olonne

Fontenay-le-Comte

Saint-Pourçain

Vierzon

Sancerre Menetou-Salon

Pouilly Fumé et Pouilly-sur-Loire

La Rochelle

Côte Roannaise

Château-Meillant

Quincy

Clermont-Ferrand

Côtes du Forez

Reuilly

Bourges

Montluçon

Côtes d'Auvergne

Champagne

Neither democracy nor recession can affect this most famous of sparkling wines. Its flair for luxury remains unimpaired. Its bubbles, which were at that time quite restrained, first fascinated the London society of the 17th century. The enthusiasm for its sparkle then bubbled over and spread to France. Louis XV, a right royal spendthrift, allowed himself be seduced by his mistresses into drinking champagne. Since then, champagne has been a must at every feast, whether attended by the nobility, bourgeoisie or demi-monde. And not only there, but also every celebration, every ball, every special occasion gains that extra bit of class by its presence. To open a bottle of champagne is indeed a celebration in itself. It is often forgotten, of course, that champagne is a wine and that it comes from the most northerly vineyards in France. The growing area and the method of production are very much part of its diverse makeup. With no other wine are there so many possibilities of variation. They all influence its taste. There are champagnes which are slim or ample, fruity or flowery, fresh or mature, simple or complex, sweet or bone dry, young or developed. As is the case everywhere, there are good and bad, fine and ordinary, harmonious and rough, expensive and cheap. Some are suitable as an aperitif, others go well with seafood. Some accompany fish or white meats, some the dessert. Champagne fits all occasions – but it must be the right one.

Most of the 60,000 acres (25,000 hectares) of the Champagne vineyards are in the Départements of Marne and Aube. Mineral-rich chalk soils and a cool climate endow the two red grapes Pinot Meunier and Pinot noir, as well as the white Chardonnay with crispness, fruitiness and refinement. The situation of the vineyards also have a decisive influence. They are divided into Grands Crus and Premiers Crus as well as other categories, according to which the grapes are annually priced. Prices usually reach between eighty and one hundred percent of this figure. Most wine growers deliver their harvest to the firms or cooperatives.

Champagne Glossary

Blanc de blanc
Made from the white Chardonnay grape
Blanc de noir
From red grape varieties Pinot noir or Pinot Meunier
Cuvée
A blend of various wines to produce a champagne unvarying in quality, character or flavor
Dégorgement
Removal of the yeast residues
Dosage
The addition of a sugar-wine mixture known as *liqueur d'expédition* which determines the type of champagne:
Brut non dosé, brut nature, ultra brut, brut zéro: not dosed, no addition of sugar.
Brut: less than 1/2 oz (15 g) sugar added
Sec: 1/2 to 1 oz (17–35 g) sugar added
Demi-sec: 1 to 2 oz (33–50 g) sugar added
Doux: more than 1 oz (50 g) sugar added
Méthode champenoise
The process of bottle fermentation
Remuage
The shaking process on specially designed racks during which the yeast collects in the bottle neck
Millésimé
Vintage champagne which has matured for a minimum of three years
Pupitre
Specially designed rack for shaking the bottles
Rosé
Produced from basic wines from red grapes or a mixture of red and white grapes.

The ideal champagne glass made from the finest, clear crystal glass, with a long stem and a slender, elongated bo[...] Its upper rim should be bending inwards slightly in order to fully concentrate the aromas of the champagne.

Well-known brands of champagne

1 **Ayala Brut**
Fine bouquet, good sparkle, harmonious
2 **Taittinger**
Fruity, lingering on the palate
3 **Salon**
1982, full-bodied and of astonishing freshness
4 **Philipponat Royal Reserve**
Tangy, elegant, full of expression
5 **Mercier Brut**
Pleasant and well-balanced
6 **Abel Lepitre**
Fine sparkle and very harmonious
7 **Heidsieck Monopole**
Intense bouquet, well structured
8 **Audoin de Dampierre**
Spicy, mature and full of character
9 **Henriot Souverain Brut**
Very big, dry style
10 **Besserat de Bellefon**
Well balanced and refreshing
11 **De Venoge**
A pleasant aperitif with a distinctive fruity note
12 **Lanson**
Very fruity, with a hint of citrus fruit and a delicate acidity

1   2   3   4   5   6   7   8   9   10   11   12   13   14   15

During the *remuage*, each bottle is given a short, sharp turn every two or three days and is gradually placed in an increasingly steep position with the neck pointing downwards. In this way, all the yeast residue is collected in the neck of the bottle.

The yeast residue is a sign of the traditional method of bottle fermentation known as *méthode champenoise*. Before the final bottling, the residue is removed by means of dégorgement.

After that, the champagne is topped up with *liqueur d'expédition*, a mixture of sugar and wine, and labeled ready for the market.

As soon as harvesting is allowed at the end of September, speed is called for, since the grapes must neither oxidize nor should the red varieties color the must. A so-called *charge* weighs 8,300 lbs (4,000 kg). According to current thinking only 210 pints (100 liters) of must may be pressed from 330 lbs (160 kg) of grapes. After the pressing, the fermentation process begins in a controlled temperature. This produces the foundation wine. Now begins the art of champagne making which was first developed by Dom Pérignon, the famous cellar master of the Abbey of Hautvilliers. Unless a vintage champagne is being made, wines from various grapes, vineyards and years are blended in the vat and bottled. The brand name, its success and the reputation of the champagne house rely on the character and consistent quality of the finished product. Just under an ounce (twenty-four grams) of sugar and yeast are put in each bottle, which is then sealed with a crown cork. In the spring following the harvest, the second fermentation, the bottle fermentation, begins. This is the so-called *méthode champenoise*, which gives the wine its bubbles. Fermentation of the yeast sediment in the bottle takes a year for simple champagnes and three for vintage champagnes. During this time the bottles are stored in the labyrinths of cellars dug in the chalk cliffs of Reims or Epernay. The best will be allowed to age for considerably longer.

After the sediments have been allowed to settle in the bottle neck, they are removed by a process known as *dégorgement*. This involves rapidly freezing the neck of the bottle. The pressure of the bubbles forces out the frozen sediment and at the same time leaves enough room for the *liqueur d'expédition*, a mixture of wine and sugar, the *dosage* of which will determine the sweetness and type of the champagne. If it is a dry wine, it will be *brut non dosé*, *brut nature*, *ultra brut*, etc. The scale ranges from the *brut* with the lowest dosage to the *doux* with the highest. It is important here that the final product is harmoniously balanced. Sweeter champagnes are only to be recommended for desserts. Vintage champagnes, those with a year on the label, are only possible in good or excellent years. There are some wonderfully complex and subtle wines to be found amongst champagnes and they should be treated with the respect which is their due. This means removing the cork carefully by turning the bottle and separating the cork without any noise. It is best served in crystal clear, tulip-shaped glasses which collect and concentrate the aroma of the champagne. They also promote the play of the bubbles to maximum effect.

13 **Pommery**
Winey, fresh and harmonious

14 **Veuve Clicquot Ponsardin**
Aromatic with a fine fruitiness; strong taste to the palate

15 **Laurent Perrier**
Complex, classy and distinctly fruity

16 **Pol Roger**
Distinguished by a beautiful harmony, elegance and rich variety of aromas

17 **Piper Heidsieck**
A classic, well-balanced wine

18 **Jacquart**
Marked by a strong bouquet and lingering aftertaste

19 **Deutz**
Lively and exciting; goes well with seafood

20 **Ruinart**
Light in character, refreshing

21 **Charles Heidsieck**
Fruity flavor and a characteristic buttery note

22 **Perrier-Jouët**
Pleasantly balanced taste and a fine sparkle

23 **Mumm Cordon Rouge**
Very intense nose, refinement and long aftertaste

24 **Bollinger**
Tangy, complex Cuvée with a lingering taste

25 **Gosset**
Fruity and exciting, with a good body

26 **Krug Grande Cuvée**
An excellent wine full of refinement and expression

27 **Louis Roederer**
Excellent, with a fine fruity note, very well balanced and elegant

28 **Moët & Chandon**
Fine and straight, harmonious and consistent

29 **De Castellane**
Flowery bouquet, well balanced

30 **Bricout**
Marked by a pleasant freshness and long aftertaste

16   17   18   19   20   21   22   23   24   25   26   27   28   29   30

Fruit Brandies

The strongholds of the clear fruit brandies are Alsace and Lorraine with cherry being the most popular in the former and mirabelle in the latter. The method of production is the same for both. The cherries or mirabelles are mashed and undergo a slow fermentation lasting a few weeks, before being distilled. Since they age in large glass and wicker demijohns of between ten and one hundred pints (five and fifty liters) in capacity, they remain as clear as water. The French call these bottles *Dame Jeanne*, a corruption of the English word, demijohn. Berries are treated similarly, except that they do not have sufficient sugar to ferment by themselves and are therefore soaked in pure alcohol. In this process, which is known as maceration, the alcohol releases and absorbs the aromatic substances from the fruit. They are distilled again and are used in a fine, but concentrated form, in fruit spirits. Using this technique, all berries can be made to give up their potent tastes. This is demonstrated by specialties such as hawthorn, holly, elder, sloes, or mulberries. Only in the case of Prune, made of plums, and Eau-de-Vie-de-Poire, made of crushed and fermented ripe pears, do we find master distillers in other regions such as Hardouin in Maine-et-Loire, Christian Labeau in Lot-et-Garonne, and, especially, Etienne Brana and his daughter Martine in the Pays basque with their incomparable pear schnapps.

Berries, Wild Berries, and Fruits for Fruit Brandies

The figures in brackets refer to the numbers of the illustrations

Abricot – apricot
Alisier – hawthorn, rowan
Baies de houx – holly berries
Cassis – black currant
Coing – quince
Eglantier – wild rose, dog rose
Fraise – strawberry (3)
Framboise – raspberry
Genevrier – juniper
Gratte-cul – rose hip
Kirsch – cherry
Mirabelle – mirabelle, cherry plum (4)
Mûre – mulberry
Mûre sauvage – blackberry
Muscat – muscat grape (6)
Myrtille – blueberry, bilberry
Nefle – medlar
Pêche blanche – white peach
Poire Williams – William's pear (1, 2)
(Pomme) golden – Golden Delicious
Pomme verte – green apple
Prunelle – sloe
Prune – plum (5)
Quetsch – a variety of damson plum
Reine-claude – Reine-claude (plum variety)
Sorbier des oiseaux (oiseleurs) – rowan tree, mountain ash
Sureau – elder

1

2

3

Glossary of Fruit Brandies – Eaux-de-vie de Fruits

Degré alcoolique – alcohol content
This refers to the degree expressed in percent by volume; for fruit brandies it is usually somewhere between 40 and 50 percent.

Distillation – distillation
Fruit brandies are normally distilled twice: first to produce a raw brandy with a lower alcohol content, and then to produce the refined brandy; this is also known as "distilling by fraction."

Eau-de-vie
Literally, this means "water of life"; a term used to refer to distilled drinks which also include Armagnac and Cognac.

Eau-de-vie de fruit
This term usually refers to spirits distilled from one single type of fruit whose flavor is greatly concentrated by the alcohol. The most popular of these digestifs, usually enjoyed after a meal, are Poire William (William pear), Framboise (raspberry), Kirsch (cherry), Mirabelle (cherry plum) and Quetsch (damson plum).

Elévage en fût – maturation in wooden casks
In the case of fruit brandies this tends to be the exception rather than the rule. However, plum distillations in particular improve if left to mature in wooden casks.

Fermentation – fermentation
Fruit with a sufficiently high natural sugar content is crushed and fermented as mash. Distillation takes place once the alcoholic fermentation is completed.

Macération – maceration
Fruit or berries that do not have a sufficiently high sugar content are first soaked in alcohol and distilled afterwards. This applies particularly to raspberries and other wild fruits.

Vieillissement – aging
The flavor and aroma of fruit brandies are at their most intense the younger they are; they do, however, usually need a few months in the glass demijohn in order to acquire balance. Cherry brandy tends to improve on further aging, but this is not the case for all fruit brandies.

Regions

Alsace
The stronghold of the production of fruit liquor; here many distillers produce the most astonishing specialties, in addition to the well-known classic concoctions.

Lorraine
Famous above all for its excellent Mirabelle.

Loire
The long valley of the Loire is home to a number of distillers who distill good-quality regional fruit such as pears, apples, cherries, and blackcurrants. In the rest of the country, master distillers are only few and far between.

4   5   6

Cider

Apple trees grew in Normandy long before the Normans established themselves here. It is still the case today that the meadows and pastures are dominated by their tall trunks and branches loaded down with apples. The apple tree, of which botanists have identified hundreds of sorts, very much determines the character of the Norman landscape. Four dozen of these have been used for cider and Calvados. Most of them produce only small shriveled fruits, and clearly nature destined them for the manufacture of these alcoholic beverages. Cider is like a liquid jigsaw, each sort of apple being one of the pieces. There are three categories of apple: sweet, bitter, and sour. The proportion worked to is usually two sweet and two bitter apples to one sour apple. The latter lends freshness and bite, the bitter ones provide body and tannins, and the sweet ones contribute mildness and alcoholic strength. Fortunately the good cider farmers appreciate variety. Like wine growers, they will swear by particular slopes. Eric Bordelet, a trained wine grower from the Somme, insists on the superiority of the slate soil of Charchigné on the border between Normandy and Brittany. It is there that he produces a sparkling and highly refined *sidre* made from twenty sorts of fermented apple. The harvest begins in September and extends over three months. In the farms which set great store by quality, they wait patiently for the first frosts which prevent the fermentation starting too early. After washing and sorting the fruit is crushed and placed in layers in the press. The freshly pressed must is left to ferment naturally in barrels and steel vats. Because of the winter cold, it ferments very slowly over two to three months. Whilst the big producers filter and pasteurize it, and possibly add carbon dioxide, the farmers, *fermiers*, bottle the cider unfiltered. Depending on how much of the fermentation is complete, there remains a certain amount of sugar, which breaks down in the bottle into alcohol and carbon dioxide, producing a natural fizziness. When completely fermented *cidre brut*, dry cider, has 4.5 percent by volume. Some cider will mature over a year and have a correspondingly higher level of alcohol. Cider is the base for Calvados. Whilst the large producers are supplied with cider from various regions and even sometimes with young apple brandy, the small-scale and farm distillers rely on cider from apples of their own or the immediate neighborhood.

The crushed apples are put into the press, which is operated by hand and pressed hydraulically.

As soon as sufficient pressure is applied the raw must begins to flow.

Background: Cider production begins after the first frost with the crushing of the fruit.

The cider press is opened and the apple residue removed; the raw must is fed into tanks.

The "Sidre" is now bottled without filtering and without any additives.

Such noble packaging is fully justified: Eric Bordelet's "Sidre" is a natural product.

Apple Desserts

Whilst France is the fourth largest apple producer in the world, it is the leading exporter. The Golden Delicious dominates this market, and accounts for sixty-four percent by quantity and fifty percent in terms of the number of apple trees. Because of its good storage characteristics it is available throughout the year. In second place, a long way behind, is the Granny Smith with eleven percent whose season is from November through April. The traditional variety Reine des Reinettes is also very popular, but its season lasts only from August to the end of October. As regards cooking apples, the russet from the north of France is one of the best.

**Symphonie Autour d'une Pomme –
Symphony on an Apple**

In the old town center of Caen, immediately by the château, Françoise and Michel Bruneau run *La Bourride*, one of the best restaurants in Normandy. Fish and other seafoods, prepared with skill and finesse, of course find their proper place on the menu. However, it is Michel Bruneau's apple desserts that enjoy the most enthusiastic approval. One of the most renowned is his "Symphonie," the recipe for which is to be found on this page.

Aumonières de Pommes
Apple Turnovers

2 apples (Granny Smith)
Butter
Sugar
4 Tbs Crème pâtissière (p. 435), flavored with Calvados
4 crêpes, made according to the traditional recipe (p. 432)
4 green leaves of a leek

Peel and core the apples and cut them into pieces; lightly fry the apple pieces in a little butter and sugar. Allow them to cool before mixing them with the cream. Arrange the apple cream on the crêpes.
Cut the leek leaves lengthwise into narrow strips and glaze them in boiling sugar syrup. Fold up the crêpes above the filling, tie each one with strips of leek and then serve.

Tartelettes Tatin
Apple Tartlets

Short pastry
4 apples (Granny Smith)
1½ Tbs (20 g) butter
½ cup (100 g) sugar

Prepare the short pastry from the flour, cold butter and sugar in a proportion of 3:2:1 and 1 or 2 eggs and a pinch of salt. Wrap the pastry in cling film and put it in the refrigerator for at least 60 minutes.
Peel and core the apples and cut them into pieces; cook them lightly in butter and sugar. Grease the tartlet tins with butter, sprinkle them with sugar and line with the pastry. Bake them in the oven at a temperature of 350 °F (180 °C) for 8–10 minutes. Spoon the stewed apple into the pastry cases and serve.

Gâteau "Grandmère"
Grandmother's Stewed Apple Compote

2 tsp (10 g) powdered gelatin
5 apples (Granny Smith)
1½ Tbs (20 g) butter
½ cup (100 g) sugar
5 eggs
Granulated sugar

Dissolve the gelatin in 3 tablespoons of water. Peel and core the apples and cut them into pieces; stew them in the butter with the sugar.
Take the apples off the heat and mix the gelatin in with the hot apples; then gradually stir in the eggs.
Butter an oven proof pudding or soufflé dish and sprinkle it with sugar. Spoon the stewed apple into the dish and let it set for about 40 minutes in a bain-marie in the oven at about 340 °F (170 °C).
Finally turn it out of its dish, sprinkle with sugar and caramelize under the grill.

Sorbet Pomme Verte
Green Apple Sorbet

2 large apples (Granny Smith)
½ cup (100 g) sugar syrup
Juice of 1 lemon
1 pinch black pepper

Cut the washed apples into pieces and place them in the deep-freeze.
Once they are firm, purée them in a blender together with the sugar syrup, the lemon juice, and the pepper. Store in the deep-freeze.

Sorbet Pomme Rouge
Red Apple Sorbet

Prepare the sorbet as for *sorbet pomme verte* but replace the Granny Smith apples with a red-skinned apple variety, for instance Ida Red or Jubilee.

The *symphonie autour d'une pomme* (symphony on an apple) is served as follows: one *aumonière de pomme*, one *tartelette Tatin* and one *gâteau "Grandmère"* are heated up in the microwave and arranged on a large plate, together with two spoonfuls of stewed apple and one scoop each of Green and of Red Apple Sorbet. Serve hot.

Calvados

Calvados is produced in an area which extends from Cherbourg in the north, almost to Le Mans in the south and across to the Seine estuary. It is also produced in an area around Beauvais. As an appellation Calvados is strictly confined to the area bearing its name. It is mostly distilled using the continual distillation process, the same as for Armagnac. The Calvados of the Pays d'Auge, regarded as a top Cru, has received its own appellation. Also within its kingdom, around Lisieux, some of the most renowned cheeses in France are to be found, such as Pont L'Evêque and Livarot. Its high reputation is related to the fact that it is distilled using the double, fractional method, the same method as is employed for Cognac. The *petites eaux*, the thirty percent rough brandy, are collected after the first distillation. The second follows and allows the removal of all the impurities to obtain its purest form. The water-clear apple brandy flows out of the cooling coil with a percentage by volume of sixty-nine to seventy-two. Its further processing is similar to the other renowned brandies. During its storage in oak casks it absorbs a dose of the aromas and tannins of the wood. It is then transferred to older and older containers as it matures. Each year of careful maturation will make it finer and finer.

It is classified by quality according to the maturation time in the casks:

- Three stars or apples: two years
- VO (Very Old): four years
- VSOP (Very Special Old Pale): five years
- Hors d'Age, Extra or Napoléon: six or more years

Sometimes the cellar master will put cider in a barrel for a year before using it again for maturing Calvados. In this way it will absorb additional fruity aromas. Recently a few of the best producers have been putting some of their noblest apple brandies in old sherry or port barrels, and bottling it as vintage Calvados. Generally, however, it is blended from brandies of various ages and origins, in order to be able to offer the greatest possible harmony and consistency of taste.

Calvados undergoes a maturing process in wooden casks for several years to improve its flavor.

Background: An original traveling still; the art of the master distiller consisted above all in his ability to regulate the fire correctly.

Desserts

Œufs à la Neige
"Snow Eggs"

4 egg whites
1 pinch salt
1 tsp sugar
1¹/₂ pints (750 ml) milk

Crème anglaise – custard

Pulp of ¹/₂ vanilla bean
4 egg yolks
4 oz (100 g) sugar

Beat the egg whites with the salt and the sugar until they form stiff peaks. Put the milk into a wide saucepan and bring it almost to boiling point.
Using two dessert spoons, cut egg-shaped pieces out of the stiff egg whites. Carefully place them onto the hot milk, but ensure that they do not touch each other. Cook each piece for one minute, then turn it over and cook for a further minute. Remove and drain well on kitchenroll.
To prepare the custard, pass the milk through a sieve into a smaller saucepan and heat it up again, adding the vanilla. Stir together the egg yolks and the sugar in a bowl. Stirring continuously, add the hot milk to this mixture – first a spoonful at a time, then gradually in larger quantities. Pour the mixture into the saucepan and, over a low heat, stir continuously until the cream begins to thicken. Do not boil the mixture. As soon as it has thickened pass the cream through a sieve and allow it to cool. Serve the snow-eggs arranged on top of the cream.

Bavarois au Chocolat
Chocolate Blancmange

4 sheets gelatin
4¹/₂ oz (120 g) chocolate
2¹/₂ cups (500 ml) milk
Pulp of ¹/₂ bean vanilla
4 egg yolks
4 oz (100 g) sugar

Soak the gelatin in cold water. Melt the chocolate in a bain marie. Add the vanilla to the milk and bring this to the boil.
In a bowl, mix together the egg yolks and the sugar. Add the hot milk, first a spoonful at a time, then in larger quantities, stirring all the time. Pour the mixture back into the saucepan and, on a low heat, stir continuously until the mixture begins to thicken. Do not boil. Once thickened, remove the cream from the heat and pass it through a sieve.
Squeeze out the gelatin. Stir the gelatin and the melted chocolate into the cream. Pour the cream into a greased blancmange mold and allow it to cool, then chill it further in the refrigerator.
Now turn the blancmange out of its mold. Garnish it to taste with fruit and whipped cream and serve.

Crème Caramel
Caramel Custard
(Illustration opposite)

5 oz (150 g) sugar
4 cups (750 ml) milk
4 oz (100 g) sugar
1 packet vanilla sugar
6 eggs

Heat up 4 tablespoons of sugar with 2 tablespoons of water. Remove the sugar from the heat when it has turned brown. Put the caramel into an oven proof blancmange mold, and shake the mold so that the mixture is well distributed all over the dish. Take great care during this process not to get burned!
Mix the milk with the remaining sugar and the vanilla sugar and bring to the boil. Whisk the eggs in a bowl. Gradually add the hot milk to the eggs, stirring the mixture constantly.
Preheat the oven to 450 °F (225 °C).
Pass the egg cream through a sieve into the blancmange mold. Place the filled mold into the oven in a bain-marie for about 30 minutes until the mixture has set. Allow it to cool completely in the mold before turning the custard out onto a flat plate.

Soufflé au Grand Marnier
Grand Marnier Soufflé

3 Tbs flour
1¹/₂ cups (300 ml) milk
2 oz (50 g) sugar
3 egg yolks, 3 egg whites
2 oz (50 g) butter
3 Tbs Grand Marnier
1 pinch salt
2 Tbs confectioner's sugar

Mix the flour with a little of the cold milk. Bring the remaining milk to the boil and thicken it with the flour. Now remove the milk from the heat. Beat in the egg yolks and just over half (30 g) the butter, then add the Grand Marnier. Beat the egg whites and the salt until stiff and fold into the egg cream.
Preheat the oven to 400 °F (200 °C).
With the remaining butter, grease four small oven proof soufflé dishes and dust them with the confectioner's sugar.
Pour the egg cream into the dishes, smooth the tops and bake in the oven for 25 minutes. Sprinkle with confectioner's sugar and serve at once.

Beignets de Pommes
Apple Doughnuts

5 oz (150 g) flour
2 egg yolks, 2 egg whites
1 Tbs sunflower oil
1 pinch salt
¹/₂ cup (100 ml) milk
4 large tasty apples
3 Tbs Calvados
Oil for deep-frying
Granulated sugar

Sieve the flour into a bowl. Add the egg yolks, salt and sunflower oil and mix everything well with the flour. Gradually stir in the milk. Cover the batter and leave it for 60 minutes.
Peel and core the apples and cut them into narrow rings about ¹/₈ inch (5 mm) thick. Sprinkle with Calvados. Beat the egg whites until stiff and fold them into the batter. Coat each individual apple ring in the batter and fry in the hot oil until golden brown. Allow the doughnuts to drain and sprinkle them with sugar.

Tarte Tatin
Apple Upside-down Tart

1¹/₄ lbs (600 g) slightly sour apples
4 oz (100 g) butter
4 oz (100 g) sugar
1 packet vanilla sugar
7 oz (200 g) short pastry (see Tartelettes Tatin, p. 144)

Peel and core the apples and cut them into slices. Melt half the butter in a high-sided, flat cake tin and sprinkle with half the sugar and the vanilla sugar. Cover the bottom of the tin with evenly arranged apple slices and put the remaining apples on top in layers. Stew for 15 minutes, then remove the tin from the heat.
Preheat the oven to 400 °F (200 °C).
Roll out the short pastry in the shape of a circle, put it on top of the apple and press the pastry firmly onto the sides of the tin. Bake in the oven for 30 minutes. Carefully turn the tart out of its tin. Put little flakes of the remaining butter onto the apples, sprinkle them with the remaining sugar and caramelize under the grill. Tarte Tatin should be served hot.

Clafoutis aux Cérises
Pancake with Cherries

1 lb (500 g) black cherries
5 oz (150 g) flour
2 eggs
1¹/₂ oz (40 g) sugar
1 pinch salt
1³/₄ cups (350 ml) milk
Granulated sugar

Wash the cherries and remove the stalks but not their stones. Whisk together the flour, eggs, sugar, and salt and add enough milk to obtain a smooth and not too runny pancake batter.
Preheat the oven to 350 °F (175 °C).
Grease a round baking dish, distribute the cherries on the bottom of the dish and pour the pancake batter over them. Bake in the oven for about 60 minutes. Allow to cool and carefully turn the pancake out of its dish. Sprinkle with sugar and serve while still warm.

Poires au Vin Rouge
Pears in Red Wine
(Illustration right)

4 ripe but firm pears
4 oz (125 g) sugar
½ bottle strong red wine
1 Tbs lemon juice
1 piece untreated orange peel
Pulp of ½ vanilla bean
1 large pinch cinnamon
2 cloves

Peel the pears, taking care to remove as thin a layer of skin as possible and leaving the stalks in place. Put the sugar and the red wine into a saucepan and heat them up slightly until the sugar has dissolved. Add the lemon juice, orange peel, and spices. Place the pears upright into the red wine syrup, cover the saucepan and cook the pears over a low heat for about 30 minutes. Allow them to cool in the syrup.

Arrange the cold pears in little dishes. Pass the sauce through a sieve and pour it over the pears. Decorate with macaroons according to taste and serve.

Poires au vin rouge – Pears in red wine

Crème caramel – Caramel custard

Crêpes

Crêpes were not always so wafer thin, so glisteningly golden like small suns, or topped with so many different things. In short they were not always as fine and delicate as we know them today. Their primeval form is reminiscent of the gray cliffs of Brittany. Summer wheat would not grow easily on their granite soil. On the other hand buckwheat, or black wheat as it is known to the Bretons, flourished there. Its gray flour was simply kneaded with water and salt to form a dough which was baked on hot stones to make *galettes*. They served as a bread substitute and, together with curdled milk and potatoes, formed the staple diet of the Bretons. During bad times there was nothing else to eat. The tasty galettes have retained their place until the present day as savory crêpes, which are garnished with cheese or ham, fish or meat, vegetables or mushrooms. Alternatively you can simply break an egg which will cook on the hot crêpe dough. Finally when the egg is ready the crêpe is folded over.

The finer crêpes require white wheat flour, eggs, butter, and milk. Often a shot of beer or cider is added to make the dough lighter and looser. They are fried in hot fat in iron frying pans which distribute the heat evenly. It was only in the middle of the last century, when haute cuisine was becoming ever more fashionable in France, that the popularity of crêpes really took off. It was not as a fast food or snack, as one might imagine from the numerous crêperies today, but as a dessert.

It was Crêpes Suzette that became the most famous. Like all crêpes they occur in the plural and are folded twice. The late British King Edward VII, a great admirer of France, rated them most highly. As was fashionable around the turn of the century, he would spend the winter on the Côte d'Azur. One day he invited Suzette, an attractive French lady whom he was courting, to dinner. When the crêpes were being prepared for dessert, the orange liqueur caught fire by mistake. The chef had the clever idea of serving up this mishap as his own new creation. The Prince of Wales was enthusiastic and christened the flambéed crêpe with the name of his lady guest.

1

2

3

4

Basic Recipe for French Pancakes
(Illustrations 1–4)

1 lb (500 g) flour
6 eggs
Peel of 2 untreated lemons
3 Tbs sugar
4 oz (100 g) melted butter
5 cups (1 l) milk
Butter for cooking

Sieve the flour into a bowl and make a hollow in the center. Put the eggs, the lemon peel, sugar and melted butter into the hollow. Gradually mix everything together with the flour to make a runny batter. Allow the batter to stand at room temperature for about 30 minutes. To cook the pancakes, heat up a little butter in a frying pan. For each crêpe, put one ladleful of batter into the frying pan (1). Distribute the batter evenly over the bottom of the frying pan by shaking the pan or by means of a scraper (2). Put a small piece of butter on top of the batter and allow it to melt (3). Fry the pancake until it is a golden yellow color on the bottom interspersed with a few brown patches. Now turn it over and fry the other side. Continue this process until all the batter is used up. Stack the crêpes on a preheated plate. Fold them into crescents or quarters (see illustration on the right-hand side).

The Most Popular Crêpes

Crêpes au sucre
The classic amongst crêpes: sprinkled only with sugar and a little lemon juice

Crêpes aux confitures
Spread with jam and rolled up

Crêpes aux marrons
Spread with sweet chestnut paste and rolled up

Crêpes bretonnes
The batter contains buckwheat flour and rum

Crêpes fourrées
Filled with confectioner's custard and raisins and dried fruit soaked in rum

Crêpes Georgette
A crêpe folded around a slice of pineapple

Crêpes soufflées
A small amount of soufflé – preferably praliné – is wrapped up in the crêpe which is then put in the oven for about 15 minutes

Crêpes Suzette
Derives its flavor from the batter mixture which consists of butter, sugar, mandarin juice, grated lemon peel, and flambéed bitter orange liqueur

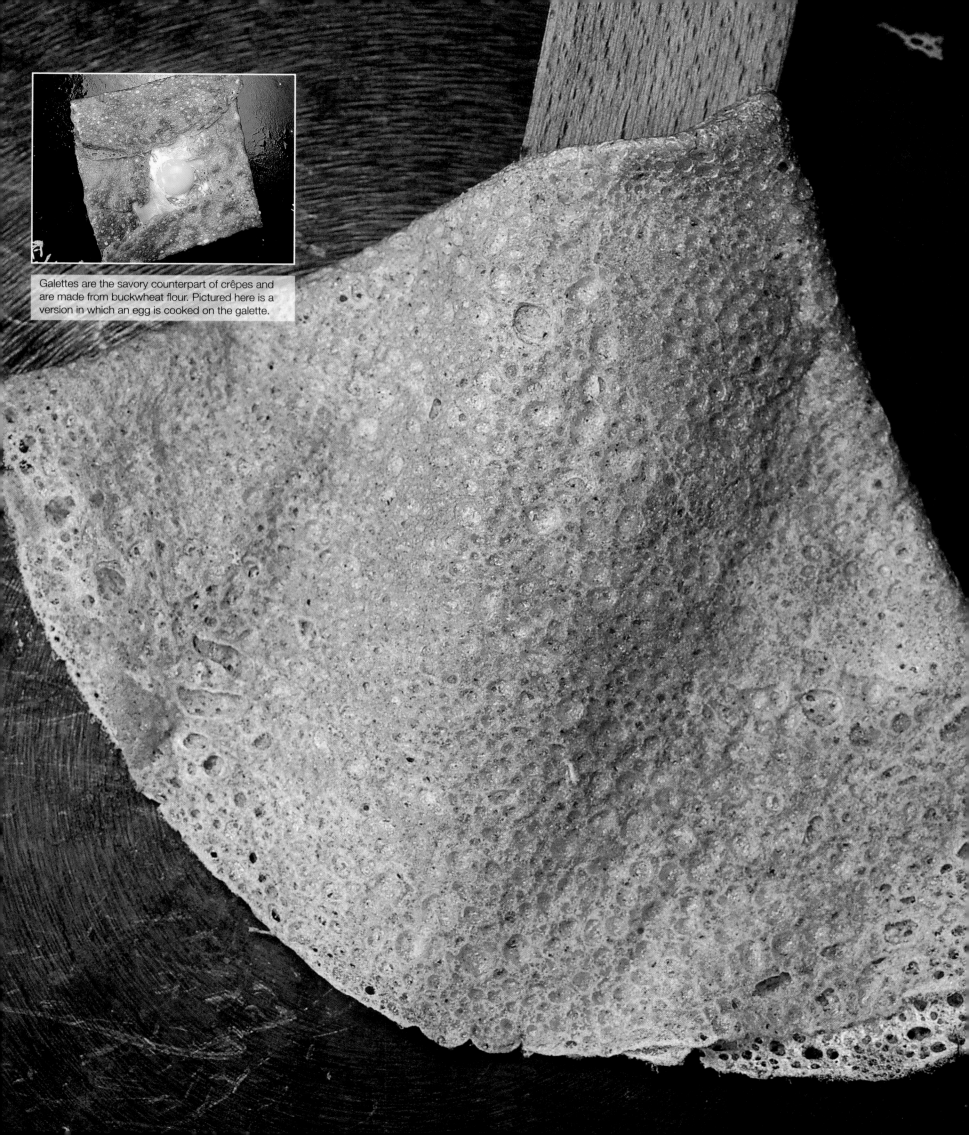

Galettes are the savory counterpart of crêpes and are made from buckwheat flour. Pictured here is a version in which an egg is cooked on the galette.

Patisserie

Patisseries resemble jeweler's shops. Their interiors glisten with gold and glass and their wares are laid out like precious jewels. The clientele carefully choose from the range of *gourmandises*, as if they were purchasing a diamond ring. The reason is that a good meal is not over without a feast for the eyes and the palate, whether it be gâteaux or tarts, cakes or buns, Charlottes, Bavarois or ices, petits fours or chocolates. Patisseries provide the French with their desserts and often a guest will take some such little offering to the host's house when invited for a meal. Great restaurants need excellent patissiers, otherwise they will be ignored by the critics and gourmets.

France would not today be the land of the refined taste, if it had not revered such sweet temptations in its past. In the 13th century wafer bakers received official status and baked waffles on feast days. Nevertheless there was no clear distinction between the various professions which catered for the nourishment and well being of the body. Pastry makers, *pâtéiers*, would mainly make savory baked products and pâtés, but would also supply the very popular doughnuts. The trade which catered for the sweet tooth really took off thanks to Catherine de Medici who married Henri II in 1533. In her retinue, which came to Paris, there were Italian patissiers and chefs who, amongst other things, made ice cream and invented choux pastry. The use of two basic ingredients, sugar and almonds, spread. In 1566 the pâtissier was recognized as a profession in its own right. Nuns in Nancy at the end of the 16th century dreamt up macaroons whilst the painter Claude Lorrain a few decades later pioneered puff pastry. Roasted almonds were credited to the Count of Plessis-Praslin, to which he gave the name pralines. Once it was discovered how to produce valuable sugar from beet, there was nothing to stand in the way of the spread of sweets and cakes. The great chef and reformer Carême defined the principles of the craft in his writings *Le pâtissier royal*. The invention of chocolate, ice cream, and dragée machines as well as refrigerating machines considerably eased the difficulties of pursuing this trade. Brilliant cooks and patissiers dreamed up new dishes – glacéed chestnuts, the Swiss roll, peach melba, to name but a few. Nowadays a master of his trade must be able to make all categories of sweets. After all, the successful conclusion of a meal lies in his hands.

Background: Patisseries present their delicacies in much the same way as valuables are displayed.

The most Important Crèmes used by the Patissiers

The taste of cakes and pastries depends on the kind of cream which fills or covers them.

Basic ingredients
Eggs, milk, butter, sweet cream, crème fraîche, vanilla beans, sugar

Flavoring ingredients
Cocoa, chocolate, coffee powder, almond paste, liqueurs or liquor

Crème anglaise – "English cream"
Made from egg yolk, milk, confectioner's sugar, vanilla. May be flavored with cocoa, chocolate, coffee, almond paste, liqueur or liquor; used for mousses, Bavarois, Parfaits, ice cream desserts

Crème au beurre – butter cream
Made from butter, sugar, water, egg yolk, vanilla. May be flavored with cocoa, chocolate, coffee, almond paste, liqueur or liquor; used in Swiss rolls and Petit fours and for decoration

Crème bavaroise – Bavarian cream
Made from egg yolk, sugar, vanilla, milk, gelatin, and whipped cream. Variations may include vanilla, chocolate, coffee, almonds, fruit, and alcohol

Crème Chantilly – whipped cream with vanilla
Made from crème fraîche, sugar, and vanilla. Used for Choux (cream puffs), Savarins (yeast cakes baked in a ring mold and soaked with rum), Bavarois, ice cream, and bombe glacées,

Crème d'amandes – almond cream
Made from butter, sugar, eggs, ground almonds, flour, rum, and vanilla. Used for Jésuites (puff pastry cakes) and Pithiviers (round puff pastry cakes)

Crème pâtissière – confectioner's custard
Made from eggs, milk, flour, vanilla, sugar. May be flavored with cocoa, chocolate, coffee powder, almond paste, liqueur or liquor; used in Choux and Eclairs, Savarins, Millefeuilles (a puff pastry cake), soufflées. Basis for: Crème Saint-Honoré (with gelatin), Crème frangipane (with ground almonds), Crème mousseline (mixed with butter cream)

Ganaches – Ganache cream
Made from crème fraîche, chocolate or covering chocolate, and sometimes butter or milk. May be flavored with lemon or orange peel, tea, coffee, liqueur, liquor, peppermint; used to cover and decorate cakes and as a filling for chocolates

Petit fours: a delicious, bite-sized pastry creation

Succès au chocolat: a rich morsel made from chocolate and vanilla

Eclairs au chocolat: a treat made from choux pastry with a chocolate cream

Choux à la crème: cream puff filled with confectioner's custard

Chocolate from Lyon

The better the quality of the cocoa, the more delicious and tasty the chocolate. As is the case with coffee, the aromatic potential, however, is only released during roasting.

The covering or basic chocolate has to be stirred for between 24 and 72 hours before it reaches the required smooth consistency and balanced taste.

"What the great lovers of chocolate are searching for is the taste of cocoa" says Maurice Bernachon, grand master of the French *chocolatiers* in Lyon. Being a purist, he makes his own chocolate from the cocoa bean. Only five French confiseries still uphold this traditional art and shape the taste of the chocolate according to their own recipes. Forty years ago there were still 400 in France; around 1900 there were 300 in Lyon alone. However, this type of production is mostly too time-consuming and costly for the small enterprise.

Cocoa trees were first cultivated by the Mayas, and later by the Aztecs, to whom they were sacred and precious. Their beans were not only used for preparing a strengthening drink, but also as a means of payment, a currency. When Columbus landed on the island of Guanaja in 1502, he was the first European to taste cocoa, which the natives gave him as a greeting present. Hernando Cortés brought cocoa to Spain. From the 17th century onwards its popularity spread all over France. Although Rotterdam is the traditional trading place for cocoa and coffee beans, Bordeaux is the traditional stronghold of cocoa experts. Just like wine, cocoa has high and low quality sorts, cultivation areas which are first class and those which are poor. It flourishes everywhere there is a tropical climate, but it is only on good soils such as in its native central and south American lands as well as in the Caribbean and on Madagascar that it attains its very best quality. In ripe pods the beans are enclosed by the plant flesh in which they begin to ferment. Then, before being exported as the raw material for chocolate, they are dried, either in the sun or in holes in the ground. First they are roasted, separated by type, in a process similar to that for coffee. This is done at a temperature of between 350 and 400 °F (180 to 200 °C) for twenty minutes. This process serves to release the taste of the cocoa. The often violet skin can then be separated from the bean. Weighed according to type, they are then mixed in a grinder whose revolving cylinders crush the bean. In order to obtain a paste, cocoa butter is added to the pressed-out fat of the cocoa beans. In the next stage the sugar and vanilla pods are mixed in and crushed. In order to remove any bitterness and acid, and to give the chocolate its smoothness, it is stirred in a mixing machine for between one and three days, for some of the time in a vacuum. The chocolate is then ready and is molded into large bars whose cocoa content is between sixty-three and seventy percent. Only first-class beans will make first class chocolate coatings. They are the pride of every *chocolatier*, as they form the basis of all the subsequent work, whether it be bars of chocolate, pralines, crèmes or cakes. They are also the favorite of true connoisseurs.

Every *chocolatier* gives free play to his creativity. Whether he depends more on classical associations such as cinnamon, tea, and coffee, or composes with ginger, licorice or peppermint, nuts or dried fruit, creams or liqueurs, what is vital is the quality of the ingredients, and his sensitivity in the preparation and mixing of tastes and textures. All this will determine his success with the chocolate enthusiast. As in other areas of cuisine, the French know how to distinguish and exploit subtle tastes. They also know that such artistic and noble miniatures are well worth their high price. They should not be put in the refrigerator as they go white. Instead they should be kept at a temperature of about 68 °F (20 °C) and should not lie around for more than three weeks. But then no lover of chocolate could resist for that long!

The chocolate is used for the molding of all chocolate shapes. Here, nuts are put into a bar of chocolate. Amongst renowned chocolatiers, most carry out the majority of the work by hand.

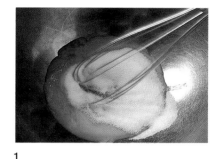
1

2

3

4

5

6

7

8

Mousse au Chocolat
Chocolate Mousse
(from a recipe by Jean-Marie Patroueix)
(Illustrations 1–8)

10 oz (300 g) bitter chocolate	
4 egg yolks	
4$^1/_2$ oz (130 g) sugar	
3 Tbs (50 ml) cream	
1 cup (250 g) egg white	

Melt the chocolate in a bain marie.
Beat the egg yolks with 2 tablespoons of sugar until frothy (1, 2).
Now stir in the cream (3). Mix the chocolate in with the egg yolk and sugar mixture (4).
Beat the egg white and the remaining sugar until stiff (5) and fold it into the chocolate mixture (6, 7). Put the mousse into glasses or small molds and allow to cool.

Nougat

"Tu nous gâte" – "You are spoiling us" – the children shouted as grandmother once again prepared the traditional treat from Montélimar made of honey, sugar, and almonds. This is allegedly how the sweet specialty acquired its name. Language researchers, on the other hand, refer to the Latin name for nut cake, *nux gatum*. The nuts, of course, were replaced by almonds, for without them white nougat would not have its characteristic aroma and taste.

Almond trees were imported from western Asia to the south of France at the end of the 16th century by the widely traveled agronomist Olivier de Serre. Large plantations developed quickly around the small village of Villeneuve-de-Berg in the Ardèche, twenty miles (thirty kilometers) west of Montélimar. It cannot have been long before the first sugar baker mixed almonds with honey, the base, since time immemorial, for so many sweets. In order to promote their product the *confisiers* would make large quantities of it available whenever some important person was traveling through the Rhône valley. The first to be mentioned in this context were the Ducs de Berry and Bordeaux. A certain Monsieur Miche founded the first factory in 1778.

The quality of the nougat depends on the quality of its ingredients. Apart from good almonds, the honey is also important, the finest and most characteristic scent being provided by lavender honey. Production always begins with this product. It is poured into a large cauldron and heated in a bain marie, so that the water content of the honey evaporates. Egg white and sugar are added, the latter having previously been boiled with a little glucose (grape sugar). This prevents crystalization. If its temperature does not exceed 250 °F (120 °C), the nougat will be soft. If, on the other hand, the temperature increases to 300 °F (150 °C), it will be hard. It is, therefore, important to catch the right moment, when the mixture is light and airy. Albert Escobar, renowned for the finest nougat, uses his finger to test the consistency in the mixer. He then reduces the speed and adds ground or half almonds and pistachios or other nuts such as hazelnuts and walnuts, and dried fruits such as oranges or lemons. Once all the ingredients are thoroughly mixed, the viscous mass is spread and rolled out evenly in frames covered with special paper. The nougat is cut into small dominoes, bars or cubes and packed. As nougat with too high a sugar and glucose content is too sweet and lacks taste, it is surprising how successfully Escobar's little masterpieces combine gentle sweetness, delicate consistency, fine almond and pistachio flavors, and an unmistakable hint of lavender.

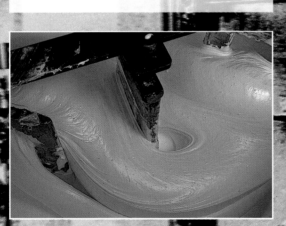
The basic mixture for nougat consists of honey, egg white, and sugar.

The mixer has to keep stirring hard until the mixture becomes light and airy.

Now the speed is reduced and the almonds, pistachios, and dried fruits are added.

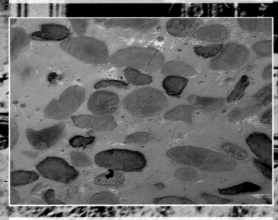
Once all the ingredients are mixed together well, the nougat is poured into frames and smoothed over.

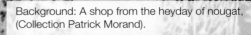
Background: A shop from the heyday of nougat, (Collection Patrick Morand).

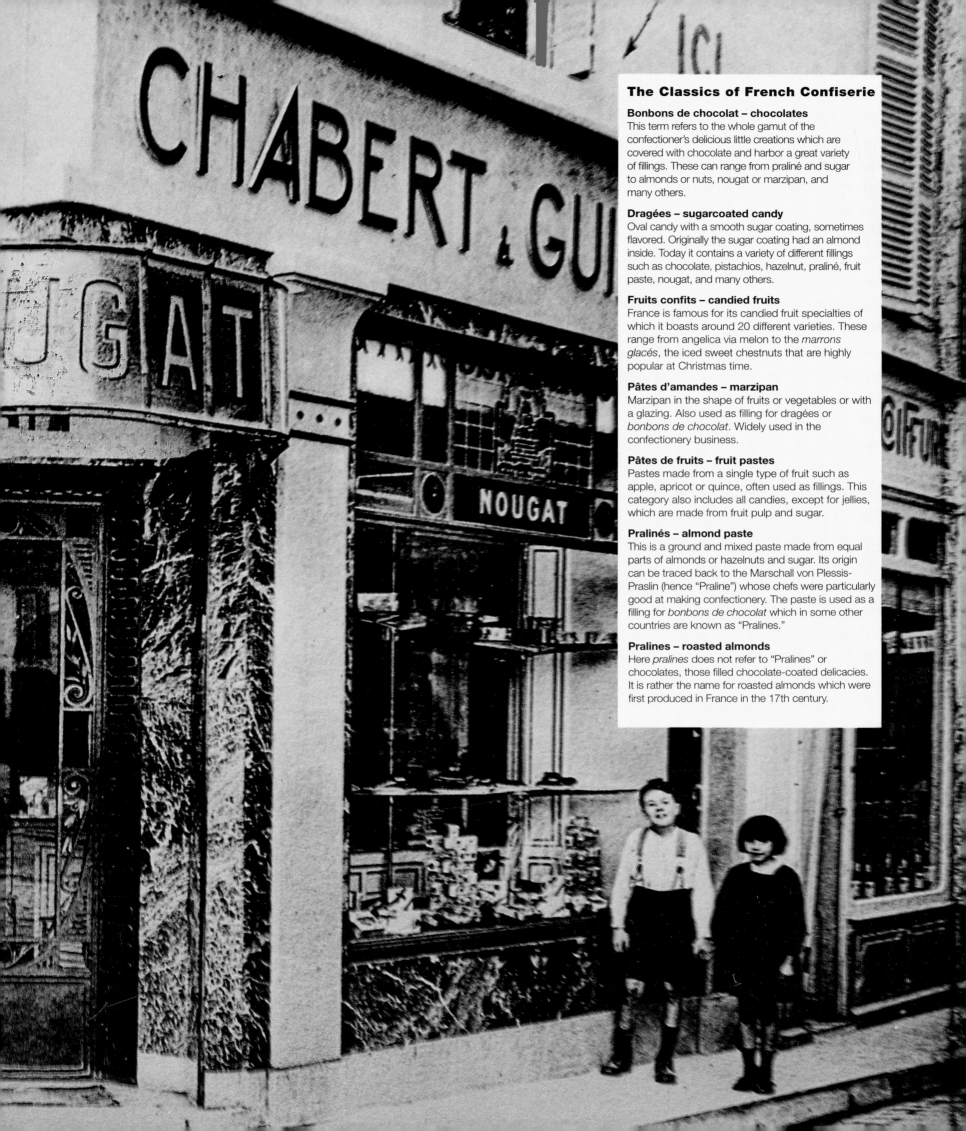

The Classics of French Confiserie

Bonbons de chocolat – chocolates
This term refers to the whole gamut of the confectioner's delicious little creations which are covered with chocolate and harbor a great variety of fillings. These can range from praliné and sugar to almonds or nuts, nougat or marzipan, and many others.

Dragées – sugarcoated candy
Oval candy with a smooth sugar coating, sometimes flavored. Originally the sugar coating had an almond inside. Today it contains a variety of different fillings such as chocolate, pistachios, hazelnut, praliné, fruit paste, nougat, and many others.

Fruits confits – candied fruits
France is famous for its candied fruit specialties of which it boasts around 20 different varieties. These range from angelica via melon to the *marrons glacés*, the iced sweet chestnuts that are highly popular at Christmas time.

Pâtes d'amandes – marzipan
Marzipan in the shape of fruits or vegetables or with a glazing. Also used as filling for dragées or *bonbons de chocolat*. Widely used in the confectionery business.

Pâtes de fruits – fruit pastes
Pastes made from a single type of fruit such as apple, apricot or quince, often used as fillings. This category also includes all candies, except for jellies, which are made from fruit pulp and sugar.

Pralinés – almond paste
This is a ground and mixed paste made from equal parts of almonds or hazelnuts and sugar. Its origin can be traced back to the Marschall von Plessis-Praslin (hence "Praline") whose chefs were particularly good at making confectionery. The paste is used as a filling for *bonbons de chocolat* which in some other countries are known as "Pralines."

Pralines – roasted almonds
Here *pralines* does not refer to "Pralines" or chocolates, those filled chocolate-coated delicacies. It is rather the name for roasted almonds which were first produced in France in the 17th century.

Fede Falces

Spain

What is fascinating about Spanish specialties and Spanish cuisine is their genuineness and rich variety. These are a result of the structure of the country that takes in the major part of the Iberian Peninsula. In the northwestern regions bordering on the Atlantic Ocean, the climate and vegetation are very different from those on the tip of Andalusia, which also borders the Atlantic, at the Strait of Gibraltar and at the Gulf of Cádiz. Different plants grow, different animals can be reared, and even fish and seafood, which in both regions are of first class quality, seem to differ in character – a difference that arises from the distinctive atmosphere in which they are encountered. The same is true for all the seventeen regions of Spain. The differences between Catalonia and Castile, between La Mancha and Navarre are truly extraordinary!

Like other southern people, the Spaniards place no great importance on breakfast, *desayuno*. However, they like going down to their regular bar where they sip hot chocolate and eat freshly baked *churros*, the ubiquitous fancy cakes made from dough squeezed through a piping bag and then deep-fried. People in the country and workmen who start work early attach great importance to the *almuerzo* or *las once*, a hearty second breakfast consisting of bread, eggs, and sausage. Lunch, the main meal of the day, is known as *comida* and starts late by European standards, in most families not until two or three o'clock in the afternoon. The meal is a substantial affair, consisting of three or four courses and, of course, including wine and bread as well. For those who feel like a snack or something sweet in the late afternoon, there is *la merienda*, an opportunity to enjoy cakes, biscuits, sweets, and *café solo* or *con leche*, that is, black coffee or coffee with milk.

La cena, the evening meal, really does not start until ten o'clock at night. If eaten at home, supper tends to be a less substantial meal which can nevertheless consist of soup, fish, vegetables and fruit. But the Spanish often forego supper at home. Instead, they go out to some bar where they have a few drinks and enjoy a few tasty morsels. Known as *tapas*, these irresistible tidbits are splendid representatives of the rich variety Spanish cuisine has to offer.

Left: Grocer in Barcelona with Serrano ham.

Tapas

There are literally hundreds of these small snacks available in Spain. They reflect the Spanish lifestyle with its love of socializing and variety. The time before lunch and before supper are devoted to the daily ritual of the *tapeo* – going out to eat *tapas*. The Spanish tend to eat very late, particularly in the summer, so there is plenty of time – hours, in fact – for the *tapeo*. Depending on the region, it is also known as *tasqueo*, *ir de vinos*, *poteo* or *chiquiteo*.

Rather than settling down in one regular bar, Spaniards move from one bar to the next accompanied by friends or colleagues. They visit *tascas* and *mesones*, pubs and simple restaurants specializing in tapas.

Some are renowned for their vast choice of tapas. Others depend for their fame on a single specialty such as *champiñones a la plancha*, for example, mushrooms fried on an iron hob, *calamares fritos*, deep-fried squid, or *pinchos morunos*, kebabs with marinated and grilled meat. Some specialize in seafood, others in traditional dishes braised for hours on end. However, even the simplest restaurant has at the very least salted almonds, olives, mussels or tinned tuna fish, or *tortilla española*, potato omelet. Occasionally a restaurant's reputation is also based on the quality of the drink served there, either of the Fino, the lightest and driest sherry, the *vino joven*, young wine, or the *sidra*, cider.

All Mediterranean countries have been subject to Moorish influence, which is still reflected in their fondness for a great variety of starters. The customary *tapas* and the *tapeo*, however, are thought to have begun around the mid-19th century in Andalusia. In the hot regions of Spain, barkeepers used to protect their sherry against dust and insects by covering the slender glasses with a piece of bread, cheese, sausage or ham. *Tapa* literally means lid. So customers were able to satisfy their hunger by eating the salty morsels, which in turn made them want to drink more. Soon the *tapas* became an attraction in themselves, with barkeepers starting to compete as to the quality and variety of the tasty tidbits on offer. As the outstanding selections in Seville, Córdoba or Cádiz prove, Andalusia is still regarded as the *tapas* stronghold.

The *tapas* custom has long since spread throughout the whole of Spain. Particularly in cities, eating *tapas* has become a way of life and of socializing. Whether at the start of the lunch-break or right after work, it provides an informal atmosphere in which to meet, to talk, to joke, and to debate or discuss, or to have a drink and to try out whichever little nibbles one fancies. It does not matter whether the *tapa* consists of merely a handful of olives or is a lavish mini-dish in itself: eating is only one aspect of this life-enhancing custom.

Tapas can be divided into two main categories: cold ones, and *tapas* served hot. The cold *tapas* on offer can easily be recognized since they are arranged in rows of bowls and plates behind the counter, together with any nibbles and cold dishes. It is always worthwhile having a good look around the whole bar in order to take note of any ham or sausage that might be hanging from the ceiling, for they, like the cheese, are all part of the scene.

Special hot dishes are either written up and displayed on boards or in menus. Sometimes one has to ask the innkeeper or waiter

who are usually more than happy to tell you what is available, and often recommend a particular dish whether asked or not. Then delicious little meals cooked in tasty sauces are served in small brown earthenware bowls known as *cazuelitas*. Freshly grilled meats such as *pinchos* (kabobs), *costillas* (cutlets), or chops are often served on bread. Another popular specialty is seafood grilled on an iron hob, *a la plancha*.

But no matter where you are in Spain, if you would like to taste some really good *tapas*, your best bet is to go to those bars and restaurants that are frequented by the locals from about 12 o'clock, that is lunch time, and 7 o'clock in the evening.

Firmly established in the lives of Spanish city-dwellers, *tapas* bars add gourmet delights to people's everyday routine.

Anchovies, a smaller variety of sardine, are a classic amongst *tapas* particularly in the north of Spain.

Tapas do not have to be extravagant: a few olives and some slices of *chorizo* are often enough.

Background: A rich selection of dishes on the counter, designed to whet the customers' appetite, is the hallmark of a *tapas* bar.

Albóndigas
Meat balls – a classic amongst *tapas* – with various, sometimes spicy, sauces

Almejas
Clams, often marinated in white wine with garlic and parsley

Atún fresco con judías en escabeche
Fresh tuna fish with beans in marinade

Bacalao
Dried salt cod, either as filling or prepared in various ways; particularly popular *pil pil*, with garlic paste

Berberechos – clams
Fresh clams, with garlic and parsley, in herb, tomato, sherry, or other sauces

Boquerones
Anchovies or smelt; especially nice when deep-fried

Buñuelos
Little parcels of choux pastry filled with vegetables, cheese, sausage or ham and then deep-fried

Calamares rellenos
Stuffed squid; their bag-like bodies are often filled with chopped meat, ham or mushrooms

Champiñones
A la plancha, fried on an iron hob, filled or as a salad

Cigallas
Langoustes, brushed with olive oil and broiled *a la plancha* on the iron hob

Conejo
Rabbit braised in a clay pot or broiled

Croquetas
Made from flour and bread crumbs, with added vegetables, fish, meat, egg or cheese

Anchoas
Pickled anchovies, a specialty of the Costa Brava; also available freshly marinated or deep-fried, with black olives

Aceitunas
Olives, green or black and of various sizes; green olives stuffed with anchovy paste, almonds or peppers; in herb marinade

Dátiles de mar
Sea dates, simply steamed they are a delicacy

Ensalada mixta
A mixed salad with lettuce, tomatoes, olives, tuna fish

Ensalada del salmón marinada
Marinated salmon, deliciously arranged on a variety of lettuce leaves

Esqueixada
Catalonian dried salt cod salad with fresh pepper, tomato, and onion

Jamón
Ham, often eaten raw, also served with vegetables, fish or other meat

Mejillones
Mussels, either prepared in a variety of ways or eaten cold as a preserve

Navajas
Razor shells, popular in canned form or fresh; broiled until they open, then sprinkled with lemon juice

Pa amb tomáquet
A Catalonian specialty: bread toasted with olive oil and garlic and then rubbed with ripe tomatoes

Pescados fritos
Fried fish (right), particularly delicious in the ports of Andalusia and Galicia; just as tasty are the following: deep-fried *chipirones*, baby squid, *rabas*, pieces of

squid, *pulpitos*, baby octopus, *calamares*, fried squid rings (left), as well as shrimps, mussels, and other seafood

Pimientos
Peppers, these are most delicious when simply broiled with garlic or stuffed with dried cod

Tortilla
Omelet, especially *tortilla española* with potato (recipe p. 457)

Atún
Tuna fish, canned a Spanish specialty; used in various salads, also fresh

Gambas
Shrimps seasoned with garlic, brushed with olive oil and broiled *a la plancha*, on the iron hob

445

Sherry

Sherry comes from Andalusia, from the province of Cádiz. The area where the wine for the sherry is grown borders on the Atlantic and extends to about ninety square miles (23,000 hectares). Its center lies between the towns of Jerez de la Frontera (from which the wine takes its name), Puerto de Santa María on the Guadalete, and Sanlúcar de Barrameda on the Guadalquivir estuary. The vineyards stretch across low, gently undulating hills whose lime soil – the famous *albarizas* – strongly reflects the blazing southern sun. More than ninety percent of the vineyards are planted with the Palomino vine, while the other two varieties of the Jerez, the Pedro Ximinez and the Moscatel, are used as sweeteners.

The wine-growing tradition in the region can be traced back to the Phoenicians and was developed further under the Romans and the Visigoths. From the 8th century onwards the area was ruled by the Moors who introduced the secrets of distillation from the Orient. With Alambiques and Alquitaras they distilled "al-Kuhl" which they used for medicinal and cosmetic purposes. Andalusian wine producers later discovered that the wine could be preserved by adding alcohol – and sherry was born.

The fame of sherry spread throughout the Middle Ages. When, in 1587, Sir Francis Drake attacked Cádiz he carried off 300 barrels of wine and took them back to England. They laid the foundation for the great love of the English for *sack*, as it was then called. The drink in question was, presumably, a heavy sweet wine. Later they called it sherry, in line with how they pronounced the name of its home town, Jerez de la Frontera (in France the wine is called Xeres).

Despite its long history, it is only over the past few decades that the actual special feature of sherry, Jerez, or Xeres has really been appreciated and preserved. For its real secret is the flor, a special kind of yeast which in certain conditions forms a cotton wool-like layer on top of the wine and protects it against oxidation.

Flor yeasts are tricky. If they are not provided with the special environment they need, they die. They thrive only on wines that are completely fermented through and through and have been fortified to between fifteen and a maximum of sixteen percent by volume, and in a damp and moderately warm climate. These weaknesses on the part of the yeasts have been given full consideration in the construction of the *bodegas*, the wine cellars. The sherry vats are stored in cellar vaults with high ceilings and a good air supply, providing them with a cool environment during the hot summers and allowing in the Poniente wind which brings humidity from the Atlantic Ocean. The closer the *bodegas* are to the water,

the more consistent is the "flowering" of the yeasts which impart their flavors to the initially neutral wine.

No matter into which type of sherry the wine is later developed by the *bodegas* (also synonymous for wine firm), all new wine pressed from Palomino grapes is thoroughly fermented at the beginning. The young, dry wine is fortified to 15.5 percent by volume and poured into oak barrels. The *capataz*, or master cellarman, leaves the wine for one year, after which every barrel is inspected. He checks the flor, dips his *venenzia* (usually a slim silver cup on a rod – only

Types of Sherry (left to right): Fino, Amontillado, Oloroso, Pedro Ximinez.

Right: Fino Sherry is protected by a thin layer of yeast mold, the flor, and in this way develops its characteristic fresh and fragrant flavor.

Types of Sherry

Almacenista Sherry
Rarities from small, private producers

Amontillado
Well-aged, amber-colored Finos that are developed by oxidation

Cream Sherry
Oloroso which has been enhanced with sweet wine made from Pedro Ximinez or Moscatel; very full-bodied and smooth

Fino
A very dry, pale Sherry matured under the yeast mold (flor). It is best during the first six months after bottling. Serve well chilled as aperitif, and to accompany *tapas* or fish dishes

Manzanilla
The particularly light and pale Fino from Sanlúcar de Barrameda which also boasts a subtle hint of iodine

Manzanilla Pasada
This rarity is an excellent variety of Amontillado from Sanlúcar; multi-layered and elegant

Oloroso
Wines that have undergone a long maturation by oxidation, without yeast mold; they are complex and full-bodied, with flavors of dried fruit and nuts

Palo Cortado
A very rare, dry, extremely delicate, and complex Sherry matured without flor; it is somewhere between Amontillado and Oloroso

Pedro Ximinez
Rarely found as a pure variety, this extremely sweet dessert wine is normally blended with Oloroso.

in Sanlúcar is it made of bamboo) into the wine, tastes it, and decides about the future development of each individual barrel, marking his judgment onto the wood with chalk. The best wine with the best flor is destined to become Fino. In the case of wine with a thinner layer of flor the final decision is deferred. Wine without flor is destined for several years of improvement so it can turn into (fragrant) Oloroso, and is therefore fortified to eighteen percent by volume. This ensures that any yeast is killed. Amontillados are made from aging Finos whose flor dies off after several years. To produce sweet sherry, Amontillado or Oloroso are mixed with special sweet wines.

Sherry producers are never interested in vintage wines. They are always concerned with constant quality and to ensure this they created the unique Solera system. It always involves several rows of 140 gallon (500 liter) oak barrels of different ages. The bottling is done only from the oldest barrel, the solera, which rests on the ground (in Spanish *suelo*). The amount lost through the bottling is replaced by wine from the next-oldest row, or *criadera*. The system means that row after row is refilled in turn, with new wine always being poured in the youngest barrel which is at the top. In this way the older wines pass on their qualities to the younger ones, with the result that the solera never loses its character.

Fino has existed as long as there has been sherry. In the past it used to be left in the barrel until it had turned an amber color and had almost turned into Amontillado. It is only since modern wine techniques have opened up new perspectives that Finos have become younger, fresher, lighter, and have had the chance to make more of their peculiar yeasty character and their taste of fresh almonds. They are the type of sherry most popular in Andalusia and in Madrid.

Brandy de Jerez

Considerable amounts of brandy were produced in Jerez as early as the 16th century. It was essential for the sherry production, but soon a new market opened up for it. Dutch traders eager to do business had invented liqueurs and spirits for which they needed fortified wine. Soon the Jerezanos named it after their main buyers, "Holanda." Luckily for Jerez, the Holanda trade did not run without a hitch. The most famous example is the case of Pedro Domecq Loustau. One day Domecq was left with 500 barrels of young brandy. Everyone in the oldest *bodega* of Jerez was at a loss as to what to do with it, so they simply poured it into barrels that had been used for sherry. It was not until five years later that the cellar master remembered and tasted it and gave some to Pedro Domecq to try. What a transformation! The coarse Holanda had turned into a delicate brandy. Domecq realized its potential and at the beginning of 1874 launched the first brandy under the name of "Fundador."

At first brandy was distilled from sherry grapes. Now the bodegas obtain young fortified wines from grapes predominantly pressed in La Mancha. The best one, which is still known under the name of "Holanda," is made in traditional copper distilling vats, is rich in aromatic flavor and has a strength of only 65 percent. After Cognac and Armagnac, Brandy de Jerez is the third fortified wine which was recognized as guaranteed in 1989 and given the label Denominación especifica (specially nominated). In the case of Cognac and Armagnac, the soil of the vineyards considerably influences their character. Brandy de Jerez, on the other hand, really only begins to develop from the moment fortified wine is filled into barrels in the *bodegas* of the sherry region. Only its special maturing gives it its color, bouquet, and taste. Preference is given to those barrels which were used to mature Oloroso and whose wood is impregnated with the Oloroso's distinctive aromas. After all, the wood of a 140 gallon (500 liter) barrel absorbs 4 gallons (17 liters) of sherry! Brandy has to have between 36 and 45 percent alcohol per volume. The maturation takes place in soleras (casks; pictured on the left).

One of the most renowned Finos undergoes maturation in the famous Bodega La Ina in Jerez de la Frontera.

The ideal sherry glass is a narrow, tall sampling glass. The samples of the *venenzia*, which is silver in Jerez, are taken from the barrels for tasting.

The *capataz*, the cellar master, pours a sherry sample in a great arc from the *venenzia* into the glass.

Iberian Ham

Cerdo ibérico, Iberian pig, is the name of the long-legged creature without which the world would be lacking one of its most sought-after ham specialties: the *jamón ibérico*. These Mediterranean pigs, which have been kept for thousands of years and are similar to their wild cousins, are found in the *dehesa* in the southwest of Spain, from Andalusia via Extremadura right into the two provinces of Castile. *Dehesa* refers to a light, southern woodland consisting of evergreen holm-oaks or cork-oaks which grow quite a distance apart from each other so that there are only about eighteen trees per acre (thirty-five per hectare). The Iberian pig has adapted brilliantly to its natural environment. It can survive for long periods with very little food and water and thus tide itself over the dry summers. But when the acorns fall from the trees in the fall the animal's appetite knows no bounds. Each individual pig then consumes between twelve and twenty pounds (six and ten kilograms) of acorns per day. In addition to that, the animals devour all kinds of weeds and roots which impart extra flavor to their meat. In the past, Iberian pigs were "sacrificed," as is the profound way the Spanish put it, when they had reached the age of two. Today they are slaughtered when they are between fourteen and eighteen months old and weigh between 320 and a maximum of 360 pounds (160 and 180 kilograms). In the summer their food is supplemented with cereals, so that in the fall they enter the *montanera*, their traditional fattening period, weighing about 200 pounds (100 kilograms). The fattening with acorns helps the agile animals to put on a thick layer of fat which penetrates right into the muscle fibers. This later accounts for the fine grain of the meat and its incomparable taste.

Two factors are of the utmost importance in order to achieve this: the animals have to be pure-bred with at least seventy-five percent *cerdo ibérico*, and their fattening process must be supported with no more additional food than a maximum of thirty percent.

Slaughtering takes place in late fall and winter. After the hams are thoroughly bled they spend the first phase of their transformation covered all over with coarse sea salt. For each two pounds (one kg) of weight they are reckoned to be left from about one day in the colder regions to a day and a half in the warmest areas. They are then stored in cold rooms for another four to six weeks before they are hung up in the airy drying halls known as *secaderos*.

The most important centers of Iberian ham production are Valle de los Pedroches, Sierra de Aracena, Dehesa de Extremadura, and Guijuelo in Salamanca. They are all situated in mountainous regions at relatively high altitudes which makes them particularly suitable for curing ham. The warmer it gets the stronger becomes the *sudado*, the sweating process during which the ham gradually secretes moisture and fat and develops its flavor. By the end of the summer each ham has lost about one third of its original weight in this manner. In the early fall when it gets colder, the hams are moved into dark cellars with constant low temperatures of around 50 °F (10 °C) for the final stage in their maturing process, the *curado*. The special fungal process of the *penicillium roquefortis* is now given a minimum of six months to play its part in the completion of the unique, nutty quality of the ham. Then the *calador* reaches for his tool, the *cala*, a punch made from high-grade wood or from cow or hare bone, and pierces each individual ham at roughly the height of the bone joint. The smell guides his decision as to whether the ham is ready for consumption. At that stage at least eighteen, but in most cases twenty or twenty-four months have passed since the moment of the "sacrifice." The outer appearance of a properly matured ham takes the characteristic shape of a "V." The leg itself is covered with pale yellow to bluish-gray patches of mold. The weight is between eleven to sixteen pounds (5.5–8 kg). The labels carry additional names which refer to the fattening feed stuff that has a decisive influence on the ham's quality:
• *bellota* refers to animals that were fattened exclusively with acorns;
• *recebo* indicates pigs whose feed consisted of cereals up to a maximum of thirty percent;
• *pienso* denotes hams from Iberian pigs that were fed only on cereals.

The name *pata negra* is often used in Spain as a synonym for Iberian ham. It is, however, not an official quality label, but refers to the black feet that are a feature of some, but by no means all, Iberian pigs. Of all the pigs slaughtered throughout Spain, a mere five percent are Iberian pigs, and today these are used exclusively for the production of ham and sausages. *Jamón serrano* – the generic term for mountain ham – on the other hand is produced from the ordinary bred pigs which must be at least eight months old. Jamón serrano is also produced along traditional lines and has to be left to dry for a minimum of twelve months. The best serrano hams have matured for eighteen months.

Opposite (from top to bottom): pigs of the *cerdo iberico* type live in light oak forests.
After salting, the hams are dried in airy curing halls.
During the ensuing maturation process in cool cellars, a special mold develops.
Hams hanging from the ceiling of a *bodega*.

How to Slice and Eat *Jamón Ibérico*

In Spain a *jamonera* is used for slicing ham. This is a kind of rack made of wood or metal in which the legs of ham are placed and held in such a way that one of the two flat sides always faces upwards. In addition to that a long knife with a thin, narrow, flexible blade is required. First the rind and the excess fat are removed. Then wafer-thin slices – the *lonjas* – are cut in the direction of the meat fibers, as evenly and thinly as possible. A lot of practice is required to achieve this.

Anyone who cannot cope with a whole ham and who is not very skilful should buy the ham ready-sliced. Beware if you shop in markets: the traders do not always possess the skill or patience necessary for cutting the ham correctly by hand. Once a ham has been cut, it should be used up within two weeks, otherwise it will dry out and its flavor will evaporate. Whole hams should be kept for no longer than three months, since the drying process is continued while the ham is exposed to the air. Naturally, the ham loses not only its juiciness, but the intense flavor is also impaired. *Jamón ibérico* is an unusual, rare, and expensive delicacy. For that reason it should be enjoyed on its own, accompanied by nothing but a little bread, and at a temperature of no lower than 74 °F (23 °C).

The blade of the knife has to be long and flexible so that the ham can be cut into wafer-thin slices.

Sausages

Spanish sausages are of particular quality. As the example of the *jamón ibérico* illustrates, one reason for this is the fact that the meat of the *cerdo ibérico*, the genuine Iberian pig, is used to produce the best quality sausages. After all, the specially matured hams of the front and hind legs account for a mere quarter of the animal's weight. The remaining three-quarters are designated for sausage production in the same regions. It is, however, very well understood by Spanish farmers far beyond the western provinces – from Andalusia to Salamanca – that the pig feed, too, is a major contributory factor to the quality and taste of the pork. The advent of modern breeding methods and animal foods which threatened to undermine traditional animal husbandry in the 1970s did not succeed in eliminating the knowledge that had been accumulated over centuries.

The example of high-quality, expensive, and well sought-after Iberian hams and sausages meant that all regions of Spain experienced a new awareness of fundamental natural quality. This strong connection with tradition is emphasized by the great significance which, in many areas, is still attached to the traditional slaughtering feast, the *matanza*. The Spanish language, too, bears testimony to the fact that the Spanish are very well aware of the difference: a clear distinction is made between sausages that are produced commercially and referred to as *charcutería*, and those which are home produced and known as *chacinería*.

The most popular Spanish sausages are the *chorizos*. There is a great wealth of regional variations and of different qualities. The basic ingredients are usually pork, bacon, paprika, garlic, and oregano. During drying and curing a fermenting process takes place which lends to the sausages their characteristic, slightly sour flavor. Depending on their culinary destination, the *chorizos* are dried for a shorter or a longer period, and are either used soft or left until they harden. They are often served raw and sliced as tapas – but this is by no means the only way to enjoy them. *Chorizo* is an indispensable ingredient in many traditional recipes, especially in stews.

Number two in the Spanish sausage selection are the *morcillas*, the black puddings. They, too, have their firm place in a variety of different dishes, and can be braised, boiled, broiled or fried, and also served raw. The basic mixture often contains a high percentage of rice or onions and is enriched with spices.

A special position is occupied by sausages from Galicia and the northern provinces at the Bay of Biscay – Asturias, Cantabria, and the Basque country. In the humid climes of those regions, smoke-curing is widely practiced. Not only does it have an aseptic effect, but also contributes to the characteristic and delicate flavor of the products thus treated. The Spanish verb for filling sausages is *embuchar*. *Embuchados* or *embutidos* are generic terms for sausages. Often they denote particular specialties, the finest and most popular of which is *lomo embuchado*. This is a whole fillet of pork, that is left in a delicately seasoned marinade in which paprika is a main ingredient. The *lomo* is then stuffed into the natural skins and put into the drying chamber.

Yet another category of sausages is the *salchichones*, which are made from ground meat and can also be fried. Their main producing centers are Salamanca, Boloñas, Lorca, and Vic in the Catalonian hinterland.

Sausage Shapes

Ristras
Small sausages in large loops consisting of natural skins which have been filled and tied off at intervals to form the sausages; they are usually meant for broiling

Sarta
A popular horseshoe shape usually used for sausages, which can either be eaten raw or prepared in various ways

Vela
Dead straight sausages which usually contain largish pieces of meat and fillet; thin slices of *vela* are served raw as a *tapa*

Most Spanish sausages develop their characteristic flavor due to being left to mature in airy drying chambers for several months.

Only specialties produced from first-class pork and bacon are smoke-cured in the traditional manner.

Spain boasts a wealth of sausage specialties. Each region contributes its own variations of *chorizos*, *morcillas*, pepper sausage, and black pudding.

Meat

In Spain, meat is comparatively rare. However lavishly and abundantly vegetables, fruit, and olives may grow, there are only few lush pastures in the northwestern regions. To eat meat, therefore, used to carry at the same time a certain social prestige. Veal and beef in particular used to be regarded as delicacies that were a privilege only of the rich. The magnificent bulls, however, that sacrificed their lives in the bullrings, were not intended for consumption. It is only recently that their meat has gained some recognition in culinary terms.

Lamb and mutton hold a special position in Spain. For these undemanding creatures manage to find sufficient food even in the barren regions that have characterized the interior of Spain. It is, in fact, exactly the flora existing there, with its many aromatic wild-growing herbs, which gives the meat its excellent flavor. But there are additional reasons why Spanish lamb can be an incomparable culinary treat. In Spain, young lambs, known as *lechazos*, are slaughtered earlier than in other countries, namely when they are only three or four weeks old. And in traditional restaurants they are then braised, often in centuries-old clay ovens that are fired with brushwood and wood, at a low temperature until they literally melt in one's mouth. This traditional, mouthwatering cooking method is also used to prepare kid and sucking pig.

With very few exceptions, Iberian pigs are today used only for producing ham and sausages. Apart from that, pig-breeding has largely been brought into line with European methods, and the same goes for poultry-breeding. Spain, however, has remained a hunters' paradise. Wild boar hunting plays an important role, as is the case in all Mediterranean countries. However, the fact that Spain attracts large numbers of hunting tourists must be put down to the presence of the Red-legged Partridge. It occurs in large numbers in New Castile, La Mancha, and Extremadura. Other species of wildfowl, as well as hares and rabbits, today remain as popular as ever.

Meat Glossary

Albóndigas – meatballs
Ajillo – Andalusian stew
Asado – roast
Buey – ox or beef
Cabrito – kid
Caldereta – stew
Callos – tripe
Carne – beef or veal
Cerdo – pork
Chuleta – chop, cutlet
Cochinillo – sucking pig
Conejo – rabbit
Codorniz – quail
Cordero – lamb
Cordero lechal – sucking lamb
Corzo – deer
Estofado – braising steak
Filetes – thinly cut steaks
Gallina – hen, fowl
Hígado – liver
Lacón – knuckle of pork
Lechazo, cordero lechal – sucking lamb
Lengua – tongue
Liebre – hare
Lomo – loin of pork
Magras – roast ham
Molleja – sweetbreads
Oca – goose
Pastenco – Easter lamb, older than eight weeks
Pato – duck
Pavo – turkey
Pelota – meatball
Perdiz – partridge
Pichón – pigeon
Pierna – leg
Pinchito – kabob
Pollo – chicken
Rabo de toro – oxtail
Redondo – rolled roast meat
Riñones – kidneys
Solomillo – fillet
Ternera – veal
Toro – ox
Tronzón – slice, steak

A sucking pig roasted on the spit makes the mouth of any Spaniard water.

Cochinillo Asado
Roasted Sucking Pig

Serves about 12

2¹/₂ cups (500 ml) olive oil	
5 garlic cloves, finely chopped	
Salt, black pepper	
1 sucking pig	

Stuffing

Piglet's liver	
7 oz (200 g) pig's liver	
5 oz (150 g) raw ham	
Salt, black pepper	
1 pinch of nutmeg	
3 onions	
3¹/₂ oz (100 g) black olives, stoned	
3 hard-boiled eggs	

Prepare a sufficiently large charcoal grill.
Mix together the olive oil, garlic, salt, and pepper and brush it over the sucking pig.
For the stuffing, make a hash of the livers and the ham; season with salt, pepper and nutmeg.
Peel and finely chop the onions. Chop the olives and the eggs. Add to the hash and mix everything together well.
Now fill the sucking pig with the stuffing and sew it up with cotton thread. Brush again with the oil mixture and place the piglet on a rotating spit. Broil over charcoal embers for about 3 hours, basting the meat frequently, until the skin is golden brown and crusty.
Serve the sucking pig with white bread and *ensalada mixta* (p. 445). This dish is best accompanied by beer.
Note: Alternatively, the sucking pig can be roasted in the oven at 350 °F (180 °C).

Typical ingredients for a fortifying stew are chickpeas, carrots, potatoes, sausage, bacon, and meat. The broth is usually enriched with noodles or rice.

Soups and Stews

The soups and stews of Spain reflect the variety of the country, of its landscapes and of its people. Until well into the 19th century, the main meal of the day for the majority of the population consisted of a dish which combined all the available ingredients in one saucepan. Then water was added and the food was left to cook over the fire for several hours. The situation was similar in most European countries. These *potajes* or *ollas* constituted comparatively opulent meals. Sometimes, however, the pots were left hanging over the fire for too long, with the result that one had to eat *olla podrida*, spoilt stew, like Cervantes' Don Quixote.

An example of how simple the soups could be is garlic soup, *sopa de ajo*, which today is as popular as ever. All this soup consisted of was bread, olive oil, garlic, salt, and a pinch of paprika. Eggs were beaten into it, if one was lucky enough to possess some, and any piece of bacon or sausage at hand was added and cooked in it too. If the region was rich in vegetables, evidence of this could be found in the soup. If only few varieties were grown in the area concerned, the soup would be a correspondingly frugal one or be based on pulses such as chickpeas, lentils or usually white beans. In coastal areas fish and shellfish would be added to the soup. In areas where pigs were bred and ham and sausages were produced, this would leave its enriching mark on the soup in the form of leftovers or small bits of meat or ham, and also of lard and bacon.

Olla is the original name for the stewing pot in which the food was cooked. The term was then extended to refer to those types of stew where first the broth is eaten with a spoon before consuming the vegetables and/or the meat.

The *cocido*, the Spanish version of *pot-au-feu*, has undergone much the same development. It, too, exists in numerous regional variations, the best-known of which is the *cocido madrileño*. In the past, this used to be a humble stew that the men took along to work so they could heat it up at lunch time and have a source of warmth and of sustenance. Today, it is fashionable to turn this dish into an extremely opulent meal that consists of two and often three courses and has its firm place on the menus of many restaurants in the capital. It always contains several types of meat, but at the very least a piece of beef and a chicken. Added to this are bacon, ham – and a nice bone, if at all possible – and sausages, *chorizo* as well as *morcilla*. Absolutely imperative are chickpeas, potatoes, and cabbage, and nearly always it includes garlic.

As with a traditional *olla*, the meat and the vegetables used to be cooked together in the same pot. Now, however, it is customary to prepare the vegetables separately, with the exception of the chickpeas. The meal starts with the broth which is usually served with noodles. The second course consists of the vegetables, while the highlight of the meal is the meat dish that follows. Here, everything is served in slices or small pieces. Some Madrilenians prefer, however, to have the vegetables as their third course.

Sopa de Ajo
Garlic Soup

9 oz (250 g) stale white bread
1/4 cup (50 ml) olive oil
Juice of 5 garlic cloves
5 cups (1 l) bouillon or water
4 eggs
Salt, black pepper

Dice the white bread and fry it in the oil until golden brown. Add the garlic juice and then add the stock; season with salt and pepper. Cover and simmer for 20 minutes. Preheat the oven to 400 °F (200 °C). Pour the soup into 4 oven-proof soup-bowls and break one egg into each of them. Leave to set in the oven for 15 minutes, then serve.

Fabada Asturiana
Asturian Bean Stew

1 lb (500 g) dried haricot beans
2 onions
6 garlic cloves
3 Tbs olive oil
2 bay leaves
7 oz (200 g) lean bacon
1 ham bone
Salt, black pepper
1 pinch each saffron and hot paprika
7 oz (200 g) each of chorizos and morcillas (p. 170)

Soak the beans overnight in plenty of water. Peel and finely chop the onions and the garlic and fry lightly in the oil. Add the beans and the bay leaves.
Coarsely dice the bacon and put it together with the ham bone into the saucepan. Add salt and pepper. Add 4 1/2 cups (1 1/2 l) of water and bring to the boil. Skim off the surface scum and cook for 60 to 90 minutes, adding more hot water if necessary.
Cut the *chorizos* and *morcillas* into chunks and add them to the beans, together with the saffron; simmer for 60 minutes. Season to taste with paprika, salt and pepper.

Cocido Madrileño
Stew à la Madrilenia

1 1/2 lb (700 g) chickpeas
1 tsp soda
1 ham bone
1 lb (500 g) beef
5 oz (150 g) bacon
1 onion, 1 carrot
8 garlic cloves
1 bay leaf
1 Tbs coarse sea salt, black pepper
3 potatoes
3 1/2 oz (100 g) chorizos (p. 170)

Soak the chickpeas in lukewarm water to which the soda has been added and leave overnight. Pour off the water and drain the chickpeas. Cover them with plenty of cold water and add the ham bone, the beef and the bacon. Peel or wash and prepare the onion and carrot, cut into slices and add to the chickpeas. Add also the garlic, bay-leaf, salt and pepper. Cover and simmer for about 3 hours.
Peel the potatoes and cut into chunks. Cut the chorizos into pieces. Add both potatoes and chorizos to the stew and cook for a further 15 minutes.
Serve the meat and the vegetables in separate bowls.

Egg Dishes

Every good Spanish cookery book has a separate chapter dedicated to egg dishes. Even the *tortillas* alone merit such attention. It is with justification that the *tortilla de patata* has become established under the name *tortilla española* since it must be regarded as a national institution. The translation "potato omelet" conveys an inadequate idea of the tortilla and does not remotely capture any sense of the unique flavor typical of this potato cake which is made from raw potatoes and eggs, and although baked until it has a golden brown crust outside, remains deliciously juicy inside.

Eggs are a highly valued food and are often added in order to enrich a dish. If they cannot be stirred in they are boiled until hard, diced and used as garnish. But eggs also constitute a respectable dish in themselves, particularly in the shape of fried eggs. Spaniards can spend hours discussing the art of frying eggs so that they achieve just the right degree of crispness.

Eggs play an important part in many other dishes where they are combined with vegetables or meat. And without eggs, many Spanish desserts would be inconceivable.

Popular Tortillas

A la payesa
Peasant omelet with a variety of vegetables, green beans, and peas, but often containing also ham, chorizo or morcilla

Al sacre-monte
With offal from lamb or calf; a specialty of the gypsies of Granada

Catalana
Usually with haricot beans and botifarra

De alcachofas
With artichoke hearts and ham

De angulas
With baby eels (elvers), which in Spain are regarded as a delicacy and whose flavor excellently complements that of eggs

De cebolla
Only with onions which give the tortilla a mildly spicy taste

De espárragos trigueros
With thin, wild-growing asparagus which imparts an incomparable flavor to the dish

De espinacas
A version from Catalonia, with spinach and pine nuts

De habas
With thick beans

De hierbas finas
With finely-chopped herbs

De jamón
With Serrano ham

De lechuga
With steamed romaine lettuce

De pimientos verdes
With green peppers cut into strips

De riñones
With slices of calf's kidney and a dash of sherry

De setas
With oyster mushrooms, or preferably even with wild mushrooms

De tomate y atún
With onions, tomato and white tuna fish

De tres pisos
Three different tortillas on top of each other, with mayonnaise

Española
With raw potato and a little onion

Mariscos
A variation with seafood, usually mussels

Murciana
With plenty of vegetables

Valenciana
With rice and ham or Paella leftovers

For a proper *tortilla española* you need potatoes, onions, eggs, pepper, salt, and, of course, olive oil.

Fry the raw potatoes together with the onions in plenty of hot oil over a medium flame until they are soft.

Now beat the eggs until frothy and add the potatoes and onions to the egg.

Put the mixture into the frying pan (which must be cleaned in the meantime) with a little oil and allow it to set.

The tortilla is turned over with the aid of a plate so that both sides can be baked until golden brown.

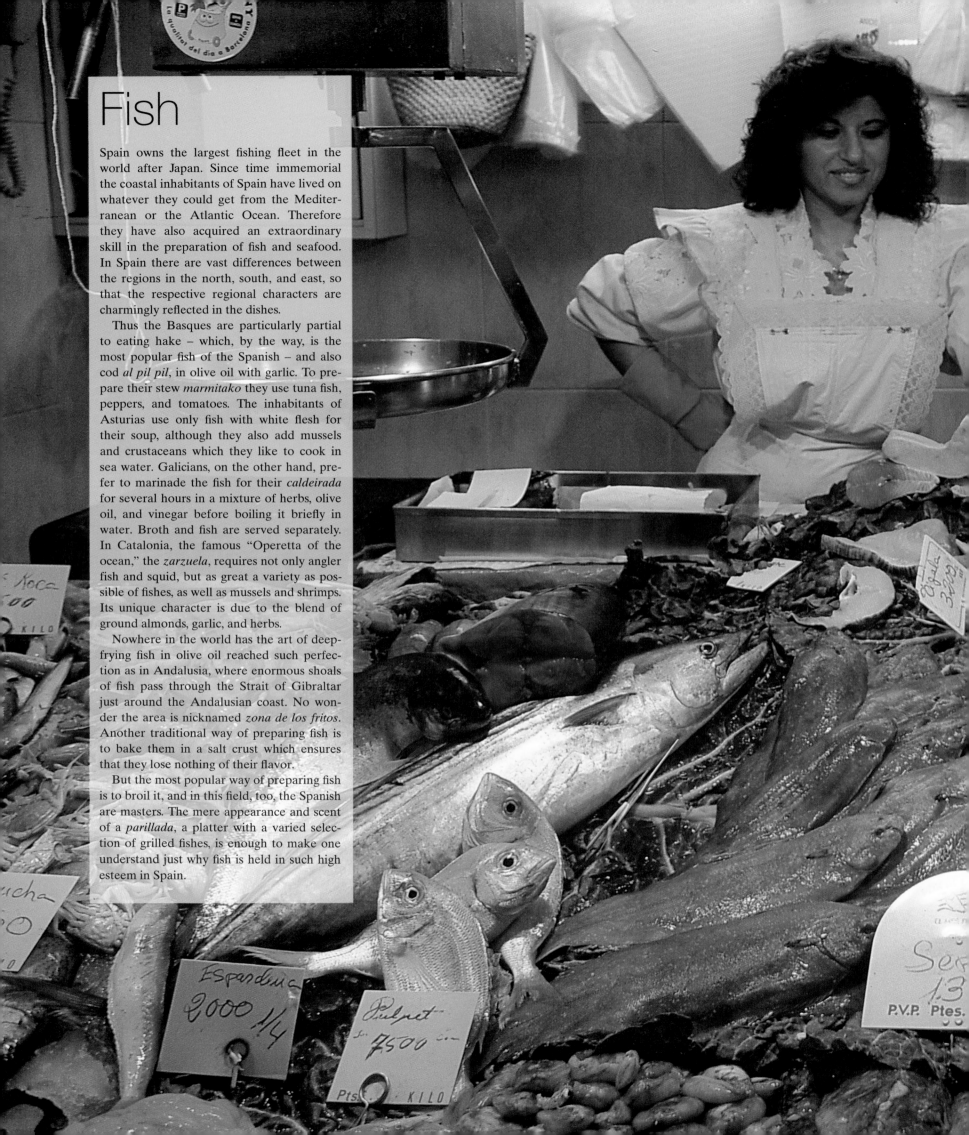

Fish

Spain owns the largest fishing fleet in the world after Japan. Since time immemorial the coastal inhabitants of Spain have lived on whatever they could get from the Mediterranean or the Atlantic Ocean. Therefore they have also acquired an extraordinary skill in the preparation of fish and seafood. In Spain there are vast differences between the regions in the north, south, and east, so that the respective regional characters are charmingly reflected in the dishes.

Thus the Basques are particularly partial to eating hake – which, by the way, is the most popular fish of the Spanish – and also cod *al pil pil*, in olive oil with garlic. To prepare their stew *marmitako* they use tuna fish, peppers, and tomatoes. The inhabitants of Asturias use only fish with white flesh for their soup, although they also add mussels and crustaceans which they like to cook in sea water. Galicians, on the other hand, prefer to marinade the fish for their *caldeirada* for several hours in a mixture of herbs, olive oil, and vinegar before boiling it briefly in water. Broth and fish are served separately. In Catalonia, the famous "Operetta of the ocean," the *zarzuela*, requires not only angler fish and squid, but as great a variety as possible of fishes, as well as mussels and shrimps. Its unique character is due to the blend of ground almonds, garlic, and herbs.

Nowhere in the world has the art of deep-frying fish in olive oil reached such perfection as in Andalusia, where enormous shoals of fish pass through the Strait of Gibraltar just around the Andalusian coast. No wonder the area is nicknamed *zona de los fritos*. Another traditional way of preparing fish is to bake them in a salt crust which ensures that they lose nothing of their flavor.

But the most popular way of preparing fish is to broil it, and in this field, too, the Spanish are masters. The mere appearance and scent of a *parillada*, a platter with a varied selection of grilled fishes, is enough to make one understand just why fish is held in such high esteem in Spain.

Popular Fish

Anchoa, anxoa – anchovies
Anguila – eel
Angula – baby eel, elver
Atún – tuna fish (particularly the red variety)
Atún blanco – small white tuna fish
Atún claro (albacares) – large tuna fish with yellow
    fins, from subtropical waters
Bacalao – cod, dried salt cod
Besugo – sea bream
Bonito – striped tunny (a variety of tuna fish)
Boquerón – fresh anchovies
Caballa, verat (Catalonian) – mackerel
Cóngrio – conger
Dentón – dentex
Dorada – gilt-head, sea bream
Lenguado – sole
Lubina – sea bass
Melva – small tuna fish with pink flesh
Merluza – hake
Mero – grouper
Rape, pixin (Asturian) – angler fish
Raya – ray, skate
Reo – sea trout
Rodaballo – turbot
Salmón – salmon
Salmonete – red mullet
Sardinas – sardines
Sardinillas – small sardines
Trucha – trout

At the heart of the Boqueria, Barcelona's indoor
market, is the large, round stand with fish, mussels,
and crustaceans from the Mediterranean and Atlantic.

Seafood

The Spanish province of Galicia is the leading mussel-breeding area in the world. For half a century, mussels have been cultivated in the wide bays of the *rías bajas* which extend into the interior of the country for dozens of miles. Today there are more than 3,000 so-called *bateas*, a kind of latticed raft, which can each reach a size of up to 500 square yards (500 square meters). The new generation of mussels is sown during the first months of each year. Since they are not yet capable of clinging onto anything, tiny mussels are tied to ropes by means of cotton thread. The mussel breeders attach hundreds of lines to the struts of the rafts before lowering them into the water. It is not long before the mussels have developed their beards and can cling on by their own efforts.

The water of the *rías* provides ideal conditions if they are part of a river estuary. This results in the bay containing a mixture of fresh water and sea water which particularly agrees with (almost) all crustaceans and shellfish. Accordingly, the *mejillones* (mussels) thrive in such conditions, needing, after all, up to thirty-eight pints (eighteen liters) of water per hour to filter through their bodies. After four months they have grown so much that they no longer have enough space on the original line. Now they have to be placed on new lines at a convenient distance from each other. After nine to twelve months they are ready for the market, having reached a size of between $2\frac{1}{2}$ and $4\frac{1}{2}$ inches (seven to eleven centimeters) – considerably bigger than the common mussel. Despite the harsh climatic conditions in which they grow, they are a real southern species: so instead of their northern competitors' pallid complexion, the Galician mussels have beautifully orange flesh. That they also have a more distinctive flavor goes without saying.

The annual mussel harvest averages 220,000 tons (200,000 metric tons). This figure accounts for nearly the total of the Spanish production and for half of the mussel production worldwide. 110,000 tons (100,000 metric tons) reach the market as fresh mussels. The same amount is preserved in cans, thirty percent of which are destined for export.

Other shellfish varieties cultivated in the coastal waters of southern Galicia are oyster, clams, and pilgrim cockles. There used to be a rich supply of the latter in the past, whereas today they are a rare and expensive delicacy. Shellfish cultivation is obviously very important in terms of the national economy. In addition to that, however, fishing along the Galician coast still provides the fishermen with a variety of sea creatures unique in Europe. Only the most experienced connoisseurs know the names of the three dozen or more varieties of seafood – and more than six dozen varieties of fish – that occur in that area. Every single Galician, however, is an expert when it comes to dealing with such a treasure of such rich and varied flavors.

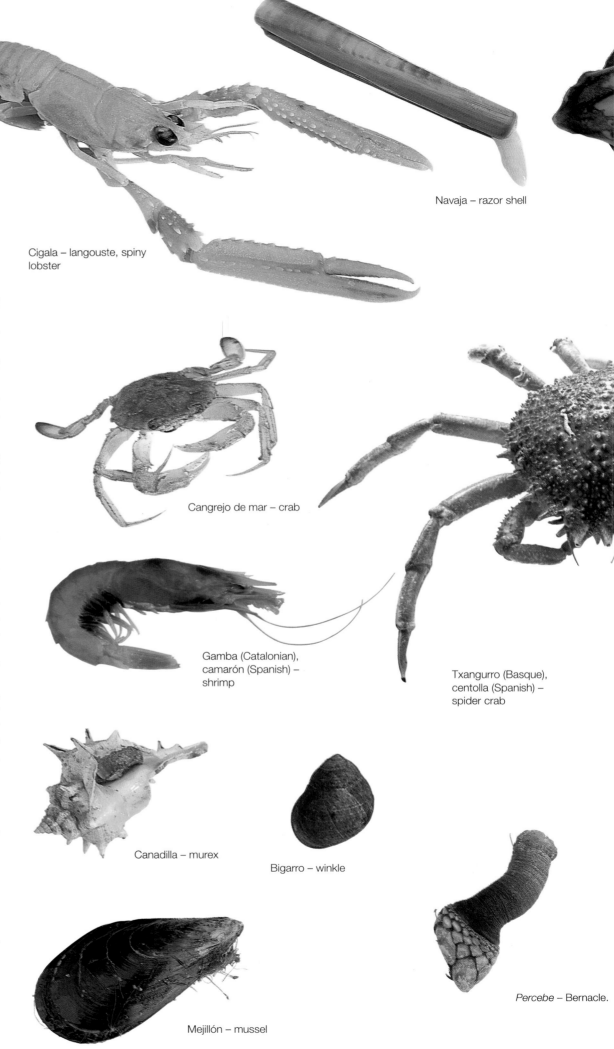

Navaja – razor shell

Cigala – langouste, spiny lobster

Cangrejo de mar – crab

Gamba (Catalonian), camarón (Spanish) – shrimp

Txangurro (Basque), centolla (Spanish) – spider crab

Canadilla – murex

Bigarro – winkle

Percebe – Bernacle.

Mejillón – mussel

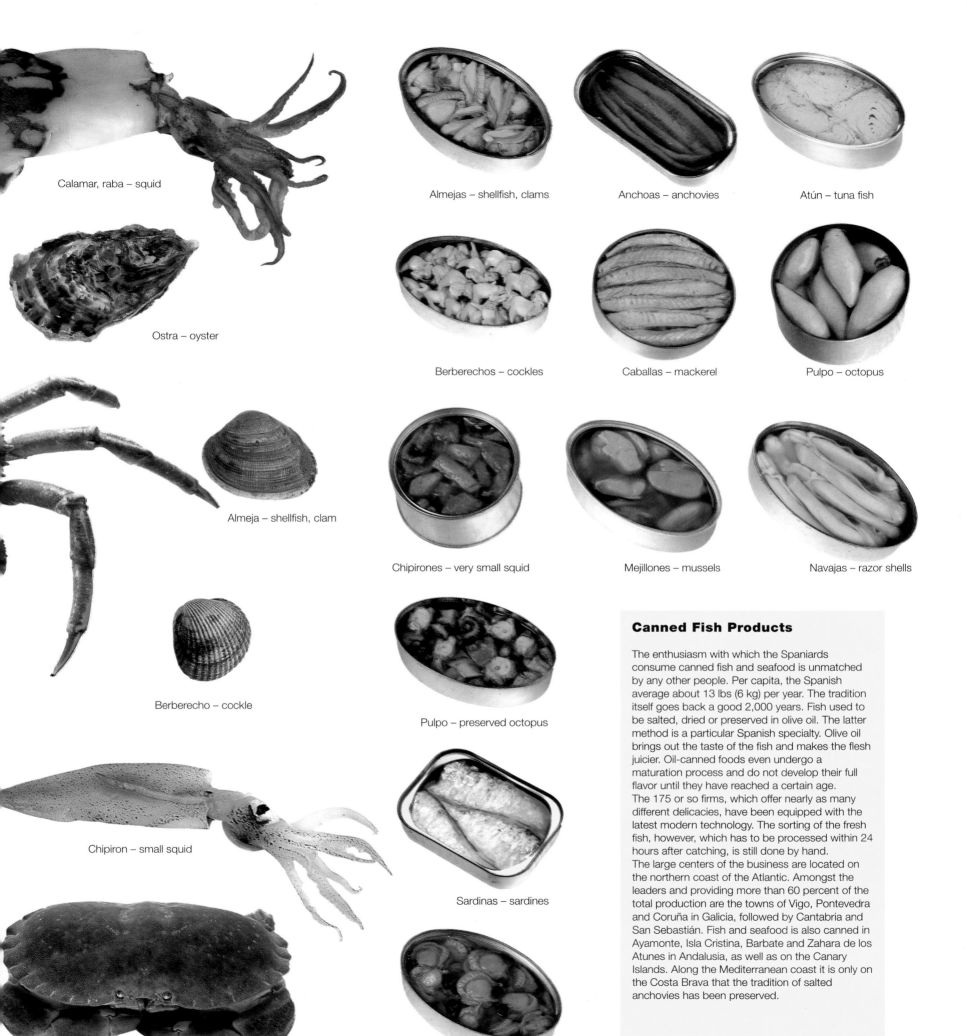

Calamar, raba – squid

Ostra – oyster

Almeja – shellfish, clam

Berberecho – cockle

Chipiron – small squid

Cambaro masero –
edible crab

Almejas – shellfish, clams

Berberechos – cockles

Chipirones – very small squid

Pulpo – preserved octopus

Sardinas – sardines

Zamburiñas – scallops

Anchoas – anchovies

Caballas – mackerel

Mejillones – mussels

Atún – tuna fish

Pulpo – octopus

Navajas – razor shells

Canned Fish Products

The enthusiasm with which the Spaniards consume canned fish and seafood is unmatched by any other people. Per capita, the Spanish average about 13 lbs (6 kg) per year. The tradition itself goes back a good 2,000 years. Fish used to be salted, dried or preserved in olive oil. The latter method is a particular Spanish specialty. Olive oil brings out the taste of the fish and makes the flesh juicier. Oil-canned foods even undergo a maturation process and do not develop their full flavor until they have reached a certain age.

The 175 or so firms, which offer nearly as many different delicacies, have been equipped with the latest modern technology. The sorting of the fresh fish, however, which has to be processed within 24 hours after catching, is still done by hand.

The large centers of the business are located on the northern coast of the Atlantic. Amongst the leaders and providing more than 60 percent of the total production are the towns of Vigo, Pontevedra and Coruña in Galicia, followed by Cantabria and San Sebastián. Fish and seafood is also canned in Ayamonte, Isla Cristina, Barbate and Zahara de los Atunes in Andalusia, as well as on the Canary Islands. Along the Mediterranean coast it is only on the Costa Brava that the tradition of salted anchovies has been preserved.

Fish and Seafood Dishes

Zarzuela
"Operetta of the Ocean"

4 slices of angler fish
4 small squid
8 langoustes (spiny lobsters)
1/2 cup (100 ml) olive oil
3 lbs (1.5 kg) mussels
1 large onion
1 lb (500 g) tomatoes
4 garlic cloves
1 pinch of saffron threads
Salt, black pepper
2 tsp (10 ml) brandy
1 cup (200 ml) dry white wine
1/4 cup (60 g) ground almonds
2 Tbs finely chopped parsley
4 slices of bread

Wash and prepare the fish and langoustes. Put a little oil in a large saucepan, cover and lightly braise the fish and langoustes in it for 10 minutes.
Brush and wash the mussels and remove their beards. Put them into a separate saucepan, add a little water and simmer over a low heat until their shells open. Drain. Remove the mussels from their shells but retain some shells for garnish.
Peel and chop the onion. Put 2 Tbs (20 ml) olive oil in a large frying pan and fry the onion until transparent. Remove the fish and langoustes from the saucepan and, together with the mussels, add to the onion in the frying pan. Skin the tomatoes, remove the seeds, and chop up the flesh. Add to the fish and onion mixture, together with 2 crushed cloves of garlic and the saffron. Season with salt and pepper and add the brandy. Cook at a low heat for 15 minutes. Add the white wine and leave to reduce. Then stir in the almonds.
Rub the remaining garlic cloves into the slices of white bread and toast in the remaining oil until golden brown. Place the bread into preheated soup-plates, and pour the zarzuela over it. Serve garnished with parsley. This flavorsome seafood dish is best enjoyed when accompanied by the sparkly and very dry Blanc Pescador from the Cavas del Ampurdán, the best-known white wine from the Costa Brava.

Truchas a la Navarra
Trout with Ham

4 trout, gutted, with head (8 oz/250 g each)
Salt, black pepper
4 thin slices of Serrano ham
3 Tbs flour
2 1/2 oz (70 g) lean bacon
1/4 cup (50 ml) olive oil
Lemon quarters

Rinse the trout and pat dry. Roll up the slices of ham and put one inside each of the trout. Turn the trout in flour. Dice the bacon and fry in the oil until crisp. Place the trout in the frying pan and fry for 10 minutes on each side over a low heat. Pour some of the frying oil over the fish from time to time during cooking.
Arrange the trout on pre-heated plates, garnish with the lemon quarters and serve.
This dish goes well with a cooled fruity rosé from Navarra.

Dorada a la Sal
Sea Bream in a Salt Crust
(Illustration below)

1 sea bream prepared ready for cooking (about 3 lbs/1.5 kg)
Juice of 1 lemon
3 garlic cloves
1 twig of thyme
4–6 lbs (2–3 kg) coarse sea salt
2 untreated lemons

Romesco sauce

1/4 cup (50 g) almonds
3 garlic cloves
1 tomato
Salt, black pepper
1/4 cup (50 ml) olive oil
1 Tbs (10 ml) wine vinegar

Preheat the oven to 460 °F (250 °C). Rinse the fish and season inside with lemon juice. Cut the garlic cloves in half and place inside the fish together with the thyme. Cover the bottom of a fireproof dish with a layer of salt as thick as a finger. Place the fish on top of this and then add enough salt for the fish to be completely covered.
Bake in the oven for 40 minutes.
Now break open the salt crust and carefully remove the fish from it. Take off its skin and fillet the fish. Place on pre-heated plates and serve with a garnish of lemon quarters.
This dish is often accompanied by a romesco sauce. To prepare the sauce, peel and lightly roast the almonds and crush them in a mortar together with the garlic. Skin the tomato, remove the seeds, and add it to the almonds. Work everything into a smooth paste. Season with salt and pepper and add the olive oil and the vinegar, mixing everything together thoroughly.

Bacalao pil pil
Dried Cod in a Spicy Garlic Sauce

1½ lbs (700 g) dried salt cod
1 whole bulb of garlic
1 dried red pepper pod
¼ cup (50 ml) olive oil
Black pepper

Soak the salt cod in cold water for at least 24 hours, during which time the water has to be changed several times. Then cut the fish into small pieces, rinse well, and drain.

Peel the garlic cloves and chop them finely. Break up the pepper pod into several pieces. Lightly fry the garlic and pepper in the oil, then remove the pieces of pepper. Now add the pieces of fish to the garlic in the pan. Place them skin-side down and cook them for 20 minutes over a low heat, stirring continuously. (The stirring causes the olive oil, the gelatin in the fish skin, and the garlic to combine into a sauce which reaches the consistency of a mayonnaise.) Add pepper to taste. Serve with boiled potatoes.

A suitable drink to accompany this dish is Txakoli, a fresh, tingling white wine from the Basque country.

Marmitako
Tuna Fish Ragout

1 onion
3 garlic cloves
1 green and 1 red pepper
2 Tbs (30 ml) olive oil
14 oz (400 g) tomatoes
Salt, black pepper
1 pinch of hot paprika
6 potatoes
1 cup (200 ml) dry white wine
1¾ lbs (800 g) fresh tuna fish
Juice of 1 lemon

Peel and finely chop the onion and garlic. Wash the peppers, remove the seeds and cut the peppers into strips. Heat the oil in a stewing pot and lightly fry the vegetables in it for 5 minutes. Skin the tomatoes, remove the seeds, cut the flesh into small pieces, and add it to the peppers. Season with salt, pepper, and paprika. Cover and simmer on a low heat for 15 minutes.

Peel the potatoes, cut into chunks and add to the vegetables. Add the white wine. Cover and leave everything to cook for a further 30 minutes.

Clean the tuna fish and rinse it under cold water. Cut it into small cubes, sprinkle with lemon juice and season with salt and pepper. Add the fish to the vegetables and cook for 5 to 10 minutes until done. Season to taste. Serve with a rosé from Navarra.

Almejas a la Marinera
Clams Mariner Style

1 onion
2 garlic cloves
2 Tbs olive oil
1 lb (500 g) tomatoes
1 cup (200 ml) dry white wine
1 bay leaf
Salt, black pepper
1¾ pounds (800 g) clams (shellfish)
2 Tbs finely chopped parsley

Peel and finely chop the onion and garlic and fry lightly in the oil. Skin the tomatoes, remove the seeds, and cut the flesh into pieces. Add to the onion and garlic, together with the white wine, the bay leaf, the salt and the pepper. Cover and simmer for 10 minutes.

Wash and brush the clams thoroughly. Add them to the onion and tomato mixture and cook for 10 minutes over a low heat, until all the clams have opened. Discard any unopened ones. Serve sprinkled with parsley.

Langostinos al Ajillo
Langoustes in Garlic Oil

2 lbs (1 kg) fresh langoustes (spiny lobsters)
¾ cup (150 ml) olive oil
Salt, black pepper
5 garlic cloves
2 Tbs finely chopped parsley

Preheat the oven to 400 °F (200 °C). Brown the langoustes in the hot oil over a high heat. Season with salt and pepper. Set aside and keep warm in an oven-proof dish.

Finely chop the garlic and braise lightly in the oil in which the langoustes were fried for five minutes, stirring the mixture continuously.

Pour the garlic oil over the langoustes and bake them in the oven for 10 minutes. Sprinkle with parsley and serve immediately.

Serve with Cava or Manzanilla.

Dorada a la sal – sea bream in a salt crust

Arroz negro –
black rice

Rice

Spain has to thank the Moors for the introduction of rice in the 8th century. Since rice was already an important ingredient on the Moorish menu, they grew it where natural conditions were most suitable for its cultivation. Since then, the conditions have remained unchanged. Rice cultivation is therefore still practiced in the same places as before, and in some cases even irrigation channels and devices for regulating distribution which were installed by the Moors more than 1,200 years ago have been preserved.

In the 13th century, however, with the Reconquista (reconquest), the catholic rulers drove out the Moors and with them the specialists in irrigation cultivation. Rice-growing was beset by yet another problem which even led to its prohibition: malaria. The swamps of Catalonia and the lagoon of Albúfera south of Valencia provided favorable conditions not only for growing rice but also for encouraging mosquitoes. For centuries people believed that the rice plants were responsible for causing the fever, and the ban was not lifted until 1860.

Rice cultivation had, nonetheless, started spreading well before that date, in particular around Valencia. Now people even began to drain the delta area of the River Ebro so that rice could be grown there, too. Working conditions were extremely harsh, with the incidence of malaria being a daily occurrence. "*Terra de arroz,*

terra de plos," as the locals used to say – country of rice, country of tears.

The region that developed into the most important rice-growing area of Spain was the Spanish Levant with its four provinces of Murcia, Alicante, Valencia, and Castellón de la Plana. Calasparra on the upper reaches of the River Segula in the hilly region northwest of Murcia is regarded as the Eldorado of rice, outshining even Albúfera and the Ebro delta. The traditional method of mixed cultivation at Calasparra makes for well-balanced, healthy soil, and the regulated water supply makes conditions ideal. Although the yield is decidedly lower, the rice produced here – some of it grown along organic lines – is of high quality and includes old varieties which have become rare, such as Bomba. Large centers

of rice cultivation have been established in Andalusia and Extremadura over the past thirty years which specialize in growing long-grain rice for export.

The main thing Spaniards expect from the rice they use is that it is absorbent, for it is supposed to absorb the flavors of the other ingredients. Far from being a side-dish, rice constitutes the most important part of the dish – be it prepared with fish, meat or vegetables, or as a sweet dessert.

Originally, short-grain rice used to be perfectly adequate and, moreover, corresponded to Spain's culinary tradition. In the end, however, it proved too susceptible, and the farmers began to plant new varieties. These combine a medium grain with the special qualities that are needed for Spanish cooking.

Caldero murciano –
Rice stew with fish,
Murcia style

Arroz con costra – rice
with a crust

Arroz Negro
Black Rice
(Illustration opposite)

3 Tbs olive oil
4 garlic cloves
1 tomato
1 Tbs chopped parsley
1 large octopus inclusive of its ink sac
Salt, black pepper
1 pinch of cinnamon
1¹/₂ cups (250 g) short-grain rice

Heat the oil in a large frying pan. Finely chop the garlic and add to the oil. Then skin the tomato, remove the seeds and chop up the flesh. Add to the oil and garlic. Sprinkle with parsley.
Clean the octopus (take off the tentacles, remove eyes, hard mouth parts, and entrails); put the ink sac to one side. Wash the octopus and cut it into pieces. Add to the tomatoes and season lightly with salt, pepper, and cinnamon. Cover and simmer over a low heat for 30 minutes.
Add the rice, mix in well and cook briefly in the sauce. Add 2 cups (500 ml) of hot water and cook everything at a high temperature. Holding it over a cup, cut open the ink sac. Collect the ink and mix it with ¹/₂ cup (100 ml) of the cooking stock. Add to the rice and mix well, adding some more hot water if necessary. Cover and cook over a low heat for 20 minutes, until the rice has absorbed all the liquid and has turned black. (In the winter the rice turns more of a grayish color since the octopus has less ink in that season.)

Caldero Murciano
Rice Stew with Fish, Murcia Style
(Illustration center)

4 lbs (2 kg) fresh Mediterranean fish
(red mullet, sea bream, scorpion fish)
1 whole bulb of garlic
2 Nora pods (p. 189) or deseeded chilies
1 lb (500 g) tomatoes
1 onion
1 carrot
Salt, black pepper
1 pinch of saffron threads
2 cups (350 g) short-grain rice

Clean and prepare the fish and put to one side, retaining the leftovers. In a mortar, crush the garlic and Nora pods, add a little water and mix to a paste. Put into a *caldero*, a large, cast iron stew pot, and add 4 pints (2 l) of water. Skin the tomatoes, remove the seeds and cut the flesh into pieces; peel and quarter the onion; clean and slice the carrot. Put the vegetables and the fish leftovers into the pot and season with salt and pepper. Bring to the boil and simmer for about 60 minutes.
Pass the fish stock through a sieve. Rinse the pot, then pour half of the fish stock back into it. Add the saffron. Bring the fish stock to the boil and cook the rice in it for just under 20 minutes to ensure that it stays very juicy. Serve the rice first.
Poach the fish in the remaining fish stock. Arrange on a plate and serve as a second course with garlic sauce (see *Bacalao pil pil*, p. 463).

Arroz con Costra
Rice with an Egg Crust
(Illustration above)

1 rabbit, hen or cockerel (3 lbs/1.5 kg) with insides
8 oz (200 g) Butifarra negra (p. 170)
1 lb (500 g) tomatoes
³/₄ cup (150 ml) dry white wine
1 pinch of saffron threads
Salt, black pepper
1¹/₂ cups (250 g) short-grain rice
11 eggs

Take the meat off the bones and cut into smallish pieces. Put the oil in a fireproof pan and brown the meat in it. Skin and de-seed the tomatoes and cut into small pieces. Add to the meat together with the insides and the Butifarra negra. Add the chicken stock, the white wine, and the saffron. Season with salt and pepper and stew everything for 60 minutes. Add 2 cups (500 ml) of hot water, season once more with salt to taste, and bring to the boil. Then stir in the rice and let it simmer for 20–25 minutes, stirring occasionally, until it has absorbed all the liquid and become soft.
Preheat the oven to 350 °F (180 °C).
Break the eggs into a bowl. Season with salt and pepper, whisk well and pour over the rice. Cover the dish with aluminum foil and bake in the oven for a good 10 minutes. Then remove the foil and serve the food in its dish. Do not break open the eggy crust until the dish is being served at the table.
A lightly chilled red wine from the Mancha or from Valdepeñas goes well with this dish.

465

Different Qualities of Olive Oil

Aceite de oliva virgen extra
Top-quality cold-pressed oil, with perfect flavor

Aceite de oliva virgen
High-quality cold-pressed oil, very good flavor

Aceite de oliva
Normal, medium-grade cooking oil produced from
a blend of refined and cold-pressed oils

The producers divide the oils into six categories
according to a different system:
1. Virgin – cold-pressed olive oil available in four
   different grades (first to fourth pressing)
2. Refined olive oil – refined virgin oil
3. Olive oil – a blend of refined and virgin oils
4. Raw crushed olive skin oil – extracted from
   pressed skins with the aid of solvents
5. Refined crushed olive skin oil
6. Olive skin oil – a blend of refined olive skin oil,
   virgin, and other olive oils

Olive Oil

Ever since Roman times olive oil has been one of the most important products and export goods of Spain. As far back as the first century, the Iberian Peninsula was the main supplier to the Roman Empire. Olive oil was sent to the remotest corners of the empire in amphorae (jars) sealed with seals of origin. Today Spain – probably the largest producer of olive oil in the world – has more than 190 million olive trees.

In the past, the best olives used to be bought up by Italian oil producers who sold the oil under their own labels. Recently, however, the self-confidence of the Spanish producers has experienced a considerable boost. Today there exists a number of estates, private enterprises and cooperatives that have established reputations for themselves with their own bottled oils on both the national and international markets. What is remarkable about this is that several of them have specialized in organically grown produce.

Take the province of Jaén as an example, where nine tenths of all arable land – nearly 1.1 million acres (435,000 hectares) – is planted with olive trees, arguably the largest continuous olive growing area in the world. New plantations are planted with single-stemmed tree cuttings, about sixty per acre (150 per hectare). In older plantations veterans with three or four trunks that are often centuries old, around eight-five trees stand on the same area.

It is true that around sixty different olive varieties exist in Spain, although Picudo and Picual are the ones that have established themselves as the main varieties used for oil production. Of the two, Picual has been preferred in Jaén which is situated some forty miles (seventy kilometers) north of Granada. It is an extremely dry area with temperatures soaring to undreamed-of heights in the summer. Of course, it is perfectly possible for olive trees to thrive in such conditions. But in order to produce a good yield they require a lot of water during their main growing season of two months. Today growers attempt to supply the water via irrigation systems, although it is worth remembering that prime quality olives often come from steep locations where the trees are left to themselves.

Growing olive trees is similar to growing vines. Like vines, they have to be carefully pruned since their fruit forms mainly on the young wood. As with wine, restricting the yield ensures better concentration and better quality as well as longer living, healthier plants.

Harvesting lasts for over three months, from November until well into February. Quality-conscious producers avoid using machines for harvesting since they damage the trees. Instead,

Left page: When the olive oil comes out of the press it is still mixed with the fruit juice and is, therefore, cloudy.

With few exceptions, the practice of knocking ripe olives off the trees with poles is still employed today.

Nets spread out under the trees make gathering in the harvest easier.

Olives ripen between the end of November and the middle of February, a process during which their color becomes increasingly intensified.

The olives are pressed between disks made of plastic or coconut fiber, the *capachos*.

the olives are knocked gently off the trees by means of poles called *gaules*, picked up by hand and gathered in small baskets.

To begin with, the freshly harvested olives are washed. Then they are sorted and their leaves and stalks removed before the olives are pressed in order to make them burst open. All the flavor is fully retained if large, old, stone millstones are used which hardly warm up at all. In traditional presses the olives are distributed onto *capachos* (disks) made of coconut fibers, and then pressed by means of hydraulic pressure. Modern machines can process up to one hundred tons (one hundred metric tons) per day. To ensure prime quality oil, the temperature must not exceed 86 °F (30 °C). About ten pounds (five kilograms) of olives are required to produce two pounds (one kilogram) of oil.

The next step is to clarify the reddish-looking oil in order to separate it from the plant sap, the *alpechín*. The most natural form of clarification is based on the principle of overflow basins in which the lighter olive oil slowly rises to the surface. There is, however, a danger that the sap might begin to ferment and then pass its bad flavor on to the oil. Therefore, rapid rotating machines are used today. The oil is stored traditionally in large clay vessels, the so-called *trujales*. Before bottling the olive oil is also filtered.

Olive oils from Catalonia have a smoother taste, a more refined character, and tend to be distinguished by a subtle aroma of almonds or nuts. The oils from Andalusia, on the other hand, are usually distinguished by a more pronounced olive taste illustrated by their fruitiness. In Spanish cooking olive oil is used not only for salads and as cooking fat, it also features in many sauces and mayonnaises. Above all it is a favorite for deep-frying fish or vegetables and even some sweet delicacies. It is also used as a natural preservative for sausage and cheese, fish, and meat.

Olive oil oxidizes easily, which results in the loss of its delicate flavors. It should, therefore, be stored in tinted glass bottles or in tin cans to protect it from light and air, and should be kept cool, but not in the refrigerator.

Alioli
Garlic and Olive Oil Paste

1 bulb of fresh garlic
1³/₄ cups (350 ml) of olive oil
¹/₂ tsp salt
1 tsp lemon juice

Peel the garlic cloves and mash them to a pulp in a mortar. Add the olive oil, at first drop by drop, then in a thin trickle, stirring all the time. Stir in the salt and lemon juice.
Note: This is the original, traditional version of Alioli. It is spicy and aromatic and is a suitable seasoning for broiled fish and for seafood, as well as for snails and grilled or cold meat. Nowadays the paste usually consists of a mayonnaise on a egg yolk base, with the egg yolks being mixed with crushed garlic before the olive oil is added.

Vegetables

That Spain is a vegetable paradise is a fact already acknowledged by the Romans. They irrigated large stretches of land in Murcia and Valencia and established vegetable gardens, *huertas*. Fruit and vegetables were also appreciated by the Moors who cultivated them in the Spanish Levant and in Andalusia using progressive gardening and irrigation techniques.

Today the most significant vegetable-growing regions still stretch all along the Mediterranean coast from Gerona to Malaga. The most extensive and most varied areas of cultivation can be found here in the provinces of Valencia, Murcia, Almería, and Málaga.

At about two million tons (2.5 million metric tons), tomatoes are the most frequently grown vegetable, followed by onions at one million tons (about 1.2 million metric tons) and potatoes at 800,000 tons (about 850,000 metric tons). Other important vegetables grown include peppers and lettuces, cucumbers, artichokes, green beans, garlic, white cabbage and cauliflower, carrots, broad beans, zucchini, and eggplants. As far as quantity is concerned, asparagus is of little consequence with a mere 100,000 tonnes or so produced. It has, however, a relatively large profit margin. Other important produce grown in Spain are endives, leeks, peas, celery, gherkins, broccoli, Brussels sprouts, fennel, and chicory. The Spanish prefer a salad or vegetables as the first course of a meal. Particularly popular for this purpose is the romaine or cos lettuce with its elongated leaves and slightly sweetish taste. The Spanish also prefer firm tomatoes that are still slightly unripe, and scallions in their salads. Salad is never served with a ready-made dressing. Instead, everybody helps themselves according to their taste, adding first a dash of wine vinegar to the salad, then salt, and some olive oil at the end.

Peppers occupy a special place amongst Spain's vegetable specialties. There are very different varieties, some of which are completely unknown abroad, such as the *pimientos del piquillo de Lodosa* – the only peppers that can boast a registered label of origin. The *piquillos* are of triangular shape tapering to a point, are always harvested when they are red, and must be no longer than four inches (ten centimeters). Although they are widely cultivated in Navarra and in the Rioja region where they are grown for canning, the best quality ones come from Lodosa. In contrast to the moisture content usually permitted (up to thirty-eight percent), theirs must not exceed three percent, and they are roasted above the embers of an open fire.

Other varieties include the *choriceros* which are dried and ground to add piquancy to sausages. *Ñoras*, on the other hand, are round, red, spicy dried pods often added to sauces and fish and rice dishes. A rather more fiery taste is achieved by using *guindillas verdes* or *rojas*, green or red chilies which the Basques call *piparras*. *Bichos* pickled in vinegar are added to souvlakis for spiciness. The green, small-podded Galician variety with their tender flesh are called *de Padrón* and are deep-fried to be enjoyed as an aperitif or with meat dishes. Murcia and Almería are the main regions where the *morrones* are grown. They are a large variety often square in shape and come on the market when are fully-ripe and deep red in color. They are best enjoyed grilled.

Sofrito
Tomato Sauce

1 large onion
½ cup (100 ml) olive oil
2 ripe tomatoes
5 garlic cloves
½ each of a red and a green pepper
1 Tbs chopped parsley
Salt, black pepper

Peel and chop the onion. Steam in about ½ cup (100 ml) of water until all the water has evaporated. Add the oil and lightly brown the onion in it. Remove skin and seeds from the tomatoes and cut the flesh into quarters. Finely chop the garlic; clean and prepare the peppers and cut them into strips. Add the vegetables to the onion and simmer until all ingredients have combined to form a creamy sauce. Season to taste with salt and pepper.
Note: This basic sauce, which provides the base for many stews and meat dishes, may also be prepared without the peppers.

Samfaina
Summer Vegetables

1 large green and 1 large red pepper
3 eggplants
4 Tbs olive oil
4 tomatoes
3 garlic cloves
Salt, black pepper

Clean the peppers and eggplants, remove the seeds and cut into large chunks. Heat the oil in a saucepan and brown the eggplants in it. Remove the eggplants and set them aside. Then add the peppers to the oil and fry them lightly.
Remove the skin and seeds from the tomatoes and chop up the flesh. Crush the garlic. Add the tomatoes and garlic, together with the eggplants, to the peppers. Add salt and pepper and cook over a low heat for about 30 minutes.

Espinacas con Pasas y Piñones
Spinach with Raisins and Pine Nuts

7 lbs (3.5 kg) fresh spinach
5 oz (150 g) raisins
5 Tbs olive oil
7 oz (200 g) pine nuts
Salt, black pepper

Sort and clean the spinach and wash it thoroughly. Blanch it in boiling salted water for 10 minutes. Drain through a colander and press out excess liquid.
Soak the raisins in lukewarm water for 30 minutes, then pour off the liquid and leave the raisins to drain.
Heat the oil in a frying pan and lightly roast the pine nuts. Add the raisins, stir well and then add the spinach. Mix everything together thoroughly and add salt and pepper. As soon as the spinach is heated through, serve the meal from the frying pan.

Pisto Manchego
Vegetable Ragout from La Mancha

1 onion
3 Tbs olive oil
4 garlic cloves
2 green peppers
6 zucchini
1½ lbs (700 g) ripe tomatoes
Salt, black pepper
2 Tbs finely chopped parsley

Peel and chop the onion and fry in the oil until transparent. Crush the garlic, clean the peppers and the zucchini and cut them into strips. Add the garlic and vegetables to the onion and steam for 5 minutes. Remove the skin and seeds from the tomatoes, chop up the flesh and add to the vegetables. Season with salt and pepper. Stew, uncovered, over a low heat until all the liquid has evaporated (about 25 minutes). Now sprinkle with parsley.
The ragout can be served hot or cold.

Escalivada
Ovencooked Vegetables

2 small eggplants
2 red peppers
2 tomatoes
2 onions
2 garlic cloves
Salt, black pepper
5 Tbs olive oil
2 Tbs wine vinegar

Preheat the oven to 350 °F (180 °C).
Clean and prepare the eggplants and peppers and cut them into large, long chunks. Skin the tomatoes, remove the seeds and cut the flesh into halves. Peel and slice the onions and crush the garlic.
Put the vegetables in layers in an oven proof dish, season with salt and pepper and sprinkle with the olive oil. Cook in the oven for 25 minutes and serve warm. If the vegetables are to be served cold, mix in the vinegar after cooking and leave the dish to cool.

Opposite: Farmers and gardeners supply a magnificent variety of lettuces, vegetables, and fruit which can be bought at the weekly markets and in the market halls in the towns and cities.

Cheese

Amongst the greatest culinary delicacies still waiting to be discovered are Spanish cheeses. Due to its ancient shepherd traditions, which are as varied as the landscapes, the Iberian Peninsula offers a wealth of cheese specialties. With the exception of the internationally renowned Manchego, the remaining one hundred or so types of cheese that are available in Spain are largely unknown outside the country's boundaries. Many cheeses nowadays are produced in factories. Most of these varieties are, however, also available as unpasteurized cheeses produced by hand in the same way as it has been done for centuries.

Which type of cheese is produced where, and from what milk, depends on the conditions. Sheep are kept wherever the climate may be extreme and food may be in short supply at times – for example in central Spain and in the western Pyrenees. Dairy cows are kept in regions where the higher rainfall provides lusher pastures, for example on the slopes of the Pyrenees and in the northwest of Spain as far as Galicia. Goats, on the other hand, adapt very well to the arid and barren Mediterranean climate and the rugged mountain regions, which are found in places such as the Balearic and the Canary Islands. Fresh goats' cheese is very popular in the Levant and in Andalusia.

The rind patterns often found on Spanish cheeses are the result of the rings made from esparto grass which are initially placed around the soft cheese dough in order to hold it together. Some dairies pasteurize hard cheeses, especially those made from sheep's milk. As far as taste is concerned, however, cheeses that are made from raw unpasteurized milk, *lecha cruda*, are far superior.

Depending on the proportion of sheep's, cows' and goats' milk, the following distinctions are made:
• Hispánico: contains a minimum of thirty percent sheep's and fifty percent cows' milk as well as forty-five percent of fat by dry weight;
• Ibérico: contains a minimum of ten percent sheep's, thirty percent goats' and fifty percent cows' milk as well as fat content of forty-five percent by dry weight;
• de la Mesta: contains a minimum of seventy-five percent sheep's and fifteen percent cows' milk, with five percent goats' milk being permitted; has a fat content of fifty percent by dry weight.

Cabrales – blue-veined cheese from Asturia

Every Spanish grocer offers a good selection of cheeses to his customers.

Manchego – the best-known sheep's cheese from La Mancha

Idiazabal – a hard cheese from the Basque country

Tetilla – a creamy cows' milk cheese from Galicia

Spanish Cheese Varieties

Burgos – originated in the region around Burgos but is now produced from sheep's milk everywhere in Spain – a moist, fatty fresh cheese low in salt. *Pata de mulo*, a cheese made from donkeys' milk, is also popular.

Cabrales – a blue-veined cheese from the Picos de Europa in Asturia, the region which produces the greatest variety of cheeses. The handmade Cabrales is a mixture of variable proportions of sheep's, cows', and goats' milk that has to mature in caves for at least three months. A very distinctive and slightly spicy taste.

Cantabria – a mild, semi-firm cheese made from the milk of cows that graze on the lush pastures of Cantabria between the Atlantic Ocean and the mountains.

Cebreiro – a fatty cows' milk cheese from Galicia in a distinctive soufflé shape; matured for two weeks.

Cendrat, Montsec – Catalonian goats' cheese from Montsec, the mountain range near Lérida. Produced in the village of Clúa, it is shaped into large whole cheeses weighing 4 lbs (2 kg) each, sprinkled with ash and left to mature for two months. It has a creamy consistency with a characteristic flavor.

Garrotxa – a Catalonian goats' cheese the outside of which is formed by a gray, velvety layer of mold; soft texture and a delicate, nutty flavor.

Ibores – a cylindrical goats' cheese from Extremadura, northeast of Cáceres of cylindrical shape; it weighs about 2 lbs (one kg), takes at least two months to mature, and has an orange rind and a distinctive flavor. Comparable cheeses are Acehuche, Fredenal, Hurdes, and Siberia.

Idiazabal – a hard cylindrical cheese from the Basque country, made mainly from raw milk from Latxa sheep; smoked or unsmoked varieties available; strong, slightly spicy flavor. A similar cheese is the Quesucos which comes in 2 lb (one kg) portions.

Mahón – a rectangular cows' milk cheese from the island of Menorca. It can be eaten fresh but reaches a firm consistency and distinctive flavor after having its rind brushed with oil and being left to mature for three months.

Majorero – the best matured goats' cheese of the Canary Islands, with a pleasant and slightly nutty taste. The inhabitants of the Canaries are the greatest cheese lovers in the whole of Spain, producing large quantities of goats' cheese for their own consumption.

Manchego – the best-known of all Spanish goats' cheeses, it is made only from whole milk from Manchego sheep that graze on the dry plains of La Mancha. A densely structured hard cheese with a fresh and full-bodied flavor.

Picón – a blue-veined cheese made from three types of raw, unpasteurized milk; it is produced within the region of the Picos de Europa national park and offered for sale wrapped in leaves. Dozens of very different cheeses made by hand come from that area. Another well-known variety is the Gamonedo, which is a cheese weighing 80 lbs (40 kg) with a marble-like mold.

San Simón – a pear-shaped, semi-firm cheese with a smoked rind from the slopes of the mountains of the Cordillera Cantabrica in northern Spain. It is made from raw cows' milk and matured for two months.

Serena – a handmade cheese with a tradition going back centuries; made from the milk of Merino sheep whose famous wool is in less demand today than it used to be. It is pressed by hand and salted, matured for one month, and is produced only in spring. An expensive specialty from 21 communities of the province of Badajoz in the southwestern part of Extremadura.

Tetilla – a young, creamy and very mild Galician cheese produced from cows' milk and named after its udder shape. The related Ulloa is somewhat more mature and stronger.

Tronchón – a hard cheese made from sheep's milk from the provinces of Castellón and Teruel in the east of Spain. It is distinguished by its conical shape decorated with traditional motifs.

Zamorano – a hard cheese weighing 4–6 lbs (2–3 kg) produced from sheep's milk mainly from the Churra breed; it matures for three to twelve months and has a distinctive flavor. Look out for cheeses made from raw milk! Comes from the region around Castile-León. A similar cheese is the Castellano.

Fruit

When in the 11th century the Moors first introduced bitter orange trees to Andalusia, they were used to decorate the gardens of their palaces. The fruit, which originally comes from South-East Asia, was long regarded as a symbol of luxury. When Columbus set off on his voyage of discovery he took with him on board bitter orange trees which he introduced to America. Orange trees were soon found all along the Mediterranean coast in Spain, although only the flowers and the dried peel of the fruits were used for medicinal purposes. It was not until about 1780 that people in the province of Valencia began to cultivate sweet oranges as an edible fruit. Only a few years later 7,500 acres (3,000 hectares) of land had been planted with orange trees, with the figure rising to over 91,000 acres (37,000 hectares) twenty-five years later, while today nearly 500,000 acres (over 200,000 hectares) of land are used for that purpose. Three-quarters of the total production come from Valencia which has been the main orange growing area since the 19th century.

Other fruits cultivated include mandarins. Growers saw in the satsuma from Japan the hope that it might rescue them after an epidemic disease known as *tristeza* (sadness) had destroyed thousands of orange trees after the Second World War. This seedless variety of mandarin had the advantage that trees could reach full capacity in seven years, compared to a navel orange tree which needed twice as long as that. Their season lasts from October to January. Satsumas are also preserved in cans, with an annual turnover of more than 300 million.

The selection of fruit on offer in Spain is simply heavenly, due to the extensive fruit growing areas along the Mediterranean coast and in Andalusia.

Spanish Fruit

Aguacate – avocado
Grown in Andalusia and on the Canary Islands; available throughout the year; dominant is the late variety Hass with its thick, wrinkly skin (until July).

Caqui – date plum
Grows along the Mediterranean, often as an ornamental tree, and has been cultivated in Granada for a long time. It has soft, pleasant flesh with a very individual aroma and is available from October through to the end of the year.

Cerezas, mollares – cherries
These are for sale either with stalks or without, in which latter case they are known as *picotas* or *garrafales*; their season is from May through August.

Chirimoya – custard apple
Granada is the origin of this little-exported fruit with its aromatic white flesh and its dark seeds. It is harvested from September through March. Do not keep in the refrigerator or the fruit will turn black.

Fresas – strawberries
Spain is the biggest strawberry exporter in the world, with a total annual production of more than 200,000 tons (180,000 metric tons). More than nine tenths of this is produced in the province of Huelva in southwest Andalusia, where the climate is so favorable that the strawberries ripen early in the spring before all its competitors.

Granada – pomegranate
Grown on the Levant and in Andalusia, although most come from Alicante. This is a very juicy fruit with garnet-colored vesicles around elongated seeds, and is available from July through January.

Higo – fig
There are many varieties, ranging from yellow to near-black. Available fresh from mid-July through to Christmas.

Higo chumbo – prickly pear
This plant grows wild everywhere in the warm Mediterranean climate and has also been cultivated as a fruit. Since a non-prickly variety was cultivated the flesh of the fruit has been a reddish color.

Limón – lemon
The main growing areas are Murcia, Alicante and Málaga. The fleshy, richly-yellow variety Verna is available from February through July, while paler varieties come onto the market during the winter months.

Manzana – apple
North Catalonia and Zaragoza are the producers of varieties such as Golden Delicious, red Starking and Starcrimson.

Melocotón – peach
Peaches and nectarines are cultivated above all in the northeastern provinces as well as in Murcia.

Melones – honeydew melons
Available in summer and fall is the sweet yellow *amarillo liso* melon with its green flesh. The crunchy *tendral* variety has green peel. Apart from these two varieties, the very sweet yellow Galia melon from the Cantaloupe family is becoming increasingly popular.

Níspero – medlar
This special, orange-yellow fruit the size of an apricot comes on the market as early as March and is available until the beginning of June. It has brown, oblong seeds and a pleasantly aromatic flavor.

Pera – pear
Lemon-yellow, finely-spotted pears from Lérida, Zaragoza and Huesca are available from June through to October.

Plátano – banana
A specialty from the Canary Islands, above all from Tenerife. It is sweet and tasty; available throughout the year.

Sandía – watermelon
Watermelons come mainly from Almería, Valencia and Seville and are available from April. Meanwhile, a seedless variety has been cultivated.

Uva – grape
Dessert grapes are cultivated in all four provinces of the Levant and in the western part of Badajoz. The most popular variety in Spain are the muscatel grapes. The season is from July through February.

Desserts and Sweets

Desserts do not generally represent the strongest point of Spanish cuisine. This has probably something to do with the mouthwatering abundance of fresh ripe fruit that is available throughout the year. Ice cream, on the other hand, is very popular as a dessert. With pride the Spaniards look back over 1,000 years to the time when the Moors had blocks of ice brought down from the heights of the Sierra Nevada in order to prepare their *granizados* (drinks mixed with ice) or sorbets.

The choice of desserts is, therefore, relatively small. Nevertheless, there are some classic desserts which have lost none of their appeal, and they include several variations of vanilla and caramel blancmange. A popular way of caramelizing the sugar on the *crema catalana* is the traditional method of melting it with a great hiss by means of a special red-hot iron. At home, blancmange cubes are dipped in flour and egg and then fried in oil. They are known as *leche frita* or *torrijas*, "poor knights." The sweet delicacies baked in fat constitute a category of their own, with the *churros* being the most popular. Churros are made from simple choux pastry which is piped into hot oil by means of a piping bag with a star-shaped

spout. As soon as the pastry is browned on both sides it is lifted out of the oil with a pair of tongs and cut up into pieces the length of a finger. The churros are then put into open paper bags and sprinkled with sugar. They are best consumed immediately after cooking, either for breakfast or as a sweet snack.

The Moors were also responsible for introducing candy made from egg yolk and sugar. The *yemas* are egg confectionery in the shape of little round balls, and there are also the little rounded forms of the heavenly *tocino de cielo*. They are a favorite at Christmas time, which is also the season of the *turrones* which are traditionally made from roasted almonds, honey and sugar. The Turrón of Alicante is a firm variety, a *turrón duro*, in which the almonds are left whole. A bar of it weighs about 6½ oz (200 g). For the soft *turrón blando*, the ingredients are thoroughly ground and mixed and molded into bars of 10 oz (300 g) each. Both the cradle and the stronghold of this turrón is Jijona, situated near Alicante. Other classic turrones may also contain walnuts, hazelnuts, pistachios, dried fruits, and egg yolk. Another optional ingredient is marzipan, which was first produced by the Moors in Toledo. Toledo has

remained the capital of marzipan until today, and Spain its most significant producer. The Spanish are passionate nibblers of cookies and small cakes. Cream cakes such as the *tarta de Santiago* consisting of an almond paste and decorated with a Jacob's cross in icing sugar are reserved for more significant occasions. Even at breakfast they dunk María or Madeleine cookies in their coffee. Many places have their own regional specialties, such as the *ensaimada mallorquina*. This is a very light yeasty bun that is baked in lard and sprinkled with confectioner's sugar. Variations of this bun contain a jam made from pumpkin and blancmange called *cabell d'angel* (angels' hair), or its savory counterpart, the famous paprika sausage from the island of Mallorca known as *sobrasada*.

Fine breads, cakes, and pastries are often associated with ecclesiastic feast days. An example of this is the *panellets* from Catalonia. The pastry is a mixture of boiled, mashed sweet potato and finely ground almonds. It is formed into little balls which are rolled in ground pine nuts before baking. The people of Barcelona like a variety of such *panellets*, adding dried fruits, spices, ground chestnuts or cocoa to the basic mixture. The *panellets* are baked for All Saints Day on the first of November. Then the people of Valladolid piously eat their *huesistos de santo* (little bones of the holy), tiny pastry cylinders made from almonds, sugar, and honey, and baked in oil.

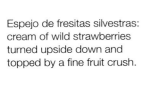

Espejo de fresitas silvestras: cream of wild strawberries turned upside down and topped by a fine fruit crush.

Petit fours: those delicious fancy pastries inspired Spanish confectioners to come up with their own creations.

Profiteroles con chocolate: filled cream puffs with chocolate sauce are a popular dessert in any restaurant.

Fresitas silvestras con nata: wild strawberries with whipped cream. These strawberries ripen superbly well in Spain and are generally a very popular dessert ingredient.

Crema Catalana
Catalonian Custard
(Illustration right and below)

2 cups (500 ml) milk
1 cinnamon stick
Peel of ¹/₂ an untreated lemon
3 egg yolks
About ¹/₂ cup (150 g) sugar

Add the cinnamon stick and the lemon peel to the milk and bring to the boil over a low heat, then take off the heat. Mix just under ¹/₂ cup (100 g) of sugar with the egg yolks and stir until creamy. Remove the cinnamon and lemon peel from the milk. Gradually stir the egg yolk and sugar mixture into the milk. Place it back on the hob and at very low heat, stir until the custard thickens.
Fill the custard into oven proof dishes, let it cool down. Then place the dishes into the refrigerator for a minimum of 30 minutes. Now take out of the refrigerator and sprinkle with sugar. Caramelize briefly under the grill.
Note: the traditional way of caramelizing the sugar was to heat up a spiral-shaped, coiled iron over an open flame and then place it briefly onto the sugar.

Flan de Naranja
Orange Custard

2–3 oranges
3 egg yolks, 3 egg whites
¹/₄ cup (70 g) sugar
1 heaped Tbs (20 g) cornstarch
4–6 slices crystallized oranges

Squeeze the oranges and heat up the juice, then remove from the hob. Whisk the egg yolks together with the sugar and cornstarch and gradually stir the mixture into the warm orange juice. Put it back on the heat and over a very low temperature, stir until the custard thickens. Then take it off the heat and allow to cool.
Whisk the egg whites until stiff and fold into the custard. Allow to cool. Serve well chilled, garnished with the slices of crystallized orange.

Arroz con Leche
Rice Pudding

³/₄ cup (125 g) short-grain rice
Salt
3¹/₂ cups (700 ml) milk
Peel of 1 untreated lemon
¹/₄ cup (70 g) sugar
1 heaped Tbs (20 g) butter
1 tsp cinnamon (optional)

Blanch the rice in boiling salted water for 5 minutes. Drain and rinse with lukewarm water, leave to drain well.
Heat the milk with the lemon peel in it. Melt the butter and the sugar in the hot milk. Remove the lemon peel, add the rice to the milk and bring to the boil. Then reduce the heat, cover and cook, without stirring, for 25 minutes. Pour into a serving bowl and – if desired – dust with cinnamon. Serve either hot or cold.

Even today some cooks caramelize the sugar on top of the *crema catalana* by placing a hot iron coil on it.

Crema catalana – Catalonian custard

Leche Frita
Fried Custard

¹/₂ cup (125 g) butter
2 cups (250 g) flour
¹/₃ cup (100 g) sugar
1¹/₄ cups (250 ml) milk
1 stick of cinnamon
1 piece untreated orange peel
1 piece untreated lemon peel
4 egg yolks, 4 egg whites
¹/₃ cup (100 g) very fine white bread crumbs
8 Tbs olive oil
Confectioner's sugar and cinnamon for dusting

Slowly melt the butter. Retain one Tbs of the flour; sift the remaining flour into the melted butter, add the sugar and mix well. Add the cinnamon stick and the orange and lemon peel to the milk and bring to the boil. Then remove the flavoring ingredients from the milk.
Add the milk to the flour mixture gradually and stir everything together well. Beat the egg yolks into the mixture one by one.
Cut the pastry into squares with sides of about 3–4 inches (8–10 cm) in length, then cut the squares diagonally into triangles. Whisk the egg whites until they form stiff peaks. Turn the pastry triangles lightly first in the flour retained, then in the stiffly-beaten egg white, and lastly in the bread crumbs. Fry on both sides in very hot oil. Dust with confectioner's sugar and cinnamon. Serve hot or cold.

Suspiros de Monja
Nun's Sigh

1¹/₄ cups (250 ml) milk
Just over ¹/₂ cup (150 g) butter
1 pinch of salt
1 pinch of sugar
2 cups (250 g) flour
6 eggs
Oil for deep-frying
Confectioner's sugar for dusting

Add 1¹/₄ cups (250 ml) of water, the butter, salt and sugar to the milk. Bring everything to the boil and remove from the hob. Quickly mix in the flour. Put the saucepan back on the hob and stir until the mixture comes away from the sides of the saucepan. Now beat in the eggs one by one.
Heat up the oil. Cut out portions of the mixture with a teaspoon and put them into the hot oil. When they rise increase the temperature and cook for 4 to 5 minutes. Remove them from the oil with a ladle and leave to drain on some kitchenroll. Continue this process until all the dough mixture is used up. Serve immediately dusted with confectioner's sugar, or leave to cool.

Rioja

The Spanish are very demanding when it comes to enjoying wine. Be it in a restaurant or in a shop: when they ask for a bottle of wine they expect it to be ready for drinking. It is by this unwritten law that almost all bodegas (wineries) abide, no matter what their position is amongst the now thirty-nine guaranteed registrations of origin, the Denominaciones de Origen.

A good example was set by the Rioja region. Its leading position resulted from the phylloxera crisis at the end of the 19th century. After the vineyards of Bordeaux had fallen prey to this greedy insect, the merchants had to look for alternatives. The area along the River Ebro in the northwest of Spain provided ideal growing conditions. The wine growers set up wineries and brought all their expertise with them. The boom came to an end, however, when Spain, too, became a victim of the epidemic. Throughout the Franco regime the Rioja had no competition whatsoever within Spain. The bodegas took to heart what their loyal customers wanted and brought onto the market only such wines that were ready to consume.

This new upswing was related to renewed demand from abroad and to the economic development of Spain, and from 1970 it turned the attention of (mainly local) investors towards the area. New, and often spectacular, wineries were built. While wine production was modernized, the well-proven principles on which cultivation and marketing had been based were retained. Other great wine growing regions throughout the world leave it up to their customers to wait patiently for their noble vintages to mature – or to open them too early. The customer service in the Rioja and the Spanish wine growing regions in general is excellent by comparison. They market wine categories of different quality. But no matter to which category it belongs, every wine is suitable for immediate consumption, even if good vintages may mature to even greater perfection if left longer (see right-hand page).

A wine that is drunk with much enthusiasm in the Rioja region itself and also in the Basque country is the Vino joven. This is a very fruity, young red wine comparable to the Beaujolais nouveau which is bottled by small independent wine growers, the *cosecheros*. Its preparation is based on traditional methods and takes place in open concrete tanks known as *lagos*. In these *lagos*, the whole grapes are fermented, a process during which the development of carbonic acid causes intracellular fermentation. Whilst this extracts color and aroma from the skins, it extracts only little tannin – which is exactly what is expected in a wine that is meant to be drunk when it is young. Some bodegas carry out this carbonic acid maceration process in modern tanks to ensure that wines that come onto the market after only a brief maturing period are as fruity as possible. In the case of all other red Rioja wines, the bodegas carry out a pulp fermentation, the duration of which is determined by the grapes available and the quality desired. All higher quality wines are then matured in sixty-gallon (225-liter) oak casks. For many decades these *barricas* used to be made from American oak. During the last twenty years, however, the more refined French *barriques* with their distinct hint of vanilla have gained considerable acceptance. The wine then has to mature further either in the tank before the final bottling, or in the bottle. The Rioja's economic organization is reminiscent of that of the Champagne. It is more or less practiced in many other regions of Spain. The bodegas buy the major part of their grape requirements from wine-growers who are either independent or in organized cooperatives. The grapes are paid for by weight, per kilogram. In the past, there often used to be a demand for new or young wine. Now, the bodegas tend to be quite well supplied with modern wine processing equipment, so that they accept only the grapes, and prepare their own wines under their own control. This step has led to a considerable improvement in both technique and quality. Quite a number of bodegas have also invested in buying their own vineyards. The marketing side is looked after by wineries, the majority of which belong to successful companies predominant in other economic sectors. Independent vineyards that bottle their own production exclusively are the exception in the Rioja. The best-known are Rémelluri, Contino, Barón de Ley, Amezola de la Mora, and the great veteran Marqués de Murrieta.

Rioja Vintages

In the Rioja, vintages are classed officially according to their quality as follows:
5 = outstanding – 4 = very good – 3 = good – 2 = satisfactory – 1 = poor

1994 5	1980 3	1966 2
1993 3	1979 2	1965 1
1992 3	1978 4	1964 5
1991 4	1977 2	1963 2
1990 3	1976 3	1962 4
1989 3	1975 4	1961 3
1988 3	1974 3	1960 3
1987 4	1973 3	1959 4
1986 3	1972 1	1958 5
1985 3	1971 1	1957 2
1984 2	1970 4	1956 3
1983 3	1969 2	1955 5
1982 5	1968 4	1954 3
1981 4	1967 2	

Categories of Quality

• Vino sin crianza: wine that has not been matured in wooden casks; the label states only the year of the vintage or *vino de cosechero*; these are fruity young wines bottled at the wine-growers' and are known as *vino joven* (primeur).
• Vino de crianza: wine that is matured in wooden barrels for up to one year and does not come onto the market until it is at least two years old; its flavor is still fruity but more rounded and complex.
• Reserva: during its minimum three years of maturation, this wine has spent at least one year in oak casks. The wines are made from selected grapes and are well structured and may often improve if left to mature even longer. Their bouquets are already well developed with hints of ripe fruit and natural woodland. The rosé and white wines mature for a minimum of two years, six months of which are in barrels.
• Gran reserva: selected red wines from exceptionally good harvests; they have enough body and structure to develop during a minimum of two years in wooden casks and another three years in bottles. From the moment they are released onto the market they boast a multi-layered bouquet and a velvety flavor. The better vintages can reach perfection if left for several years or even decades. It is upon these wines that a bodega's prestige rests.

Background: The vineyards of the Rioja produce only a small yield. This imparts strength and character to the most famous red wines of Spain.

Rioja wines mature in oak barrels (*barricas*) that hold sixty gallons (225 liters). The storage cellars or *bodegas* have to be very large.

The Spanish expect the Rioja wines on the market to be ready to drink. No price is too high for the excellent vintage Reserva or Gran Reserva.

Airen – produces pleasant white wines in the region La Mancha

Tempranillo – the star amongst the red grape types of Spain

Cariñena – a widespread variety that gives color and structure to red wines

Garnacha – lends body to red wines, and a delicate fruity quality to rosados

Background: Palomino – the grape used to make all the best sherry

Important Grape Varieties

Red grapes

Cariñena (Mazuelo) – Carignan produces dark, robust wines.

Garnacha – Spain's most important type of grape with regard to quantity; thrives in arid conditions; rich in alcohol; often used for blended wines.

Monastrell – a widespread and hardy variety which tolerates warm climates very well; produces strong, rich, and rather pale wines and is also partly used for liqueur wines.

Tempranillo (Cencibel, Ull de Llebre, Tinta del País a.o.) – a highly renowned early ripening variety that grows on chalky ground; main variety in the Rioja and in Ribera del Duero.

White grapes

Airen – main grape type in the vast wine-growing area of La Mancha, accounting for 30 percent of all Spanish vines; extremely resistant to dry and hot conditions; provides special wines for distilling brandy.

Albariño – the star amongst the white grape types of Galicia is fermented without adding any other types of grape; the bouquet is aromatic and exciting.

Garnacha blanca – widely cultivated in the north of Spain, this robust vine is the white version of the Grenache (Garnacha).

Macabeo (Viura) – the main type of white grape in northern Spain; can grow in arid conditions; important in Catalonia where it is used for the production of Cava and light white wines.

Moscatel – produces sweet, heavy wines rich in alcohol, especially Málaga.

Palomino – Andalusian variety which reaches unique distinction only in sherry.

Parellada – lends fruitiness and refinement to Cava and the dry white wines of the Penedés; the best qualities are grown at high altitudes.

Pedro Ximénez – a sweet grape variety that ripens early in the season and is dominant in Montilla-Moriles and important in Málaga; no longer of importance in Jeréz.

Verdejo – A variety of Rueda which is full of character and matures well in the bottle.

The map shows the following Spanish wine-growing regions and cities:

Chacoli de Guetaria, San Sebastián, Rias Baixas, Vigo, Ribeiro, El Bierzo, Valdeorras, Méntrida, Valladolid, Ribera del Duero, Rioja, Logroño, Navarra, Somontano, Ampurdán-Costa Brava, Zaragoza, Costers del Serge, Barcelona, Alella, Toro, Rueda, Calatayud, Cariñena, Penedés, Tarragona, Terra Alta, Priorato, MADRID, Méntrida, Madrid, Utiel-Requena, Valencia, Palma, La Mancha, Almansa, Valencia, Valdepeñas, Jumilla, Alicante, Córdoba, Murcia, Condado de Huelva, Sevilla, Montilla-Moriles, Sta. Cruz de Tenerife, Jerez, Málaga, Tacoronte-Acentejo, Málaga, Tajo, Guadiana, Guadalquivir

Wine

Spanish Wine-growing Regions

El Bierzo
An interesting red wine area in the very northwest of Spain where the Galician variety Mencia provides aroma and complexity.

Cariñena
Near Zaragoza, this area produces full-bodied red wines that keep well from the variety Garnacha Tinta; the Carignan grape plays a subordinate role.

Jerez (Xerez, Sherry)
An area comprising nearly 57,000 acres (23,000 hectares) in Andalusia, world famous for its Palomino Fino which accounts for 90 percent of the cultivation (see pp. 446–447).

La Mancha
The largest wine-growing region in the world, situated in the arid central part of Spain. It produces special wines for Brandy de Jerez, and nowadays also light, pleasant white wines from Airen grapes as well as distinctly fruity red wines from the Tempranillo variety.

Montilla-Moriles
A hot area with excellent limy soil south of Córdoba which produces interesting wines of the sherry type but has difficulties in making a name for itself. Favorable prices.

Navarra
A province that borders Rioja and extends further north as far as the Pyrenees; recently it has been amongst the most successful wine-growing regions with its fruity, strong rosé and smooth, characterful red wines.

Penedés
This is the home not only of Catalonian Cava, but also of well-balanced white wines of Macabeo, Xarel-lo and the refined Parellada as well as Chardonnay. It is reestablishing its importance as a red wine region, above all thanks to the popularity of Cabernet Sauvignon and Merlot.

Priorato
An area in the hilly hinterland of Tarragona where *vino generoso*, dessert wine, is produced; it is however famous for its partly concentrated and full-bodied red wines from Garnacha and Cariñena.

Rías Baixas
This label from Galicia is highly esteemed and therefore expensive. The area consists of the three sub-regions El Rosal and Condado del Tea in the south, and Valle del Salnés in the north of Pontevedra. The white wines are fresh and sparkling, with pure Albariño being the best.

Ribera del Duero
Home of the cult wine Vega Sicilia which is a blend of French grape varieties and Tinto del País (Tempranillo) and white Albillo. The area south of Burgos produces a number of other great red wines, including Pesquera, and is undergoing a dynamic development. Cabernet Sauvignon, Malbec and Merlot are now officially registered.

Rioja
The best-known and still the leading wine region of Spain extending over about 112,000 acres (45,000 hectares) along the River Ebro and divided into three zones: the warmer and more arid Rioja Baja in the east where a lot of Garnacha is grown; the Rioja Alta west of Logroño and south of the Ebro, where the well-known little wine town of Haro is situated; and further to the north the Rioja Alavesa which is part of the Basque country and where a high percentage of Tempranillo is cultivated. According to tradition, wines from the three zones are blended with one another, although exceptions are on the increase. So far this is the only region with the superior Denominación de Origen Calificada (DOC, awarded by the *Instituto de Denominaciones de Origen*.)

Rueda
A region situated south of Valladolid and famous for its white wine thanks to the remarkable Verdejo vine.

Somontano
A region east of the city of Huesca, in the foothills of the Pyrenees. It is planted with Mediterranean varieties and Tempranillo, while the future of this up and coming area may well lie with French vines.

Valdepeñas
Situated in the province of Ciudad Real, the major part of this region is enclosed by La Mancha. Nowadays it specializes in modern, light, fruity white and rosé wines; there is also a new generation of velvety, full-flavored red wines made from Cencibel (Tempranillo) and matured in the *barrique*.

Cava

Translated literally, cava means cellar. In Spain the term is also used to refer to sparkling wine produced according to the *méthode champenoise* (p. 420). It is a popular drink enjoyed in generous quantities and on many occasions. In its home province of Catalonia in particular it is drunk not only as an aperitif or with a dessert, but as an accompaniment to the whole meal. A firmly established institution in Barcelona are the Xampagnerias, bars where different types of cava are sold by the glass.

The first sparkling wine produced according to the champagne method of double fermentation was launched in 1872 by José Raventos. His family still owns the wine firm Codorniu and has done so since it was first recorded in 1551. Others soon followed, notably Freixenet, a firm that was established in 1889 and has now overtaken Codorniu as the biggest producer.

The largest and most significant Denominación de Origen, Penedés, became the center for the production of Cava, Sant Sadurni d'Anoia its capital. Here, more than ninety percent of all Cavas are produced. The hilly area southwest of Barcelona and the foothills of Montserrat provide good ripening conditions for grapes. They form enough sugar in a natural way so that – unlike in the Champagne – no artificial measures have to be employed to produce basic wines. And good weather during the harvest is virtually guaranteed.

In Catalonia, Cava was initially produced exclusively from a strong grape type rich in alcohol and known as Xarel-lo. Then Macabeo was added which imparted fruitiness to both the wine's bouquet and taste. It was not until forty years ago that the Parellada variety was rediscovered, originally known as Montonac – "he from the mountains." His contribution to Cava is refinement and freshness.

In September, the wineries come to life. This is the time when thousands of wine-growers deliver their grapes to the Cava producers. A strictly defined procedure is followed to ensure that any oxidation in the harvested grapes is avoided so that good sparkling wines can be produced. Immediately after checking weight, sugar content, and condition, the grapes are put into the presses (predominantly of the continuous type). The next step is usually a clarification of the must before it is fermented at a controlled temperature to produce dry wines, divided up according to type of grape. The various Cava types are produced by the cellarers using the basic wines derived from Xarel-lo, Macabeo, Parellada, and Chardonnay. To some of them they add a part of reserved wine from earlier vintages. The further development of the Cava follows along the same lines as that of all sparkling wines of above-average quality. The still wine is now filled into bottles made from specially thick glass. To each bottle is added an exactly measured dose of sugar and yeast. Then the bottles are closed with crown caps and stored in the cellar where the wine undergoes its second fermentation which will turn it into sparkling wine.

The wine spends a minimum of nine months – and the best vintages up to five years – fermenting on the yeast which helps develop its taste. Then the time comes for its transformation into Cava, and the *remuage*, or the shaking process, begins. In the case of top quality Cava, this is still done by hand. Otherwise a special kind of rack is used.

After about a month and a half all yeast residues will have collected in the neck of the tilted bottle. Then the neck of the bottle is frozen and the frozen lump of sediment is pushed out as soon as the crown cap is removed. A dash of *liqueur d'expédition*, a mixture of wine and sugar, is now added to the Cava, determining its sweetness or dryness. At last the bottle is sealed by means of the final wired cork with its metal cap.

Cava Quality Categories

Extra Brut – less than 3 g sugar per pint (per 500 ml)
Brut – up to 7 g sugar per pint (per 500 ml)
Extra seco – between 6 to10 g of sugar per pint (per 500 ml)
Seco – between 8 to 35 g sugar per pint (per 500 ml)
Semi-seco – between 16 to 25 g sugar per pint (per 500 ml)
Dolce – more than 25 g sugar per pint (per 500 ml)
Cava with no vintage year stated – matured on yeast for a minimum of nine months
Cava with vintage year stated – matured on yeast for a minimum of 24 months

A constant, cool temperature is required in the cava ("cellar").

The second phase of fermentation takes place in the bottles.

All remaining yeast particles have to collect in the bottle neck.

The permanent corks are put in place after disgorging.

Background: During the disgorging process the frozen yeast sediments are forced out by the pressure of the wine when the temporary cap is removed.

Sidra

Sidra is the Spanish name for cider. The home of Sidra is the northwestern part of the Iberian Peninsula, mainly the Basque country and Asturia. The Atlantic climate provides ideal conditions in which not only several types of natural crabapples thrive, but also sweeter varieties such as the Danziger Kant. The art of the cider producers, the sidrerias, lies in their blending skills. A harmonious taste is achieved by an alcohol content of five to six percent by volume. As the various apple varieties are ripe at different times, harvesting is from September through November.

The actual production of the cider starts with the washing and chopping up of the apples. The fruit is then soaked overnight in plenty of water to make it swell up before it is put into the presses. The apple pulp must not become too compact since it would yield no juice. In order to avoid this, the layers of fruit are alternated with layers of straw, linen or woven cane. The juice from the fruit is put into large open barrels and tubs and left to ferment for a couple of months. The onset of fermentation is slow because of the low temperature. During this time, the so-called "pomace hat" or *sombrero* forms gradually on the surface. From its coloring the experienced Sidra maker will be able to judge the quality of the cider. If the color varies between dark red and dark brown the producer may rest content, whereas a whitish or yellowish tint suggests a mediocre quality.

At the end of the first stage of fermentation, only part of the sugar has been converted into alcohol, and the Sidra master now pours the raw cider into sealed oak or chestnut casks. While the Sidra producers in Asturia prefer to clarify the juice, their Basque counterparts leave it on the yeast, resulting in a Sidra of more aromatic strength and character. It is now left to ferment thoroughly until May. The fresh Sidra is ready in time to reach the tapas bars and sidrerias (cider bars) before the start of the summer season.

In the coastal regions of the north, Sidra has been a traditional drink for 2,000 years. Landlords and waiters can be seen performing the traditional way of pouring Sidra: in a majestic gesture difficult to imitate, one arm is stretched out above the head, and the Sidra streams out in a thin, amber-colored arc into the pint-glass held low in the other hand, so that it comes up in a delicious golden foam. The cider with its pleasant sparkle and its refreshing, slightly sour taste is a favorite accompaniment for tapas, but is also often enjoyed with bacalao dishes, sardines, and the Asturian dish *fabada* (page 456).

Background: The correct pouring of the apple cider is an art which has reached perfection in the public houses in the northwest of Spain.

If the cider has been poured correctly, the bubbles will rise in an exemplary fashion.

The traditional drink is produced by hand by firms in the Basque country and in Asturia.

Fede Falces

Portugal

Portugal is well worth the trip for those who have a love of authentic foods – for real gourmets. There are, in all areas of agriculture, species and varieties that have developed, or been developed, over the course of centuries and millennia in harmony with their natural surroundings. The same is true of many of the ways of preparing food such as ham, sausage, cheese, dried fruits, and candy, or one of the large range of recipes; all of these are firmly rooted in tradition. There are historical reasons why Portugal still has such a wealth of culinary delights. The country was cut off from the outside world for over forty years until 1974, when the dictatorship founded by Salazar came to an end. There was no change to rural systems throughout this period, which meant that hardly any Portuguese managed without some means of self-sufficiency. Since Portugal joined the European Community, a section of its agriculture is being increasingly pressurized to adopt the uniform range of products favored by Brussels' bureaucrats. It has taken a while for these standardized Euro-products to reach the more remote parts, however. A result of this is that cuisine is better in the country than in the cities, as it uses regional produce. The inhabitants of Oporto are nicknamed *tripeiros*, tripe eaters, but they enjoy a richer, more extensive cuisine than those of Lisbon, the city of *alfacinhas* or lettuce eaters. Cooking in the Algarve is adversely affected by the need to cater for the tourist industry, coupled with a rather less fertile supply area. All coastal areas, however, offer a wealth of first-class fish and shellfish. Breakfast is a rather unimportant meal in Portugal. Workers or people in the country will often snack on one or two *petiscos* (a range of delicacies) before lunch, and these are traditionally eaten with wine straight from the cask. Dinner, the *jantar*, is eaten between seven and eight pm, and is frequently the proper family meal. It is cooked specially and is usually served in an attractive manner. Meals in restaurants are more or less extravagant, depending on the occasion. Two things are a vital part of every meal: plenty of bread, and wine. Any restaurant that takes pride in its reputation will list several wines from a variety of regions.

Left: A Portuguese restaurateur examining a lobster and crayfish.

Caldo Verde

The national dish of Portugal is *caldo verde*, green soup; it comes from the same region as *Vinho verde*, green wine. It is based on one particular variety of cabbage from Galicia, *couve galega*. This cabbage is one of the elements that shapes the entire look of the landscape in Minho and northern Portugal. It often grows successfully underneath vines, and is a regular feature of gardens, even backyards in Lisbon. It is one of the standard vegetables on sale at all markets. This extremely green, long-stemmed cabbage is even frequently sold ready to use in bags – it needs to be chopped very finely for use in soups. *Couve galega* is only available in Galicia and Portugal, and it is used almost without exception to make green soup.

The traditional accompaniment for green soup is freshly-baked *broa de milho*, a typical, thick-crusted northern maize bread. A few slices of sausage, such as *chouriço* or *salpicão*, should also be placed in each bowl or plate before the soup is poured over it.

Caldo Verde
Green Soup
(Illustrations 1–4)

10 oz (300 g) Galician cabbage (alternatively kale or spring cabbage)
1 large onion
2 garlic cloves
1 lb (500 g) mealy potatoes
3 Tbs olive oil
5 oz (150 g) Chouriço (p. 222)
Salt, black pepper
Maize bread

Wash the cabbage; let it drain and then cut into very thin strips (1, 2). Peel the onion and garlic and dice finely. Peel the potatoes and cut into thin slices.

Heat the olive oil in a large pan, fry the onion and garlic gently until the onion is transparent; add the slices of potato and brown them gently, turning them over occasionally. Add enough water to cover the ingredients.

Simmer gently for about 25 minutes, until the potatoes are cooked. Remove the pan from the heat and mash the potatoes.

Cut the sausage into slices and fry for about 10 minutes; drain the fat away.

Return the pan to the heat. Add the sausage and re-warm slowly; season to taste with salt and pepper.

Add the cabbage and simmer for about 5 minutes until tender; add a dash of olive oil if desired.

Pour the soup into bowls (3, 4) and serve with chunks of maize bread.

1

2

Background: The main ingredients of *Caldo Verde* are cabbage, sausage, onions, and potatoes. It is eaten with *broa de milho*, maize bread.

Vegetable Glossary

Agrião – watercress, either in a salad or on its own; available all year round

Abóbora – large type of pumpkin with orange flesh; an important ingredient in vegetable soups

Batata – potato; there are native, often purple-skinned varieties of a very high quality consumption per capita per annum about 360 pounds! (150 kg)

Batata doce – sweet potato; popular fried, though seldom served in restaurants

Bróculo – broccoli; popular side dish; sometimes accompanies boiled fish, in which case it is dressed with oil and vinegar

Cebola – onion; perhaps the most important vegetable, used to add flavor or as a side dish; native varieties are large and flat in shape, and taste delicious in a salad

Cenoura – carrots; Portuguese carrots are especially sweet, which is why they are often used in recipes for cakes and desserts

Couve-flor – cauliflower; either just cooked or as part of home-made mixed pickles

Couve galega – the tall-growing Galician cabbage, cut into thin strips to make *Caldo Verde*

Couve portugesa – Portuguese cabbage; less tall, aromatic; used for *cozido*, stew; whole leaves are cooked and served with meat and fish

Ervilhas – peas; exceptional quality when fresh between March and May; served with and in meat dishes

Espinafres – spinach; served on its own or with other green leaf vegetables, usually steamed in oil with garlic

Fava – broad beans; particularly popular in the north

Feijão verde – green beans; large number of varieties; used in soups with peppermint, or boiled with cilantro

Feijão – dried beans, whether white, black, brownish red or spotted, are one of Portugal's basic foods

Grelos – green cabbage shoots with flower buds; a delicate native vegetable that is usually served steamed with garlic

Nabiças – young leaves of small turnips; a popular side dish when steamed

Nabo – small white turnips; used in stews and soups, and mixed with potatoes in purée

Pimento – sweet peppers, *verde* (green) or *vermelho* (red); available all year round, though in season outdoors from the end of June through the middle of November; sweet red peppers are popular broiled in salads

Tomate – tomato; used in salads, numerous dishes and sauces; a large crop, planted on a total of 17,000 hectares; in season from June through October

Sopa de pedra – Stone soup.

Caldeirada à algarvia –
Fish stew, Algarve style.

Soups and Stews

Soups are an important part of every meal in Portugal. To this day, housewives up and down the country, as well as chefs of both small and large restaurants, start the day by cutting up potatoes and vegetables, the important ingredients of most soups. Portuguese soups, if freshly cooked to traditional recipes, are tasty and of good quality, and unlikely to be omitted willingly. Together with the classic *caldo verde* and the usual chicken broth, *canja*, another firm favorite is the straightforward *sopa de legumes*, which is a puréed vegetable soup. It can be made out of practically any vegetables that are fresh from the garden or market. If there is only a limited range of fresh material available, dried beans are sometimes added. Like *caldo verde*, it is often thickened using potatoes. Vegetable soup has a typical yellowish colour, due usually either to carrots or the brilliant orange-coloured flesh of pumpkins. Cabbage is also added to many soups. Out in the country, rice or noodles are often added to make the soups more filling – these tend to be overcooked, but do not ruin the taste of the soup which is usually enhanced with olive oil.

Soups in Portugal are usually divided into two categories:
• *Sopas* – thick, puréed soups
• *Caldos* – clear broths.

There are exceptions to this rule, as the creamy *caldo verde* proves; others are the *sopa à alentejana*, which is a bouillon, and the *sopa de cozido*, which is the broth in the Portuguese national dish *cozido à portuguesa* (recipe p. 493).

There are three terms generally applied to stews:
• *Cozido* – the name for the modified, though fundamentally similar, versions of the national dish, the meat stew *cozido à portuguesa*.
• *Açordas* – the term used for bread soups, whose consistency can vary from runny to very thick. As bread was the only special thing added to the soups, they were simple meals eaten in the poorer areas, such as Alentejo. Other ingredients were olive oil, garlic, fresh cilantro leaves, and – if available – eggs as well. Mussels were added in the region around Lisbon. Modern refined versions are prepared using lobster or other more expensive shellfish.
• *Caldeiradas* – the generic term for fish stews. They are sometimes based on just one type of fish, but more usually contain a number of different varieties and are served as a main course. Lighter and frequently excellent fish soups are, in contrast, simply called *sopa de peixe*. The creamed soups made out of crustaceans or shrimps, *creme de mariscos*, are normally not of the same quality.

Sopa de Pedra
Stone Soup
(Illustration)

Serves 8

1 pig's ear
5 oz (150 g) streaky bacon
2 onions
3 garlic cloves
1 black Chouriço (black pudding)
1 Chouriço (see p. 502)
1 lb (500 g) fresh red or black beans
2 bay leaves
Salt, black pepper
1 lb 10 oz (750 g) potatoes
1 carrot
1 small white turnip
1 tomato
2 Tbs finely-chopped cilantro

Scald the pig's ear and bacon. Peel the onions and garlic, dice finely and place in a large pan together with the meat, bacon, sausages, beans and bay leaves; add salt and pepper. Cover with water and bring to the boil. Simmer gently with the lid on for 45 minutes.
Take out the meat and bacon and reserve. Remove some of the beans, purée them and reserve. Peel and dice the potatoes, carrot, and turnips, and skin and dice the tomato. Add the vegetables to the soup and simmer for a further 30 minutes, until the vegetables are tender.
Mix in the puréed beans, bring to the boil and season to taste. Cut the meat, bacon, and sausage into pieces or

Sopa à alentejana –
Soup, Alentejo style.

slices and place in a soup tureen. Pour in the hot soup, add the cilantro and allow to stand for a few minutes. Traditionally, a large, thoroughly washed and cleaned stone is placed in the soup before serving, and the soup is served with fresh maize bread.

Sopa à Alentejana
Soup, Alentejo Style
(Illustration)

Serves 4

4 slices of light sourdough bread
2 bunches of cilantro
4 garlic cloves
Salt
$^{1}/_{2}$ cup (100 ml) cold pressed olive oil
4 eggs

Cut the slices of bread into large pieces. De-stalk the cilantro leaves and chop finely; also chop the garlic and mix with the coriander, salt and olive oil. Place the bread in a soup tureen and drizzle the mixture of herbs and oil over it. Boil 5 cups (1 liter) of water. Slip the eggs into it and poach for 3 minutes; reserve. Pour boiling water over the bread in the soup tureen and mix in the ingredients. Add the eggs carefully and salt them lightly. Cover and allow to stand for 5 minutes.
Tip: In Portugal *pão caseiro*, a white country sourdough bread, is used.

Caldeirada à Algarvia
Fish Stew, Algarve Style
(Illustration)

Serves 6–8

4 lb (2 kg) fresh assorted fish
(such as anglerfish, ray, perch, shark)
Coarse sea salt
$1^{1}/_{2}$ lb (750 g) cockles
3 large onions
1 lb 12 oz (800 g) ripe tomatoes
1 green pepper
5 garlic cloves
1 lb 10 oz (750 g) potatoes
2 Tbs parsley
$1^{1}/_{4}$ cups (250 ml) olive oil
1 or 2 piri-piri (chillies)
1 pinch nutmeg
White pepper
1 cup (200 ml) dry white wine
2 bay leaves

Gut, descale and wash the fish. Cut it into 2 inch (5 cm) pieces and sprinkle with sea salt. Brush and wash the cockles, rejecting open ones. Peel the onions and cut into rings; wash and slice the tomatoes and peppers, chop the garlic cloves, peel and slice the potatoes. Place a layer of onions, tomatoes, peppers, some garlic and parsley, and potatoes into a large pan. Add a layer of fish and cockles, and cover this in turn with another layer of vegetables and potatoes. Mix the olive oil with the crushed piri-piri (remove the seeds to make them less sharp), nutmeg and pepper and stir in the wine. Spread out over the contents of the pan and place the bay leaves on top.
Simmer with the lid on for about 35 minutes. Occasionally turn the pan gently to make sure that the broth is evenly spread out. Serve immediately, with white Bairrada.

Cozido à Portuguesa
Portuguese Meat Stew

Serves 8

2 lb (1 kg) brisket
1 lb (500 g) belly of pork
1 pig's ear
7 oz (200 g) streaky bacon
1 boiling fowl about $2^{1}/_{2}$ lb ($1^{1}/_{2}$ kg)
2 heads of Galician cabbage
(see illustrations on pp. 490–491)
3 small white turnips
5 medium carrots
8 large potatoes
2 Chouriços (see illustration on p. 222)
2 black Chouriços (black pudding)
2 garlic sausages
1 lb (500 g) white rice
Salt, black pepper

Place the beef, pork, bacon, and chicken in a large pan. Cover with plenty of salted water and simmer gently, with the lid on, for about $2^{1}/_{2}$ hours. Remove some of the broth after 90 minutes and put in another pan. Wash the cabbage and cut it into strips; peel or scrub the turnips, carrots, and potatoes, cut into pieces and put together with the cabbage into the broth. After a further 45 minutes, boil the sausages, add them to the vegetables and simmer for a further 15 minutes. When the sausages have been added to the vegetables, remove 5 cups of broth from the meat pan, salt it if necessary and use it to boil the rice until it is done. Take the meat and sausages out of the pans. Cut the meat into pieces and the sausage into slices, and divide the chicken into eight portions. Put the cooked rice into a bowl and decorate with the sausage slices. Place the meat on a warmed serving dish. Using a ladle, spoon the vegetables out of the broth and place around the meat; spoon some of the broth on top. A red Ribatejo wine is a suitable accompaniment to this meal.
Tip: The rich meat and vegetable broth is used to make the famous *sopa de cozido*, often served as a starter.

Sardines

King João II of Portugal reigned towards the end of the 15th century and had a taste for good food, parties, and stimulating entertainment; he had the following to say about the sardine: "There are plenty of sardines, they taste very good and are very cheap." These words, uttered by the man who was considered by his subordinates to be the embodiment of perfection, sum up the reasons why the sardine became Portugal's favorite fish. The king's words remain true to this day. While other fish has become more expensive, even in Portugal, sardines have remained at a reasonable price. The annual Portuguese catch of sardines is about 100,000 tonnes, about forty percent of the country's entire catch of fish. It is precisely because of their great love of sardines that the Portuguese are good at telling when sardines are going to be fresh, good, and tasty. The sardines are specially rich and aromatic when the schools of fish first approach the coastline in April, after overwintering in deeper waters further south. This is the start of the season, which lasts until the end of October. They are caught along the entire Portuguese coastline, from the Algarve to the Minho province. Because sardines taste so very exquisite when they are absolutely fresh, they can be found all along the coast, but are rarely eaten further inland; dried, salted cod and (even deep-frozen) hake are more likely to be served – and sometimes sardines tinned in oil.

A large part of Portugal's catch is tinned. The canning industry has an excellent reputation, which dates back to the practice of only using olive oil, or *azeite*, for preserving the sardines – a practice which continues to this day for the best quality levels.

One way of preparing fresh sardines is to make *sardinhas assadas*, which entails broiling them over charcoal. The gutted, descaled fish are laid in salt for at least two hours, and are then washed, dried, and brushed with olive oil. They are placed onto the broiler over the glowing charcoal and are broiled on both sides, two to three minutes according to size. They are especially delicious if grilled with ripe peppers and then drizzled with olive oil and vinegar. Another favorite is *sardinhas fritas*, sardines that are coated in flour (with or without egg) and fried. In the Algarve, *carapaus*, which are a type of mackerel, are often used instead of sardines. Very small ones are nicknamed *carapauzinhos*, and large ones, more than ten inches (25 cm) long, are called *chicharro*.

In coastal towns, the women frequently prepare sardines on small clay broilers, and these can also be seen in the streets of Lisbon on

Opposite: In April, schools of sardines swim near the coast, and the fishing season starts. At this time of year the fish is especially rich and aromatic.

A large part of the sardine catch is canned. Here the fish are being gutted.

Sardines continue to be canned in oil by hand; this is an important source of jobs in coastal towns.

Before the fish are preserved, they have to be descaled and cleaned.

Sardines in oil develop a quite individual, particularly delicate flavor.

June 12, the feast of St. Anthony. Street vendors sell fresh *sardinhas* or *carapaus*. They simply set up shop on the pavement with a wooden crate full of fish. This immediately attracts the attention of any passers-by, and if the fish are of good quality, they will soon be sold. A race of fish lovers is hardly like to pass by on an opportunity to buy some fresh, delicious sardines.

Sardinhas Assadas com Pimentos
Grilled Sardines with Peppers

Serves 6

2 lb (1 kg) medium and large-sized sardines
Coarse sea salt
Olive oil
4 green and/or red peppers
1 onion
Wine vinegar

Descale the sardines, but do not gut them. Wash in salty water and rub with sea salt. Allow to stand for at least two hours. Rub off some of the salt and brush with olive oil.
Wash the peppers, remove the seeds, cut them into strips, and oil and salt them slightly. Broil both sides of the fish and peppers over a charcoal fire. Peel the onions and cut them into rings. Arrange the sardines on warmed plates, and decorate with the onion rings and broiled peppers. Drizzle olive oil over them and, optionally, vinegar. They are served with boiled potatoes and a green salad, accompanied by a fresh, dry Alentejo white wine.

Sardinhas de Escabeche
Marinated Sardines

Serves 4–6

2lb (1 kg) small to medium-sized sardines
Vegetable oil for frying

Marinade
3 onions
1 tomato
5 Tbs olive oil
1 bunch flat leaf parsley
2 garlic cloves
2 bay leaves
1/2 cup (100 ml) dry white wine
2 Tbs white wine vinegar
Salt, black pepper
1 tsp ground paprika

Descale the sardines, gut and wash them, pat them dry and then fry them a portion at a time. Allow to cool on paper towels.
To make the marinade, peel the onions and cut them into rings, skin the tomatoes, remove the seeds and cut them into pieces; chop the parsley and garlic up finely. Heat the olive oil in a frying pan and brown the onions slowly. Then add the garlic, bay leaves, tomato, and parsley, and season with salt. Finally add the white wine and vinegar, cook for five minutes and allow to cool. Put the sardines into a bowl, season with salt and pepper and sprinkle the paprika over them. Pour on the marinade and place in the fridge for two days. Before serving, garnish the sardines with onion rings and parsley, and pour some of the marinade over each portion. Serve a well-chilled Vinho Verde with this dish.

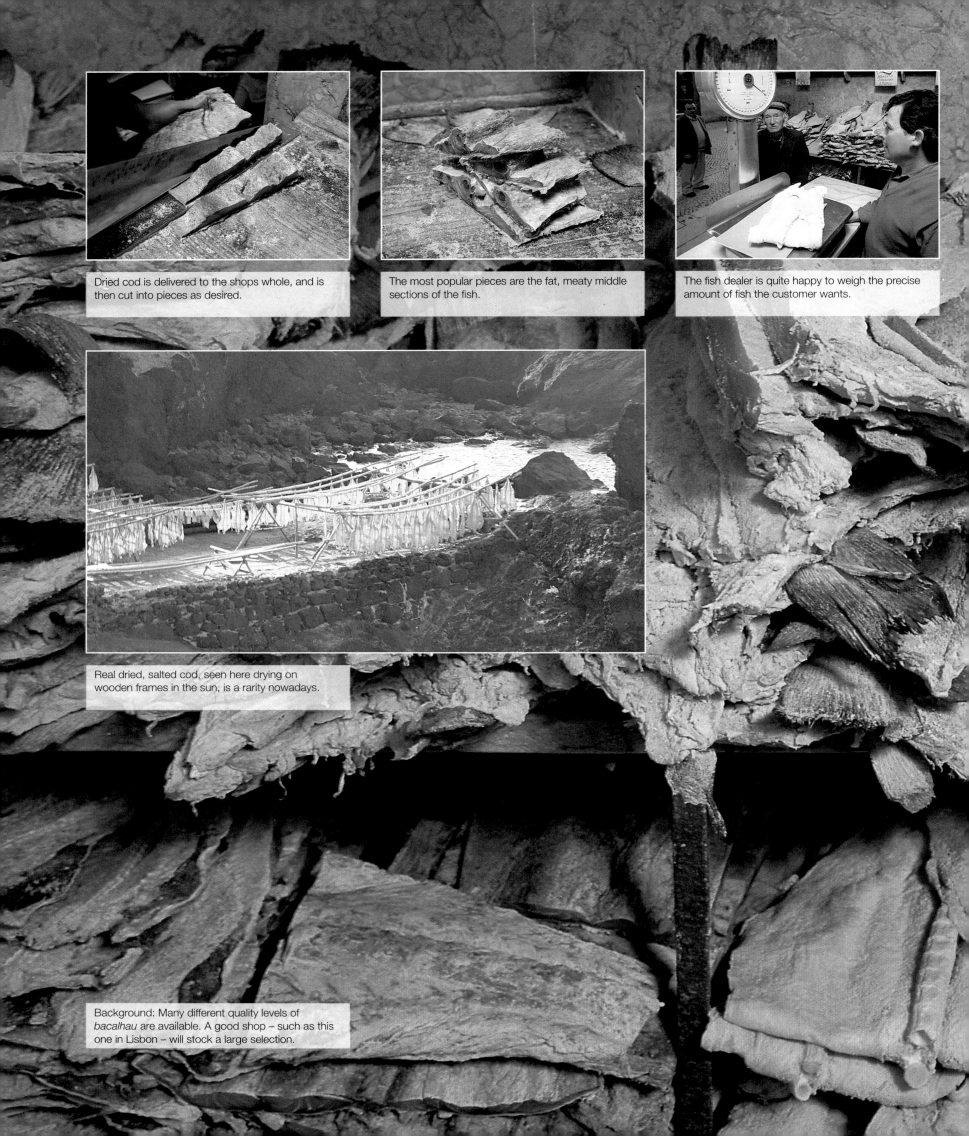

Dried cod is delivered to the shops whole, and is then cut into pieces as desired.

The most popular pieces are the fat, meaty middle sections of the fish.

The fish dealer is quite happy to weigh the precise amount of fish the customer wants.

Real dried, salted cod, seen here drying on wooden frames in the sun, is a rarity nowadays.

Background: Many different quality levels of *bacalhau* are available. A good shop – such as this one in Lisbon – will stock a large selection.

Bacalhau

Columbus had scarcely discovered America when the first Portuguese fishermen were already sailing into the waters of Terranova, Newfoundland, to catch cod (*bacalhau*) and related species. They processed their catches every day, cutting off the heads of the fish, removing the spines and fishbones, and then salting them. This preserved the fish and prevented it going bad, and ships were able to remain off the Atlantic coast of Canada as long as it took to process a full cargo. The salted cod was not dried in the sun until the return home to Portugal.

Less than a decade after America had been discovered, dried salted cod made up a tenth of the total fish sold in northern Portuguese harbors. It was a particularly important commodity at the time, as it was used as provisions on board ships setting off on voyages of trade and discovery. To this day, Portuguese ships continue to leave port in order to catch cod and similar fish and process them on board.

Nowadays, however, a considerable amount of the dried salted cod eaten in Portugal is imported from Norway, England, and Canada.

Bacalhau is normally sold whole in Portugal (although dried cod, unlike dried salted cod, is dried immediately and not salted, the term "dried cod" has come to be used for both dried and salted cod):

• *Especial* is the name given to the biggest, heaviest and best pieces, weighing about eleven pounds (5 kg)
• *Graúdo* is a thinner piece
• *Lombo* or *meio* is the name given to the much sought-after fat middle pieces
• *Barbatanas* are the fins, which are good value for money and can also be used to prepare some excellent meals.

The first thing that needs to be done, before any of the numerous recipes are attempted, is to get rid of the salt in the fish. Dried cod needs to be soaked in cold water – best of all in the fridge – for at least twenty-four hours to remove the salt. The water will need changing about four or five times during this period, although the time needed can vary according to the thickness of the pieces. Very thin pieces may only need twelve hours, whereas thirty-six hours may be needed for thick pieces. If not enough salt has been soaked out of the fish, it will spoil the taste of any dish cooked with it; if it has been soaked for too long, the fish becomes insipid and tasteless. The clearest indication of whether the fish is ready is usually the condition of the last change of water. Fresh cod is seldom used in Portugal.

Bacalhau com Natas
Dried Cod and Cream

1 lb 10 oz (750 g) dried cod	
1 lb (500 g) potatoes	
5 Tbs olive oil	
3 onions	
Black pepper	
1¹/₂ oz (40 g) butter	
2 Tbs flour	
3 cups (600 ml) milk	
1¹/₂ cups (300 ml) light cream	
1 bay leaf	

Soak the cod in cold water for 24 hours, changing the water regularly. Drain the fish, skin and bone it and pull the flesh apart into small pieces. Peel the potatoes, cut them into thin slices and fry them in 3 tablespoons of olive oil until they are golden brown; dry them on paper towels.
Peel the onions and cut them into rings; fry them in the rest of the olive oil. Add the pieces of fish and season with pepper.
Pre-heat the oven to 350 °F (180 °C).
Melt the butter, stir in the flour, and add the milk slowly whilst stirring. Bring to the boil, then remove from the heat and stir in the cream.
Place the dried cod and onions into an ovenproof dish and cover with the fried potatoes. Pour the cream sauce over the top and add the bay leaf. Cook in the oven for 30 minutes and serve immediately.

Bolinhos de Bacalhau
Dried Cod Rissoles
(Illustrated on p. 489)

10 oz (300 g) dried cod	
9 oz (250 g) mealy potatoes	
1 onion	
2 garlic cloves	
2 Tbs finely chopped flat leaf parsley	
1 pinch cayenne pepper	
1 pinch nutmeg	
4 eggs	
Salt, black pepper	
Olive oil for frying	

Soak the dried cod in cold water for 24 hours, changing the water regularly. Place the cod into a pan, pour on boiling water and cook gently for 10 minutes. Take fish out of the pan and remove the skin and bones. Pull the flesh apart into small pieces and mince it. Boil the potatoes in their jackets, then peel and mash them.
Peel the onion and garlic, chop them finely and place them in a bowl together with the parsley, spices, potato, and dried cod purée. Mix well, then slowly add the eggs and season with salt and pepper to taste.
Use two tablespoons (dip them into cold water before use each time) to make the dough into oval balls, and fry them in hot oil. The rissoles can be served cold as *petiscos* or warm, with a salad, as a main course.
Vinho Verde goes very well with *bacalhau* dishes.

Fish and Shellfish

Portugal is a paradise for people who love fish. This has nothing to do either with the numerous ways of preparing dried cod or the abundance of sardines, one of the very best of fresh fish. Rather, it is due to the large number and excellent quality of fish, shellfish and crustaceans on offer, a fact that has led to the great popularity of Portugal amongst experts throughout Europe. Many of the sea bass and red mullet served in the best restaurants in France, Italy, and Germany will have been caught in Portuguese waters.

Although some types of fish, such as gilt head bream, are missing, as almost all of them end up on French tables, the huge variety on offer along Portugal's coastline is overwhelming. The better restaurants display fish nestling on ice underneath glass panes. Diners choose the individual fish that they want and also say how they want it to be prepared:

- assado na brasa · · · · broiled over charcoal
- assado no forno · · · · oven-baked
- cozido · · · · · · · · · boiled
- frito (na frigideira) · · pan-fried
- frito (na fritadeira) · · deep-fried
- grelhado · · · · · · · · broiled
- guisado · · · · · · · · · steamed

The bill is worked out according to the cost of the fish per kilogram. Potatoes, rice, salad or vegetables are usually included in the price.

Pescada, or hake, used to be good value for money, but because it is so good and popular it has become one of the most expensive fish. Any hake that is on offer cheaply is certain to have been deep-frozen. The Algarve is famous for its mussels, and its coastal waters are an El Dorado for crustaceans. Near to Lisbon, places with a good reputation as regards the quality of their crustaceans include Sesimbra, Setúbal, Cascais, and Ericeira.

Further north are Portugal's two largest fishing ports, Peniche and Matosinhos near Oporto. Long sandy beaches mean that most of the former fishing communities in the north have turned into tourist resorts. Northern Portugal is also famous for its fresh water fish. The eel-like lamprey has only survived in Europe's cleanest rivers, and as a result has become an expensive specialty; gourmets travel up to 250 miles north from the capital at weekends, just in order to enjoy a dish of *lampreia à bordelesa*, lamprey in red wine.

Robalo – sea bass

Pescada – hake

Tamboril – angler fish

Faneca – poor cod

Peixe-galo – John Dory

Pargo – sea bream

Corvina – meagre

Salmoneta – red mullet

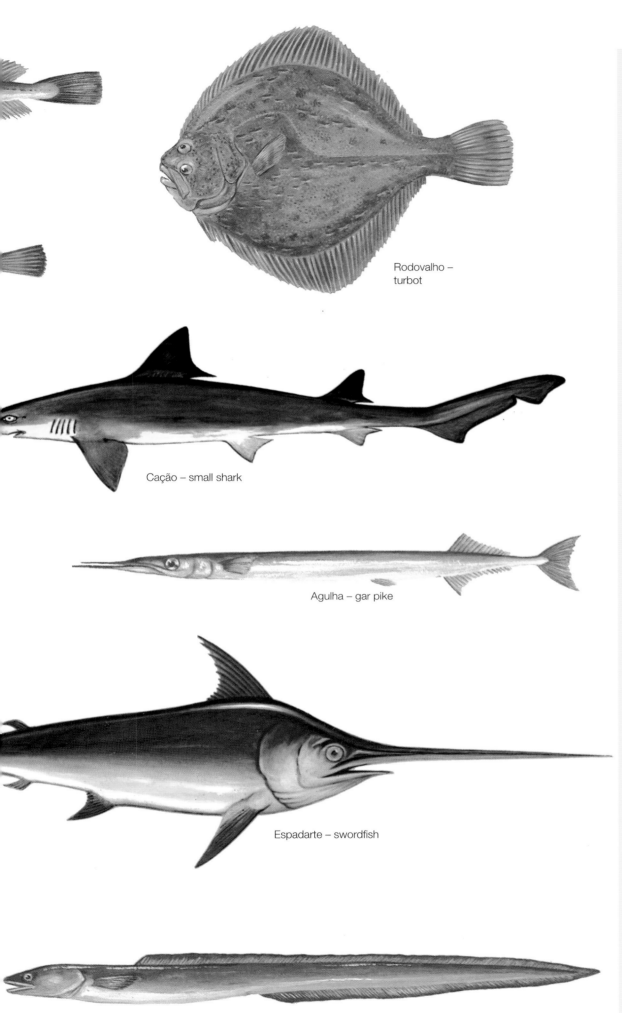

Rodovalho – turbot

Cação – small shark

Agulha – gar pike

Espadarte – swordfish

Congro, safio – sea eel

Found in Portuguese Waters

Amêijoas – Venus'-shell; served either on its own, or as part of a variety of fish, and even meat, dishes
Berbigão – heart-shell, cockle; cheap; often spiced as a *petisco* or hors d'œuvre
Besugo, goraz – grey bass; fine flavor, still affordable
Búzios – whelks; especially popular in the Algarve
Cabras cegas – very small variety of crab; rare, delicate and expensive
Cação – type of small shark; important ingredient of *caldeiradas*, fish stews
Camaroes de costa – small shrimps; much sought-after and fairly expensive; used in pastries
Carapau – saurel; similar to mackerel; like sardines, is cheap and tasty, served grilled with potatoes
Cherne – grouper, together with sea bass and turbot Portugal's most valuable fish; main fishing grounds off Lisbon and the Algarve
Choco – cuttlefish; normally broiled or fried; often served in its own ink
Choquinhos – small cuttlefish; sometimes served as *petiscos*
Congro, safio – sea eel; used in stews
Corvina – meagre; used to be cheap, but now is more highly prized; tasty, usually about 2 foot (60 cm) long
Dourada – gild head bream; excellent, delicious fish, most of which is exported
Enguias – eels; much sought-after; famous in Aveiro; used mainly in *caldeirada de enguias*
Espadarte – sword fish; usually smoked
Faneca – poor cod; cheap; quite tasty flesh, normally steamed
Gamba – large shrimp; very popular, frequently imported
Lampreia – lamprey; found in northern Portugal's rivers; rare, delicious, and very expensive
Lavagante – lobster; increasingly rare; annual catch just five tonnes
Lagosta – crayfish; high quality; Ericeira near Lisbon is famous for its crayfish
Lagostim – Norway lobster; mainly caught off the Algarve; frequently more expensive than crayfish
Linguado – sole; broiled or fried in butter
Lula – calmar (type of squid); rarer than octopus or squid; prepared in a number of different ways; sometimes stuffed
Navalheira, caraguejo – small types of crab
Pargo – sea bream; slightly red body; delicate flavor; classic method of preparation is to bake it
Peixe-espada preta – ribbon fish; only broiled or fried; very tasty, and relatively cheap
Peixe-galo – John Dory; excellent; very rare, and therefore exported
Perceves – goose barnacle; delicious, and increasingly rare, therefore expensive
Pescada – hake; very popular
Polvo – octopus; excellent in a salad with *molho verde*, a herb vinaigrette
Robalo – sea bass of exceptional quality; from Portugal's northern Atlantic coast
Rodovalho – turbot; excellent quality; mainly exported
Salmoneta – red mullet; normally broiled; mainly found in Setúbal and along the Algarve
Santola – spider crab; excellent quality; found north-west of Lisbon
Sável – sea saibling; very fine fish, which like the lamprey swims from the sea up rivers
Tamboril – angler fish; used to be used in fish stews; often used in seafood rice dishes or roasted on the spit; has become fashionable over the last few years and is expensive
Truta – trout; it is frequently wild trout that are caught in northern Portugal

Meat

There are two particularly remarkable circumstances that turn Portuguese meat dishes into both a culinary adventure and an exceptional pleasure. The first is that the unbroken tradition of shepherding and hill farming means that old breeds have remained unchanged, something which is regrettably the exception rather than the rule in modern Europe. Secondly, Portugal's countryside, climate and former political conditions have combined to produce a poor country, whose inhabitants nonetheless know how to conjure up a delicious meal out of low quality cuts of meat. The cuts used range from variety meats and blood to feet and ears, as well as old hens, goats, and mutton. Many of the favorites such as *ranchos*, stews with chick-peas, *feijoadas*, bean stews, and *ensopados*, thick ragouts, owe their intense flavors to these ingredients.

The Portuguese use a special term that proves that they have a special attitude towards stock-breeding and the production of meat, especially where their *to inhos* or cattle are concerned. This term is *solar*, and is used to describe the quality of meat much as the French would use the term *terroir* to talk about wine. *Solar* encompasses all the natural factors that combine in the proper raising of an animal, all of which will have a very specific effect on the quality of the meat. These factors are not simply a matter of the animal's breed, but of the biosphere, climate, vegetation, and feed, to name but a few. The special quality of Portuguese beef was already recognized last century. England, in particular, imported *Barrosão* cattle, and Londoners considered them to be the ultimate in beef. Fortunately, there is still widespread knowledge and respect of the achievements of these traditional agricultural methods in Portugal. The *Denominação de Origem* (DO) quality mark has not just been restricted to certain varieties of cheese, but has also been given to several old, valuable breeds.

Portuguese Breeds Bearing the *Denominação de Origem* (DO) Quality Mark

Vaca – beef

Alentejana
Alentejo breed; best-known Portuguese cattle breed which produces first-class beef

Arouquesa
Old breed from northern Portugal; small animals, up to 600 lbs (300 kg) when fully grown

Barrosão
Famous breed of cattle; current numbers 5,000–6,000; widely exported to England in the 19th century

Cachena
Very small, rare breed found in the mountains near Arcos de Valdevez in northern Minho; numbers around 200 at present; weigh about 300 lbs (150 kg) when fully grown; high fat levels in milk

Marinhoa
Rare, exquisite breed from the Bairrada region

Maronês
Rare, excellent breed from northern Portugal

Mertolenga
Found mainly in Alentejo; small animals; rare

Mirandesa
Small cattle from northern Portugal, which produce little beef

Borrego – lamb
Terrincho
Lambs of the Churra de Terra Quente breed from Trás-os-Montes, which are normally slaughtered when they reach a weight of about 24 pounds (12 kg)

Serra da Estrela
Sheep of the adapted Bordaleira breed, which produce the best cheese

Cabrito – kid
Cabrito Serrano Transmontano
The kids born of the goats whose milk is used to produce the well-known goatsmilk cheeses

Cordeiro Bragançano
Kids of both sexes of the northern Portuguese breed of Churra Galego Bragançano, which are slaughtered when aged three to four months

Other breeds were given an *Indicação Geográfica*, a lower award than the DO.

Ensopado de Borrego
Lamb Ragout
(Illustration)

Serves 8

4 lbs (2 kg) lamb
1/2 cup (100 ml) olive oil
5 garlic cloves
Salt, black pepper
3 onions
1 Tbs ground paprika
2 bay leaves
1 Tbs white wine vinegar
1 1/4 cups (250 ml) dry white wine
2 1/2 cups (500 ml) bouillon
8 thin slices of light sourdough bread

Cut the lamb into large pieces (each about 2 oz or 50 g). Peel the garlic and chop it finely. Put the meat and garlic together with the olive oil into a large pan, season with salt and pepper, and turn the heat on.
Peel and chop the onions and add them to the meat once it has been browned gently all over. Sprinkle on the paprika, add the bay leaves, vinegar and wine and half the bouillon. Stir and simmer the meat for about 30 minutes. Then stir again and add the remaining stock. Simmer for a further 20–30 minutes and season with salt and pepper to taste.
Put one thin slice of sourdough bread into the bottom of each of eight deep plates. Place the pieces of lamb on top and pour over the thin meat sauce. A young Alentejo red wine goes very well with this dish.

Bife à café – Steak served in the style of Lisbon's cafés

Ensopado de borrego – Lamb ragout

Bife à Café
Steak Served in the Style of Lisbon's Cafés
(Illustration)

Serves 1

1¹/₂ oz (40 g) butter
1 steak about 7 oz (200 g)
Coarse sea salt, black pepper
1 Tbs potato flour
3 Tbs milk
1 Tbs mustard
A few drops of lemon juice

Heat half the butter in a heavy-based frying pan. Quickly brown the meat on both sides and season with salt and pepper.
Reduce the heat. Mix the potato flour and milk and add to the meat with the remaining butter, stir thoroughly and continue to simmer according to preference. Finally, stir the mustard and lemon juice into the sauce. Serve with home-made french fries. A red Reserva wine from the Douro goes well with this meal.

Iscas com Elas
Marinated Calf's Liver
(Illustration)

Serves 3–4

1 lb (500 g) calf's liver
2 garlic cloves
Salt, white pepper
1 bay leaf
1 Tbs white wine vinegar
¹/₂ cup (100 ml) dry white wine
1 lb (500 g) potatoes
1¹/₂ oz (40 g) pork fat
1 Tbs coarsely chopped flat leaf parsley

Cut the liver into very thin slices and spread out on a large plate (not metal). Chop the garlic finely and sprinkle it over the liver, and season with salt and pepper. Add the bay leaf and pour the vinegar and wine over the liver. Marinate for at least two hours, preferably overnight, turning the slices of liver occasionally.
Boil the potatoes in their skins, peel and slice them. Heat the pork fat in a frying pan and add the liver slices (without draining them). Brown them briefly on both sides and remove immediately.
Take the bay leaf out of the marinade, add the marinade to the frying pan and boil it down. Dip the liver slices in the resulting sauce and arrange on a pre-heated plate. Coat the potato slices in the remaining sauce and arrange around the liver. Sprinkle on the parsley and serve with a red Dão.

Meat Glossary

Boi – ox
Borrego – lamb
Cabrito – goat
Carneiro – mutton
Codornizes – quail; popular either as *petiscos* or broiled as a main course
Coelho – rabbit; in the north, in particular, of high quality and prepared in many different ways
Frango do campo – free-range chicken
Galo – cockerel; if this is on the menu, it will be the genuine article
Galinha do campo – free-range hen; usually bought from small farms
Ganso – goose; not frequently eaten
Javali – boar; excellent quality, usually braised
Leitão – sucking pig; very popular dish
Novilho – young cow; not older than 30 months, and not weighing more than 650 pounds (300 kg)
Pato – duck; rare, but famous served with rice as *arroz de pato*
Perdiz – partridge; expensive, first-class game often served in top restaurants
Peru – turkey; the typical Portuguese Christmas dinner
Vaca – cow, beef
Vitela – veal from a calf aged between six and nine months, weighing about 300 pounds (150 kg)

Iscas com elas – Marinated calf's liver

Sausages and Ham

Pigs are an extremely important resource in Portugal. For centuries they have formed a fundamental part of people's nutrition, whether living in the mountainous regions of the north or the hot plains of the south. They were not just kept in a big way on farming estates or guarded by herdsmen in the forests of cork oaks. Nearly every family living in the country kept one or two pigs for its personal use. Methods of preserving pork by salting and smoking were passed on from generation to generation.

While Portugal has restricted itself to the paprika sausages and black pudding that are traditionally produced throughout the Iberian peninsula, there are an immense number of regional specialties. Sausages are even occasionally still home made. One example is Barrancos, a small enclave on the eastern edge of the Alentejo, where it juts into Spain. Pedigree black pigs are bred here, and the best hams and sausages in Portugal are made with their meat. It was not, however, until a group of producers got together that this produce was made more widely available, and is available bearing the "*Casa do Porco Preto*" trademark. The Portalegre region in northern Alentejo is also well known for its sausages, and black pigs, which they call *porco alentejano*, are enjoying something of a renaissance there.

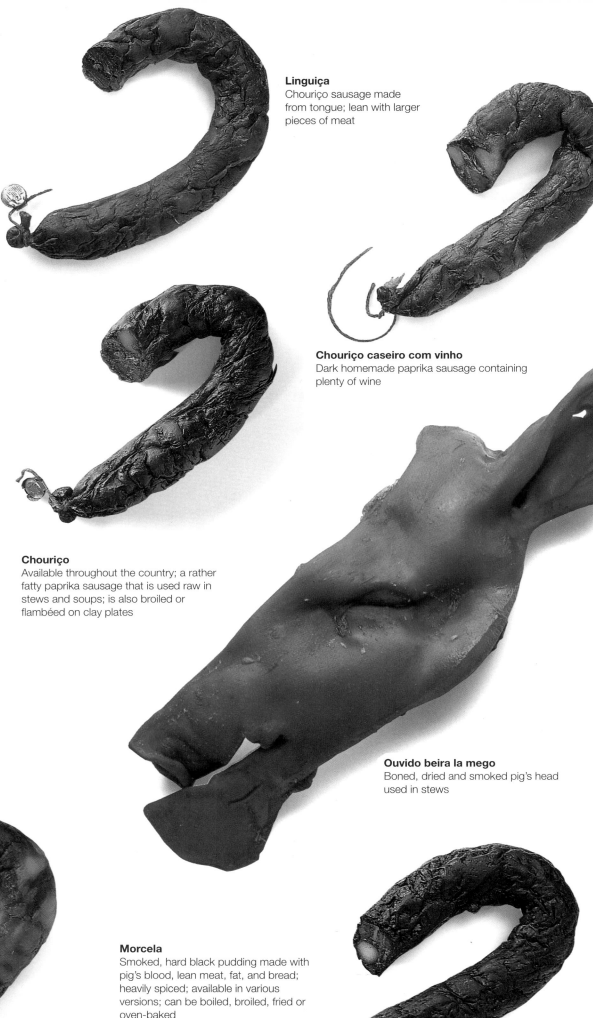

Linguiça
Chouriço sausage made from tongue; lean with larger pieces of meat

Chouriço caseiro com vinho
Dark homemade paprika sausage containing plenty of wine

Chouriço
Available throughout the country; a rather fatty paprika sausage that is used raw in stews and soups; is also broiled or flambéed on clay plates

Ouvido beira la mego
Boned, dried and smoked pig's head used in stews

Chouriço caseiro
Pale homemade paprika sausage

Morcela
Smoked, hard black pudding made with pig's blood, lean meat, fat, and bread; heavily spiced; available in various versions; can be boiled, broiled, fried or oven-baked

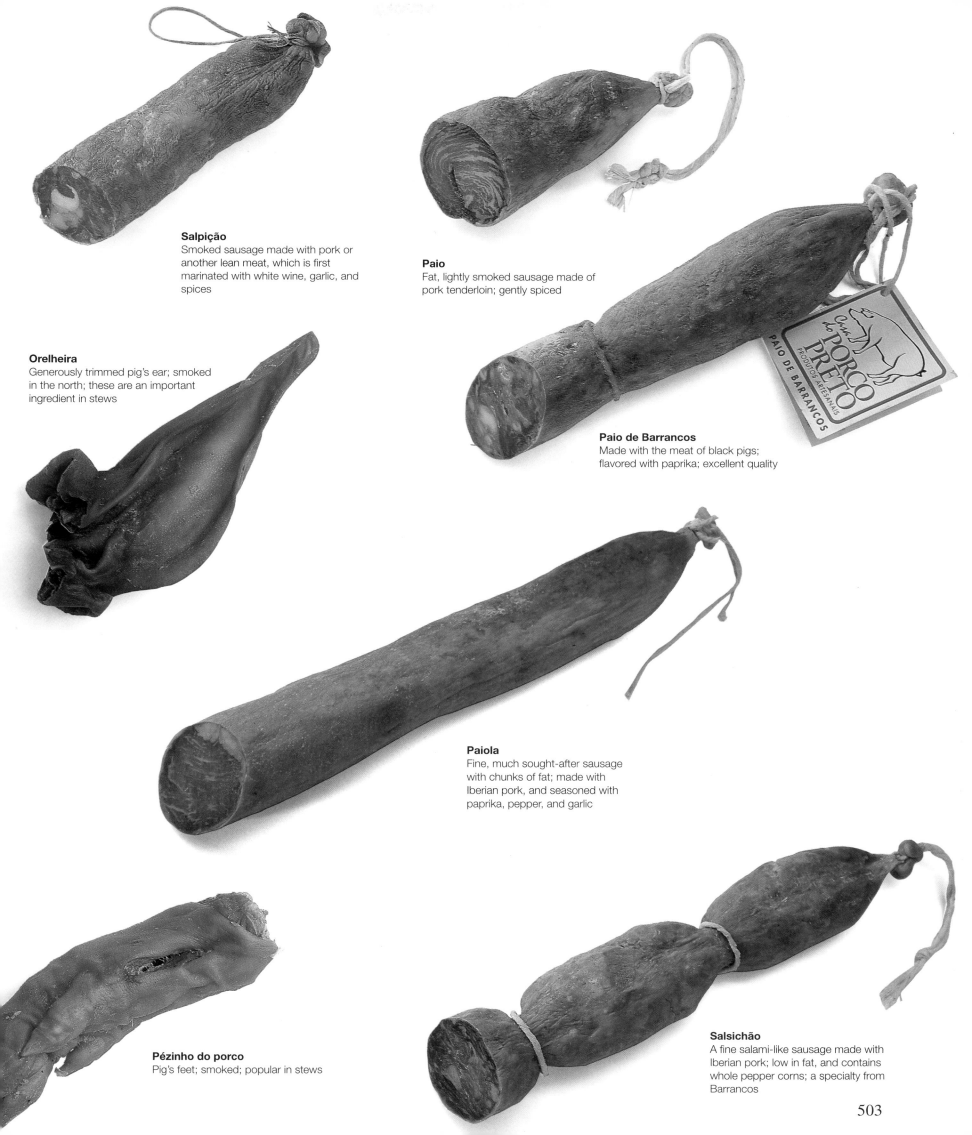

Salpição
Smoked sausage made with pork or another lean meat, which is first marinated with white wine, garlic, and spices

Paio
Fat, lightly smoked sausage made of pork tenderloin; gently spiced

Orelheira
Generously trimmed pig's ear; smoked in the north; these are an important ingredient in stews

Paio de Barrancos
Made with the meat of black pigs; flavored with paprika; excellent quality

Paiola
Fine, much sought-after sausage with chunks of fat; made with Iberian pork, and seasoned with paprika, pepper, and garlic

Pézinho do porco
Pig's feet; smoked; popular in stews

Salsichão
A fine salami-like sausage made with Iberian pork; low in fat, and contains whole pepper corns; a specialty from Barrancos

503

Bread

Bread, *pão*, is an essential food in Portugal. There is scarcely a country in southern Europe that has such a robust, even archaic type of bread as Portugal. Its importance is unchallenged, even though nearly every meal is served with either potatoes and/or rice. *Pão caseiro*, the classic, home-made bread, is utterly delicious. It is easy to find in the countryside, and in the towns it can be found if one follows signs or notices labelled *pão cozido na lenha*. In this case the verb *cozer*, or cook, actually means "bake," and *lenha* is firewood. Breads baked in ovens heated with pine logs produce the most delicate aromas.

Wheat is not the only flour used for bread dough; other mixtures include variably high proportions of rye flour. Yeast, natural sourdough, or both, are used as raising agents. Bakers go to great pains to knead the dough thoroughly by hand. The high temperatures in the wood-fired ovens mean

Above: *Pão*, Portuguese bread, can be seen as a symbol of the original way of cooking – whether it be *pão caseiro*, home-made bread, which appears in many different forms, *broa de avintes*, a small, tall and very compact loaf (in paper) or *broa de milho* (sliced).

that the resulting bread is very crusty. In Minho, the region where Vinho Verde is produced, they bake *broa de milho*, a yellow bread with a large proportion of corn flour, which is served with *Caldo verde*, the famous green soup. Each village has its own recipe. *Broa de a intes* has a singular shape, which has earned it a special position – it looks like a small, domed tower. The dough, which contains honey, is black. It is cut into thin slices and its distinctive taste means that it is goes very well with sausage and ham.

Piri-Piri is a condime made out of red pep that is available throughout Portugal

Olive Oil

The Portuguese love their olive oil. It is not only used copiously for frying and steaming, but is also frequently drizzled onto the finished dish, in particular fish and vegetables. It is believed that olives were pressed for their oil in Portugal before the Romans. During their rule, and subsequently that of the Moors, the olive orchards spread. Later, the Knights Templar encouraged oil production by building presses. The ground beneath the trees was usually used in some other way. Even today, every other orchard still produces a second crop, such as wheat, potatoes, corn and cabbage.

In Portugal as a whole, a total of 316,000 hectares are planted with olive trees, cared for by some 190,000 farmers. There are about thirty varieties altogether. About three-quarters of the fifty million trees are extremely old. The majority, which grow in mountainous areas, are left to fend for themselves and are harvested by hand.

The most important areas for the production of *azeites extra irgem* bearing the designation of origin, or *Denominação de Origem* (DO), are:
- Trás-os-Montes – comes from the Douro valley, where the grapes for port are grown; a high quality, light and very fine olive oil. Scent of fresh olives and herbs; very fruity taste
- Beira Alta and Beira Baixa or Beira Interior – eastern regions south of the Douro; includes the wine regions of Pinhel and Castelo Rodrigo; usually a greenish-yellow, very aromatic and fruity oil
- Ribatejo – grown in the Ribatejo wine region; this is a famous area on the banks of the River Tagus with a highly regarded quality oil; low production; golden color, somewhat viscous; very fruity
- Norte Alentejo – the northern Alentejo, including the wine regions of Portalegre, Borba, and Redondo; includes plantations of more modern, standard varieties; more viscous; strong flavor
- Moura – communities near the town of Moura and the Serpa regions, as well as the wine region of Granja in southern Alentejo; made using the varieties Galega and Verdeal; greenish-yellow, with an intense aroma of olives; delicate bitter flavor.

Piri-Piri and other spices

Piri-Piri, which are very sharp, small red peppers from Angola, is one of the most popular spices in Portugal. At first tiny Malagueta pods were used, and these are still grown in many gardens. Piri-Piri is particularly popular with shellfish, and is also used with poultry, stews, and marinades. It is also diced finely and mixed with olive oil, vinegar, and coarse sea salt, to be used as a condiment at the table. This is available ready-made in shops (see illustration left).

Due to Portugal's long history as a colonial power, the Portuguese have developed a taste for exotic flavors. *Caril*, curry, is used frequently, though sparingly. *Canela*, cinnamon, is used in desserts and cakes instead of vanilla. The favorite herb is *coentros*, fresh cilantro leaves, but *hortelã*, mint, *louro*, bay leaves, *oregão*, oregano, and *salsa*, flat leaf parsley, are also popular. Meat dishes are seasoned with *nozmoscada*, nutmeg, *cominho*, cumin, and/or *cravinho*, cloves. Needless to say, *alho*, garlic, is also much used.

Gallo-Azeite Novo-Colheita: vintage oil; olive oil is at its most aromatic when young

Romeu, Casa Menéres: a well-known family estate that produces oil from organically cultivated olive groves

Moura, Cooperativa Agricola de Moura e Barrancos: a *virgem extra especial* from the Alentejo

Vilaflor: This is the trade name of a fine oil with just 0.5° acidity

Santa Rosa: from the best olive region, Terra Quente, a premium oil refined using traditional methods

Quinta Domoste: a more popular quality level with 0.7° acidity, which is produced by a single estate

Portugal's hand-made cheeses are a culinary treasure. The milk is frequently curdled using a type of thistle; three examples are the ripe, mild Amarelo (top left), the pure sheep's milk cheese Ovelheira (top right), both from the Castelo Branco region, and the semi-hard cheese from Nisa in northern Alentejo (below right). Queijo da Serra Estrela (below left) is a famous mountain cheese which is marvelously fine, spicy, and runny at the *amanteigado* stage and can be eaten with a spoon.

Cheese

Cheese that is made by hand using unpasteurized milk is experiencing something of a comeback in Portugal. This centuries-old tradition had been threatened by standardized mass production, but in 1985 it was protected by the awarding of ten designations of origin. Just a few years ago these cheeses were almost impossible to find. They were at best available from regional market stalls or the few exceptionally well-stocked *charcutarias*, Lisbon's delicatessen shops. Nowadays, supermarket chains such as Pingo Doce and Continente hold a cheese festival or *Feira de Queijo* when the cheese is at its best and most plentiful in March. For two to three weeks, up to fifty different varieties of cheese are on offer, affording a comfortable and delicious glimpse into a world of cheese. Pure sheep's milk cheese is the most highly prized. But no matter what the specific qualities of their regions, all these cheeses have an incomparable, home-made character.

Types of Portuguese Cheese

Azeitão
A famous sheep's milk cheese from the Arrábida mountains near Setúbal; a rarity made by four producers; curdled using a fermentation from a special variety of thistle; at its best between January and April, later on sale as *amanteigado*, a runny soft cheese; weight 4 to 9 ounces (100–250 g).

Cabreiro
Goat's milk cheese and cheese containing a proportion of goat's milk from Castelo Branco and Beira Baixa; a very popular soft, salty fresh goats' milk cheese which is a regional specialty; mature and pungent.

Evora
Sheep's milk cheese from the Alentejo; usually sold as a firm and tart miniature weighing 2 to 3 ounces (60–90 g); popular snack for laborers; also available up to 10 ounces (300 g), as a fresh, soft, and lightly salted cheese.

Nisa
A semi-hard sheep's milk cheese from northern Alentejo; curdled using *cardo*, a type of thistle; weighs either 7 to 14 ounces (200–400 g) or 1 lb 12 oz to 3lbs (800–1,300 g).

Ovelheira slang name for Queijo de Ovelha
Mature, pure sheep's milk cheese from the communities around Castelo Branco and neighboring regions of Beira Baixa; hard rind; spicy flavor; used for grating.

Queijo amarelo da Beira Baixa
Dark yellow cheese; either pure sheep's milk, or mixed with goats' milk; mature, but mild, buttery, with an intense flavor.

Queijo da Ilha or São Jorge
The only named pressed, crumbly cows' milk cheese in Portugal; comes from the Azores; bears the DO mark as an untreated milk product; cylindrical shape; weighs $17\frac{1}{2}$ to $26\frac{1}{2}$ pounds (8–12 kg); either very spicy or mild; often grated.

Queijo da Serra Estrela or Queijo da Serra
The king of sheep's milk cheeses; comes from the plateau which rises to a height of nearly $1\frac{1}{4}$ miles (2,000 m); mountain cheese made using the milk of Bordaleira sheep; weighs 2 to $3\frac{3}{4}$ pounds (1–$1\frac{1}{2}$ kg) – sold as *amanteigado*, buttery, with a fine, creamy texture, gentle spiciness and acidity; runny, held together in linen, and often eaten with a spoon – *meio-curado*, available semi-mature from May onwards, firm enough to cut – and as *curado*, mature, after one year, with an intense flavor but keeping its creamy taste.

Queijo de cabra Serrano Transmontano
Very hard goat's milk cheese from northern Portugal, made from the milk of a local breed of goats; weighs 1 lb 5 oz to 2 lbs (600–900 g); not well known. The term *cabras* is also used for fresh goats' cheese, which is especially popular in Alentejo.

Queijo de Castelo Branco
Sheep's milk cheese from the Serra Estrela region; curdled using *cardo*, a type of thistle; usually sold semi-mature, or *meio-curado*; medium soft to medium hard; also sold mature, when it is firm and used for grating.

Queijo picante da Beira Baixa
Hard or medium hard mixed milk cheese; as the name suggests, tastes sharp and spicy; frequently rather salty; weighs 14 oz to 2 lb 4 oz (400–1,000 g).

Rabaçal
Produced south of Coimbra; about 80 percent sheep's and 20 percent goats' milk; curdled using goat rennin; weighs 11 oz to 1 lb 2 oz (300–500 g); at its best medium soft in March and April; pleasantly sharp.

Serpa
Pure sheep's milk cheese from the area around the town of Serpa in Baixo Alentejo; made using the milk from Merino ewes; sold in all manner of forms, usually weighing 3 to $4\frac{1}{2}$ pounds ($1\frac{1}{2}$–2 kg), though also as *merendeira* at about 8 ounces (250 g); available from January through April in a runny, soft form, *amanteigado*; also popular *meio-curado*, semi-mature, and *curado*, firm; complex, striking yet creamy flavor; white woollen cloths are used in the production process.

Terrincho
Creamy, white cheese from Trás-os-Montes; made solely from the milk of the Churra da Terra Quente breed; weighs $1\frac{3}{4}$ to $2\frac{3}{4}$ pounds (800–1200 g).

Sweets and Cakes

The Portuguese have a sweet tooth. There is no other area of culinary specialties that they worked and continue to work on with such an abundance of enthusiasm and inventiveness as *doces*, sweets. There are endless variations on the basic theme of egg yolks and sugar. There was a practical reason for using egg yolks and sugar so frequently: yolks were leftovers, in a manner of speaking, as egg white was needed in large amounts to clarify red wine and to brush on the rigging of sailing ships.

The art of making sweet things originated in the convents distributed right across the country. Nuns continually conjured up new delicacies, either in order to win over prominent clerical or secular figures on behalf on their convents, or simply in order to sweeten their own rigidly-controlled convent lives. When the monasteries were dissolved, the recipes, which were often many hundreds of years old, were passed on to lay people. In addition, families guarded the secrets of their sweets over generations, until they were firmly established as local specialties. Nearly every town and many villages base their culinary pride on special *doces de o os*, sweets

made with eggs, which they alone make and which can only be bought and enjoyed in their communities.

The Portuguese way of getting to know a new place is to go into the local *pastelaria*, which is the cake shop. The place is judged by its sweets and cakes, and the sense of touch is just as important to their enjoyment as taste. The body and texture of the dough, case as well as filling give rise to sensations of lightness or weight. Some Lisbon cafés attract customers by displaying small cakes bearing regional names. They are

delivered fresh every day, from all over the country, for no baker would be able to copy these labor-intensive regional masterpieces. Quite apart from that, many recipes are still closely-guarded secrets, though every traditional Portuguese cookbook devotes more space to *doces* than anything else.

Apart from the countless *doces de o os*, another firm favorite is *pudim*, or pudding. It is one of the indicators of the standard of a restaurant – whether it be a simple *pudim flan* with caramel sauce, a *pudim de leite* with caramelized

sugar and sometimes lemon, or a *pudim de abóbora*, with orange-coloured pumpkin, *de limão*, lemons, or *de laranja*, oranges.

One favorite is *pudim de amêndoa*, almond pudding, and another which is common in northern Portugal is *pudim do abade de priscos*, with smoked bacon, cinnamon, lemon peel, and port. The gently sweetened *arroz doce*, milk pudding, is usually served in clay bowls, and the straightforward *leite creme*, a cream made with milk, egg yolk, sugar, and grated lemon peel, is every bit as popular as *pudim flan*. In many regions there are

sweet *broas*, bread-like cakes made with corn meal. On Madeira, a very rich *bolo de mel* is baked using spices, nuts, dried fruits, and Madeira. Seasonal specialties include the light *pão de ló*, which is served in many different forms throughout the country at Easter, and *bolo rei*, or king's cake, which is made at Christmas. It is considered lucky to find a broad bean, toy or piece of jewellery, in amongst the dried fruits and nuts of this yeast cake; however, whoever finds it has to give everyone else at the table a king's cake next year.

Cakes and Pastries
Numbers in brackets refer to the picture on the left.

Bolinhos de amêndoa
Small almond cake; many variations

Bolo de coco
Small coconut cakes

Dom Rodrigo
Algarve specialty; made with egg yolk and ground almonds

Morgado
Made with egg yolk, sugar, almonds and occasionally figs; Algarve specialty

Ovos moles (1, 2)
Aveiro specialty; a mixture of egg yolks, sugar, and sometimes rice and sugar, is filled into rice paper; a variety of forms are produced, such as shells, snails, fish, barrels, and these are sold in cardboard boxes; the mixture is also sold plain, from 4 ounces to several pounds (100 g–1 kg), in painted wooden boxes

Papos de anjo
"Angels' stomachs," shapes made using an egg yolk and sugar dough, covered with syrup or jam

Pastel de nata (5)
Light, flaky pastry case filled with a pudding made of eggs, cream and sugar; in Lisbon they are called *pastel de Belem* after a part of the town; this is where, centuries ago, these cakes were invented in the famous Jerónimo monastery

Pastéis de brasão (9)
"Coat of arms" cakes; trademark used by a pastelaria for its *pastéis de feijão*, bean pastries

Pastéis de cenoura (4)
Pastry with a filling of carrots, eggs, sugar, and sometimes nuts

Pastéis de feijão (3)
Small cakes made with white beans; famous in Torres Vedras near Lisbon, where almonds are added

Pastéis de grão
Small cakes made with chick pea flour

Pastéis de laranja (7)
Small short-crust pastries; the egg and sugar filling is flavored with orange peel

Pastéis de Santa Clara or de Tentugal
Famous, oblong cakes with a thin, transparent case, filled with *oves moles*, rice; when eaten, crackle like paper

Pinhoadas
Slices of pine kernels, bound with honey, sugar, and butter; a specialty from Alcácer do Sal in Alentejo

Queijadas
Small cakes made with fresh cheese and egg yolk; in the area around Lisbon there are marvelous *queijadas de sintra* with chopped almonds, coconut, and cinnamon

Rabanadas
Fried rolls or bread slices, which are dipped in milk, eggs, sugar, honey, lemon peel, and wine

Tarte de amêndoa (8)
Small tarts covered with almond pieces

Tigeladas (6)
Light, fluffy, thick, pancake-like pudding made with milk, eggs, sugar, and then baked in a clay dish in the oven

Toucinho do céu
"Heavenly bacon"; the term used throughout the country for sweets made with eggs, almonds, pumpkin, and butter, though rarely with real bacon

Nuts and Nibbles

The numbers in brackets refer to the pictures at the bottom of the pages.

Amêndoa (3, 5) – almonds; a typical Portuguese product; exceptionally high quality from the Douro region, complete with designation of origin; also from the Algarve and Alentejo; grown on a total of 43,000 hectares, producing 19,000 tonnes; used mainly in cakes; a popular nibble when roasted and salted

Azeitona de mesa – sweet olives; grown on 12,500 hectares in Trás-os-Montes, Beira Interior and Alentejo, producing 16,500 tonnes, of which 23 percent is exported; several independent varieties; eaten marinated or with various fillings;

Castanha – sweet chestnuts; 17,500 hectares are planted with sweet chestnuts, mainly in Trás-os-Montes and Beira Interior; at least 30 percent of the annual production of 30,000 tonnes is exported making chestnuts the most important exported fruit; a traditional food, that is used chiefly in soups; they are roasted and sold by the dozen, wrapped in old newspaper, on every street corner in Lisbon

Fava frita (6) – deep-fried broad beans; salted and spiced quite sharply with Piri-Piri; a popular snack

Miolos de pevide (1, 2) – pumpkin seeds; either peeled or unpeeled

Miolos de pinhão (4) – pine kernels; harvested in coastal pine forests; frequently Portugal's most important exported fruit; strong flavor; salted or used in cakes

Fruit and Nuts

Portugal has remained true to its origins where fresh and dried fruit are concerned. There are many native varieties of oranges and chestnuts, apples and olives, cherries and pine kernels, apricots and almonds. Modern varieties cannot begin to compare with their flavors, although they are less productive. Nearly all of these fruits are also imported, and there are only a few types that produce a surplus for export.

In the markets, native produce, even though it often looks less attractive on the outside, is more expensive than imported fruit – and rightly so, because they are grown naturally, produce low yields, but compensate with more intense flavors. They are normally very labor-intensive to grow, and this is appreciated by customers who are looking for good quality. Portugal has a very long tradition of drying fruit. It is the Algarve in particular, with its hot climate, that is really expert in this field. Influenced by the Moors, houses were built with flat roofs, which could be used as *açoteia* or terraces, and were ideally suited to drying figs, grapes, apricots, and other fruit. The Algarve is also famous for the quality of its almonds.

One of the most popular nibbles is *tremoços*, a type of pickled bean.

Delicious figs grow in the Algarve and are dried in its strong sunlight.

1 Peeled and salted pumpkin seeds

2 Unpeeled pumpkin seeds

3 A different quality of unpeeled pumpkin seeds

Mel – Honey

The flora in the more remote and wild parts of the Portuguese interior is often quite unique. The sun shines down on the wild herbs, enabling their flowers to develop plenty of nectar and fragrance. Portuguese bees produce the highest amounts of honey in western Europe. There are a total of 210,000 colonies, looked after by 70,000 beekeepers. The best honeys are produced in the National Parks. A marvelous heather honey is made in the Serra da Malcata in the Beira Baixa region. The main regions that are known for their honey are Trás-os-Montes, Beira, Estremadura, Alentejo, and the Algarve. Festive orange blossom honeys are made in the Algarve, which also produces mead. A total of thirteen Designations of Origin have been introduced so far.

Portugal can thank its wild and natural landscapes for its high quality honeys, which are often sold in jars like this.

Rosemary honey, from wild bushes, has an incomparable spicy flavour.

A type of heather grows in the Serra da Malcatat, which is used to produce this honey, famous for its therapeutic powers.

The heathers of the arid Serra da Estrela give this honey its intense flavor.

Almonds in honey – a delicious marriage of two Portuguese specialties.

An irresistible and marvelously aromatic treat: pine kernels in honey.

4 Pine kernels

5 Unpeeled almonds

6 Deep-fried broad beans

Port

The Portuguese seldom drink port; they keep it for special occasions such as Christmas and other celebrations. This is because port was, from the start, produced for the export market rather than local consumption.

In the middle of the 17th century, England secured a privileged trading status with Portugal. Attitudes to the consumption of claret from Bordeaux varied: it was occasionally forbidden altogether, and at other times was considered politically undesirable – it was always, however, extremely popular. This meant that people would have been quite happy to drink Portuguese red wine instead; the only problem was that it was of rather indifferent quality at that time. All this was changed by the Marquis de Pombal when he classified the vineyards in 1756. These were the first official limits ever given to any wine, and they introduced clear quality grades that remain reliable to this day. The practice of fortifying wine with brandy in order to make it keep better also dates back to that time. It was at least a hundred years later, however, that the sweet port that we are familiar with today became popular.

Port, like any other wine, owes its potentially exceptional properties to the quality, and perfect ripeness, of the harvest. The grapes thrive up to

In Vila Nova de Gaia, opposite Oporto, port wines are laid down to age in casks in the *caves*, lodges built on the slopes of the town.

Ports can age for decades and attain a remarkable complexity and intensity of flavors.

Below: From the very beginning, port was produced for export, and many firms were founded by the English.

an altitude of 700 yards (700 m) on the steep, terraced slate hillsides along the banks of the River Douro and its tributaries; the vineyards start about sixty-two miles (100 km) east of the seaport of Oporto and end just short of the Spanish border. In the summer, the slate protects the vines from the extreme heat of the sun, and then releases warmth during the relatively cool nights. This ensures that the grapes ripen at a steady rate. The yields produced by the stony ground are very small, however. There are a large number of grape varieties, and the five main ones are the Touriga Nacional, Touriga Francesca, Tinta Roriz, Tinta Barroca, and Tinto Cão. The grape harvest normally starts towards the end of September, when the grapes have reached a potential alcohol level of twelve to fourteen percent by volume.

Port is produced in three stages: these are the treading of the grapes, fermentation, and fortification with brandy. The most important is fermentation. It is during this stage, which in the case of port lasts at most for forty-eight hours, that the fermenting wine absorbs aromas, pigments, and tannins from the grape skins. This process traditionally takes place in a *lagar*, an open, low, and broad stone trough. The surface area is very much greater than that of a fermenting vat; this means that there is much closer contact between the grape skins and juice, and at the same time the temperature at which fermentation takes place is more controlled. In addition, treading in *lagares* is done with the naked foot, which is the perfect instrument for extracting the juices. Due to the high labor cost of this process, however, the use of fermenting vats has become the norm. Despite this, some of the best vintages continue to receive additional body, tannins and character in *lagares*.

After one and a half to two days, the partially fermented wine is run off and carefully mixed with a quarter barrel of young, neutral, seventy-seven percent vol. brandy. This raises the alcohol level to twenty percent vol. and stops the fermentation process so that the port retains its natural sweetness.

From January onwards, the wine is taken downriver to Vila Nova de Gaia. This town, whose houses and shippers' warehouses (lodges) stretch up the hillside on the shore opposite Oporto, is the real home of port. It is here, in the lodges, that decisions are made about the individual wines, they are aged in dark cellars, and eventually distributed and sold.

Madeira

Zarco, a Portuguese captain in the service of Henry the Navigator, landed on this island 400 miles (600 km) from the coast of Morocco in 1420. Madeira is a small chain of mountains in the Atlantic, starting two and a half miles below and rising to 12,000 feet (4,000 m) above sea level; he cleared its dense forests and planted sugar cane, together with Malvasia, an extremely sweet grape variety that had been brought from Crete, and would later be called Malmsey. After the discovery of America, Madeira became an important supply port on the best sea route over the Atlantic. It was the only port where English ships were allowed to call. It was soon discovered that Madeira wine improved tremendously when exposed to the heat of the tropics. British traders had taken over much of the wine business, and from 1750 onwards they quite intentionally shipped casks to the East Indies and back, although the wine was fortified with brandy to twenty percent by volume as a precaution. More recently, the eight wine merchants that remain of the original seventy have taken to simulating this tropical effect. The wines are kept in *estufas*, that is heated tanks, at a temperature of 120 °F (45 °C) for at least three, and preferably five months. Then the wines are aged in sometimes quite massive soleras.

There are 2,100 hectares of vineyards on the island, and they produce about 2,600,000 gallons (100 million litres) of wine per year; unfortunately, only a tenth of this area is planted with the four noble white grape varieties, Sercial, Verdelho, Bual, and Malvasia. They are the ones that produce the great wines. Madeiran vines tend to be grown in terraces over low pergolas. The wine growers can then make use of the valuable ground underneath them. Harvesting has to be done either by bending or kneeling, and the grapes frequently have to be carried up to the road 600 to 1,000 feet (200–300 m) above.

The most wide-spread grape variety is the Negra-Mole; wine growers and merchants do what they like with this grape and produce cheap madeira of all types, altogether forty percent of the total production. This is a pity, because the madeiras aged from the four noble grape varieties are one of the great specialties in the world. They have a quite remarkable quality: they seem to be able to age forever and only get better. The proof can be found in several vintages dating from the nineteenth and early twentieth centuries – they are all delicious.

Background: The most spectacular vineyards in Madeira are situated on its wild northern coast, close to the foaming waves of the Atlantic.

Exceptional Madeiras

Boal or **Bual**
Medium-sweet madeira; increasingly rare grape variety with small, amazingly hairy leaves; develops interesting aromas at a comparatively early age, reminiscent of dried apricots, raisins, nuts, caramel, and rancio, the tang by which all madeiras are recognized.

Malvasia or **Malmsey**
Sweet madeira; not as common as Verdelho; a very popular dessert wine in Anglo-Saxon countries.

Sercial
The driest madeira, which develops its very complex and elegant bouquet after about ten years; it becomes more subtle, with greater finesse, as the decades pass; very rare.

Terrantez
A legendary grape variety that has almost disappeared as a result of phylloxera; very rare old wines of almost unbelievable finesse and liveliness.

Verdelho
Medium-dry madeira; early-ripening, much-grown variety that produces a pleasant wine with a hint of sweetness; when aged, can end up, rather unconventionally, tasting of iodine and smoke.

Bettina Dürr

Italy

The great differences in Italy's climate and geography are favorable to many different agricultural forms. This means that while a superb cheese is produced from cow's milk in the north, the south has cheese made from sheep's milk, just as excellent as its northern counterpart. Northern Italian recipes often use butter and cream, whereas olive oil dominates the more southern cuisine. Northern Italians have mastered the art of turning risotto and polenta into delicious dishes, yet their southern compatriots prefer to indulge in numerous tasty pasta variations. What all Italians do have in common, however, is their *ars vivendi* – their art of living. Despite modern city lifestyles and busy jobs, good food is today just as highly valued as it always has been.

Respect for the basic product and a feeling for the freshness and quality of the ingredients determines the lively, seasonal variety of dishes. Consequently, the range of products on offer is extensive and high in quality. Unadulterated taste and inspired simplicity are the main characteristics of the Italian cuisine, as well as a healthy and economical attitude towards food and eating habits. In the cities, breakfast is usually just an espresso, drunk quickly on the way to work; the morning break at about 10 am is far more important, when Italians like to slip into a bar for a *spuntino*, a bite to eat. The rather luxurious-sounding *pranzo*, or lunch, used to be the main meal of the day, when the entire family gathered together around the table; today, Italians prefer a *seconda colazione*, or a second breakfast at lunch time, where they eat considerably less. Only people in the suburbs and in the country, where a lunch break from 1–4 pm is still common, take time for a substantial meal with three or four courses. Thus more extensive meals with additional *antipasti* and *dolci* tend to be saved for Sundays or special occasions.

In the cities, the evening meal is usually eaten at about 8 pm and consumed more quickly than it used to be. Italians allow themselves a warm main meal with vegetables and a dessert. An extra snack around midnight seems to be becoming a habit, however, as it is never too late for some exquisite Italian ham, choice salumi or other specialties.

Left: A proud butcher in front of his shop in Greve in Chianti.

Bread

No Italian meal is imaginable without bread, *pane*, whether eaten with soup, vegetables, fish or meat. In Southern Italy, bread is even served with pasta, and people also like to eat it with grapes or melon.

Italian bread crumbs are white, soft, and have a fine texture, especially in northern Italy. The simple yeast dough, made of flour and water and sometimes enriched with olive oil or fat, has to be kneaded for a long time to obtain the desired, smooth texture.

Italians are masters in the art of creating diverse and sophisticated uses for bread and bread dough. This is not just true in the case of pizza, a dish known all over the world. They toast and bake slices of bread with cheese, they fill dough and dough parcels, sprinkle or brush round flat loaves with herbs, olive oil or cheese, season loaves with sage or rosemary, bake soft and crusty, white and brown, salted and unsalted breads, not to mention the abundance of sweet breads. Stale bread is not inevitably turned into bread crumbs, but can be used in soups and salads.

A common saying just goes to prove how highly Italians regard their bread. When speaking of a kind, good-natured person, he or she is described as *buono come il pane*, "as good as bread."

Bruschetta
Toasted Garlic Bread

4 slices of coarse, white, Italian bread
2 garlic cloves, pressed
4 Tbs cold-pressed olive oil
Salt and black pepper

Toast the slices of bread in the oven on both sides. Rub in the garlic, sprinkle with the oil, season well with the salt and pepper and serve immediately while still hot. Tip: Often a skinned and seeded medium-sized tomato is pressed onto each slice of bread.

To make crocette, the *panettiere*, the baker, twists the rolled oil dough into one length.

This dough is then rolled into small, thin, croissant-type fingers of the same length.

Several of these dough fingers are knotted together.

Here the dough is being made into a star; crosses and knots are also popular.

Bread Specialties

The numbers in brackets refer to the numbers in the picture on the next page, bottom right.

Biovetta (10), **Filonciono** (7), **Mantovana** (9), **Montasù** (3), **Rosetta** (8), **Soffiato** (11) – various bread rolls, made from a yeast dough.

Bruschetta – toasted slices of coarse, white Italian bread with garlic and olive oil (for recipe, see left).

Carta da musica (6) – literally, this is "manuscript paper," flat, wafer-thin bread rounds made from durum wheat semolina. A Sardinian specialty.

Cilindrati – croissants from very thin bread dough which has been rolled out repeatedly before being formed into croissants. A specialty from Ferrara; rolls made from the same dough are called *cazzottini*.

Crocette (4) – literally "cross," artistically formed from a soft oil dough.

Crostini – pieces of white bread, toasted with liver, sage, black olives or other toppings.

Filascetta – a thicker, flat bread round made from a yeast dough, sprinkled with fried onions and then baked. Sometimes caramelized with sugar. A specialty of Lombardy.

Focaccia – thin, flat, round bread made from a yeast dough, seasoned with oil, salt, herbs, and olives. A specialty of Liguria. Often eaten as a "double-decker" with various fillings, also sweet ones.

Grissini (12, 13) – bread sticks from Turin, baked until the dough made from flour and water becomes a crust. The thicker *grissini del pannetiere*, baker's grissini, are rolled out by hand.

Michette – bread rolls from Milan, crusty on the outside and hollow on the inside. Filled with cheese or salami.

Pan sciocco – a classic from Tuscany, made without salt. Used as replacement for pasta when stale. Also found in the well-known salad dish *panzanella*, with soaked bread crumbs, tomatoes, onions, and other ingredients.

Pane (1, 2) – Italy's daily bread is basically a simple, smooth, yeast dough made with wheat flour. In Central and Southern Italy it has a rustic-looking crust with a lighter inside. In Naples it is a large loaf with a dark crust.

Pane alla salvia – sage bread, a favorite in Tuscany, where a little white wine and sage steamed with oil is kneaded into the yeast dough. Often found with rosemary as *pane al rosmarino*.

Pane casareccio (5) – literally, this is "bread baked on the premises," a round, very light loaf from Apulia with a light, crisp crust.

Pane di segale – rye bread.

Pane nero – black bread made from a mixture of rye and wheat flour. Particularly typical for the Aosta Valley region.

Panzarotti – parcel loaf, made either from a simple yeast dough or high-fat, short-crust pastry. Rolls are always long, and have squared corners when filled.

Piadina – a round, flat loaf from Emilia-Romagna. Usually eaten with ham or sausage while still warm; sometimes filled.

Schiacciata – literally "squashed flat," this is a round, flat loaf made from a yeast dough using wheat flour and oil. Often simply sprinkled with coarse grains of salt, brushed with oil and then baked. A Tuscan specialty.

Crusty and golden, the baker takes his bread – here,
pane casareccio – out of the oven.

There are numerous kinds of breads and rolls – the numbers here refer to the
list of bread specialties on the left.

Pizza

When a homesick Neapolitan opened the first pizzeria in New York in 1895, little did he suspect that the flat, round yeast bread from his home town would soon conquer the world. About sixty years later, Americans, Australians, and Northern Europeans were consuming pizzas with enthusiasm, at a time when Naples' staple diet was only hearsay to most Italians. It was only from 1970 onwards that pizza started to reach the rest of Italy. Today, pizza is the hamburger's only serious opponent, and pizza can boast greater gastronomic perspectives and penetration.

In Naples, the pizza has been valued as a tasty, low-cost snack for over 200 years. It was baked in the narrow streets in wood-fired ovens and seasoned with herbs, a few drops of olive oil, and, at best, a few salted anchovies. Pizza was literally accepted at court on June 1, 1899, when Italy's royal couple paid a visit to Naples. In order to demonstrate an affinity with the public, the couple ordered pizza. The commissioned baker garnished the flat yeast dough round with white Mozzarella made from buffalo milk, red tomatoes, and bright green basil leaves, the colors of the Italian flag.

Unfortunately, the optically attractive aspect of this national pizza, named after the queen at that time, Margherita, often suffers considerably. Its harmony of flavors, however, has made it the favorite not just of Italy's some 30,000 pizzerias, but of the whole world.

Basic Recipe for Pizza Dough

Makes 3–4 pizzas

1 oz (30 g) yeast
1 pinch sugar
1¾ cups (350 ml) lukewarm water
1 lb (500 g) flour
½ tsp salt

Crumble the yeast into a small bowl and sprinkle with the sugar. Stir in 5 tablespoons of the lukewarm water and 3 tablespoons of the flour. Cover with a clean tea towel and leave to rise in a warm, draft-free place for about 30–60 minutes.

Sieve the rest of the flour onto the work surface, make a well in the center and add the yeast mixture prepared above. Add the salt. Gradually work in the flour from the edges, adding the rest of the lukewarm water (the amount of water depends on the type of flour used) until the dough no longer sticks.

Knead the dough for at least 15 minutes, stretching it with the balls of the thumb and folding it back on itself, until it is smooth and elastic.

Roll the dough into a ball, cover and leave to rise in a warm place for 1–2 hours. Briefly knead again before dividing up into portions and rolling out to form flat dough rounds. Place these on well-greased pizza tins or baking trays and press down the edges to form a thick crust.

Brush with a thin layer of oil and add toppings.

Bake at 460 °F (250 °C) at the bottom of the oven for 15–20 minutes.

Pizza is best baked in a traditional Italian stone oven, fired with wood. In these conditions the temperature can reach 645 °F (340 °C) and the pizza only needs to be baked for 4–5 minutes.

Pizza alla napolitana – Pizza Napoli
With tomatoes, Mozzarella, anchovy fillets, oregano, and olive oil.

Pizza alla romana – Roman pizza
With tomatoes, Mozzarella, oregano (like the Pizza Napoli), and anchovies, the classic pizza.

The flat dough rounds are baked at extremely high temperatures for a few minutes in the pizzeria's stone oven.

Calzone
"Half-moon" pizza folded over and filled with ham and Mozzarella, and often also with Ricotta and oregano.

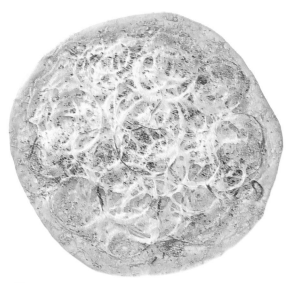

Pizza pugliese – Apulian onion pizza
With finely-chopped onions, oregano, grated Pecorino, and olive oil.

Pizza calabrese – Calabrian pizza
With tomatoes, tuna, anchovies, olives, capers, and – sticking to the original recipe – lard instead of olive oil.

Pizza alle vongole – Clam pizza
With tomatoes, oregano, clams, parsley, and garlic.

Pizza spinaci – Spinach pizza
With fresh spinach and lots of garlic.

Pizza al prosciutto – Ham pizza
With tomatoes, Mozzarella, and cooked ham.

Pizza con funghi – Mushroom pizza
With tomatoes, Mozzarella, sliced mushrooms, parsley, and garlic.

Pizza quattro stagioni – "Four Seasons" pizza
With tomatoes and Mozzarella, and, each covering a quarter of the pizza, mushrooms, cooked ham, finely-chopped artichokes, and olives.

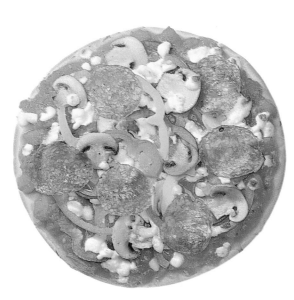

Pizza alla siciliana – Sicilian pizza
With tomatoes, Mozzarella, pieces of yellow, green and red peppers fried in olive oil, and slices of salami and mushroom.

Pizza Margherita
With tomatoes, Mozzarella, and fresh basil, so that with a bit of creativity your pizza proudly displays the national colors of Italy.

521

Prosciutto di Parma

The five-pronged crown of the former Duchy of Parma is emblazoned on its hide. Italy's most famous ham comes from the province of the same name, north-west of Bologna. Its strictly limited territory begins three miles south of the Via Emilia and stretches into the first foothills of the Apennines up to a maximum altitude of 3,000 feet. The center and historical birth place of Parma ham is Langhirano. The village with its mere 3,000 inhabitants is sixteen miles away from the provincial capital and lies at the end of the valley of the River Parma. Enormous warehouses dominate the little town, their façades split by long columns of high, tall windows, shaded by Venetian blinds. These blinds can be adjusted to allow various quantities of the particularly tangy air into the buildings. This winds its way around millions of legs of pork, maturing them to produce aromatic ham. The quality of Parma ham is created with the pigs themselves, which are fed on forage barley, corn, and fruit. They live in controlled sties in Northern and Central Italy. When slaughtered, they must be at least ten months old. This ensures that the meat is firm and rosy and surrounded by a considerable layer of fat protecting the ham, which after a year's drying and maturing is particularly soft and tender.

First, the raw legs of pork, which weigh about twenty-two pounds (ten kilograms), are salted. For the first salting phase, they are left in cold cells of about 32–40 °F (0–4 °C) for six to seven days. They are then resalted and left for a period of fifteen to eighteen days. Cold air and salt draw the moisture from the meat which is indispensable for preservation. After this second salting phase, the legs of pork are thoroughly kneaded (this is now done by machines). This allows the salt to enter into the meat more quickly over a third period of sixty to seventy days in the cells. The legs of pork are washed in tepid water and then left to dry (*prosciutto* comes from *prosciugare*, which means "to dry").

Over a period of six months, in their early maturing stages the legs of Parma ham are transferred between carefully designated cold stores, climatized drying rooms, and airy warehouses. Without their rind, they are then completely coated in a paste made from lard, ground rice, and pepper. This prevents the meat from drying out and hardening. Once coated, the ham is moved to cellars with a limited air supply and cooler temperatures. There, natural, biochemical processes can be completed, it is these that give the ham its exquisite taste.

Ten to twelve months later, according to whether it weighs fifteen to twenty or over twenty pounds, the Parma ham is ready to eat. With favorable storage conditions, however, it can improve its flavor and finesse over a maximum of a further fourteen months. In the final maturing stages the ham is regularly checked with a needle-shaped horse bone. When inserted into the ham, tiny particles stick to its porous surface. The ham curer knows just by breathing in the aroma whether the ham has sufficiently matured.

Fifty percent of Parma ham is eaten in Italy itself. The remaining fifty percent is exported and, unlike its native country, ninety-five percent of export sales require the ham unboned.

Prosciutto di San Daniele

The most north-easterly peak of Italy proffers the country's second largest specialty ham, San Daniele from the Friuli region, sixteen miles from Udine. This, too, enjoys a long tradition. Its commercial development started later than that of Parma ham. San Daniele ham requires legs of pork that weigh at least twenty-four and at the most thirty-three pounds, whereby the average weight is around twenty-eight pounds. The hams are bought up from various regions in Italy. They owe their particularly delicate, sweetish flavor and characteristic shape to the following factors:

- The ham is only salted for a short period of time; this is basically one day per two pounds, whereby two days are often added, bringing the average to fourteen to sixteen days
- It is then pressed, which not only gives the ham its attractive guitar shape, but also distributes the fat around the ham
- The trotter is left on the leg to prevent the lower parts of the joint from drying out.

San Daniele ham matures for a minimum of ten and for an average of thirteen months. Its trade mark is the SD monogram on the stretched leg of ham pointing to the right.

As a trade mark and guarantee, every genuine Parma ham bears the five-pronged crown and the name of its region of origin.

The ham curer inserts a needle-shaped horse bone into the ham. He can tell by the aroma whether the desired level of maturity has been reached.

Fifty percent of Parma ham is eaten in Italy itself. The remaining fifty percent is exported where it is mostly required unboned.

The exquisite taste of Parma and San Daniele ham is best brought out when it is thinly sliced.

Pasta Secca

What would an Italian meal be without *il primo*, the first course? And who can imagine it without pasta? On average, an Italian consumes half a hundredweight of *pasta secca*, dried (bought) pasta, per annum, not including fresh pasta. As a comparison, an average American eats only eighteen pounds (8 kg) and an average German twelve pounds (5.6 kg) in a year.

Italy has about 300 different kinds of this staple food. Pasta, which is an overall term for noodles made with durum wheat semolina, can be divided into three general categories:

● *Pasta corta* – short noodles, which include everything from the tiniest soup noodles to the rather more substantial *penne*, and also shapes such as spirals, wheels, stars, snails, ears, shells, and short tubes

● *Pasta lunga* – long noodles, which include the entire spaghetti and tagliatelle family. Anything longer than about four inches belongs to this group

● *Pasta ripiena* – filled pasta parcels; tortellini and ravioli are perhaps the best known examples of this group.

The origin of pasta has been the subject of much argument. One would like to picture the Etruscans as *mangia maccheroni*. They weren't just "macaroni-eaters," however; *maccheroni* was used as a general term for any kind of pasta for a long time. It is supposedly derived from the Greek *macarios*, meaning "happy." Macaroni's more recent history began in Sicily. According to ancient documents, strips of pasta dough were drying in the sun as early as the 12th and 13th centuries. It did not take long for pasta to reach the mainland, where Naples soon became a pasta stronghold. The wider availability of durum wheat semolina, *grano duro*, from the 15th century onwards, proved significant in securing pasta's success.

Today, Sicily, Apulia, and Calabria supply the majority of the sun-hungry grain. Its high percentage of binding protein makes it extremely suitable for pasta. This allows the dough, which is only mixed with water, to bond without adding any extra binding agents. It also creates the right *tenuta alla cottura*, that is that the dough does not dissolve when being cooked. Without this characteristic, we would not be able to eat our pasta *al dente*, with that desired firmness "to the tooth."

When in the 18th century the *trafila* was invented – an iron utensil with holes in it through which the pasta dough could be pressed into long ribbons – spaghetti conquered the land. It was only one hundred years later, however, that its current name, derived from *spago* "string" became the standard term.

There are many reasons for *pasta secca*'s success:

● It keeps for up to three years
● It is simply cooked in boiling salted water, using three cups of water per 1/2 cup of noodles
● It only needs 4–12 minutes' cooking time, according to noodle thickness
● 1/2 cup of noodles made from durum wheat semolina has a mere 346 calories; fresh pasta only has 140.

When cooked *in sugo*, "in sauce," whether the sauce be with vegetables, tomatoes or meat, such as *ragù alla bolognese*, any ingredients to hand can be used:

● Even if just tossed in butter or oil, and sprinkled with cheese, herbs, and pepper, it is delicious!
● In order to justify the wine which goes so well with pasta, it can often be heard said that wine is indispensable, as water would make the noodles swell in the stomach (which, of course, isn't true!).

Pasta Sauces

Salsa di Pomodoro
Tomato Sauce

1 onion
1 garlic clove
3 Tbs olive oil
2 lbs (1 kg) ripe tomatoes
1 tsp basil, finely chopped
Salt, black pepper

Peel the onion and the garlic clove, chop finely and gently fry in the oil. Cut the tomatoes into small pieces and add to the onion and garlic.
Bring to the boil and simmer, covered and over a low heat, for 45 minutes. Press through a sieve, add the basil and season well. Leave to stand for 10 minutes.
This classic pasta sauce goes well with all kinds of pasta. Serve the pasta with 3–4 tablespoons of sauce and one knob of butter per portion.

Pesto alla Genovese
Pesto – Genoese Basil sauce

1 small pot of fresh basil
4 crushed garlic cloves
2 oz (50 g) pine nuts
3/4 cup (150 ml) olive oil
Salt
2 oz (50 g) grated Pecorino or Parmesan cheese

Purée the basil leaves, garlic, and pine nuts. Gently whisk in the olive oil, a pinch of salt – do not add too much salt, as the cheese is very salty – and the Pecorino until the mixture forms a creamy sauce. Traditionally, Ligurian noodles such as trenette, spaghetti, tagliatelle, and fettuccine are eaten with pesto; cook them al dente. In a warmed bowl, dilute the pesto with 4 tablespoons of boiling noodle water. Drain the pasta, add to the pesto, stir well and serve.
Tip: Pesto will keep in the refrigerator for several weeks in an airtight jar. When used, make sure that enough olive oil is added to the jar so that the basil remains covered. Otherwise it will oxidize and discolor or go moldy. Pesto can also be used to season minestrone and gnocchi or can be spread on toast and served as an antipasto.

Ragù alla Bolognese
Bolognese Sauce

1 small onion
1 garlic clove
1 medium-sized carrot
1 stick celery
2 Tbs butter
2 oz (50 g) fatty bacon
4 oz (100 g) raw ham
4 oz (100 g) chicken liver
4 oz (100 g) ground pork
4 oz (100 g) ground beef
1 cup (200 ml) red wine
1 cup (200 ml) beef stock
3 Tbs tomato paste
1 tsp oregano
Salt, black pepper

Peel or wash the onion, garlic, carrot, and celery and chop finely. Melt the butter in a saucepan, finely slice the bacon and gently fry with the vegetables and garlic. Finely slice the ham, finely chop the chicken liver and add this and the ground meat to the vegetables. Fry, stirring continuously. Add the wine, stock, tomato paste, and oregano. Bring to the boil and season to taste. Cover and simmer over a very low heat for 2 hours; season once more.
This sauce goes well with almost any kind of pasta and can also be used as a filling for either lasagna or cannelloni.

Which Sauce for Which Pasta?

Pasta should only be allowed to swim in the much-loved clear broths and soups. Otherwise the sauce should be portioned so that the pasta completely absorbs the liquid; if the sauce is thin, then the pasta must be more absorbent and hollow than for a thicker sauce.

Aglio e olio – crushed garlic, parsley, and cold-pressed olive oil, with spaghetti, spaghettini, vermicelli, and linguine.

Ai frutti di mare – with seafood; served with capelli d'angelo, fidelini, spaghetti, and lingue.

All'amatriciana – bacon and tomato sauce, with bucatini, spaghetti, gramigna.

Alla napolitana – see *sugo di pomodoro*.

Alla panna – in cream (with lots of pepper), with tortellini and rigatoni.

Alla siciliana – tomato sauce with fresh sardines, with vermicelli and bucatini.

Allo spezzatino – with braised fish; eaten with maccheroni, marelle, fusilli, penne, rigatoni, pappardelle, and other ribbon noodles.

Burro e salvia – sage butter, made from butter and crispy, fried leaves of sage. Goes well with all kinds of pasta.

Carbonara – bacon, cheese, and eggs, with spaghetti and other long noodles.

In brodo – clear broth, usually chicken; with anolini, cappelletti and tortellini, and also capelli d'angelo or tagliolini.

Pesto – basil sauce, eaten with filled or unfilled noodles, especially with trenette, fettuccine, tagliatelle, linguine, and farfalle.

Ragù alla bolognese – with ground meat, a universal sauce for all kinds of long pasta such as spaghetti, tagliatelle or maccheroni; also used as a filling for lasagna.

Salsa cruda – "raw," i.e. an uncooked sauce, with raw eggs or uncooked tomatoes, parsley, basil, and Parmesan; eaten with ribbon noodles.

Salsa di noci – sauce with walnuts and Ricotta, with fettuccine and other ribbon noodles.

Sugo d'agnello – lamb ragout, with penne, rigatoni, marelle, orecchiette, pappardelle, and tortiglioni.

Sugo di asparagi – asparagus sauce, with fresh tagliatelle or other ribbon noodles which are not too wide; can also be served with gnocchetti.

Sugo di pesce – fish sauce with tomatoes, with maccheroni, penne, and rigatoni.

Sugo di pomodoro, alla napolitana – tomato sauce, with all kinds of pasta, regardless of shape and consistency.

Background: Spaghetti being dried in a pasta factory on a special frame.

Cappelletti
Little hat-shaped pasta parcels, filled with meat and/or cheese, either eaten boiled in a clear broth, *in brodo*, with butter or with a meat sauce.

Tortelli
A general term for filled pasta, especially used to refer to 2 inch (5 cm) square parcels.

Lasagne
Rectangular sheets of pasta, approximately three by four inches (8 by 12 cm) in size. The simplest kind of homemade pasta, this can be used in many different ways for oven dishes. Also available dried.

Pansôti
From handmade pasta dough, these parcels are filled with Ricotta, egg, Parmesan, and herbs. They are served with sage butter and Parmesan.

Panzarotti di magro
From the area around Piacenza, these parcels are filled with spinach and Ricotta – *di magro* means "lean," without meat. Baked as a gratin in the oven with butter and Parmesan.

Ravioli
Pasta parcels, the favorite of its kind. Usually filled with ground meat and served with a tomato sauce.

Ravioli alle noci
Ravioli filled with a nut paste.

Tortellini
The best known variety of pasta parcel, filled with cheese or ground meat; can also be bought as *pasta secca*.

Triangoli al salmone
Decorative *pasta negra*, dyed with octopus ink and filled with salmon.

Gnocchi

Gnocchi – little dumplings – are a passion of the Italians. Among a wealth of variations, the most common type is made with mashed potatoes, mixed with milk while still hot to form a dough. Often (but not always) eggs are added. Gnocchi are usually served with lots of Parmesan and often with a tomato or meat sauce.

Gnocchi do not have to be made with potatoes, however; they are almost as popular with durum wheat semolina. Other variants use cornmeal or chestnut flour; one specialty from Mantua uses pumpkin as a potato replacement.

Gnocchi di Patate
Potato Gnocchi

Serves 6–8

3 lb (1.5 kg) mealy potatoes
2 eggs
Salt
2¹/₂ cups (300 g) flour

Boil the potatoes in their skins until soft. Drain, leave until cool enough to handle, then peel and mash. Mix in the eggs and salt and then add the flour and knead into a dough.
Divide the potato mixture into 10 equally-sized portions and roll each portion into long strings about as wide as your thumb. Cut up the dough string into pieces of about 1 inch (2¹/₂ cm) in length and dust with flour. Using the back of a fork, pattern the pieces with the typical ribbed gnocchi design.
Cook the gnocchi in moderately sized portions in boiling salted water. They are done when they rise to the surface. Remove from the water with a slotted spoon and drain well.
Serve with sage butter, or a tomato or meat sauce (p. 527).
Tip: The amount of flour needed depends on the kind of potato used. New potatoes are unsuitable for gnocchi, as they absorb far more flour than older varieties.

Gnocchi alla Romana
Roman Gnocchi

Serves 4

5 cups (1 l) milk
1 tsp salt
2¹/₂ cups (300 g) durum wheat semolina
3 egg yolks
¹/₂ cup (125 g) butter
4 oz (125 g) grated Parmesan

Bring the milk with the salt to the boil. Sprinkle in the semolina, stirring continuously. Simmer for 20 minutes over a low heat; leave to cool in the saucepan.
Stir in the egg yolks and 2 oz (50 g) of the butter and Parmesan. Pour the semolina mixture onto a damp baking tray and spread out until it is ³/₈ inch (1 cm) thick. When cooled, use a glass to cut out circles of about 2 inches (5 cm) diameter.
Preheat the oven to 350 °F (180 °C).
Grease a flat ovenproof dish well with butter. Layer the gnocchi like brick tiles in the dish and sprinkle with the remaining Parmesan. Melt the rest of the butter and pour over the gnocchi. Bake in the oven for about 45 minutes.
Serve in the ovenproof dish. A chilled Frascati is a suitable accompaniment to this dish.

Malfatti
Spinach and Ricotta Gnocchi

Serves 6

1³/₄ lb (800 g) spinach
1 onion
¹/₂ cup (125 g) butter
8 oz (250 g) Ricotta
4 oz (125 g) grated Parmesan
3 eggs
¹/₄ tsp nutmeg
Salt, black pepper
2 cups (250 g) flour

Wash and trim the spinach and cook in the water clinging to the leaves over a medium heat until reduced. Place in a sieve and allow to drain well; squeeze dry and chop. Peel the onion, chop and fry in half of the butter until transparent. Add the spinach and stir; fry for a further two minutes and then leave to cool.
Mix the Ricotta with half of the Parmesan and the eggs and season with the salt, pepper, and nutmeg. Add the spinach and stir together well. Gradually add the flour until a workable dough is formed.
Bring plenty of salted water to the boil in a large, wide saucepan. Add small teaspoon-sized portions of the spinach and Ricotta mixture to the boiling water. Reduce the heat and allow the malfatti to simmer until they rise to the surface. Remove from the water with a slotted spoon and drain.
Preheat the oven to 400 °F (200 °C).
Grease a flameproof dish well with butter and tip the malfatti into it. Melt the rest of the butter and pour over the malfatti. Sprinkle with the remaining Parmesan and bake in the oven for 5–8 minutes.
A Cabernet is an excellent wine to go with this dish.
(The literal translation of *malfatti* is "badly made"; here it means "irregular in shape").

Gnocchi alla Zafferano
Sardinian Gnocchi with Saffron

Serves 4

For the dough
1 cup (100 g) flour
2¹/₂ cups (300 g) durum wheat semolina
A few saffron strands

For the sauce
1 onion
3 Tbs olive oil
7 oz (200 g) Sardinian garlic sausage
2 garlic cloves
1lb (500 g) tomatoes
1 bunch fresh basil
Salt, black pepper
2 oz (50 g) grated Pecorino

Mix the flour and semolina. Dissolve the saffron in 4 tablespoons of tepid water, add to the flour mixture and with a little salt, knead to form a smooth dough. Divide the dough into small portions and shape into dough rolls 2 inches (5 cm) thick. Cut the rolls into pieces ¹/₂ inch (1 cm) in length and lightly dust with flour. Flatten each piece of dough with your fingertips and give them their typical curved shape and ribbed pattern by pressing against a large-meshed sieve. Leave to dry overnight on floured kitchen towels.
To make the sauce, peel and chop the onion and fry in the oil until transparent. Slice the sausage and finely chop the garlic and basil; add to the onion. Skin, de-seed and chop the tomatoes. Add to the onion and sausage and season with salt and pepper. Simmer over a low heat until the sauce thickens.
Bring plenty of salted water to the boil and cook the gnocchi for 1–15 minutes until *al dente*. Leave to drain in a sieve. Add to the hot sauce, mix well and serve. Serve with the Pecorino and a Sardinian red wine, for example a Cannonau.
Tip: In the north Sardinian town of Sassardi, where this specialty comes from, saffron gnocchi are made with bacon and ground lamb and pork, and are called *ciciones*.

Gnocchi di patate – Potato gnocchi

Polenta

Polenta was northern Italy's basic foodstuff long before Columbus brought corn to Europe. In those days, the rural population had to make do with a porridge made from grain cooked in water, whether this be millet, buckwheat or common spelt. Polenta was also made from chick-peas or broad beans.

Northern Italy provided *mahiz*, corn cobs with their crunchy yellow kernels, with a suitable climate and enough water. Corn harvests were prosperous, where other cereals yielded miserable amounts. It soon became the most economically viable product grown in the area.

Finely-ground corn first hit the Venetian market. In a more coarsely-ground form, it spread first to Lombardy, then to Piedmont and the other northern provinces. Polenta began to replace bread and pasta. Each region developed its own variations in accordance with available ingredients.

Polenta was always cooked in a *paiolo*, a huge copper cauldron hanging over the fire in an open fire place. When the water in the cauldron came to the boil, the corn meal was sprinkled into it. Then the hard work began. Housewives needed to be equipped with an *olio di gomito*, a well-oiled elbow, and a sturdy *bastone*, a long wooden stick, for the polenta had to be stirred continuously.

Northern Italy's filling, golden porridge became such a daily feature that southern Italians began to mockingly refer to their northern cousins as *polentoni*, polenta-eaters; the Northerners' cutting answer to this was *mangia-maccheroni*, maccheroni-eaters.

Polenta may once have fallen into disrepute as the food of the poor, but has since won many loyal followers. True polenta devotees insist that it be stirred in the traditional way and not ooze out of the pressure cooker as happens when using more modern, time-saving cooking methods.

Once the polenta begins to curl away from the sides of the saucepan, it is tipped out onto a wooden board and sliced with a piece of string. It is usually eaten when still warm instead of bread. Polenta is delicious with rabbit, lamb, game or forest mushroom ragout. Italians also like to eat it with sausages or cream cheese and in Veneto it is an obligatory accompaniment to all fish dishes. Polenta can also be served as a *primo*, a first course, spread with a little butter and topped with freshly grated Parmesan. Favorite uses for left-overs are grilling, frying or polenta *gratin* with a sauce.

Corn is mostly found in northern Italy, where it produces greater yields than other cereals.

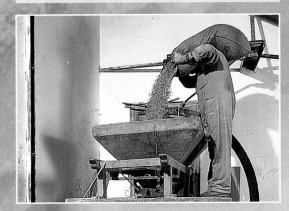

The ground yellow kernels determine the texture of the polenta.

When making polenta, a tall saucepan and a sturdy, wooden *bastone* are needed.

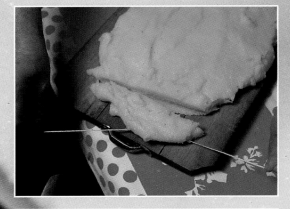

Once the polenta has cooled, it is cut into slices about 3/8 inch (1 cm) wide with a length of string.

Basic Recipe for Polenta

Serves 8
(These quantities can be halved or quartered).

In a tall, heavy saucepan, bring 7$^1/_2$ cups (1$^1/_2$ l) of salted water and a pinch of finely-ground hominy (this reduces the lumpiness later on) to the boil. Slowly sprinkle 1 lb (500 g) hominy grits into the boiling water, stirring continuously. The thicker the polenta becomes, the more it needs to be stirred. Should lumps form, break them up against the side of the saucepan.
When all of the grits have been added, reduce the heat and simmer the mixture for 45 minutes, stirring continuously. Be careful, as the mixture is very hot and will form bubbles which will burst and could splash over the sides of the pan.
A crust will gradually form on the bottom of the saucepan; this is normal. The polenta is ready when it has detached itself from the crust.
Turn the polenta out onto a wooden board and pat down using the flat of a wet knife. Hot polenta is cut with a piece of string; when cold, a knife is used.

Polenta con Gorgonzola
Polenta with Gorgonzola

Polenta
2 oz (50 g) butter
7 oz (200 g) Gorgonzola

Prepare polenta following the above recipe, using 8 oz (250 g) hominy grits and 4 cups (750 ml) water. Leave to cool.
Preheat the oven to 350 °F (180 °C).
Grease a flameproof dish with some of the butter. Cut the polenta into strips about $^3/_8$ inch (1 cm) wide and line the dish with them. Crumble a little Gorgonzola onto each slice and cover with a second slice of polenta. Cover with knobs from the rest of the butter. Bake in the oven for 15–20 minutes and serve hot.
A fresh Soave is a good accompaniment to this dish.

Polenta e Fontina
Polenta with Fontina cheese

Polenta
6 oz (150 g) Fontina
4 oz (100 g) butter

Cut the cheese into small pieces.
Prepare polenta following the above recipe, using 8 oz (250 g) hominy grits and 4 cups (750 ml) salted water. When the mixture starts to curl away from the sides of the saucepan, add the cheese and 2 oz of the butter and stir for a further 5 minutes.
Turn out onto a plate and smooth with a wet knife. Brown the rest of the butter and pour this over the polenta.
Open a bottle of red Bardolino and serve!

Background: Cooking polenta is a test of strength, as the mixture has to be stirred continuously.

Parmigiano-Reggiano

The most famous of all Italian cheeses, which as Parmesan has countless imitators, has been produced using the same method for seven centuries. One even suspects that it was known to the Etruscans. To qualify for a guaranteed certificate of origin, this cheese can only be produced in a stipulated area which encompasses the provinces Parma, Reggio Emilia, Modena, and Mantua on the right bank of the River Po and Bologna on the left bank of the River Reno. There are also rules set out to secure the high quality of Parmigiano-Reggiano, the main one being that the cows either be put out to graze on a meadow or be fed not on silo cattle fodder but on alfalfa.

The milk from the evening's milking is left to stand overnight and the next morning the cream is skimmed off. Then, together with the morning's milk, it is poured into the traditional, bell-shaped copper vats. Whey is added to it from previous cheese-making processes as a fermentation serum. Stirring slowly, the cheese maker heats up the milk to 91 °F (33 °C) in order to add rennin – calves' stomach enzymes – to it. The milk curdles after twelve to fifteen minutes. The curd, the cagliata, is broken with the *spino*, a spike, until its grains are about the size of wheat germ. The cheese maker now gradually reheats the vat to 113 °F (45 °C), and then more fiercely to 131 °F (55 °C). After the heat has been turned off, the cheese mass sinks to the bottom of the vat and is removed with linen cloths. Still in the cloth, the cheese is deposited in wooden or metal molds, *fasceri*. It is lightly squeezed to accelerate the discharge of the remaining whey. A few hours later, the cloth is removed and a stencil is pressed onto the cheese, labeling it with the "Parmigiano-Reggiano" mark of origin and the date of production. The cheese remains in this mold for a few days, after which it has become a solid, slightly bulbous cylinder. This is left in a salt solution for 20–25 days. The cheese is then dried in the sun for a short period before finally being moved to the store, the *cascina*. Lying on stable wooden shelves, the cheeses mature slowly, during which process they are regularly turned and brushed.

It is mostly at the end of the year that the cheese maker transfers his annual production to specially-built store rooms. These stores can hold between 50,000 and 100,000 cheeses and usually belong to banks or cooperatives, which also provide some financial support. Each year, the region produces 90,000 tons of cheese, that is 2.4 million cylinders of Parmigiano-Reggiano, for which they use 400,000 gallons of milk; two gallons of milk are needed to make one pound of this excellent cheese. Parmigiano-Reggiano belongs to the category of medium-fat, cooked hard cheese. It is made between April 1 and November 11. Maturing, which with Parmigiano-Reggiano is a completely natural process, must last until at least the end of the summer of the year following the year of production. Often this lasts much longer, however. The following characteristics are typical for Parmigiano-Reggiano:

- Weight: between a minimum of 50 and a maximum of 100 pounds (24–44 kg); mostly between 70 and 80 pounds (33–36 kg)
- Diameter: between 14 and 18 inches (35–45 cm)
- Height: between 7 and 9 ¹/₂ inches (18–24 cm).
- Rind thickness: about ¹/₄ inch (6 mm)
- Fat content of dry matter: at least 32 percent.
- Color of the rind: dark with paraffin wax or a natural golden yellow
- Color of the cheese: light to straw yellow
- Cheese structure: fine-grained and scaly, with minute, barely visible holes
- Aroma: mild and full-bodied; never strong
- Age: *fresco* (fresh) – less than 18 months; *vecchio* (mature) – 18 to 24 months; *stravecchio* (very mature) – 24 to 36 months.

Opposite: After maturing for several months, the cheese has formed a rind and developed its characteristic taste.

The cheese maker uses a ladle to check if the curdled milk is thick enough to cut the curd.

After the curd has been reheated, the cheese is deposited on the bottom of the vat, covered by the whey, as demonstrated here in a bowl.

The cheese mass is lifted out of the vat with a cloth.

The cheese is then tipped into a mold and gently squeezed to accelerate the discharge of the remaining whey.

In the *fasceri*, wooden or metal molds, the Parmigiano-Reggiano takes on its final shape.

The famous hard cheese has a fine-grain texture and looks rather scaly.

Pecorino

There are cheeses called "Pecorino" all over Italy. Nobody actually stipulates how and from which kind of milk farmers and dairies should make it, meaning that many different versions of Pecorino can be found, ranging from fresh to ripe, and from mild to mature. In principle, however, Pecorino is a hard cheese made from sheep's milk. It is therefore hardly surprising that its most well-known representatives come from central and southern Italy, and from Sardinia and Sicily, where the largest flocks of sheep graze. Rennin is added to the milk so that a soft gel is quickly formed. The cheese maker usually cuts the curd until it is the size of wheat germ. This is then heated to just under 122 °F (50 °C). The mixture is poured into basket-work cylinders which are woven in Sardinia. Pecorino takes eight months to mature, during which time it is regularly washed with salt water and turned. Once matured, the rind is oiled; this is mostly hard and dark. The cheese itself is light in color, often with a gray tinge, and tastes pleasantly tangy. The most famous types of Pecorino are Pecorino romano (or latiale), Pecorino toscano, Pecorino siciliano, and Pecorino sardo or Fiore sardo.

Young Pecorino is popular for the cheese-board, whereas when matured, it is grated. In southern Italy, Pecorino is used instead of Parmesan.

Pecorino is made from the fresh milk of peaceful sheep, contented to graze on mostly barren

Pecorino can be eaten when young and mild, but when used for grating, it must be aged for longer to give it a hard consistency and mature taste.

Pecorino is produced in many regions and its shape varies as much as its weight, which can be anything between 3 and 50 pounds (1.5–22 kg).

Gorgonzola

Originally only produced in the little town of the same name near Milan, Gorgonzola is today made in the provinces of Lombardy and Piedmont. Its basic ingredient is full-cream, pasteurized cows' milk.

The milk is heated to a temperature between 82 °F and 90 °F (28–32 °C) and curdled using calves' rennin. Milk enzymes and spores of *penicillium glaucum*, a special mold, are added to the milk with the rennin. Once the curds and whey have been separated, the cheese is poured into molds of ten to twelve inches in diameter, salted and left to settle for two weeks.

To allow the blue veining to spread through it, the cheese is punctured with long, high-grade steel needles first from one side and then from the other a week later.

In special stores, where the temperature and humidity correspond to that of the natural caves of the Valsassina Valley, the cheese matures for up to three months, producing the following grades:

- *bianco* – very young, before the blue veining starts
- *dolce* – slightly marbled, very mild
- *piccante* – with developed greenish-blue veins and a characteristic strong taste

Gorgonzola should be stored in a cool place but eaten at room temperature to allow its full aroma to be appreciated.

In the large vat, through the addition of curdling enzymes the milk has formed a soft gel which will be reduced to curd.

The cheese maker rolls the cylindrical cheese in salt.

Needles puncture the cheese to allow enough air in and enable the blue veining to spread.

Gorgonzola's coat of arms is stamped into every cheese, guaranteeing its authenticity.

On sturdy wooden shelves in cellars with an ideal climate, the cheese matures for up to three months.

With its typical marbling, this Gorgonzola will taste deliciously creamy and rich.

Italy's Cheeses

The numbers in brackets refer to the numbers in the picture at the bottom of the next page.

Asiago d'Allevo
A firm, semi-hard to hard cheese, weighing 18 to 26 pounds (8–12 kg). It originates from the Alpine plateaus and has small and mid-sized holes. Straw yellow in color, with a young, mild, tangy taste after nine or more months; it is used mostly for grating when older.

Asiago pressato
Semi-cooked and pressed, young, milky cheese from Vicenza and Trento. Available medium-fat or full-fat.

Bel Paese
Soft cheese made from pasteurized milk since 1929. Soft and yellow, it is sweetish and very mild.

Caciocavallo (3)
Hard cheese made from cooked *pasta filata*. Widely available in Central and Southern Italy. Smooth, often golden yellow rind; a mild cheeseboard cheese. When mature, it can be grated, fried or broiled, mixed with rice, eggs or vegetables.

Caciotta (9)
Small, full-fat, semi-hard cheese from Central Italy; often made from cow's and sheep's milk. Thin rind, mild.

Crescenza
Fresh, uncooked, full-fat soft cheese without a rind. Soft, homogeneous texture, with a fresh, mild taste.

Fiore sardo
A Sardinian specialty; raw, hard cheese from sheep's milk, weighing 3 to 9 pounds (1.5–4 kg). Deep yellow or nut-colored rind. Mild if ripened for up to 6 months; if matured for longer, it has a stronger taste and is mostly grated.

Fontal

Predestined for use in many different dishes, as it melts evenly when heated. Mild, delicate cheese from Northern Italy. It is flat and cylindrical in shape.

Fontina (2)

Fatty cheese from the Aosta Valley made from full-cream milk. It often has an orange rind and a soft, melting texture. Popular for the cheeseboard.

Gorgonzola (1)

Soft, marbled cheese; produced in parts of Lombardy and Piedmont. *Penicillium glaucum* is added to the cheese mixture, later punctured with needles. It is green-veined and very creamy (see left).

Grana padono

Medium-fat, cooked hard cheese, slow maturation. Parmigiano-Reggiano's counterpart from the Venetian and Lombardian side of the Po plateau. It has a dark, paraffin-waxed or natural golden yellow rind, stamped with the mark of origin. Used for grating, but also as a mild cheeseboard cheese with a strong aroma.

Italico

Full-fat soft cheese from Lombardy in the style of the famous Bel Paese. Matures for 20 to 40 days, with a very thin, smooth rind. It has a soft and elastic texture, with a buttery, very mild taste.

Marzolino (12)

Sheep's cheese produced in Tuscany with a mild to tangy taste. Also available made from a mixture of sheep's and cow's milk.

Mascarpone

Cream cheese made from real cream and often used instead of cream in cooking.

Montasio

Full-fat, cooked, pressed cow's cheese from the plateaus and the Alps of Friuli and Veneto. Used on the cheeseboard as a tangy cheese if matured for five months or less; otherwise grated.

Mozzarella

Cream cheese made from buffalo milk from Campania and Lazio. Cooked in water; has a *pasta filata* elastic consistency and only keeps if stored in a cool place. Used on pizzas and called *fior di latte* if made from cow's milk.

Paglietta (10)

Soft cheese from Piedmont.

Parmigiano-Reggiano (4)

Medium-fat, cooked hard cheese with a slow, natural maturation process. Perhaps Italy's most renowned grated cheese (p. 536).

Pecorino romano

Cooked hard cheese from full-fat sheep's milk in tall cylinders, mostly about 37 pounds (17 kg) in weight. Matures for at least five months. It comes from Sardinia (Pecorino sardo) and the area around Rome.

Used for grating if matured and on the cheeseboard if younger. Large quantities are exported.

Pecorino siciliano (6)

Uncooked, yellowish-white hard cheese made from sheep's milk, only produced in Sicily. It has a strong taste.

Pecorino sardo (5)

See Fiore sardo and Pecorino romano.

Provolone

Semi-hard cheese from *pasta filata*, which takes on an elastic consistency when dipped in boiling water. Bound with string into the shape of a pear, melon or sausage and hung up to mature.

Ragusano

Sicilian hard cheese from *pasta filata*. Served as a mild cheeseboard cheese when young; has a more full-bodied taste when matured.

Ricotta (7)

Made in many regions, this is cream cheese made from whey. Snow-white and soft, with a vaguely sour, milky taste. Used in cooking as a filling for pasta and cakes.

Scamorza (11)

Pear-shaped cheese from cow's milk with a thin, smooth rind. Also made mixed with sheep's milk.

Taleggio (8)

Full-fat, uncooked soft cheese in a classic brick shape. Produced in Lombardy, Piedmont and Veneto, with a reddish, soft rind and a mild taste.

Pasta e fagioli – Pasta and beans

Minestrone alla milanese
Milanese minestrone

Soups

Italy's soups are a reflection of the country's different landscapes and seasons; the latter is a prime determiner of the kinds of vegetables available at any one time. The ingredients of many vegetable soups disclose the region they come from. Thus soups in Tuscany are made with dried white beans and toasted slices of white bread, whereas tomatoes, garlic, and olive oil play an important role in soups from more southern climes. Recipes from Liguria favor lots of fresh herbs or pesto. Where rice is a major component in minestrone from the Milan area, pasta is used in Veneto. Adding noodles to soups is a common trait in Italy and there is a wonderful selection to choose from. When pulses were introduced to Europe – and initially to Spain and Italy – after the discovery of America, they were quickly adopted as a main ingredient in soups and broths, being so filling. There are great varieties from region to region; in the north, bean soup is always cooked with brown, speckled borlotti, yet in the south small, white cannellini are preferred. Other specialties include *zuppa di ceci* with chick peas from southern Italy, *zuppa di lenticchie* with lentils, and *jota* from Trieste. This is a dish considered rather exotic by the rest of Italy, as this soup is made from sauerkraut, white beans, and garlic sausage.

Minestrone alla Milanese
Milanese Minestrone
(Illustration right)

3 Tbs olive oil
5 oz (150 g) fresh belly of pork
2 oz (50 g) fatty bacon
1 Tbs chopped onions
1 Tbs flat-leaved parsley, finely chopped
1 tsp garlic, finely chopped
2 sticks celery
2 carrots
3 mealy potatoes
2 zucchini
1 lb (500 g) tomatoes
1 Tbs basil, roughly chopped
8 oz (250 g) borlotti beans, shelled
1 small savoy cabbage
8 oz (250 g) freshly-shelled peas
5 oz (150 g) arborio or vialone rice
2¹⁄₂ oz (60 g) grated Parmesan
Salt

Heat up the oil in a large soup saucepan. Gently fry the belly of pork, bacon, onion, parsley, and garlic in the oil. Wash and peel the celery, carrots and potatoes, and chop the vegetables. Wash and cube the zucchini, skin and de-seed the tomatoes and cut into small pieces. Add the vegetables, basil and beans to the saucepan and cover with 10 cups of water. Cover and leave to simmer for 2 hours.
Wash the cabbage and cut into thin strips. Add with the peas to the saucepan; 15 minutes later, add the rice. Simmer for a further 20 minutes or until the rice is cooked. Stir in the Parmesan and season with salt. Minestrone is eaten hot, but can be served lukewarm in the summer.
A chilled Soave or Pinot grigio would go well with this dish.

Zuppa Pavese
Soup from Pavia

5 cups (1 l) beef stock
2 oz (60 g) butter
4 slices of sandwich loaf
4 eggs
4 Tbs grated Parmesan

Warm up the beef stock. Melt the butter in a frying pan and fry the bread on both sides until golden brown. Line flameproof soup bowls with the bread and carefully break one egg onto the bread into each bowl.
Preheat the oven to 400 °F (200 °C).
Place the soup bowls in the oven until the eggs are cooked. Remove, sprinkle the Parmesan over the eggs and pour 1–2 ladlefuls of stock into each bowl. A white Franciacorta Pinot is a good wine to drink with this meal.

Pasta e Fagioli
Pasta and Beans
(Illustration opposite)

1 lb (500 g) borlotti beans
2 garlic cloves
2 Tbs dried rosemary
1 large onion
1 stick celery
1 small carrot
5 Tbs olive oil
Salt, black pepper
7 oz (200 g) broken linguine or small, hollow noodles

Leave the beans to soak overnight in plenty of lukewarm water. Once soaked, discard the water, pour the beans into a large soup saucepan and cover them with fresh, lukewarm water to a level 1½ inches (4 cm) above the beans.

Variety Meats

In the past, it used to be the custom to go into Genoa's offal kitchens after a night on the town and order a bowl of offal soup to chase away the hangover. It was also drunk late in the evening after a visit to the theater, and traditionally, it was also the first beverage on New Year's Day.

Not many of these hot food kitchens have survived. Preparing offal is a long process which takes up a lot of time. To make the broth, carefully cleaned cow's rumen from the stomach and stomach lining have to be boiled for three hours. Today, offal is again available in good restaurants, where it is marketed as a regional delicacy – whether from Rome, Florence, Bologna, Milan, Genoa or South Tyrol.

Minestra di Trippa alla Piemontese
Piedmont Offal Soup
(Illustration below)

2 oz (50 g) bacon
1 stick celery
2 leeks
2 mealy potatoes
2 onions
1 bayleaf
6 sage leaves
2 oz (50 g) butter
10 cups meat stock
1½ lb (700 g) precooked veal offal
14 oz (400 g) savoy cabbage
2 Tbs grated Parmesan
Salt, black pepper

Finely cube the bacon, wash the celery and leek, discarding any outer leaves, and slice. Peel and cube the potatoes and onions. Crumble the bayleaf and finely chop the sage leaves.
In a large saucepan, gently fry the bacon with the celery, sage and bayleaf in the butter, stirring continuously. Add the potato, onion, and leek and fry. Heat up the stock and add to the vegetables.
Cut the offal into thin strips and add to the broth. Season with pepper, cover and leave to simmer for one hour. Clean the cabbage, discarding any outer leaves, cut into thin strips and add to the offal. Cover and simmer for 1 hour. Stir in the Parmesan and season the soup with salt and pepper.
A Dolcetto from Piedmont is an excellent wine for this dish.

Minestra di trippa alla piemontese – Piedmont offal soup

Peel the garlic, make a bouquet garni with the garlic and rosemary and hang in the saucepan. Peel the onion, leaving the root end so that the onion does not disintegrate during cooking. Wash, peel and chop the celery and carrot and add to the beans with the onion. Add the oil and bring to the boil. Cover and simmer for 2½–3 hours until the beans are done (the length of time needed depends on the age of the beans). Extract the bouquet garni and the onion.
Remove about one third of the beans from the saucepan, mash through a sieve and return to the pan. Season well with salt and pepper. Bring the soup to the boil again, add the noodles and cook until *al dente*. This soup is eaten hot and can also be served cold in summer. A Cabernet is a good accompaniment.

Rice

Italy is not just Europe's largest producer of rice; no other Western country has cultivated such a great variety of delicious rice recipes. Alexander the Great brought rice back from his campaigns of conquest, yet it was the Arabs in Sicily who really knew how to pay homage to its culinary versatility and who gradually introduced rice to the rest of Europe. Nutritious rice pudding, *biancomangiari*, was consumed as early as 1300 in Tuscany; only in the 15th century did rice start to be grown in any quantity, however. From 1800 onwards it quickly began to gain in importance.

Rice cultivation, totaling 245,000 hectares in Italy, is concentrated almost without exception on the Po Plateau. In the triangle of land between Vercelli, Novara, and Pavia, south-west of Milan, the fields are submerged in water after sowing in March. The water is drained only in May, when green shoots start to penetrate the water surface. By the harvest in September, the rice plants are dry, brown, and bushy. Rice has an especially large role to play in the cuisine of Northern Italy and has joined pasta in equal rank in the *primi piatti*, the second starter. It is also popular in soups and salads, however, and as an accompaniment, or an ingredient in desserts or cookies. The average per capita rice consumption is about eleven pounds (5 kg) per year.

Italians know how to use rice. There are many kinds which have different properties when cooked and are thus suitable for a variety of dishes. Of great importance are the kinds belonging to the *oryza sativa japonica* family, which have rounder grains. *Oryza sativa indica*, long-grain rice, is not as common.

Rice of one type is always the same according to Italian law. The different types are divided up into four categories laid out by the Italian Rice Institute. To date, the Institute has tested over 25,000 kinds of rice.

Once the rice has been sown in the spring, the paddy fields on the Po Plateau are submerged under water.

As soon as the shoots start to penetrate the water surface the fields are drained.
The harvest is in September.

The rice is husked in this mill.

Types of Rice

In Italy, rice is split into the following categories, with the name of the rice type always printed on the packet:

- **Riso comune** – subdivided into the types *originario* and *balilla*. Round, glutinous, short-grained rice which needs 13 to 14 minutes' cooking time. Ideal for desserts.
- **Riso semifino** – subdivided into the types *padano*, *lido* and *rosa marchetti*. Has longish, round grains and needs 15 minutes' cooking time. Used in minestrone and other soups.
- **Riso fino** – subdivided into the types *vialone nano*, *ribe*, *R. B.*, *Sant'Andrea* and *ringo*. Round, medium-grain rice; non-stick and even-cooking, with 16 minutes' cooking time. Good for risottos.
- **Riso superfino** – subdivided into the types *arborio*, *roma*, *baldo* and *carnaroli*. Large, long, round grains, needing 18 minutes' cooking time. The most common types of rice for risottos.

Specialties:
Carnaroli: round, long-grain rice, lavishly cultivated without fertilizers and herbicides. Top-quality, non-stick rice. 18 minutes' cooking time; excellent for risottos.
Indica or **Thai**: long, thin grains, a non-stick rice. Makes up over one fifth of Italy's rice produce, mainly for export purposes. Needs 18 to 20 minutes' cooking time and is used in international rice dishes.

Risotto di Gamberetti
Risotto with Shrimps
(Illustration below)

5¹/₂ cups (1¹/₄ l) meat stock
1 shallot
4 oz (100 g) butter
1 lb (500 g) arborio rice
8 oz (250 g) shelled Mediterranean shrimps
1 cup (200 ml) white wine
1 Tbs chopped flat-leaved parsley

Heat up the stock. Peel the shallot, chop finely and brown in 2 oz of the butter. Add the rice and fry for 1–2 minutes. Rinse the shrimps, add to the rice and fry gently for a further 1–2 minutes, then add the white wine.
When the rice has absorbed all the liquid, gradually add the stock, stirring continuously. When the rice is *al dente* (after about 18 minutes), mix in the rest of the butter and the parsley. Leave the risotto to stand, covered, for 2 minutes and serve on warmed plates.
A Bianco Colli Euganei goes well with this dish.
Tip: Risotto with fish or shellfish is nearly always served without Parmesan.

Risotto di gamberetti – Risotto with shrimps

Risi e Bisi
Rice with Peas

1³/₄ lbs (800 g) young peas-in-the-pod
2¹/₂ oz (75 g) fresh belly of pork
1 onion
2¹/₂ oz (75 g) butter
1¹/₂ cups (300 g) arborio rice
2 Tbs parsley, finely chopped
4 oz (100 g) grated Parmesan

Shell the peas and set aside. Boil the pea pods in 7¹/₂ cups (1¹/₂ l) of salted water for 1 hour. Sieve, reserving the liquid; keep the liquid warm.
Finely cube the pork. Peel and finely chop the onion.
Melt the butter in a suitably large saucepan and gently fry the pork and onion in it. Add the rice and fry until transparent, stirring continuously. Add two ladlefuls of the pea liquid and the peas and boil for 5 minutes. When the rice has absorbed all the liquid, keep adding the pea water, stirring continuously, until after about 18 minutes the rice is *al dente.* Then add half the Parmesan and the parsley.
Leave the finished risotto to stand for 1–2 minutes and then sprinkle with the remaining Parmesan.
Serve a Tocai del Piave with this dish.

Risotto alla Milanese
Milanese Risotto

6 cups (1¹/₄ l) chicken stock
¹/₄ tsp (1 g) saffron strands
2 large bones of beef with marrow
3 oz (80 g) butter
1 Tbs chopped onion
2¹/₂ cups (400 g) vialone rice
1 cup (200 ml) dry white wine
4 oz (100 g) grated Parmesan

Heat up the chicken stock. Leave the saffron to soak in two tablespoons of the stock. Remove the beef marrow from the bones and melt in 2 oz of the butter. Add the onion and fry gently.
Add the rice and fry until transparent, stirring continuously. Add the wine. Once the wine has been fully absorbed by the rice, gradually add the hot chicken stock, using a ladle; stir continuously.
After about 10 minutes, add the saffron with its 2 tablespoons of stock. Once the rice is *al dente* (about 16 minutes), remove the pan from the heat and stir in the rest of the butter and half the Parmesan. Sprinkle the risotto with the rest of the Parmesan and serve.
A suitable wine for this dish would be a Barbaresco dell'Oltrepò Pavese.

Risotto con Asparagi Verdi
Rice with Green Asparagus

7¹/₂ cups (1¹/₂ l) meat stock
1 lb (500 g) green Italian asparagus
1 Tbs chopped onion
2¹/₂ oz (75 g) butter
2¹/₂ cups (400 g) vialone rice
1 cup (200 ml) dry white wine
4 oz (100 g) grated Parmesan

Heat up the meat stock. Peel the asparagus, removing the tips and set aside; cut into 1 inch (2 cm) pieces. Fry the onion in the butter until transparent. Add the pieces of asparagus (without the tips) and fry briefly. Then add the rice. When the rice is transparent, add the white wine. Once the rice has fully absorbed the wine, gradually add the hot stock, using a ladle and stirring continuously.
After about 10 minutes, add the asparagus tips. When the rice is *al dente* (after about 16 minutes), stir in half the Parmesan and sprinkle the rest over the risotto. Serve.
A Sauvignon Colli Berici goes well with this rice dish.

Types of Rice
(See overview opposite)
1 R. B.
2 Riso brillato
3 Riso sbramato
4 Roma
5 Riso parboiled
6 Balilla
7 Vialone nano
8 Arborio

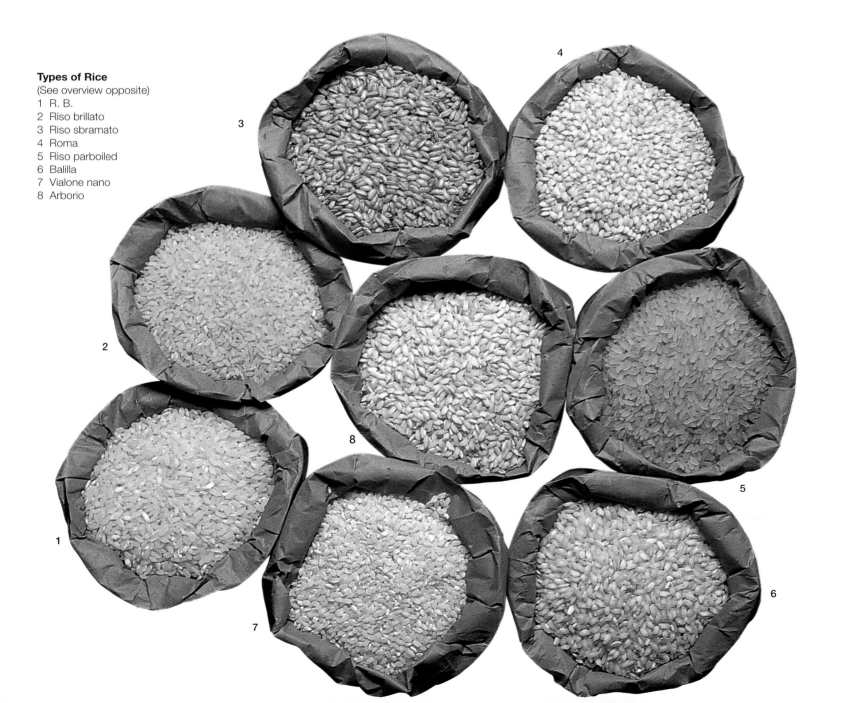

545

Salumi

Italy boasts a proud collection of salumi. This general term – in which the word *salare*, to salt, can be found – covers all kinds of ham and Italian sausage. Salumi are so popular that Italian pigs are farmed only with a view to their suitability for ham and sausage. Their use as fresh pork is considered to be a secondary factor.

Hams and sausages are divided up into two categories:

● Raw and cured products – these are made from raw meat, salted in varying degrees and then matured, whereby air-dried salumi is of great importance. Once cured, the meats can be kept at room temperature. Raw hams such as Parma or San Daniele and salamis such as Soppressa, Coppa or Bresaola belong to this category.

● Cooked products – after the initial preparation, these are cooked or heated in modern fan ovens. They should be stored in a cool place and consumed relatively quickly. Mortadella, Cotechino, Zampone, and *prosciutto cotto*, cooked ham, are part of this category; the latter probably has first place among salumi, especially as far as its usage is concerned.

1 **Coppa** – famous specialty made from pork neck-end muscle. The meat is cured wrapped in a cloth which has been soaked in white wine.

2 **Bresaola** – air-dried beef, similar to Switzerland's "Bündner Fleisch."

3 **Mortadella** – pork sausage, originally from Bologna. Comes in different grades.

4 **Zampone** – filled pig's trotters, a specialty from Modena. The filling is made from finely-ground, well-seasoned pork knuckle and shoulder.

5 **Soppressa veneta** – pressed, coarsely-grained sausage from Veneto, air-dried for up to six months in dark stores.

6 **Bondiola** – sausage from Veneto.

7 **Soppressata** – brawn sausage with a spicy taste, often lightly smoked, then pressed and air-dried.

8-10 **Salame** – possibly the best-known of all salumi, this is cured for three to six months. Northern salami has a milder taste; in the south, it is hotter and spicier.

Salami

The basis of all types of salami is raw meat, especially pork, but also beef, wild boar, goose or donkey meat can be used. Depending on the kind of salami to be made, fifty to one hundred percent lean meat is selected; with pork, this is usually from the neck end and shoulder. Belly of pork or loin can be added as a further ingredient.

The meat is first put through a meat grinder and coarsely ground. If a finer texture is required, it is reground using a smaller blade.

Lean and fatty meat is then mixed together and seasoned with finely-chopped garlic, freshly-ground pepper or whole peppercorns, with dried herbs, even fennel seeds, sometimes with a little wine, and always with plenty of salt. All the ingredients have to be stirred well to ensure that the fat and spices are evenly distributed.

The sausage skin is then bound at one end; the other end is stretched over a funnel through which the sausage meat is pushed into the skin. During this process, it is important that the meat is tightly packed to avoid the formation of air bubbles. The sausage is then bound at the desired length.

The next stage in the preparation of salami takes place in a heated chamber, where the sausage is dried for a few hours. It is then transferred to a cold store, which is neither too dry nor too damp, and left to cure.

During this period of natural maturation, normally lasting three to six months, a floury mold builds up on the outer skin of the salami. Although this is regularly washed off, it is this mold which gives the sausage its fine aroma.

Italy's Pigs

Pigs are primarily reared for ham and salami. This means that they have to fulfill specifications which are completely different from those for their northern European cousins. The latter end their days as light-weights, weighing under 220 pounds (100 kg); Italian ham and salami manufacturers require rather more sturdy candidates which should top around 350 pounds (160 kg) when slaughtered. Italian pigs are also not fattened so quickly, so that their meat is suitable for salami production. They are usually slaughtered aged between nine and twelve months.

Great value is attached to the nutritional balance of the feed, which consists of cornmeal, barley, soya, bran, and whey. For the feed gives the meat its fine aroma and solid consistency, both indispensable requirements for quality ham.

Wild boar are a much sought-after catch, as their meat not only makes excellent ragouts; it is also often used in salami, a Tuscan specialty.

The meat is put through the mixer and ground coarse or fine, depending on the type of salami.

Each butcher has his own special composition of spices and seasonings.

Once the sausage dough has been evenly mixed, it is filled into long skins.

Wild boar salami is often made into small sausages.

Salami Specialties
(See also pp. 546–547)

Salame al sugo
This owes its exceptional taste to the tongue and liver worked into the mixture, as well as to various herbs and spices, especially garlic (Lucrezia Borgia is credited with the recipe). It is cured for six months. It is eaten cooked, whereby a rich sauce, the *sugo,* is formed during the cooking process. A specialty from Ferrara, Emilia-Romagna.

Salame di Felino
This village near Parma has risen to fame through its medium-coarse *salame.* Only lightly salted, it is made from pork and belly of pork, seasoned with pepper and garlic pressed in white wine.

Salame di Milano
This is possibly the most well-known of the salami family, made from especially lean, finely-ground, evenly-mixed pork or pork and beef with a maximum of 20 percent pig's fat. Cured for at least three, but often up to six months, it can weigh up to 9 pounds (4 kg).

Salame di Montefeltro
This owes its individual character to the meat of black-haired wild pigs. Only the best cuts from loin, shoulder and leg are chosen; seasoned with finely- and coarsely-ground pepper.

Salame di Napoli
This is made from the meat of Southern Italy's smaller pigs, mixed with ground beef, lots of garlic, and peppers. Lightly smoked and air-dried.

Salame di Varzi
Coarsely-ground pork, made with 30 percent bacon and flavored with white wine, garlic and nutmeg. Usually about one foot (30 cm) long; from the borderlands between Lombardy and Emilia.

Salame d'oca
Goose determines the taste of this salami (It. *oca* means goose), although equal proportions of lean pork and belly of pork are also included in the mixture. Goose salami from Mortara, a village in Lombardy, is particularly famous.

Salame gentile
This "gentle" salami comes from Emilia-Romagna, mixed from lean pork and bacon. It is filled into especially thick skins and famed for its tenderness.

Salame nostrano veneto
Venetians love this coarse salami made from lean and fatty pork and crushed peppercorns. It is available with or without garlic and eaten in thick slices.

A selection of regionally produced salamis, coarse and fine, spicy and mild.

Meat

Italian cuts of beef

Quarto anteriore – front:
1 Costata – cutlet, chine
2 Sottospalla – fore rib
3 Pancia – thin flank
4 Fesone di spalla – thin rib
5 Reale – thick rib
6 Petto – skirt
7 Muscolo anteriore – shank
8 Polpa di spalla – brisket
9 Girello di spalla – shoulder
10 Copertina – chuck
11 Copertina di sotto – blade
12 Collo – neck

Quarto posteriore – back:
13 Lombata – sirloin
14 Filetto – fillet
15 Scamone – upper rump
16 Fianchetto – piece of loin from head of bone
17 Noce – tender cut from the lower head of bone
   and thick flank
18 a) Fesa – tender cut of topside
18 b) Sottofesa – tender cut of silverside
19 Girello – round
20 Campanello – shank
21 Muscolo posteriore – hind shank

Vitello tonnato
Veal with Tuna Sauce

Serves 6

2 lb (1 kg) tender piece of leg of veal
1 onion
1 carrot
1 stick celery
1 bayleaf
1 can tuna in oil
4 anchovy fillets
2 hard-boiled eggs
2 Tbs capers
1 cup (200 ml) olive oil
Salt, black pepper
1 Tbs lemon juice
Slices of lemon, parsley

Roll up the meat, bind with kitchen twine and place in a large saucepan. Peel or wash the onion, carrot, and celery, add to the saucepan and add enough water to cover the meat. Bring to the boil. Cover and simmer over a very low heat for 2 hours. Leave the meat to cool in the liquid.
Drain the tuna well and divide up into largish pieces. Rinse the anchovies and dry. Purée the tuna, anchovies, eggs, and one tablespoon of capers in a mixer. Gradually add the olive oil and a few tablespoons of the meat liquid until a creamy sauce is formed. Season to taste with the salt, pepper, and lemon juice.
Cut the twine away from the veal joint. Slice thinly and arrange on a large platter. Pour the tuna sauce over the meat.
Garnish with the rest of the capers, the slices of lemon and sprigs of parsley.
Cover and leave to stand in the refrigerator for at least 2 hours before serving.
A Cabernet or Bardolino goes well with this dish.

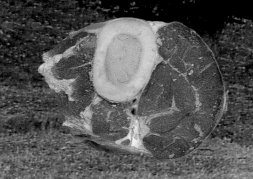

The best-known cut of meat from Tuscany is the *fiorentina* from the fillet and sirloin of Chianina cattle.

The legendary *ossobuco,* sliced leg of veal with marrow, is braised and served with polenta.

Meat Glossary

Agnello – lamb

This, and especially milk lamb – *agnello di latte*, in Rome *abbacchio* – is a favorite at Easter. It is usually cut small and braised as a ragout with vegetables such as peas or artichokes. Leg of lamb, *cosciotto d'agnello*, or lamb cutlets, *costolette di agnello*, are also popular, especially in Piedmont, Liguria, and Rome. Excellent lamb can be had in Sardinia.

Capretto – kid

Kid, much rarer than lamb, comes from the mountainous regions of central and southern Italy. It is prepared in much the same way as lamb, often braised in wine with ham; often it is seasoned with oregano. In Piedmont a good wine such as a Barolo is often used for braising.

Coniglio – rabbit

Rabbit is a savored dish everywhere in Italy. The borderlands, Le Marche, probably have the largest variety of recipes. Rabbit is prepared stuffed – *ripieno* or *farcito* – or rolled, *arrotolato*; it is also often braised in white wine with sage, garlic, and tomatoes, and usually seasoned with rosemary. The north-east like to marinade their rabbit before cooking; the south serve it with pine nuts and raisins.

Maiale – pork

Pork has traditionally always been appreciated most in the ham and salami regions of Italy, such as the Emilia-Romagna with Bologna; it is also important in Umbria with its butchers, famed since the Middle Ages. Here, unboned sucking pig, *porchetta*, is considered a great delicacy. Umbria also has a special breed of semi-wild, lean, black pigs whose meat, in a bacon jacket, is roasted on a spit.

Manzo – beef

Beef is a more common item on menus from the Po Plateau, with its many meadows. Perhaps the most famous Italian beef is from the large, white Chianina cows which graze the Chiana Valley in Tuscany; the best cut is found in restaurants as *fiorentina*, comprising parts of sirloin, fillet and bone. The steaks are approximately $1/2$ inch (1 cm) thick and weigh about 12 oz–1 lb (400–500 g).

Vitello – veal

Veal is mainly eaten when young; one famous specialty is the rare *vitello da latte*, the milk calf, which is no older than one year and no heavier than 400 lb (180 kg). A slightly older, grass-eating calf would hit up to 500 lb (230 kg) on the scales.

Vitellone – heifer, young cow

A heifer weighs 1,100 to 1,320 lb (500–600 kg) maximum and is 16 to 18 months old. A difference is made between *vitello leggero*, light heifers, weighing no more than 1,100 lb (500 kg) and *vitello pesante*, which can weigh between 1,100 and 1,320lb (500–600 kg). *Vitellone* makes up nearly 60 percent of Italy's entire meat consumption. The most popular cuts are *scaloppine*, thin cutlets from the upper leg, thick flank and loin, flattened with a steak hammer, or *ossobuco*, literally "hollow bone," which are slices of hind leg. Italians also like to make *spezzatino*, a kind of goulash, or a classic roast from *vitellone*. Delicacies such as veal offal, and liver in particular, are especially treasured by Italy's gourmets.

Saltimbocca alla Romana
Veal Cutlet with Ham and Sage
(Illustration below)

Serves 2

2 thin veal cutlets
2 slices Parma ham
4 sage leaves
2 ½ oz (70 g) butter
Salt, black pepper
½ cup (100 ml) white wine

Halve the veal cutlets and slices of ham, then carefully flatten the cutlets with a steak hammer. Using toothpicks, fix one slice of ham and one sage leaf to each halved cutlet.

Heat 2 tablespoons of butter in a large frying pan and fry the cutlets over a high heat for 2 minutes on both sides. Season with pepper and a little salt, pour in the wine and reduce the heat.

Add the rest of the butter and stir into the juice. Arrange the cutlets on warmed plates and trickle the sauce over the top of them.

Serve a chilled, dry Frascati with this dish.

Ossobuco alla Milanese
Milanese Knuckle of Veal
(Illustration opposite)

4 thick slices of knuckle of veal
Salt, black pepper
4 Tbs flour
5 Tbs olive oil
1½ oz (40 g) butter
2 onions
2 garlic cloves
2 carrots
1 stick celery
2 sprigs thyme
1 bayleaf
1 wedge untreated lemon peel
1 cup (200 ml) dry white wine
1 cup (200 ml) meat or chicken stock
3 tomatoes
1 Tbs tomato paste

For the gremolata

4 garlic cloves
Grated peel of 1 untreated lemon
2 Tbs parsley, finely chopped

Season the slices of meat with salt and pepper and coat with the flour. Heat the oil and butter in a wide braising pan and brown the meat well on both sides.

Remove and keep warm. Peel or wash and chop the onions, garlic, carrots and celery, add to the pan and fry, stirring continuously. Add the thyme, bayleaf, and lemon peel and then the wine and stock.

Skin and de-seed the tomatoes and cut into small pieces. Add to the vegetables with the tomato paste. Stir well and then return the meat to the pan. Braise over a low heat for 1½ hours. To make the gremolata, finely chop the garlic and mix with the parsley and grated lemon peel. Arrange the slices of meat on warmed plates, sprinkle with the gremolata and pour over the sauce. *Ossobuco* is traditionally served with a *risotto alla milanese* (for recipe see p. 545) and a Barbera d'Asti.

Tip: Ossobuco tastes even better reheated so that it can be prepared the day before it is needed. However, the gremolata should be sprinkled over the meat just before serving.

Beef fillet carpaccio (for recipe see p. 524)

Saltimbocca alla romana – Veal cutlets with ham and sage

Scaloppine di Maiale al Marsala
Pork Cutlet in Marsala Wine

4 pork cutlets
Salt, black pepper
2 Tbs flour
2 oz (60 g) butter
1/2 cup (100 ml) dry Marsala wine

Hammer the cutlets until they are very flat, season with the salt and pepper and dust with the flour. Heat half the butter in a frying pan and fry the cutlets on both sides for 1 1/2 minutes per side. Pour in the Marsala and leave to stand for 5 minutes. Remove the cutlets, arrange on a platter and keep warm.

Scrape together the juices from the meat and stir in the remaining butter in knobs. Season to taste and trickle while still warm over the cutlets. A well-chilled Frascati is an excellent accompanying wine.

Fegato alla Veneziana
Venetian Calf's Liver

3 Tbs olive oil
3 white onions
1 cup (200 ml) dry white wine
1 oz (30 g) butter
1 lb (500 g) calf's liver
Salt, black pepper
2 Tbs parsley, finely chopped

Heat the oil. Peel the onions, cut into rings and fry in the oil until transparent. Pour in the wine and fry for a further 20 minutes until the wine has evaporated. Remove the onion and set aside.
Melt the butter. Finely slice the liver, add to the butter and cook for 4 minutes until done, stirring continuously. Add the onions and warm through; season to taste with the salt and pepper, sprinkle in the parsley and serve immediately.

Agnello Arrosto
Roast Lamb

Serves 6
1 leg of lamb, weighing about 3 1/2 lb (1 1/2 kg)
1 sprig rosemary
4 garlic cloves
Salt, black pepper
3 Tbs olive oil
4 oz (100 g) fatty bacon
1 cup (200 ml) dry white wine
1 Tbs parsley, finely chopped
1 Tbs bread crumbs
2 Tbs grated Parmesan

Pierce the leg of lamb in various places with a sharp knife and insert rosemary leaves and halved garlic cloves into the holes. Season with salt and pepper. Preheat the oven to 400 °F (200 °C).
Heat 2 tablespoons of the oil in a large, heavy roasting pan, cube the bacon and fry until the fat has been released. Place the lamb in the roasting pan and seal well on all sides. Pour in the wine and reduce the liquid by half. Roast in the oven for about 1 1/4 hours, basting frequently with the juices.
Mix together the parsley, bread crumbs, Parmesan, and the rest of the olive oil. Brush the lamb with the paste and leave in the oven, uncovered, for a further 15 minutes, until a crust is formed. When cooked, leave to stand for 10 minutes before carving. Arrange on a plate and pour on the sauce. A Montepulciano d'Abruzzo is an ideal accompaniment.

Ossobuco alla milanese –
Milanese knuckle of veal

Pollastro in squaquaciò – Venetian chicken in tomato sauce

Poultry

Poultry, or to be more precise, chicken and guinea fowl, are among the most popular dishes to feature on Italy's menus. The Mediterranean chicken, the most common type found, has a partridge-colored plumage. The Paduan chicken is also well known and is especially stocky and heavy. The imagination of Italy's cooks has fired a wealth of poultry dishes from simple broiled chicken to the most lavish recipes. The main criteria is, however, that the bird used has had a good and relatively free life. Italians – at least in more rural areas – thus like to buy their poultry live and slaughter and pluck them at home.

Poultry Glossary

Anatra – duck
Beccaccia – snipe
Cappone – capon
Fagiano – pheasant
Faraona – guinea fowl
Galletto – spring chicken
Gallina – boiling fowl
Oca – goose
Pernice – partridge
Piccione – pigeon
Pollastra, pollastro – pullet (young chicken)
Pollastro da ingrasso – fattened chicken (poulard)
Pollo – chicken
Quaglie – quails
Tacchina, tacchino – turkey hen, turkey cock

Pollastro in Squaquaciò
Venetian chicken in Tomato Sauce
(Illustration above)

1 Tbs dried porcini mushrooms
1 poulard, weighing about 3½ lb (1.5 kg)
1 onion
1 can tomatoes
2 garlic cloves
A few basil leaves
³/₄ cup (150 ml) Cabernet (red wine)
Sugar
Salt, black pepper
2 oz (50 g) butter
4 Tbs olive oil

Preheat the oven to 400 °F (200 °C).
Soak the mushrooms in lukewarm water for 15 minutes. Separate the chicken into four pieces. Peel and quarter the onions and cut up the tomatoes into small pieces. Put the onion, tomatoes, mushrooms with their soaking liquid, garlic, basil, red wine, and a pinch of sugar into a roasting tin and mix well.
Season the poulard pieces with the salt and pepper and place in the roasting tin, skin-side up. Add the butter and olive oil. Roast in the oven for 1–1¹/₂ hours. Remove the meat from the sauce and keep warm. Press the sauce through a sieve, thicken if necessary, season to taste and serve separately.
Grilled polenta and the wine used in preparing the dish are good accompaniments.

Pollo alla Diavola
Deviled Chicken
(Illustration above right)

1 young chicken, weighing about 3 lb (1.2 kg)
2 small, dried peppers
8 sage leaves
1 sprig rosemary
6 Tbs olive oil
Juice of 1 lemon
Salt

Cut open the chicken along the spine using poultry shears and press very flat. Finely chop the peppers, sage leaves, and rosemary and mix together with the oil, lemon juice, and a pinch of salt.
Brush the chicken with half the mixture and leave to stand for one hour.
Preheat the oven to 400 °F (200 °C).
Place the chicken on a sheet of aluminum foil, fold up the sides and place this on a baking tray. Roast in the oven for about one hour until brown and crispy, basting from time to time with the remaining pepper mixture. If the chicken browns too quickly, reduce the heat. Serve with a young Chianti.

Pollo alla diavola – Deviled chicken

Faraona al vino bianco – Guinea fowl in white wine

Faraona al Vino Bianco
Guinea Fowl in White Wine
(Illustration above right)

1 guinea fowl, weighing about 3 lb (1.2 kg)
Salt, black pepper
1 onion
2 garlic cloves
8 medium-sized potatoes
1 sprig rosemary
5 sage leaves
1½ oz (40 g) butter
4 Tbs olive oil
1¼ cups (250 ml) dry white wine (Soave)
1¼ cups (250 ml) chicken stock

Preheat the oven to 400 °F (200 °C).
Cut the guinea fowl into four pieces and season with the salt and pepper. Peel and quarter the onion, halve the garlic and peel the potatoes.
Put the onion, garlic, rosemary, and sage into a flameproof casserole. Place the pieces of guinea fowl on top of this, skin-side down. Arrange the potatoes around the meat and add the butter and oil.
Put the casserole in the oven. When the fat begins to sizzle after about 15 minutes, pour in the wine and half the chicken stock. Turn the meat and potatoes after approximately 40 minutes and pour in the rest of the stock, if needed. After a total cooking time of 1½ hours, the wine and stock should have been absorbed by the meat and potatoes; the only liquid remaining should be the cooking fat and meat juices. Arrange the meat and potatoes on a platter and keep warm. Sieve the sauce. Serve this separately and as a wine, the Soave used in the preparation of the dish.

Pollo alla Marengo
Chicken Marengo

1 young chicken, weighing about 3 lb (1.2 kg)
Salt, black pepper
6 Tbs olive oil
1 lb (500 g) tomatoes
2 garlic cloves, pressed
¾ cup (150 ml) dry white wine
¾ cup (150 ml) chicken stock
8 oz (250 g) mushrooms
6 oz (200 g) pearl onions
3 Tbs butter
3 Tbs lemon juice
4 large shrimps or yabbis
4–8 slices baguette
4 eggs
A few basil leaves
1 Tbs flat-leaved parsley, finely chopped

Separate the chicken into several pieces and season with the salt and pepper. Heat 5 tablespoons of olive oil in a large frying pan and brown the chicken pieces on all sides for 10 minutes. Remove and keep warm.
Skin, de-seed, and quarter the tomatoes; add to the chicken with the garlic. Fry briefly and then add the white wine and the chicken stock. Cover and leave to simmer for 45 minutes. Wash the mushrooms and skin the onions. In a second frying pan, melt 2 tablespoons of the butter and fry the onion and mushroom in it for approximately 10 minutes. Season with salt, pepper, and 2 tablespoons of the lemon juice.
Preheat the oven to 400 °F (200 °C).
In a third small frying pan, fry the shrimps in the rest of the oil for 5 minutes. Add the last tablespoon of the lemon juice. Toast the bread slices in the oven for 10 minutes, turning once. Remove the meat from the first pan, reduce the sauce and season to taste. Add the mushroom, onion, chicken pieces, and breasts to the sauce and warm through. Melt the rest of the butter, add the eggs, season and scramble. Arrange the chicken, vegetables, and shrimps on a large warmed platter. Place the toasted bread around the edges and spoon some of the egg onto each slice. Garnish with parsley and basil and serve.
A Barbera goes well with this dish.

Game

The Italians are enthusiastic hunters. Some breeds of animal may have become rather rare, but rabbit and wild boar are still plentiful. In the past few years, the number of wild boar has actually increased considerably. Thus in the late fall and early winter in the regions of Tuscany, Lazio, the Abruzzi, and Calabria, traditional recipes with wild boar loom large on the menu. The gourmet requires rather more luck, however, when looking for restaurants serving pheasant, partridge or coot. Quail is a more common phenomenon as they are often bred. In the most northerly regions of Italy, even fallow deer can be found during the hunting season (August through January).

Fagiano Tartufato
Pheasant with Truffles

Serves 2

1 young pheasant
2 Tbs brandy
1 Tbs dry Marsala wine
1 small, black truffle
Salt, black pepper
6 slices fresh, fatty bacon
3 Tbs olive oil
1 garlic clove
1 sprig rosemary
1/2 cup (100 ml) chicken stock

Prepare the pheasant. Mix the brandy and Marsala. Finely slice the truffle and leave to marinate in the wine and brandy mixture for one hour.
Remove the sliced truffle from the marinade, reserving the liquid, and carefully insert under the skin of the pheasant. Leave the pheasant in the refrigerator overnight, covered, so the truffle can flavor the meat. Preheat the oven to 350 °F (180 °C).
Season the pheasant with the salt and pepper and cover with the bacon slices. Heat the oil in a braising pan. Finely chop the garlic and rosemary and fry gently (the garlic should not discolor). Then add the pheasant to the pan and braise in the oven, covered, for 30 minutes. Pour in the truffle marinade and chicken stock. Baste the pheasant occasionally. Remove the bacon from the meat after 15 minutes; increase the heat and brown the pheasant for 15 minutes.
Remove the bird from the pan and keep warm. Sieve the sauce, skimming off the fat, and reduce the sauce to a maximum of 6 tablespoons of liquid. Carve the pheasant and trickle the sauce over the meat.
Serve immediately while still hot.
A Barolo goes well with this dish.

Cinghiale al Barolo
Wild Boar in Red Wine

2 lb (1 kg) shoulder of wild boar
Salt, black pepper
3 Tbs olive oil
2 oz (50 g) butter
1 Tbs tomato paste

For the marinade

1 onion
1 carrot
1 stick celery
2 garlic cloves
5 cloves
10 black peppercorns
1 bayleaf
1 sprig rosemary
1 sprig thyme
1 bottle Barolo (red wine)

Skin the meat if necessary and place in a small, high-sided saucepan.
To make the marinade, peel or wash the onion, carrot and celery and cut into pieces. Add to the meat with the herbs and spices, pour in the wine and leave to marinate for 1–2 days.
Remove the meat from the marinade, dry well and season with salt and pepper. Strain the marinade. Heat the oil and butter in a heavy pan large enough to hold the joint and seal the meat on all sides in the fat. Pour in half the marinade, add the tomato paste and simmer the meat over a low heat, turning occasionally and adding more marinade if needed. The cooking time is about 2–3 hours.
Remove the joint from the pan and leave to stand for 10 minutes. In the meantime, press the sauce through a sieve, reduce if necessary and season to taste. Carve the joint and serve with the sauce in a separate jug. Fresh, soft polenta and a matured Barolo are the usual accompaniments to this dish.

Lepre in Salmi
Hare Ragout
(Illustration)

1 hare, weighing about 3 1/2 lb (1.5 kg)
Salt, black pepper
Flour
2 oz (50 g) butter
3 Tbs olive oil
1 Tbs tomato paste

For the marinade

1 onion
1 carrot
1 stick celery
2 garlic cloves
1 bayleaf
10 black peppercorns
6 juniper berries
1 sprig fresh thyme
1 sprig fresh rosemary
6 sage leaves
1 bottle Chianti

Prepare the hare and divide up. Keep the innards in a bowl in the refrigerator. Put the meat in a saucepan. Peel or wash the onion, carrot, and celery and chop. Add to the meat with the herbs and spices, pour in the wine and leave to marinate in a cool place for 2 days.
Remove the meat from the marinade, dry well, season with salt and pepper and flour lightly. Strain the marinade.
Heat the oil and butter in a heavy braising pan and fry the hare on all sides. Finely chop the innards, add to the meat and fry briefly. Pour in the marinade, add the tomato paste and simmer the meat over a low heat for about 2 1/2–3 hours.
Remove the meat from the pan and keep warm. Press the sauce through a sieve and reduce if necessary. Return the pieces of hare to the sauce, heat and serve hot. Freshly-made polenta and a Chianti go well with this dish.

Lepre in salmì – Hare ragout

The hunt is a great passion of the Italians, mobilizing old and young. In many regions it is mainly wild boar that are hunted.

Fish and Seafood

A large degree of Italy's attraction must surely be apportioned to its unbelievable coastline. Which other major country can boast such a large proportion of shoreline in relation to its surface area? The islands of Sardinia and Sicily must also be included here. Sicily's waters, for example, are considered extremely fruitful and are rich in different species. The Gulf of Venice is also famous for its great wealth of fish and seafood.

It is, therefore, hardly surprising that the Italians have at their bequest an exceptional treasury of fish recipes. This is mainly due to the fact that every coastal region swears by its own particular preparation of each type of fish or shellfish. The differences are often very small, as the gifts of the sea are loved far too much that one would want to spoil them with complex recipes.

Background: Once the seafood fishermen have brought in their harvest, they head for their raised hut, where the mollusks are sorted and packed.

Cultivated mussels like to affix themselves to posts and pillars; hence their name "post mussels."

The seafood fisherman brings his harvest inland in baskets.

Fish and Seafood Glossary

Acciuga, alice – anchovy
Anguilla – eel
Aragosta – crawfish
Astice – lobster
Baccalà – salted, also dried cod
Bianchetto, spratto, sarda papalina; gianchetto (Genoese) – whitefish
Branzino, spigola – sea bass
Calamaretto – small squid
Calamaro – squid
Canocchio – shrimp; only in the Adriatic
Cannolicchio – ascidian
Capa santa, conchiglia di San Giacomo – scallop
Carpa, carpione – carp
Cernia – sea bass
Ciecha – glass eel
Cocciola, vongola (colloquial) – cockle

Cozza, mitilo – mussel
Dattero di mare – sea date or date mussel
Gamberetto – shrimp (100 to 125 per 1 lb)
Gambero – prawn
Gamberone – king prawn; langoustine
Grancevola, granceola – sea spider or spider crab
Granciporro – edible crab
Grongo – conger eel
Lampreda – lamprey
Luccio – pike
Lumaca di mare – winkles
Merluzzo – cod
Muggine – gray mullet
Nasello – hake
Orata – sea bream
Ostrica – oyster
Pesce cappone – gurnard
Pesce San Pietro, sampiero – John Dory
Pesce spada – swordfish

Polpetto – baby octopus
Polpo – octopus
Razza – ray
Riccio di mare – sea urchin
Rombo – turbot
Rospo, rospo marino – monkfish
Salmone – salmon
Sarda, sardina – sardine
Scampo – scampi
Seppia – squid
Sgombro – mackerel
Sogliola – sole
Stoccafisso – dried cod
Tellina – bean shell, sunset shell
Tinca – tench
Tonno – tuna
Triglia – red mullet
Trota – trout
Vongole – clam

On Italian markets, and especially in fishing villages, there is a huge range of shellfish to be had:
1 *chicciole di mare* – whelks; 2–4 various clams: *vongola minore* (2), *vongola grigia* (3), *vongola fasolara* or *noce* (4); 5 *lumace di mare* – winkles.

Coda di Rospo in Umido
Monkfish in White Wine Sauce

4 monkfish fillets, each weighing about 8 oz (250 g)
1 onion
2 garlic cloves
1 stick celery
1 sprig rosemary
3 sprigs flat-leaved parsley
6 Tbs olive oil
Salt, white pepper
Flour
1 1/4 cups (250 ml) white wine

Wash the fillets and dry. Peel or wash the onion, garlic
and celery; chop these and the herbs. Fry gently in a
flameproof frying pan in the olive oil.
Preheat the oven to 400 °F (200 °C). Season the fish
with the salt and pepper, flour and fry on both sides.
Pour in the wine and cook in the oven for 20 minutes.
Arrange the fillets of fish on a platter and keep warm.
Reduce the fish liquid, sieve and pour over the fish.
Serve immediately while very hot. A Vermentino from
Liguria is an ideal accompanying wine.

Insalata Frutti di Mare
Seafood Salad
(Illustration top right)

1 lb (500 g) fresh squid
8 oz (250 g) fresh octopus
14 oz (400 g) fresh shrimps
1 1/2 lb (750 g) fresh clams

For the sauce
5 Tbs olive oil
1/4 tsp mustard powder
Juice of 1 lemon
1 garlic clove
1 bunch flat-leaved parsley
Salt, white pepper

Prepare the squid (carefully remove the tentacles, eyes,
hard masticatory organs, cuttlebone "beak," viscera,
and ink sac) and wash and cut into rings. Wash the
octopus, shell the shrimps and remove the black
intestine.
Bring 7 1/2 cups (1 1/2 l) of salted water to the boil and
boil the squid rings, octopus and shrimps for 5 minutes.
Remove and rinse in cold water.
Wash and scrub the clams and put into a saucepan
with some water. Cover, bring to the boil and leave to
stand for 5 minutes until the shells open. Drain and
remove the clams from their shells, discarding any that
have not opened.
To make the sauce, mix together the olive oil, mustard
powder, and lemon juice. Press the garlic and add the
juice to the sauce. Wash the parsley, chop finely and
add to the sauce. Season with the salt and pepper.
Put the seafood in a bowl and toss in the sauce. Leave
to stand in the refrigerator for at least 2 hours. Season
to taste before serving.
Garnish with wedges of lemon and sprigs of parsley
and serve with a chilled Chardonnay.

*Insalata frutti di mare –
Seafood salad*

Calamaretti alla Napoletana
Neapolitan Squid

1½ lb (800 g) baby squid
1 oz (30 g) raisins
1¼ cups (250 ml) dry white wine
1 Tbs chopped onion
1 garlic clove, pressed
5 Tbs olive oil
10 oz (300 g) tomatoes
4 oz (100 g) black olives
1 oz (30 g) pine nuts
2 Tbs flat-leaved parsley, chopped
Salt, white pepper

Prepare the squid, wash and cut into rings. Soak the raisins in 3 tablespoons of the wine. Fry the onion and garlic in the oil in a heavy frying pan until transparent. Add the rest of the wine and reduce the liquid by half. Skin and de-seed the tomatoes, cut into pieces and simmer in the wine for 20 minutes. Add the squid rings and raisins; cover and cook for 30 minutes.
Stone and halve the olives; roast the pine nuts in a saucepan without any fat. Add the olives, pine nuts, and parsley to the squid rings, mix well and bring to the boil. Season with the salt and pepper.
A white wine from Capri or Ischia would go well with this dish.

Grigliata Mista di Pesce
Mixed Broiled Fish
(Illustration left)

4 small sole
4 small red mullet
4 monkfish fillets
8 medium-sized shrimps, unshelled
8 Tbs olive oil
For the sauce
2 garlic cloves
1 Tbs chopped parsley
6 Tbs olive oil
Juice of ½ lemon
Salt, white pepper
Lemon slices

Preheat the broiler. Scale, gut and clean the sole and red mullet. Wash the monkfish fillets and shrimps and drain well. Brush the fish and shrimps with 4 tablespoons of the olive oil and leave to stand for 10 minutes.
Meanwhile, prepare the sauce. Finely chop the garlic and mix together with the parsley, olive oil, lemon juice, salt, and pepper.
Carefully broil the fish on both sides for about 10 minutes, and the shrimps for a maximum of only 5 minutes per side. Arrange the shrimps and fish on a platter and garnish with wedges of lemon. Serve the sauce separately. A good accompaniment is broiled polenta and a Riesling Italico.

Grigliata mista di pesce –
Mixed broiled fish

Tonno stufato – Braised tuna

Tonno Stufato
Braised Tuna
(Illustration above left)

1 onion
1 garlic clove
2 sprigs rosemary
6 Tbs olive oil
Piece of tuna, weighing 2 lb (1 kg)
Salt, black pepper
1 cup (200 ml) dry white wine
1 Tbs flat-leaved parsley, chopped

Peel the onion and garlic; finely chop these and the rosemary and fry gently in the olive oil.
Preheat the oven to 340 °F (170 °C).
Wash and dry the tuna, season with salt and pepper and quickly fry on both sides in the oil. Pour in the wine and bring to the boil. Cook the fish in the oven for 40 minutes. Remove from the pan and keep warm. Reduce the sauce, add the parsley and pour over the tuna. Serve with a slightly chilled Cabernet.

Vegetables

Every vegetable imaginable seems to flourish from the Alps to the tip of the Boot, a favorite nickname for boot-shaped Italy. Agricultural sources officially list approximately fifty different types. Without doubt, the Italian vegetable king must be the tomato, for nowhere else does this fruit enjoy such a supremacy as in Italy. It is found as a sauce for pasta and gnocchi, as a basic topping on pizzas, in salads or, ingeniously, just with Mozzarella. It is added to many fish soups and fish dishes, to ragouts of meat and poultry, and to numerous other recipes. And in order to be able to savor them all year round, tomatoes are bottled or dried, whole or as a concentrated paste, in cans and jars.

Italians know how to prepare vegetables as a matter of principle. They cook them carefully, so as not to spoil their natural aroma and color; they should always have a pleasant, *al dente* crunch.

Peperoni imbottiti – Stuffed peppers

Parmigiana di melanzane – Baked eggplant

Bagna Caôda – Vegetable Fondue

Vegetable fondue is a traditional hors d'œuvre in Piedmont. The ingredients differ from town to town, from host to host and from restaurant to restaurant, however. Sometimes large quantities of anchovies or garlic are used for the sauce; sometimes smaller portions are added. Sometimes only raw or only cooked vegetables find their way onto the fondue forks; sometimes a combination of both is preferred. In all cases, it is the seasons that determine the selection, and the vegetables should always be fresh and of the best quality.

The vegetables are dipped in an anchovy and garlic sauce, which is kept warm on a spirit burner. In Piedmont, this dish is usually prepared in winter among a group of friends or when the family is gathered together. If the meal has more than one course, the fondue is served before the main course.

Bagna Caôda
Vegetable Fondue

A variety of different vegetables, cut into bite-sized pieces

For the sauce
6–8 garlic cloves
2 oz (60 g) butter
$1^{1}/_{4}$ cups (250 ml) olive oil
4 oz (100 g) anchovy fillets in oil

Arrange the vegetable pieces on a large platter. Press the garlic and gently fry in the butter in a saucepan; do not allow the garlic to brown. Over a very low heat, gradually add the olive oil, stirring continuously. Take care that the oil does not become too hot or the garlic will turn brown and become bitter. Remove the pan from the heat. Add the anchovy fillets and mash with a fork. Return the pan to the stove and stir the sauce over a low heat until it becomes creamy. Place the pan on a spirit burner in the middle of the table within reach of all the guests, who can now select vegetable pieces and dip them into the sauce. Careful: the sauce should not come to the boil at any time! Baguette is usually served with fondue and a young, fruity red wine, for example a sparkling Bonarda Piemontese or a Dolcetto.

Parmigiana di Melanzane
Baked Eggplant
(Illustration opposite bottom left)

2 lb (1 kg) eggplant
Salt, black pepper
4 Tbs olive oil
2 garlic cloves, crushed
2 Tbs basil, finely chopped
2 lb (1 kg) tomatoes
Pure vegetable oil for frying
Flour
3 Mozzarella
5 oz (150 g) grated Parmesan

Cut the eggplant lengthwise into slices about ¹/₂ inch (1 cm) thick. Salt and leave to stand for one hour. Then rinse off the salt and dry with kitchenroll.
Meanwhile, heat the olive oil and gently fry the garlic and basil in it. Peel and de-seed the tomatoes and cut into small pieces. Add to the oil and simmer for 20 minutes. Season with the salt and pepper to taste.
Heat some pure vegetable oil in a large frying pan. Dust the eggplant slices with flour and fry a few at a time until brown. Drain them on kitchenroll to absorb any excess oil. Slice the Mozzarella.
Preheat the oven to 350 °F (180 °C).
Lightly grease a flat, flameproof dish. Layer the eggplant, tomato sauce, Mozzarella and, with each layer, 2 tablespoons of Parmesan in the dish, finishing off with a layer of Mozzarella and Parmesan.
Bake the vegetables in the oven for 30–40 minutes. This dish tastes best when served lukewarm with a Chianti Classico.

Peperoni Imbottiti
Stuffed Peppers
(Illustration opposite top left)

2 red and 2 yellow peppers
3 tomatoes
Salt, black pepper
2 garlic cloves
8 anchovy fillets (in oil)
3 Tbs cold-pressed olive oil
1 Tbs flat-leaved parsley, chopped

Preheat the oven to 400 °F (200 °C).
Wash, halve, and de-seed the peppers. Place in a flat, flameproof dish.
Slice the tomatoes. Place two slices of tomato on each halved pepper and season with the salt and pepper. Thinly slice the garlic and arrange on the tomato slices with one anchovy fillet per halved pepper. Trickle olive oil over the peppers and cook in the oven for 30 minutes. Sprinkle with the parsley and serve hot.
A chilled Trebbiano goes well with this dish.

Fiori di Zucchini Fritti
Deep-fried Zucchini Blossoms

2 egg yolks, 2 egg whites
¹/₂ cup (100 ml) mineral water
¹/₂ cup (100 ml) white wine
Vegetable oil for frying
Salt, black pepper
1¹/₂ cups (200 g) flour
16 zucchini blossoms with small fruits
Lemon wedges

Beat the egg yolks together with the mineral water, wine, one tablespoon of the oil, salt and pepper and gradually add the flour. Leave the batter to stand for about 20 minutes. Then beat the egg whites with a pinch of salt until stiff and fold into the batter.
Heat the oil for deep-frying. Carefully clean the zucchini blossoms by gently blowing through them and not washing them, dip them into the batter and deep-fry a few at a time. Drain on kitchenroll. Garnish with lemon wedges and serve immediately.

Peperonata
Peppers

2 lb (1 kg) red, green and yellow peppers
1 lb (500 g) tomatoes
¹/₂ cup (100 ml) olive oil
2 Tbs onions, finely chopped
1 tsp garlic, finely chopped
Salt, black pepper

Wash and de-seed the peppers and cut into strips. Skin and de-seed the tomatoes and chop. Heat the oil and fry the onion and garlic in it until transparent. Add the vegetables, cover, and braise for 20–30 minutes, stirring occasionally. If the sauce is too runny, reduce the liquid. Season to taste with the salt and pepper.

Carciofi alla Veneziana
Venetian Artichoke Hearts
(Illustration left)

8 fresh artichoke hearts
Lemon juice
3 garlic cloves
1 bunch flat-leaved parsley
2 oz (50 g) butter
3 Tbs olive oil
Salt, black pepper

Cover the artichoke hearts with the lemon juice until needed to stop them from discoloring. Press the garlic, wash the parsley and chop finely. Heat the butter and olive oil, gently fry the garlic and parsley in it, then add the artichoke hearts. Pour in about ¹/₂ cup (100 ml) of water and cook the vegetables for approximately 30 minutes. Season with the salt and pepper. Serve with baguette and a Sauvignon from Friuli.

Carciofi alla veneziana – Venetian artichoke hearts

Vegetable Glossary

Aglio – garlic
Asparago, bianco e verde – asparagus, white and green; also wild asparagus
Bietole, erbette – mangel
Broccoli – broccoli
Carciofi – artichokes
Cardi – teasel, cardon (thistle-like vegetable)
Carota – carrot
Castagne, marroni – chestnuts
Cavolfiore – cauliflower
Cavolo – cabbage
Cavolo capuccio – white cabbage
Cavolo verza – savoy cabbage
Ceci – chick peas
Cipolle – white onions
Fagioli – beans (in general)
Fagiolini – green or French beans
Fave – broad beans
Finocchio – fennel
Fiori di zucchini – zucchini blossoms
Funghi – mushrooms, usually porcini (pp. 286–287)
Funghi prataioli – button mushrooms
Indivia riccia – endive with crinkly leaves
Indivia scarola – endive with smooth leaves
Lattuga – lettuce (in general)
Lattuga brasiliana – iceberg lettuce
Lattuga capuccia – Webb's lettuce
Lattuga romana – roman lettuce
Lenticchie – lentils
Melanzane – eggplant
Patate – potatoes
Peperoncini – small, hot pimentos
Peperoni – peppers
Piselli – peas
Pleutrotus – Chinese mushroom
Pomodoro – tomato
Radicchio – radicchio, red chicory
Radicchio rosso di chioggia – round-headed radicchio
Sbrisa (colloquial), pleutrotus – Chinese mushroom
Scorzobianca – salsify, vegetable oyster or oyster plant (bitter, long, white roots from the Tragopogone family)
Scorzonera – scorzonera hispanica
Sedano – celery, celeriac
Spinaci – spinach
Zucca – pumpkin
Zucchini – zucchini

What is a Frittata?

A *frittata* is a kind of flat omelet and found in all regions of Italy.
It is not moist like an omelet, but dry and hard. It is also not folded over like an omelet, but baked flat with a filling. The ingredients mix in with the eggs when the *frittata* is cooked, giving the eggs extra flavor. The *frittata* is sliced like a cake and served as an hors d'œuvre.

The ingredients can include:
Artichokes – all kinds of mushrooms – peas – leftovers of meat – green beans – potatoes – cheese – ham – asparagus – spinach – zucchini – onion rings.

Porcini Mushrooms

Funghi porcini (yellow bolete) are a passion of the Italians. The star of wild mushrooms grows wherever trees such as oaks, beech, chestnut, pine, and spruce offer it ideal conditions. Porcini feel at home near the roots of conifers and deciduous trees and thus can be found in these types of forest, but also in mixed woodland, which they apparently prefer.

Porcini mushrooms are picked in Liguria and in Piedmont with just as much enthusiasm as in the southern part of the Apennines. It is Tuscany, however, which is famed for its outstandingly high-quality porcini. They have become so popular that most people no longer bother to call them by their proper name, but refer to them simply as *funghi*, mushrooms.

A cousin of the porcini, the *suillus granulatus* tastes almost as good, but has a lighter, stickier and more irregularly-domed cap and a much thinner and less delicate stem.

● When young, genuine porcini have firm, hemispherical heads which are light to dark brown. The smallest have caps which are about $2^{1}/_{2}$ inches (6 cm) in diameter; this can reach 8 inches (20 cm) with fully-grown porcini.

● As a boletus they have no lamellas, but a layer of soft, tightly-packed hollow tubes under the cap which are reminiscent of a dry sponge. These are light and pale at first, but darken with age. When fully ripe, they have the color of good olive oil.

● Porcini are easily recognized by their thick, bulbous or leg-shaped stems, which have a fine mesh pattern directly under the cap. The volume of the stem sometimes exceeds that of the cap.

● When young, the flesh of a porcini is very firm; it later becomes more fibrous, but is always white, apart from the brown directly under the rim of the cap.

● The warmer the region, the more intensive the pleasant aroma becomes, at the same time complex, nutty and subtly musty.

● Porcini appear in summer, but are really only in full season by the late fall, and can go on into the winter with mild temperatures.

Porcini have many culinary uses, whether as a salad, fried, broiled or braised. They can be marinated in white wine as an *antipasti*, served as an accompaniment with meat, or dried and used to flavor sauces, soups, and egg recipes.

Dried morel mushrooms with their distinctive aroma are also a favorite ingredient in sauces.

Truffles

Near the little town of Alba in Piedmont, a truffle unique to the whole world, the *tuber magnatum*, is to be found. This white truffle, with its rather irregular, round shape, has a smooth, gray-brown surface. When cut open, the flesh displays a brown tint rather like that of hazelnuts, marbled with whitish streaks. Truffles favor oak trees as hosts, mixing with their roots to form mycorrhizae.

The white truffle is the crowning glory of Alba's culinary reputation, a reputation wide-spread by its wines and gastronomy alone. The *tuber magnatum* especially flourishes in the hills and forests of the Langhe. Yet here many of its underground hiding places have become barren; the most fruitful areas are now in the province of Pavia.

The first truffles begin to ripen from the beginning of October. Only then do they begin to secrete their strong scent. It is so powerful that it penetrates the four to sixteen inch (10–40 cm) layer of earth under which they are buried. Specially-trained dogs are used to sniff them out. Piedmont truffle hunters are usually out at night, for in darkness the dogs are able to fully concentrate on their sense of smell.

In the Langhe, the truffle season lasts until December 31. At dawn, the truffle hunters arrive in Alba, armed with their muddy booty, to do battle with cooks, traders and gourmets for the best prices. The almost ugly roots can be nut- to fist-sized and normally weigh between one and four ounces (25–100 g). If they are in demand, offers can go up to a hundred dollars or more per four ounces. The truffles only have to be scrubbed well to free them of their earthy coating before being put to culinary use.

Alba's *tuber magnatum* retain their freshness and aroma for ten days. Some enterprising souls try to preserve the truffles and their flighty fragrance in butter, oil or vacuum-packs, in ready-made risotto or egg tagliatelle. Knowing connoisseurs prefer to undertake a pilgrimage to Piedmont in the truffle season themselves, however, longing to inhale the intensive, appetizing aromas with their definite hint of garlic and trace of mature cheese. These are best savored when the truffles are sliced very thin and strewn over risotto, pasta or scrambled eggs. They forfeit their fantastic flavor and smell when cooked, unlike the *tuber melanosporum*, black truffles. Also found in Norcia and Spoleto in Umbria, these delicacies release their full aroma only when used in cooked recipes.

Ecco il mo
cui tutta l'Ita
tirato un sos
sollievo: Dino
all'83', raccog
una respinta e
segna il gol che
piega il Portogal

The intensive aroma of Alba's white truffles, which only grow underground, enchants gourmets everywhere.
Specially-trained dogs are the best truffle seekers.

Olive Oil

In Italy, the cult of the olive tree goes back to Roman times. It was holy, a symbol of peace and fertility. Olive oil served as an ointment, as a source of light, as medicine and as a costly trading commodity. With an appreciation greater than that of any other nation, Italians have bestowed a halo – albeit a purely culinary one – upon their olive oil.

Modern food science has also taught the Italians that:

● Olive oil is not just easy to digest; it generally has a positive effect on the stomach and digestive system

● The high content of simple, unsaturated fatty acids, which with their eighty percent exceed that of any other animal or vegetable oils, reduces the risk of heart and circulatory disease

● Due to the high percentage of antioxidant agents, olive oil can be heated without producing substances which may damage your health; this is not so with animal and vegetable fats

● All in all, out of the usual household fats, olive oil is by far the healthiest oil and the fat best assimilated by the human body.

Italy's olive plantations cover 1.2 million hectares. Almost three-quarters of these are situated in higher, hilly regions where the yields are less but the quality much higher. The best time to start the olive harvest is November when the small, green fruits start to turn violet. This is when they are at their most aromatic, having acquired a full flavor and a good nutritional balance. Harvesting fully-ripened, black olives into the early spring results in harmonious, less aromatic oils which are lighter in character.

Olives for top-quality oils are picked by hand. A good olive picker can manage up to eighty-eight pounds (40 kg) in one day, about 20,000 olives, which in good years can produce up to eight quarts of oil. For other high-quality oils, the olives are knocked from the trees with sticks and caught in nets which minimizes the damage to the fruit. As in the making of white wine, it is important to lose as little time as possible between the picking and pressing of the olives.

The production of olive oil has long been industrially mastered. In Europe, Italy is generally the leader in the field of special agricultural technology, and naturally also in Elaio technology, the technical term for oil extraction. Nonetheless, olives are often still ground to a pulp by granite millstones in a pan grinder, whereas the presses and centrifuges are state-of-the-art technology. Most qualities of oil are filtered; connoisseurs cherish the unfiltered, slightly cloudy varieties, however, with their intense flavor.

When harvesting the olives, the trees are roughly shaken so that the fruit tumbles down onto the net spread out below.

The different shades of the olives, ranging from green to violet to black, indicate how ripe they are.

Heavy millstones first grind the oily fruits to a pulp.

The paste is spread onto mats which are put under literally tons of pressure in the press.

The Different Qualities of Olive Oil

Olio d'oliva extra vergine – extra virgin olive oil
Oil of the first pressing; top quality.

Olio d'oliva vergine – virgin olive oil
Oil of the second and third pressing, graded "fine" and "medium-fine"; above-average quality.

Olio d'oliva – olive oil (also: **pure olive oil**)
A mixture of native and refined oil.

Olio di sansa d'oliva – olive pomace oil
The main ingredient in this oil is pomace oil extracted using solvents from the pulp remaining after pressing.

Native olive oils have to undergo tasting. Cold-pressed oils of the first pressing are of particularly high quality and should therefore preferably only be used in the preparation of cold dishes. For cooking, a simple native olive oil is sufficient. Today, the mark of origin is often indicated on bottles of olive oil, showing that the olive plantations and processing methods for the oil are submitted to regular controls. In general, different olive-growing areas can be assigned to northern, central or southern Italy:

● In the north, the Ligurian Riviera is well known, dominated by the Taggiasco type of olive producing very light, fine, thin oils with a delicate almond flavor. The more southern areas on Lake Garda, part of Veneto, also produce very delicate oils. In Lombardy, stronger, fruitier oils that are greener in color are pressed from Casaliva, Leccino, and Moraiolo olives; they often taste of herbs.

● In central Italy, namely in Tuscany, Emilia-Romagna, Umbria, Le Marche, and Lazio, a large variety of types of olive can be found, whereby Frantoio, Leccino, and Moraiolo olives are most common in the Tuscany and Umbria areas of origin. The oils have an often spicy, herby, and nutty aroma and an occasionally peppery bite in varying degrees of intensity, according to specific growing conditions, such as soil, climate, humidity, and altitude.

● In the south, the main provider of Italy's olive oil, each region has its own main olive types, whether these be Gentile di Chieti in the Abruzzi, Cima del Bitonto in Apulia, Ottobratica in Calabria, Nocellara in Sicily or Palma in Sardinia, to name but a few. The spectrum is extremely broad, yet the oils are mostly all golden yellow and strong in character with a well-developed olive aroma; they have a fruity taste and an often nutty aftertaste.

The large differences in oil bouquet and flavor have helped initiate a distinctive gastronomical culture in Italy. Olive oil is used as a seasoning and trickled over prepared food. As with wine, an attempt is made to harmonize oil and dish. In good restaurants, an oil menu or oil trolley is provided, from which the guest can either select a suitable candidate him or herself, or use it to ask the proprietor or waiter for advice.

Tip: Olive oil is sensitive to light, heat, air, and moisture. It should thus be stored in air-tight bottles in a cool, dry, dark place. In these conditions it will keep for one-and-a-half years.

Insalata – Salad

How to prepare Italian salad dressings

In Italy, salad is made from raw or cooked vegetables. One or several kinds of vegetable can be used, served in a dressing made from salt, pepper, olive oil, and a good wine vinegar or lemon juice. Here, the selection is also determined by the seasons. In spring, for example, asparagus with green beans or boiled zucchini with potato cubes are a favorite combination. Green lettuce is predominant in the summer, decorated with strips of pepper and fennel, tomatoes, cucumbers, grated carrots, and much more.

Salad variants also include meat and fish; these are not strictly an insalata as a side or vegetable dish, however, but are meals in their own right, such as the numerous rice salads with seafood or chicken which are fully-fledged *antipasti*.

Salads are nearly always dressed at the table and according to the tastes of the consumer. Ready-made bottled dressings, so common to northern Europe, are unknown in Italy.

Dolci

Italians hardly ever prepare desserts or cakes themselves. They like fruit, which is served as a sweet dish all year round. Spring brings with it wild strawberries, and when these are no longer in season, there are cherries and melons. Peaches, grapes and pears ripen in the late summer and fall, and in winter Sicilian oranges and mandarins are ready for eating. When the winter evenings are particularly cold, roast chestnuts are a favorite. All of these desserts involve little effort and are at the same time healthy and tasty.

It is mostly only on special occasions that Italians serve a "proper" dessert after the main course. These are usually brought home from the patisserie or cake shop, stocked with exquisitely delicious *dolci*. The amount of sugar they contain is clearly determined by a north–south divide; the further south the region, the sweeter the desserts.

Tiramisù

1 cup (200 ml) heavy cream
5 Tbs sugar
4 egg yolks
1 lb (500 g) Mascarpone
7 oz (200 g) sponge fingers
4 Tbs strong Espresso
4 Tbs Amaretto
Cocoa powder

Whip the cream and one tablespoon of the sugar until stiff. Mix the egg yolks with the rest of the sugar on the highest speed of a handmixer until creamy. Add the Mascarpone in spoonfuls and then stir in the cream, using a lower mixer speed.
Line a flat ovenproof dish with the sponge fingers, putting some aside for decoration. Mix together the Espresso and Amaretto and trickle over the biscuits (not too much). Spread a layer of the cream mixture over this, then add a second layer of the sponge fingers, sprinkled with the Espresso and Amaretto mixture. Cover with a final layer of cream. Sprinkle with the cocoa powder. Leave to stand in the refrigerator for at least one hour before serving.
A Marsala all'uovo (with egg) goes well with this dessert.

Zabaione
Zabaglione

4 egg yolks
4 Tbs sugar
Pulp from 1 vanilla bean
4–6 Tbs Marsala wine

Beat the egg yolks with the sugar and vanilla pulp until foamy. Stand the egg mixture in a bain-marie of hot water. Gradually add the Marsala, beating continuously, until the consistency is that of thick, solid cream. (The zabaglione should not be allowed to boil as it will then thin out again.) Pour into glasses immediately and serve, as the zabaglione will collapse as quickly as it thickened when beaten.
A Marsala or Prosecco goes well with this dessert.

Candied fruits are a favorite with sweet tooths and are often used in sweet dishes.

These *frutta di Martorana* – named after a Sicilian monastery – are life-like, marzipan copies of fruits (the picture shows seafood).

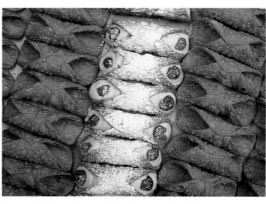
Cannoli, deep-fried, cylindrical pastries filled with Ricotta cream and little pieces of chocolate and candied fruits, are among some of the finest *dolci*.

Below: Even if *cassata* has now conquered the whole world, it cannot be found anywhere else in such splendid form as to be seen in the original, the Sicilian festive gateau.

Gelato – ice-cream (see pp. 572–573).
Krapfen – a kind of donut, this is an Austrian inheritance, which swept from Trentino across the whole of Italy. Also called *castagnole fritte*.
Macedonia di frutta – various fruits of the season, cut into pieces and prepared with sugar and Maraschino.
Monte bianco – "Montblanc": a mountain made from puréed chestnuts, topped with sweet, white cream.
Panna cotta – a sort of crème caramel, turned out before being served.
Pastiera – Neapolitan Easter cake, flavored with orange peel and orange blossom water.
Pesche ripiene – peaches with a chestnut filling, stewed in Marsala.
Semifreddo – semi-frozen, layered gateau.
Strudel di mele – South Tyrolean apple strudel.
Tiramisù – cream made from Mascarpone with flavored sponge fingers.
Zabaione – cold zabaglione, flavored with Marsala.
Zucotto – ice-cream gateau with chocolate and almond cream; a Tuscan specialty.
Zuppa inglese – sponge cake, with layers of sponge soaked alternately in Alchermes and rum and filled with vanilla cream. A specialty from Rome.
Zuppa romana – layered cake with a sponge base, vanilla cream, and candied and preserved fruit.

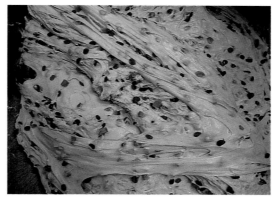

Delicious, light panettone, a must at every Italian Christmas, made from a yeast dough.

The brown paper cylinders, used by Italian panettone bakers, force the rich dough to rise vertically.

Browned, the panettone comes out of the oven sporting its characteristic "cummerbund."

Panettone

Panettone, literally "large loaf," was originally a simple, sweet bread, typical of the Lombardy region. It originated in Milan, where it is often filled with ice-cream, yet every year at Christmas panettone ceases to be just a Milanese specialty and becomes instead a traditional Christmas cake enjoyed in all parts of Italy. At this time of year, the patisseries sell over sixty million pounds of panettone.

Panettone is only successful if great care is exercised in the making of it. Using yeast as a baking agent and leaving the dough to rise for ten to twenty hours ensure that the resulting cake is tall and light in consistency. Raisins, candied fruit, and candied lemon peel are added to the moderately sugared dough. The panettone spends its final hours rising in a round container (panettone bakers use a paper cylinder, in which the cake is also sold); this forces the dough to rise vertically.

Panettone is eaten neither with a cake fork, nor is it broken up into crumbs. Instead, Italians pinch bite-sized portions out of the soft, elastic dough with their fingers. Panettone is best accompanied by a chilled, sparkling Spumante brut.

Panettone

Serves 10–12

2 oz (50 g) yeast
4 Tbs lukewarm water
5 cups (600 g) flour
¹/₂ cup (150 g) sugar
A pinch of salt
5 eggs
7 oz (200 g) butter
Grated rind of an untreated lemon
8 oz (250 g) candied fruit and candied lemon peel, cubed
5 oz (150 g) raisins
1 Tbs sunflower oil

Mix the yeast in the lukewarm water with a little of the flour. Cover and leave to rise for 30 minutes. Mix together the flour, sugar and salt and make a well in the center of the flour. Break the eggs into the well, add the yeast and knead the ingredients together to form a workable dough. Add the butter in knobs, the lemon peel, the candied fruit, and raisins and work these into the dough.
Roll the dough into a ball, cover and leave to rise in a warm place free from drafts for 8 hours. Then roll the dough into a long cylinder and place in a well-oiled Charlotte or fluted Brioche tin. Leave to rise for a further 2 hours.
Preheat the oven to 425 °F (220 °C). With a knife, make a cross on the top of the panettone and bake in the oven for about 50 minutes. Remove from the tin immediately and place on a wire rack to cool. Leave to stand for at least 12 hours before cutting.

Aceto Balsamico

This thick, radiant dark-brown essence with its extraordinarily complex fragrance has nothing at all in common with other types of vinegar. Its unique character is only truly exposed when tasted, revealing an unusual harmony of sweet and sour, of velvetiness and incomparable balsamic spice. We should point out that here we are talking about the real, the costly balsamic vinegar, which rightly bears the words *tradizionale* or *naturale*, and not of cheap imitations which are available in any supermarket.

Anyone who knows anything about aceto balsamico also knows that the only genuine flacons are those which require the purchaser to dig deep into his or her pocket, if, indeed, they can be bought at all. For in principle, this vinegar is not a mercantile product. Nine hundred years ago, the Dukes of Este and other noble families in the Modena area and Reggio Emilia were manufacturing vinegars. They were considered valuable tonics, used as remedies and spices, and were presented to important people as a mark of favor.

Unlike other vinegars, aceto balsamico's basic ingredient is wine marc, and not wine itself. This marc is taken from neutral-tasting Trebbiano grapes which ripen on the slopes near Modena or in the province of Reggio Emilia. After pressing, which produces about nineteen gallons (seventy liters) of marc from 220 pounds (100 kg) of harvested fruit, the marc is concentrated in slow motion at a maximum of 180 °F (80 °C) until a third or even half has evaporated. If not used immediately, the vinegar is corked in demijohns – a large bottle encased in wickerwork, holding about $1^1/_2$ to 13 gallons (5–50 liters) – until the following spring.

Aceto balsamico ages in rows of wooden barrels in airy attics called *acetaia*. Here, over periods lasting years and even decades, it is exposed to changes in the weather and to the seasons; it suffers the heat and the cold, dryness and damp; all are factors which support its development. A battery of barrels, a *batteria*, comprises several barrels of different volumes. This assembly often has five to twelve members, whereby the largest barrels hold twenty-seven gallons (one hundred liters) and the smallest only four (fifteen liters). The barrels are only three-quarters full, as the bacteria in the vinegar need a lot of air.

Aceto balsamico is only drawn from the smallest barrel containing the oldest vinegar, and then only a small amount. This amount is then replenished from the next-smallest barrel, which is refilled from the next size up and so on. In this way, room is made in the largest barrel for new wine marc. This needs approximately three years until the vinegar has undergone double fermentation. First the sugar is transformed into alcohol; this then becomes vinegar. About ten percent of the liquid evaporates every year.

Aceto does not just owe its broad aromatic spectrum and balsamic character to long maturation. The wood from which the barrels are made plays an important part in the process. Not only oak is used; chestnut, cherry, and ash are used for the larger barrels, whereas mulberry and juniper are reserved for the smaller ones, adding a final spice to the aceto.

The name "Aceto balsamico tradizionale di Modena" has been legally protected since 1983; that of "di Reggio Emilia" since 1987. Both vinegars have a minimum age of twelve years. They are filled into small bottles which hold half a cup of liquid. But even after a dozen years, genuine aceto balsamico is still in its early stages. Real specialties, rarely purchasable, have spent several decades in the barrel.

Aceto is used with all the respect that its career requires. It has become an aromatic concentrate. A few drops in a salad, on carpaccio, fish, veal or even ice-cream will give the dish a culinary note that it is not easily forgotten.

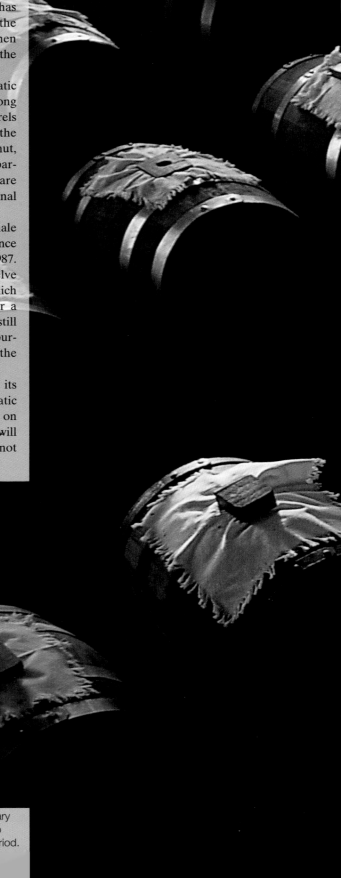

Background: Aceto balsamico acquires its culinary finesse in attics, where, barreled, it is exposed to changes in temperature during its maturation period.

The fermentation of the marc starts with the acetous ferment, a jelly-like mass which forms in the barrels.

As with wine, a sample is extracted from the barrel using a pipette.

The Consorzio de Aceto Balsamico taste each vinegar before it is sold.

Wine

No other region demonstrates the development of Italian wine as perfectly as Tuscany. Twenty-five years ago, the province used to export thousands of Chianti-filled demijohns, so-called *fiaschi*. They enjoyed a high level of popularity, but unfortunately the quality of the contents usually lived up to its name; it was literally a fiasco. Today, Chianti is not just the world's best-known Italian wine; alongside celebrated good-quality wines, the Chianti area also has a number of outstanding wines with a guaranteed certificate of origin. There is also a number of excellent Tuscan wines produced by wine-growers who have consciously freed themselves from restrictive legal regulations concerning types of grape and cultivation. These *vini da tavola*, table wines, have become symbolic of the dynamism and creativity characteristic of the new generation of Italian wine-growers and enologists. In virtually every region there are now wine-growers, cooperatives and wine merchants who have understood how important it is to go with the times. They have reduced their yields and have mastered work in the wine cellars with the aid of modern science and technology. Although Italy has an enormous fund of locally-grown grapes at its disposal, the number of types convincing to the palate which are actually used is relatively limited. Despite this, there are still marked regional differences, and it is not unusual to find the spectrum of local grapes enriched with tried-and-tested French varieties.

No other European wine-growing country offers such crass differences in wine, however. This is perhaps due to the fact that grapes are picked throughout the country from the slopes of the Alps to Sicily's coastline, facing the shores of Africa. Some years ago, the more northern regions were the driving power in the industry with their famous Piedmont, a province which has the highest concentration of classic wine-growing areas; more southerly regions, with their hotter, often more favorable climes, tended to be more responsible for quantity. But even here, the number of new, dedicated wine-growers has recently been on the increase, surprising connoisseurs with some exquisite wines.

The wine-growers of Piedmont, Tuscany, and other regions make wines that equal the quality of vintages produced in other countries, especially France; the strengths of the modern Italian wine culture, however, must surely lie in the ability to produce pleasant and easily-accessible wines.

Even the Romans, ingenious wine-growers to whom almost all the best wine-growing locations in Europe were known, realized it was best to restrict the boundaries of wine plantations. It took until 1963, however, for these areas of cultivation to be legally named and registered.

Categories of Wine

According to the new wine law, passed in 1992, Italian wines are sorted into the following categories:

Denominazione di origine controllata e garantita, DOCG

Controlled and guaranteed mark of origin, which not only determines the area, but also the type of grape, yield, cultivation etc. These wines are also rigidly checked and controlled by tasters; individual wines are often denied the DOCG appellation. This is the highest category, introduced in 1980. There are only 13 regions, including Barolo, Barbaresco, Brunello di Montalcini, Vino Nobile di Montepulciano, Chianti, Torgiano Rosso Riserva, and others.

Denominazione di origine controllata, DOC

Controlled mark of origin, which not only determines the area, but also the type of grape, yield, cultivation etc. These wines are also rigidly checked and controlled by tasters. Today there are approximately 240 DOC areas with over 1,000 different wines.

Vino da tavola con indicazione geografica

Table wine which comes from a geographically fixed area. Origin, type of grape, and year may be indicated on the label. Included in this category are all rather unusual *vini da tavola* which fail to comply with DOC regulations; their quality is often higher, however.

Vino da tavola

The lowest category of Italian wine which comprises the remainders; these are often blends. These wines are permitted to indicate neither geographical origin nor year.

Major Varieties of Grape

White grapes

Catarratto
An old, much-grown Sicilian grape whose cultivation covers over 80,000 hectares. It has some variants and is robust and high-yielding; mostly used in Marsala.

Chardonnay
Famous white wine grape from Burgundy. First planted in the north, it is now being grown in other regions.

Cortese
A delicate, traditional vine, it gives the best-known white wine of Piedmont, the Gavi, its fresh, discreetly fruity but lingering character with a good acidity.

Garganega
This is the main grape used in Soave, documented fairly early on in Veneto. It usually produces average wines, but sometimes fresh and dry or discreetly sweet and fruity wines.

Malvasia bianca
This old, very aromatic vine is grown nearly all over Italy and is full of character. Often used in blends, it is suitable for all kinds of wine from dry to sweet. It has many varieties but is not related to the red Malvasia grape.

Moscata bianco
Cultivated all over Italy, this is a Muscatel with small grapes. It has a typical nutmeg bouquet, is used in the preparation of dry to sweet wines (the latter as liqueur wines) and often used for sparkling wines.

Nuragus
A Sardinian white vine named after the Nuraghe, the characteristic towers of the island. Much-planted, it produces simple, light wines.

Pinot grigio
More important than white burgundy, Pinot Bianco, this is the gray version. Internationally famed as an Italian white wine made from one single variety of grape from the northern areas of cultivation.

Prosecco
A white vine from Friuli-Venezia Giulia, used for dry or discreetly sweet, still wines, but also for sparkling wines.

Trebbiano
Cultivated *en masse* in 40 provinces and internationally as Ugni blanc. It covers over 130,000 hectares in Italy (including variants), especially in Tuscany, Emilia-Romagna and Lazio. Usually only used in blends, it has a neutral bouquet and a good acidity. Also used as brandy.

Red grapes

Aglianico
This vine was introduced by the Greeks to the lower parts of Italy. Used on its own, it produces two great red wines, both with a high tannin content and which age well; these are the Taurasi in Campania and the Aglianico del Vulture in Basilicata.

Barbera
This is number two in Italy, but internationally is the most widely-cultivated, Italian red grape. From Piedmont, it has a high acidity, an intense color and is high-yielding. It is enjoying a renaissance as a character wine, especially as Barbera d'Alba.

Cabernet
Cabernet Sauvignon and Cabernet Franc were common in the last century in the north-east; today, Cabernet Sauvignon is fashionable and grown in many regions, also in the south.

Dolcetto
A delicate, demanding vine from Piedmont. It produces fruity, pleasant, dry wines with a low tannin content, which should be drunk when young.

Lambrusco
An age-old vine from Emilia-Romagna, this is hardy and high-yielding. It is made into sweet or dry, slightly sparkling red, rosé or even white wine.

Merlot
The famous Bordeaux grape is now number three among the red vines. It produces single-variety wines which are pleasantly rounded and full-bodied in the south and light and fruity in the north.

Montepulciano
A widely-cultivated vine, this is late-ripening and hardy. It produces pleasant, robust red wines, especially in Central and Southern Italy; in the Abruzzi it is used in a rosé called Cerasuolo.

Nebbiolo
This is the king of Italy's red vines. It is demanding and not often planted. It requires summer heat and ripens in late fall when it is often foggy (Italian *nebbia*). It produces deep, robust wines with a high acidity and tannin content and which are very long-lasting. It has a typical bouquet of violets and tar and characterizes Barolo and Barbaresco.

Nerello
This is common in Sicily and found as the variant Mascalese in many table wines and in the Corvo Rosso mixture. In the north-east it produces the single-variety Nerello Capuccio.

Primitivo
This and the Negro Amaro are the main grapes grown in Apulia for aromatic, fruity, balanced red wines.

Sangiovese
This is Italy's age-old, leading red vine, hardy but thin-skinned. Originally from Tuscany, it and its variants now cover over 180,000 hectares throughout the country. Sangiovese piccolo is the commonest variety and is the main grape used in Chianti. The Grosso variant produces Brunello and Vino Nobile di Montepulciano.

Vernatsch
The main red wine grape grown in South Tyrol, this is also called Schiava grosso or by its German name, Trollinger. It has four common variants which are often mixed with each other. It produces aromatic, fruity wines which are best drunk when young.

The number of available Italian wines has increased tremendously over the past two decades and today makes up a fascinating range covering all regions.

Vin Santo

Vin Santo, literally a holy wine used in the Mass, is a true Tuscan specialty. Small vineyards still produce it for home use and serve it on special occasions, and thankfully some wine growers and merchants have thought to offer it to wine aficionados as well. Vin Santo is a treasured cheerer-upper, aperitif or liqueur wine. When at home, Italians like to dunk their *cantucci*, dry almond cookies, into their glass. The cookies then melt deliciously on the tongue, yet for the pure, unadulterated palate, the taste is definitely spoiled.

Vin Santo is made mainly from Malvasia and Trebbiano grapes. Especially fine specimens from the late harvest are hung up on hooks or laid out on mats. They are then normally left to dry and to continue ripening for two months. The grapes start to shrivel to raisins, allowing the sugar content and extract values to become concentrated. Rotten fruit is discarded once a week.

When the grapes are pressed, about five to ten gallons (twenty to forty liters) of extremely rich marc are all that are left from 220 pounds of fruit. This is filled into small, old oak or chestnut barrels, *caratelli*, which have usually contained Vin Santo and which are impregnated with yeast. Alternatively, a good portion of yeast sediment, called *madre* or mother, is added from a predecessor.

The barrels are not completely filled and are sealed with cement. Vin Santo's long career is now launched in the Vinsanteria in the attic. Fermentation begins immediately, but in the closed environment of the barrel, the yeast repeatedly needs a starting point to be able to turn the fruit sugar into alcohol. This is the time of year and the temperature, which together determine whether the yeast's progress is encouraged or hindered. The fermentation and maturation processes in each individual barrel, lasting from two to six years, thus differ slightly. In one barrel, the wine ferments completely and is dry, in another it remains discreetly ripe, in a third it is decidedly sweet. In one barrel it may have taken on a dark amber coloring and a hint of oxidation typical for Vin Santo; in another, the wine may be straw-colored and fruity. The wine-grower's artistic skill and tastebuds now become decisive factors in the further fate of Vin Santo, for it is down to him to assemble the contents of the barrels in order to attain the desired character. Vin Santo is, so to speak, truly a gift from Heaven.

Italians like to dunk popular Amaretti almond cookies into Vin Santo, holy (Communion) wine. It is, however, better to savor the heavenly drink on its own.

Grappa

No other traditional European liquor has enjoyed a greater rise to fame than grappa. It has undergone a metamorphosis from a rough schnapps made from wine marc, drunk by Italian Alpine farmers to drive away the cold and fire them into life, to a classy liquor in designer bottles, jostling for space on the *digestif* trolleys of top restaurants.

Italians like to argue about when grappa was actually first distilled. One suggestion is the year 1451, when a certain Enrico in Friuli bequeathed his own particular brand of liquor to his heirs, calling it *grape*. This term is derived both from the word *rapus* or *rappe*, meaning "grape," and from *graspa*, a pressed grape.

Grappa is made from the remains of pressed grapes, from *vinaccia* or wine marc. If red grapes are used, all the stalks have to be removed first, a process called "destemming"; white grapes require a more complicated process. Red grapes are pressed after alcoholic fermentation so that the marc has also fermented; white grapes are pressed before fermentation sets in. This means that for grappa, white wine marc has to be allowed to ferment before it can be distilled. This takes place in fermenting vats, where a little water is added to the marc before being pressed.

Up to twenty percent of the yeast residue deposited at the bottom of the tank after fermentation is complete may be added to the grappa. If distillation is not begun immediately, the liquid must be stored carefully so as not to be spoiled by mold or acetic bacteria. Large quantities are required: 200 pounds of marc produce a mere one to two gallons of distillate with sixty to eighty percent alcohol per volume.

There are two possible distilling methods employed when making grappa: batch and continuous distillation. With batch distillation, the vat is filled with wine marc and heated by steam or in a water bath, *a bagnomaria,* causing alcohol and other volatile substances to evaporate and condense in a coil condensor. The distiller has to exercise great skill in capturing and separating off the first and last runnings at precisely the right moment. For *testa*, the head, and *coda*, the tail, contain not just unwanted alcohol compounds and fusel oils, but also a large percentage of the vital aromas. Only with long years of experience and a good nose can a grappa distiller separate out the *cuore*, the heart or middle runnings, with the utmost efficiency, giving the resulting spirit that certain something which determines its market value and bestows fame upon its manufacturer. Once the distillation process is finished, the vat is emptied and refilled. The best-quality grappe are produced using this method. This complex procedure is not suitable for large quantities,

Even the pressing process determines the quality of the resulting grappa. Good marc with a high juice content should be selected from the best grapes.

When distilling, the marc is filled directly into the pot still and then the lid is carefully closed.

Old marc is used to fire the distilling apparatus; the ashes serve as fertilizer for the vineyards.

The distillate precipitates in the condensor.

however. Thus, in 1960, as the demand for grappa began to increase, continuous distillation was introduced. This involves the steam-powered distilling apparatus being constantly fed with marc. The integrated column system allows the first and last runnings to be separated, albeit with less subtlety than with batch distillation.

As well as the distillation process, two other factors play a major role in the production of grappa: wine marc and maturation.

• The marc, which must be clean and have a high juice content, has a significant influence on the final aroma, depending on the type of grape or wine that is used. A difference is generally made between grappa made from unaromatic grapes and grappa from aromatic varieties, such as Muscatel or Traminer.

• The maturation process, which lasts at least twelve months, six of these in wooden barrels, refines and balances the liquor. In oak barrels, the liquid takes on an amber tint, whereas it remains clear if stored in ash. Information should also be recorded as to the age and type of storage of the grappa, such as Riserva or Stravecchia, for example. Grappa with a maturation period of a few years are a particular specialty.

As with fruit liquor, grappa unfolds its remarkable bouquet and characteristic flavor as early as a few months after distillation. Young grappa should be served in tall *digestif* glasses at a cool temperature of 46–50 °F (8–10 °C); older vintages best release their full aroma in wine-tasting or brandy glasses at 60–64 °F (16–18 °C). Grappe are classified according to their various areas of origin:

• Grappa from Friuli-Venezia Giuila
• Grappa from Lombardy
• Grappa from Piedmont and the Aosta Valley
• Grappa from Trentino and South Tyrol
• Grappa from Veneto.

Other, less common grappe come from Emilia-Romagna, Tuscany, Liguria, Sardinia, and Lazio. Hidden behind the label "Italian Grappa" are also a number of blended spirits from various different regions.

Grappa di monovitigno, grappa from one type of grape, is mainly produced by quality-conscious distillers. The most famous is Grappa di Picolit, a vine which has low yields but highly-concentrated, sweet grapes. Barolo, Verduzzo, and Moscato among others are also popular.

There are also special kinds of flavored grappe. This group includes Grappa alla ruta, grappa with a rue twig placed in the bottle and perhaps the most well known. But there is also a host of other herbs, spices and fruits which are used to flavor this Italian spirit. These include peppermint, mugwort, gentian, caraway, and aniseed, but also raspberries, blueberries, oranges, almonds, honey, and even coffee.

Not only the contents of the barrels are controlled (background); each bottle is thoroughly checked.

Labels for top-quality grappe are written by hand.

Campari

When in 1867 the Caffè Campari opened in the recently-built Galleria Vittorio Emanuele II in Milan's cathedral square, the owner, Gaspare Campari, served his guests a bright red drink, which he called "Bitter all'uso di Hollanda," a Dutch bitter schnapps. Campari made many of his drinks himself, as did most of his colleagues in those days. These included his own vermouths and aperitifs, such as Kinal, Cedro or Americano, but also Fernet, Grappa Moscato, Latte di Vecchia, Assenzio, and even Black Forest Kirsch. His elegant clientele soon developed a taste for his subtly sharp, slightly bitter aperitif, however, and began demanding Bitter Campari.

Bitters are a special category of alcoholic beverage. They are made from alcohol, water, sugar (usually caramel), and plant extracts. In Italy and France, bitters are usually aperitifs whose bitterness is primarily down to China bark and the peel of Seville oranges. Both are probably contained in Campari. This is no certainty, however, as in the main Campari factory of Sesto San Giovanni in Milan, none of the ingredients is mentioned by name. An infusion is made from herbs, fruit, and bits of plants and left to macerate for several days. Alcohol is then added which draws further flavors out of the mixture in an automatically controlled circulatory process. The aromatic concentrate is ready after three weeks. This is then measured out electronically and mixed with alcohol, a sugar solution, distilled water and crimson to produce the bitter aperitif. Originally, the typical bright coloring came from the shells of the cochineal bug; today, it is manufactured chemically.

Subtly sharp, crimson red Campari is served in stemmed glasses.

Aperitifs and Liquors

The numbers in brackets refer to the numbers under the bottles pictured at the bottom of the page.

Amaro and strong bitters (6, 7, 8)

Herbal liqueurs are an Italian specialty and are available in a huge range of varieties from strong to mild, as *aperitivos* or bitters, and from sharp to smooth. Amari are mainly drunk as a digestif.

Americano

This is a mixture of vermouth and bitters, very popular in bars in Turin around the middle of the 19th century. Its name can be traced back to a spoonerism of the word *amaricante*, meaning "bitter." Nearly all manufacturers of vermouth also make Americano.

Aperitivo

A favorite term used by many companies for bitters or Americanos; a typical *aperitivo* is Aperol with only 11 percent alcohol. It has been manufactured since 1919 using four dozen aromatic plants, including China bark, rhubarb, gentian, and Seville oranges.

Brandy (5)

Trebbiano from Romagna and Tuscany and Asprigno from Veneto are the two types of grape to feature large in the production of Italian brandy. Depending on the quality, this is distilled twice or continuously using a cognac-type process. The minimum age is six months; top-quality brandies mature over many years. The market leader is Vecchia Romagna, aged in barrels using the Spanish Solera system. With this method, old brandy extracted from the barrels is replaced with young brandy.

Liquori (1, 4, 8)

These make up a large group of often regional specialties. The most well-known are Amaretto, a sweet, bitter almond liqueur, the golden yellow Strega and the equally golden, vanilla Liquore Galliano in its characteristic long bottle. Nocini, nut liqueurs, come from Piedmont, Veneto, Emilia, the Abruzzi, and Campania. Rose liqueurs, such as Rosolio di Rose, Tè Rose, and Amarella are supposedly of Arabian origin. Centerbe (a hundred herbs) and Mentuccia, a peppermint liqueur, come from the Abruzzi.

Sambuca (2)

This is a popular clear liqueur from Central Italy, distilled with steam from aniseed and other plant extracts. It is drunk after a meal, either flambéed at room temperature, or served with ice or *con la mosca*, with flies, i.e. with an odd number of coffee beans floating on its surface.

Vermouth (3)

Vermouth was heard of even before it was first launched under the name vermouth in 1786 by Antonio Benedetto Carpano in his Turin shop. It immediately became popular as a luxury wine and other liqueur manufacturers, namely Cinzano, soon followed Carpano's example. Martini was put on the market in 1863. Other well known brands are Gancia, Filipetti, Riccadonna, Stock, Lombardo, and Cora. Vermouth is white wine, flavored with the essence of and infusions from a wealth of herbal extracts, including wormwood leaves. Further ingredients are sugar, alcohol and, for red vermouth, caramel as a colorant.

Espresso

The Italian way of drinking coffee has spread to all parts of the world. Yet there is no other country in which coffee takes up such an important place in the social life of the inhabitants. From the Alpine peaks to the tip of the Boot, nine billion cups of *caffè* are consumed every year. About one-third of these traverse the counters of Italy's some 134,000 stand-up bars and cafés, places frequented by passers-by and Italians in a hurry. Espresso's development is inextricably linked to that of coffee machines which function with steam and pressure. A further element is also imperative to Italy's coffee culture: caffè is freshly ground, portioned into a special fitting with its own individual filter and freshly prepared for the customer. Luigi Bezzera is the forefather of this system, for which he obtained a patent in Milan in 1901. In 1905, Desiderio Pavoni began producing machines based on Bezzera's invention. Other manufacturers copied this in the ensuing years. This technology enabled the birth of real *caffè espresso*, quick coffee. Its quality is dependent on a number of different factors.

- Coffee – Italian roasters prefer Brazilian coffees, from which they mix their special blends. Robusta of the finer Arabica is a favorite.
- Roasting – in Italy, the beans are roasted for much longer than in other countries, i.e. for six to twenty minutes from 400 to 450 °F (180–240 °C). The strong, dark-brown roasted beans have a powerful aroma.
- Granulation – apart from the fact that the coffee has to be freshly ground to allow it to release its full flavor, its granulation is also important. It has to have the right consistency to allow the water to be compressed by the machine in twenty-five to thirty seconds. If this takes longer, the coffee is too bitter; too short, and the coffee tastes too weak. If the beans are too finely-ground, the froth is too dark; with a coarser grind, the froth is too light.
- Amount per cup – about one teaspoon of ground coffee.
- Machine – ideally, an espresso machine should compress the water at 190 to 200 °F (90–95 °C) and with an atmospheric pressure of nine through the coffee in twenty-five to thirty seconds. This fills an espresso cup holding one fl oz (25 ml). If the temperature is too low or the pressure too high, the froth is too light; if this becomes too dark, the temperature is either too high or the pressure is too low.

A perfect espresso is almost black, hidden beneath a very light brown layer of froth.

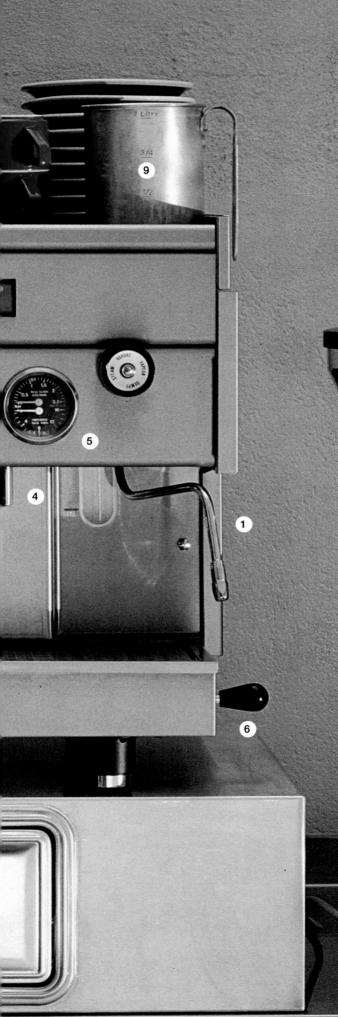

The filters contain exactly enough ground coffee for one cup of espresso.

The filter is clicked into place. The pressure determines whether the espresso is good or not.

The steam nozzle can be used to froth milk for cappuccino, for example.

Parts of an espresso machine

1 Steam nozzle
2 Pressure regulator
3 Lights
4 Filter holder
5 Manometer (pressure gauge)
6 Water feed
7 Container for ground coffee
8 Cup warmer
9 Milk container
10 Electric coffee grinder

André Dominé

Greece

It is its unmistakably Mediterranean character that gives a particular attraction to Greek cuisine and its culinary specialties. Due to the supremacy of Athens and Sparta in the ancient world, Greek cooks were able to draw on a rich abundance of ingredients whilst they gained as great a fame as did poets, philosophers, and artists. Greek merchants brought back with them from their travels spices, fruits, vegetables, poultry, pigs, cattle, and wines. Trading stations situated all around the Mediterranean made sure that there was no shortage of supply of all the diverse goods.

Oppression and poverty marked the period after that, and in particular the 400 years of Turkish occupation. Meat was scarce and usually commanded prohibitive prices, which meant that the sea was the only source of more abundant food supplies. Today, the markets and shops in Greece boast the same rich selection of ingredients as can be found all over Europe. The Greek culinary skills and customs, however, are nevertheless based on the long periods in which ingredients were scarce. While breakfast is of hardly any consequence at all, the Greeks like to partake of a snack at about eleven o'clock, or at the very least buy themselves a bag of salted pistachio nuts, pumpkin or sunflower seeds from the *pasatémpo* seller. The meal at lunch time is usually a more or less sumptuous affair when the Greeks sit down to enjoy their main meal, which may include salad and olives. After all, there is plenty of time to rest in the afternoon, at least in the summer. The evening meal, on the other hand, tends to be less substantial. The evening is the time for going out and stopping at a bar for a drink and a few *mezédes*. What is available is still dictated by the seasons. Particularly full of flavor are lamb and kid from the indigenous flocks. Herbs are used relatively sparingly, which benefits the intrinsic taste of the ingredients. Many dishes are enriched and refined by Féta and other sheep's cheeses, which also give the dishes their typically Greek flavor. The Greeks take second place in cheese consumption in Europe, being overtaken only by France. Next to the famous Retsína, an increasing number of well-produced dry wines have helped this oldest wine-growing area in the world to gain a new and ever-expanding reputation.

Left: Lambs roasted on a spit are amongst the culinary highlights that Greece has to offer.

589

Vegetables

The Greek eat more vegetables than all other Europeans. The Greek orthodox faith demands of its followers to fast for about a third of each year. This includes every Wednesday and every Friday. During the days of fasting, known as *nistía*, not only is the consumption of meat prohibited, but also that of fish which bleed and of animal products such as milk, cheese, and eggs. *Nistísima*, the Lenten fare, does not, however, give instantaneous rise to miserable faces. This is due, on the one hand, to the inventiveness of the Greeks when it comes to matters culinary, and on the other, to their partiality for wild-growing foodstuffs such as asparagus, dandelion, endives, teasels, bulbs, and herbs. Today the rules about fasting are treated far more leniently in Athens, Salonika, and other cities, although many Greeks still observe the rules as always. But even those who are not strong believers are very fond of eating plenty of *laderá*, or cooked vegetables. That is the reason why the vegetable dishes in restaurants in the menus are listed not as side dishes but always as meals in their own right. The rich variety of salads, however, are regarded in Greece either as mezédes or as accompaniment to meat or fish dishes, bearing in mind that with the latter the Greeks prefer lightly-cooked vegetables.

Kolokithokeftédes
Zucchini Rissoles
(Illustrations 1–4)

1 lb (500 g) small zucchini
1 onion
1 Tbs olive oil
1/2 cup (100 g) grated Kefalotíri
3/4 cup (150 g) bread crumbs
1 egg
1 Tbs parsley, finely chopped
1 Tbs mint, finely chopped
Salt, black pepper
Vegetable oil for frying the rissoles

Wash and prepare the zucchini, chop them into pieces and boil them in salted water for 8 minutes; drain well (1). Peel and finely chop the onion and fry in the oil until transparent. Purée the zucchini in a blender and mix the purée thoroughly with the cheese, onion, two thirds of the bread crumbs, the egg, parsley, mint, salt, and pepper (2). Leave in a cool place for 30 minutes. Use your hands to shape the zucchini purée into small rissoles (3), coat them in the remaining bread crumbs and fry them in the hot vegetable oil until they are golden brown (4). Remove the rissoles from the oil and drain them on kitchenroll. Serve hot.

1

2

3

4

Angináres alá Politá
Artichokes Constantinople Style

8 fresh artichokes
4 Tbs lemon juice
5 Tbs olive oil
1 onion
4 young carrots
8 scallions
2 leeks
8 small potatoes
1 Tbs dill, finely chopped
Salt, black pepper

Cut the top two-thirds off the artichokes and remove the stalks. Then remove all the hard tips of the outer leaves and pick out the fibers. Now arrange the artichokes in a bowl, sprinkle with half the lemon juice and cover them with water to avoid discoloration.

Horiátiki saláta – Country salad

Peel and finely chop the onion. Heat up the olive oil in a stewing pot and fry the onion until transparent. Clean the carrots and cut them into half lengthwise, clean and prepare the scallions and leeks and cut them into rings. Add the carrots and scallions to the onion and braise them briefly.

Peel the potatoes; add them to the vegetables together with the artichokes and the dill. Season with salt and pepper, add just under one cup (200 ml) of hot water. Cover and cook over a low heat for about 60 minutes. Arrange everything in a bowl and season with the remaining lemon juice. Serve hot or cold.

Horiátiki Saláta
Country Salad
(Illustration below)

2 large, firm tomatoes
1 untreated cucumber
1 green pepper
1 onion
5 oz (150 g) Féta, in cubes
$^1/_2$ tsp dried oregano
1 tsp fresh thyme, finely chopped
5 Tbs olive oil
2 Tbs red wine vinegar
Salt, black pepper
Black olives

Wash and dry the vegetables. Cut the tomatoes into eighths; chop the unpeeled cucumber into cubes; deseed the pepper and cut into narrow strips; peel the onion and cut into rings. Put the vegetables and the Féta into a salad bowl, retaining a few of the Féta cubes and onion rings. Add the herbs.

Mix the oil, vinegar, salt, and pepper together thoroughly and pour over the salad. Mix everything together carefully and sprinkle with the remaining Féta. Garnish the salad with onion rings and black olives.

Briámi
Baked Vegetables

2 eggplants
3 zucchini
$^1/_2$ pint (300 ml) olive oil
2 onions
2 garlic cloves
2 green peppers
5 tomatoes
1 tsp dried oregano
1 Tbs parsley, finely chopped
$^3/_4$ lb (400 g) small potatoes
7 oz (200 g) green beans
Salt, black pepper

Cut the eggplants and zucchini into chunks, sprinkle with salt and – in separate dishes – leave them in water for 30 minutes. Then rinse them and squeeze them lightly. Put a little olive oil in a frying pan and brown the eggplants and zucchini. Peel the onions and cut them into rings; chop the garlic; clean and deseed the peppers and cut them into strips; skin, de-seed the tomatoes and cut the flesh into cubes. Put the vegetables, the oregano, and the parsley into the frying pan and braise everything for 10 minutes.

Preheat the oven to 350 °F (180 °C). Peel the potatoes and cut them into halves; clean the beans and cut into pieces. Put the potatoes and beans together with the braised vegetables into an oven proof dish; add seasoning. Pour the remaining olive oil over everything and add $^3/_4$ cup (150 ml) of water. Cover and cook in the oven for 60–70 minutes, stirring the vegetables once or twice. Serve hot or cold.

Moussakás
Eggplant Casserole

Serves 8

4 lbs (2 kg) eggplants
2 onions
2 lbs (1 kg) lean ground lamb
4 garlic cloves
Salt, black pepper
1½ lbs (750 g) tomatoes
1 cup (200 ml) dry white wine
2 Tbs tomato paste
1 tsp dried oregano
1 Tbs parsley, finely chopped
¼ cup (50 g) bread crumbs
¼ cup (60 g) butter
6 Tbs flour, 10 cups (1 l) milk
1 pinch nutmeg
2 egg yolks
2½ oz (75 g) grated Kefalotíri cheese

Wash and dry the eggplants and remove the stalks. Cut lengthwise into slices ½ inch (1 cm) thick. Sprinkle with salt and leave for 60 minutes. Then rinse the slices, squeeze them out gently and pat them dry. Brown the eggplant slices lightly in hot oil from both sides, then drain (1).

Peel and chop the onions and fry them until transparent; brown the ground meat. Finely chop the garlic and add to meat; season with salt and pepper. Skin and de-seed the tomatoes, stir into meat mixture and braise for 5 minutes.

Mix the wine in with the tomato paste and add to the meat. Leave to simmer over a low heat for 30 minutes until the sauce has thickened (2). Add the herbs and season to taste.

Preheat the oven to 350 °F (180 °C).

Grease a baking dish with olive oil and sprinkle the bottom with bread crumbs. Arrange a layer of eggplants in the dish, then tomato-meat sauce, and alternate until full, with eggplants on top (3).

Use the butter and flour to prepare a roux, brown it lightly, and mix in the milk, stirring continuously. Bring slowly to the boil and simmer for 5 minutes, stirring all the time, until the sauce is smooth and creamy (4). Now take it off the heat and season it with nutmeg, salt, and pepper. Beat the egg yolks into the grated cheese and add to the sauce; pour the sauce over the eggplants (5).

Bake in the oven for about 60 minutes. Let it cool (6).

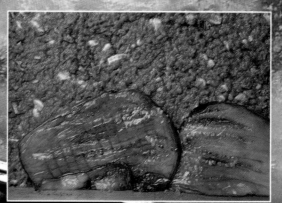

①

②

③

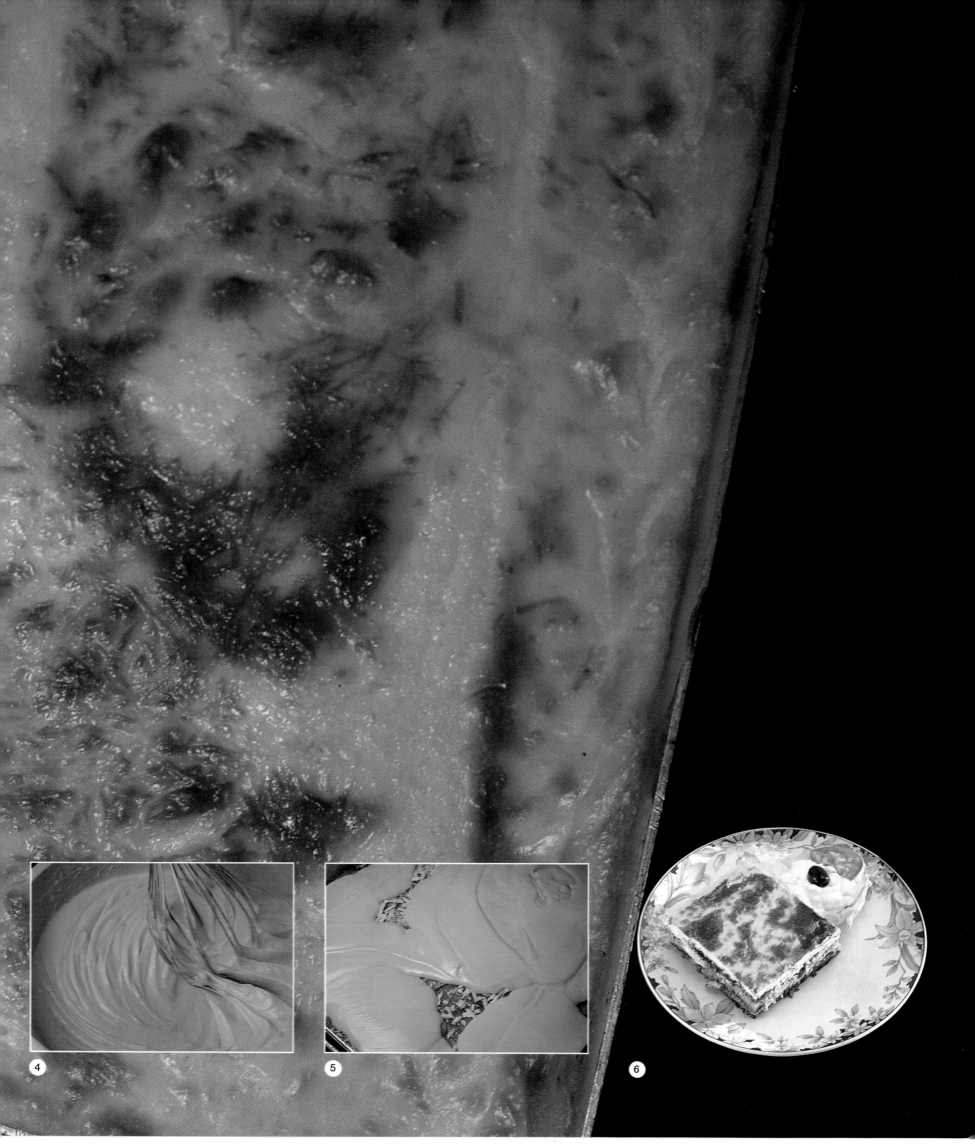

Meat

The hilly, barren landscape of Greece does not provide naturally favorable conditions for cattle-breeding. Sheep and goats adapt best to the often steep, stony, and meager mountain pastures which account for forty percent of the whole country. However much the Greeks appreciate the meat provided by lambs and kids, they are not the primary reasons for keeping them. It is the milk, rather, which is used for the production of cheese and yogurt and is thus a central element in the Greek diet. The processing of wool and leather, too, is still an important sector of the economy. In those areas where the pastures are somewhat more lush, mostly in the north of the country, rearing cattle is common practice.

The Greeks prefer meat from young animals, be it veal, lamb, kid, or sucking pig, while they are not very keen on mutton or goat. Meat used to be a scarce and expensive commodity since it had to, and still has to be, mainly imported. Many meat dishes are therefore regarded as meals for special days and thus associated with Feast days – the roast used to be regarded as a feast in itself. From such necessity sprang the wealth of ideas with which meat is used in soufflés, pies, and sauces, together with plenty of other ingredients. Hens and chicken were less difficult to come by. Like all their meat, the Greeks prefer their poultry to be cooked until it is thoroughly done so that the meat falls off the bones and melts in the mouth.

Arní kléftiko – Lamb cooked in grease-proof paper together with peas, carrots, tomatoes, and potatoes

Keftédes – Rissoles made from ground meat

Kotópoulo me bámies – Chicken with okra

Kotópoulo piláfi – Pilaf with chicken, onion, and tomato sauce

Worldwide, *Gyros* is one of the best-known products of the Greek cuisine. The vertically arranged pieces of meat give off a mouth-watering aroma as they cook on a rotating spit. A long-bladed knife is used to cut the meat off in thin slices. The name of this meat specialty is derived from the word *gyre*, the Greek term for a rotating axis.

Souvlákia
Meat Kabobs
(Illustration opposite)

1³/₄ lb (800 g) lamb or other tender meat
Salt, black pepper
1 Tbs dried oregano
¹/₂ cup (100 ml) olive oil
Juice of 1 lemon
2 onions
2 green peppers
2 large, firm tomatoes
Wooden kabob skewers

Cut the meat into cubes of about one inch (2¹/₂ cm) and put them into a bowl. Season well with pepper on all sides and sprinkle with oregano; then pour over the olive oil and lemon juice.
Leave the meat to marinate in a cool place for at least 6 hours.

Peel and quarter the onions; wash and de-seed the peppers and the tomatoes and cut the flesh into bite-sized pieces.
Remove the meat from the marinade and pat it dry. Put the meat cubes onto the skewers, alternating them with chunks of vegetables.
Place the kabobs on the hot charcoal grill and cook them for about 15 minutes, turning them over several times. When the meat is done, season the kabobs with salt and serve with pitta or rice.

Kokinistó – Beef (or preferably veal) *moskari*, i.e. braised in tomato sauce

Kotópita – Chicken pie, seasoned with fresh herbs

Kotópoulo me avgolémono – Chicken in a lemon-egg sauce

Pastítsi – Pasta au gratin with ground meat and a cheese sauce

Sutzukákia – Ground meat sausages

Stifádo – Stewed beef or veal with onions

Souvlákia – Kabobs, usually with lamb, marinated before broiling (see recipe opposite)

Souvlákia – Kabobs with pork and vegetables

Youvarlákia – Egg-lemon soup with dumplings made from ground meat and rice

Cheese

The Greeks are very fond of cheese, ranking second only after the French in cheese consumption in Europe. By far the most popular Greek cheese is Féta, which translated means simply "piece." Since this cheese used to be pressed into blocks it was only ever possible to take along a piece of it, but never the whole cheese.

Féta is a country cheese that is made from curdled sheep's milk. The shepherds must have very early on been faced with the problem of preserving their cheese. On the one hand, they did not as a rule have the opportunity to sell their products on the spot but instead had to travel long distances to reach the nearest market-town. On the other hand, their customers demanded fresh white cheese. A further problem was having to bridge the gap when no milk was produced without having to go without Féta. The method of preserving it in salt water is an ancient one. In this brine the cheese keeps for months, and as a result the Féta destined for export is put in an especially strong brine. In order to be able to enjoy it, the cheese should be put in cold water and left for several hours.

With the addition of a few black olives and a piece of bread, Féta constitutes one of the most customary mezédes. It is also an indispensable ingredient in every Greek country salad. Its role in Greek cooking goes beyond that, however: Féta is used just as much for au gratin dishes as for enriching numerous varieties of pie and pastry fillings. When buying Féta it is important to make sure that you obtain a cheese made from sheep's milk with possibly some added goats' milk. Attention should also be paid to its fat content which ideally should be forty-five or fifty percent by dried mass. Féta produced from cows' milk has a completely different flavor.

Féta
This soft or medium sheep's cheese comes in blocks; it is marinated, stored in brine and has many uses.

Kasséri
Recognized by its yellow color and shiny appearance; it is reminiscent of Cheddar and mild in taste.

Myzíthra
A soft curd cheese used primarily in the preparation of cakes and pastries.

Kefalotíri
A hard and salty cheese made from raw, unpasteurized milk; often used grated for cooking purposes; the best types come from a mixture of goats' and sheep's milk.

Manoúri
A creamy curd cheese made from sheep's, goats' or cows' milk, depending on the region; unsalted for cakes or with honey.

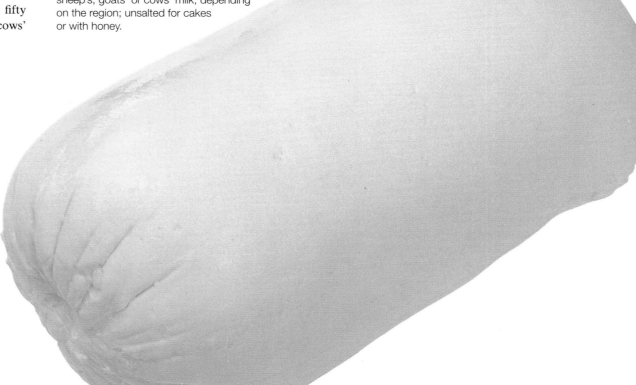

Easter in Greece

Easter is the most important religious festival for the Greeks. Full of joy and enthusiasm and accompanied by fireworks, the population remembers the resurrection of Christ, exchanges gifts, and celebrates together with all the family. No wonder that Easter also represents the culinary climax of the whole year. The women invest a lot of time and loving energy preparing food for this feast, which means that some of the most famous specialties of the Greek cuisine are associated with Easter.

Since the start of the orthodox ecclesiastical year differs from the Roman Catholic calendar, Easter is celebrated up to five weeks later in the Greek orthodox church of the east. In fact, the time when Easter is celebrated in both churches coincides only once every three years. The Lent period of forty days has already started by the last week of Carnival time in which the only animal-derived food allowed is cheese. The day before Shrove Tuesday is marked with a popular family picnic consisting of *lagána*, the unleavened bread, *taramosaláta*, squid, and plenty of sweet *halwá*. It is also the first day on which strict fasting rules have to be observed. The climax of Christ's Way of the Cross is marked on Good Friday by His deposition and entombment. The Mass in church on the Saturday night is attended by practically every Greek family. When the bells ring at midnight and the new light has been lit the congregation greet each other with the words "Christ is risen." Now *majirítsa* is served, Greece's famous Easter soup. It is cooked only once a year and for this particular occasion. The soup includes the offal of the freshly slaughtered lamb that is destined to be the Easter roast. The popular egg-lemon sauce *avgolémono* is used as a thickener. On Easter Sunday, whole lambs are roasted on spits over the open fire, a delicacy known as *arní sti soúvla*. Most people prefer to eat outdoors after the morning service. Everyone is given hard-boiled eggs, the *kókkina avgá*. Following an ancient tradition, they are colored red, with the color of the shell symbolizing the blood of Christ, and the egg eternal life. The eggs are also used to play the traditional Easter game *tsoúgrisma*: each player takes his egg in his hand and knocks it against the egg of his neighbor at table. Easter Sunday comes to a close with mezédes, music, and dancing.

After the morning service, the traditional Easter festival begins with eggs that have been dyed red.

Whole lambs are broiled (see background photo) to celebrate an Easter open air feast.

Music and dancing on Easter Sunday, here performing their world-famous Sirtáki.

Oúzo

Like all nations bordering on the Mediterranean, the Greeks have a pronounced predilection for the taste of aniseed, which is reminiscent of licorice. This is not surprising since the umbelliferous, white-flowering herb has its origin in the eastern Mediterranean region and in the Middle East. Anise was regarded as sacred by the Egyptians and as a panacea by the Greeks. Once the Arabs had invented the art of distilling alcohol, its practice quickly spread around the Mediterranean. As a result, all countries adopted the method of soaking anise in alcohol and using it for fortifying liqueurs. In Greece, with its ancient wine-growing tradition, grape skins were used for this purpose, and distilled into pure brandy. But in order to extract all of the flavor from the aniseed it has first to be soaked in a mixture of alcohol and water. It is only the distilling process, sometimes repeated, that brings out the pure character of the flavorings desired.

Oúzo is produced almost everywhere in Greece, usually in small quantities on a do-it-yourself basis. Everyone takes great care to guard his or her own recipe like a treasure; even the well-known brand names do not give away their secrets. In the big factories today, each aromatic mixture is calculated down to the smallest detail in order to avoid any deviation in taste. The aromatic distillation is then mixed with a flavorless alcohol, sugar, and distilled water to produce aniseed liqueur. Oúzo is often drunk cold with added ice-cubes and diluted with water. This causes it to turn a milky-white color, a reaction caused by the aniseed oil dispersing itself in minute droplets. Despite all the signs of its popularity, Oúzo would not be regarded as the national drink of Greece if it were not for the fact that it is usually drunk at the end of a meal – and in a restaurant it is often served as an amiable gesture on the part of the landlord.

Digestifs

Metaxá
The most famous Greek alcoholic spirit is classed amongst the brandies, although Metaxá is not a pure brandy. It is a blend of brandy, other base liquor, natural flavorings, and distilled water that is matured in barrels. The base quality has five stars and an alcohol content of 38 percent by volume. The Amphora brand has seven stars, 40 percent by volume and has to mature in a special bottle for seven years. More superior still are the Grand Olympian Reserve and the exquisite Centenary.

Tsípouro
Tsípouro is distilled from grape skins or from grapes, and despite its origins in Macedonia, it has increasingly rivaled the Italian Grappa. Nonetheless, prime products made from only one type of grape have so far been very rare. Instead, the version flavored with aniseed has blurred the difference between itself and Oúzo.

Tsikoudiá
A strong alcoholic drink made from grape skins; it is also referred to by the more general term Rakíya.

The white flowering anise herb has its origin in the eastern Mediterranean region and the Middle East.

In order to extract all their flavoring, the aniseeds have to be macerated in a mixture of alcohol and water.

Oúzo, the Greek national strong alcoholic drink, is drunk neat with ice, or diluted with cold water.

Retsína

Wine was said to have been given to the Greeks – and thus ultimately to all Europeans – by Dionysus, the God of viniculture. On Crete there is an ancient clay bowl that was used for pressing grapes. It possesses a spout through which the juice dripped into the fermenting jug underneath it. The bowl is an estimated 3,600 years old. Even all that time ago, the cultivation of vines and the pressing of grapes was widely practiced both on the mainland and on the islands of Greece. Resin residue has been found in the oldest amphorae (jars) so far discovered. In Antiquity when wines were enriched with herbs and honey, the resin of the Aleppi pine was used to seal the clay vessels in which the wines were stored. The resin had the added advantage of acting as a natural preservative. It is possible that it was Dionysus himself who revealed that secret, for as a mark of his dignity he used to carry a staff known as Thyrsos and decorated with pine cones. Be that as it may, the Greeks have at any rate kept their partiality for this distinctive resinous taste that overpowers any other flavors.

Retsína is by far the most popular wine. Being produced at an annual rate of over thirteen million gallons (500,000 hectoliters) it alone represents more than ten percent of the country's total wine production which amounts to about 120 million gallons (4.5 million hectoliters). Most of the Retsína is produced in the Attica wine-growing area near Athens. Mainly used is the white grape of the Savatiano vine because it is not susceptible to drought. During fermentation, resin crystals are added to the juice which protect it from oxidation and give it its distinct taste. The unique Retsína enjoys the special status of "traditional wine," a term which defines the method by which it was produced and Attica, Viotia, and Euboa as its three areas of cultivation. If a Retsína is classified as a vin du pays it means that it has, in addition to the above, complied with the stipulations laid down for that classification both to the more restricted area of origin and the guaranteed higher wine quality.

Viticulture

Ever since Greece joined the European Community in 1979, its wine-growing sector has been in a state of upheaval. Controlled labels of origin have been awarded to precisely defined areas since the year 1971. In the meantime twenty-eight appellations have been established defining the range of wine varieties, the yield, and the wine preparation. The major part of wine preparation is done by the cooperative societies – and the few large wine firms – and has been thoroughly modernized, due to considerable subsidies. Given the hot Greek climate, refrigeration is obviously of prime importance. A large selection of clean and pleasant white and red wines has been available ever since excessively

Retsína derives its characteristic flavor from the pine resin that drips from the cuts in the bark and is collected in cans.

The resin is added to the wine in order to protect it against oxidation.

The major Retsína growing areas are found near Athens. The grape variety most commonly used to make Retsína is Savatiano.

The popular traditional wine is also available in bottles with crown caps.

high temperatures have been avoided during fermentation and preservation, and since the wine making has been carried out by qualified experts. The most important wine-growing regions are the Peloponnese, Attica and Crete: between them they account for almost eighty percent of the 170,000 acres or so (70,000 hectares) cultivated for wine production. Of course Macedonia in the north offers the best natural conditions for growing great wines, but a good deal still remains to be done in the vineyards. Of the large number of grape varieties available there are only a very few that are really suitable for producing wines of convincing quality. Local traditional grapes are often only good enough for heavy country wines, and the market for those is on the decline even in Greece. There have, however, for some time now been positive developments in high-quality vines such as the Agiorítiko from Neméa, the Xynómavro from Náoussa, or the white Robóla varieties from the island of Kefalloniá, and Assýrtiko on Santorin.

The wines of Greece are becoming increasingly popular abroad – a fact for which the dynamic wine producers must take most of the credit. An early pioneer in this movement was the German Gustav Clauss who founded the estate of Achaia Clauss in 1861. The estate is situated within the region above Patras, an area richly steeped in the wine-growing tradition. The Achaia Clauss estate brought the well-known red wine Deméstica onto the market in 1902 and for many decades put down standards of quality and turnover that were unmatched by anyone. Today the estate remains one of the most successful and innovative wine concerns. Proof of this is Peloponnesiakós, a fresh white country wine produced from the varieties Rodítis and Chardonnay and introduced in 1991.

Three further enterprises have in the meantime joined the ranks of the main marketing concerns. Boutáris specializes in guaranteed wines and has gained a particularly strong following in Macedonia, in the north. The firm's principal wine there is Náoussa, produced from the black, distinctly sour Xynómavro grape. Boutáris' Grande Reserve Náoussa is one of the best Greek wines. Another interesting wine is the white Santoríni. In the 1980s, the well-known Oúzo producer Tsántalis began to expand its wine production and established an exemplary 250-acre (100 hectare) estate situated in the monastic state of Athos. This estate is planted primarily with Agiorgítiko vines. The firm has achieved enormous export successes with Retsína and Imíglykos. Fourth in line is the Retsína giant Kourtákis, an enterprise which has invested in a large-scale winery with all the latest technical equipment.

White and red country wines from Crete based on traditional varieties enjoy particular success. The largest private wine-growing estate was founded twenty-five years ago by the ship owner John Carrás in the northern Côtes de Meliton. The prestige of the Château Carras rests on a selection of wines produced from Bordeaux grapes.

Mavrodáphne Grapes reach a high sugar content and are suitable for producing sweet liqueur wines.

Mavrodáphne wines are left to mature for years to develop a smooth and harmonious flavor.

Liqueur Wines

The wine-growing tradition on Sámos can be traced back to the 9th century before Christ. The Muscat vine found throughout the Mediterranean region was planted there even then, and of course its highly esteemed variation, the small, white Muscatel grape. Today an area of about 3,700 acres (1,500 hectares) on Sámos is used to grow grapes for muscatel wine. The majority of the traditional vineyards are set out in narrow terraces that can only be worked by hand. Although some wines are sweetened during maturation, the proper Sámos is a wine that is naturally sweet. In the hot Mediterranean climate of the Aegean, the muscatel grapes can reach an extraordinarily high juice content. In the past, the most traditional way of processing the grapes involved exposing them to the sun by spreading them on straw or cloths in order to increase their concentration further. Today they are placed on lengths of paper or plastic for that purpose. The sugar content of the grapes then increases to such an extent that the yeast cultures manage to convert only about half of it into alcohol. This Sámos, referred to as Nectar, has a strength of fourteen percent by volume with a residual sugar content of up to eight ounces (250 g). In the case of other sweet or semi-sweet wines fermentation is arrested through the addition of alcohol to ensure that the desired proportion of natural glucose is preserved in the wine. Traditionally the wines are matured in large oak barrels during which their color quickly darkens to take on a deep golden or amber hue. These wines always have a bouquet that combines the typical Muscat scent with traces of honey, wax, raisins, and other dried or preserved fruit. Other recognized muscatel wines come from Patras and Ríon and from the islands of Kefalloniá, Rhodes, and Límnos.

The golden-colored muscatel has a red relative that is produced from the variety Mavrodáphne, the "black laurel." It can be developed into a full-bodied, strong, dry wine, but as a naturally sweet wine it is available in two appellations: the Mavrodáphne from Patras and the other from Kefalloniá. In its preparation, too, alcohol is used to stop fermentation and preserve the glucose. Then follows a period of maturing in wooden barrels which during the first year are generally left out of doors so that heat and fluctuations in temperature speed up its development. Mavrodáphne yields a complex, naturally sweet wine that is an excellent accompaniment to goat's or sheep's cheese.

Opposite: An old and naturally sweet red wine from Patras or Kefalloniá that has a rich aroma reflecting the wild countryside in which it grew and reached maturity. Such a wine provides a rare feast for both nose and palate of any wine lover.

Grape Varieties, Wines, and Wine-growing Regions

Agiorgítiko – a very good Greek variety of red grape which produces velvety, well-balanced wines. However, it needs to be grown at high altitudes and has a low yield. Main growing area is Neméa

Assýrtiko – a white grape variety grown on the island of Santorin for the production of fine, fresh wines with a pleasant acidity

Cáva – not a sparkling wine but red or white table wines which mature for two and three years respectively; in the case of red wine part of this period has to be spent in barrels

Chíma – general term for wine from the wood

Epitrapézio – table wine, usually offered under brand names

Gouménissa – a red wine growing region where Xynómavro is predominant

Kántza – a dry Savatiano white wine with a low acidity and no resin added; the best one of its kind in central Greece

Kefalloniá – an island in the Ionian Sea where three quality wines are produced: the good, dry, white Robóla, the dark, heavy Mavrodáphne, and Muscatel

Kokkinéli – a dark, resinated rosé

Kotsifáli – Crete's dominant red grape which leaves its mark on Pezá and Archánes; pleasant aromatic character

Kreta – an important wine-growing region with four appellations: Archánes, Dafnés, Pezá, and Sitía

Mantínia – fruity white wines and sparkling wines predominantly from the Moscho and Filero grapes

which grow on the plateau of Mantínia in the center of the Peloponnese peninsula

Mavrodáphne – a red grape used particularly for naturally sweet liqueur wines, registered in Patras and Kefalloniá

Muscatel – wines produced from the white, small-fruited muscatel grape were already famous in Antiquity; apart from Sámos, Límnos and Kefalloniá they are produced also in Patras and Ríon on the Peloponnese peninsula

Náoussa – a wine-growing region in Macedonia where Xynómavro obtains top results

Neméa – the largest continuous wine-growing area of the Peloponnese; Agiorítiko is used to produce some interesting, velvety wines, but the majority of wines are of average quality and referred to as Hercules' blood

Patras – port and capital of the province situated on the gulf of the same name; also a significant wine-growing region of high repute in the northern Peloponnese for the production of liqueur wines as well as dry wines

Rapsáni – a rustic red wine from the area around Mount Olympus

Retsína – a resinated white wine, mostly made from Savatiano grapes

Rodítis – pink-colored grapes that produce resinated Kokkinéli or pleasantly dry wines from Patras

Sámos – famous sweet muscatel wines from the island of the same name in the Aegean Sea

Topikós oínos – the Greek term for country wines

Vilaná – a white grape variety from Crete which is used to produce well-balanced country wines or the white Pezá

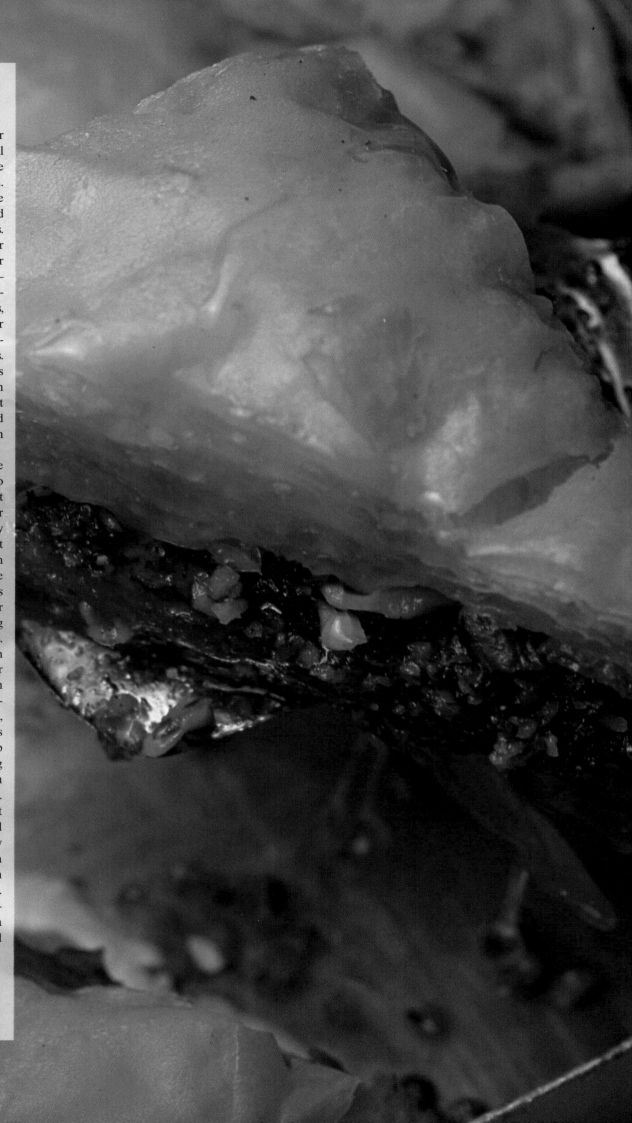

Sweets

The Greeks do not like sweets or puddings for dessert. Instead, they prefer to end a meal with fresh fruit, which is understandable since they can choose from a magnificent selection. The oranges and mandarins that ripen in the winter are followed by medlars, which herald the spring and whose fruits resemble apricots. Excellent strawberries and the very popular cherries are next in season. Early summer brings apricots, plums, and the first peaches – their main season is in July. Then virtual pyramids of melons are displayed in the markets, and there are also small bananas with their distinctive flavor. Apples and pears are available quite early, and the same goes for grapes. The production of light raisins and currants is still of considerable importance – more than 150,000 acres (60,000 hectares) of vines are set aside for that purpose. Figs are also dried and still wound into wreaths, as they were in Antiquity. Fresh, they are a real delicacy.

Of course, Greece is familiar with a large variety of sweet specialties. The Greeks do not, however, eat them as a pudding, but instead consume them in the afternoon or later in the evening. Or, accompanied by Greek coffee, they are offered to visitors that drop by – relatives, neighbors or friends. Often sweets that have to be eaten with a spoon are served to start with, the *gliká koutalioú*. As custom demands, they are served in a silver bowl known as the *glikothíki*. From it hang spoons with which the guests help themselves. The bowl usually contains fruit preserved in syrup – figs, cherries, grapes, or apricots, for instance, though there may also be green tomatoes, bitter oranges or miniature eggplants. With it is always served a glass of water, as it is with other sweets or cakes. The Greeks like to sit in or in front of a confectionery shop making the most of the occasion by choosing from the numerous cakes and cream pies on display, or with a Fíllo pastry or a yeast ball. Many sweets are made with honey, and yogurt with honey – probably the most classic of all sweet dishes of Greece – continues to enjoy great popularity. Thyme honey from Attica has been in demand since ancient times, when honey was the most sought-after sweetener. Thyme honey remains one of Greece's delicacies, even in the face of competition from other specialty honeys such as lemon and orange blossom, or pine.

Background: Bakláwas, the ultra-sweet puff pastry slices, are not served for dessert: instead, they are the Greeks' favorite sweet for all occasions.

Baklawás
Nut Pastry

1 cup (250 g) butter
1 lb (500 g) sheets of Fillo pastry (p. 317)
2 lbs (1 kg) almonds, finely chopped
3 tsp powdered cinnamon
2¹/₂ cups (625 g) sugar
Peel of 1 untreated orange
3 cloves 1 cinnamon stick
¹/₂ cup (125 g) honey
2 tsp rose-water

Melt the butter. Grease a rectangular baking dish with butter, line it with a sheet of Fillo and brush the Fillo with melted butter. Butter another 9 pastry sheets and add them one by one to the dish. Cover the remaining pastry with a damp cloth to prevent it from drying out. Preheat the oven to 325 °F (160 °C).
Mix together the almonds, powdered cinnamon, and ¹/₂ cup (125 g) of the sugar. Spread a thin layer of the almond mixture over the layered pastry and cover with 3 sheets of Fíllo, each brushed with butter. Spread another layer of the almond mixture over this, cover again with Fíllo as before and proceed in this manner until all the almond filling has been used up. The top layer must be one of Fíllo. Brush any overhanging pastry with butter and tuck it in. Mark the portions with a diamond-shaped pattern. Brush more butter over the top layer of pastry and moisten with a little water. Bake for about 75 minutes until golden brown.
In the meantime, mix the remaining sugar with the orange peel, the cloves and the cinnamon with 2 cups (400 ml) of water and bring slowly to the boil. Simmer for 15 minutes. Then remove the spices and orange peel, add the honey and the rose-water and stir well; leave to cool. Pour the syrup over the finished pie and leave overnight (do not put it in the refrigerator). Cut into slices as marked and serve.
Note: Baklawás may also be prepared with other nuts.

Popular Sweets

Amygdalotá – little almond balls, flavored with rose-water or orange-blossom water
Baklawás – Fíllo pie, filled with a nut or almond mixture and with syrup poured over it
Díples – pastry bows fried in oil with a honey-syrup poured over and sprinkled with finely-chopped walnuts
Galaktoboúreko – Fíllo pie filled with vanilla cream
Gliká koutalioú – fruit preserved in syrup and served in bowls
Halwás – semolina pudding, usually enriched with finely chopped or ground almonds, walnuts, pistachios or pine kernels; or it may also consist of a mixture of crushed sesame seeds with sugar syrup or honey
Karidópita – walnut cake soaked with brandy syrup
Kataífi – little rolls made of the fibrous angels' hair – pastry filled with a nut mixture and soaked with lemon syrup
Kourabiédes – almond pastry flavored with Oúzo or brandy; served on feast days
Loukoumádes – yeast balls deep-fried in oil, dunked into honey-syrup and sprinkled with cinnamon
Moustalevriá – a grape-harvest pudding, made from grape juice
Tiganítes – small cakes fried in oil, usually flavored with orange

To prepare Greek coffee, first put the sugar into the saucepan.

Then add the exact amount of finely ground coffee.

Now add the required amount of water and bring everything to the boil.

Once the coffee is ready it has to stand for a moment to allow the grounds to settle at the bottom of the cup.

Gliká Koutalioú
Preserved Fruit

Makes 2–3 jars
2 lbs (1 kg) fruit (cherries, apricots, grapes, figs, green tomatoes)
2 lbs (1 kg) sugar
Juice of 1 lemon
Untreated lemon peel

Wash the fruit thoroughly, remove stones and seeds if required and skin or peel as necessary.
Mix the sugar with 2¹/₂ cups (500 ml) of water and bring to the boil slowly, stirring all the time. Put the fruit into the syrup, add the lemon juice and peel and simmer over a low heat for 10 minutes. Pour into a bowl, cover and leave to soak overnight.
Bring to the boil again and simmer for 5 minutes, then leave to soak for another 12 hours. Bring to the boil once more; leave the fruit to cool down a little before removing the lemon peel. Now pour the fruit into sterilized, warm screw-top jars and seal. Store in a dark, cool place.

Loukoumádes
Deep-fried Yeast Balls

Serves 8
3¹/₄ cups (400 g) flour
1¹/₂ oz (30 g) yeast
1 tsp sugar
¹/₂ cup (100 ml) lukewarm milk
1 tsp salt
10 cups (1 l) peanut oil for deep-frying
1 cup (250 g) honey
1 Tbs lemon juice
Powdered cinnamon

Sieve the flour into a bowl and form a hollow in the center. Put the crumbled yeast into the hollow, sprinkle it with sugar and add the milk, stir in a little flour. Cover and leave to rise for 30 minutes.
Now add the salt and gradually stir in about 1¹/₂ cups (300 ml) of lukewarm water. Knead the dough well until it has reached a very light and fluffy consistency. Cover and leave to rise for 2 hours.
Heat up the peanut oil. With a teaspoon, cut out little balls of dough, and with the aid of a second teaspoon, let them glide into the hot oil. Deep-fry each batch of yeast balls for about 4 minutes until the outside turns brown; turn each yeast ball over once. Remove from the oil with a slotted spoon and leave to drain on kitchenroll.
Heat up the honey together with 1¹/₂ cups (300 ml) of water and the lemon juice and cook until it turns into syrup. Dip the yeast balls into the honey-syrup one by one, heap them up on a plate, and sprinkle with powdered cinnamon. Pour the remaining syrup into a bowl and serve with the yeast balls.

Halil Gülel

Turkey

Turkey can look back on an extraordinary culinary heritage. Due to a number of early writings dealing in some detail with food and cuisine, we know that many a specialty still popular today was already whetting appetites 700 years ago. *Halva* is one example, or the wedding rice dish flavored and colored with saffron. Under the Ottoman empire, the Palace Cuisine, as it was known, led to a specialization that had a lasting influence on culinary art and craft in general. Thus, particular guilds developed for each culinary "sector": the *lokmacı* supplied everything fried, the *köfteci* supplied meatballs, savory pastries were the province of the *börekci*, and rice dishes that of the *pilavcı*. Turkey has a wide range of fruit and vegetables at her disposal, as well as fish and meat dishes. The reason can be found in the country's geographical structure, with its rich and fertile maritime regions. On the Black Sea, for instance, where fishing plays an important role, almost every variety of garden vegetable is grown, along with tea and tobacco. Hazelnuts are a further economic factor of importance. The Marmara region, in particular the European side, with Thrace, is the centre of Turkish viticulture, while most Turkish olive oil comes from the Aegean coastal region, as do the tastiest figs. The Mediterranean coast, by contrast, specializes in citrus fruits, bananas, tomatoes, paprika, and other vegetables, along with cotton. The interior of the country presents a quite different picture. Anatolia, for example, is a barren region, the home of shepherds and cowherds, while fertile Cappadocia, with the town of Kayseri (Caesarea in Roman times) is famous not only for its carpets, but also for *pastırma* – dried meat – and *sucuk*, a spicy garlic sausage. Eastern Anatolia is dominated by stockbreeding, and produces the best kabobs in Turkey. With her variety of vegetables, her individual spices, her cooking methods and her eating customs, her refreshing sauces, her aromatic grills, her abundance of hors d'œuvres, and irresistible sweetmeats, Turkey can give the gourmet a foretaste of Asia.

Left: A convivial round, where Turkish men pass around the hookah. Mostly they first fill it with damp tobacco, on to which they then place glowing charcoal.

611

Flat Bread

Flat bread has been eaten in Turkey for as long ago as the country's culinary memory reaches. It was an important element in the diet even for the nomadic tribes, and during the Seljuk period from the 11th to the 13th century there were, for example in Anatolia, religious communities that maintained inns and kitchens where they would feed their own members as well as travelers with two main meals a day, as prescribed by the Koran, at which each person would receive four unleavened loaves.

A bread oven is not part of classical Turkish kitchen equipment, because the advantage of unleavened bread – whose ingredients are just flour, salt, and water – is that it can be baked on a round griddle, the *saç*, over a fire, and when dry will keep for weeks. It could be regarded as the original form of *yufka* – paper-thin sheets of dough. It is sometimes called *yufka ekmeği*, or sometimes, after the griddle, *saç ekmeği*.

A particularly tasty version of flat bread though, is *pide*, known internationally as the typical Turkish flat bread. This is a yeast bread and, in Turkey, eaten only during the fast of Ramadan. It is an obligatory part of the Iftar meal, eaten in the evening when the rules of the daylight fast no longer apply.

Pide
Flat Bread

1 oz (30 g) yeast
Sugar
1¼ cups (250 ml) lukewarm water
4¼ cups (500 g) flour
1 egg yolk
1 Tbs olive oil
1 oz (30 g) sesame seeds

Dissolve the yeast with a pinch of sugar in half of the water. Sift the flour into a bowl, add the salt and the dissolved yeast and stir well.
Add the remaining water, and knead the dough until smooth and elastic and no longer sticky. Cover, and leave in a warm place to rise for at least 20 minutes.
Pre-heat the oven to 400 °F (200 °C).
Shape the dough by hand on a floured surface, making a slight hollow in the middle. With a finger dipped in oil, press a lozenge pattern on the surface of the dough. Place the dough on a well-oiled baking tray. Paint the surface of the dough with a mixture of the egg-yolk, olive oil and one teaspoon of sugar, and scatter the sesame seed over it. Bake for about 20 minutes, until the bread is golden brown.

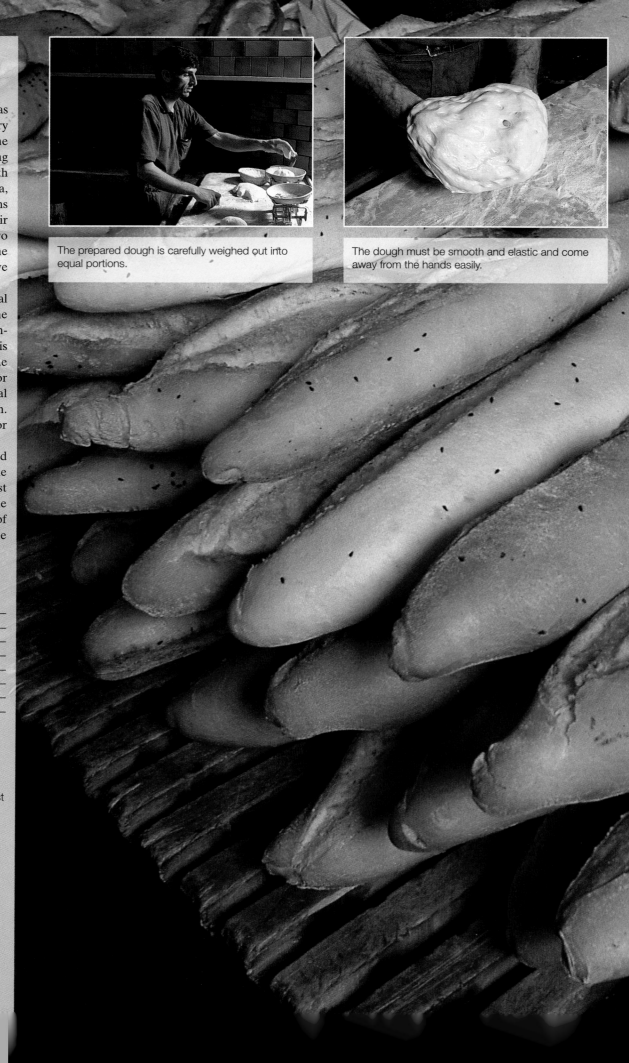

The prepared dough is carefully weighed out into equal portions.

The dough must be smooth and elastic and come away from the hands easily.

The baker pushes the bread into the oven using a wooden shovel.

Delicious flat loaves, which rise beautifully as they bake, while developing a good crust.

Background: Crusty bread is one of Turkey's favorite staple foods.

A cut is made in each individual loaf to make it rise better and give it a crisp crust.

There is a wide variety of shapes, ranging from flat loaves to rolls and baguettes.

Meze

It is in *meze* – hors d'œuvres – that we see the whole wealth of Turkish cuisine spread before our eyes. On special occasions, guests are offered a large choice of small delicacies, and since they are washed down with raki, the popular aniseed flavored liquor, the whole spread is known as a "rakı table." Istanbul and other large cities have restaurants specializing in rakı tables. While the focus in such places is on the meze, there are several other courses too – a variety of main courses with meat, fish, and poultry dishes, vegetables and pasta, dessert, fruit, and coffee. A rakı table gives the impression that the sophisticated variety under the Ottoman sultans has come back to life.

Domates Salatası
Tomato salad

2 beef tomatoes
1 onion
1 Tbs finely chopped mint
2 garlic cloves
6 Tbs olive oil
2 Tbs lemon juice
2 Tbs wine vinegar
Salt, black pepper

Peel, slice, and mix the tomatoes and onion, and scatter with chopped mint. Squeeze the garlic, and mix the juice with the remaining ingredients until a homogeneous sauce is obtained. Pour it over the tomato-onion mixture, and serve.

Hummus
Chick-pea purée

8 oz (250 g) chick-peas
5 oz (150 g) tahini (sesame paste)
Juice of 2 lemons
3 garlic cloves
1 tsp salt
6 Tbs olive oil
1 tsp hot paprika
Parsley

Soak the chick-peas overnight. Rinse, and boil in salted water for one hour. Strain and leave to cool. Remove the skins (these will come off easily) and beat to a purée.
Add the tahini, lemon juice, garlic, salt, and 2$\frac{1}{2}$ tablespoons of olive oil, and mix all the ingredients thoroughly. Put the hummus into a bowl and smooth the surface. Stir the paprika into the remaining olive oil and spread over the hummus. Garnish with parsley.

Typical Turkish Hors d'œuvre
(Illustration below)

1 **Bezelyeli havuçlu patates yemeği** – mixed vegetables with potatoes, peas, and carrots

2 **Karnabahar köftesi** – cauliflower fritters

3 **Haydari** – sheep cheese and herb cream

4 **Salatalık turşusu** – pickled gherkins

5 **Soğuk mantar buğulama** – pickled mushrooms

6 **Karides güveci** – shrimps in clay pots

7 **Cacık** – yogurt with cucumber, garlic, and dill

8 **Turşu** – pickled vegetables such as carrots, pimentos, eggplants, beans or cucumbers

9 **imam bayıldı** – "The Imam's Delight": baked eggplants

10 **Beyin köftesi** – calf's brain fritters

11 **Midye dolması** – stuffed mussels

12 **Domatesli karışnik kızartma** – fried vegetables in tomato sauce

13 **Beyaz peynir** – sheep cheese

14 **Mücver** – zucchini fritters with mint and dill

15 **Çiğ köfte** – raw ground meat with hot spices

16 **Patates piyazı** – potato and onion salad

Yufka, Bulgur, and Rice

Turkish cuisine uses three basic ingredients, which endow many dishes with a particular charm.

- Yufka are sheets of pastry rolled out very thinly, and correspond to the fíllo pastry in Greek cuisine (see p. 593). Sometimes, Turkish housewives make them themselves. This being extremely time-consuming, the job is often left to the *yufkacı*. The sheets of pastry can also be bought ready-made, wrapped in foil, in Turkish shops. As a rule, the one pound (500 g) packs contain five sheets measuring about twenty inches (50 cm). The best-known use for yufka (which resembles western flaky pastry) is in *baklava*, the Turkish national dessert. However, yufka is also used for a number of savory pastries, which take their place among the meze on the rakı table.

- Bulgur is parched crushed wheat, made from boiled grains. In its coarse form, it is used, boiled, as a side-dish to minced meat dishes or kabobs, or else forms a main dish along with vegetables and diced meat. Finely crushed bulgur is shaped, along with other ingredients, into little rolls, which are eaten raw or baked, or else used in salads and soups.

- Rice is a component of most main dishes in Turkey. It is cooked by the pilaff or absorption method (as are bulgur and wheat.) The amount of liquid is all-important: the rice – preferably long-grain rice – is first fried in butter for a few minutes; then hot bouillon is poured over it. When the liquid has been absorbed, the resulting pilaff is smeared with butter, and covered with a cloth or kitchen paper. The lid is put on the pot, which is stood in a warm place for fifteen minutes, so that any surplus liquid is absorbed. This makes the rice particularly fluffy. The art of a cook or the skills of a housewife are measured by the quality of their pilaff.

Ispanak böreği – Pasty (börek) with a filling of sheep cheese and spinach

Right: *Pide böreği* – Bread-dough pasty with a filling of ground meat (left) or sheep cheese

Left: *Su böreği* – Pasta dough pasty, with a spinach and sheep cheese filling

Kısır
Bulgur Salad

5 oz (150 g) finely crushed bulgur
2 onions
2 tomatoes
1 yellow Turkish pimento
2 small mild green Turkish peperoni
2 Tbs finely chopped parsley
1 Tbs finely chopped mint
1/2 teaspoon hot paprika
3 Tbs olive oil
3 Tbs lemon juice
Salt, black pepper

Place the bulgur in a bowl and gradually stir in 3/4 cup (150 ml) boiling water. Leave to stand for 20 minutes. Peel and finely chop the onions; peel and dice the tomatoes; wash and dice the pimentos and peperoni. Add the vegetables with the remaining ingredients to the bulgur, and mix well. Leave to stand for 15 minutes, and season to taste. Serve the kısır on lettuce leaves of your choice.

Sigara Böreği
Cigarette Böreği

7 oz (200 g) sheep cheese
1 egg
2 Tbs finely chopped parsley
1 Tbs finely chopped dill
Black pepper
2 sheets of yufka (pastry)

Crumble the cheese into a bowl. Add the egg, herbs, and some pepper and mix thoroughly. Cut each sheet of pastry into four strips of equal size. Cut each strip into three triangles of equal size.
Spread one tablespoon of the cheese mixture along one of the long sides of each pastry triangle, and roll up like a cigarette. Moisten the edges with water, and lightly press to seal. Fry in hot oil for about 5 minutes, until the cigarettes are golden-brown. Drain on kitchenroll and serve warm as a starter.

iç Pilav
Mixed Rice

1 cup (200 g) long-grain rice
1/4 cup (60 g) butter
1 onion
1/4 cup (30 g) pine-nuts
5 oz (150 g) lambs or chicken liver
Salt, black pepper
1/4 cup (30 g) currants
1/2 teaspoon cumin
11/2 cups (300 ml) chicken bouillon
1 Tbs finely chopped dill

Pour boiling salted water over the rice, allow to cool and strain. Melt half the butter. Peel and chop the onion, and soften in the butter. Add and lightly brown the pine-nuts.
Dice the liver, add to the onion and fry. Season to taste and put to one side. Melt the remaining butter, add the currants and cumin, and pour in the chicken stock. Bring to the boil and add the rice, stir, and boil for 10 minutes.
Carefully stir in the liver and the dill, and cook for a further 10 minutes. Cover the pot with a cloth, and allow the rice to stand for 10 minutes.

Rakı

A substantial Turkish evening meal is almost unthinkable without rakı. Turks drink this spicy aniseed-flavored liquor with its characteristic licorice-like taste to accompany any of the numerous courses, and also between the courses. Some like it neat, washing it down with a sip of cold water. However, most prefer it in the form of *aslan sütü*, or "lion's milk," the poetic name given to the cloudy liquid that results when rakı is mixed with water. The classical method of making rakı involves putting chopped figs and raisins into fermenting vats, adding four times the amount of water, and soaking the fruit until soft. The fermentation process is then started by adding yeast. In four to five days, the sugar in the fruit has turned to alcohol, producing a fermented mash with an alcohol content of seven to eight percent by volume. This is then distilled in a continuous process, producing a clear, highly alcoholic liquor known as soma. Aniseed is then soaked in *soma* and water, which is distilled a second time. The resulting liquor is diluted to drinking strength (forty to forty-five percent by volume) with distilled water, mildly sweetened and matured in barrels for one to two months before bottling.

The first officially licensed rakı distillery, Bomomti Nektar, was opened in Izmir Halka Pazar in 1912. Today, production has been taken over by state monopoly distilleries. Nowadays rakı is largely distilled from Turkish wine.

There are two varieties:
• Yenı Rakı: eighty grams of aniseed per liter, plus four grams of sugar; matured for at least one month
• Kulüp Rakı: one hundred grams of aniseed per liter, plus six grams of sugar; matured for at least two months.

The Turks love the pleasant aniseed taste of "lions' milk," as they like to call their national drink, and will drink it both with and between the courses of a meal.

Vegetables

The range of vegetables available in Turkey is very substantial. While many meat dishes are prepared with vegetables, there is also an independent category of vegetable dishes prepared with domestically produced olive oil. They are eaten cold and served as either a starter or as a between-courses dish. Such recipes often begin with the description *zeytinyağli*, which means "in olive oil." Pickled vegetables – *turşu* – are popular; they are used to supplement the range of meals in winter especially.

Karışık Turşu
Pickled Vegetables
(Illustration)

6 carrots
¹/₄ head of celery
3 green, 3 yellow and 3 red pimentos
12 gherkins
6 small, very firm tomatoes
12 garlic cloves
2 Tbs chick-peas
6 sprigs dill
6 leaves mint
2 oz (50 g) vine leaves
5 cups (1 l) white wine vinegar
4 oz (125 g) salt

Wash, clean or peel the vegetables. Cut the carrots, celery, and pimentos into bite-sized pieces. Make a number of slits in the tomatoes and gherkins. Peel the garlic.

Arrange the vegetables decoratively in a large glass jar. Distribute garlic, chick-peas, dill, and mint among them, cover with a layer of vine leaves.
Boil 10 cups (2 l) of water together with the vinegar and the salt, and pour enough over the vegetables to cover them. Shake the jar a little, to remove any air bubbles. Place a suitably sized plate on top of the vegetables, weighing it down with a stone to prevent them rising above the surface of the liquid. Close the jar, and stand it in a cool dark place for about five weeks. Serve as required, either as a starter or as an accompaniment to broiled meat.

Karişik Turşu – Pickled vegetables

Zeytinyağlı Pırasa
Leeks in Olive Oil

2 lbs (1 kg) leeks
2 onions
1/2 cup (100 ml) olive oil
2 carrots
3 Tbs long-grain rice
1 tsp sugar
2 Tbs lemon juice
Salt
Slices of lemon

Cut away all the green from the leeks, wash them thoroughly and allow to drain. Then cut them into sections of approximately 2 1/2 ins (5 cm).
Peel and chop the onions and gently fry in the oil until transparent. Clean the carrots, cut them into thin slices and add to the leeks. Gently fry for 10 minutes, stirring from time to time.
Add the rice, sugar, lemon juice, and salt, and about 3/4 cup (150 ml) of water.
Cover the pan, and simmer for about 25 minutes. Place in a dish, allow to cool and garnish with slices of lemon.

Yoğurtlu Kabak Kızartması
Fried Zucchini in Yogurt Sauce

1 lb (500 g) small zucchini
1 1/4 cups (125 g) flour
3/4 cup (150 ml) beer
Oil for frying
Salt
1 garlic clove
1 1/4 cups (250 g) yogurt

Wash, dry and rim the zucchini, and cut them into strips about 1/4 in (5 mm) thick. Sift the flour into a bowl and make a batter with the beer.
Coat the zucchini slices with the batter and fry in hot oil for about 3 minutes on each side, until they are golden brown.
Serve on a warm plate and sprinkle with salt. Press out the garlic, and mix the juice into the yogurt with a little salt. Serve in a separate bowl.

imam Bayıldı
"The Imam's Delight"
(Eggplants in Olive Oil)

4 medium-sized eggplants
Salt, black pepper
3/4 cup (150 ml) olive oil
4 onions
4 garlic cloves
2 tomatoes
1 tsp sugar
2 Tbs finely chopped parsley
1 tsp hot paprika
4 mild green Turkish peperoni
2 sprigs flat-leaf parsley

Wash and trim the eggplants and peel off strips of peel lengthways about 3/4 in (2 cm) apart. Soak in salted water for 15 minutes and pat dry.
Make deep lengthways cuts in the eggplants on one side, to produce pockets. Brown on all sides in 1/2 cup (100 ml) olive oil for about 5 minutes. Remove from the oil, and with the opening on top, place them in a heatproof dish.
Peel and thinly slice the onions, chop the garlic, skin and dice the tomatoes. Gently fry the onions and garlic in the remaining oil.
Remove from the heat and add tomatoes, sugar, chopped parsley, and paprika, season with salt and pepper. Pre-heat the oven to 350° F (180° C). Fill the eggplants with the vegetable mixture, distribute surplus vegetables among the eggplants, and place a seeded and cored half-peperoni on each. Mix the liquid from the vegetables in the pan with 1 1/4 cups (250 ml) of water and pour into the dish with the eggplants. Bake for 30–40 minutes, allow to cool in the dish, garnish with sprigs of parsley and serve from the dish.

Fish

Turkey is surrounded on three sides by the sea. To the north she is bordered by the Black Sea, whose fish specialty is *hamsi,* anchovies. Numerous recipes make use of these inexpensive, very tasty fish as their main ingredient. A smaller relative of the sardine, they are so popular along the Black Sea coast that the local people are jokingly accused of making anchovy jam. The high-grade *kalkan* – turbot – by contrast has become rare, as has the popular *levrek* – sea-bass – and the typical *zargana* – pipefish. Particularly important is the *mersin balığı* – sturgeon – of which there are a number of species in the cooler waters of the Black Sea, and which is famous not only for its caviar but also for its excellent flesh.

The Sea of Marmara, between the Bosphorus and the Dardanelles, is home in particular to *karides* – shrimp – and other crustaceans, as well as *midye* – mussels. But all the swarms of fish migrating from the Mediterranean to the Black Sea or vice versa have to pass through the Sea of Marmara and squeeze through the Bosphorus. On both shores of these straits between the continents, fishing villages have consequently sprung up in some profusion. In view of this, it is not surprising that Istanbul has for centuries enjoyed a particularly rich supply of fish, or that its inhabitants set high standards of quality and freshness.

The Aegean is famous for its various species of bream and for its squid. But tuna and the much sought-after bonito, the popular swordfish and the delicate gray mullet, as well as mackerel and sardines are caught here as well as in the Mediterranean, which forms the country's southern border. Thus, Izmir too can boast of interesting fish markets and its restaurants serve many specialties which reflect the wealth of Turkish fish cuisine. Often the fish are barbecued over charcoal, sprinkled with lemon juice, and served with tomatoes and lettuce. However, they are for preference previously marinated for a short time by painting them outside and in with a mixture of olive oil, lemon juice, and the juice of a crushed onion. Sometimes marinated portions of fish are broiled on a skewer, while larger fish or fillets of *levrek* – the popular sea-bass – are cooked in grease-proof paper. What all the cooking methods have in common is that the fish are prepared as simply as possible and without an excess of other ingredients, so that they lose nothing of their authentic taste.

Fish from Three Seas

Ahtapot – Squid	Karides – Shrimp
Ayna – Spider crab	Kefal – Grey mullet
Barbunya – Barbel	Kılıç (balığı) – Swordfish
Berlam – Hake	Kırlangıç – Gurnard
Böcek – Crayfish	Levrek – Sea bass
Çipura – Gilthead	Lüfer – Bluefish
Deniz kestanesi – Sea hedgehog	Mercan – Red bream
	Mersin balığı – Sturgeon
Dil (balığı) – Sole	Midye – Mussel
Dülger – John Dory	Magri – Conger eel
Fenerbalığı – Angler fish	Morina – Cod
Hamsi – Anchovy	Orkinos – Tuna
iskorpit – Stingfish	Palamut – Bonito
Istakoz – Lobster	Sardalye – Sardine
Kalamar – Cuttlefish	Som – Salmon
Kalkan – Turbot	Uskumru – Mackerel
	Yengeç – Crab
	Zargana – Pipefish

Background: Against the Istanbul skyline, a good catch. Large swarms of fish migrate through the narrows of the Bosphorus.

Meat

The Muslim faith requires care in the choice and preparation of meat. There are four strict principles: one forbids the eating of pork, another the consumption of blood. The two others require the animal to be slaughtered according to Muslim ritual, by cutting its throat in the name of God. Meat is a highly regarded ingredient in Turkey. Lamb and mutton are the favorite sorts, but veal, beef, and chicken are also popular. "Milk lambs" – slaughtered at the age of two or three weeks – are regarded as a great delicacy in the spring. Sheep's tails – which in Turkey are not docked – contain a great deal of fat, which is used for frying on account of its aroma.

One legacy of the nomadic past is a predilection for variety meats. Boiled sheep's head is a common sight. In the countryside, guests are still honored by being given the "bells of good luck" – that is grilled sheep's testicles. Long nights on the town are rounded off with a bowl of tripe soup. But since meat was – and is – not always plentiful, economy and skill in the preparation of meat dishes were always hallmarks of Turkish cuisine. Meat is often cut into cubes, as the nomadic tribes used to do a thousand and more years ago. These pieces are known as *kebap*. They can be prepared in countless ways, of which *şiş kebabı* – where they are broiled on a skewer alternating with pieces of tomato, onion, and pimento – is only one, albeit internationally the best known.

A particular expression of the Turkish culinary art is the combination of meat with vegetables. This can be seen not only in the stuffings for eggplants, zucchini, pimentos, tomatoes, vine-leaves, and globe artichokes, but also in the method of preparation, whereby meat and vegetables are cooked together. In order to maintain the succulence of the dish, it is a good idea not to use meat that is too lean. Totally lean, by contrast, is *pastırma*, dried meat, for which the best cuts of beef are used. Fillet or entrecôte is rubbed with *çemen*, a spicy paste of paprika, allspice, cumin, pepper, garlic, and salt, and then dried in the air. *Pastırma* is eaten, cut into paper-thin strips, with rakı, as a filling for börek, in stews or fried with eggs.

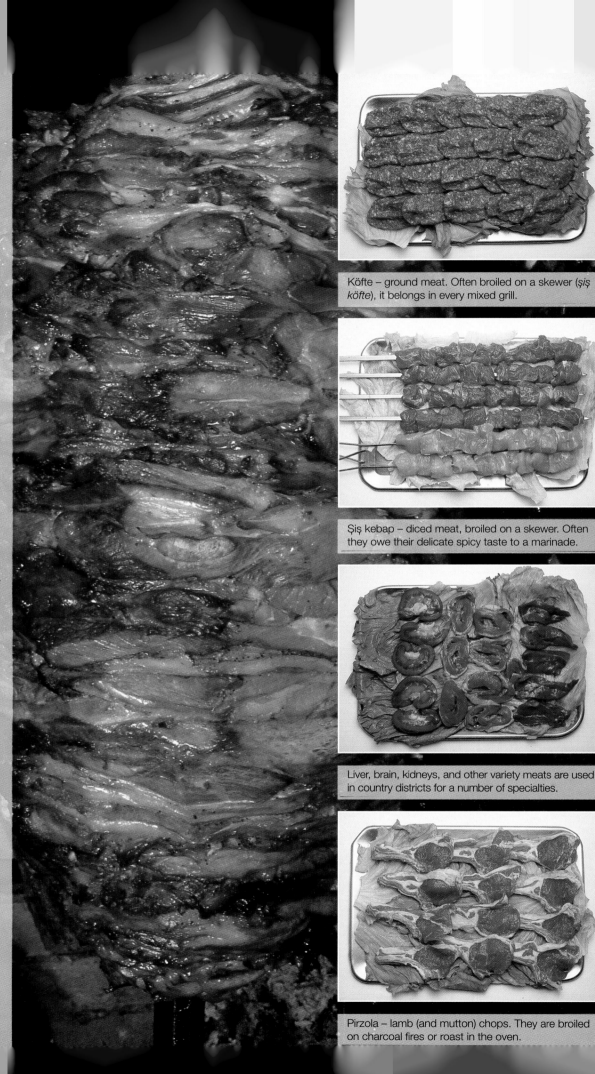

Köfte – ground meat. Often broiled on a skewer (*şiş köfte*), it belongs in every mixed grill.

Şiş kebap – diced meat, broiled on a skewer. Often they owe their delicate spicy taste to a marinade.

Liver, brain, kidneys, and other variety meats are used in country districts for a number of specialties.

Pirzola – lamb (and mutton) chops. They are broiled on charcoal fires or roast in the oven.

Şiş kebap – diced meat, broiled on a skewer and often served with a salad

Opposite (background): Döner kebap. It consists of paper-thin slices of lamb or mutton, which are marinated for a long time before being wound around a spit to form a thick roll which is rotated in front of a vertical grill.

Koyun pirzolası – roast mutton chops, a classic of Turkish cuisine

Sebze soslu köfte – Beef rissoles in sauce, with vegetables à la ménagère

Hünkar beğendi – "The sultan's joy" – braised cubes of lamb with eggplant purée

Çoban saç kavurması – Broiled meat *à la bergère*; cubes of meat with various vegetables

Yoğurt Tatlısı – Yogurt cake

Ayran – Yogurt drink

Cacık –
Yogurt with cucumber

Yogurt and Cheese

Yogurt is one of the most characteristic foods in Turkish cuisine. It, too, dates back to those ages long past when the Turks were still a nomadic people. Yogurt is used in particular as a sauce or else to refine spicy dishes. It is made from goats', sheep's or cows' milk, mostly at home. A liter of milk is brought to the boil, simmered for ten minutes and poured into a bowl. When it has cooled to lukewarm, a tablespoon of yogurt is stirred into some warm milk, and added to the milk in the bowl. With the bowl covered, wrapped in a cloth and stood in a warm place, the yogurt should develop in about five hours. The result is *sıvı tas yoğurt*, which is quite runny. If it is strained through a cotton cloth for two to three hours, the thick *süzme yoğurt* will be obtained, which is eaten with fruit as a dessert.

Turkish Cheeses

Beyaz peynir
Sheep cheese (known in Greece and Bulgaria as féta), either marinated in brine and matured for six weeks before consumption, or otherwise used fresh and unsalted.

Kaşar peynir
Best quality firm pale hard cheese, made from sheep's milk or cow's milk or a mixture of sheep's and goat's milk. Matured in a round mold. Can be used for grating.

Dil peyniri
A kind of mozzarella, eaten with flat bread.

Tulum peyniri
White, crumbly, salted cheese made from sheep's or goat's milk.

Çılbır – Poached eggs with yogurt

Yoğurt Tatlısı
Yogurt Cake
(Illustration opposite)

Serves 6

1¼ cups (250 g) full-fat yoghurt
3 eggs
1¾ cups (200 g) confectioner's sugar
1 tsp grated lemon-rind
5 Tbs (75 g) butter
2½ cups (250 g) self-raising flour
2 cups (500 g) sugar
5 Tbs lemon juice
3 Tbs finely chopped pistachios

Mix the yogurt with the eggs, confectioner's sugar, and lemon rind. Melt 3 Tbs (60 g) of butter and stir this into the yogurt mixture. Gradually add flour and work into a batter.
Pre-heat the oven to 350 °F (180 °C)
Use the remaining butter to grease a high-sided rectangular cake-pan, fill with the cake mixture and bake for 45 minutes.
Meanwhile mix the sugar and lemon juice with 3 cups (600 ml) of water, and bring to the boil, stirring all the time until the sugar has completely dissolved. Simmer for a further 10 minutes. When the cake is ready, drench it in the syrup while still in the cake tin, and allow to cool.
Serve in slices garnished with the chopped pistachios.

Ayran
Yogurt Drink
(Illustration opposite)

Serves 4–6

5 cups (1 kg) yoghurt
2½ cups (500 ml) iced water
1 tsp salt

Chill the yogurt and stir till smooth. Gradually add the iced water and then the salt. Beat in a mixer or with an egg-whisk until frothy. Salt further, or dilute, to taste. *Ayran* is a popular accompaniment to food.

Çılbır
Poached Eggs with Yogurt
(Illustration above)

Serves 2

2 garlic cloves
Salt
1½ cups (300 g) full-fat yogurt
3 Tbs vinegar
4 eggs
2 Tbs (30 g) butter
1 tsp paprika
Pinch of cayenne pepper

Crush the garlic with the salt, add to the yogurt and stir. Put into a serving dish and stand in a warm place. Add vinegar to salted water and bring to the boil. Slide eggs in and poach for 3 minutes. Remove with a straining ladle, and place on the yogurt. Melt the butter. Stir in paprika and cayenne, and pour over the eggs. Serve immediately.

Cacik
Yoghurt with Cucumber
(Illustration opposite)

Serves 4

1 large cucumber
Salt
3 cups (600 g) full-fat yogurt
3 garlic cloves, crushed
3 Tbs olive oil
2 Tbs finely chopped dill
1 Tbs finely chopped mint
Paprika

Peel the cucumber, remove the seeds, dice or grate, and salt. After about one hour, squeeze out. Place in bowl with yogurt. Add garlic, herbs, and 2 tablespoons of olive oil, if required, dilute with a little cold water. Mix well and season to taste. Divide into separate portion bowls and chill. Before serving, pour over the remaining olive oil and sprinkle with paprika.

Sweetmeats

The culinary arts fall over themselves in splendour and variety when it comes to sweetmeats; small wonder, then, that they are not confined to just one sweet course at the end of a meal. They are also enjoyed with tea in the afternoons, and for breakfast. The general appreciation of sweetmeats has given them an additional function: namely as a sign of respect and affection. Thus, it is customary for guests to take sweetmeats to their host, and conversely, visitors are offered sweetmeats as well. Celebrations for whatever cause are also an occasion for sharing sweetmeats with one's friends and neighbors.

"Strongholds" of Sweetmeats and Desserts

- Tatlıcı – confectioner's: here you can buy all the many varieties of *baklava*, the national dessert – a flaky sweetmeat drenched in syrup and enriched with nuts; *lokum*, Turkish delight; *halva*; and specialties with such oriental-sounding names as "lady's navel," "girl's bosom," "nightingale's nest" or "lady's lips"
- Pastahane – patisserie: these specialize above all in cakes and pastries, but usually also sell a small range of other sweetmeats
- Muhallebici – dairy: here you can buy sweetmeats and desserts based on milk products; the best-known are the Istanbul dessert *tavuk göğsu* and *kazandibi*, made from chicken-breast, rice, milk, and sugar
- İşkembeci – these restaurants specialize in variety meat and tripe-soup, but also serve *zerde*, "wedding rice" aromatized with saffron, and *aşure*, "Noah's pudding" – named after the feast with which Noah celebrated his deliverance from the Flood.

Halva – a sweetmeat made from sesame paste, honey, and pistachios

Şekerpare – a sweet pastry made from semolina and almonds

Baklava – a cake made from flaky pastry, here with honey and pistachios

Lokum – Turkish delight; made from sugar (or sometimes honey), nuts, and rice flour

Bülbülyuvası – "nightingales' nests": flaky pastry with pistachios, drenched in syrup perfumed with rose-water and lemon

Muhallebili baklava – a version with a sweet, milky cream filling in syrup

Sade Lokum
Turkish Delight

For about 3 lbs (1.2 kg)

2 cups (250 g) rice flour
4¹/₂ cups (1 kg) sugar
¹/₄ tsp citric acid crystals (from pharmacy)
8 oz (250 g) pistachio kernels
3 Tbs rose-water

Take a cake pan or pie dish measuring about 10 x 10 ins (25 x 25 cm) and line it with a muslin cloth large enough to overhang the sides all round. Sprinkle it with about half of the rice flour. Mix the rest of the rice flour with the sugar and just over 5 cups (1¹/₄ liters) of water, and bring to the boil in a large pan. Add the citric acid, and continue to boil, stirring continuously. When the mixture begins to foam, reduce heat and continue to simmer, but continue stirring from time to time to prevent sugar settling and caramelizing.

After about 2 hours take the pan from the heat and test as follows: put one teaspoon of the mixture into iced water and shape into a ball. If it is elastic and can be squeezed, then the Turkish delight is ready.

Toast the pistachios and stir them into the syrup with the rose-water. Pour the hot mixture into the pan or dish with the muslin, and smooth the surface. Stand for at least 24 hours, then turn out on to a baking tray which you have sprinkled liberally with confectioner's sugar. Use a very sharp knife to cut it into squares or rectangles, and turn each in icing confectioner's sugar.

Tip: instead of pistachios, chopped hazelnuts or walnuts can be used.

Pastry-honey-balls, dipped in syrup

Gözleme tatlısı – rolled sheets of pastry, fried in oil, and drenched in syrup

Tulumba tatlısı – piped batter, fried in oil, and dipped in syrup

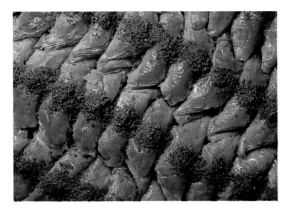

Cevizli ay – croissants with sultana-and-walnut filling

Baklava – a flaky-pastry confection with honey and walnuts or hazelnuts

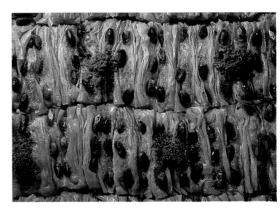

Tel kadayıf – a confection made from vermicelli, drenched in syrup and sprinkled with pistachios and other chopped nuts

Left: There are countless variations of *halva*, and not just regional variations. Many are specialties made for particular religious festivities with particular ingredients. One of the most delicious versions is made with sesame seeds.

Tea and Tea-houses

In the northeasternmost tip of Turkey, on the Black Sea coast and its immediate hinterland, the climate is humid and tropical. It rains almost every day, and the foothills of the Pontic Mountains are shrouded in warm fog. It is here, in the surroundings of Rize, that conditions are ideal for growing tea.

Tea, *çay*, is not just the Turk's constant companion through the day, but on all important occasions. This is true of business meetings at all levels as well as for appointments with officialdom and of course also for service in shops, where it is usual to provide customers with tea. The *çayhane* or tea-house is the meeting place for Turkish males. Here they go to exchange news, chat, and play, while letting the *tespih* – the Turkish rosary – glide between their fingers and all the time sipping their tea, several cups of it. Women are not seen in tea-houses. Islam forbids them from being together with strange men in one room. The problem is solved by resorting to *çaybahçesi*, or tea-gardens, in which the whole family are welcome.

If tea is not brewed in a samovar, a kettle and tea-pot are used. While the water is being heated in the kettle, the pot is placed on the open lid of the kettle to warm while the tea-leaves are inserted. Then a small quantity of boiling water is poured on to the leaves, the teapot is returned to the kettle, and the heat reduced. After the tea has brewed for eight to ten minutes, it is poured into the characteristic small glasses – more or less according to taste – and the glass is then filled with hot water. The glass is always served on a saucer with two lumps of sugar and a spoon.

The best tea in Turkey grows near Rize in the hinterland of the Black Sea coast.

When the buds open, the harvest can begin.

Background: The tea-house, *çayhane*, is a firm part of Turkish social life – but it is reserved just for men.

Tea is made very strong before being poured into glasses.

The tea in the glass is diluted to taste with hot water.

Tea is the Turk's constant companion.

Glossary

Adding water/wine
Adding liquid such as water or wine to a dish and stirring to remove any meat residue stuck to the bottom of the pan.

Affinage or maturation
With cheese, this is the level of maturation at which it is best consumed; with wine, this is the process of maturation in the bottle.

Aftertaste
Also used describe the aftertaste of a wine, especially in relation to its length.

Al dente
An Italian expression, referring to the firm bite to the tooth" of pasta and vegetables.

Appetizer
An appetizer or a snack.

Aspic
A jelly made from stock and a gelling agent into which other ingredients such as meat or vegetables are set.

Assemblage
A wine term used to describe a mixture of different varieties of grape or grapes from different locations; a blend.

Au gratin
Finishing off dishes under the broiler so that they form a crust, often with cheese or breadcrumbs.

Bain-marie
Cooking of ingredients in a container or pan which is stood in a saucepan of boiling water, or in special double-sided saucepans. This cooking method prevents food from burning.

Barding
Wrapping meat in thin rashers of bacon. This is usual with poultry or lean meat such as game.

Basting
Repeatedly pouring meat juices or other liquid over meat or poultry when being roasted or broiled to prevent them from drying out.

Béchamel sauce
A white sauce made with a flour and butter roux, milk, and seasoned with nutmeg and salt.

Binding
Using flour or cornstarch, or egg yolk and cream, to thicken liquids and roux.

Blanching
Adding ingredients, and especially vegetables, to boiling water and cooking for a few minutes. This destroys all bacteria and enzymes.

Boiling up
Increasing the heat for a short period to bring liquid to the boil.

Bouquet garni
A small posy of herbs, which always includes thyme and bayleaf and often parsley. It may also contain rosemary, marjoram, lovage, and celeriac, according to the dish and region.

Bouquet
A French word used to describe the aroma of a matured wine, its "nose."

Braising
Food to be braised is first seared (fried quickly to preserve its juices) before liquid is added to it for further cooking.

Breading
The coating of ingredients in a mixture of flour, egg, and bread crumbs before frying or deep-frying.

Broiling
Cooking and browning food either under the broiler or on a barbecue.

Browning
Frying ingredients in fat over a low heat until brown.

Buttering
Greasing the inside of an ovenproof dish or baking tray with butter.

Caramelize
Specifically, this describes the smearing of the insides of a (cake) tin with caramel sugar, but is also used in a broader sense to refer to the browning of foods with sugar and butter.

Carcass
A poultry carcass, used to make a sauce or – as in the southwest of France – broiled whole.

Clarifying
The process of removing sediments and binding broths and sauces by adding lightly-beaten egg white. The mixture is carefully heated and then strained.

Confit
French preserve, "conserve," used to describe pieces of meat and poultry, and especially goose and duck, that are preserved in their own fat.

Coulis
A sauce made from puréed fruit or vegetables.

Court bouillon
A seasoned stock in which ingredients, and especially fish, are cooked with onions, carrots, leek, and perhaps even celery, herbs and spices.

Croûtons
Fried cubes of bread.

Cuvée
Used with wine and sparkling wine to describe a product mixed from various tanks or barrels; a blend.

Deep-frying
Frying and browning ingredients which are totally immersed in hot oil or fat.

Dégorger
French "to cleanse," used with sparkling wines. The bottle is shaken to discharge the yeast residue at the bottom of the bottle to the neck of the bottle.

Degustation
This is a tasting session, especially of wine, undertaken to fathom out the aromatic characteristics of the item to be tasted.

Dusting or dredging
Sprinkling a layer of (usually) flour over ingredients; with desserts, this is usually confectioner's sugar.

Flambé
Flavoring a dish by pouring spirits with a high alcohol content over it and igniting.

Flouring and deep-frying
Frying floured or battered ingredients which are totally immersed in hot oil or fat until brown.

Folding in
Adding ingredients to a mixture without stirring rigorously.

Forcemeat or farce
This is a mixture of ground meat or fish or mushrooms with herbs, spices and other ingredients; used to fill pies and pastries, poultry, fish etc. Also used as a spread on toast or bread.

Frying
Cooking fish and meat at a high temperature in fat or oil in a frying pan.

Fumet
French, meaning literally "smell" or "aroma," this describes a concentrated residue remaining after fish or shellfish have been boiled, reduced or strained, and can be used as a basis for soups or sauces.

Garnishing
Arranging accompaniments around the main ingredient or decorating the dish.

Gently frying
Frying ingredients in fat over a low to medium heat until transparent or lightly browned.

Hack or grind
Mainly used with meat, this means to chop finely with a knife or grind.

Julienne
Vegetables cut into thin strips.

Marinating
Soaking ingredients, and especially game, in a sauce made from oil or wine, vinegar or lemon juice, and herbs and spices and leaving to stand for a length of time.

Maturation
Maturation process of fermented wine in barrels or neutral containers.

Meat juices
These are left after meat or fish has been cooked; they form the base of sauces.

Mirepoix
Small, gently-fried vegetable cubes such as carrots, onions, spring onions with herbs, and a little raw bacon, used to flavor sauces.

Moistening
This can refer to the careful addition of liquid when preparing or cooking a meat dish, for example, to make sure the ingredients do not dry out.

Parfait
Frozen dessert.

Persillade
A mixture of finely-chopped garlic and parsley.

Poaching
Carefully cooking food in liquid kept just below the boil.

Puncturing
Inserting rashers of bacon, slices of truffle or garlic clove under the skin or surface of poultry or meat; this is best done with a special needle.

Purée
Raw or cooked soft food reduced to a thick mass.

Rancio
A certain bouquet and taste which wine and brandy acquire when aged over a long period of time. It is reminiscent of fresh walnuts.

Reducing
The reduction of a liquid by putting it to boil over a high heat to evaporate it.

Rendering down
Frying bacon or other ingredients until the fat in the bacon melts.

Rinsing
This is usually done with cold water; also recommended after food has been blanched.

Roasting
Cooking fish and meat at a high temperature in the oven.

Roux
This is made by stirring flour into melted butter to form a smooth paste to which liquid is then gradually added; used to bind liquids or sauces.

Rumpot, marinated fruit
Fruit or other ingredients left to soak in alcohol, wine or marc.

Sautéing
From French *sauter*, this is the process of quickly browning food in a small quantity of fat in a wide-bottomed frying pan.

Scoring
Cutting narrow lines into the surface of fish or meat so that it cooks evenly and does not blister. Also used for decorative purposes.

Seasoning
Tasting a dish and, if necessary, adding salt, pepper, and/or other suitable herbs.

Simmering
Cooking a dish or food in liquid over a low heat just below boiling point until cooked.

Skimming
Removing the froth, scum or fat which is formed when cooking meat for soups and stews. This is best done with a slotted spoon or a skimmer; also used with fruit and butter.

Skinning and filleting
Removing the skin, bones, head, and tail from a fish.

Soaking
Leaving dried vegetables or fruit in water or any other liquid to soak until they swell up and become soft.

Steaming
Cooking food in the steam of boiling water using a special sieve or attachment.

Stewing
Cooking dishes either in their own juice or with a minimum of added liquid.

Stock
Flavored liquid used for cooking meat.

Straining
Draining food through a sieve or pressing through a cloth.

Sweating
Cooking vegetables, and in particular onions, in butter or any other kind of fat over a low heat so that they do not brown.

Tannins
Tannic acids in wine which come from the skin and stalks of grapes and function as a natural preservative. They guarantee red wine a long life.

Thickening
Thickening and binding of non-boiling sauces by stirring in egg yolk and cream, milk or butter. Also used to refer to the heating of egg mixtures until they thicken or curdle or using a gelling agent to thicken liquids.

Toasting
Browning of food with little or no fat.

Trimming
The removal of fat, gristle, and other superfluous matter from pieces of meat or fish.

Vinaigrette
A salad dressing based on a mixture of vinegar (French *vinaigre*), oil, and perhaps a little (Dijon) mustard.

Zabaglione
A creamy dessert made from egg yolks, sugar, and marsala.

Bibliography

Accademia Italiana della Cucina: Cucina Italiana, Das große Buch der Italienischen Küche. Köln 1993

Albonico, Heidi und Gerold: Schweizer Tafelfreuden. Zürich 1974

Alexiadou, Vefa: Greek Cuisine. Thessaloniki 1989

Anderson, Burton: Atlas der italienischen Weine. Bern – Stuttgart 1990

Anderson, Jean: The Food of Portugal. New York 1994

Andrae, Illa: Alle Schnäpse dieser Welt. Herford 1988

Aris, Pepita: Rezepte aus einem spanischen Dorf. München 1991

Arnaud, Tony: Wildtiere. Stuttgart 1975

Ayrton, Elizabeth/Fitzgibbon, Theodora: Traditional British Cooking. London 1985

Bailey, Adrian: Die Küche der Britischen Inseln. Time Life International, 1974

Bailey, Adrian, u.a.: Die Speisekammer. München 1993

Bati, Anwer: Zigarren –Der Guide für Kenner und Genießer. München 1994

Beer, Otto F.: Wien – Reise durch eine Stadt. München 1977

Bernard, Françoise: Le Livre d'or. Paris 1985

Beyreder, Adelheid: Küchen der Welt – Österreich. München 1993

Beyreder, Adelheid: Böhmisch kochen. München 1994

Bobadilla, Vicente F. de: Brandy de Jerez. Madrid 1990

Bocuse, Paul: Bocuse dans votre cuisine. Paris 1982

Bocuse, Paul: Die Renaissance der Französischen Küche. München 1991

Brown, Catherine: Scottish Cookery. Edinburgh 1985

Brown, Dale: Die Küche in Skandinavien. Time Life International, 1971

Bugialli, Giuliano: Classic Techniques of Italian Cooking. New York 1989

Buren, Raymond: Le Jambon. Grenoble 1990

Cadogan, Mary: Delikate Meeresfrüchte. Hamburg 1992

Campbell, Georgina: Good Food from Ireland. London 1991

Cantin, Christian: Les Fromages. Paris 1978

Carluccio, Antonio: Passion for Pasta. London 1993

Casas, Penelope: Tapas. New York 1991

Casparek, Gustav: Das Kochbuch aus dem Rheinland. Münster 1976

Casparek-Türkhan, Erika: Küchenlexikon für Feinschmecker. München 1989

Casparek-Türkhan, Erika: Kulinarische Streifzüge durch die Türkei. Künzelsau 1989

Casparek-Türkhan, Erika: Kulinarische Streifzüge durch Europa. Künzelsau 1994

Casparek-Türkhan, Erika: Griechisch kochen. München 1994

Chaudieu, Georges: Le livre de la viande. Paris 1986

Christl-Licosa, Marielouise: Antipasti. München 1991

Connery, Claire: In an Irish Kitchen. London 1992

Cousteaux/Casamayor: Le Guide de l'Amateur d'Armagnac. Toulouse 1985

Cùnsolo, Felice: Italien tafelt. München 1971

Darwen, James: Das Buch vom Whisky. München 1993

Das große Buch vom Kochen. Köln 1986

Das große Koch- und Backbuch. Frankfurt/Main 1983

Das Land Bremen. Monographien deutscher Wirtschaftsgebiete. Oldenburg 1984

Davids, Kenneth: Espresso – Ultimate Coffee. Santa Rosa 1993

Davidson, Alan: Mediterranean Seafood. Middlesex 1981

Davidson, Alan/Knox, Charlotte: Seafood. London 1989

Degner, Rotraud: Fische und Meeresfrüchte. München 1989

Döbbelin, Hans Joachim: Kulinarische Streifzüge durch Skandinavien. Künzelsau 1990

Dominé, André: Die Kunst des Aperitifs. Weingarten 1989

Döpp, Elisabeth: Griechisch kochen. München 1993

Dr. Oetker: Lexikon Lebensmittel und Ernährung. Bielefeld 1983

Duch, Karl: Handlexikon der Kochkunst. Linz 1989

Enciclopedia della cucina. Novara 1990

Engin, Funda: Türkei. München 1994

Erdei, Mari: Ungarisch kochen. München 1993

Eren, Neset: The Art of Turkish Cooking. New York 1969, 1993

Faist, Fritz: Fondue und Raclettes. Niedernhausen/Ts. 1986

Falkenstein, Peter-Paul: Das Wein-Buch. Köln o.J.

Ferguson, Judith: Polish Cooking. New York 1991

Freson, Robert: Italien – Eine kulinarische Entdeckungsreise. München 1992

Freund, Heidemarie: Backen mit Obst. München 1993

Gay, Lisa: Eloge de l'huître. Paris 1990

Gericke, Sören: Smörrebröd und rote Grütze. Berlin 1993

Getränke. Time Life International, 1982

Gööck, Roland: Ein kulinarisches Rendezvous mit Deutschland. Künzelsau 1985

Gorys, Erhard: Das neue Küchenlexikon. München 1995

Grösser, Hellmut: Tee für Wissensdurstige. Gräfelfing 1992

Großbritannien – Landschaften und Rezepte. London 1991

Halıcı, Nevin: Das Türkische Kochbuch. Augsburg 1993

Hamann, Ulla: Norddeutscher Kuriositätenführer. Königstein/Ts. 1981

Haroutunian, Arto de: Middle Eastern Cookery. London 1982

Harris, Andy: Grèce Gourmande. Paris 1992

Hering, Richard: Lexikon der Küche. Gießen 1978, 1987

Hess/Sälzer: Die echte italienische Küche. München 1990

Hillebrand/Lott/Pfaff: Taschenbuch der Rebsorten. Mainz 1990

Horvath, Maria: Spanische Küche. München 1964

Imhoff, Hans: Kakao – Das wahre Gold der Azteken. Düsseldorf 1988

Inzinger, Max: Die gute deutsche Küche. Köln 1991

Jackson, Michael: Bier international. Bern 1994

Jackson, Michael: Das große Buch vom Bier. Bern 1977

Jacobs, Susie: Die schönsten Rezepte aus der griechischen Inselwelt. Köln 1992

Johnson, Hugh: Der große Weinatlas. Bern – Stuttgart 1995

Johnson, Hugh: Der neue Weinatlas. Bern 1994

Juling, Petra: 100 schwedische Gerichte. Köln 1994

Kaltenbach, Marianne: Ächti Schwyzer Kuchi. Bern 1977

Kloos, W.: Bremer Lexikon. Bremen 1977

Knich, Hubert (Hrsg.): Türkisch kochen. München 1993

Ková, Eva Hany: Westböhmisches Kochbuch. Berlin 1992

Kramer, René: Büffets und Empfänge in der internationalen Küche. München 1977

Kramer, René: Wild und Geflügel in der internationalen Küche. München 1974

Lang, George: Die klassische ungarische Küche. Budapest 1993

Le Divellec, Jacques: Les Poissons. Paris 1990

Lechner, Egon: Jagdparadiese in aller Welt. München 1991

Lempert, Peter: Austern. Düsseldorf 1988

Likidis-Königsfeld, Kristina: Griechenland. München 1994

Lissen/Cleary: Tapas. London 1989

Löbel, Jürgen: Parmaschinken & Co. Düsseldorf 1989

Loberg, Rol: Das große Lexikon vom Bier. Wiesbaden o.J.

Lombardi, Liliana: Le ricette regionali italia ne. Mailand 1969

Luard, Elisabeth: The La Ina Book of Tapas. Cambridge 1989

Luján, Néstor und Tin: Spanien – Eine kulinarische Reise durch die Regionen. München 1991

Marcenta, A.: Suppen, die die Welt bedeuten. München 1978

Marchesi, Gualtiero: Die große italienische Küche. München 1984

Marstrander, Sigrid: Norwegian Recipes. Iowa 1990

Maxwell, Sarah: Meze Cooking. London 1992

McLeod-Grant, Ameli: Scottish Cookbook. Münster 1979

McNair, James: Pizza. Berlin 1990

Medici, Lorenza de' (Hrsg.): Italien – Eine kulinarische Reise. München 1989

Mehlspeisen und Teigwaren von A bis Z. Köln 1985

Meurville/Creignou: Les fêtes gourmandes. Paris 1989

Meuth/Neuner-Duttenhofer: Toskana. München 1993

Meyer-Berkhout, Edda: Die spanische Küche. München 1985

Meyer-Berkhout, Edda: Kulinarische Urlaubs-erinnerungen. München 1981

Mitchell, Alexandra, u.a.: Frankreich – Das Land und seine Küche. München 1992

Mittelberger, Karl: Das Aachener Printenbuch. Aachen 1991

Moisemann, Anton/Hofmann, H.: Das große Buch der Meeresfrüchte. Füssen 1989

Monti, Antonia: Il nuovissimo cucciaio d'argento. Rom 1991

Musset, Danielle: Lavandes et plantes aromatiques. Marseille 1989

Norman, Jill: Das große Buch der Gewürze. Aarau 1993

Ojakangas, Beatrice: Fantastically Finnish. Iowa 1985

Olivier, Jean-François: Huiles et matières grasses. Paris 1992

Ott, Alexander: Fische. Künzelsau 1981

Papashvily, Helen und George: Die Küche in Rußland. Time Life International, 1971

Paradissis, Chrissa: Das beste Kochbuch der griechischen Küche. Athen 1972

Pebeyre, Pierre-Jean et Jacques: Le Grand Livre de la Truffe. Paris 1987

Perry, Sara: The Tea Book. San Francisco 1993

Priewe, Jens: Italiens große Weine. Herford 1987

Read, Jan: Sherry and the Sherry Bodegas. London 1988

Reck, Heinz: Käse-Lexikon. München 1979

Rezepte aus deutschen Landen. Herrsching o.J.

Rios/March: Große Küchen – Spanien. München 1993

Riza Kaya, Ali: Die Türkische Küche. München 1995

Rob, Gerda: Ein kulinarisches Rendezvous mit Griechenland. Künzelsau 1990

Rob, Gerda: Kulinarische Streifzüge durch Österreich. Künzelsau 1990

Rob, Gerda/Teubner, O.: Ein kulinarisches Rendezvous mit Portugal. Künzelsau o.J.

Robinson, Jancis: Reben, Trauben, Weine. Bern – Stuttgart 1987

Röger, Michael: Alles aus Lebkuchen. Augsburg 1990

Römer, Joachim/Schmidt, Gérard: Kölsch Kaviar un Ähzezupp. Köln 1990

Römer, Joachim: Kölsches Kochbuch. Köln 1994

Rossi Callizo, Gloria: Las Mejores Tapas. Barcelona 1985

Samalens, Jean et Georges: Le livre de l'amateur d'Armagnac. Paris 1975

Scheibenpflug, Lotte: Das kleine Buch vom Tee. Innsbruck 1992

Schindler, Hedwig: Die unbekannte türkische Küche. Berlin 1990

Schmöckel, Peter: Das große Buch der Getränke. München 1993

Schokolade und Kakao. Über die Natur eines Genusses. Neuwied 1991

Schoonmaker, Frank: Das Wein-Lexikon. Frankfurt/Main 1990

Schuhbeck, Alfons: Das neue bayerische Kochbuch. Steinhagen 1990

Schwäbisch-alemannische Küche. Offenburg 1982

Schwarzbach, Berti: Das Kochbuch aus Wien. Tirol 1978

Scott, Astrid Karlsen: Ekte Norsk Mat. Lake Mills, Iowa 1983

Stender-Barbieri, Uschi: Wanderung durch Italiens Küche. Herrsching 1974/75

Steurer, Rudolf: Vino – Die Weine Italiens. Rüschlikon–Zürich o.J.

Steurer, Rudolf/Thomann, Wolfgang/Schuller, Josef: Welt Wein Almanach. Wien – München – Zürich 1992

Supp, Eckhard: Enzyklopädie des italienischen Weins. Offenbach 1995

Taubert, H. G.: Kaviar. Düsseldorf 1989

Teubner, Christian: Die 100 besten Kochrezepte. Füssen 1994

Teubner (Hrsg.), Christian: Das große Buch vom Fisch. Füssen 1987

Teubner (Hrsg.), Christian: Das große Buch vom Käse. Füssen 1990

Teubner, Christian/Wolter, Annette: Spezialitäten der Welt – köstlich wie noch nie. München 1982

Theoharous, Anne: Griechisch kochen. München 1981

Thurmair, Elisabeth: Teigtaschen aus allen Ländern. München 1988

Torres, Marimar: The Spanish Table. London 1987

Toussaint-Samat, Maguelonne: La cuisine de Maguelonne. Paris 1988

Uecker, Wolf: Brevier der Genüsse. München 1986

Uecker, Wolf: Deutschland, deine Küchen. Steinhagen 1988

Volokh, Anne: The Art of Russian Cuisine. New York 1983

Walden, Hilaire: Portuguese Cooking. London 1994

Ward, Susann: Russische Küche. Köln 1995

Widmer, Peter/Christ, Alexander: Schweiz – Kulinarische Tafelfreuden. Künzelsau 1993

Wien und Umgebung. Grieben-Reiseführer

Willan, Anne: Die Große Schule des Kochens. München 1990

Willinsky, Grete: Gemüse – international serviert. Berlin 1976

Wolter, Annette, u.a.: Spezialitäten der Welt – köstlich wie noch nie. München 1993

Wolter, Annette: Geflügel. München 1987

Zoladz, Marcia: Portugiesisch kochen. St. Gallen – Berlin – Sao Paulo 1987

Acknowledgments

The publishers would like to thank all those concerned for their support and assistance. The publishers would also like to express their gratitude to all of those people and institutions who helped to realize this project without being known by name to us.

Birgit Beyer, Cologne
Ilona Esser Schaus, Cologne
Rebecca Hübscher, Cologne
Peter Khow, Cologne
Annette Nottelmann, Cologne
Julia Mok, Cologne
Andreas Pohlmann, Cologne

England

Mitch Farquharson, The Cheese Company, Melton Mowbray
Chris Lynch, Colman's of Norwich
The Coronation Tap, Bristol
Fortnum & Mason, London
Shaun Hill, Gidleigh Park
Lea & Perrins International, Worcester
Meat and Livestock Commission, Milton Keynes
Jason Hinds, Neal's Yard Dairy, London
Patak's (Spices) Ltd., Haydock
Harry Ramsden's, White Cross
Bill Scott, The Riverhouse, Thornton-le-Fylde
Smiles, Bristol
Simpson's-in-the-Strand, London
Ann Taylor, Taunton Cider Company, Taunton
Paula MacGibbon, The Tea House, Covent Garden, London
Thornton's, Cheapside, London
Twinings, Andover

Scotland

The Aberfeldy Water Mill, Aberfeldy
C. Alexander & Son, Lanark
Mr. Young, The Breadalbane Bakery, Aberfeldy
Denrosa Apiaries, Coupar Angus
Dunsyre Blue Cheese, Carnwath
Glenturret Distillery, Crieff
John Meterlerkamp, The Chesterfield Hotel, Mayfair, London
John Milroy, London
Nancy Ewing and Arthur Bell, The Scottish Gourmet, Thistle Mill, Biggar

Ireland

Maureen O'Flynn, R. & A. Bailey & Co., Dublin
Maureen O'Flynn, Boxty House, Dublin
John Meterlerkamp, The Chesterfield Hotel, London
Guinness Ireland, Dublin
McCartney's Family Butchers, Moira, Co. Down
Patrick Doherty, Mulligan's of Mayfair, London
Jason Hinds, Neal's Yard Dairy, London
Sheila Croskery, The Old Bushmills Distillery, Bushmills, Co. Antrim
Scally's Supermarket, Clonakilty, Co. Cork
Veronica and Norman Steel, Eyeries, Co. Cork
Michael Stafford, Co. Cork
Ulster-American Folk Park, Omagh, Co. Tyrone

Denmark

Carlsberg Brewery, Copenhagen
Royal Danish Embassy in Germany
Hjorth's Røgeri, Ansdale, Bornholm
Gert Sørensen and Employees, Konditoriet i Tivoli, Copenhagen

Norway

Jens-Harald Jenssen, Finnmark Travel Association, Alta
Norske Meierier, Oslo
Torger Pedersen, City Café, Alta
SAS Hotel, Varasjok
Vinmonopolet, Oslo
Harald Volden, Volden Fiskeoppdrett

Sweden

Lauri Nilsson and Karl-Heinz Krücken, Ulriksdals Wärdshus, Solna
Vete-Katen Bakery, Stockholm
Vin + Sprithistorika Museet, Stockholm
Wasa, Celle

Finland

Annan Kotikukko Bakery, Sorsasalo
Finnish Embassy; Press and Cultural Department; Marita Schulmeister
Lohimaa Trout Farm, near Kuopio
Hotel Rahalaati, Kuopio

Russia and other member states of the former Soviet Union

Svetlana Dadasheva, Moscow
Hotel Lux, Cologne

Poland

Metzgerei Beim Schlesier, Mr Wieschollek, Kerpen
Restaurant Dwór Wazów, Mr Malec Wroctaw
Mr. & Mrs. Klęsk, Duszniki Zolrój
KPPL "Las", Mr. mgr. ini. Marek Rojek, Kłoc'zko
Dr. Henryk Rola, Duszniki Zolrój

The Czech Republic · Slovakia

Juraj Heger, Bratislava

Hungary

Zander Fishing Fleet Balaton, Kesztheim
Barneval, Kishunhalas
Restaurant Fogas, Tihany Peninsula
Magda Molnár and Gabór Vince, Kulturtrade
Thomas Niederreuther GmbH, Munich
Peppermill, Kalocsa
Tokay Vineyard Gundel, Mád

Austria

Café Hawelka, Vienna
Frau Jell, Gasthaus Jell, Krems a. d. Donau
Hietzinger Bräu, Vienna
Josef Jamek, Weingut Jamek, Joching, Wachau
Heurigen Maier-Resch, Stein a. d. Donau
Barbara and Manfred Pichler, Krems a. d. Donau
Heinz Prokop, Traismauer
Café Reuter, Stein a. d. Donau
Bailoni, Stein a. d. Donau
Hotel Sacher, Vienna

Switzerland

Fleisch Trocknerei Brügger, Parpan
Landsbeck Bakery, Aarau
Leckerli Hus, Basle
Kuttel-Tabaco, Berne
Konditorei Meier, Zug
Confiserie Schiesser, Basle
Raclette-Stube, Zürich
Schaukäserei Switzerland, Seenen bei Schwyz
Zunfthaus Zur Waage, Zürich

Germany

Aachener Printen- und Schokoladenfabrik Henry Lambertz, Aachen (Aix-la-Chapelle)
Auswertungs- und Informationsdienst für Landwirtschaft und Forsten (AID)
Bäckerei Allkofer, Regensburg
Bergische Forellenzuchtanstalt, Lindlar
Hans Dieter Blume, Lohne
Centrale Marketinggesellschaft der deutschen Agrarwirtschaft (CMA)
Deidesheimer Hof, Deidesheim
Deutscher Brauerbund
Deutscher Weinfonds/Deutsches Weininstitut
Deutsches Teigwaren-Institut
Dikhops Hof, Wesseling
Metzgerei Hans Dollmann, Regensburg
Konditorei und Bäckerei Fassbender, Siegburg
Restaurant Friesenhof, Kiel
Weingut Gunderloch, Nackenheim
Brauerhaus Heller, Cologne
Weingut Juliusspital, Würzburg
Horst Mayer, Hotel Steigenberger *Graf Zeppelin*, Stuttgart
Fürst von Metternich, Johannisberg
Microgrill, Cologne
Niederegger Marzipan, Lübeck
Päffgen, Cologne
Simex, Jülich
Verband der deutschen Binnenfischerei
Vereinigung Getreide-, Markt- und Ernährungsforschung (GMF)
Weissbräu, Cologne
Fischräucherei Wiese, Kiel

The Netherlands

Abrahams Mosterdmakerij, Eenrum
Restaurant Auberge Maritim, Maroel, Ziriksee
Droppie, Groningen
Fassbender, Siegburg
Fish Market, Sheveningen
Hooghoudt, Groningen
Café Theo Könegracht, Maastricht
Muschelkantor, Yerseke
J. T. Neeleman, Cheese Factory, Scheemda
Dutch Office for Milk Products
Van De Lei, Groningen

Belgium

Fabienne Velge, Brussels, for her contribution, especially for recipes and detailed information, but also for her great help with the organization of the research.
André Leroy, Charleroi, for his wonderful hospitality and great help with the organization of the research, as well as for his recommendations of wine for the recipes.

Abbey Notre-Dame-de-Scourmont, Chimay
Bières de Chimay; Michael Weber
Brauerei Lindemans; Gert Lindemans, Vleezenbek
Brugge Tourist Office; J.P. Drubbel
Jacquy Cange, Péruwelz
Chocolaterie Sukerbuyc; M. Depreter, Bruges
Marc Danval, Brussels
De Gouden Boom; Paul Vanneste, Bruges
Detry Frere, Aubel
Ferme Colyn, Bruyères-Herve
Fritterie Eupen
Fromagerie Vanderheyden, Pepinster
Gaufrerie La Doyenne Liégeoise; F. Joiris, Herstal
Dominique Gobert, Oigniès-en-Thiérache
Godiva, Chocolats, Brussels
Herve Société, Herve
Hostellerie Pannenhuis, Brussels
Hotel- en Toerismeschool; Eddy Govaert, Bruges
Maison Dandoy; Jean Rombouts, Brussels
Maison Matthys & Van Gaever; Patrick van Gaever, Brussels
Office National des Débouchés Agricoles et Horticoles, Jambes
Office des Produits Wallons, Montignies-sur-Samble
Pub Aquarell, Eupen
Restaurant Le Brabançon; Marie-Jeanne Lucas, Brussels
Restaurant Café des Arts, Bruges
Restaurant Le Joueur de Flûte; Philippe van Capellen, Brussels
Restaurant Le Sanglier des Ardennes; Jacky Buchet-Somme, Oignies-en-Thiérache
M. Ryckmans, Kortenberg
L. Ryckmans-Vrebos, Kortenberg
Siroperie Nyssen, Aubel
Van De Goor, Leevdaal

France

M. Astruc, Roquefort
Auberge de la Truffe; Mme. Leymar, Sorges
Guy Audouy, Ansignan
Roland Barthélemy, Paris
M. Bernachon, Lyon
René Besson, Saint-Jean d'Ardière
Gabriel Boudier, Dijon
Boulangerie-Pâtisserie Jean Baptiste Waldner, Erstein
Bureau Interprofessionnel des Vins de la Bourgogne; Dominique Lambry, Beaune
La Cargolade; Eheleute Fourriques, Argeles Surbeer
Le Chalut; Jean-Claude Mourlane, Port-Vendres
Le Chardonnay; Jean-Jacques Lange, Reims
Château de Monthélie; Eric de Suremont, Monthélie
Chocolaterie Valrhona, Tain-l'Hermitage
Cidrerie Château d'Hauteville; Eric Bordelet, Charchigné
La Cognathèque, Cognac
Jeanne und Michel Colls, Perpignan
Comité Interprofessionnel de la Volaille de Bresse, Louhans
Comité Interprofessionnel des Vins du Languedoc; Christine Behey-Molines, Narbonne
Coumeilles, Boucherie du Faubourg
Au Couscoussier D'Or, Lyon
Crémerie Henri Reynal, Perpignan

632

Crêperie Ty-Coz; Familie Lejollec, Locronan
Cru Minervois; Yves Castell, Olonzac
Martine Cuq, Roquefort
Distillerie des Fiefs Sainte Anne; Christian Drouin, Calvados
Ecole Hôtelière de Moulin-à-Vent, Perpignan
Ecomusée de la Truffe, Sorges
Albert Escobar, Montélimar
L'Estaminet au Bord L'Ill, Erstein
Edmont Fallot, Beaune
Ferme Auberge du Grand Ronjon; Pierre Emanuel Guyon, Cormoz
Anse Gerbal, Côte Catalane, Port Vendres
Claude Gineste, Izarra, Bayonne
Laiterie de Saint-Hilaire-de-Briouze; Jacques de Longcamp, Gillot
La Littorine; Jean-Marie Patroueix und Jean Sannac, Banyuls
Maison Samalens; Philippe Samalens, Laujuzon
Maurice de Mandelaeré, Flörsheim-Dalsheim
Moët & Chandon; Laurence Le Cabel und Philippe de Roys de Roure, Epernay
Mairie de Montélimar
Patrick Morand, Montélimar
Gérard Mulot Pâtissier, Paris
Pierre und Dominique Noyel, St. Claude Huissel, Amplepuis
Les Pêcheries Côtières; Daniel Huché, Paris
Restaurant Auberge de Bergeraye; Pierrette Sarran, Saint-Martin d'Armagnac
Restaurant La Bourride; Michel Bruneau, Caën
Restaurant Chez Philippe; Philippe Schadt, Blaesheim
Restaurant Robin; Daniel Robin, Chénas
M. Rivière, Anjeal-Charente
Fa. Roque, Collioure
Claude Rozand, Montrevel en Bresse
Sopexa; Katja Bremer, Brigitte Engelmann und Christa Langen, Düsseldorf
Robert Telegoni, Montbrun Les Bains
La Tremblade; François Patsuris
Union Interprofessionnelle des Vins du Beaujolais; Michel Deflache, Villefranche
Le Vintage, Reimes

Spain

Maité Schramm, Calce, who contributed the recipes.

Bodegas Marques de Caceres, Cenicero, Rioja
Cava Freixenet, San Sadurni de Noya
Charcuteria La Pineda; Antonio Segovia, Barcelona
Pedro Domecq S.A., Jerez de la Frontera
Fábrica de Sanchez Romero Carvajal, Huelva, Jabugo
Hostal Montoro; Rafael Majuelos y Bartolomé Garcia, Cordoba
Angel Jobal S.A., Barcelona
Klemann, Wachenheim
El Mirador De Las Cavas, San Sadurni de Anoy
Patrimonio Communal Olivarero, Montoro, Cordoba
Pescaderia Garcia, Mercado Galvany, Barcelona
Restaurant Cal Pep; Josep Manubens Figueres, Barcelona
Restaurant Los Caracoles, Barcelona
Don Manuel Roldan, Sevilla
Sidra Escanciador, Villaviciosa
Sidra Trabanco Lauandera, Gijon
Spanisches Generalkonsulat; Handelsabteilung, Vicente Salort, Juan Carlos Sanz und Barbara Wehowsky, Düsseldorf
Oliver Strunk, Barcelona
Tapas Bar El Xampanyet, Barcelona

Portugal

Joachim Krieger, Piesport, who in Portugal sought out excellent and original specialties, collated material and information and drew up drafts for much of the text.

Cervejaria da Trindade, Lissabon
Cockburn Smithes & Comp.; Gina Nonteiro, Villa Nova de Gaia
Isabel Gambino, Trier
Konservenfabrik Idamar, Matosinhos
Manteigaria Silva, Lda., Lissabon
Portuguese Consulate General; Commercial Section, António Teixeira, Düsseldorf
Quinta de Ancede, Amares (Braga)
Restaurant Búzio; Luis Matens, Sintra

Italy

Uschi Stender-Barbieri, Herrsching, for recipes, information, corrections and additions; Nico Barbieri for countless tips and recommendations.

Acetaia Raffaele Piccirilli, Cavriago (R.E.)

Al Castello Romano, Cologne
Al'Dorale Ristorante, Cologne
Antica Macelleria Falorni, Greve, Chianti
Antica Sciamadda, Genoa
Associazione dei trifulau; Agostino Aprile, Montà, Alba
Azienda Agricola Corbeddu Santino e Pasqualino, Castelnuovo Berardenga (SI)
Azienda Agricola Oberto Egidio, La Morra (CN)
Azienda Turistica; Federica Bono, Vercelli
Bar Camparino, Milan
Barilla Alimentare S.P.A., Parma
Giuditta Besana, Calce
Camera Di Commercio, Modena
Castello Di San Paolo in Rosso; Stefan Giesen, Gaiolo in Chianti
Conservificio Allevatori Molluschi, Chioggia
Consorzio del Parmigiano Reggiano; Leo Bertazzi, Reggio Emilia
Consorzio per la tutela dell'Aceto Balsamico tradizionale di Moden, Modena
Consorzio per la tutela del formaggio Gorgonzola, Novara
Distillerie Sibona, Piobesi d'Alba
La Fungheria, Milan
Gastronomie Service Dahmen GmbH, Cologne
Gelateria Mickey Mouse, Parma
Gelateria Pasticceria Etnea, Bergamo
Frantoio Giachi, Mercatale Val Di Pesa (FI)
Ghibellino, Castelnuovo Berardenga (SI)
Italian Institute for Foreign Trade, ICE; Gertrud Schmitz and Dr. Vittorio Taddei, Düsseldorf
Romano Levi, Neive
Lidero Truccore, Montà
Macelleria Falcinelli, Arezzo
Marcella Tognazzi, Radda
Mario Marchi, San Casciano
Mazzucchelli Goretti Piero, Bologna
Molino Sobrino, La Morra (CN)
Moto Nautica Nordio, Chioggia
Panetteria Paolo Atti e Figli, Bologna
Pasticceria Panarello; Francesco Panarello, Milan
Pizzeria La Conchiglia, Novellara, Reggio Emilia
Prosciuttificio Pio Tosini, Langhirano bei Parma
Riseria Tenuta Castello, Desan, Vercelli
Ristorante Picci, Cavriago
Salsamenteria Bolognese Tamburini, Bologna
San Giusto A Rentennano; Bettina und Luca Martini, Gaiole, Chianti
Sansone, Cologne
Michele Scrofani, Bergamo
Serafina Laboratorio Artigianale, Genua
La Sfogliatella, Bologna
A.B. Sre tripperia, Genua
Tartuflanghe di Bertolussi, Piobesi d'Alba
Torrefazione Faelli; Angela Biacchi, Parma
Uniteis, Seligenstadt

Greece

Achaia Clauss, Patras
Simos Countouris, Markagoulo, Attica
Dimitriadis, Attica
Greek Consulate General; Commercial Section, Mr. Alexandrakis, Bonn
Hotel Poseidon, Patras
Taverne Delphi; Eheleute Pavegos, Köln
Taverne Delphi; Mr. and Mrs. Pavegos, Cologne

Turkey

Bazar Kebap, Cologne
Çinar Restorant, Istanbul
Grillrestaurant Bandirma, Colgne
Ahmet Yavas, Istanbul

Picture Acknowledgments

All photos by Günter Beer with the exception of the following:
Food Foto Köln, Brigitte Krauth and Jürgen Holz: 12/13, 18/19 (large photo), 50/51, 58–61, 68/69, 78/79 (large photo), 81–85, 102/103, 106–107, 108/109, 112/113, 120/121, 124/125, 129/130, 132/133, 135, 137 (small photo), 139 (small photo), 140–143, 146/147, 150 (bottles), 160/161, 168, 177, 184/185, 189, 200/201, 210/211, 236/237, 244/245, 256–258, 262–266, 278/279 (bottles), 288/289, 298/299 (large photo), 314–317, 340/341, 352/353, 358/359, 362/363, 370–373, 382/383, 396/397 (large photo), 424/425, 430/431, 462/463, 488/489, 492/493, 500/501, 504/505 (large photo), 506–511, 542/543, 552–555, 560–563, 572/573, 590–593, 618–619, 624–625
agrar-press, Fachbildagentur für Agrar- und Naturfotografie Dr. Wolfgang Schiffer: 253
Andrej Reiser/Bilderberg: 134 (all photos)
© Johannes Booz/Benedikt Taschen Verlag, Cologne: 144/145 (all photos)
Mary Evans Picture Library: 30/31
Dr. Rainer Berg/Fischereiforschungsstelle des Landes Baden-Württemberg: 121 top center, 121 top right, 222 (Burbot, Grayling, Laube, Whitefish), 223 (Pike)
© Garden Picture Library/Brian Carter: 19 (no. 6)
© Garden Picture Library/Vaughan Fleming: 19 (no. 7)
© Garden Picture Library/Lamontagne: 19 (no. 1, 4, 5)
© Garden Picture Library/Clive Nichols 19 (no. 3)
© Garden Picture Library/J. S. Sira: 19 (no. 8)
© Garden Picture Library/Brigitte Thomas: 19 (no. 2)
© Raimund Cramm/Verlags-Service K.G. Hütten: 34 (Grouse), 121 (top left), 222 (Tench), 222/223 (Brook char)
© Kriso/Verlags-Service K.G. Hütten: 222 (Redeye, Freshwater bream), 269 (Red feather, River perch)
© Horst Niesters/Verlags-Service K.G. Hütten: 199 (no. 7, 9)
© H. Schrempp/Verlags-Service K.G. Hütten: 155 (Shallow-pored Boletus, Turban fungus, Cep, Yellow-cracked Boletus, Large Morel)
© Günther Schumann/Verlags-Service K.G. Hütten: 198 large photo and no. 1–6, 8, 10
© The Hulton Deutsch Collection: 34/35 (background), 40/41
Jürgens Ost u. Europa-Photo: 148 (all photos)
© G.J. Keizer: 154 (all photos), 155 (Brown Birch Boletus, Poplar Boletus, Horn of Plenty, Larch Boletus, Sand Boletus, Saffron Milk Cap, The Blusher, Honey Fungus, Field Mushroom, Chanterelle, Common Morel)
Kelterei Possmann KG 274/275
Archiv Brigitte Krauth: 258
Magyar Nemzeti Muzeum Történeti Fényképtára: 188/189 (large photo)
Österreich Werbung: 204 (large photo)
Fachbuchverlag Dr. Pfannenberg & Co., from "Lexikon der Küche" by Richard Hering Giessen 1987, 23rd. edition, p. 744: 196 (illustration)
Christl Reiter: 277 top
Scandinavian Fishing Year Book, Bækgaardsvej, DK-2640 Hedehusene: 96/97
Hans Schmied: 277 below
Ruprecht Stempell, Cologne: 254/255, 389 (fennel), 410, 411 (5 wine bottles), 604 (Aniseed)
Thomas Veszelits: 171 (Trèboň — Catching Carp)
Vinmonopolet: 99 (small photo and map)
VISUM/Günter Beer: 116/117
VISUM/Gerd Ludwig: 126/127, 138/139, 149
Christa Wendler: 135 (all illustrations)
© WILDLIFE/K. Keilwerth: 223 (Pike-perch)
Till Leeser/Bilderberg: 392/393 (large photo)
© Claus Photography 1994 and 1995: 416/417, 418/419
André Dominé: 496 (small photo, below), 512
Bishop/FOCUS: 588/589
Kalvar/magnum FOCUS: 610/611
Manos/magnum/FOCUS: 603 (small photos)
Snowdon/Hoyer/FOCUS: 603 (large photo)
© Hans Reinhard/Verlags-Service K.G. Hütten 604 (aniseed plant)
Scandinavian Fishing Year Book, Baekfgaardsvej, DK-2640 Hedehusene: 498/499, 600/601
Spanish Consulate General; Commercial Section, Düsseldorf; 480 (© Carlos Navajas: Palomino, Tempranillo)
SOPEXA: 347 (3 oysters), 350/351, 381, 384, 385, 407 (Vacherin de Mont d'Or)

Index